U•X•L Encyclopedia of

Native American Tribes

THIRD EDITION

U•X•L Encyclopedia of
Native American Tribes

THIRD EDITION

VOLUME 2

SOUTHEAST

GREAT PLAINS

Laurie J. Edwards, Editor

U·X·L
A part of Gale, Cengage Learning

GALE
CENGAGE Learning·

Detroit • New York • San Francisco • New Haven, Conn • Waterville, Maine • London

U•X•L Encyclopedia of Native American Tribes, 3rd Edition

Laurie J. Edwards

Project Editors: Shelly Dickey, Terri Schell

Rights Acquisition and Management: Leitha Etheridge-Sims

Composition: Evi Abou-El-Seoud

Manufacturing: Wendy Blurton

Imaging: John Watkins

Product Design: Kristine Julien

For product information and technology assistance, contact us at
Gale Customer Support, 1-800-877-4253.
For permission to use material from this text or product,
submit all requests online at **www.cengage.com/permissions.**
Further permissions questions can be emailed to
permission request@cengage.com

Cover photographs reproduced by permission of Standing Eagle Dancers, ©Mark Romesser/Alamy; War Dance, ©Sylvain Grandadam/Robert Harding Picture Library Ltd/Alamy.

While every effort has been made to ensure the reliability of the information presented in this publication, Gale, a part of Cengage Learning, does not guarantee the accuracy of the data contained herein. Gale accepts no payment for listing; and inclusion in the publication of any organization, agency, institution, publication, service, or individual does not imply endorsement of the editors or publisher. Errors brought to the attention of the publisher and verified to the satisfaction of the publisher will be corrected in future editions.

LIBRARY OF CONGRESS CATALOGING-IN-PUBLICATION DATA

U•X•L Encyclopedia of Native American Tribes / Laurie J. Edwards ; Shelly Dickey, Terri Schell, project editors. -- 3rd ed.
   5 v. . cm.
   Includes bibliographical references and index.
   ISBN 978-1-4144-9092-2 (set) -- ISBN 978-1-4144-9093-9 (v. 1) -- ISBN 978-1-4144-9094-6 (v.2) -- ISBN 978-1-4144-9095-3 (v.3) -- ISBN 978-1-4144-9096-0 (v. 4) -- ISBN 978-1-4144-9097-7 (v. 5),
   1. Indians of North America--Encyclopedias, Juvenile. 2. Indians of North America--Encyclopedias. I. Edwards, Laurie J. II. Dickey, Shelly. III. Schell, Terri, 1968-

E76.2.U85 2012
970.004'97003--dc23   2011048142

Gale
27500 Drake Rd.
Farmington Hills, MI, 48331-3535

978-1-4144-9092-2 (set)	1-4144-9092-5 (set)
978-1-4144-9093-9 (v. 1)	1-4144-9093-3 (v. 1)
978-1-4144-9094-6 (v. 2)	1-4144-9094-1 (v. 2)
978-1-4144-9095-3 (v. 3)	1-4144-9095-X (v. 3)
978-1-4144-9096-0 (v. 4)	1-4144-9096-8 (v. 4)
978-1-4144-9097-7 (v. 5)	1-4144-9097-6 (v. 5)

This title is also available as an e-book.
ISBN 13: 978-1-4144-9098-4 ISBN 10: 1-4144-9098-4
Contact your Gale, a part of Cengage Learning, sales representative for ordering information.

Printed in U.S.A.
1 2 3 4 5 6 7 16 15 14 13 12

Contents

Tribes Alphabetically

First numeral signifies volume number. The numeral after the colon signifies page number. For example, 3:871 means Volume 3, page 871.

Reader's Guide

Long before the Vikings, Spaniards, and Portuguese made land-fall on North American shores, the continent already had a rich history of human settlement. The *U•X•L Encyclopedia of Native American Tribes, 3rd Edition* opens up for students the array of tribal ways in the United States and Canada past and present. Included in these volumes, readers will find the stories of:

- the well-known nineteenth century Lakota hunting the buffalo on the Great Plains
- the contemporary Inuit of the Arctic, who in 1999 won their battle for Nunavut, a vast, self-governing territory in Canada
- the Haida of the Pacific Northwest, whose totem poles have become a familiar adornment of the landscape
- the Anasazi in the Southwest, who were building spectacular cities long before Europeans arrived
- the Mohawk men in the Northeast who made such a name for themselves as ironworkers on skyscrapers and bridges that they have long been in demand for such projects as the Golden Gate Bridge
- the Yahi of California, who became extinct when their last member, Ishi, died in 1916.

The *U•X•L Encyclopedia of Native American Tribes, 3rd Edition* presents 106 tribes, confederacies, and Native American groups. Among the tribes included are large and well-known nations, smaller communities with their own fascinating stories, and prehistoric peoples. The tribes are grouped in the ten major geographical/cultural areas of North America in which tribes shared environmental and cultural connections. The ten sections, each beginning with an introductory essay on the geographical area and the shared history and culture within it, are arranged in the volumes as follows:

- Volume 1: Northeast and Subarctic
- Volume 2: Southeast and Great Plains
- Volume 3: Southwest
- Volume 4: California and Plateau
- Volume 5: Great Basin, Pacific Northwest, and Arctic

The *U•X•L Encyclopedia of Native American Tribes, 3rd Edition* provides the history of each of the tribes featured and a fascinating look at their ways of life: how families lived in centuries past and today, what people ate and wore, what their homes were like, how they worshiped, celebrated, governed themselves, and much more. A student can learn in depth about one tribe or compare aspects of many tribes. Each detailed entry is presented in consistent rubrics that allow for easy access and comparison, as follows:

- History
- Religion
- Language
- Government
- Economy
- Daily Life
- Arts
- Customs
- Current Tribal Issues
- Notable People

Each entry begins with vital data on the tribe: name, location, population, language family, origins and group affiliations. A locator map follows, showing the traditional homelands and contemporary communities of the group; regional and migration maps throughout aid in locating the many groups at different times in history. Brief timelines in each entry chronicle important dates of the tribe's history, while an overall timeline at the beginning of all the volumes outlines key events in history pertinent to all Native Americans. Other sidebars present recipes, oral literature or stories, language keys, and background material on the tribe. Color photographs and illustrations, further reading sections, a thorough subject index, and a glossary are special features that make the volumes easy, fun, and informative to use.

A note on terminology

Throughout the *U•X•L Encyclopedia of Native American Tribes, 3rd Edition* various terms are used for Native North Americans, such as *Indian, American Indian, Native,* and *aboriginal.* The Native peoples of the Americas have the unfortunate distinction of having been given the wrong name by the Europeans who first arrived on the continent, mistakenly thinking they had arrived in India. The search for a single name, however, has never been entirely successful. The best way to characterize Native North Americans is by recognizing their specific tribal or community identities. In compiling this book, every effort has been made to keep Native tribal and community identities distinct, but by necessity, inclusive terminology is often used. We do not wish to offend anyone, but rather than favor one term for Native North American people, the editors have used a variety of terminology, trying always to use the most appropriate term in the particular context.

Europeans also had a hand in giving names to tribes, often misunderstanding their languages and the relations between different Native communities. Most tribes have their own names for themselves, and many have succeeded in gaining public acceptance of traditional names. The Inuit, for example, objected to the name Eskimo, which means "eaters of raw meat," and in time their name for themselves was accepted. In the interest of clarity the editors of this book have used the currently accepted terms, while acknowledging the traditional ones or the outmoded ones at the beginning of each entry.

The term *tribe* is not accepted by all Native groups. The people living in North America before the Europeans arrived had many different ways of organizing themselves politically and relating to other groups around them—from complex confederacies and powerful unified nations to isolated villages with little need for political structure. Groups divided, absorbed each other, intermarried, allied, and dissolved. The epidemics and wars that came with non-Native expansion into North America created a demographic catastrophe to many Native groups and greatly affected tribal affiliations. Although in modern times there are actual rules about what comprise a tribe (federal requirements for recognition of tribes are specific, complicated, and often difficult to fulfill), the hundreds of groups living in the Americas in early times did not have any one way of categorizing themselves. Thus, some Native American peoples today find the word *tribe* misleading. In a study of Native peoples, it can also be an elusive defining term. But in facing the challenges of maintaining traditions and heritage in modern times, tribal or community identity is acutely important to many Native Americans. Tremendous efforts have been undertaken to preserve native languages, oral traditions, religions, ceremonies, and traditional arts and economies—the things that, put together, make a tribe a cultural and political unit.

Comments and suggestions

In this third edition of the *U•X•L Encyclopedia of Native American Tribes* we have presented in-depth information on 106 of the hundreds of tribes of North America. While every attempt was made to include a wide representation of groups, many historically important and interesting tribes are not covered in these volumes. We welcome your suggestions for tribes to be featured in future editions, as well as any other comments you may have on this set. Please write: Editors, *U•X•L Encyclopedia of Native American Tribes, 3rd Edition,* U•X•L 27500 Drake Road, Farmington Hills, Michigan 48331-3535; call toll-free 1-800-877-4253; or fax 248-699-8097; or send e-mail via http://www.gale.com.

Words to Know

Aboriginal: Native, or relating to the first or earliest group living in a particular area.

Activism: Taking action for or against a controversial issue; political and social activists may organize or take part in protest demonstrations, rallies, petitioning the government, sit-ins, civil disobedience, and many other forms of activities that draw attention to an issue and/or challenge the authorities to make a change.

Adobe: A brick or other building material made from sun-dried mud, a mixture of clay, sand, and sometimes ashes, rocks, or straw.

Alaska Native Claims Settlement Act (ANCSA): An act of Congress passed in 1971 that gave Alaska Natives 44 million acres of land and $962.5 million. In exchange, Alaska Natives gave up all claim to other lands in Alaska. The ANCSA also resulted in the formation of 12 regional corporations in Alaska in charge of Native communities' economic development and land use.

Allotment: The practice of dividing and distributing land into individual lots. In 1887 the U.S. Congress passed the General Allotment Act (also known as the Dawes Act), which divided Indian reservations into privately owned parcels (pieces) of land. Under allotment, tribes could no longer own their own lands in common (as a group) in the traditional ways. Instead the head of a family received a lot, generally 160 acres. Land not alloted was sold to non-Natives.

American Indian Movement (AIM): An activist movement founded in 1966 to aggressively press for Indian rights. The movement was formed to improve federal, state, and local social services to Native Americans in urban neighborhoods. AIM sought the reorganization of the Bureau of Indian Affairs to make it more responsive to Native American needs and fought for the return of Indian lands illegally taken from them.

Anthropology: The study of human beings in terms of their populations, culture, social relations, ethnic characteristics, customs, and adaptation to their environment.

Archaeology: The study of the remains of past human life, such as fossil relics, artifacts, and monuments, in order to understand earlier human cultures.

Arctic: Relating to the area surrounding the North Pole.

Assimilate: To absorb, or to be absorbed, into the dominant society (those in power, or in the majority). U.S. assimilation policies were directed at causing Native Americans to become like European-Americans in terms of jobs and economics, religion, customs, language, education, family life, and dress.

Band: A small, loosely organized social group composed of several families. In Canada, the word band originally referred to a social unit of nomadic (those who moved from place to place) hunting peoples, but now refers to a community of Indians registered with the government.

Boarding school: A live-in school.

Breechcloth: A garment with front and back flaps that hangs from the waist. Breechcloths were one of the most common articles of clothing worn by many Native American men and sometimes women in pre-European/American settlement times.

Bureau of Indian Affairs (BIA): The U.S. government agency that oversees tribal lands, education, and other aspects of Indian life.

Census: A count of the population.

Ceremony: A special act or set of acts (such as a wedding or a funeral) performed by members of a group on important occasions, usually organized according to the group's traditions and beliefs.

Clan: A group of related house groups and families that trace back to a common ancestor or a common symbol or totem, usually an animal such as the bear or the turtle. The clan forms the basic social and political unit for many Indian societies.

Colonialism: A state or nation's control over a foreign territory.

Colonize: To establish a group of people from a mother country or state in a foreign territory; the colonists set up a community that remains tied to the mother county.

Confederacy: A group of people, states, or nations joined together for mutual support or for a special purpose.

Convert: To cause a person or group to change their beliefs or practices. A convert (noun) is a person who has been converted to a new belief or practice.

Coup: A feat of bravery, especially the touching of an enemy's body during battle without causing or receiving injury. To "count coup" is to count the number of such feats of bravery.

Cradleboard: A board or frame on which an infant was bound or wrapped by some Native American peoples. It was used as a portable carrier or for carrying an infant on the back.

Creation stories: Sacred myths or stories that explain how Earth and its beings were created.

Culture: The set of beliefs, social habits, and ways of surviving in the environment that are held by a particular social group.

Dentalium: Dentalia (plural) are the tooth-like shells that some tribes used as money. The shells were rubbed smooth and strung like beads on strands of animal skin.

Depletion: Decreasing the amount of something; depletion of resources such as animals or minerals through overuse reduces essential elements from the environment.

Dialect: A local variety of a particular language, with unique differences in words, grammar, and pronunciation.

Economy: The way a group obtains, produces, and distributes the goods it needs; the overall system by which it supports itself and accumulates its wealth.

Ecosystem: The overall way that a community and its surrounding environment function together in nature.

Epidemic: The rapid spread of a disease so that many people in an area have it at the same time.

Ethnic group: A group of people who are classed according to certain aspects of their common background, usually by tribal, racial, national, cultural, and language origins.

Extended family: A family group that includes close relatives such as mother, father, and children, plus grandparents, aunts, and uncles, and cousins.

Fast: To go without food.

Federally recognized tribes: Tribes with which the U.S. government maintains official relations as established by treaty, executive order, or act of Congress.

Fetish: An object believed to have magical or spiritual power.

First Nations: One of Canada's terms for its Indian nations.

Five Civilized Tribes: A name given to the Cherokee, Choctaw, Chickasaw, Creek, and Seminole during the mid-1800s. The tribes were given this name by non-Natives because they had democratic constitutional governments, a high literacy rate (many people who could read and write), and ran effective schools.

Formal education: Structured learning that takes place in a school or college under the supervision of trained teachers.

Ghost Dance: A revitalization (renewal or rebirth) movement that arose in the 1870s after many tribes moved to reservations and were being encouraged to give up their traditional beliefs. Many Native Americans hoped that, if they performed it earnestly, the Ghost Dance would bring back traditional Native lifestyles and values, and that the buffalo and Indian ancestors would return to the Earth as in the days before the white settlers.

Great Basin: An elevated region in the western United States in which all water drains toward the center. The Great Basin covers part of Nevada, California, Colorado, Utah, Oregon, and Wyoming.

Guardian spirit: A sacred power, usually embodied in an animal such as a hawk, deer, or turtle, that reveals itself to an individual, offering help throughout the person's lifetime in important matters such as hunting or healing the sick.

Haudenosaunee: The name of the people often called Iroquois or Five Nations. It means "People of the Longhouse."

Head flattening: A practice in which a baby was placed in a cradle, and a padded board was tied to its forehead to mold the head into a desired shape. Sometimes the effect of flattening the back of the head was achieved by binding the infant tightly to a cradleboard.

Immunity: Resistance to disease; the ability to be exposed to a disease with less chance of getting it, and less severe effects if infected.

Indian Territory: An area in present-day Kansas and Oklahoma where the U.S. government once planned to move all Indians, and, eventually, to allow them to run their own province or state. In 1880 nearly one-third of all U.S. Indians lived there, but with the formation of the state of Oklahoma in 1906, the promise of an Indian state dissolved.

Indigenous: Native, or first, in a specific area. Native Americans are often referred to as indigenous peoples of North America.

Intermarriage: Marriage between people of different groups, as between a Native American and a non-Native, or between people from two different tribes.

Kachina: A group of spirits celebrated by the Pueblo Indians; the word also refers to dolls made in the image of kachina spirits.

Kiva: Among the Pueblo, a circular (sometimes rectangular) underground room used for religious ceremonies.

Lacrosse: A game of Native American origin in which players use a long stick with a webbed pouch at the end for catching and throwing a ball.

Language family: A group of languages that are different from one another but are related. These languages share similar words, sounds, or word structures. The languages are alike either because they have borrowed words from each other or because they originally came from the same parent language.

Legend: A story or folktale that tells about people or events in the past.

Life expectancy: The average number of years a person may expect to live.

Linguistics: The study of human speech and language.

Literacy: The state of being able to read and write.

Loincloth: See "Breechcloth".

Longhouse: A large, long building in which several families live together; usually found among Northwest Coast and Iroquois peoples.

Long Walk of the Navajo: The enforced 300-mile walk of the Navajo people in 1864, when they were being removed from their homelands to the Bosque Redondo Reservation in New Mexico.

Manifest Destiny: A belief held by many Americans in the nineteenth century that the destiny of the United States was to expand its territory and extend its political, social, and economic influences throughout North America.

Matrilineal: Tracing family relations through the mother; in a matrilineal society, names and inheritances are passed down through the mother's side of the family.

Medicine bundle: A pouch in which were kept sacred objects believed to have powers that would protect and aid an individual, a clan or family, or a community.

Midewiwin Society: The Medicine Lodge Religion, whose main purpose was to prolong life. The society taught morality, proper conduct, and a knowledge of plants and herbs for healing.

Migration: Movement from one place to another. The migrations of Native peoples were often done by the group, with whole nations moving from one area to another.

Mission: An organized effort by a religious group to spread its beliefs to other parts of the world; mission refers either to the project of spreading a belief system or to the building(s)—such as a church—in which this takes place.

Missionary: Someone sent to a foreign land to convert its people to a particular religion.

Mission school: A school established by missionaries to teach people religious beliefs as well as other subjects.

Moiety: One of the two parts that a tribe or community divided into based on kinship.

Myth: A story passed down through generations, often involving supernatural beings. Myths often express religious beliefs or the values of people. They may attempt to explain how the Earth and its beings were created, or why things are. They are not always meant to be taken as factual.

Natural resources: The sources of supplies provided by the environment for survival and enrichment, such as animals to be hunted, land for farming, minerals, and timber.

Neophyte: Beginner; often used to mean a new convert to a religion.

Nomadic: Traveling and relocating often, usually in search of food and other resources or a better climate.

Nunavut: A new territory in Canada as of April 1, 1999, with the status of a province and a Inuit majority. It is a huge area, covering most of Canada north of the treeline. Nunavut means "Our Land" in Inuki-tut (the Inuit language).

Oral literature: Oral traditions that are written down after enjoying a long life in spoken form among a people.

Oral traditions: History, mythology, folklore, and other foundations of a culture that have been passed by spoken word, often in the form of stories, from generation to generation within a culture group.

Parent language: A language that is the common structure of two or more languages that came into being at a later time.

Parfleche: A case or a pouch made from tanned animal hide.

Patrilineal: Tracing family relations through the father; in a patrilineal society, names and inheritances are passed down through the father's side of the family.

Per capita income: The average personal income per person.

Petroglyph: A carving or engraving on rock; a common form of ancient art.

Peyote: A substance obtained from cactus that some Indian groups used as part of their religious practice. After eating the substance, which stimulates the nervous system, a person may go into a trance state and see visions. The Peyote Religion features the use of this substance.

Pictograph: A simple picture representing a historical event.

Policy: The overall plan or course of action issued by the government, establishing how it will handle certain situations or people and what its goals are.

Post-European contact: Relating to the time and state of Native Americans and their lands after the Europeans arrived. Depending on the part of the country in which they lived, Native groups experienced contact at differing times in the history of white expansion into the West.

Potlatch: A feast or ceremony, commonly held among Northwest Coast groups; also called a "giveaway." During a potlatch goods are given to guests to show the host's generosity and wealth. Potlatches are used to celebrate major life events such as birth, death, or marriage.

Powwow: A celebration at which the main activity is traditional singing and dancing. In modern times, the singers and dancers at powwows came from many different tribes.

Province: A district or division of a country (like a state in the United States).

Raiding: Entering into another tribe or community's territory, usually by stealth or force, and stealing their livestock and supplies.

Ranchería: Spanish term for a small farm.

Ratify: To approve or confirm. In the United States, the U.S. Senate ratified treaties with the Indians.

Red Power: A term used to describe the Native American activism movement of the 1960s, in which people from many tribes came together to protest the injustices of American policies toward Native Americans.

Removal Act: An act passed by the U.S. Congress in 1830 that directed all Indians to be moved to Indian Territory, west of the Mississippi River.

Removal Period: The time, mostly between 1830 and 1860, when most Indians of the eastern United States were forced to leave their homelands and relocate west of the Mississippi River.

Repatriation: To return something to its place of origin. A law passed in the 1990s says that all bones and grave goods (items that are buried with a body) should be returned to the descendants. Many Native American tribes have used that law to claim bones and other objects belonging to their ancestors. Museums and archaeological digs must return these items to the tribes.

Reservation: Land set aside by the U.S. government for the use of a group or groups of Indians.

Reserve: In Canada, lands set aside for specific Indian bands. Reserve means in Canada approximately what reservation means in the United States.

Revitalization: The feeling or movement in which something seems to come back to life after having been quiet or inactive for a period of time.

Ritual: A formal act that is performed in basically the same way each time; rituals are often performed as part of a ceremony.

Rural: Having to do with the country; opposite of urban.

Sachem: The chief of a confederation of tribes.

Shaman: A priest or medicine person in many Native American groups who understands and works with supernatural matters. Shamans traditionally performed in rituals and were expected to cure the sick, see the future, and obtain supernatural help with hunting and other economic activities.

Smallpox: A very contagious disease that spread across North America and killed many thousands of Indians. Survivors had skin that was badly scarred.

Sovereign: Self-governing or independent. A sovereign nation makes its own laws and rules.

Sun Dance: A renewal and purification ceremony performed by many Plains Indians such as the Sioux and Cheyenne. A striking aspect of the ceremony was the personal sacrifice made by some men. They undertook self-torture in order to gain a vision that might provide spiritual insight beneficial to the community.

Sweat lodge: An airtight hut containing hot stones that were sprinkled with water to make them steam. A person remained inside until he or she was perspiring. The person then usually rushed out and plunged into a cold stream. This treatment was used before a ceremony or for the healing of physical or spiritual ailments. Sweat lodge is also the name of a sacred Native American ceremony involving the building of the lodge and the pouring of water on stones, usually by a medicine person, accompanied by praying and singing. The ceremony has many purposes, including spiritual cleansing and healing.

Taboo: A forbidden object or action. Many Indians believe that the sacred order of the world must be maintained if one is to avoid illness or other misfortunes. This is accomplished, in part, by observing a large assortment of taboos.

Termination: The policy of the U.S. government during the 1950s and 1960s to end the relationships set up by treaties with Indian nations.

Toloache: A substance obtained from a plant called jimsonweed. When consumed, the drug causes a person to go into a trance and see visions. It is used in some religious ceremonies.

Totem: An object that serves as an emblem or represents a family or clan, usually in the form of an animal, bird, fish, plant, or other natural object. A totem pole is a pillar built in front of the homes of Natives in the Northwest. It is painted and carved with a series of totems that show the family background and either mythical or historical events.

Trail of Tears: A series of forced marches of Native Americans of the Southeast in the 1830s, causing the deaths of thousands. The marches were the result of the U.S. government's removal policy, which ordered Native Americans to be moved to Indian Territory.

Treaty: An agreement between two parties or two nations, signed by both, usually defining the benefits to both parties that will result from one side giving up title to a territory of land.

Tribe: A group of Natives who share a name, language, culture, and ancestors; in Canada, called a band.

Tribelet: A community within an organization of communities in which one main settlement was surrounded by a few minor outlying settlements.

Trickster: A common culture hero in Indian myth and legend. tricksters generally have supernatural powers that can be used to do good or harm, and stories about them take into account the different forces of the universe, such as good and evil or night and day. The Trickster takes different forms among various groups; for example, Coyote in the Southwest; Ikhtomi Spider in the High Plains, and Jay or Wolverine in Canada.

Trust: A relationship between two parties (or groups) in which one is responsible for acting in the other's best interests. The U.S. government has a trust relationship with tribal nations. Many tribes do not own their lands outright; according to treaty, the government owns the land "in trust" and tribes are given the use of it.

Unemployment rate: The percentage of the population that is looking for work but unable to find any. (People who have quit looking for work are not included in unemployment rates.)

Urban: Having to do with cities and towns; the opposite of rural.

Values: The ideals that a community of people shares.

Vision quest: A sacred ceremony in which a person (often a teenage boy) goes off alone and fasts, living without food or water for a period of days. During that time he hopes to learn about his spiritual side and to have a vision of a guardian spirit who will give him help and strength throughout his life.

Wampum: Small cylinder-shaped beads cut from shells. Long strings of wampum were used for many different purposes. Indians believed that the exchange of wampum and other goods established a friendship, not just a profit-making relationship.

Wampum belt: A broad woven belt of wampum used to record history, treaties among the tribes, or treaties with colonists or governments.

Weir: A barricade used to funnel fish toward people who wait to catch them.

Timeline

25,000–11,000 BCE Groups of hunters cross from Asia to Alaska on the Bering Sea Land Bridge, which was formed when lands now under the waters of the Bering Strait were exposed for periods of time, according to scientists.

1400 BCE Along the lower Mississippi, people of the Poverty Point culture are constructing large burial mounds and living in planned communities.

500 BCE The Adena people build villages with burial mounds in the Midwest.

100 BCE Hopewell societies construct massive earthen mounds for burying their dead and possibly other religious purposes.

100 BCE**–400** CE In the Early Basketmaker period, the Anasazi use baskets as containers and cooking pots; they live in caves.

1 CE: Small, permanent villages of the Hohokam tradition emerge in the southwest.

400–700 In the Modified Basketmaker period, Anasazi communities emerge in the Four Corners region of the Southwest. They learn to make pottery in which they can boil beans. They live in underground pits and begin to use bows and arrows. The Anasazi eventually design communities in large multi-roomed apartment buildings, some with more than 1,200 rooms.

700 CE The Mississippian culture begins.

700–1050 The Developmental Pueblo period begins. The Anasazi move into pueblo-type homes above the ground and develop irrigation methods. A great cultural center is established at Chaco Canyon. Anasazi influence spreads to other areas of the Southwest.

800–950 The early Pecos build pit houses.

900 The Mississippian mound-building groups form complex political and social systems, and participate in long-distance trade and an elaborate and widespread religion.

984 The Vikings under Erik the Red first encounter the Inuit of Greenland.

1000–1350 The Iroquois Confederacy is formed among the Mohawk, Oneida, Onondaga, Cayuga, and Seneca nations. The Five Nations of the Haudenosaunee are, from this time, governed by chiefs from the 49 families who were present at the origin of the confederation.

1040 Pueblos (towns) are flourishing in New Mexico's Chaco Canyon. The pueblos are connected by an extensive road system that stretches many miles across the desert.

1050–1300 In the Classic Pueblo period, Pueblo architecture reaches its height with the building of fabulous cliff dwellings; Acoma Pueblo is a well-established city.

1200 The great city of Cahokia in the Mississippi River Valley flourishes.

1250 Zuñi Pueblo is an important trading center for Native peoples from California, Mexico, and the American Southwest.

1300–1700 During the Regressive Pueblo period, the Anasazi influence declines. The people leave their northern homelands, heading south to mix with other cultures.

1350 Moundville, in present-day Alabama, one of the largest ceremonial centers of the Mound Builders, thrives. With twenty great mounds and a village, it is probably the center of a chiefdom that includes several other related communities.

1400s Two tribes unite to start the Wendat Confederacy.

1494 Christopher Columbus begins the enslavement of American Indians, capturing over 500 Taino of San Salvador and sending them to Spain to be sold.

1503 French explorer Jacques Cartier begins trading with Native Americans along the East Coast.

1524 The Abenaki and Narragansett, among other Eastern tribes, encounter the expedition of Giovanni da Verrazano.

1533 Spaniards led by Nuño de Guzmán enter Yaqui territory.

1534 French explorer Jacques Cartier meets the Micmac on the Gaspé Peninsula, beginning a long association between the French and the Micmac.

1539–43 The Spanish treasure hunter Hernando de Soto becomes the first European to make contact with Mississippian cultures; De Soto and Spaniard Francisco Coronado traverse the Southeast and Southwest, bringing with them disease epidemics that kill thousands of Native Americans.

1540 Hernando de Alarcón first encounters the Yuman.

1570 The Spanish attempt to establish a mission in Powhatan territory, but are driven away or killed by the Natives.

1576 British explorer Martin Frobisher first comes into contact with the central Inuit of northern Canada.

1579 Sir Francis Drake encounters the Coast Miwok.

1590 The Micmac force Iroquoian-speaking Natives to leave the Gaspé Peninsula; as a result, the Micmac dominate the fur trade with the French.

1591 Spanish colonization of Pueblo land begins.

1598 Juan de Oñate sets up a Spanish colony and builds San Geronimo Mission at Taos Pueblo. He brings 7000 head of livestock, among them horses.

1602 Spanish explorer Sebastián Vizcaíno encounters the Ohlone.

1607 The British colonists of the Virginia Company arrive in Powhatan territory.

1609 The fur trade begins when British explorer Henry Hudson, sailing for the Netherlands, opens trade in New Netherland (present-day New York) with several Northeast tribes, including the Delaware.

1615 Ottawa meet Samuel de Champlain at Georgian Bay.

1621 Chief Massasoit allies with Pilgrims.

1622 Frenchman Étienne Brûlé encounters the Ojibway at present-day Sault Sainte Marie.

1634–37 An army of Puritans, Pilgrims, Mohican, and Narragansett attacks and sets fire to the Pequot fort, killing as many as 700 Pequot men, women, and children; Massacre at Mystic ends Pequot War and nearly destroys the tribe.

1648–51 The Iroquois, having exhausted the fur supply in their area, attack other tribes in order to get a new supply. The Beaver Wars begin, and many Northeast tribes are forced to move west toward the Great Lakes area.

mid-1600s The Miami encounter Europeans and provide scouts to guide Father Jacques Marquette and Louis Joliet to the Mississippi River.

1651 Colonists establish first Indian reservation near Richmond, Virginia, for what is left of the Powhatans.

1675–76 The Great Swamp Fight during King Philip's War nearly wipes out the tribe and the loss of life and land ends a way of life for New England tribes.

1680 The Hopi, Jemez, Acoma, and other Pueblo groups force the Spanish out of New Mexico in the Pueblo Revolt.

1682 Robert de la Salle's expedition descends the Mississippi River into Natchez territory.

1687 Father Eusebio Francisco Kino begins missionary work among the Tohono O'odham and establishes the first of twenty-eight missions in Yuman territory.

1692 The Spanish begin their reconquest of Pueblo land; Pecos make peace with Spaniards, in spite of protests from some tribe members.

1700 Pierre-Charles le Sueur encounters the Sioux.

1709 John Lawson discovers and writes about the "Hatteras Indians."

1729 French governor Sieur d' Etchéparre demands Natchez land for a plantation; Natchez revolt begins.

1731 The French destroy the Natchez, the last Mississippian culture. Most survivors are sold into slavery in the Caribbean.

1741 Danish-born Russian explorer Vitus Bering sees buildings on Kayak Island that likely belong to the Chugach; he is the first European to reach the Inuit of Alaska.

1760–63 The Delaware Prophet tells Native Americans in the Northeast that they must drive Europeans out of North America and return to the customs of their ancestors. His message influences Ottawa leader Pontiac, who uses it to unite many tribes against the British.

1761 The Potawatomi switch allegiance from the French to the British; they later help the British by attacking American settlers during the American Revolution.

1763 By the Treaty of Paris, France gives Great Britain the Canadian Maritime provinces, including Micmac territory.

1763 England issues the Proclamation of 1763, which assigns all lands west of the Appalachian Mountains to Native Americans, while colonists are allowed to settle all land to the east. The document respects the aboriginal land rights of Native Americans. It is not popular with colonists who want to move onto Indian lands and becomes one of the conflicts between England and the colonies leading to the American Revolution.

1769 The Spanish build their first mission in California. There will be 23 Spanish missions in California, which are used to convert Native Californians to Christianity, but also reduces them to slave labor.

1769–83 Samuel Hearne and Alexander Mackenzie are the first European explorers to penetrate Alaskan Athabascan territory, looking for furs and a route to the Pacific Ocean. Russian fur traders are not far behind.

c. 1770 Horses, brought to the continent by the Spanish in the sixteenth century, spread onto the Great Plains and lead to the development of a new High Plains Culture.

1776 Most Mohawk tribes side with the British during the Revolutionary War under the leadership of Thayendanégea, also known as Joseph Brant.

1778 The Delaware sign the first formal treaty with the United States, guaranteeing their land and allowing them to be the fourteenth state; the treaty is never ratified.

1778 The treaty-making period begins when the first of 370 treaties between Indian nations and the U.S. government is signed.

1786 The first federal Indian reservations are established.

1789 The Spanish establish a post at Nootka Sound on Vancouver Island, the first permanent European establishment in the territory of the Pacific Northwest Coast tribes; Spain and Great Britain vie for control of the area during the Nootka Sound Controversy.

1791 In the greatest Native American defeat of the U.S. Army, the Miami win against General Arthur St. Clair.

1792 Explorer George Vancouver enters Puget Sound; Robert Gray, John Boit and George Vancouver are the first to mention the Chinook.

1805 The Lewis and Clark expedition ecounter the Flathead, Nez Percé, Yakama, Shoshone, Umatilla, Siletz, and are the first to reach Chinook territory by land.

1811 Shawnee settlement of Prophet's Town is destroyed in the Battle of Tippecanoe.

1813 Chief Tecumseh is killed fighting the Americans at Battle of the Thames in the War of 1812.

1816 Violence erupts during a Métis protest over the Pemmican Proclamation of 1814, and twenty-one Hudson's Bay Company employees are killed.

1817 The First Seminole War occurs when soldiers from neighboring states invade Seminole lands in Florida looking for runaway slaves.

1821 Sequoyah's method for writing the Cherokee language is officially approved by tribal leaders.

1827 The Cherokee adopt a written constitution.

1830 The removal period begins when the U.S. Congress passes the Indian Removal Act. Over the course of the next thirty years many tribes from the Northeast and Southeast are removed to Indian Territory in present-day Oklahoma and Kansas, often forcibly and at great expense in human lives.

1831 Some Seneca and Cayuga move to Indian Territory (now Oklahoma) as part of the U.S. government's plan to move Native Americans westward. Other Iroquois groups stand firm until the government's policy is overturned in 1842.

1832 The U.S. government attempts relocation of the Seminole to Indian Territory in Oklahoma, leading to the Second Seminole War.

1838 The Cherokee leave their homeland on a forced journey known as the Trail of Tears.

1846–48 Mexican-American War is fought; San Juan lands become part of U.S. territory.

1847 Another Pueblo rebellion leads to the assassination of the American territorial governor. In retaliation U.S. troops destroy the mission at Taos Pueblo, killing 150 Taos Indians.

1848 Mexico gives northern Arizona and northern New Mexico lands to the United States. Warfare between the Apache people and the U.S. Army begins.

1850 New Mexico is declared a U.S. territory.

1851 Gold Rush begins at Gold Bluff, prompting settlers to take over Native American lands. As emigration of Europeans to the West increases, eleven Plains tribes sign the Treaty of Fort Laramie, which promises annual payments to the tribes for their land.

1851 Early reservations are created in California to protect the Native population from the violence of U.S. citizens. These reservations are inadequate and serve only a small portion of the Native Californians, while others endure continued violence and hardship.

1854 The Treaty of Medicine Creek is signed, and the Nisqually give up much of their land; the treaty also gives Puyallup lands to the U.S. government and the tribe is sent to a reservation.

1858 Prospectors flood into Washoe lands after the Comstock lode is discovered.

1859 American surveyors map out a reservation on the Gila River for the Pima and Maricopa Indians. It includes fields, but no water.

1861 Cochise is arrested on a false charge, and the Apache Wars begin.

1864 At least 130 Southern Arapaho and Cheyenne—many of them women and children—are killed by U.S. Army troops during the Sand Creek Massacre.

1864 The devastating Long Walk, a forced removal from their home-lands, leads the Navajo to a harsh exile at Bosque Redondo.

1867 The United States buys Alaska from Russia for $7.2 million.

1870 The First Ghost Dance Movement begins when Wodzibwob, a Paiute, learns in a vision that a great earthquake will swallow the Earth, and that all Indians will be spared or resurrected within three days of the disaster, returning their world to its state before the Europeans arrived.

1870–90 The Peyote Religion spreads throughout the Great Plains. Peyote (obtained from a cactus plant) brings on a dreamlike feeling that followers believe brings them closer to the spirit world. Tribes develop their own ceremonies, songs, and symbolism, and vow to be trustworthy, honorable, and community-oriented and to follow the Peyote Road.

1871 British Columbia becomes part of Canada; reserve land is set aside for the Nuu-chah-nulth.

1874–75 The Comanche make their last stand; Quanah Parker and his followers are the last to surrender and be placed on a reservation.

1875 The U.S. Army forces the Yavapai and Apache to march to the San Carlos Apache Reservation; 115 die along the way.

1876 The Northern Cheyenne join with the Sioux in defeating General George Custer at the Battle of Little Bighorn.

1876 The Indian Act in Canada establishes an Indian reserve system, in which reserves were governed by voluntary elected band councils. The Act does not recognize Canadian Indians' right to self-government. With the passage of the act, Canadian peoples in Canada are divided into three groups: status Indian, treaty Indian, and non-status Indian. The categories affect the benefits and rights Indians are given by the government.

1877 During the Nez Percé War, Chief Joseph and his people try fleeing to Canada, but are captured by U.S. Army troops.

1879 The Ute kill thirteen U.S. soldiers and ten Indian agency officials, including Nathan Meeker, in a conflict that becomes known as the "Meeker Massacre."

1880s The buffalo on the Great Plains are slaughtered until there are almost none left. Without adequate supplies of buffalo for food, the Plains Indians cannot survive. Many move to reservations.

1884 The Canadian government bans potlatches. The elaborate gift-giving ceremonies have long been a vital part of Pacific Northwest Indian culture.

1886 The final surrender of Geronimo's band marks the end of Apache military resistance to American settlement.

1887 The General Allotment Act (also known as the Dawes Act), is passed by Congress. The act calls for the allotment (parceling out) of tribal lands. Tribes are no longer to own their lands in common in the traditional way. Instead the land is to be assigned to individuals. The head of a family receives 160 acres, and other family members get smaller pieces of land. All Indian lands that are not alloted are sold to settlers.

1888 Ranchers and amateur archaeologists Richard Wetherill and Charlie Mason discover ancient cliff dwellings of the Pueblo people.

1889 The Oklahoma Land Runs open Indian Territory to non-Natives. (Indian Territory had been set aside solely for Indian use.) At noon on April 22, an estimated 50,000 people line up at the boundaries of Indian Territory. They claim two million acres of land. By nightfall, tent cities, banks, and stores are doing business there.

1890 The Second Ghost Dance movement is initiated by Wovoka, a Paiute. It includes many Paiute traditions. In some versions the dance is performed in order to help bring back to Earth many dead ancestors and exterminated game. Ghost Dance practitioners hope the rituals in the movement will restore Indians to their formal state, before the arrival of the non-Native settlers.

1896 Discovery of gold brings hordes of miners and settlers to Alaska.

1897 Oil is discovered beneath Osage land.

1907 With the creation of the state of Oklahoma, the government abolishes the Cherokee tribal government and school system, and the dream of a Native American commonwealth dissolves.

1912 The Alaska Native Brotherhood is formed to promote civil rights issues, such as the right to vote, access to public education, and civil rights in public places. The organization also fights court battles to win land rights.

1916 Ishi, the last Yahi, dies of tuberculosis.

1920 The Canadian government amends the Indian Act to allow for compulsory, or forced, enfranchisement, the process by which Indians have to give up their tribal loyalties to become Canadian citizens. Only 250 Indians had voluntarily become enfranchised between 1857 and 1920.

1924 Congress passes legislation conferring U.S. citizenship on all American Indians. This act does not take away rights that Native Americans had by treaty or the Constitution.

1928 Lewis Meriam is hired to investigate the status of Indian economies, health, and education, and the federal administration of Indian affairs. His report describes the terrible conditions under which Indians are forced to live, listing problems with health care, education, poverty, malnutrition, and land ownership.

1934 U.S. Congress passes the Indian Reorganization Act (IRA), which ends allotment policies and restores some land to Native Americans. The IRA encourages tribes to govern themselves and set up tribal economic corporations, but with the government overseeing their decisions. The IRA also provides more funding to the reservations. Many tribes form tribal governments and adopt constitutions.

1940 Newly opened Grand Coulee Dam floods Spokane land and stops the salmon from running.

1941–45 Navajo Code Talkers send and receive secret messages in their Native language, making a major contribution to the U.S. war effort during World War II.

1942 As hostilities leading to World War II grow, the Iroquois exercise their powers as an independent nation to declare war on Germany, Italy, and Japan.

1946 The Indian Lands Commission (ICC) is created to decide land claims filed by Indian nations. Many tribes expect the ICC to return lost lands, but the ICC chooses to award money instead, and at the value of the land at the time it was lost.

1951 A new Indian Act in Canada reduces the power of the Indian Affairs Office, makes it easier for Indians to gain the right to vote, and helps Indian children enter public schools. It also removes the ban on potlatch and Sun Dance ceremonies.

1954–62 The U.S. Congress carries out its termination policy. At the same time laws are passed giving states and local governments control over tribal members, taking away the tribes' authority to govern themselves. Under the policy of termination, Native Americans lose their special privileges and are treated the same as other U.S. citizens. The tribes that are terminated face extreme poverty and the threat of loss of their community and traditions. By 1961 the government begins rethinking this policy because of the damage it is causing.

1955 The Indian Health Service (IHS) assumes responsibility for Native American health care. The IHS operates hospitals, health centers, health stations, clinics, and community service centers.

1958 Alaska becomes a state; 104 million acres of Native land are taken.

1960 The queen of England approves a law giving status Indians the right to vote in Canada.

1964 The Great Alaska Earthquake and tsunami destroys several Alutiiq villages.

1965 Under the new U.S. government policy, the Self-Determination policy, federal aid to reservations is given directly to Indian tribes and not funneled through the Bureau of Indian Affairs.

1968 Three Ojibway—Dennis Banks, George Mitchell, and Clyde Bellecourt—found the American Indian Movement (AIM) in Minneapolis, Minnesota, to raise public awareness about treaties the federal and state governments violated.

1969 Eighty-nine Native Americans land on Alcatraz Island, a former penitentiary in San Francisco Bay in California. The group calling itself "Indians of All Tribes," claims possession of the island under an 1868 treaty that gave Indians the right to unused federal property on Indian land. Indians of All Tribes occupies the island for 19 months while negotiating with federal officials. They do not win their claim to the island but draw public attention to their cause.

1971 Quebec government unveils plans for the James Bay I hydroelectric project. Cree and Inuit protest the action in Quebec courts.

1971 The Alaska Native Claims Settlement Act (ANCSA) is signed into law. With the act, Alaska Natives give up any claim to nine-tenths of Alaska. In return they are given $962 million and clear title to 44 million acres of land.

1972 Five hundred Native Americans arrive in Washington, D.C., on a march called the Trail of Broken Treaties to protest the government's policies toward Native Americans. The protestors occupy the Bureau of Indian Affairs building for a week, causing considerable damage. They present the government with a list of reforms, but the administration rejects their demands.

1973 After a dispute over Oglala Sioux (Lakota) tribal chair Robert Wilson and his strong-arm tactics at Pine Ridge Reservation, AIM leaders are called in. Wilson's supporters and local authorities arm themselves against protestors, who are also armed, and a ten-week siege begins in which hundreds of federal marshals and Federal Bureau of Investigation (FBI) agents surround the Indian protestors. Two Native American men are shot and killed.

1974 After strong protests and "fish-ins" bring attention to the restrictions on Native American fishing rights in the Pacific Northwest, the U.S. Supreme Court restores Native fishing rights in the case *Department of Game of Washington v. Puyallup Tribe et al.*

1978 U.S. Congress passes legislation called the Tribally Controlled Community College Assistance Act, providing support for tribal colleges, schools of higher education designed to help Native American students achieve academic success and eventually transfer to four-year colleges and universities. Tribal colleges also work with tribal elders and cultural leaders to record languages, oral traditions, and arts in an effort to preserve cultural traditions.

1978 The American Indian Religious Freedom Act is signed. Its stated purpose is to "protect and preserve for American Indians their inherent right of freedom to believe, express, and exercise their traditional religions."

1978 The Bureau of Indian Affairs publishes regulations for the new Federal Acknowledgement Program. This program is responsible for producing a set of "procedures for establishing that an American Indian group exists as an Indian tribe." Many tribes will later discover that these requirements are complicated and difficult to establish.

1982 Canada constitutionally recognizes aboriginal peoples in its new Constitution and Charter of Rights and Freedoms. The Constitution officially divides Canada's aboriginal nations into three designations: the Indian, the Inuit, and the Métis peoples. Native groups feel that the new Constitution does not adequately protect their rights, nor does it give them the right to govern themselves.

1988 The Federal Indian Gambling Regulatory Act of 1988 allows any tribe recognized by the U.S. government to engage in gambling activities. With proceeds from gaming casinos, some tribes pay for health care, support of the elderly and sick, housing, and other improvements, while other tribes buy back homelands, establish scholarship funds, and create new jobs.

1990 Two important acts are passed by U.S. Congress. The Native American Languages Act is designed to preserve, protect, and promote the practice and development of Indian languages. The Graves Protection and Repatriation Act provides for the protection of American Indian grave sites and the repatriation (return) of Indian remains and cultural artifacts to tribes.

1992 Canadians vote against a new Constitution (the Charlotte-town Accord) that contains provisions for aboriginal self-government.

1995 The Iroquois request that all sacred masks and remains of their dead be returned to the tribe; the Smithsonian Institution is the first museum to comply with this request.

1999 A new territory called Nunavut enters the federation of Canada. Nunavut is comprised of vast areas taken from the Northwest Territories and is populated by an Inuit majority. The largest Native land claim in Canadian history, Nunavut is one-fifth of the landmass of Canada, or the size of the combined states of Alaska and Texas. Meaning "Our Land" in the Inukitut (Inuit) language, Nunavut will be primarily governed by the Inuit.

2003 The first official Comanche dictionary is published, compiled entirely by the Comanche people.

2004 Southern Cheyenne Peace Chief W. Richard West Jr. becomes director of the newly opened National Museum of the American Indian in Washington, D.C.

2006 The United Nations censures the United States for reclaiming 60 million acres (90%) of Western Shoshone lands. The federal government uses parts of the land for military testing, open-pit gold mining and nuclear waste disposal. The Shoshone, who have used it for cattle grazing since the Treaty of Ruby Valley in 1863, have repeatedly had their livestock confiscated and fines imposed.

2011 The government gives the Fort Sill Apache 30 acres for a reservation in Deming, New Mexico.

2011 Tacoma Power gives the Skokomish 1,000 acres of land and $11 million.

N

Makah
Skokomish   Duwamish
Puyallup
Nisqually   Lake   Spokane
Umatilla   Colville   Salish   Blackfoot
Chinook   Flathead
                  Yakama
Siletz   Nez   Nakota
                              Percé
                                                        Crow   Lakota
Yurok
Chilula
Hupa   Modoc   Northern   Northern
         Pit River   Northern Paiute   Shoshone   Cheyenne   Arikara
Cahto Maidu   Western   Arapaho
Pomo   Shoshone   Eastern
                                      Shoshone   Pawnee
         Washoe
Miwok
Costanoan   Kawaiisu
         Yahi and Yana
                                                 Ute   Southern
                    Southern Paiute   Cheyenne
Chumash   San Carlos
                                      Anasazi
                              Hopi   Navajo   Pueblo   Kiowa
         Cahuilla   Jemez   Jicarilla
         Luiseño   Mohave   Apache   San Juan Taos
                                                                        Kiowa
                    Yuman   White Mountain Zuñi   Apache
PACIFIC   Yaqui   Acoma
OCEAN   Tohono O'odham   Pecos
                            Pima   Comanche
                                      Chiricahua

California
Great Basin
Great Plains
Northeast
Pacific Northwest
Plateau
Southeast
Southwest

Abenaki

Menominee

Mohawk

Sauk

Iroquois

Fox

Narraganset

Dakota

Wyandot

Pequot

Potawatomi

Wampanoag

Delaware

Hopewell

Miami

Powhatan

Missouri

Shawnee

Mississippian
(Mound Builders)

Lumbee

Osage

Cherokee

Quapaw

Chickasaw

Caddo

Creek

Choctaw

Natchez

Seminole

ATLANTIC
OCEAN

Gulf of Mexico

0   100   200 mi

0   100 200 km

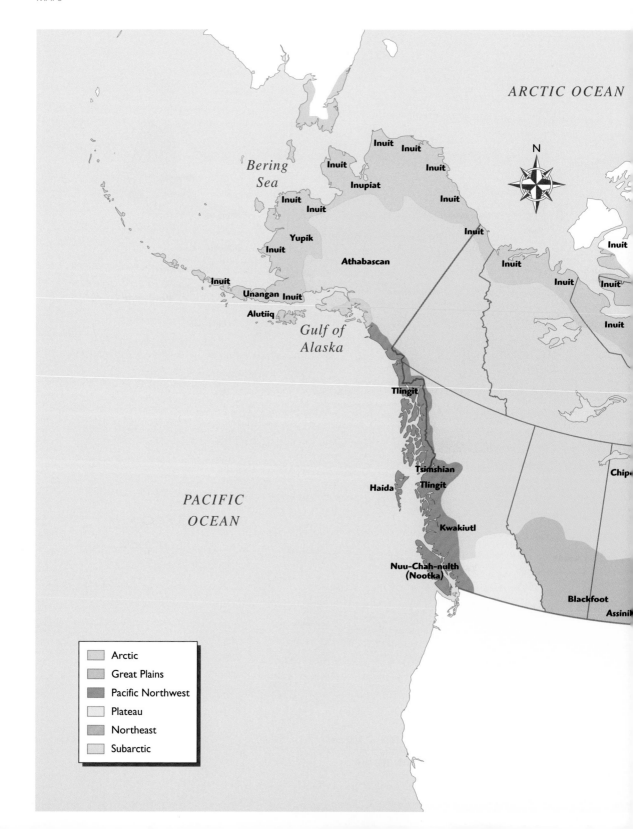

ARCTIC OCEAN

N

Bering Sea

Inuit
Inuit
Inuit
Inuit
Inuit
Inupiat
Inuit
Inuit
Inuit
Inuit
Inuit
Inuit
Inuit
Inuit
Yupik
Inuit
Athabascan
Inuit
Inuit
Inuit
Inuit
Unangan
Inuit
Alutiiq

Gulf of Alaska

Inuit

Tlingit

PACIFIC OCEAN

Tsimshian
Haida
Tlingit

Chipe

Kwakiutl

Nuu–Chah–nulth
(Nootka)

Blackfoot
Assinib

- Arctic
- Great Plains
- Pacific Northwest
- Plateau
- Northeast
- Subarctic

Baffin
Bay

Labrador
Sea

Inuit

Inuit

Inuit

Inuit   Inuit

Inuit

Inuit

Inuit

Inuit   Inuit   Inuit

Inuit

Inuit   Inuit

Inuit

Hudson
Bay

Innu

Cree

ATLANTIC
OCEAN

étis

Micmac

Ojibwa   Algonkin

Ottawa

Huron

Wyandotte

| 0 | 250 | 500 mi |
| 0 | 250 | 500 km |

Southeast

Southeast

The Native tribes of the Southeast region lived in the warm, temperate part of eastern North America where, year after year, sufficient rain fell for reliable agriculture. This includes not only the states east of the Mississippi River and south of the Mason-Dixon Line (the boundary between Pennsylvania and Maryland once used to distinguish between the South and the North), but also west of the Mississippi in Louisiana and considerable portions of Arkansas and Texas. These areas are included in the Southeast region of tribes because the Caddoan and other native peoples who lived in them maintained a lifestyle similar to Native people east of the Mississippi, and quite different from the tribes of the Great Plains to the west.

The Southeast region generally had two types of Native economies. The interior peoples emphasized raising vegetables—corn, beans, and squash—supplemented by hunting and fishing. On the coast, where fish, shellfish, and marine mammals were plentiful, the tribes relied less on farming and more on gathering. Shellfish were a staple, and all around the coast, especially on the Gulf side of the continent, there are enormous mounds of shells discarded by hundreds of generations of coastal Native people.

The interior also contains the remains of great mounds—earthen structures built as ceremonial and political centers. The oral traditions of the Southeastern tribes say that the mound-builders were their ancestors, and in fact the 1540–42 chronicles of the Spanish explorer Hernando de Soto (c. 1496–1542) reveal descriptions of the mounds and the temples built on top of them when they were in regular use. As late as the 1700s, the Natchez Indians, who lived near the present city of Natchez, Mississippi, were still using their mounds and temples.

Coastal Southeastern tribes encounter Europeans

The coastal Native Americans are not as well known as the interior tribes because they were quickly attacked, dispersed, and sometimes enslaved by the invading Europeans, beginning with de Soto. Along with the

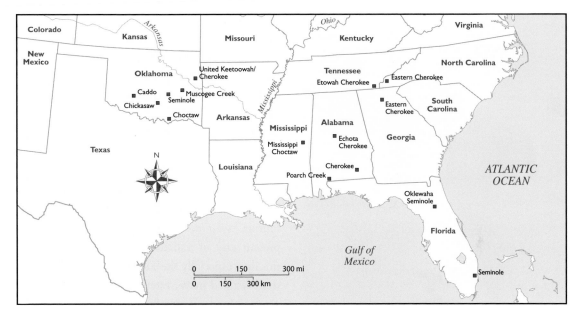

A map of some contemporary Native American communities in the Southeast region. MAP BY XNR PRODUCTIONS. CENGAGE LEARNING, GALE. REPRODUCED BY PERMISSION OF GALE, A PART OF CENGAGE LEARNING.

violence they met, they rapidly became victims of deadly European diseases to which they had no natural resistance. When de Soto entered Florida searching for gold, he brought with him chains and manacles for enslaving Natives to serve as porters (who were forced to carry the Spaniards' gear) and as concubines (women who were forced to serve as sexual partners and to take care of domestic tasks for de Soto's men). As they marched through Georgia, Alabama, and Mississippi, de Soto's soldiers killed thousands of Native people; however, the Natives fought back. In a well-coordinated night attack in 1541, the Chickasaw and their allies burned Spanish dwellings, destroying much of the European's equipment and running off their horses. After wandering through Arkansas and Texas, de Soto died on the banks of the Mississippi River in 1542, leaving his men to flee down the river toward the Gulf of Mexico, pursued by thousands of angry Natives in canoes.

Farther north, British colonists also tried to enslave Natives, not as porters and concubines, but to work on their plantations. This attempt was unsuccessful, since the Native workers could easily escape to join their own or other tribes in the interior. So in the eighteenth century, the remaining Native slaves were sold or traded to Jamaica and other Caribbean islands and

A watercolor titled Village of Secoton *by John White gives an idea of the way of life that developed throughout the Southeast prior to European contact in the 1500s.* ©THE ART ARCHIVE/BRITISH MUSEUM/ EILEEN TWEEDY.

were replaced by African slaves, who were more easily identified as slaves because of their skin color.

Around the mouth of the Mississippi River, the initial European presence was French. French traders acquired furs and other goods that were sent down the Mississippi and back to France. The French also established plantations on both sides of the Mississippi upriver toward the present city of Memphis, Tennessee. In the meantime, the Spanish had mobilized many of the Florida Natives into a line of missions from St. Augustine, Florida, west across the peninsula toward the present city of Tallahassee. The tribes south of this line, especially the Timucua and Calusa, were so devastated by warfare and disease that the survivors joined other tribes or migrated to Cuba or other Caribbean islands. The three European powers—Great Britain, France, and Spain—then contested for control of the Southeast region from the middle 1600s until the United States took over the area in the beginning of the nineteenth century. At the same time, the coastal tribes were caught up in the European struggle for control of "Greater Florida," which included everything south of Virginia and west to Alabama.

Interior Southeast tribes

While the Europeans fought for control of the coastal areas, the interior tribes were reorganizing to face them. The northernmost interior tribe was the Cherokee, related historically to the Iroquois of New York, who at some point had migrated to the Appalachian Mountains. Living in the interior valleys of the Great Smoky Mountains, the Cherokee and their mountains got in the way of the southward expansion of British colonies in the eighteenth century, so the coastal region was settled first.

The "fall line" of the major rivers is an important concept for understanding the history of this period. Coastal boats and some oceangoing vessels could only travel up the coastal rivers until they reached a waterfall or rapids. The locations of these falls in the various streams, connected together by a fall line on a map, essentially defined the areas where Europeans could live successfully, because they needed a dock to receive supplies and to ship out their agricultural produce. Upstream from the fall line, trade goods and produce had to be carried in packs or on horseback, so this area was left to the Native peoples. In the early colonial period, then, the Cherokee occupied the area above the fall line in what are present-day North Carolina and Tennessee.

Social and political organization

The interior tribes shared a social and political structure that was useful for integrating their societies and creating alliances with other tribes. The essential building block of the tribes was the matrilineal clan (a group of extended family members who trace their descent through the mother's line). All tribal members received their clan identity from their mother, and tribal law declared that one's mother and father had to be from different clans. Alliances among towns, and also among the different nations of the interior, were often based on intermarriage.

The Native tribes of the interior tended to locate their villages along streams and rivers, needing access to water for drinking and bathing as well as for transportation in dugout canoes where possible. Villages were arranged around a ceremonial center. The center was usually an outdoor square surrounded by four arbors, with a large, enclosed roundhouse on one side that served for tribal meetings and sometimes as a refuge during cold weather. Log houses with small gardens were located near the center. Around the village were large cultivated fields, some of which belonged to families, whereas others, called "town fields," were cultivated for the benefit of the whole village. Periodically the entire village moved when local soil and other resources had been depleted.

The interior tribes had elaborate military organizations. Typically, war leaders were assigned ferocious military titles, which were carried as personal names. For example, a principal chief of the Cherokee from the late 1990s into the early 2000s was Wilma Mankiller (1945–2010), who bears a personal name derived from a military title. As a Southeastern warrior gained more experience and performed brave deeds, he was awarded higher and more prestigious titles and given the responsibility of leading war expeditions.

Adopting new members into tribes

Wars inevitably created refugees, and although all Southeastern tribes occasionally adopted such people, this became a matter of national policy with the Creek Indians. Under the rules of the Creek Confederacy, families, villages, and even whole tribes could be adopted and take up residence with the Creek. The remnants of the Calusa, Timucua, Yamasee, and later the Natchez were taken in as individuals and families. Larger groups of Alabama, Coushatta, and Hitchiti were given the status of clans or towns, depending on size, whereas multiple villages of the Yuchi and Shawnee were taken in so that they became "nations within nations," but subject to the laws of the confederacy.

Similarly, people of European and African ancestry acquired citizenship in some Native nations of the Southeast. In early colonial times, European indentured servants broke the bonds of servitude by "running away to join the Indians." Later, African American slaves escaped to form "Freedman" communities among the villages of Southeastern tribes.

One special circumstance among the Creek was the birth of the Seminole nation. Originally constituting the southernmost villages of Creek in southern Alabama and Georgia, the Seminole experienced a large increase in population when they took in refugees from the Creek Wars of the early nineteenth century. Migrating farther into the Florida peninsula when the Spanish withdrew, they became a separate nation and are the ancestors of the present-day Seminole of Oklahoma and Florida.

Languages in the Southeast region

The Creek and Seminole both speak languages that are quite different from the Cherokee language, which is part of the Iroquoian family of languages. The Creek and Seminole, along with the Choctaw, Chickasaw, Alabama, and several other Southeastern tribes, speak dialects from the most prominent language family of the Southeast, the Muskogean family. Besides the Muskogean family and the Iroquoian, other language families represented in the Southeast region include Caddoan, Algonquian, and Siouan, as well as four languages that are not related to a language family. Some scholars believe that the Southeast region probably represents the ancient homeland of the Siouan peoples, who migrated north and west in prehistoric times, finally spilling out onto the Plains as Lakota and Dakota people.

The Choctaw and Chickasaw were originally one people, and the languages are still only dialectically different. Sometime in the late prehistoric period, according to oral tradition, the Chickasaw withdrew from their brethren in central and southern Mississippi and Alabama, and established themselves as traders in the area south of present-day Memphis, Tennessee. From that location, they traded up and down the Mississippi River, dominating other groups not only by their economic power, but also with their military power. As a disciplined, well-organized military force, the Chickasaw not only defeated de Soto in 1541 but also repulsed an Iroquois attack and a French invasion in later years. Their automobile license plates still proclaim them to be the "Unconquered Chickasaws."

Trade and other relations

As soon as European trade goods became available in the seventeenth century, the Chickasaw allied with the British, establishing a busy trade route toward the east, just north of Creek territory in Alabama and Georgia. The Choctaw, on the other hand, established trade relations with the French in New Orleans and allied with them in wars against the Chickasaw, the Creek, and other tribes of the vicinity.

The Choctaw, who were much more numerous than the Chickasaw, were never able to unite themselves as strongly as the other Southeastern tribes, largely because of geographical problems. The watersheds of the Pearl and Tombigbee Rivers contain numerous swamps, which divided the Choctaw towns from one another and made it difficult for them to act collectively in war or politics.

West of the Mississippi, the Quapaw, or Arkansaw Indians, are often included as part of the Southeast Region, as are the Caddo of the west and the various tribes of Louisiana, notably the Houma and Chitimacha. The Quapaw are a small tribe whose cultural relationships are with the Osage and Kansa to the northwest. The Caddo and their ancestors built mounds in earlier times and relied on agriculture, like other Southeastern peoples, but later they lived in earthen lodges, kept horses, and hunted buffalo, although still maintaining their corn fields. Their cultural relationships were with the Wichita and Arikara to the north.

Two tribes that moved around in this period were the Shawnee, sometimes considered as part of the Northeast Region, and the Alabama. Originally located on the Savannah River, the Shawnee for a time occupied the area of Kentucky. Then, some of the Shawnee towns joined the Creek Confederacy. Later, the Shawnee preceded the other Southeastern nations westward, ultimately coming to occupy reservations in

Oklahoma and Kansas. The Alabama and the Coushatta, in early historic times, occupied the area near the mouth of the Alabama River, where they were strongly allied with the French. After the French withdrawal, the Alabama and Coushatta towns migrated singly toward the west, coming to rest in Louisiana and Texas, although several towns joined the Creek Confederacy.

Traders and mixed bloods

As soon as there were Europeans in North America, there were traders. Most were British traders who traveled among the Native nations, bartering guns, knives, and kettles for furs, deerskins, and other products of the forest. Some of these men married the daughters of chiefs. Their offspring became members of a newly created mixed-blood aristocracy, which is still important in the culture and politics of the Southeastern Native nations. Familiar with the ways of the Europeans, and most often bilingual in English and a native language, the mixed-bloods came to dominate trade. They soon established farms and ranches in their tribal areas and hired their own people as workers or purchased African slaves from the colonies. The status of African American people within the nation was always a source of political dispute.

Although one might expect that mixed bloods in the various nations would be sympathetic toward European interests, this was not always the case. Some of the most militant Native leaders had European ancestry, including John Ross (1790–1866) of the Cherokee and Alexander McGillivray (1750–1793) of the Creek. Such leaders were instrumental in navigating their nations through the treaty period, when the interior tribes gradually gave up land in exchange for peace and the benefits of trade.

Land crises

A crisis point was reached in the Southeast region just after 1800, when the Native nations were crowded onto small parcels of land and surrounded by a steadily increasing number of land-hungry settlers. By that time, each of the interior nations had matched its own army and defenses against those of the United States and been forced to withdraw farther into the interior. The Cherokee had been defeated in 1794 and the Creek in 1814. The Chickasaw were firm U.S. allies, but the Choctaw were in political disarray after their French sponsors withdrew from North America upon the Louisiana Purchase of 1803.

By this time, the Native populations had been devastated, but there were still enough warriors available to cause some worry on the part of the U.S. government. By 1800, the Cherokee numbered about twenty-five thousand persons, the Creek about the same, the Choctaw twenty thousand, and the Chickasaw about three thousand.

Indian Removal Act and Indian Territory

Even including wars and disease, perhaps the most traumatic injury inflicted on the Southeastern tribes was the passage of the Indian Removal Act in 1830. Although negated by a ruling of the U.S. Supreme Court, the act was nonetheless implemented by President Andrew Jackson (1767–1845; served 1829–37) on behalf of the land-hungry frontier people who had elected him to office. The federal government demanded that Eastern and Midwestern tribal groups be moved to an area west of the Mississippi River. The administration set aside an area in what is now Oklahoma for Native settlement that came to be known as Indian Territory.

Although all Native American people removed to Indian Territory suffered death and disease along the "Trail of Tears" in the period 1831 to 1848, some groups suffered more than others. The least affected tribe was probably the Chickasaw, who were by that time a highly integrated and sophisticated group with important allies in the federal government. Anticipating the certainty of removal, they explored Indian Territory, the eastern half of what is now Oklahoma, and selected an area at the western edge of the territory where they could establish themselves as traders with the Plains Indians while farming and ranching along the creeks and rivers near what is now Tishomingo, Oklahoma. After a period of thoughtful negotiations with the federal government, they made an orderly migration in 1837.

The Choctaw were a much larger group and politically divided among themselves about whether to resist removal or not, and if they did emigrate, which lands they wanted to occupy in Indian Territory. The mixed-blood elite wanted to occupy lowlands along the Red River where they could take their slaves and start plantations. Ordinary Choctaw wanted to occupy the rolling hills farther north where they could establish small family farms. For the entire decade of the 1830s, each Choctaw town was embroiled in controversy and, although Choctaw migration began in 1831, it did not end until 1847. Many Choctaw avoided removal by retreating to the hills and valleys of Mississippi.

The Creek essentially formed two factions, the mixed-blood elite on the one hand and the ordinary Creek and their Freedman allies on the other hand. The elite proceeded to move in wagons with their slaves and supporters to organize plantations near the Arkansas River, while the other or "traditional" faction built family farms and ceremonial grounds farther south and west.

This kind of factionalism between "traditionals" and "mixed-bloods" was even more emphatic and much more complicated among the Cherokee, who were split among regional as well as class, clan, and marriage alliances. Treaties between the Cherokee and the U.S. government had promised the Cherokee a permanent homeland and self-government on that part of their ancestral territory that was located in Georgia. When faced with the prospect of losing their rights and lands, the Cherokee Nation sued in federal court. Having important friends in the federal government and among the Christian clergy, they fully expected to win their case before the Supreme Court and stay in the East. When President Jackson sent federal troops to remove the Cherokee by force, they were not ready to go. Many were dragged from their houses by soldiers and set on the road to walk 600 miles (1,000 kilometers) to Indian Territory. Thousands of Cherokee and other Native peoples, especially the very young and very old—died along the way.

The special targets of Indian Removal were those Native people occupying desirable farmland or areas with mineral resources. After they had been removed, the government became less thorough in searching for the remaining Natives in rough, mountainous terrain. Several thousand Cherokee hid in the Great Smoky Mountains, feeding themselves from small gardens. They gradually emerged from their hiding over the next several decades. In Mississippi the pattern was the same, and the Choctaw were recognized by the federal government in 1918. In addition, other small groups of Native American people had avoided removal because they occupied state reservations, such as the Catawba in South Carolina, or because they were so dispersed into the general population, as were the Lumbee of North Carolina.

The Seminole were a special case. Living in the wetlands of Florida at the time other groups were being removed, they occupied land that was not especially desired and, therefore, might not have been subjected to any forced removal. The Seminole continued to open their community to escaped slaves. To those who benefited from the slave system, this was intolerable, so a series of federal armies invaded the Seminole

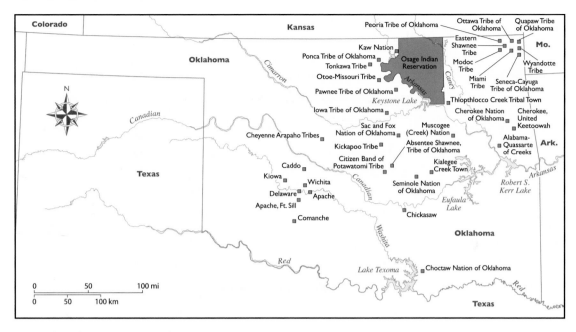

A map of Oklahoma reservations today. MAP BY XNR PRODUCTIONS. CENGAGE LEARNING, GALE. REPRODUCED BY PERMISSION OF GALE, A PART OF CENGAGE LEARNING.

between 1830 and 1845. The Seminole turned the forces back and inflicted great casualties on the U.S. troops, finally forcing the federal government to pay off certain bands to remove themselves to Indian Territory, whereas other bands were left in peace in Florida, such the Chickasaw, still unconquered.

Life and culture after removal

In Indian Territory, the Southeastern nations were reorganized, although in different ways. For the Cherokee, the struggle was over a national government as different factions contested for power. The elite struggled against the emerging traditional or "Keetowah faction," and they quarreled among themselves in other complex ways. The polarization of the Creek continued, with periodic outbreaks and protests of the traditional faction during the Green Peach War (1882–83) and the Crazy Snake Rebellion (1897–98). The traditional Choctaw, living in the eastern Oklahoma hills, essentially abandoned the federally sponsored tribal government and left it to the mixed-blood elite. The Chickasaw remained united, but increasingly married and mixed with the local white population. The Seminole tenaciously maintained the chief-and-band political system they had developed in Florida.

The Southeastern tribes in Indian Territory adopted plows instead of hoes for agriculture, and they raised increasing numbers of horses, cattle, and hogs. Their diet and economy improved, and their populations multiplied. Solicited by Christian missionaries, they experienced patterns of conversion that reflected their political structure. The Creek traditionalists became Baptists, whereas the elite became Methodists. The traditional Choctaw became convinced, teetotalist (not drinking any alcohol) Methodists, while the elite Choctaw joined a variety of Protestant denominations in the small towns. The Keetowah (traditional) Cherokee remained non-Christian and even took to burning Christian churches and punishing anyone who became baptized.

Southeast Native nations today

After settling in Indian Territory or back in their eastern homes, the Southeast Native nations faced more disruptions at the hands of inconsistent government policy. The American Civil War (1861–65; a war between the Union [the North], which was opposed to slavery, and the Confederacy [the South], which was in favor of slavery) forced an adjustment of reservation boundaries, depending on whether a group had sided with the Confederacy or the Union. More traumatic was the government's allotment policy. The 1887 General Allotment Act (also known as the Dawes Act) required that communally held tribal land be partitioned into lots owned by individuals. The Curtis Act of 1898 dismantled tribal governments in Oklahoma. On the brighter side, the Indian Reorganization Act (1934) and the corresponding Oklahoma Indian Welfare Act of 1836 brought some civil rights and religious freedom to Native Americans, although the constitutional Bill of Rights was not extended to Native American citizens until 1968. In the last several decades, tribal governments have received federal funds, so that they can supply social services to their citizens. Some tribes have benefited by sponsoring casinos, bingo halls, or other gaming facilities.

Meanwhile, the eastern remnants of recognized Southeastern tribes have become more organized and have likewise attracted federal funds. In addition, new groups have emerged and sought formal acknowledgment from the federal government. The Office of Federal Acknowledgement of the Bureau of Indian Affairs has a list of more than twenty groups located in the Southeast region that claim ancestry among the aboriginal tribes of the area, and who seek official recognition of their status. And so, after a long period of hardship and oppression, the immediate prospects of the descendants of the aboriginal tribes of the Southeast region seemed brighter in the 2000s. Not only were there more Native people than there have been since the seventeenth century, but also more tribes.

BOOKS

Bartram, William, and Gregory A. Waselkov. *William Bartram on the Southeastern Indians.* Lincoln: University of Nebraska Press, 2002.

Braund, Kathryn E. Holland. *Indians of the Greater Southeast: Historical Archaeology and Ethnohistory.* New York: Southern Historical Association, 2002.

Brown, Virginia Pounds, Laurella Owens and Nathan Glick. *The World of the Southern Indians: Tribes, Leaders, and Customs from Prehistoric Times to the Present.* Montgomery, AL: NewSouth Books, 2011.

Crawford, James M., ed. *Studies in Southeastern Indian Languages.* Athens: University of Georgia Press, 1975.

Doherty, Craig A. *Southeast Indians.* Minneapolis, MN: Chelsea House, 2007.

Foreman, Grant. *Indian Removal.* Norman: University of Oklahoma Press, 1972.

Frank, Andrew K. *Creeks and Southerners: Biculturalism on the Early American Frontier.* Lincoln: University of Nebraska Press, 2005.

Green, Michael D., and Theda Perdue. *The Columbia Guide to American Indians of the Southeast.* New York: Columbia University Press, 2001.

Hobson, Geary, Janet McAdams, and Kathryn Walkiewicz, eds. *The People Who Stayed: Southeastern Indian Writing after Removal.* Norman: University of Oklahoma Press, 2010.

Hrdlicka, Ales. *The Anthropology of Florida.* Classics Southeast Archaeology. Tuscaloosa: University Alabama Press, 2007.

Hudson, Charles. *The Southeastern Indians.* Knoxville: University of Tennessee Press, 1976.

Johnson, Michael. *American Indians of the Southeast.* Oxford: Osprey Publishing, 1995.

Kelton, Paul. *Epidemics and Enslavement: Biological Catastrophe in the Native Southeast, 1492–1715.* Lincoln: University of Nebraska Press, 2007.

Kniffen, Fred B., Hiram F. Gregory, and George A. Stokes. *The Historic Indian Tribes of Louisiana.* Baton Rouge: Louisiana State University Press, 1987.

Lacquement, Cameron H., ed. *Architectural Variability in the Southeast.* Tuscaloosa: University of Alabama Press, 2007.

McEwan, Bonnie G., ed. *Indians of the Greater Southeast: Historical Archaeology and Ethnohistory.* Gainesville, FL: University Press of Florida, 2000.

Paredes, J. Anthony, ed. *Indians of the Southeastern United States in the Late 20th Century.* Tuscaloosa: University of Alabama Press, 1992.

Peterson, Herman A. *The Trail of Tears: An Annotated Bibliography of Southeastern Indian Removal.* Lanham, MD: Scarecrow Press, 2011.

Porter, Kenneth W. *The Black Seminoles.* Gainesville: University Press of Florida, 1996.

Wallis, Michael, and Wilma P. Mankiller. *Mankiller: A Chief and Her People.* St. Martin's Press, 1994.

Waselkov, Gregory A., Peter H. Wood, and Tom Hatley. *Powhatan's Mantle: Indians in the Colonial Southeast.* Lincoln: University of Nebraska Press, 2006.

Wright, Muriel H. *A Guide to the Indian Tribes of Oklahoma.* Norman: University of Oklahoma Press, 1951.

Caddo

Name

The name Caddo is an abbreviation of the Caddoan word *Kadohadacho*, meaning "the real chiefs." The term comes from the word *Kaadi* (chief) and designates not only the Caddo people but the Caddoan language family, the original group of twenty-five tribes within the Caddo Nation, and the lands they occupied.

Location

Groups of Caddo lived in parts of Arkansas, Louisiana, Oklahoma, and Texas, with the Red River valley as the center of their territory. Present-day Caddo live in Oklahoma (near Fort Cobb and Fort El Reno) and in other southwest-central states.

Population

In the 1700s, there were about 8,000 people from Caddo nations, including about 2,500 Caddo, 3,000 Hasinai, and 1,800 Natchitoches (the three main tribes in the Caddo Nation). By 1910, their numbers had dropped due to diseases, warfare, and removal to only 452. In the 1990, U.S. Census, 2,935 people identified themselves as Caddo; an additional 49 people identified themselves as Oklahoma Caddo. In 1998, the Caddo Tribe of Oklahoma claimed 3,200 enrolled members. The 2000 census recorded 2,768 Caddo living in the United States. These statistics differ somewhat from the official roll of the Caddo Nation, which in 2006 listed 4,774 members. The Oklahoma Indian Affairs Commission listed total tribal enrollment as 5,757 in 2011.

Language family

Caddoan.

Origins and group affiliations

Most experts agree that the Caddo Nation lived in the Red River region since at least 800 CE, if not longer. The nation consisted of about

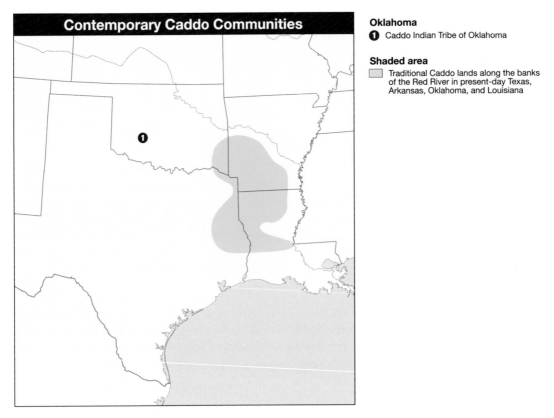

Contemporary Caddo Communities

Oklahoma
❶ Caddo Indian Tribe of Oklahoma

Shaded area
Traditional Caddo lands along the banks of the Red River in present-day Texas, Arkansas, Oklahoma, and Louisiana

A map of contemporary Caddo communities. MAP BY XNR PRODUCTIONS. CENGAGE LEARNING, GALE. REPRODUCED BY PERMISSION OF GALE, A PART OF CENGAGE LEARNING.

twenty-five tribes with similar languages and cultures that lived along the Red and Arkansas Rivers in present-day Oklahoma, Texas, Louisiana, and Arkansas. Until they were removed from their homelands in the nineteenth century, the groups were not united and operated mostly on their own. The three powerful members of the Caddo confederacies were the Hasinai, the Natchitoches, and the Kadohadacho, or Caddo proper.

The Caddo lived comfortable lives as farmers and livestock tenders in the beautiful, fertile lands along the Red River before Europeans arrived in their lands. According to their tribal history, they had lived in this same place since the beginning of time. After the Europeans arrived, the Caddo became embroiled in three centuries of disputes. Through it all, the Caddo remained true to their treaties and to their traditions. Although brave when they had to fight, they preferred to live in peace.

HISTORY

Before Europeans

Early writings about the Caddo describe the people as "industrious, intelligent, sociable, and lively; courageous and brave in war, and faithful to their … word." These records also told of the friendly welcome the Caddo extended to European visitors, giving them the best food and places to sleep.

The Caddo built their homes, temples, and burial mounds in villages with central open areas for social gatherings and ceremonies. These were the villages found by the first Europeans who explored their region.

Around the mid-1500s, the Caddo acquired horses from other tribes who had gotten them from Spanish explorers. They learned to hunt buffalo on the western Plains. This changed Caddo life, and the tribe adopted some traits of the Plains cultures (see Great Plains entries). They became skilled horsemen and hunted farther west than ever before.

Relations with Europeans

In 1541, when the Spanish explorer Hernando de Soto (c. 1496–1542) led his treasure-hunting expedition into Caddo territory, the tribe controlled lands in Louisiana, Arkansas, Texas, and parts of Oklahoma. Yet de Soto did not mention in his journals that he had seen the Caddo people. When the French explorer René-Robert Cavelier de La Salle (1643–1687) arrived in 1686, he began a French association with the Caddo that lasted until 1762.

From the beginning of their arrival in Caddo territory, France and Spain vied for control of the land and its people. The French sought to do this by trading and giving gifts, whereas the Spanish felt the best way to control the people was to convert them to the Catholic faith. The Caddo preferred the French approach and established friendly relations with them, thwarting initial Spanish efforts to control the tribe.

Important Dates

1714: The French found a trading post in Caddo territory and begin a half-century of control.

1763: The Spanish take control of Caddo territory.

1803: The United States takes control of Caddo territory with Louisiana Purchase.

1835: A treaty gives more Caddo territory to the United States; some Caddo move to Texas, where a reservation is established for them in 1846.

1859: The Caddo relocate to Indian Territory to escape murderous white Texans.

1938: The Caddo organize as the Caddo Tribe of Oklahoma.

1963: The Caddo, Delaware, and Wichita tribes are given land in Oklahoma, which the three tribes now hold in common.

1976: The tribe amends original constitution and bylaws.

2002: Name of the tribe is changed to the Caddo Nation of Oklahoma.

Between 1714 and 1719, the French built several trading posts and forts along the Red River. The Caddo learned to speak the French language, and the French developed a great respect for the tribe. Troubles back in Europe distracted the French, though, and they never succeeded in building the Louisiana territory or attracting settlers. The war that raged between France and Spain in Europe carried over into Caddo territory. Caddo villages became European forts, and European soldiers marched along Caddo trails. The Native people suffered and died from European diseases; survivors were sometimes forced to abandon their villages.

In 1763, France ceded Louisiana to Spain, and the Caddo came under Spanish control. The Caddo were angry at being "given away" by the French as if they were cattle and threatened to resist Spanish control. The Spanish were quick to realize that they had to adopt French ways of dealing with the Caddo. They built up a relationship based on trade, the giving of gifts, better treatment, and friendship with the Caddo. The relationship between the Caddo and the Spanish did not last long, however.

Under U.S. control

Caddo territory passed into the hands of the United States with the Louisiana Purchase of 1803, in which France sold to the United States territory extending from the Mississippi River to the Rocky Mountains, an area that doubled the area of the United States. The Caddo were enthusiastic about the change, not because they disliked the French or the Spanish, but because the Americans paid more for furs. The U.S. government continued the policies of their European predecessors by giving the Caddo gifts, and they promised that no Americans would settle on their lands.

Meanwhile other tribes from the East were being driven out of their lands by American settlers, who never seemed to have enough land to satisfy them. In the 1820s, the U.S. government allowed small groups of displaced Native peoples to settle on Caddo lands. At first, the Caddo did not object—they wanted the cooperation of the Choctaw, Delaware, and Cherokee against the Osage (see entries), who raided Caddo hunting expeditions and camps, stole horses, and killed Caddo people. But the Caddo did object when the U.S. government worked out a treaty in 1825 that required thousands of Native peoples from many different tribes to move onto Caddo lands and become part of the Caddo nation.

Next settlers set their sights on Caddo lands and moved there, even though it was against the law. The game supplies in their traditional hunting territory were now seriously depleted, and the Caddo population was decreasing due to war and disease. For the first time, Caddo people thought about moving away from their ancient villages.

The Caddo sell their homeland

The Caddo signed a treaty with the United States in 1835, selling about one million acres of land in Louisiana for $80,000 worth of cash and goods. They agreed to move within one year—at their own expense—to land outside the boundaries of the United States, never to return.

Some Caddo joined their relatives in Texas, which was then part of Mexico. In the 1820s, Mexico invited American settlers to move to Texas because it was sparsely populated. By the mid-1830s, those settlers were revolting against Mexican rule. Before more Caddo could move to Texas, settlers there asked the U.S. government to prohibit Native movement to the territory. They feared that angry tribes who had been forced out of their homelands would band together to fight against Americans in Texas.

Short residence in Texas

By 1836, the settlers had won control of Texas. Some Caddo joined the Texas Cherokee, who battled the Texans in 1839 and lost. A series of peace treaties followed, the last being the Council Springs Treaty (1846) between the Caddo and the U.S. government. In exchange for "perpetual peace," the Caddo agreed to move to a Texas reservation.

The Caddo lived peacefully on the reservation for a short time, but Texans' resentment and hostility toward all tribes grew stronger. In 1858, white men attacked a group of Native peoples who were grazing their horses. The U.S. government decided to move the Caddo to Indian Territory for their own safety. (Indian Territory was the land that now forms most of the state of Oklahoma.) During the 1800s, many tribes were moved to Indian Territory as part of a government plan to make the area into a state governed by those tribes.

Texans did not think the government was acting quickly enough to rid the state of its Native population, and they threatened to massacre every person on the Caddo reservation. To avoid such a tragedy, Indian Superintendent Robert S. Neighbors (1815–1859) hurriedly took 1,500 people from the reservation across the Red River in the scorching heat of the summer of 1859. In fifteen days, they marched to what would become the new Caddo County along the Washita River in Oklahoma. There the Wichita Agency and Reservation was established near Fort Cobb. (The Wichita were Caddoan speakers.) Superintendent Neighbors was murdered when he returned to Texas.

Settling in Oklahoma

At the Wichita Reservation, the Caddo cultivated land and built homes. Other settlers soon cast their eyes on Indian Territory, demanding that it be opened up for settlement. The U.S. government gave up efforts to keep settlers out of the territory. In 1887, the government passed a law that divided tribal land into 160-acre parcels, one parcel for each family. Instead of tribes cultivating their land as a community, as was traditional, families had to farm their own parcels. This policy, called allotment, was intended to turn the people into farmers so they could assimilate, or become more like American society. After the parcels had been allotted, the leftover land was opened to settlers. Thousands of acres of Native land passed into the hands of settlers in the early 1900s.

The Caddo managed to retain much of their culture throughout the allotment period, which lasted until the 1930s. At that point, the U.S. government concluded that allotment was not working. It passed laws to end the policy, to restore lands to the various tribes, and to organize their governments so tribes would oversee themselves. The Caddo organized in 1938 as the Caddo Tribe of Oklahoma. In 1963, land in Oklahoma was restored to the Caddo, Wichita, and Delaware tribes. The land, jointly owned by the three tribes, was a 487-acre reservation spread throughout Grady, Canadian, and Caddo counties.

RELIGION

Traditional beliefs and practices

The Caddo worshipped a Great Spirit they called Ayanat Caddi ("the great captain"), as well as many spirits and powers, including the sun, the moon, and animal spirits. They believed that long ago the Great Spirit placed a family (carrying corn and pumpkin seeds) near a lake in Caddo territory, and from that family sprang all the Caddo people.

According to Caddo belief, everything in nature had power for both good and evil. Natural forces had to be kept happy so they would not turn their powers against the tribe.

The religious leader of the community was a high priest known as the *xinesi* (pronounced *che-ne-see* or *hee-ne-see*), who informed the people of the wishes of the spirits. The xinesi conducted ceremonies, maintained the temple, and performed religious services. Fire was especially sacred to the Caddo, and a perpetual fire was kept burning in the temple, tended by the xinesi.

Because fire was an important part of the Caddo religion, each house also kept a sacred fire burning at all times. The Caddo built these fires by placing four logs in the shape of a cross, pointing north, south, east, and west. As the ends of the wood closest to the fire burned, families pushed the logs toward the center. Fire symbolized the sun, or highest god.

Native religions

The Caddo began performing the Ghost Dance in 1890. The Ghost Dance was a revitalization movement that had arisen in the 1870s to return to traditional lifestyles. Ghost Dance practitioners hoped to bring back the buffalo and their dead ancestors and to free the continent from the white invaders. The Caddo held the Ghost Dance two or three times a year, usually during the summer months. They composed songs, often after being in trances, to use as prayers that the world would become as fruitful and peaceful as it had been in the past.

Meanwhile, a man named John Wilson (c. 1840–1901) was spreading the Peyote (pronounced *pay-OH-tee*) religion among the Caddo and other Native groups. (Peyote is a cactus plant that causes hallucinations when chewed or eaten.) Wilson was of mixed Delaware, Caddo, and French parentage but considered himself Caddo and spoke only that language. He claimed to have had several visions while under the influence of peyote, and these visions allegedly revealed the "rightway" for the people to worship Jesus Christ. According to Wilson, those who followed the Peyote Road would be set free from their sins.

A Caddo named Enoch Hoag (c. 1856–1920) served as Wilson's assistant and then developed his own version of Wilson's Big Moon Peyote ceremony. Hoag began a thirty-year reign as a Caddo chief in 1896.

Religion today

The Baptists started missions after the Caddo moved to the Oklahoma reservation, and they still maintain an Indian Baptist Church there. Later, both the Episcopalians and Catholics established missions.

In the early twenty-first century, many Caddo belonged to various Christian denominations, whereas others belong to the Native American Church.

LANGUAGE

Many tribes spoke varieties of the Caddoan language, including the Wichita and the Pawnee (see entry). The Caddo were the southernmost tribe speaking the language. They also used a sign language, and many Caddo spoke several different dialects to communicate with other tribes.

The Hasinai language has two distinct forms: a common form used in ceremonial songs and a prayer language that only a few Caddo men now living in Oklahoma still use. Since the 1970s, the common form of Hasinai has been taught outside the home in places such as the Caddo Tribal Complex in Oklahoma.

GOVERNMENT

The Caddo Nation consisted of twenty-five small, loosely organized groups with similar languages and cultures. The Caddo had not united as a people before the government removed them from their homelands in the nineteenth century. Each tribe remained independent of the others.

Village leadership and power passed through the mother, making it a matrilineal society. Several officials, led by the xinesi, or priest, ruled each tribe. Beneath the priest were the *caddi* (the village headmen or chiefs) and the *canahas* (subchiefs and village elders). The caddi governed the community, making important political decisions, conducting peace pipe ceremonies, and leading war councils. The canahas assisted the caddi, performing tasks like lighting peace pipes and preparing their beds during a hunt.

Caddo war leaders were called *amayxoya*. They were elected from those who had achieved success in combat. When the tribe engaged in battle, the war leader had absolute authority.

The Caddo Nation of the late 1990s was a union of the Kadohadacho, Hasinai, and Natchitoches peoples. The Caddo are governed by a constitution and an eight-member elected tribal council, although every tribal member has a say in the decision-making process. The tribe is headquartered in Binger, Oklahoma. The Caddo also co-own land with the Delaware and Wichita tribes spread over three counties.

In 2009, the nation started with an Indian Child Welfare Act (ICWA) Court as the first step in establishing a Caddo Nation Tribal Court System. The goal of the ICWA Court is to support families in raising their children. Building on this foundation of the ICWA court, the Caddo Nation will move into other areas, such as divorce, adoption, and civil court, as well as mediation services.

ECONOMY

Throughout history, the Caddo have been noted for their work ethic (a guiding philosophy that stresses the importance of hard work). No one was allowed to be idle, and those who refused to work were punished. Long ago, the Caddo economy was based mostly on agriculture, although the people did some hunting and fishing. After about 1700, when the Caddo became expert horsemen, hunting and trading grew even more important than farming. The Caddo traveled as far north as Illinois to trade with other tribes. Their most prized trade items were the salt they extracted from boiled spring water and the wood from the Osage orange tree, which only grew in their area. The French called it *bois d'arc* (pronounced *bwah-dark*), meaning "bow wood," because it was so popular for making bows.

The Caddo are cooperating with the Delaware and the Wichita to help members of all three tribes achieve economic independence. They jointly own WCD Enterprises, which leases the oil, gas, and grazing lands that provide much of their income. The tribe manages farming operations, a factory, a smoke shop, and a bingo enterprise. The Caddo also work in fields such as health care, education, banking, ranching, farming, sports, and construction.

DAILY LIFE

Families

Several Caddo families—as many as eight to ten—lived in the same house in traditional times. Each family had its own space within the dwelling, but the entire household owned and cultivated the land around the house. An elderly woman in the household took charge of distributing food supplies to each family.

The Caddo lived in conical grass-covered homes. © LINDSAY HEBBERD/CORBIS.

Buildings

The Caddo built two kinds of houses: grass-and-cane-covered or earth-covered. Grass-covered houses were conical in shape and could be as large as 60 feet (18 meters) in diameter and up to 50 feet (15 meters) high. They were well insulated and kept out wind, snow, and rain. The tribe used their enclosed houses all winter but built open shelters for summer. These open-air homes had raised woven platforms to allow air to circulate through the holes in the floor.

Villages were arranged around a central open area used for ceremonies and other gatherings. Caddo communities also held a variety of public buildings, including the temple for the sacred fire and meeting places for tribal leaders.

Clothing and adornment

The Caddo made their clothes out plant fibers that they wove into cloth. One of their most impressive garments was a mantle decorated with feathers. They also used deerskin and buffalo hide to make clothes. In summer both men and women wore only breechcloths, garments with front and back flaps that hung from the waist. They often went barefoot, wearing moccasins only for travel. In the winter, they wore leggings, buckskin shirts, and moccasins that they painted with intricate designs. The Caddo decorated their clothing with fringe and adorned themselves with bead necklaces, collars, nose-rings, and earrings.

Some Caddo tribes removed their body hair completely, including their eyebrows. Others cut their hair short with one long section tied off to the side, or left it uncut and untended. The Caddo wore tattoos with designs featuring animals and birds. At puberty, Caddo girls received tattoos of large, brilliantly colored flowers.

Food

Caddo life revolved around farming, hunting, fishing, and gathering wild plants. Corn was their most important crop, with two harvests per year. The early crop, "little corn," was much like modern-day popcorn; it was planted in April and picked in July. "Flourcorn" was planted in June and harvested in September in a celebration called the Harvest of the Great Corn.

The Caddo ate corn baked as bread and in a variety of other ways. They also cultivated squash, beans, melons, sunflowers, and tobacco. The tribe hunted deer, buffalo, bear, raccoon, turkey, and other animals and gathered nuts, acorns, berries, and fruits such as pomegranates and wild grapes. (A painting by the American artist George Catlin [1796–1872], who traveled among the various tribes, is titled *Caddo Indians Gathering Wild Grapes*.) At some point before the turn of the nineteenth century, the Caddo began to raise livestock.

Farming, Caddo-style

An early European onlooker once wrote down his observations of the Caddo style of farming. He said that when it was time to ready the fields for planting, word went around the entire village. On the chosen day, the men gathered their tools, met at one family's field, and prepared it, while the women went to the home to prepare a feast. If there was no meat, he wrote, "they [would] bake Indian bread in the ashes, or boil it, mixing it with beans." After the feast, the men socialized until the next day, when they moved on to the next household's field. The women of the house did the planting.

Education

The Caddo prized the virtues of honesty, fair dealing, and hospitality, and they passed these beliefs on to their children. Built in the late twentieth century, the Adai Indian Nation Cultural Center in Louisiana, and the Caddo Heritage Museum in Oklahoma stand as a reminder to tribal members of their proud and ancient heritage. Two organizations—the Hasinai Society and the Caddo Culture Club—meet regularly to pass on tribal culture. Attendees practice songs and dances or learn storytelling, so these arts will not be lost.

Healing practices

In addition to their roles as political and religious leaders, the xinesi served as the tribes' healers. They cured the sick or wounded with fire, snakeskins, feathers, necklaces, and musical instruments. Another aspect of the xinesi healing ritual involved sucking foreign objects and blood from victims to rid them of disease-causing evil spirits. Illnesses, called *aguian* (meaning "arrowtip"), were thought to stem from an object shot into a victim by an evil spirit or a witch.

The Caddo also practiced a limited number of natural remedies with special brews and used sweat baths to cure the sick. Elsie Clews Parsons wrote in her article "Notes on the Caddo" that doctors had different rules for curing, depending on their supernatural guide. For example, she wrote: "Tsa'bisu… [was] a famous doctor. His supernatural partner was a red-headed woodpecker." The powers these animals provided helped the doctors in curing the sick or wounded.

ARTS

Caddo women were skilled at crafts; they decorated their houses with handmade, beautifully colored rugs, baskets, and clay pottery. Caddo potters were known for their creativity. Pottery ranged in size from huge three-foot-tall vessels for storage to tiny child-sized cups. The potters also made ear spools (worn through slits in the ear lobe), pipes, and ceremonial objects. Archaeologists have found ancient Caddo pottery hundreds of miles away from their homelands, leading them to believe that other tribes also valued these distinctive pieces.

The Spanish described many intricate carvings in wood, including masks, bowls, and chests. Unfortunately, because wood rots, few wooden artworks survive into modern times. The Caddo also carved designs into

False Bridegroom

In this Caddo tale, two twin girls desire to marry a rich chief they have never met. They set off but need directions along the way. The man they ask tells them he is the chief and has them wait while he informs his grandmother.

> The man, who was no other than Owl, ran on to his home and, calling his grandmother, said, "Clean up the lodge and put it in order. I am going to bring home two girls whom I am playing a joke on. They think I am the rich chief and want to marry me." After they had cleaned the lodge, for it was very disorderly, Owl said, "I am going to put this turkey which I have brought home over my bed; when you get up in the morning ask me which turkey you shall cook and pretend to point to one, and I will say, "No, take this." Then the girls will think that we have many turkeys and many good things to eat."
>
> Owl went back for the girls and brought them to his grandmother's lodge. They were pleased, for everything looked neat and nice, and so they married Owl. Every day Owl came in with the turkey, and he always pretended to have been out hunting. Really he had been at the council, and the chief gave him the turkey for allowing him to sit on his back. At all the councils the chief always sat on Owl's back, and so he gave Owl a turkey every time to repay him for his trouble and the pain of holding him so long.
>
> After many moons the twins grew weary of nothing but turkey and they began to suspect something, so one day they followed Owl when he went away. They followed and saw him go to a large grass lodge. They peeped through an opening, and there they saw Owl sitting in the middle of the lodge with the chief sitting on his head. They gave a scream. Owl recognized their voices and jumped up, throwing the chief off his head, and ran home. He gave his grandmother a terrible scolding for letting the girls follow him and find him out. The girls felt so ashamed when they discovered how they had been fooled that they slipped off to their home and told their father and mother their experience.

SOURCE: McNeese, Tim. *Illustrated Myths of Native America: The Southwest, Western Range, Pacific Northwest, and California.* London: Blandford, 1999.

shells, some of which were used for jewelry or utensils. Cups made of conch shells had detailed designs on the bottom.

Dance

The Caddo have preserved many of their traditional dances. In addition to those that have ceremonial significance, they have many social dances.

Some of the most well known are the Alligator Dance, the Duck Dance, and the Bear Dance. Songs are connected with each dance, and some, like the Bell Dance, have dozens of songs, many more than the two or three songs that most tribes have.

Oral literature

The sun and fire were central characters in the stories of tribes of the Southeast. Sacred fires were the centers of their towns and homes, and Caddo tales reflect the importance of the sun as a figure of power. Like many other North American tribes, the Caddo told stories that centered on the trickster figure, Coyote.

Tribal history was shared largely through song. The song that accompanies the Drum Dance tells of the tribe's beginnings, and the song that accompanies the Turkey Dance tells of events both ancient and modern. These and other songs have been recorded and preserved in the collections of the Hasinai Cultural Center and the Duke Collection of American Indian Oral History, part of the Western History Collections at the University of Oklahoma.

CUSTOMS

Festivals and ceremonies

Of all the Caddo ceremonies, the most important were centered on hunting, warfare, and harvest. The Turkey Dance celebrated victory and was performed in the afternoon; it ended by sunset, when turkeys come home to roost. A Drum Dance began an evening ceremony, and a Morning Dance ushered in the dawn. Since corn was the major crop, it was often the central focus of ceremonies.

The Caddo have worked hard to maintain their culture, and they still perform traditional dances and ceremonies. Since the 1970s, the Caddo Culture Club has worked to pass along traditional stories, songs, dances, and customs.

War and hunting rituals

Before going to war, some Caddo warriors sang and danced around a fire for a week or more, offering gifts, such as corn or bows and arrows, to the Great Spirit. Warriors rubbed their bodies with smoke from the fire so the Great Spirit would grant their wish to slay their enemies.

Some Caddo groups tortured prisoners of war, then killed and ate them. They considered this practice necessary to "feed" the Caddo gods. Caddo warriors also took the scalps, and sometimes the heads, of their enemies for trophies.

The people took special care with the burial of dead warriors. They buried those who died at home with the scalps they had taken from enemies over their lifetimes; the Caddo believed this granted them power over their foes in the House of the Dead. They also buried food, water, tools, and weapons with the bodies. A fire burned near graves for six days until the spirit passed on to the next world. Those who died in battle were either cremated (their bodies were burned) or left to be eaten by wild beasts, which was a great honor.

Before a hunt, Caddo men prayed to animal spirits, asking that the animals would allow themselves to be slain.

Courtship and marriage

A Caddo man who wished to marry presented the woman of his choice with the finest gift he could manage. If she accepted it, then they were married. Sometimes these marriages lasted only a few days. If a man came along and offered a better gift, a woman was free to leave her husband and marry the new man. Men had only one wife at a time, though few stayed with their wives for long.

CURRENT TRIBAL ISSUES

In 2003, the Caddo Nation received a grant from the National Park Service Historic Preservation Fund to do a cemetery documentation project. Many old cemeteries dot their homeland, but the small houses that marked the plots are now gone. Some elders know the approximate locations, but do not know who is buried there. Tribe members were trained to use new technology such as global positioning systems (GPS) and ground-penetrating radar (GPR) to help with them find and document the gravesites.

The people who called themselves the Adai Caddo (Natchitoches Parish), who have been recognized by the state of Louisiana, ran into difficulty with the Caddo Nation of Oklahoma, who did not want them to use the name "Caddo." The Caddo Nation said that the Adai were not one of the many loosely connected bands who had an original connection to the Caddo. Nonetheless, the Adai listed themselves as one of the

George Washington, also known as Sho-we-tat and Little Boy, was a Caddo chief who served with the Confederacy during the American Civil War.
© NATIONAL ARCHIVES AND RECORDS ADMINISTRATION.

five main groups of Caddo, and they maintained that although most of the Caddo people moved to Arkansas, then Texas, and finally to Oklahoma, they remained behind in their traditional homeland, where they hunted bison, fished, and traded.

NOTABLE PEOPLE

George Washington (Sho-we-tat, Little Boy) was chief of the White Bead, or Indian Territory Caddo, before that band and the Texas band were merged. During the American Civil War (1861–65; a war between the Union [the North], who were opposed to slavery, and the Confederacy [the South], who were in favor of slavery), he served the Confederacy as commander of the Caddo Frontier Brigade.

Carol Cussen McDonald Hampton (1935–) is a teacher, tribal historian, writer, and activist for the Caddoan people. She taught Native American Studies at the University of Science and Arts of Oklahoma. Hampton has been active in the Caddo tribal council since 1976 and in many state and national programs concerning education and Native American development.

Other notable Caddo include highly regarded Caddo-Kiowa artist T. C. Cannon (1946–1978); Richard Donaghey, who operates the internationally known First Nations Dance Company; and Dayton Edmonds, a Methodist minister and storyteller whose tales combine elements of traditional spirituality with Christian teachings.

BOOKS

Berlainder, Jean Louis. *The Indians of Texas in 1830.* Washington, DC: Smithsonian Institution, 1969.

Bolton, Herbert Eugene. *The Hasinais: Southern Caddoans as Seen by the Earliest Europeans.* Reprint. Norman: University of Oklahoma Press, 2002.

Bowen, Jeff. *Kiowa, Comanche, Apache, Fort Sill Apache, Wichita, Caddo and Delaware Indians Birth and Death Rolls, 1924–1932.* Signal Mountain, TN: Mountain Press, 2005.

Bruchac, Joseph. *Flying with the Eagle, Racing the Great Bear: Tales from Native North America.* Golden, CO: Fulcrum, 2011.

Dorsey, George A. *Traditions of the Caddo.* Lincoln: University of Nebraska Press, 1997.

Duval, Kathleen. *The Native Ground: Indians and Colonists in the Heart of the Continent.* Philadelphia: University of Pennsylvania Press, 2006.

Kissock, Heather, and Rachel Small. *Caddo: American Indian Art and Culture.* New York: Weigl Publishers, 2011.

Harrington, Mark Raymond. *Certain Caddo Sites in Arkansas.* Charleston, SC: Johnson Press, 2011.

Jackson, Helen Hunt. *The Indian Reform Letters of Helen Hunt Jackson, 1879–1885.* Edited by Valerie Sherer Mathes. Norman: University of Oklahoma Press, 1998.

La Vere, David. *Life among the Texas Indians: The WPA Narratives.* Austin: Texas A&M University Press, 2006.

Lankford, George E., ed. *Native American Legends of the Southeast: Tales from the Natchez, Caddo, Biloxi, Chickasaw, and Other Nations.* 5th ed. Tuscaloosa: University of Alabama Press, 2011.

Parsons, Elsie Clews. "Notes on the Caddo." *Memoirs of the American Anthropological Association.* No. 57. Menasha, WI: American Anthropological Association, 1941.

Stacy, Liz Chrysler. *Caddo Lake Tales.* Shreveport, LA: Ritz Publications, 2009.

Swanton, John R. *Source Material on the History and Ethnology of the Caddo Indians.* Norman: University of Oklahoma Press, 1996.

PERIODICALS

Haurwitz, Ralph. "Selling the Beauty of Caddo." *Austin American-Statesman,* March 26, 1993.

WEB SITES

"Arkansas Indians: Arkansas Archeological Survey." *University of Arkansas.* http://www.uark.edu/campus-resources/archinfo/ArkansasIndianTribes.pdf (accessed on June 12, 2011).

"Caddo Indian History." *Access Genealogy.* http://www.accessgenealogy.com/native/tribes/caddo/caddohist.htm (accessed on June 12, 2011).

"The Caddo Confederacies." *El Centro College.* http://pw1.netcom.com/~wandaron/caddo.html (accessed on June 12, 2011).

Glover, William B. "A History of the Caddo Indians." Formatted for the World Wide Web by Jay Salsburg. Reprinted from *The Louisiana Historical Quarterly,* 18, no. 4 (October 1935). http://ops.tamu.edu/x075bb/caddo/Indians.html (accessed on June 12, 2011).

Official Website of the Caddo Nation. http://www.caddonation-nsn.gov/ (accessed on June 12, 2011).

"Texas Beyond History: Caddo Fundamentals." *The University of Texas at Austin,* created by Texas Archeological Research Laboratory in partnership with Southern Texas Archaeological Association. http://www.texasbeyondhistory.net/tejas/fundamentals/index.html (accessed on June 12, 2011).

Cherokee

Name

Cherokee (pronounced *CHAIR-uh-key*). The name comes from the Creek word *chelokee*, which means "people of a different speech." The Cherokee refer to themselves as *Ani'-Yun'wiya'*, meaning "the real people" or "the principal people," or *Tsalagi*, which comes from a Choctaw (see entry) word for "people living in a land of many caves." The tribe's original name was *Kituwah*, which is why the traditional group calls itself the United Keetoowah Band.

Location

The Cherokee originally lived in parts of eight present-day southeastern states: North Carolina, South Carolina, Virginia, West Virginia, Kentucky, Tennessee, Georgia, and Alabama. In the early twenty-first century, the tribal lands of the Cherokee Nation spanned 124,000 acres throughout fourteen counties in northeastern Oklahoma. Although the territory is not a reservation, the U.S. government holds it in trust and considers it a Jurisdictional Service Area. By the 2000s, most Cherokee lived in northeastern Oklahoma, North Carolina, and Tennessee.

Population

In 1674, the Cherokee population was estimated to be around 50,000. From the mid-1600s to the 1730s, the population had dropped to about 25,000. In the 1990 U.S. Census, 369,979 people identified themselves as Cherokee. By the 2000 census, that number had decreased to 281,069. Many people also claim some Cherokee blood; 729,533 people said they have a Cherokee ancestor. The 2010 census counted 284,247 Cherokee, with a total of 819,105 people claiming some Cherokee ancestry, making it the largest tribal grouping in the United States. In 2011, the Oklahoma Indian Affairs Commission showed a tribal enrollment of 299,862 for the Cherokee Nation and one of 14,300 for the United Keetoowah Band.

Language family

Iroquoian.

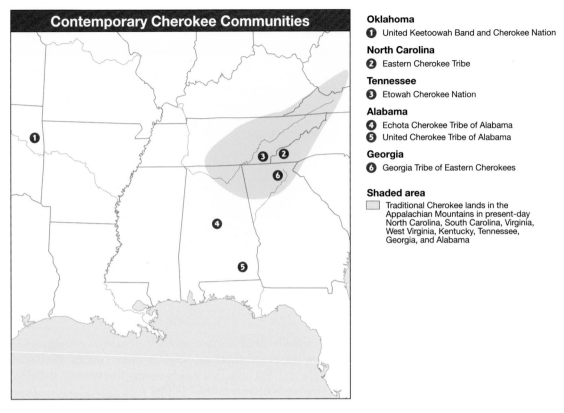

Contemporary Cherokee Communities

Oklahoma
1. United Keetoowah Band and Cherokee Nation

North Carolina
2. Eastern Cherokee Tribe

Tennessee
3. Etowah Cherokee Nation

Alabama
4. Echota Cherokee Tribe of Alabama
5. United Cherokee Tribe of Alabama

Georgia
6. Georgia Tribe of Eastern Cherokees

Shaded area
Traditional Cherokee lands in the Appalachian Mountains in present-day North Carolina, South Carolina, Virginia, West Virginia, Kentucky, Tennessee, Georgia, and Alabama

A map of contemporary Cherokee communities. MAP BY XNR PRODUCTIONS. CENGAGE LEARNING, GALE. REPRODUCED BY PERMISSION OF GALE, A PART OF CENGAGE LEARNING.

Origins and group affiliations

Many historians believe that the very early ancestors of the Cherokee moved from territory that is now Mexico and Texas to the Great Lakes region. Between three thousand to four thousand years ago, after enduring conflicts with the Iroquois and the Delaware (see entries) tribes, the Cherokee moved again—this time to the southeastern part of the present-day United States. Their traditional enemy was the Chickasaw (see entry) tribe. By the early 2000s, three major tribal groups and more than fifty other organizations in at least twelve states claimed to have Cherokee origins.

Before the arrival of Europeans in their territory in 1540, the Cherokee were an agricultural people numbering about 50,000 who controlled 40,000 square miles (103,600 square kilometers) of land. Over the years, the tribe lost many of its people to wars and to diseases brought by the settlers. The Cherokee became known as one of the "Five Civilized Tribes" along with the Chickasaw, Creek, Choctaw, and Seminole nations (see entries). Settlers coined this term because these groups had formed institutions that American culture valued, such as constitutional governments and school systems. This, however, did not help the Cherokee and their allies when settlers wanted their land.

During the nineteenth century, the U.S. government forced many Cherokee to move westward, away from their homeland on the sad journey known as the Trail of Tears. The Cherokee formed a new government and school systems in Indian Territory, but the U.S. government abolished those when the state of Oklahoma was created in 1907. In spite of these tragedies, the Cherokee went on to become the largest Native American group in the United States and to enjoy a high standard of living.

HISTORY

Trade with Europeans

The Cherokee people made up a confederacy consisting of as many as two hundred separate towns nestled in the river valleys of the southern Appalachian Mountains. The people in these towns shared a common language and customs, but each town had its own chief, and no overall chief or government existed for the confederacy. The Cherokee had been farming in the southern Appalachian region for one thousand years when they first encountered Europeans in 1540, as the Spanish explorer Hernando de Soto (c. 1496–1542) led a party through Cherokee lands. After that, the Cherokee had very little contact with outsiders until the 1600s, when European traders moved into the region. The tribe traded with them for manufactured goods such as metal tools, glass, cloth, and firearms. In exchange, the Cherokee supplied the settlers with deerskins, which became an important source of leather in Europe. This partnership changed the Cherokee culture. The people no longer farmed and hunted for survival. Instead, they engaged in buying and selling, and hunters replaced priests as the leaders of Cherokee society.

For generations, the tribe had shown great respect for nature, but eighteenth-century Cherokee hunter-traders killed as many deer as they could to keep up with the booming trade. One report shows that the number of deerskins the Cherokee sold in a year increased from fifty thousand in 1708 to around one million in 1735. Further changes took place when traders built stores near Cherokee towns and married Cherokee women. Instead of remaining with their people, women often went

Important Dates

1540: The Cherokee are first visited by Europeans.

1821: Sequoyah's method for writing the Cherokee language is officially approved by tribal leaders.

1827: The Cherokee adopt a written constitution.

1846: The Ceremonial Day of Unity ends internal tribal conflict.

1838: The Cherokee leave their homeland on a forced journey known as the Trail of Tears.

1907: With the creation of the state of Oklahoma, the government abolishes the Cherokee tribal government and school system, and the dream of a Native American commonwealth dissolves.

1984: The first modern-day meeting between the Eastern Band and the Cherokee Nation is held.

2006: The Cherokee Nation adopts a new constitution.

to live with their white husbands. Traditional Cherokee people did not accumulate possessions, but the children of these couples inherited personal wealth.

The Cherokee allied with the British in the French and Indian War (1755–63; a war fought in North America between England and France involving some tribes as allies of the French) and the American Revolution (1775–83; the American colonists' fight for independence from England). In the peace treaties that followed each of these wars, the Cherokee lost large portions of their lands.

Divisions among the Cherokee

Between 1790 and 1817, several groups of Cherokee moved westward in an attempt to hold their culture together against the threat of increasing numbers of settlers. One Cherokee group settled in Arkansas and became known as the Western Band (today's United Keetoowah Band). By 1820, this group had five thousand members. The majority of the Cherokee people, however, stayed in their southeastern homeland. Terrible smallpox epidemics raged in the mid-1700s, killing nearly half the Cherokee population. A series of treaties between 1785 and 1806 resulted in the loss of even more Cherokee land. Christian missionaries and government forces tried to make the Cherokee assimilate to, or adopt, white culture. Many Cherokee had already turned away from traditional ways in the hopes that the government would let them stay in their homelands.

Two conflicting factions arose within the Cherokee Nation. One was called the Treaty Party. Its members, who were mostly well-to-do slaveholders, merchants, and plantation owners, believed in assimilation. They thought the Cherokee should sell their homelands in Georgia to the U.S. government and voluntarily move to lands west of the Mississippi River. Resistance, they warned, would be a disaster for the Cherokee.

The Ross Party of Cherokee, led by Principal Chief John Ross (1790–1866), thought the Cherokee should negotiate with the government and use the U.S. court system to stay in what was left of their ancestral lands. They created a law under which selling or bargaining away Cherokee land was an offense against the tribe punishable by death.

The fight for the southeastern homelands

In the 1820s, a warrior named Sequoyah (pronounced *suh-KWOY-ah*; c. 1770–1843) showed tribal leaders a method he had invented for writing the Cherokee language. His system used a syllabary—a writing code using symbols for syllables rather than for single letter sounds as in the English alphabet. Many Cherokee quickly learned to read and write in the Cherokee syllabary. From 1828 to 1834, the *Cherokee Phoenix*, a weekly newspaper printed in both English and Cherokee, was published and widely read.

In the early 1820s, the Cherokee established a capital in New Echota, Georgia. They wrote a constitution for a government in 1827 that was, in many ways, similar to the U.S. Constitution. They wished to establish their own government and the right to preserve their homelands in Georgia, Tennessee, and Alabama. The Georgia legislature, however, passed a series of laws that abolished the Cherokee government and appropriated (took for itself) Cherokee land.

When the state of Georgia tried to remove the Cherokee from their lands, the Cherokee took the case to the U.S. Supreme Court. They based their defense on a clause in the Constitution that allows foreign nations to seek redress (compensation or remedy) in the Supreme Court for damages caused by U.S. citizens. The court ruled that Native American nations are not foreign nations but dependent, domestic nations. Until that time, U.S. law had treated Native nations as separate, or foreign, nations. Although the Cherokee lost this case, in a case in 1832, the Supreme Court ruled that Georgia could not remove the Cherokee from their land, stating that only the federal government had the right to

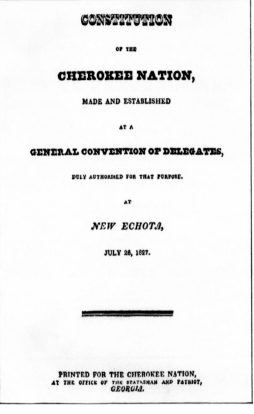

The Cherokee Nation outlined its government in a constitution published in 1827.

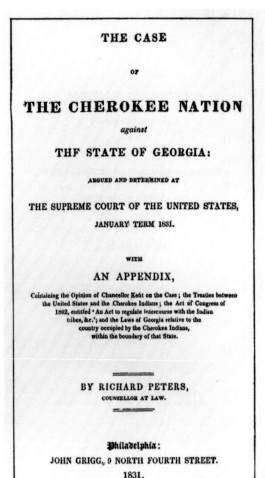

THE CASE

OF

THE CHEROKEE NATION

against

THE STATE OF GEORGIA:

ARGUED AND DETERMINED AT

THE SUPREME COURT OF THE UNITED STATES,

JANUARY TERM 1831.

WITH

AN APPENDIX,

Containing the Opinion of Chancellor Kent on the Case; the Treaties between
the United States and the Cherokee Indians; the Act of Congress of
1802, entitled 'An Act to regulate intercourse with the Indian
tribes, &c.'; and the Laws of Georgia relative to the
country occupied by the Cherokee Indians,
within the boundary of that State.

BY RICHARD PETERS,

COUNSELLOR AT LAW.

Philadelphia:

JOHN GRIGG, 9 NORTH FOURTH STREET.

1831.

The title page of the Cherokee Nation case against the state of Georgia, which was argued in the U.S. Supreme Court in 1831. © NORTH WIND/NORTH WIND PICTURE ARCHIVES. ALL RIGHTS RESERVED.

regulate their affairs; states could not extend their laws over Native governments. However, this Cherokee victory was temporary.

The dispute deepens

During the 1800s, the U.S. government moved many tribes to Indian Territory, where, they were told, they could govern themselves and not be bothered by settlers. In 1830, the U.S. government passed the Indian Removal Act, which required the Cherokee and other tribes living east of the Mississippi to trade their homelands for property in Indian Territory. (Indian Territory at the time was comprised of what are now Oklahoma, Kansas, and parts of Colorado, Nebraska, and Wyoming.)

Two years later, Cherokee Principal Chief John Ross argued before the U.S. Supreme Court that the Removal Act went against the terms of the U.S. Constitution. Although the Supreme Court agreed with Chief Ross, President Andrew Jackson (1767–1845; served 1829–37) refused to accept the court's decision. Instead, he made plans to enforce the Removal Act. Angry Cherokee leaders refused to talk with government agents about an exchange of their land for land in Indian Territory.

In direct opposition to the wishes of most Cherokee, the Treaty Party signed the Treaty of New Echota in 1835. The treaty agreed to the exchange of the tribe's land in the East for property in Indian Territory and some money to aid the relocation process.

The majority of the Cherokee people were outraged at the signing of such a treaty. The Treaty Party was a small group with neither the authority nor the right to represent the entire tribe. In response, Chief Ross and sixteen thousand tribal members signed a petition of protest against the treaty. The U.S. Senate passed the treaty anyway, however, and ordered the tribe to move west within two years. Most of the Cherokee refused to leave voluntarily.

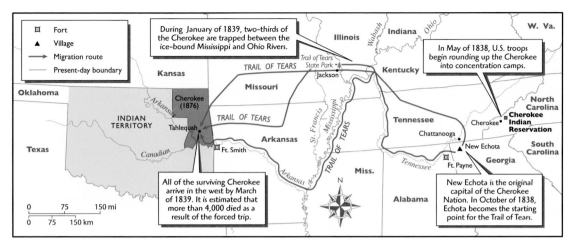

The routes taken by Native Americans on the forced trip to their new home in Oklahoma, now known as the "Trail of Tears," 1838– 39. MAP BY XNR PRODUCTIONS. CENGAGE LEARNING, GALE. REPRODUCED BY PERMISSION OF GALE, A PART OF CENGAGE LEARNING.

The Trail of Tears

In 1838, the U.S. government launched a program of forced removal against Native groups. Seven thousand government troops removed the Cherokee from their homes, gathered them in disease-infested camps, and forced them to travel about 800 miles (1,300 kilometers), many on foot, for three to five months to reach what was to be their new homeland.

The Cherokee set off on their journey without food, supplies, or shelter. Once the Cherokee were on the trail, whites attacked them and stole the few possessions they managed to carry along. About 17,000 Cherokee began the tragic march, and before it was over, about 2,500 of them had died. Some were left unburied at the side of the road. The route of the forced march—a painful reminder of an agonizing experience in history—was later named the Trail of Tears.

In North Carolina, about one thousand Cherokee escaped removal with the help of state officials who were sympathetic to them. One North Carolinian, William H. Thomas (called Wil-Usdi by the Cherokee), bought land in his name for the Cherokee, went to court in their defense, and even visited Washington, D.C., on their behalf.

Conflicts followed by "Golden Age"

Conflicts among the Cherokee were initially intense once they moved into Indian Territory. On June 22, 1839, three Cherokee leaders—John Ridge,

Major Ridge, and Elias Boudinot—who had signed the despised removal agreement were killed. As the Cherokee groups settled into their new home, a new leadership (sometimes called the National Party) arose and worked to establish an effective form of government. The National Party invited the full participation of the two other Cherokee groups already living in Indian Territory—the Treaty Party and the Old Settlers, the group of Cherokee who had moved to Arkansas from North Carolina in the early 1800s, hoping to settle there permanently. In 1828, settlers had forced them to move farther west to Indian Territory, where they set up their community according to their old ways.

The Old Settlers resented the arrival of the newcomers, and the three Cherokee groups could not reach any agreement. Several years of violent conflicts came to an end with a ceremonial day of unity in 1846, during which the Cherokee people dedicated themselves to making the best of their circumstances. They did this to avoid being divided into two tribes by the U.S. government. Although tensions persisted, in the 1850s, the differing groups enjoyed a period of peace and prosperity known as the "Golden Age."

America's Civil War divides Cherokee

The American Civil War (1861–65; a war between the Union [the North], which was opposed to slavery, and the Confederacy [the South], which was in favor of slavery) threatened to divide the tribe once again. Chief John Ross at first favored neutrality (not taking sides). In time, however, he agreed to fight on the side of the Confederacy, a move encouraged by wealthy Cherokee landowners who held a lot of power in the Cherokee Nation and favored the South. The Old Settlers and many others, however, joined the Union army. Experts estimate that 25 percent of the entire Cherokee population died in the Civil War.

More broken promises

At war's end the U.S. government punished Cherokee supporters of the South by invalidating all treaties made with the Cherokee people. In new treaties signed in 1866 and 1868, large portions of Cherokee lands were taken for use by the railroads, for American settlements, and to house other tribes. The U.S. government had promised the Cherokee people that land in Indian Territory would be set aside solely for Native American use and that no non-Natives would be allowed to settle there. Thus began a series of broken promises that the government made to the Cherokee. Within fifteen years, settlers outnumbered Natives in Indian Territory.

For years, the Cherokee earned money by providing grazing land to ranchers for their cattle. Without explanation, the government halted the grazing land practice in 1890. The poverty-stricken Cherokee were forced to sell their land to white settlers. Worse luck followed when terrible dust storms forced many Cherokee farmers to leave Oklahoma in the 1930s.

In the 1970s, after years of hardship for the Cherokee, the U.S. government made federal money available to Native American tribes. The Cherokee Nation in Oklahoma adopted a new constitution in 1975, elected their own officials, and began governing themselves once again. Since that time, the Cherokee Nation has become a national leader in education, health care, housing, and economic matters.

Eastern Band of Cherokee Indians

While the Cherokee Nation adapted to their western home, the Cherokee who had remained in North Carolina organized in the East. The people called themselves the Eastern Band of Cherokee Indians. In 1924, the tribe reached an agreement with the U.S. government to make sure that Eastern Cherokee lands would remain forever in the possession of the tribe.

In 1984, more than thirty thousand people attended a two-day meeting at which representatives of the Cherokee Nation of Oklahoma and the Eastern Band discussed common concerns. The two groups continued to meet for cultural exchange programs and joint Tribal Council meetings to address issues of concern for all of the Cherokee people.

United Keetoowah Band

The United Keetoowah Band (UKB) traces its history back to 1817. At that point in time, a group of Cherokee refused to adopt the white way of life and instead agreed to trade their lands in North Carolina for lands farther west in Arkansas, where they lived for the next eleven years. In 1828, however, the federal government removed them from Arkansas to Indian Territory, where they set up their headquarters in Tahlequah, Oklahoma. Because they did not intermarry with whites as other Cherokee groups did, the descendants of the UKB represent the largest group of full-blood Cherokee people in the United States. (They prefer the name Keetoowah

From Indian Territory to the State of Oklahoma

As part of the Indian Removal Act of 1830, the Western Territory Bill called for the establishment of an Indian commonwealth or territory in the removal area. It was to be governed by a confederation of tribes and was to be composed of present-day Kansas, Oklahoma, parts of Nebraska, Colorado, and Wyoming. As other states were organized, the U.S. government decreased the area reserved for Native peoples until the boundaries were almost identical to present-day Oklahoma. By 1868, this territory, known as Indian Territory, was the only unorganized territory (without a state government) in the lower forty-eight states.

In 1890, the Oklahoma Organic Act reduced Indian Territory to the eastern portion of the territory and established a U.S. territorial government called Oklahoma Territory in the western portion. After much dispute, the U.S. government made Oklahoma into a state in 1907. The promise of a free Native American state dissolved.

In *Chronicles of Oklahoma,* historian Edward E. Dale described one Cherokee woman's pain as she spoke of the passing of her nation to statehood. Thirty years later, with tears in her eyes, she recalled, "It broke my heart. I went to bed and cried all night long. It seemed more than I could bear that the Cherokee Nation, my country and my people's country, was no more."

Since Oklahoma became a state, the tribes have kept their status as self-governing and independent communities, except for limitations placed on them by treaties, agreements, or laws. Throughout the next decade, Oklahoma Indians suffered from the lowest income level and the highest unemployment rates of any of the population of Oklahoma.

Native peoples once owned all the land in the state of Oklahoma. At the turn of the century, the "Five Civilized Tribes" owned 19.5 million acres of land. By 1975, Oklahoma tribal lands amounted to only 65,000 acres. Individual Natives owned about one million acres.

In the early twenty-first century, about four hundred thousand Oklahomans identify themselves as Native peoples—more than in any other state. A 65-mile (105-kilometer) radius around the city of Tulsa contains the highest nonreservation population of Native peoples anywhere in the world.

to Cherokee.) The UKB have retained traditional ways to a greater extent than other groups, and many still speak the Keetoowah language.

RELIGION

As far back as the 1600s, the Cherokee tribe was divided in its religious beliefs. The majority believed that the world had been created by several "beings from above," who then abandoned it. The sun took over and created plants, animals, and people, then continued to watch over and preserve the earth. The Cherokee holding these beliefs worshipped various heavenly bodies, animals, and fire.

The other group of Cherokee believed in "three beings who were always together and of the same mind." The three beings created all things and were present everywhere. They had messengers who visited the world to take care of human affairs.

The two groups of believers participated in the same ceremonies. For both, the primary god was the Creator, who was called *Yo wah* or *Ye ho waah.* Where there was order, there was goodness; where there was disorder and confusion, there was evil, represented by *Uktena*, a creature who was part snake, part deer, and part bird.

Religion was part of the Cherokee people's daily life and a part of their interpretation of nature. The annual cycle of festivals followed the earth's seasonal rhythms. During times of peace, the head priest also functioned as the community's chief. Cherokee ways changed when Europeans came, and many Cherokee converted to Christianity. Today, many belong to Protestant Christian churches.

During the early 1900s, some Cherokee chose not to adopt the Christian religion and ideas. The elders formed a secret society to keep the old ways alive. This group, the Keetoowah Nighthawk Society, preserved traditional ceremonies and rituals. The Keetoowah tribe in Oklahoma still practices the Stomp Dance religion. In the early twenty-first century, the various Keetoowah groups have ceremonial dance grounds in Oklahoma, where traditional ceremonies are held. (See "Festivals.")

LANGUAGE

The Cherokee language is the southern branch of the Iroquoian language. It is quite different from northern Iroquoian languages like Mohawk (see entry). In the Cherokee language, verbs and nouns are not single words, but phrases that include descriptions of an action or object. For example, *so qui li*, the term for "horse," is translated as "he carries heavy things." Some words have several meanings, and meaning is sometimes shown by the way a word is spoken.

Cherokee differs from English and other European languages by placing the subject of a sentence after the object. For example, in the sentence "The girl caught a fish," "girl" is the subject, "caught" is the verb, and "fish" is the object. If the sentence were in Cherokee, "girl" would appear

Cherokee Words

OH-see-yoh	"hello"
gog-GEE	"summer"
wah-DOH	"thank you"
HOH-wah	"you're welcome"

after "fish" in the sentence. Cherokee believe that humans (often the subjects of sentences) are not superior to other living things (often the objects of sentences) but rather are equal to and partners with all creation.

The Cherokee language has its own unique written form. In the early 1800s, a Cherokee man named Sequoyah invented a system for writing the Cherokee language. Shortly thereafter, most Cherokee could read and write their language.

In the late 1990s, at least fourteen thousand people spoke Cherokee, and schools in Cherokee communities offered classes in both English and Cherokee. Those who sought to preserve the language shot video footage of Native speakers, who were careful to pronounce words properly and assume the correct facial expressions as they spoke. In 2001, the Cherokee Nation began a program to increase language usage in the home and community and instituted classes at several levels of proficiency. Although only 15 percent of the people spoke the language at that time, their fifty-year goal was for 80 percent to become fluent.

GOVERNMENT

In traditional times, each Cherokee town had a chief who led in wartime and a priest who led in peacetime. Chiefs sought the guidance of a town council, made up of men and women who discussed issues until they reached an agreement. Initially, the Cherokee did not have a single chief who ruled over all, and the entire group came together only for ceremonies and wars. During the nineteenth century, they created the post of principal chief to unify the nation, especially in its dealings with the Americans and government agencies.

The Eastern Band of Cherokee formed in 1889. Its current government is made up of a principal chief, a vice chief, and a twelve-member tribal council whose members are elected to two-year terms. The council deals with tribal issues, while another group runs the court system.

Before removal, the Cherokee Nation had created a constitutional government based on the U.S. government model. A couple of decades after removal, the Cherokee formed a new government with an executive, legislative, and judicial system. This government successfully led its people, providing many high-quality services, particularly in education.

In 1906, as Oklahoma was about to be made a state, the U.S. government dissolved the government of the Cherokee Nation and took over tribal affairs. From then until the 1970s, when the Cherokee Nation organized a new government, the presidents of the United States appointed the principal chiefs of the tribe, who had little authority.

By the end of the twentieth century, the Cherokee Nation tribal government consisted of a fifteen-member elected tribal council whose members served four-year terms and worked with a principal chief. The Cherokee Nation District Court handled judicial matters. An agreement made with the U.S. Congress in 1990 gave the tribe even more control over its own affairs.

In 1999, a committee met to create a new Constitution. The people voted to accept it in 2003, and it was enacted in 2006. A seventeen-member legislative council works with the executive branch of a Principal Chief and Deputy Principal Chief and four cabinet members. A five-member Cherokee Nation Supreme Court is now the highest tribal court and oversees the District Court system.

ECONOMY

Early economy

Prior to contact with Europeans, the Cherokee economy was based on farming and hunting. Women did most of the farming, took care of the animals, prepared the food, made clothing, and cared for the house and children. Men served as warriors and hunters. They cleared fields for farming and built houses and canoes. They also hunted many types of animals.

The Cherokee used all parts of a captured animal. Bears supplied meat and grease for food, fur for clothing, and claws for jewelry. The tribe used the flesh of deer for food, the skin and hide (tanned with a solution made from deer brains) for clothing and other objects, the bones and antlers for tools and ornaments, the tendons for thread, and the hooves for glue.

Before trade with Europeans began, the Cherokee did not generally accumulate possessions or wealth. By the 1820s, however, many Cherokee had intermarried with whites and become landowners. Many had even become slave owners. They raised cotton and other crops on large farms and plantations and sold the crops for profit. For most of the Cherokee people, the period of removal meant the loss of most of the wealth they had accumulated.

The creation of the Great Smoky Mountains National Park in the 1930s helped to improve the economic condition of Cherokee living in North Carolina. After World War II (1939–45; a war in which Great Britain, France, the United States, and their allies defeated Germany, Italy, and Japan), the park had become the main industry at the Eastern Cherokee Reservation in North Carolina.

Modern economy

The Cherokee Nation owns multiple casinos along with hospitality, retail, and tourism businesses. In addition, the tribally owned Cherokee Nation Industries (CNI) employed many tribal members in its electronic parts factory; aerospace and defense manufacturing divisions helped the economy grow and added new jobs. The nation also operated a variety of other businesses, including ranches, poultry farms, tobacco shops, arts and crafts outlets, a cabinet factory, and a construction company.

Both the Cherokee Nation in Oklahoma and the Eastern Band of Cherokee in North Carolina opened gaming facilities and used tourism to help finance tribal services. The Eastern Band of Cherokee, in its efforts to broaden the economy, invests in businesses through its Sequoyah Fund. In 2011, the band's Cherokee Preservation Foundation gave out more than $2.7 million in grants for economic development, job creation, cultural preservation, and environmental protection. The goal of one grant is to develop renewable-energy sources and model energy-efficiency projects on the Qualla Boundary.

DAILY LIFE

Families

The Cherokee people were organized into seven clans (family groups) according to the ancestry of the mother. Usually a woman lived with her husband, their children, her parents, her sisters, her sisters' children, and any unmarried brothers. Fathers felt close to their children but were not considered their blood relatives.

Women's roles

The Cherokee were a matrilineal society, meaning that family lines were traced through the women of the tribe. Women controlled the fields and often worked behind the scenes to help make major decisions. They also often served as warriors in battle. Women who had great influence or power were known as *Ghighua*, or "Beloved Women." The most noted Cherokee Beloved Woman was Nan'yehi (Nancy Ward; c. 1738–1824), a brave warrior and tribal leader of the late seventeenth century who tried to warn her people against signing away their land rights to the invading culture.

Buildings

A Cherokee town was made up of a council house, a town square, and thirty to sixty private homes. A fence made of vertical poles placed close together surrounded the town to protect the people from attack. The circular council house was large enough to hold all four hundred to five hundred citizens for council meetings and major religious ceremonies. The square was used for ceremonies, meetings, and social events.

It remains unclear whether traditional Cherokee dwellings consisted of a single building or multiple buildings. It is known, however, that the walls of the structures were formed by weaving small tree branches between support posts and then plastering clay and grass over the framework. The roofs were thatched with bark shingles. By the nineteenth century, the log cabin had become the most popular type of house among the Cherokee.

Clothing and adornment

Deerskin was used for clothing and moccasins. Members of the tribe who made the clothing sewed the garments together with bone needles and animal tendons. Cherokee men wore breechcloths—garments with front and back flaps that hung from the waist. In cold weather, they added deerskin leggings, fringed shirts, and robes made of fur or feathers. Beneath their deerskin dresses, women wore long, fringed petticoats (slips) woven or knitted from the wild hemp plant.

For festive occasions, the Cherokee wore accessories made from turkey or eagle feathers, dyed porcupine quills, mulberry-root bark, or thread spun from the hair of bear or opossum. They also wore wristbands and armbands decorated with horn and shell rattles. Bones, shells, and copper were used to make jewelry.

Men often decorated their bodies and faces with paint or tattoos. They wore earrings and elongated their earlobes by cutting holes in them and inserting stones or bone in the holes. In early times, Cherokee men grew beards, sometimes braiding them in three sections. By the time the Europeans arrived, though, it was common for the men of the tribe to pluck out all of their facial hair.

Hairstyles for Cherokee men were quite distinctive. A man plucked out a two-inch-wide ring around a palm-sized section of hair on the crown of his heads. Then he pulled the long top section through a decorated, two-inch piece of hollowed deer antler, and painted any loose ends around the topknot with a thick, colored paste. The hair below the plucked ring was cut short. Women used bear grease to make their hair glossy and decorated it with yellow or red dust. They either wore it loose or tied it in a high knot.

Food

The Cherokee farmed, hunted, and gathered their food. They grew beans, squash, sunflowers, melons, pumpkin, other food crops, and tobacco on their group farms. They gathered wild nuts, roots, and fruits from the surrounding countryside, and preserved food for winter months by drying it.

Women of the Cherokee tribe kept a kettle of soup or stew bubbling at all times. It was their method for using up leftovers. A particular favorite was a mixture of game or fowl, usually squirrel, rabbit, or turkey, mixed with corn, beans, and tomatoes. The settlers in Jamestown, Virginia, called it Brunswick stew.

Corn was the primary Cherokee crop. One variety was used for roasting, another for boiling, and a third for grinding into cornmeal. Ingredients such as dried beans and chestnuts were often added to cornmeal bread, which was topped with bear grease or oil from pounded nuts. *Kanuche*, a rich broth made by boiling crushed hickory nuts in water, could be mixed with corn or rice.

Fishing provided much food for the tribe. To catch fish, the men made use of hooks, nets, traps, bows, and even poison designed to stun the fish long enough for the people to simply pick up the ones they wanted. Although the Cherokee ate bear, turkey, rabbit, and other small game, deer was the most important source of animal food. When hunting deer, Cherokee men disguised themselves by wearing entire deerskins with antlers. This allowed them to sneak up on their prey without being noticed. Using blowguns, they could hunt small animals from a distance of 60 feet (18 meters) or more. A blowgun was made by hollowing out a long cane stem, 7 or 8 feet (2 to 2.5 meters) in length. Wood splints, balanced with feathers or thistles, were used as darts and blown through the hollow tube.

Education

From the time they were small, Cherokee children were taught lessons in bravery by having to endure hunger and pain. They also learned to respect the earth and other creatures and to honor their elders. A boy was instructed in male roles by his mother's brothers. From them he learned to hunt, make war, and carry on ceremonies. A girl learned to care for the house and children by assisting her mother and her mother's sisters. She also learned to weave, garden, and make baskets.

In the late 1700s, the Cherokee Nation developed its own schools. When Sequoyah's writing system spread through the nation, the Cherokee people had a higher literacy rate (meaning more people could read and write) than the settlers who lived nearby in the Southeast. After being forced to move to what is now Oklahoma, the Cherokee reestablished their unique educational system. In the 1840s, they started 144 elementary schools and two high schools (called seminaries)—one for men and one for women. The Cherokee Female Seminary was modeled after the innovative programs at Mount Holyoke Seminary (later Mount Holyoke College) in Massachusetts. Financial problems later led to the closing of both Native high schools. When the state of Oklahoma was created in the early 1900s, the U.S. Congress abolished the Cherokee school system.

Many Native groups in the late twentieth century modeled their own community schools on the school systems created by the Cherokee. In the early 2000s, the Cherokee Nation offered job training and assistance, vocational-technical schools, and programs for children, teens, and adults. An education department oversaw educational opportunities for Cherokee students of all ages.

Healing practices

The Cherokee believed that illness came into the world when animals became angry with humans for intruding on their territory and killing them for food. Plants friendly to humans helped cure these animal-caused diseases. The root of white nettle, for instance, was used on open sores; a tea brewed from witch hazel bark was said to cure fevers; tobacco juice was used to treat bee stings and snake bites. Tobacco was looked upon as a powerful medicine—so powerful, in fact, that a lotion made from it could make unhappy wives fall in love with their husbands again.

The Cherokee believed that spiritual help promoted healing. Priests served as doctors; they knew all the proper prayers and chants and the correct methods of applying medicines. Healers sometimes massaged patients with hands warmed by sacred fire, told them to plunge into a cold stream immediately after a sweat bath, or scratched the victim's body and sucked out the cause of the illness.

The arrival of Europeans in the New World brought a variety of new diseases to which the Native peoples had no natural immunity. After a series of epidemics killed half the Cherokee population in the first half of the eighteenth century, many people lost confidence in their doctor-priests. Tribal members sought medical treatment from non-Native doctors, believing that it took European doctors to cure these illnesses. Still, many of the traditional medicines were effective for other sicknesses and are still in use.

ARTS

Oral literature

The Cherokee have always used legends to teach children about the history of the tribe and the proper way to live. Stories also explain the workings of the natural world. To preserve this storytelling past, the Tsalagi Library of the Cherokee Nation developed puppet shows based on traditional characters.

Carving and basketry

The Cherokee were known for the beauty of their carvings and basketry. They made tools and pipes from materials such as stone and wood. Canoes were made of poplar, a craft that is still demonstrated at the Oconaluftee Indian Village in Cherokee, North Carolina. For baskets, the women used honeysuckle vine, cane, and a vine called wild hemp, then painted the finished baskets with dyes from various plants and roots.

Theater and museums

Unto These Hills, a modern-day pageant honoring Cherokee history, is performed every year at the Eastern Cherokee Reservation in Cherokee, North Carolina, which also operates the Qualla Arts and Crafts Center.

A Cherokee Myth of Good and Evil

To the Cherokee, Uk'ten', a horned, snake-like monster, embodies evil. The tribe tells this tale to explain why Lightning (Uk'ten') follows Thunder.

Long ago there was a boy out walking, hunting with his bow and arrows. He was on the top of a rough, rugged hill. From where he was, he heard, somewhere down below where it was even more rugged, a thundering, and he was very anxious to find out what caused it.

In looking for it, he arrived down in the valley, and in the ruggedest place Thunder and an Uk'ten' (he was from the sea) had hold of each other in a fierce fight. Thunder was underneath: the Uk'ten' was so long and so strong—that's why he was able to overcome Thunder.

The boy looked at them fighting. (It was thundering very low.) When the boy was seen, when Thunder looked at him, Thunder said, "Nephew, help me! When he looks at you, he will kill you!"

And then the Uk'ten' said, "Nephew, help me! When he thunders, he will kill you!"

They both kept saying these things.

Because Thunder was being bested, the boy felt sorry for him. He decided to shoot at the Uk'ten'. When he shot the Uk'ten', he [the Uk'ten'] was weakened.

Then a second time he pulled his bow. The Uk'ten' was weakened even more and Thunder was becoming stronger. He made his thunders louder, and on the fourth thunder, the fiercest ever heard, he killed the Uk'ten'.

Thunder won, and the boy had helped him [to win]. That is the reason why to this day it thunders [all] around us: we [Thunder and man] are still together. A human being helped him.

Thunder is not fierce, but is very friendly and kind of heart because he knows that it was a little boy who saved him. (But he can become fierce if he does not like something.) He is really very friendly because he knows that it was a human being who saved him.

If the Uk'ten' had overcome Thunder, if Thunder had been shot, I suppose that the Uk'ten' would be lurking about everywhere. I wonder what it would have been like: Thunder would have killed us whenever it thundered, and an Uk'ten' can kill you just by smelling you.

SOURCE: Kilpatrick, Jack F., and Anna G. Kilpatrick. *Friends of Thunder: Folktales of the Omaha Cherokee.* Norman: University of Oklahoma Press, 1994. Reprinted in James D. Torr, ed. *Indigenous Peoples of North America: Primary Sources.* San Diego: Lucent Books, Inc., 2002.

For decades the Cherokee Nation of Oklahoma presented the drama *Trail of Tears* at their open-air theater in Tahlequah, Oklahoma. The Sequoyah Birthplace Museum, Tennessee's only Native-owned historic attraction, celebrates the life of the man who invented the Cherokee writing system.

CUSTOMS

Festivals

The Cherokee held six major ceremonies each year, following the course of the earth's growth and resting periods. The major ceremony, the Green Corn Dance, took place at harvest time and celebrated harmony and renewal. At this time, all crimes of the past year (except murder) were forgiven.

Cherokee ceremonies are celebrated at "stomp grounds," for religious dances. During Stomp Dances, people of all ages perform songs and rhythmic movements that create a sense of peacefulness. The dance is a type of prayer performed before a fire. The flame is lit from an ember of a sacred fire—one that never goes out. The stomp ground chief begins a dance and the dancers follow, moving in a winding line and twisting into a spiral as they circle the fire. Girls and women provide the rhythm by shaking turtle shell rattles attached around their legs.

The annual Cherokee Indian Fair has been held on the Eastern Cherokee Reservation since 1912. Cherokee National Holiday, a week-long celebration of Cherokee history and culture, takes place each year in Tahlequah, Oklahoma. Held since 1839 to commemorate the signing of the Cherokee Constitution, the event includes a parade, rodeo, arts and crafts, traditional singing and dancing, games, sports tournaments, and foods.

War and hunting rituals

The Cherokee held dances before hunting expeditions. The Buffalo Hunt Dance and Bear Dance, performed by both men and women, showed respect for the animals the hunters would kill.

Cherokee war parties consisted of two to a hundred men. Before going off to war, warriors performed special songs and dances and drank a beverage high in caffeine known as "black drink" to purify their systems by causing them to vomit.

Cherokee warriors sent ahead a team of spies wearing animal disguises. When they spotted the enemy, the spies made the sounds of the animal whose costume they were wearing to alert their companions to the locations of their foes.

In times of war, Cherokee women could accompany men into battle. If a man fell, his wife sometimes took his place in battle. Women warriors were known as "War Women." This status gave them the right to decide if prisoners lived or died.

Marriage and divorce

Men and women married outside their clan. If a couple divorced, the husband moved back to his mother's home. Adultery was a serious offense that resulted in a public whipping.

Birth

Two days after birth, a baby was passed over a fire four times by a priest, who asked for blessings for the child. Two to five days later, the priest took the infant to a creek or river, offered it to the Creator, prayed for its long and healthy life, then plunged the infant into the water seven times. An elder woman of the tribe would then give the child a name that reflected some physical or personality trait of the infant or that recalled an event that happened at the time of the birth. The child might keep the name for life or take another later, after some great personal achievement.

Funerals

Burials among the Cherokee took place promptly after death. Female relatives cried long and loudly, wailing the name of the departed one, and male relatives put on old clothes and placed ashes on their heads. Relatives observed a weeklong mourning period, during which they ate little and could not show anger or good cheer. The deceased's belongings were buried with the body or destroyed.

A priest performed a cleansing ritual at the house of the deceased and supervised the family's ceremonial bathing. A special hunting party set out to get meat for a feast to help ease the mourners' sorrow. Family and friends prepared and ate a meal seven days after the death. Widows were expected to mourn for several months and to neglect their personal grooming. Friends decided when a widow had grieved enough; then they washed her hair and dressed her in clean clothes.

CURRENT TRIBAL ISSUES

According to some Native sources, growing numbers of people are falsely claiming Cherokee ancestry to take advantage of federal government programs designed for tribal members. The Keetoowah tribe insists that its members must be one-quarter Cherokee to join, but the Cherokee Nation is less stringent with its requirements. In 2006, Cherokee Nation's spokesperson Mike Miller said, "People usually don't identify with something they don't like, so we take it as a good thing: People like Cherokees."

More than two hundred groups, in addition to the three federally recognized tribes, claim to have Cherokee heritage. Some have only banded together to celebrate their ancestry, but others are seeking federal recognition. Tribes that receive this recognition are entitled to financial help from the government and are recognized as independent nations. The Cherokee Nation maintains a list of the groups claiming to be Cherokee; many of these were not listed on the Dawes Rolls but trace their heritage to other Cherokee rolls. A few of these bands have received state recognition, but none has been granted federal recognition.

A controversy that has led to national publicity concerned the Cherokee Freedmen, an African American group, many of them descendants of escaped slaves who sought refuge with the Cherokee. In early 2006, the Cherokee Nation Judicial Appeal Tribunal announced that members of this group were official Cherokee citizens. That decision met with opposition from tribe members, and a year later, the Cherokee Freedman's citizenship was revoked. Many other groups protested, and the Cherokee Nation courts reinstated the Freedman's citizenship, but as of mid-2011, a Supreme Court appeal was still pending.

Since the 1890s, the United Keetoowah Band in Oklahoma has set itself apart from the Cherokee Nation. In 1978, the Cherokee Nation tried without success to make the Keetoowah people part of their tribe. In the late 1990s, as part of their efforts to keep their identity separate from other Cherokee, the Keetoowah planned to move back to Arkansas, the territory from which they had been forcibly moved more than 175 years earlier. In 2011, the Bureau of Indian Affairs agreed to take 76 acres of land in Tahlequah, Oklahoma, into trust for the United Keetoowah Band of Cherokee Indians. That same year, the band was also selected to participate in the U.S. Department of the Interior's tribal self-governing program beginning in 2011.

NOTABLE PEOPLE

Sequoyah (c. 1770–1843), who is believed to have been the son of a part-Cherokee woman and a white man, went by the English name George Guess. He grew up without any formal education and spoke no English. Despite a crippled leg, he fought in two European-led wars. He later observed whites using written forms of communication. He decided to give his people the same advantage and invented a written language. Sequoyah traveled far and wide teaching the language to his people, and soon thousands of Cherokee could read and write.

Wilma Mankiller (1945–2010) was elected principal chief of the Cherokee Nation of Oklahoma, making her the first woman to lead a major tribe. She was reelected twice. Robert Latham Owen (1856–1947) was the second American Indian elected to the U.S. Senate, serving from 1907 to 1925, and one of the first two senators to represent the state of Oklahoma.

BOOKS

Basel, Roberta. *Sequoyah: Inventor of Written Cherokee.* Minneapolis, MN: Compass Point Books, 2007.

Donlan, Leni. *Cherokee Rose: The Trail of Tears.* Chicago, IL: Raintree, 2007.

Fariello, Anna. *Cherokee Basketry: From the Hands of Our Elders.* Charleston, SC: History Press, 2009.

Foster, Sharon Ewell. *Abraham's Well: A Novel.* Minneapolis, MN: Bethany House, 2006.

Glancy, Diane. *Pushing the Bear: After the Trail of Tears.* Norman: University of Oklahoma Press, 2009.

Green, Michael D., and Theda Perdue. *The Cherokee Nation and the Trail of Tears.* New York: Viking, 2007.

Josephson, Judith Pinkerton. *Why Did Cherokees Move West? And Other Questions about the Trail of Tears.* Minneapolis: Lerner Publications, 2011.

Lefler, Lisa J. *Under the Rattlesnake: Cherokee Health and Resiliency.* Tuscaloosa: University of Alabama Press, 2009.

Lumpkin, Wilson. *The Removal of the Cherokee Indians from Georgia.* Mansfield Center, CT: Martino, 2008.

Marsi, Katie. *The Trail of Tears: The Tragedy of the American Indians.* New York: Marshall Cavendish Benchmark, 2010.

Mooney, James. *Myths of the Cherokee.* New York: Dover Publications, 1996.

Moore, Stephen L. *Last Stand of the Texas Cherokees: Chief Bowles and the 1839 Cherokee War in Texas.* Garland, TX: RAM Books, 2009.

Naylor, Celia E. *African Cherokees in Indian Territory: From Chattel to Citizens.* Chapel Hill: University of North Carolina Press, 2008.

Power, Susan C. *Art of the Cherokee: Prehistory to the Present.* Athens: University of Georgia Press, 2007.

Sneve, Virginia Driving Hawk. *The Cherokee.* New York: Holiday House, 1996.

Sonneborn, Liz. *Wilma Mankiller.* New York: Marshall Cavendish Benchmark, 2010.

Wade, Mary Dodson. *Amazing Cherokee Writer Sequoyah.* Berkeley Heights, NJ: Enslow, 2009.

Ward, Jill. *The Cherokees.* Hamilton, GA: State Standards, 2010.

WEB SITES

Cherokee Nation. http://www.cherokee.org/ (accessed on June 12, 2011).

Hicks, Brian. "The Cherokees vs. Andrew Jackson." *Smithsonian.* Available online from http://www.smithsonianmag.com/history-archaeology/The-Cherokees-vs-Andrew-Jackson.html (accessed on June 12, 2011).

"History and Culture." *Cherokee North Carolina.* http://www.cherokee-nc.com/history_intro.php (accessed on June 12, 2011).

Indian Country Diaries. "Trail of Tears." *PBS (Public Broadcasting Service).* http://www.pbs.org/indiancountry/history/trail.html (accessed on June 12, 2011).

Redish, Laura, and Orrin Lewis. "Cherokee Indian Fact Sheet." *Native Languages of the Americas.* http://www.bigorrin.org/cherokee_kids.htm (accessed on June 12, 2011).

Sultzman, Lee. "Cherokee History." *First Nations Histories.* http://tolatsga.org/Cherokee1.html (accessed on June 12, 2011).

United Keetoowah Band. http://www.unitedkeetoowahband.org/ (accessed on June 12, 2011).

Whisnant, Anne Mitchell. "Parkway Development and the Eastern Band of Cherokees." *The University of North Carolina at Chapel Hill.* http://docsouth.unc.edu/blueridgeparkway/overlooks/cherokee-1/ (accessed on June 12, 2011).

Chickasaw

Name

The name Chickasaw (pronounced *CHICK-uh-saw*) may come from a story of two brothers, Chisca and Chacta, from whom the Chickasaw and the Choctaw tribes are said to be descended. The British called the Chickasaw "Flat Heads" because of an ancient tribal custom of flattening the skulls of children by putting a weight on their heads.

Location

The Chickasaw thrived in northeastern Mississippi at the head of the Tombigbee River. They controlled the entire Mississippi River Valley as well as parts of western Tennessee and Kentucky and eastern Arkansas. One group was invited by South Carolina officials to settle on the Savannah River near Augusta, Georgia, and did so in 1723. By the beginning of the twenty-first century, the Chickasaw Nation territory included a multicounty area of more than 7,640 square miles (19,800 square kilometers) in south-central Oklahoma.

Population

In 1693, there were an estimated 10,000 Chickasaw. In 1890, that number had decreased to 6,400. In the 1990 U.S. Census, 21,522 people identified themselves as Chickasaw, although the Chickasaw Nation had 35,000 enrolled members at that time. In the 2000 census, 20,887 people said they were Chickasaw, and 41,974 people claimed some Chickasaw ancestry. According to tribal sources, 38,000 Chicasaw were enrolled in the tribe in 2005. That number had reached 49,000 by 2011, according to the Oklahoma Indian Affairs Commission.

Language family

Muskogean.

Origins and group affiliations

The Chickasaw tell stories of originating in the West, possibly the Red River valley in Texas, where they were part of the Choctaw tribe. About

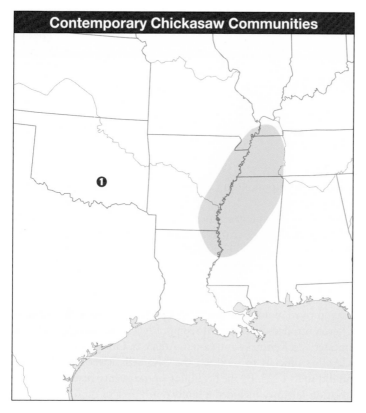

Contemporary Chickasaw Communities

Oklahoma
❶ Chickasaw Nation

Shaded area
Traditional Chickasaw lands along the Mississippi River Valley in present-day Mississippi, as well as parts of western Tennessee and Kentucky, eastern Arkansas, northeastern Louisiana and southeastern Missouri

A map of contemporary Chickasaw communities. MAP BY XNR PRODUCTIONS. CENGAGE LEARNING, GALE. REPRODUCED BY PERMISSION OF GALE, A PART OF CENGAGE LEARNING.

1300, they crossed the Mississippi River and separated from the Choctaw (see entry), who alternated between being their allies and enemies. In fact, the Chickasaw fought with many tribes, including the Creek, Caddo, Cherokee, Iroquois, Menominee, Potawatomi, and Shawnee (see entries).

The Chickasaw were a fierce, warlike people who struck fear into the hearts of all who crossed their path. Their longtime allies, the British, recognized their courage and willingness to take on any foe, no matter how superior the enemy's numbers. The British supplied the Chickasaw generously with weapons and relied on their help to take over the North American continent. In the late 1700s, when American colonists seized control of the eastern part of North America, they drove the tribe from its ancestral lands. The Chickasaw became part of a group known as the "Five Civilized Tribes," which was forced to move to Oklahoma.

HISTORY

Troubled encounter with the Spanish

Long before the arrival of the Europeans, the Chickasaw defended their fertile territory in the Mississippi River Valley against any newcomers who dared set their sights on it. Chickasaw men thought of themselves first as warriors, then as hunters, and last as farmers.

In the late winter of 1540, Spanish explorer Hernando de Soto (c. 1496–1542) led an expedition into Chickasaw territory, making the first recorded contact with the tribe. The relations between the two groups were uneasy, with distrust on both sides. The Spanish demanded food and a place to set up a winter camp. Chief Miculasa reluctantly agreed. According to historian Lee Sultzman, the Spanish shared some of their roast pork from the herd of pigs that traveled with them. The Chickasaw reportedly "loved it" and began to help themselves to Spanish pigs. The Spanish responded by killing two of the thieves and cutting off the hands of the third. Tensions mounted, and the Chickasaw eventually launched a surprise attack on the Spanish, driving off de Soto's party. Their victory over the Spanish earned the Chickasaw a reputation across Europe as bloodthirsty warriors. The Spanish left the region in March 1541, never to return.

Allies of the British

British traders based in South Carolina established trading posts along the Mississippi River in 1700, and the Chickasaw became their allies and trading partners. The traders had heard of the tribe's superior fighting ability. In exchange for animal skins and slaves, they supplied the Chickasaw with guns, metal tools, knives, and cotton cloth. The Chickasaw people used the guns for hunting and for carrying out assaults on the French, who were battling Spain and England for control of the North American continent.

To get more skins for trade, the Chickasaw expanded their hunting expeditions into the territory of neighboring tribes, kidnapping their

Important Dates

1540: The Chickasaw meet their first European, Spanish treasure-hunter Hernando de Soto.

1698: The Chickasaw make their first contact with the British, who build trading posts two years later.

1786: The Treaty of Hopewell, the first treaty between the Chickasaw and the U.S. government, is signed.

1837: The Chickasaw agree to lease land in Indian Territory from their old enemies, the Choctaw, and begin the move from their homeland.

1856: The Chickasaw Nation is created.

1906: The Chickasaw Nation is dissolved.

1970: The present-day Chickasaw Nation is granted the right to regroup and to elect its own leaders.

women and children to trade as slaves as they went along. Meanwhile, distant tribes, pushed westward by American colonists, tried to take over Chickasaw land. Throughout the eighteenth century, the Chickasaw people engaged in almost constant fighting. Frequent contact with the British led many Chickasaw to adopt European ways. The makeup and culture of the tribe changed dramatically as many Chickasaw women married British men and gave birth to children of mixed blood. More cultural changes took place as the tribe willingly adopted refugees from other tribes who had been defeated by the French.

The Chickasaw remained allies of the British (but saw little actual fighting) until England's defeat by the freedom-seeking colonists in the American Revolution (1775–83). After the war, the tribe signed a treaty with the victorious Americans. The Treaty of Hopewell (1786) established the boundaries of Chickasaw territory, and American settlers agreed to stay off the land. However, future conflicts with settlers—who never seemed to have enough land—were almost guaranteed.

Treaties reduce homeland

In 1784, a measles epidemic struck the Chickasaw and killed many of their leaders. Weakened but still ready to defend their territory, the tribe engaged in a four-decade battle with the Creek, the Osage (see entries), and others, who were stealing from them and attacking their hunting parties.

U.S. officials assured southern tribes that they did not want their land—the settlers already had plenty. In time, however, all confidence in this pledge to respect Native land rights was dashed. First, neighboring tribes such as the Cherokee, Choctaw, and Creek (see entries) gave up land to the U.S. government. Then in 1801, the Chickasaw granted the Americans permission to build a road through their homeland. Within eight years, some five thousand Americans were living on Chickasaw land illegally. The U.S. government pressured the Chickasaw to leave and make way for more settlers. The tribe could see that their control of the region was nearing an end.

In 1832, the first in a series of treaties giving all Chickasaw lands east of the Mississippi River to the U.S. government was signed. The treaties called for the removal of the Chickasaw to Indian Territory, the land that now forms most of the state of Oklahoma. Over the remaining decades of the nineteenth century, the U.S. government moved many other tribes to Indian Territory.

The Great Seal of the Chickasaw Nation. © BETTMANN/ CORBIS.

The Chickasaw wanted their own land in Oklahoma but could find nothing to suit them. They finally decided to lease a portion of land from the Choctaw, their old enemies. The Chickasaw thereby became part of the movement of the "Five Civilized Tribes" to Indian Territory. (The Five Civilized Tribes were the Chickasaw, Choctaw, Seminole, Creek, and Cherokee [see entries]. The settlers gave them this name because they had established institutions that were valued in American society.)

Removal to Indian Territory

The removal of these five tribes to Indian Territory took nearly twenty years. The Chickasaw were the wealthiest of the five tribes and had greater access to wagons and other timesaving equipment that made relocation easier. They accomplished their move more quickly than other groups, in only two years (1837–38). A count of the tribe's population taken just before their departure showed 4,914 Chickasaw and 1,156 black slaves. The Chickasaw also took five thousand horses with them and were plagued most of the way by would-be horse thieves. Throughout the journey, many of the tribe's members died from smallpox, malnourishment, or illness brought on by eating spoiled government-supplied food. Among the dead was Chief Tishomingo, the last great Chickasaw war chief, who had lived to the age of 102.

Conditions in Indian Territory were far from ideal. The region was filled with unhappy ex-warriors from numerous different tribes, many of them longtime enemies. An atmosphere of tension and chaos reigned. Living in Indian Territory on Choctaw land, the Chickasaw argued among themselves and with the Choctaw, whom they feared would come to control them. The conflicts were resolved in 1855 when the Chickasaw signed a treaty with the United States that created the land boundaries of an independent Chickasaw district. The next year the Chickasaw people formed their nation. They adopted a constitution and laws, elected Cyrus Harris (1817–1888) as their first governor, established a capital city at Tishomingo, and erected various government buildings.

Division over America's Civil War

Though unified as a tribe by 1856, the Chickasaw people soon found themselves divided by conflicting political views. Some members of the tribe were mixed-blood slaveholders who had attained great wealth in American business. Others were more traditional full-blooded Chickasaw who took a strong stand against slavery. Matters came to a head with the outbreak of the American Civil War (1861–65; a war between the Union [the North], which was opposed to slavery, and the Confederacy [the South], which was in favor of slavery). Many Chickasaw joined Union forces, whereas the "official" Chickasaw Nation signed a treaty with the Confederacy. Many Chickasaw warriors lost their lives in the bloody struggle.

After 1865, with the Civil War over and no longer a distraction, settlers cast their eyes on Indian Territory and began to move in, despite laws restricting such actions. They called for a reevaluation of the reservation system, arguing that too much land had been set aside for Native Americans and that the assimilation process (the Natives' adoption of American ways) was moving far too slowly.

Allotment of Chickasaw lands

The Chickasaw were the wealthiest and most advanced of the five nations living in Indian Territory. They had developed their oil resources and moved into the cattle industry. However, internal feuds continued to turn the Chickasaw against each other. After one conflict-filled election, intermarried white Chickasaw citizens were stripped of their citizenship in the Chickasaw Nation. These conflicts did not last long, as the U.S. Congress moved forward with its allotment plans. Allotment called for reservations to be divided into small parcels of land. Each person would be given an allotment to tend on his or her own, instead of large plots being tended by an entire tribe, as was their custom. Leftover land was opened up to settlers.

Chickasaw lands were allotted in 1897. Each full-blooded Chickasaw (then 1,538 of the 6,319 Chickasaw population) received 320 acres of land. In 1907, Oklahoma was admitted as the forty-sixth state of the United States. Just prior to this, the federal government dissolved the Chickasaw Nation, along with the governments of all five nations of the Civilized Tribes. By 1920, about 75 percent of Chickasaw lands had been either sold or leased to settlers. The Chickasaw Nation continued only as a tribal council led by a federally appointed governor. Many of the Chickasaw people moved away or assimilated into the local population.

Finally, Congress granted the Chickasaw tribe the right to elect its own leaders in 1970, and the people were able to regroup. Only in the 1990s did the tribe begin to recover from the blow of losing its land to allotment.

As the twentieth century drew to a close, a majority of Chickasaw lived scattered throughout several counties in southern Oklahoma. Although Chickasaw Nation is federally recognized, no Chickasaw reservation exists. (Federally recognized tribes are those with which the U.S. government maintains official relations. Without federal recognition, the tribe does not exist as far as the government is concerned and therefore is not entitled to financial aid or other assistance.) They do have Kullihoma, which is not a reservation, but a tribal reserve. In the past, it held a stomp ground for dances, along with a school and a community. Presently, it is used for Chickasaw reunions.

RELIGION

Everything in the Chickasaw world was filled with religious meaning. Rituals were closely tied to the moon and its phases, and the tribe celebrated the beginning of each lunar cycle. The Chickasaw believed in a supreme being called *Ababinili*, a combination of the Four Beloved

Things Above: Sun, Clouds, Clear Sky, and He That Lives in the Clear Sky. The tribe also recognized a host of other lesser powers, witches, and evil spirits. In the old times a priest called a *hopaye* conducted religious ceremonies and explained the meaning of signs, symbols, dreams, and other events to his followers.

The Chickasaw believed in a life after death. They buried their dead facing west—toward the pathway to judgment. The good were said to journey on to a world where they were rewarded for their life's work; the evil, however, would be trapped between worlds, destined to wander in the Land of the Witches.

Baptist, Presbyterian, and Methodist missionaries worked among the Chickasaw after 1819, and today most Chickasaw belong to either Baptist or Methodist churches.

The Chickasaw came into contact with a variety of religious philosophies late in the nineteenth century. Among them were the Ghost Dance and Peyote (pronounced *pay-OH-tee*) religions. A Paiute (see entry) named Wovoka (c. 1856–1932) initiated the Ghost Dance movement. Among the messages it spread were that the Native peoples should love and help one another, and return to their traditions. Followers hoped that its dances would bring dead ancestors and game back to Earth and would restore the world to the way it had been before the settlers arrived.

Followers of the Peyote religion developed their own ceremonies, songs, and symbols. Peyote is a cactus native to the Southwest. When eaten, it brings on a dreamlike feeling and often produces visions, which followers of the Peyote religion felt moved them closer to the spirit world. Followers took peyote as a sacrament and vowed to follow the Peyote Road. They promised to be trustworthy, honorable, and community-oriented. Chickasaw people may have participated in Ghost Dance and Peyote ceremonies held by other Oklahoma tribes.

LANGUAGE

In the eighteenth century, the Chickasaw branch of the Muskogean language was the common language used between settlers and all Native peoples living along the Lower Mississippi River. Only about 550 people spoke this language in the 1990s, but many of these speakers were working to teach and preserve the language.

GOVERNMENT

Traditional Chickasaw villages and towns were fiercely independent; only during times of war did the people put aside their differences and unite. A chief called a High Minko (an inherited position) and a war chief called a Tishu Minko led the villages. Tribal elders and priests served as advisers.

After 1800, Chickasaw leaders authorized mixed-blood members of the tribe to oversee dealings with U.S. officials. The mixed-bloods were well versed in the ways of the settlers, and throughout the nineteenth century they advocated the idea of giving up Chickasaw lands to the settlers. Some mixed-blood supporters even received money from the U.S. government for backing that plan.

The U.S. government dissolved the Chickasaw Nation in 1906, despite protests by the Chickasaw and even their attempt to form a separate state. The United States appointed tribal governors until Congress granted the Chickasaw the right to elect their own in 1970. At that time, the Chickasaw elected Governor Overton James, and under his leadership, the modern Chickasaw Nation was born.

The Chickasaw Nation describes its current government as a democratic republic, modeled after that of the federal government. Registered

The U.S. Cavalry suppresses an uprising by the Chickasaw people in 1906. © MARY EVANS PICTURE LIBRARY/THE IMAGE WORKS.

voters elect a governor and lieutenant governor to four-year terms. The voters also elect thirteen members to the tribal legislature. Three Chickasaw Supreme Court justices perform duties much like those of the justices of the U.S. Supreme Court (the highest court in the United States). The seat of the Chickasaw government is Ada, Oklahoma.

ECONOMY

In traditional times, the Chickasaw were mainly hunters; farming was a secondary occupation. After the British arrived, though, the tribe's way of life changed. Extensive trading was carried on, and Chickasaw hunter-warriors became dependent on British guns for their livelihood. The Chickasaw developed their own breed of horse (the Chickasaw Horse, known for its endurance and its long, graceful stride) for conducting trade with the British. In addition, some mixed-blood Chickasaw grew very wealthy running large plantations (farms) powered by slave labor.

Chickasaw life was thoroughly disrupted after the tribe's removal to Indian Territory, and again by allotment and the abolishment of the tribal government. After a period of readjustment, though, some Chickasaw prospered as the wealthiest and most advanced members of the Five Civilized Tribes. Many remain farmers or cattle and horse raisers.

In the 1970s and 1980s, under the strong leadership of Governor Overton James, the Chickasaw took advantage of state and federal loan programs to encourage tribal self-sufficiency through business ownership. The Chickasaw Nation later began operating several gaming centers with bingo—a primary source of money and employment. In the late 1990s, the nation employed about 1,300 people in its various enterprises, which include a motel, restaurant, smoke shops, a computer equipment and supply company, and trading posts. By the early 2000s, the tribal government employed six thousand people. The Chickasaw also operate businesses that catered to tourists at the tribe's historic capital city, Tishomingo, and at sites such as the Chickasaw National Recreation Area, Oklahoma's only national park.

The tribe began Chickasaw Nation Industries, Inc. (CNI) in 1996 to manage government contracts. Within a decade, CNI had become a large and successful corporation and employed more than two thousand people. It owned and managed many different businesses in a variety of fields such as aviation, mining, construction, information technology, manufacturing, and medical services. The income from these various ventures provides millions of dollars in revenue for the tribe.

DAILY LIFE

Families

The Chickasaw is a matrilineal tribe; family lines are traced through the women of the tribe. Children usually take their mother's house or clan-name. Men and women of the same house or clan-name may not marry.

Cleanliness was important to the Chickasaw, and they bathed daily, even in winter when there was ice on the water. They believed bathing removed the evil and trouble of the previous day. Women were expected to keep the house clean. If a woman did not, the tribe punished her by scratching her on the arms and legs with dried snake teeth.

Buildings

Centuries ago, Chickasaw families typically owned three buildings: a winter house, a summer house, and a storage building. Some also

Replicas of the thatched-roof summer homes used by the Chickasaw people stand in Memphis, Tennessee. © NORTH WIND PICTURE ARCHIVES.

built special steam rooms called sweathouses, used for purification rites.

The Chickasaw dug to a depth of 3 feet (1 meter) into the ground to build their winter houses. They constructed the frame from pine logs and poles and then covered it with clay and plaster made from dried grass for added protection against the cold. These houses were so warm, in fact, that visiting British traders often complained about the heat.

The Chickasaw summer house was rectangular. Walls were made of a combination of woven mats and clay plaster, and roofs were made of thatch or bark. The houses had porches, balconies, and a central partition dividing the interior into two rooms. The pioneers later adopted this design for their log cabins.

A house at the center of the community was used for meetings and ceremonies. The Chickasaw used the grounds surrounding this house for ceremonies, ball games, and other gatherings.

Chickasaw villages changed in size based on the politics of the time. In times of peace, the villages tended to spread out. In times of war, the houses and buildings were clustered more closely in fewer, larger villages, often situated in the hills to discourage attackers.

Clothing and adornment

Europeans noted that Chickasaw men were uncommonly tall for Native peoples, averaging six feet in height, while women were a foot shorter. Children's heads were flattened in infancy, a look considered attractive. Mothers put a weighted cushion on a baby's forehead and bound that to the cradle with a band.

Men wore breechcloths, garments with front and back flaps that hung from the waist. In cold weather, they topped these with deerskin shirts, robes of bear fur, and deerskin boots. Deerskin leggings protected them when they rode through the underbrush. During special ceremonies and when preparing for war, men painted their faces. The most outstanding warriors wore a cape-like garment made from swan feathers. The men usually removed their body hair and shaved away the hair along the sides of their heads, leaving a tuft of hair down the center that they kept fixed in place with bear grease. Chickasaw women simply tied up their long hair and wore dresses made of deerskin.

Food

In traditional Chickasaw society, men hunted and women gathered food and raised crops; some Chickasaw women also supervised slaves. The men of the tribe were extremely skilled trackers and trappers. They used animal calls and decoys to lure wild game such as deer, buffalo, and bear. They coaxed fish out of deep waters with poisoned nuts, then easily speared or netted them.

The women gathered and cultivated a variety of wild foods, including strawberries, persimmons, onions, honey, and nuts. They also dried fruits and made tea from different wild roots and herbs.

Education

At birth, infant boys were placed on a panther's skin in the hope that they would acquire the animal's fierceness and power. This ritual marked the beginning of their training as warriors. Male children were trained and disciplined by their mother's brother.

At the turn of the twenty-first century, the Chickasaw Nation placed a strong emphasis on the education of its people. Children and adults attended public schools, vocational training centers, and colleges. Many students receive scholarships for higher education, and by 2001, 15.3 percent of the tribe had college degrees.

To encourage their youth to become future business owners, the tribe sponsors an Entrepreneurship Academy, where students learn business management and write their own business plans. Other educational programs the tribe has implemented include Head Start, Arts in Education, Chickasaw Nation Aviation and Space Academy, Upward Bound, Youth Leadership Camp, and internship programs that give students opportunities to gain experience in their chosen professions.

Healing practices

The Chickasaw believed that evil spirits caused sickness. Traditional Chickasaw healers, known as *aliktce*, fought these spirits with potions, teas, and poultices (soft, moist substances that are heated, spread on a cloth, and applied to inflamed parts of the body). Healers also conducted the Picofa Ceremony, performing special rites over the sick person four times a day for three days. During the ceremony, a fire was kept before the victim's front door; it usually faced east, opposite the Land of the

Dead. Only the family members of the sick person attended this service, and they danced around the fire at night. The name "Picofa" is taken from the cracked corn and pork casserole that participants ate on the third day of the ceremony.

ARTS

Oral literature

Like many other Native peoples, the Chickasaw have a long storytelling tradition that centers on tales of world-ending floods. The Chickasaw also tell creation stories—accounts of their origin in the Far West and their migration from there to the New World in ancient times. Tribal lore holds that the Choctaw and the Chickasaw—then one tribe known as the Chickemacaw—migrated over a long period of time, not all at once. They followed two brothers, Chisca and Chacta, who carried a magical pole that leaned eastward. The people settled on the eastern side of the Mississippi River, the place at which the pole stopped its eastward leaning. In *The True Story of Chief Tishomingo*, Cecil Sumners traces the origin of the name "Mississippi" to the cry of a tribal elder. Upon seeing the river the elder is said to have shouted, *Misha-sipo-kni,* meaning both "beyond the ages" and "father of waters."

CUSTOMS

Festivals, games, and ceremonies

Like the Seminole and other Southern tribes, Chickasaw men performed a purification ceremony in which they consumed a "black drink," a potion that contained a large amount of caffeine and made them vomit. In the summer, they entertained themselves by playing a particularly violent type of football. The games lasted a full day and involved hundreds of players.

The Chickasaw held two major annual festivals. One, called the Renewal of Traditions, lasted for two days in July and featured the Stomp Dance, ball games, storytelling, and traditional foods and crafts. The Chickasaw Nation Festival and Annual Meeting—a weeklong affair held each September—included a Princess Pageant, Chickasaw Nation Junior Olympics, and a powwow (a traditional song and dance celebration).

The Hunter and His Dog

One winter a man of the Red Skunk people went off hunting with his dog and made camp near a mountain. After several days he had killed lots of deer and bear, and he began to think of returning home.

On the very morning he was to begin his journey home, the mountain began to smoke. He set off, but after a time he saw that he was back in the same spot where he had camped at the foot of the mountain. For several days he tried desperately to get home, but he always ended up where he had started.

Finally he decided to stop and sleep. As he was dozing, he looked up to see a strange creature, about the size of a man, approaching him. The creature said nothing to the hunter and eventually went away.

The hunter's dog said, "You cannot stay here all night. If you do you will surely die."

"What shall I do?" the man said.

"If you want to escape," said the dog, "when the creature comes back, shoot an arrow as far as you can. The creature will chase the arrow.

Then begin running for home, and get ready to shoot another arrow if he catches up with you again."

Soon the creature appeared again, and the hunter shot an arrow far away. While the creature ran after it, he and his dog ran in the other direction.

When the creature found the arrow, he turned around and followed the man and his dog. As he got close, the man shot off another arrow. This continued until the hunter ran out of arrows and the creature was close behind. "Quick," the dog said, "let's get in this hollow tree."

They crawled in, and the dog licked at the opening until he had licked it closed. The creature could not get to them in the tree and finally left. The next morning the dog licked again at the hole until it was open.

Free of the creature at last, the man and his dog made their way home.

SOURCE: Brown, Virginia Pounds, and Laurella Owens, eds. *Southern Indian Myths and Legends.* Birmingham, AL: Beechwood Books, 1995.

War and hunting rituals

Chickasaw war parties in traditional times were small, consisting of thirty to fifty men. The warriors were best known for their sneak attacks on the enemy. Even after acquiring horses, Chickasaw warriors often traveled on foot because the landscape was heavily wooded.

They believed that the ghost of a dead warrior would haunt his family until his death was avenged (the person responsible for his death was punished). The widows of warriors killed in battle often slept directly over the tombs of their dead husbands.

Courtship and marriage

Women arranged all marriages. If a man decided to take a bride, he sent his mother and/or sister to the chosen girl's family, carrying enough cloth to make at least one dress. If her family agreed to the proposal, the bundle of cloth was presented to the bride-to-be, who sealed the pact by accepting the material. Then a marriage ceremony was held.

The man returned, dressed in his best clothes and his face painted. He and his future father-in-law ate dinner alone. After the meal, the groom joined his wife in her bed.

When a Chickasaw man married a woman, in a sense he married all of her sisters as well. He could choose to live with all of them. Likewise, if a man died, the man's brother had the right to marry the widow.

The tribe had a strict moral code. Unfaithfulness to a spouse was a serious offense among the Chickasaw, especially if the wife did the cheating. Women who bore children out of wedlock (without being married) were considered a disgrace to their families.

Funerals

In many ways, Chickasaw traditions were nearly identical to those of the Choctaw, but the tribes differed in their way of burying the dead. Chickasaw buried their dead beneath their houses with all their worldly possessions. They painted the faces of the dead red, and arranged the bodies in a sitting position, facing west (the direction of the land of the afterlife).

CURRENT TRIBAL ISSUES

Only in the last quarter of the twentieth century was the landless Chickasaw Nation able to move toward self-sufficiency and away from interference by the federal government. The tribe is making great strides in employing its people and educating its children.

Along with the Choctaw Nation, the Chickasaw are embroiled in a dispute about water rights with the state government of Oklahoma. In the 1970s, the state constructed the Sardis Lake Reservoir on Choctaw-Chickasaw land without consulting the tribe. The government forcibly removed the Native peoples, and the project flooded a Choctaw town and a Caddo cemetery. After the government could not pay the loan on the project, they decided to sell the water. The state of Texas, which needed water for agriculture, put in the highest bid. Chickasaw and Choctaw rights to the water were ignored. Although an earlier treaty gave Native peoples the rights to the water, a 2001 court decision split the water rights among the state (50 percent), Choctaw (37.5 percent), and Chickasaw (12.5 percent). Although this agreement did not recognize sovereignty (self-government) or tribal rights, the Chickasaw and Choctaw accepted it because they needed the money and water. As Oklahoma City grew and needed a larger water supply, the rights became a greater issue. In 2010, Oklahoma City claimed 90 percent of the water, but the Chickasaw and Choctaw said the state did not have the rights to the water. The Choctaw Nation offered to cover the state's $5.2 million debt to give everyone involved a chance to work things out. The tribes are willing to share the water, but they want to keep as much water as they can in the lake and preserve the environment.

Writer Linda Hogan represents the ideas and images of Chickasaw life in her work.
© CHRISTOPHER FELVER/CORBIS.

Another federal project that affected area tribes was the Pick-Sloan Missouri Basin Program in 1944. Some tribes lost lands and were forced to relocate as a result of the thousands of levees and dams built along the Missouri River system. Ecosystems were damaged as well. In 2008, representatives from many tribes, including the Chickasaw, joined forces with federal, state, and local agencies to develop a plan for Missouri River recovery. This Missouri River Recovery Implementation Committee (MRRIC) hopes to restore the environment and give the tribes more say in the planning process in the future.

NOTABLE PEOPLE

The esteemed Native American studies professor Linda Hogan (1947–) is a writer and poet whose works reflect ideas and images of Chickasaw life. Other notable Chickasaw include Puc-caiunla (c. 1760–1838), the last Chickasaw chief to inherit his position from his father; Cherokee/Quapaw/Chickasaw writer and educator Geary Hobson (1941–), a staunch supporter of Native American writing; painter and sculptor Bert D. Seabourn (1931–); and anthropologist and museum curator Towana Spivey (1943–).

BOOKS

Barbour, Jeannie, Amanda J. Cobb, and Linda Hogan. *Chickasaw: Unconquered and Unconquerable*. Ada, OK: Chickasaw Press, 2006.

Brown, Virginia Pounds, Laurella Owens, and Nathan Glick. *The World of the Southern Indians: Tribes, Leaders, and Customs from Prehistoric Times to the Present*. Montgomery, AL: NewSouth Books, 2011.

Cashin, Edward J. *Guardians of the Valley: Chickasaws in Colonial South Carolina and Georgia*. Columbia, SC: University of South Carolina Press, 2009.

Cobb, Amanda J. *Listening to Our Grandmothers' Stories: The Bloomfield Academy for Chickasaw Females, 1852–1949*. Lincoln: University of Nebraska Press, 2007.

Ethridge, Robbie. *From Chicaza to Chickasaw: The European Invasion and the Transformation of the Mississippian World, 1540–1715*. Chapel Hill: University of North Carolina Press, 2010.

Green, Richard. *Chickasaw Lives: Explorations in Tribal History*. Ada, OK: Chickasaw Press, 2009.

Green, Richard. *Chickasaw Lives: Profiles and Oral Histories*. Ada, OK: Chickasaw Press, 2009.

Larsen, Mike, Martha Larsen, and Jeannie Barbour. *Proud to Be Chickasaw*. Ada, OK: Chickasaw Press, 2010.

Morgan, Phillip Carroll. *Chickasaw Renaissance*. Ada, OK: Chickasaw Press, 2010.

Paige, Amanda L., Fuller L. Bumpers, and Daniel F. Littlefield, Jr. *Chickasaw Removal*. Ada, OK: Chickasaw Press, 2010.

Snyder, Clifford Gene. *Ghost Trails: Mythology and Folklore of the Chickasaw, Choctaw, Creeks and Other Muskoghean Indian Tribes*. North Hollywood, CA: JES, 2009.

St. Jean, Wendy. *Remaining Chickasaw in Indian Territory, 1830s–1907*. Tuscaloosa: University of Alabama Press, 2011.

Sumners, Cecil L. *The True Story of Chief Tishomingo*. Amory, MS: Amory Advertiser, 1974.

Swanton, John R. *Chickasaw Society and Religion*. Lincoln: University of Nebraska Press, 2006.

WEB SITES

Ager, Simon. "Chickasaw (Chikasha)." *Omniglot*. http://www.omniglot.com/writing/chickasaw.htm (accessed on June 17, 2011).

Armstrong, Kerry M. "Chickasaw Historical Research Page." *Chickasaw History*. http://www.chickasawhistory.com/ (accessed on June 16, 2011).

"Chickasaw Indian History." *Access Genealogy*. http://www.accessgenealogy.com/native/tribes/chickasaw/chickasawhist.htm (accessed on June 16, 2011).

The Chickasaw Nation. http://www.chickasaw.net (accessed on June 12, 2011).

"Chronicles of Oklahoma, Volume 2, 1924." *Oklahoma State University Library Electronic Publishing Center*. http://digital.library.okstate.edu/chronicles/contents/v002toc.html (accessed on June 12, 2011).

"Historic Diaries: Marquette and Joliet." *The Wisconsin Historical Society*. http://www.wisconsinhistory.org/diary/001407.asp (accessed on June 12, 2011).

Redish, Laura, and Orrin Lewis. "Chickasaw Indian Fact Sheet." *Native Languages of the Americas*. http://www.bigorrin.org/chickasaw_kids.htm (accessed on June 16, 2011).

Sultzman, Lee. "Chickasaw History." *First Nations Index*. http://www.tolatsga.org/chick.html (accessed on June 16, 2011).

"2011 Oklahoma Indian Nations." *Pocket Pictorial Directory*. Oklahoma City: Oklahoma Indian Affairs Commission. Available from http://www.ok.gov/oiac/documents/2011.FINAL.WEB.pdf (accessed on June 12, 2011).

Ullrich, Dieter C. "The Chickasaw People." *University of Tennessee at Martin*. http://www.utm.edu/departments/acadpro/library/departments/special_collections/wc_hist/chksaw.htm (accessed on June 16, 2011).

Choctaw

Name

The Choctaw (pronounced *CHOCK-taw*) traditionally called themselves the Chata'ogla or Chata'. The word *Choctaw* may have come from the name *Chahta* or *Chata* (see "History"), one of the Choctaw's legendary leaders. Some other spellings of the tribal name include Chahta, Chactas, Chactaw, Chato, and Tchakta.

Location

The Choctaw nation thrived in what is now the southeastern United States, largely eastern-central Mississippi. In modern times, major Choctaw communities are found in southeastern Oklahoma and Mississippi, with some smaller ones in Louisiana, Tennessee, and Alabama.

Population

The Choctaw numbered about 20,000 before the coming of the Europeans. During the 1830s, more than 15,000 Choctaw people were removed to Oklahoma on the Trail of Tears, but only about 12,500 survived. In the 1990 U.S. Census, 65,321 people identified themselves as Choctaw. In 2000, that number had risen to 88,692. A total of 158,774 people claimed to have some Choctaw heritage. By 2010, the census counted 103,910 Choctaw, with 195,764 people claiming some Choctaw ancestry, making it the third-largest tribal grouping in the United States. In 2011, Oklahoma Indian Affairs Commission indicated that Choctaw tribal enrollment was 223,279.

Language family

Muskogean.

Origins and group affiliations

The Choctaw ancestral homeland is in eastern-central Mississippi. During the 1830s, a majority of the tribe moved to a large block of land west of the Mississippi. A popular theory holds that many of the Native groups of the southeastern United States were once Choctaw.

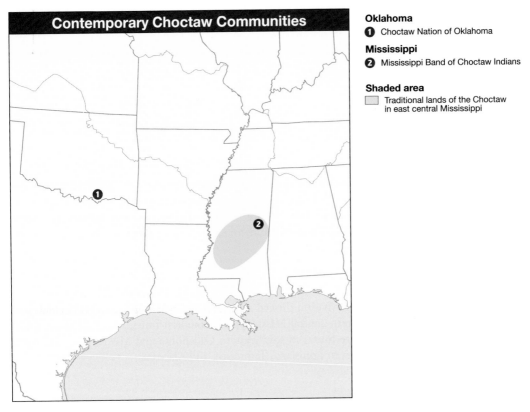

Contemporary Choctaw Communities

Oklahoma
1 Choctaw Nation of Oklahoma

Mississippi
2 Mississippi Band of Choctaw Indians

Shaded area
Traditional lands of the Choctaw in east central Mississippi

A map of contemporary Choctaw communities. MAP BY XNR PRODUCTIONS. CENGAGE LEARNING, GALE. REPRODUCED BY PERMISSION OF GALE, A PART OF CENGAGE LEARNING.

The Choctaw were known as a peaceful people. Although ready to defend themselves when challenged, they seldom initiated warfare against neighboring tribes. Choctaw territory at one time covered more than 23 million acres in Mississippi and parts of Alabama and Louisiana. As a result of their forced move to Oklahoma in the 1830s, the people now live on two main reservations in Oklahoma and in Mississippi.

HISTORY

A popular Choctaw legend tells how in the distant past a Choctaw leader named Chata led his people on a journey. Chata carried a sacred pole that he placed in the ground at the end of each day's journey. Each morning, they found the pole leaning eastward and they continued on, eventually crossing the Mississippi River. One morning, they awoke to find the pole standing upright. There they made their sacred mound by burying the remains of their ancestors, which they had carried along with them. Archaeologists (people who study the cultures of ancient peoples by looking at the things they left behind) believe that the mound was the site of tribal political and religious meetings for centuries up until the early 1700s.

The Spanish explorer Hernando de Soto (c. 1496–1542) was the first European known to encounter the Choctaw. De Soto and members of his expedition came upon the Choctaw in the 1540s. De Soto demanded women and baggage carriers of the Choctaw, and a fight broke out. Having never seen horses before, the Choctaw were frightened by those of the Spaniards. Choctaw losses were heavy in the battle, but the Choctaw people inflicted some major wounds on the Spanish as well. Afterward, the Spaniards crossed Choctaw land without further incident.

Relations with Europeans and Americans

The Choctaw had a better relationship with the French, who established their colony of Louisiana in 1700. British slave raiders operating out of the Carolinas took thousands of Choctaw into slavery in the early eighteenth century. In the 1730s, the French wiped out a neighboring tribe, the Natchez (see Natchez and the Mound Builders entry). The Choctaw, with a newly wary view of the French, took in the survivors.

A Choctaw Civil War occurred from 1747 to 1750, pitting those tribal members who wanted to maintain trading relations with the French against those who wanted to begin trading with the British. The war was so severe it wiped out entire villages and severely weakened the Choctaw.

During the American Revolution (1775–83; the American colonists' fight for independence from England), the Choctaw sided with the colonists. They entered into their first treaty of friendship with them in 1786. After they signed a second treaty in 1801, Americans began

Important Dates

1540: Hernando de Soto encounters the Choctaw and a battle arises between them.

1786: The Choctaw enter into their first formal treaty with the U.S. government.

1820: Some Choctaw agree to trade a portion of their land for territory west of the Mississippi River.

1830: The Treaty of Dancing Rabbit Creek is signed, resulting in the forced migration of the Choctaw to lands west of the Mississippi.

1918: The Bureau of Indian Affairs establishes the Choctaw Indian Agency in Philadelphia, Mississippi.

1975: Choctaw national administrative offices are established at a historic school building.

1983: The 1860 Choctaw Constitution, by which the Choctaw Nation of Oklahoma governs itself, is ratified.

1995: The Jena Band of Choctaw in Louisiana receives federal recognition.

The Promise

The Choctaw were forced to give up the rest of their lands east of the Mississippi River and move as a nation to Indian Territory by the terms of the Treaty of Dancing Rabbit Creek. Article IV of that treaty secured them this guarantee:

> The Government and people of the United States are hereby obliged to secure to the said Choctaw Nation of Red People the jurisdiction and government of all the persons and property that may be within their limits west, so that no Territory or State shall ever have the right to pass laws for the government of the Choctaw Nation of Red People and their descendants; and that no part of the land granted them shall ever be embraced in any Territory or State.

to appear in Choctaw country in increasing numbers. In 1805, the U.S. government pressured the Choctaw to move to new homes west of the Mississippi. Yet the Choctaw remained loyal to the United States. In 1811, the tribe expelled Shawnee (see entry) leader Tecumseh (1768–1813) from their lands when he tried to get them to join a confederacy (alliance) against the United States. They then fought against the Creek (see entry) in a war that arose when a faction of Creek decided to join Tecumseh's confederacy. The Choctaw also fought against the British in the War of 1812 (1812–15; a war in which the United States defeated Great Britain). Despite all this, in 1816, the United States demanded that the Choctaw people give up a large portion of tribal land.

A painful journey

By 1820, many of the Choctaw agreed to trade some of their traditional territory and move to a large tract of land west of the Mississippi River. About six thousand Choctaw, however, chose instead to remain on the more than ten million acres of original homeland they retained east of the Mississippi River. In 1830, however, under the terms of the Treaty of Dancing Rabbit Creek, the Choctaw were forced to give up those remaining lands east of the Mississippi and move as a nation to the West. Their relocation spanned the years from 1831 to 1834. This was part of a larger forced Native American journey from the southeast that came to be known as the Trail of Tears for the terrible suffering the Native peoples faced. During their journey westward to Indian Territory (land that now forms most of the state of Oklahoma where the U.S. government once planned to move all Native peoples), many Choctaw children and adults endured starvation and bitter cold. More than one-half of the tribe died along the way.

During the mid-1850s, the Choctaw in the West built a stable economy, started a public school system, and governed themselves by their own laws, in a process similar to that of their American neighbors.

Choctaw resettle in Oklahoma

Because they sided with the South during the American Civil War (1861–65; a war between the Union [the North], which was opposed to slavery, and the Confederacy [the South], which was in favor of slavery), the U.S. government forced the Choctaw to sell their western lands. The treaty they signed in 1866 granted a right-of-way for railroad companies to build tracks that crossed over the territory where the Choctaw lived. News of a railroad brought additional settlers. By 1890, settlers outnumbered tribal members on Choctaw land by three to one.

Around 1900, the government forced the Choctaw, along with other tribes, to resettle in a different region of the rapidly changing territory. Each person had to accept individual allotments, rather than holding the land in common as was the tribe's tradition. By 1907, when Oklahoma became a state, the Choctaw Nation was dissolved, and its members were required to become citizens of that state.

Choctaw in the twentieth century

Once they settled in Indian Territory, the language and culture of the Choctaw flourished. However, the outbreak of influenza from 1914 to 1918 killed 20 percent of the Choctaw population in Oklahoma. The country's allotment policies, which divided tribal lands into individual parcels that could be sold, proved to be disastrous for the Choctaw. Within one generation, most of the allotted land passed from Choctaw ownership to white ownership, often through fraud.

The Mississippi Choctaw

Although the Indian Removal Act (1830) forced the majority of the tribe to move west, about six thousand Choctaw stayed in Mississippi. Under the terms of the removal treaty, the remaining Choctaw could take individual parcels of land. Only sixty-nine Choctaw heads of households, however, were allowed to register for the Mississippi land. Most of the Choctaw in Mississippi lost everything they owned and became squatters in their former land. Many eventually moved west to join the relocated tribe.

In 1918, the U.S. Bureau of Indian Affairs opened the Choctaw Indian Agency in Philadelphia, Mississippi. The agency established schools in impoverished Choctaw communities and offered other forms of financial assistance. During the early twentieth century, the boll weevil (a type of beetle that destroys cotton plants) infested the crops in eastern-central Mississippi, depressing the economy of the region and inflicting great hardship on the Choctaw who lived there. In the second half of the twentieth century, wise and dynamic tribal leadership helped improve the economic conditions of tribal groups in both the East and West.

Choctaw in the twentieth century

During the 1970s, the tribe struggled to reestablish the sovereign (independent and self-governing) political authority of the Choctaw Nation. In 1975, they established Choctaw national administrative offices at the historic Presbyterian College building in Durant, Oklahoma, which had once served as a school for Native youth. In 1981, the federal government finally recognized the 1860 Choctaw Constitution, and the Choctaw people ratified (approved) it in 1983.

In the 1990s, lawyer Jack Abramoff began lobbying for several Native groups, including the Mississippi Band of Choctaw Indians. Abramoff was supposed to represent the tribes' gaming interests in Congress. Although he helped defeat a bill that would have taxed casinos, Abramoff cheated the tribe out of $15 million. In 2006, he was convicted of fraud and ordered to pay back the $25 million he had taken from various clients, mainly various tribes.

RELIGION

Although the Choctaw believed in spiritual beings, they did not worship a single Supreme Being. They considered the sun to be a very powerful force. Tribal members often consulted with certain people who were said to possess special powers. These included healers, rainmakers, and prophets. Medicine men were expected to predict future events, instill bravery in warriors, and help inspire a successful hunt.

The Choctaw believed that two kinds of souls survived after a person's death. The first frightened survivors at night or assumed the form of an animal. The second was an inner spirit, which began its journey to the afterworld immediately after death.

The afterworld had two sections, a good and a bad, separated by a mountainous barrier. An individual could be damned to the bad section for offenses such as murder, telling lies that led to another person's committing murder, divorcing a pregnant wife, or gossiping.

LANGUAGE

The Choctaw language is also called Choctaw-Chickasaw. It is closely related to the Creek language. Both are classified as Western Muskogean and are part of the Great Algonquian language family. The Choctaw language was an oral (spoken) language until the early 1900s. Reverend Cyrus Byington (1793–1868), who spent almost fifty years working with the tribe, wrote a dictionary of the language that was published in 1909. He also translated the Bible and several other books into the Choctaw language, including a grammar book. Some of those books are still used to study the language.

When they were questioned in 1987, half of the Choctaw people (about 12,000) said they still spoke their native language. In the mid-2000s, there were about 9,000 speakers of the Choctaw language, most of whom lived in southeastern Oklahoma. Others resided on the Pearl River Indian Reservation in central Mississippi.

The Choctaw have always excelled at public speaking. They often indicate their agreement to a proposal by saying "hoka hay." A popular legend claims that during negotiations with the Choctaw, President Andrew Jackson (1767–1845; served 1829–37), imitating this phrase, would frequently say "okay," and that expression is now used by people all around the world.

Common Choctaw Expressions

HO-ka hay	"all right"
a-LI-to	"hello"
chim a-CHUK-ma	"Are you well?"
A, chim-sha-NA-to	"Yes, are you?"
Yo-KU-ke	"Thank you"

GOVERNMENT

The traditional Choctaw tribe had many subgroups, or bands. The eldest male of each band, or *ogla*, was recognized as the chief. The ogla provided wisdom and teaching and played a major role in ceremonies and celebrations. Yet Choctaw culture was, in many respects, matriarchal (the mother ruled the family). Although men were warriors, war chiefs, and diplomats, women made the decisions during times of peace.

In modern times, the government of the Oklahoma Choctaw is run by the tribal council, made up of a chief and twelve representatives. A sixteen-member council governs the Mississippi Choctaw Reservation. Their chief, who is also the chief executive, serves for four years and presides over meetings of the council, which take place four times a year.

ECONOMY

For centuries, Choctaw men, women, and children cultivated the river floodplains on which they lived. The Choctaw tribe held all their land in common, but individuals could claim a field as long as they could cultivate it and did not interfere with fields already claimed by other members of the tribe. If an individual abandoned a field, control reverted to the tribe.

By 2011, the Choctaw Nation of Oklahoma had established businesses that brought in hundreds of millions of dollars every year and provided jobs for thousands of people. Some of their enterprises included casinos, travel plazas, smoke shops, a manufacturing plant, and a printing company. Funds from these businesses assisted the people with many social services, including education, health care, and housing.

In the late 1900s, the Mississippi Choctaw lived in extreme poverty, but by 2006, they owned many businesses and were the tenth largest employer in the state, with businesses that brought in millions. In addition to operating casinos, they chose to attract manufacturing firms. One of the advantages for businesses is that operating on reservations is tax free, so many firms took advantage of the opportunity. Average family income rose from $2,000 to $13,000 during those years, and the unemployment rate fell from 75 percent to 4 percent. By the second decade of the 2000s, the tribe had a diversified economy that included tourism, manufacturing, forestry, robotics, environmental services, retail and service industries, and engineering.

DAILY LIFE

Families

The rhythm of Choctaw family life was based on the growing season. In midwinter, the men cleared the fields by burning the underbrush. In the spring, they planted crops using cedar spades and shovels, and hoes made of flint or bone. When they were not farming, the men fished and hunted wild game. Boys learned to hunt with bows and arrows. Children, women, and the elderly gathered fruits, plants, and nuts.

Mothers brought up their daughters. Sons were raised by their mothers' brothers because they were the closest of male relatives within the clan (a group of related families that forms the basic social unit of the Choctaw society).

Buildings

The Choctaw lived in circular lodges. The frames were made of sticks, and palmetto thatch covered the tops and sides. Each lodge had one door that generally faced south. There was an open fire in the middle of the structure, with an opening in the roof to allow smoke to escape. Many persons lived in one lodge.

Clothing and adornment

Choctaw men wore belts and loincloths, adding moccasins, leggings, and garments from feathers or mulberry bark in winter. Women wore short deerskin skirts, adding deerskin shawls and moccasins when the weather got colder. The Choctaw wore decorated garments, earrings, and feathers

A Choctaw family poses at the Chucalissa Indian Town and Museum in Memphis, Tennessee, in 1961. LIBRARY OF CONGRESS, NEW YORK WORLD-TELEGRAM AND THE SUN NEWSPAPER PHOTOGRAPH COLLECTION.

of bright colors. Both men and women wore face paint and tattoos. Below their knees, men wore strings of bells they obtained from traders. Men wore their hair long, with bangs and braids. Women had long hair and wrapped it into a roll at the backs of their heads.

By the early 1900s, most Choctaw had adopted European-style clothing. A long cotton dress with a fitted bodice and full skirt was adorned with one of three traditional designs—circles and crosses, diamonds, or half diamonds. A white apron edged with designs wrapped around the waist. Men's shirts had similar designs on the front, sleeves, and collar, or around the round neckline. Many people still wear these outfits for dancing or on special occasions.

Food

The Choctaw hunted bear, turkey, deer, and other animals. They also caught trout and shrimp, which, along with bear, were eaten fresh or were dried for future consumption. The people also gathered berries that were eaten fresh, and grapes and crabapples that were dried. Their primary crops were squash and corn, which were used in their most common dishes.

Two favorite traditional dishes are hominy and banaha. Hominy is made from dried corn. Cooks simmered it in water over the fire until it was soft. Meat, such as chicken or pork, is added for flavor. Banaha is made from a mush of cooked peas and cornmeal. It is shaped into rectangles that are wrapped in wet cornhusks. The cakes are boiled for a few minutes. Banaha is often accompanied by salt pork.

Education

In earlier times, Choctaw boys and girls were trained to use blowguns for hunting small game, such as squirrels, rabbits, and birds. The blowguns were pieces of cane, about seven feet long, out of which they blew sharp cane darts. Until firearms were introduced, Choctaw youth were taught to use bows and arrows to hunt larger game. They also learned to catch fish with traps.

From the mid- to late 1800s, the Oklahoma Choctaw group had a thriving school system. Unfortunately, when the Choctaw Nation was abolished in 1907, the Choctaw became citizens of Oklahoma, and their school system ended.

The U.S. government started schools for the impoverished Mississippi Choctaw people in the 1920s. Yet until the late twentieth and early twenty-first centuries, the educational level of the average Mississippi

Choctaw remained low. In the late 1970s, most students had only a sixth-grade education. By 2006, the average educational level had reached twelfth grade. Over the next few years, money from the casinos helped fund scholarships so Choctaw teens could attend college.

Healing practices

The Choctaw treated diseases with plants and herbs, sometimes through the aid of medicine men. They boiled various roots to make medicines, wash wounds, treat snakebites, fight pneumonia, treat fever, and guard against smallpox.

The Choctaw wrapped themselves in several layers of cloth and drank hot tea to sweat disease out of the body. To cure stomach pains and arthritis, they pressed a small compress onto the area of discomfort. They treated broken bones with wraps and splints.

ARTS

Choctaw music stresses the importance of living in harmony with nature. Most Choctaw dances took place in an open field to the beat of drums and striking sticks. Three major types of Choctaw dances have been preserved. Animal dances honor various birds and animals. The Green Corn Dance, held in late summer, looks forward to a bountiful corn harvest. Both men and women participate in the Choctaw war dance, which in past centuries took place for the eight days prior to a battle. A chanter, often a young man, leads songs for dances. He begins with a shout, and the other dancers join in the song.

Collectors prize Choctaw swamp-cane baskets. The double-weave basket, a sort of basket within a basket, is the most favored. Family members usually pass down basketry skills.

For centuries Choctaw women have created a unique style of beadwork design that features double-curved scrolls and other elements of prehistoric Choctaw ceramics and shells.

CUSTOMS

Festivals

Traditionally, the Choctaw did not go in for spectacular ceremonies, religious or otherwise. In modern times, though, they host one of the top events in the Southeast, July's Choctaw Indian Fair, held in Philadelphia,

Mississippi. The fair features traditional tribal ceremonies and dances, ethnic foods, stickball games, and a craft fair. It takes place at the historic Old Capitol building that now serves as a council house and museum. Activities include a princess pageant, cultural ceremonies, Native foods, arts and crafts, sports, and musical entertainment.

In 2009 the Mississippi Band made Nanih Waiya an annual celebration in place of Columbus Day. Rather than marking a day that brought destruction to their people, the Choctaw decided to hold a ceremony that honored their Mother Mound, a sacred religious site for the tribe. They choose the second Friday in August for this annual event.

Commemoration

Every year in Skullyville, Oklahoma, members of the Choctaw tribe meet to commemorate the forcible removal of their people from their eastern homelands in Mississippi and Louisiana. They honor the thousands of Choctaw people who suffered and died in the early 1830s during the relocation journey that is called the Trail of Tears. In addition to a symbolic reenactment of the walk, present-day Choctaw listen to speakers, eat traditional foods, and perform tribal dances.

A Native American ball-player holds sticks for playing a game similar to lacrosse that was enjoyed by the Choctaw people. © NORTH WIND PICTURE ARCHIVES.

Public speaking

The Choctaw were especially accomplished public speakers. When a formal debate took place, they constructed a large brush arbor with a hole in the center of the roof. Those wishing to speak stood beneath the hole in the full heat of the southern sun, while the audience remained comfortably seated in the shade. The idea was that audience members could bear to listen as long as the speaker could stand in the heat and speak.

Games

Recreation was very important to the tribe. *Ishtaboli*, or stickball, was (and still is) a favorite sport and was sometimes used to settle disputes. The object of the game was to sling a leather ball from a webbed pocket at the end of a long stick so that it hit the opponent's goal at the end of the playing field, which was often a mile or longer. Tackling was one way of stopping the opponent. The Choctaw were very adept at handling, throwing, and passing the ball. The games were rough and sometimes resulted in serious injury or death, but no one was punished.

Another popular game was chunkey, where players rolled a round stone disk. Competitors tried to hit the moving circle with wooden sticks and to stop their opponents from scoring.

Courting and marriage

When a young man found himself alone with the woman he loved, he came within a few yards of her and tossed a pebble. If she smiled, it meant she approved of the courtship. If she disapproved, she gave him a scornful look. Another method a young man might use in courting was to enter the woman's lodge and lay his hat or handkerchief on her bed. If she approved, she would allow the item to remain. If she disapproved, she removed it from the bed. If both agreed to the union, the couple arranged a time and place for the marriage ceremony.

During a marriage ceremony, the families of the couple stood about 100 yards (90 meters) from one another. The brothers of the woman approached the man and seated him on a blanket. The man's sisters went to the woman and did likewise. Sometimes, for fun, the woman pretended to run away and had to be brought back. The woman's family set a bag of bread near her, and the man's family set a bag of meat next to him, indicating the man's role as hunter and the woman's as gatherer. Friends and relatives of the man then showered gifts over the head of the woman, which her family members grabbed and distributed among themselves. The gifts usually consisted of clothing, money, and household items. The couple, now man and wife, then rose together, and everyone went to a feast. Afterward, the man took his wife to his lodge.

Death

The Choctaw believed that the soul was immortal and that the spirit of the deceased person lingered near the corpse for some days after death. In ancient times, they wrapped the body in skins and bark and placed it on a platform with food and drink nearby. After some days, people who grew long fingernails especially for the task thoroughly removed the rotting flesh from the bones of the dead person. The bones were then given to grieving relatives, who painted the skull red and placed it in a coffin. The flesh and platform were often burned, or the flesh was buried.

In more recent times, Choctaw dressed the deceased in special ceremonial clothing for the viewing. The clothes, handed down from one generation to another, were not buried with the person. Often, a hunter's gun was placed in thes grave next to the body. Mourning periods were based on the age of the deceased and varied from three months for children to up to a year for parents.

CURRENT TRIBAL ISSUES

Although three Choctaw groups—the Choctaw Nation of Oklahoma, the Mississippi Band of Choctaw, and the Jena Band of Choctaw Indians—have received federal recognition, other groups, such as the Mowa Choctaw of Alabama, continue to seek federal recognition. Federal recognition entitles tribes to receive assistance and funding from the U.S. government and allows them to operate as an independent nation.

In the 1970s, the state of Oklahoma constructed Sardis Lake Reservoir on Choctaw land without consulting the tribe. The government forcibly removed the Native peoples, and the project flooded a Choctaw town and a Caddo cemetery. After the government could not pay the loan on the project, they decided to sell the water. The state of Texas, which needed water for agriculture, was the highest bidder. Again, Choctaw rights to the water were ignored. In spite of an earlier treaty giving water rights first to the Native peoples, a lawsuit in 2001 split the water rights among the state (50 percent), Choctaw (37.5 percent), and Chickasaw (12.5 percent). Although this agreement did not recognize tribal rights and sovereignty (self-government), the tribes accepted it because they needed the money and water. By 2005, the agreement still had not been ratified. The rights became a greater issue as Oklahoma City grew and needed a larger water supply. In 2010, Oklahoma City claimed 90 percent of the water, but the Choctaw Nation insisted the state did not have the rights to the water. The Choctaw Nation offered to cover the state's $5.2 million debt to give everyone involved a chance to work out the dispute. Both Oklahoma City and Texas need water for their people and agriculture. The Choctaw want to keep as much water as they can in the lake, preserve the environment, and develop recreational facilities there.

NOTABLE PEOPLE

Pushmataha (1764–1824) was a Choctaw warrior, statesman, and chief. Pushmataha was very loyal to the United States. He refused to join the Shawnee Chief Tecumseh (1768–1813) in a confederacy against the Americans, and he later signed a treaty ceding lands in Alabama and Mississippi to the United States. Along with Pushmataha, two other Choctaw chiefs, Apuckshunubbee (c. 1740–1824) and Moshulatubbee (1770–1836), went to Washington, D.C., in 1824 to negotiate for their people. Moshulatubbee was the only one to return; the other two died under suspicious circumstances during their trip. Moshulatubbee later ran for Congress.

Rosella Hightower (1920–2008), an internationally known ballerina, also directed ballet and opera companies. Educator Linda Lomahaftewa (1947–) is an award-winning painter and printmaker whose works highlight the culture of the Plains Indians. Her artwork has been featured at a variety of exhibitions throughout the country.

BOOKS

Akers, Donna L. *Culture and Customs of the Choctaw Indians*. Santa Barbara, CA: Greenwood, 2012.

Bowes, John P. *The Choctaw*. New York: Chelsea House, 2010.

Broadwell, George Aaron. *A Choctaw Reference Grammar*. Lincoln: University of Nebraska Press, 2006.

Brown, Virginia Pounds, Laurella Owens and Nathan Glick. *The World of the Southern Indians: Tribes, Leaders, and Customs from Prehistoric Times to the Present*. Montgomery, AL: NewSouth Books, 2011.

Kidwell, Clara Sue. *The Choctaws in Oklahoma: From Tribe to Nation, 1855–1970*. Norman: University of Oklahoma Press, 2007.

Lambert, Valerie. *Choctaw Nation: A Story of American Indian Resurgence*. Lincoln: University of Nebraska Press, 2007.

Mihesuah, Devon Abbott. *Choctaw Crime and Punishment, 1884–1907*. Norman: University of Oklahoma Press, 2009.

Snyder, Clifford Gene. *Ghost Trails: Mythology and Folklore of the Chickasaw, Choctaw, Creeks and Other Muskoghean Indian Tribes*. North Hollywood, CA: JES, 2009.

Sonneborn, Liz. *The Choctaws*. Minneapolis, MN: Lerner Publications, 2007.

Sprague, Donovin Arleigh. *Choctaw Nation of Oklahoma*. Chicago, IL: Arcadia, 2007.

PERIODICALS

Barringer, Felicity. "Indians Join Fight for an Oklahoma Lake's Flow." *New York Times*. April 12, 2011, A1. Available online from http://www.nytimes.com/2011/04/12/science/earth/12water.html (accessed on June 18, 2011).

Ferrara, Peter J. "Choctaw Uprising: Business Acumen of Mississippi Choctaw Indian Chief Philip Martin." *National Review*, March 11, 1996.

June-Friesen, Katy. "An Ancestry of African-Native Americans." *Smithsonian*. February 17, 2010. Available online from http://www.smithsonianmag.com/history-archaeology/An-Ancestry-of-African-Native-Americans.html#ixzz1RN1pyiD1 (accessed on June 21, 2011).

WEB SITES

Boykin, Deborah. "Choctaw Indians in the 21st Century." *Mississippi History Now*. http://mshistory.k12.ms.us/articles/10/choctaw-indians-in-the-21st-century (accessed on June 21, 2011).

Carleton, Kenneth H. "A Brief History of the Mississippi Band of Choctaw Indians." *Mississippi Band of Choctaw*. http://mdah.state.ms.us/hpres/A%20Brief%20History%20of%20the%20Choctaw.pdf (accessed on June 12, 2011).

"Choctaw Indian History." *Access Genealogy*. http://www.accessgenealogy.com/native/tribes/choctaw/chostawhist.htm (accessed on June 21, 2011).

"Choctaw Indian Tribe." *Native American Nations*. http://www.nanations.com/choctaw/index.htm (accessed on June 21, 2011).

Choctaw Nation of Oklahoma. http://www.choctawnation.com (accessed on June 12, 2011).

"Community News." *Mississippi Band of Choctaw Indians*. http://www.choctaw.org/ (accessed on June 12, 2011).

Jena Band of Choctaw Indians. http://www.jenachoctaw.org/ (accessed on June 12, 2011).

Kidwell, Clara Sue. "Choctaw." *Oklahoma Historical Society*. http://digital.library.okstate.edu/encyclopedia/entries/C/CH047.html (accessed on June 21, 2011).

Redish, Laura, and Orrin Lewis. "Choctaw Indian Language." *Native Languages of the Americas*. http://www.native-languages.org/choctaw.htm (accessed on June 12, 2011).

"2011 Oklahoma Indian Nations." *Pocket Pictorial Directory*. Oklahoma City: Oklahoma Indian Affairs Commission. Available from http://www.ok.gov/oiac/documents/2011.FINAL.WEB.pdf (accessed on June 12, 2011).

Creek

Name

The Muscogee (as they called themselves) were named "Creek" by the British because they lived along the fertile creeks of Alabama and Georgia. The term *Muscogee* identifies them with land that is wet or likely to flood.

Location

The early Creek, a union of several tribes, lived on lands in present-day Alabama, Georgia, Florida, and South Carolina. By 1832, the U.S. government pressured the tribes to move west of the Mississippi River. While some of the people remained in Alabama (and live there in modern times as the Poarch Band of Creek Indians), many eventually settled in Oklahoma, where members of the largest group, called the Muscogee Nation, now reside.

Population

There were about ten thousand Creek in the early 1700s. In the 1990 U.S. Census, 44,168 people identified themselves as members of the Creek tribe. The 2000 census showed that 40,487 Creek resided in the United States. In 2001, the Bureau of Indian Affairs recorded a total tribal enrollment of 52,169. Statistics from the Oklahoma Indian Affairs Commission in 2011 showed that number had risen to 69,162 for the Muscogee (Creek) Nation in Oklahoma.

Language family

Muskogean.

Origins and group affiliations

The early Creek may have been descendants of prehistoric people of what is now the southeastern United States. The original Creek Confederacy was composed of the Alibamu, Coushatta, Muscogee, and other groups. Modern Creek live in Alabama and are scattered around the Southeast. Oklahoma is home to four main groups of Creek.

The Creek were one of the "Five Civilized Tribes," a name the Europeans gave to the Cherokee, Chickasaw, Choctaw, Creek, and Seminole (see entries)

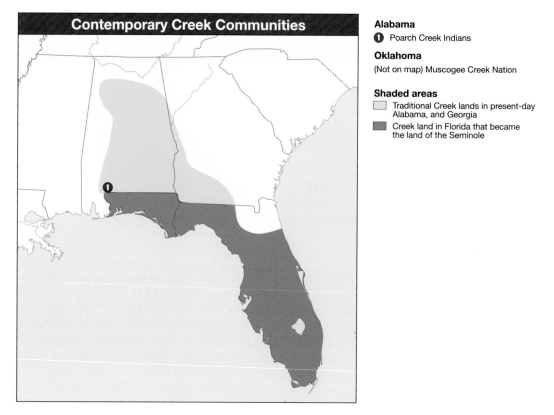

Contemporary Creek Communities

Alabama
❶ Poarch Creek Indians

Oklahoma
(Not on map) Muscogee Creek Nation

Shaded areas
☐ Traditional Creek lands in present-day Alabama, and Georgia
■ Creek land in Florida that became the land of the Seminole

A map of contemporary Creek communities. MAP BY XNR PRODUCTIONS. CENGAGE LEARNING, GALE. REPRODUCED BY PERMISSION OF GALE, A PART OF CENGAGE LEARNING.

because they established many institutions valued by Europeans. The Creek were farmers and traders and were once one of the dominant tribes in the middle South. The Creek Confederacy, an alliance of independent tribes, was established to resist attacks by northern tribes. The size of the alliance changed constantly as tribes entered or left it. Because of this, historians cannot make general statements about a "typical" Creek tribe. It is known that Creek society was balanced and harmonious, and members had a large degree of personal freedom.

HISTORY

Settling in the Southeast

Old legends of the Creek tell of ancestors who migrated to the Southeast from the Southwest. Many archaeologists (people who study ancient cultures by looking at the things that were left behind) believe that the Creek are descendants of people who moved into North America thousands of years ago. They may have been Maya Indians from Mexico and Central America who merged peacefully with other Native American people already living in what would become the United States.

The first contact with Europeans took place about 1539, when the Spanish explorer Hernando de Soto (c. 1496–1542) came to their region. Disagreements arose between the Spaniards and the Natives. Chief Tuscaloosa of the Choctaw, a member of the Creek confederacy, organized an ambush. Although it ended in a defeat for the Natives, the clash dealt a severe blow to the Europeans as well.

Creek lands reduced

In time, the Creek found themselves in the midst of territories claimed by the Spanish, the French, and the British. British traders frequently married Creek women, who taught their husbands Native customs and language. The children of these mixed marriages, who understood both cultures, often rose to positions of leadership in the tribe.

Because some of the Creek became British allies during the American Revolution (1775–83; the American colonists' fight for independence from England), the new U.S. government demanded the tribe give up some of its land. The government appointed an agent to influence the Native Americans to adapt the white lifestyle and become "civilized." A violent split developed between the Creek factions who were willing to cooperate and those who were not. The Red Stick War (1813–14) between the Creek and the whites turned into a Creek civil war, waged between those tribes who opposed the U.S. "civilization" program and those who supported it. The war ended with the Battle of Horseshoe Bend in 1814. In that conflict, some Creek joined American forces and defeated the Creek who opposed assimilation, or the adoption of white culture. In the peace treaty that followed, the Creek gave up 23 million acres of land, two-thirds of what they possessed.

Creek people move west

Treaties signed by the Creek in 1832 and 1836 gave the United States possession of virtually all Creek lands. In exchange, the Creek were given lands in present-day Oklahoma in what was then called Indian Territory.

Important Dates

1539: The Creek's first encounter with Europeans ends in defeat.

1775: Many Creek support the British during the American Revolution.

1814: With the end of the Red Stick War, the Creek lose much of their remaining land.

1830: The Indian Removal Act authorizes the U.S. government to move the Creek off their land.

1971: The Muscogee (Creek) Nation conducts its first federally recognized principal chief election in the twentieth century.

1984: Poarch Band of Creek Indians receives federal recognition.

Once again, Creek opinion was divided. Some people refused to leave their homes, while others, believing they had no choice, voluntarily left the Southeast. Finally, in 1836 and 1837, the U.S. Army oversaw forced relocation of most of the remaining Creek. Dressed in clothing that was inadequate for the winter weather, the Creek walked hundreds of miles. Thousands died—some on the journey and some during the first few months in their new home. Eventually, they learned how to adapt to the unfamiliar weather and lived peacefully beside the Plains Indians.

Muscogee adopt constitution

Historically, Creek communities had been divided geographically into upper and lower towns. The Creek lower towns in Oklahoma were located closer to Euro-American settlements. Greater interaction with the newcomers led the people of the lower town to become more open to changes in traditional ways. The upper-town Creek remained more loyal to the old ways.

Opothleyahola, also spelled Opothle Yahola (c. 1798–1863), an Upper Creek chief, worked hard to make the removal process to Oklahoma as successful as possible for his people. The American Civil War (1861–65; a war between the Union [the North], which was opposed to slavery, and the Confederacy [the South], which was in favor of slavery) interrupted the settling-in process. Although Opothleyahola spoke up for neutrality (noninvolvement), attacks by the Confederate army against his people forced the Creeks to become involved. Once again, the Creek were divided. Most lower towns allied themselves with the South, while the upper towns generally supported the North. After the war, the Creek were forced to give up half of their land in Indian Territory for supporting the Confederacy.

Tribal land broken up

Two pieces of legislation by the U.S. government disrupted Creek society. The General Allotment Act of 1887 (also known as the Dawes Act) required shared tribal land to be allotted, or divided into lots owned by individuals, a departure from traditional Creek practice of owning land in common. The Curtis Act in 1898 dismantled the tribal government in Oklahoma. This act enforced allotment, did away with tribal courts, and required that all laws passed by tribal governments be approved by the president of the United States.

Chitto Harjo and the Snake Rebellion

Tribal spokesperson Chitto Harjo (pronounced "Chit-to Ha-cho"; 1846–1911) was outraged at the notion that an external organization could dissolve his nation. Demanding that the federal government honor the Treaty of 1832 that promised the Creek a specified amount of land and self-government in Oklahoma, Harjo became part of a movement to organize an alternative government. The Snake Rebellion (named after an English translation of the name *Chitto*) was an effort to resist further encroachment by white settlers. Several years of turmoil followed, during which Harjo presented his opposition directly to a U.S. Senate select committee. Tensions, however, mounted until Harjo's death in 1911.

During the mid-1930s, the federal government did away with some of its policies designed to dissolve Native American tribes. A 1970 law opened the way for adoption of a new Creek Nation constitution in 1979. The Creek people were divided between those who supported the 1979 constitution and those who wanted to keep the 1867 constitution. Supporters of the new constitution won.

In modern times, the Creek are thriving, though many leave the reservation for work. The social services the tribe provides to its members are described by the Bureau of Indian Affairs as "the best in the nation."

RELIGION

The Creek religion centered on a single god known as the Master of Breath. All creations (such as the sun, moon, and planets) and living creatures were considered different forms of this Great Spirit. The Creek believed that living a good life would be rewarded. They had special prophets who conferred with the gods to diagnose disease and predict the future. Daily bathing in a nearby stream was an important part of their religious rites.

After Europeans arrived, missionaries of various denominations tried to convert the Creek to Christianity. Many of those who converted during the eighteenth century either concealed their conversion or left the community to escape punishment by people who honored the old ways. Eventually, some Creek towns accepted Christianity. At that point the church replaced the town square as the focal point of activity, and the Christian town preacher replaced the town chief. In modern times, Creek are still divided between those following their ancestral religion and those who have adopted Christianity. Most Christian Creek are members of the Baptist, Methodist, or Presbyterian churches.

LANGUAGE

The Creek language is part of the Muskogean group, which includes the languages of the Chickasaw, Choctaw, Tuskegee, Alabama, Natchez, Miccosukee, and Seminole tribes. It was the most common tongue among members of the Creek confederacy. Early European traders had to learn the melodious language, for most Creek showed no interest in speaking English. Early Creek words had few vowels and most contained the letter "k." During the early eighteenth century, some Creek stopped speaking their language. To be recognized as Native American meant being forced to leave their homes; therefore, some tried to hide their Native American identities.

Delegates from several tribes assemble in front of the Creek Council House in Oklahoma Territory circa 1880. © NATIONAL ARCHIVES AMERICAN INDIAN SELECT LIST PHOTO NO. 32.

Missionaries devised a system for writing the Creek language in the 1840s. The first published works were the Bible and other religious books. The Creek started a cooperative publishing company that prints a periodical called *Indian Journal* that addresses the tribes' viewpoints on current events. Most of the Poarch Creek in Alabama no longer speak the Muscogee language, but some groups in Oklahoma continue to speak it.

GOVERNMENT

For centuries, Creek towns were governed by a chief. His duties included greeting official visitors, overseeing the storage of the food supply, and representing the town before other groups. A council made up of older men assisted the chief in ceremonies and helped him make decisions about warfare.

In 1867, the Muscogee (Creek) Nation adopted a new constitution. The government consisted of an executive branch headed by the principal chief, a legislative branch composed of a House of Kings and a House of Warriors, and a judicial branch.

In 1971, the Muscogee Nation elected a principal chief who was recognized by the U.S. government (that is, the federal government agreed to have dealings with him). In 1979, they ratified a new constitution. The principal and second chief are elected every four years. Members of the national council are elected every two years. A judicial branch of the council operates the tribal court system. Mound Building, a unique modern structure built into the earth to resemble those of the ancient Mound Builders (see entry), is the tribal headquarters and houses the National Council Offices and Judicial Offices.

The Poarch Band of Creek Indians adopted their constitution in 1985. They elect a nine-member council, who, in turn, choose the Chief Executive Officer of the tribe. The tribal court handles all cases except major criminal offenses, which are the jurisdiction (authority) of the U.S. government.

There are four main groups of Muscogee in Oklahoma. The largest group of Creek, the Muscogee (Creek) Nation, is a non-reservation tribe whose people are located in eleven counties across the state. The other three are the Alabama-Quassarte Tribal Town, the Kialegee Tribal Town, and the Thlopthlocco Tribal Town. The Poarch Creek Indians are descendants of the original Creek who remained in the southeast. The Poarch Reservation is located in Atmore, Alabama. Other small groups are located throughout the Southeast.

ECONOMY

From the early days, the Creek considered the labor of men and women equally important. Women worked in the fields, tilling the soil with sharp sticks and hoes fitted with points made of stone or sharpened bone. Children helped the women gather berries, roots, nuts, herbs, and plants. Men caught fish with bows and arrows. They also trapped fish, sometimes stunning them with a special poison. Groups of men also hunted in the forests for deer, bear, and rabbit. During the seventeenth century, the Creek began to trade deerskins for guns, ammunition, cloth, metal pots, and other items.

Since the 1990s, one of the major sources of employment and money within the Muscogee Creek Nation has been from its four bingo halls. Profits have provided the people with college funds, programs for the elderly, and youth activities. By 2004, the Nation operated about 600 acres of farmland, raising mostly alfalfa. Tribal grazing lands of 1,970 acres feed about seventy cattle and a herd of buffalo. The tribal government is the largest employer.

The Muscogee Nation has also undertaken such economic development projects as operating a real-estate development office, a travel plaza, smoke shops, a museum, and tourist/recreation facilities. The federally recognized Poarch Band of Creek Indians community opened Creek Indian Enterprises (CIE) in 1988 to develop and manage tribal businesses. In the mid-2000s, CIE oversaw metal works, farmland, a wildlife reserve, a motel and service center, and three gaming centers. The farmland included crops, pecan orchards, cattle, and a catfish pond along with additional acreage they leased out to others.

DAILY LIFE

Families

Families, who lived together in groups of buildings called compounds, all belonged to the same clan (a group of related families). Creek clans included the Wind, Bird, Alligator, and Bear clans. Creek traced their family lines through the mother. Children were counted as part of their mother's clan. They were considered related to her relatives, but not to the relatives of their father.

The duties in Creek families were assigned by gender. Women performed household chores and made cooking utensils, storage vessels, and clothing. Men built houses, provided materials for clothing, and performed military functions. Women raised the children, but fathers maintained an emotional tie to their children. Hide and fur trading was a cooperative effort, with men hunting the animals and women tanning and dressing the skins.

Buildings

An open square formed the heart of every Creek town. Known as the "stomp grounds," it was the site of warm-weather meetings of the town council, the Green Corn Ceremony, and other ceremonial dances. In the winter, town council meetings were held in a circular structure about 40 feet (12 meters) in diameter with a cone-shaped roof that rose 25 feet (7 or 8 meters) into the air. It served as a social gathering place during bad weather and a shelter for the aged and homeless. Each town had a 200- to 300-yard-long playing field where a lacrosse-style game was played. (Lacrosse is a game of Native American origin played on a field by two teams of ten players each. Participants use a long-handled stick with a webbed pouch to put a ball into the opposing team's goal.) The games were also used as a way of settling disputes between towns. A pole about 40 feet (12 meters) tall stood in the center of the game field. A target on the top was used for spear or archery practice.

Each Creek family home was made up of a cluster of buildings. These may have included a kitchen, a granary/storehouse, a building for sleeping during the summer, and another for sleeping during the winter. Some had a separate warehouse. Vertical poles supported the building's peaked roof, which was made of grass or cypress bark shingles. Walls were sometimes added by weaving split saplings (young trees) between the poles and coating this framework with several inches of plaster made from clay and straw. Beginning in the late eighteenth century, the Creek began building log cabins.

Clothing and adornment

Because of the warm climate, the Creek generally did not wear much clothing. Even in the winter, they kept their windowless houses so warm with their hearth fires that there was little need for additional garments. The men wore breechcloths (deerskin pieces that hung from thin rawhide belts). They sometimes donned grass blankets or deerskin leggings in colder weather. Women wore shawls and skirts made from grass, deerskin, or bark, and sometimes added fur blankets in winter. Most children wore no clothing until they reached puberty. After seeing European products brought by traders, the Creek quickly added cotton, linen, and wool textiles to their wardrobes. They also learned to weave and dye cloth.

Although their clothing was simple, the Creek used a great deal of body ornamentation. Both men and women used porcupine needles dipped in dark blue dye to tattoo designs over most of their bodies. They also liked to paint their faces and bodies. Men removed facial hair by plucking; some also plucked hairs from their head, leaving a long lock down the middle that they braided with feathers or other decorations. Deerskin turbans were also popular among men. Women wore their long hair wrapped around the head, fastened with silver jewelry. Neck ornaments and earrings for both genders were fashioned from shell, coral, bones, silver, and copper. They added beads, silk ribbons, bells, and lace obtained from European traders to clothing, moccasins, and hair arrangements.

Food

Most Creek families had their own small gardens. They grew crops in shared fields, with each family receiving the harvest from its assigned section. Both men and women helped with the communal farming. A portion of the community harvest was set aside to provide for visitors and needy families. The Creek originally grew, gathered, and hunted only what they needed for their own use. As trade with the Europeans developed, they became commercial hunters, selling the Europeans deerskins and furs.

Corn, eaten fresh or dried, was the main Creek crop. *Sofkey,* a sour broth made of crushed corn and sometimes flavored with deer meat, was also a staple of their diet. They also raised beans, squash, pumpkins, melons, peppers, peas, cucumbers, rice, and sweet potatoes. Creek women gathered wild foods, including berries, peaches, apples, herbs, roots, hickory nuts, and acorns. They boiled mashed nuts and skimmed off the oil to make cooking oil. Deer was the most popular meat, but the Creek ate wild hogs and such small game as squirrel, opossum, and turkey. Fishermen also caught catfish and sturgeon. They preserved meat by drying or smoking it.

Abuskee, a drink made of roasted corn, was a popular beverage. People also enjoyed *ah-gee-chum-buh-gee,* a combination of boiled cornmeal, dried fruits, and brown sugar, served in cornhusk packets like dumplings.

Education

Traditionally, a woman's brothers educated and counseled her male children in hunting, fishing, and building boats and houses. Young boys were taught a game called chunkey to sharpen their skills at spear throwing. One player pushed a stone disk that rolled down the field. Other players chased it with a long stick that curved at one end. They hurled their sticks to the point where they thought the disk would stop. Sometimes whole families played the game together.

Girls were taught by their mothers, their mother's sisters, and their grandmothers. They learned to cook, weave baskets, and sew and to sing songs as they searched for edible plants.

Although the Muscogee Creek Nation now operates the Eufaula Indian Boarding School, many children attend local public schools, vocational schools, and community colleges. During the 1990s, the Muscogee Nation undertook development of a Mvskoke (Creek language) program for its elementary school students.

The tribe also operates a college that offers several majors and promotes language development. Meetings and other events are conducted in traditional Mvskoke. In an interview on the local television news station KOTV in 2007, Muscogee Creek Nation College board of regents chairwoman Ramona Mason explained the reasons for structuring the school around tribal traditions and values: "Of all the Native Americans that enroll in higher education, only 2 percent graduate.… But if they go to a tribal college, it goes up to 67, 70 percent."

Healing practices

Creek doctors used parts of many different plants to make medicine. They believed tobacco to be powerful and used it for healing and in ceremonies. For example, tobacco mixed with boiled red sumac was smoked to treat head and chest ailments. Mixed with water, it was both drunk and rubbed on the body to cure stomach cramps. Other items used as medicines were roots, tobacco blossoms, bark, milkweed, spider web, and charred coals. Medicine men concocted teas and ointments to treat burns, insect bites, fever, indigestion, diarrhea, and other ailments. Some of these potions contained morphine and salicylic acid (the active ingredient in aspirin). Doctors also helped people deal with emotional distress.

The Native Americans had no immunity or medicine to deal with diseases brought by Europeans, such as smallpox, measles, cholera, and malaria. Many people died during epidemics (uncontrolled outbreaks of disease). Alcohol abuse became another European-introduced problem, as many Creek had no physical tolerance to drinking. When the Native Americans lost their original lands, it disrupted their usual food supply. Diet-related health problems, like diabetes, became more common.

During the latter part of twentieth century attempts were made to improve the health of the Creek; the Muscogee Nation now manages its own hospital and a group of clinics.

ARTS

Weaving

Creek women learned a special type of weaving technique called finger weaving. Bands of fabric were created by weaving braided multiple strands of yarn with the fingers, sometimes with beads attached. They often left the ends unbraided to form tassels. Because they did not use looms, the women could make only those garments that could be fashioned from narrow fabric strips. These included scarves, sashes, and other types of clothing.

CUSTOMS

The Creek confederacy was made up of people from a variety of backgrounds who joined either for military protection or because they had been conquered by the Creek. Each group was an individual community. As a result, traditions and ceremonies varied among the towns. The customs described below, however, were fairly common.

Festivals

The Creek held "stomp dances" to celebrate special occasions, such as planting season, hunting season, weddings, and the approach of medicine men. Stomp dances are still held in modern times. A leader begins the dance by moving around the fire counter-clockwise. Dancers form a circle with men and women alternating; they chant as they follow the leader. Women wear pebble-filled turtle shells around their calves. Their shuffling feet set the rhythm for the dance. One of the tribe's most well-known stomp dance locations is Tallahassee Grounds.

Summer's Green Corn Ceremony, which lasted eight days, celebrated the ripening of the corn and signaled the beginning of a new year. People sang, danced, and played games. A special feature was the Ribbon Dance, which women still perform at Green Corn Ceremonies. Three or four women are selected for life to perform this function. The women fast before the dance. Then, wearing rattles and shells fastened to their legs, they wave special sticks in a certain rhythm, and male singers and gourd players accompany them.

The tribe prepared special fires holding sacred power for the ceremony. Adults drank a black herb potion that purified their bodies, and they fasted before tasting the new corn. Dances and feasting followed. In the spirit of renewal, they forgave any person who had not yet been punished for an offense (except murder) committed during the past year.

The Creek Nation Festival and Rodeo takes place annually on the third weekend in June at the Creek Nation Complex. Events include stomp and other dances, a parade, a rodeo, sporting events, and a fine arts and crafts festival. Native American food is in great abundance. The Eufaula Indian Community Powwow takes place each year over Labor Day weekend. A powwow is a celebration at which the main activities are traditional singing and dancing. In modern times, the singers and dancers at powwows come from many different tribes.

Naming

A Creek man's first name identified his town or clan, while the second name described some personal characteristic. For example, the name of the famous historical figure Chitto Harjo came from the facts that he was a member of the Snake clan (*chitto* means "snake") and that he was "recklessly brave" (*harjo*).

Hunting rituals

Before the the Europeans arrived, the Creek hunted deer for food and clothing. They painted their cheeks with ocher (dirt containing iron deposits) because they thought it improved their vision. They also sang special songs to bring the deer closer. Then they attacked them with bows and arrows, wooden spears, and blowguns.

Courtship and marriage

When a Creek man wanted to marry, he or his female relatives proposed to a woman's mother and aunts. Before the bride-to-be could accept, she needed approval from her clan elders. The wedding could not take place until the man proved his abilities by building a house and killing a deer. Likewise, the woman had to prove she could cook. The couple lived together for a year before deciding whether to make the marriage permanent. After that time, divorce was possible, but it was rare among families with children. If his wife gave her permission, a man could marry other women. He had to provide separate homes for each of them.

The Creek punished people who were unfaithful to their spouses with severe beatings or by cutting off their ears or noses. Offenders who remained hidden until the annual Green Corn Ceremony period of forgiveness, however, could escape this penalty.

Funerals

Burials took place on the floor of the deceased's home. The Creek wrapped the body in a blanket and placed it in a circular pit in a sitting position. They later dug graves outside near the family home. They kept the body in the home for a four-day period, which ended with an all-night wake. Family members put the deceased person's favorite clothing into the casket, along with bits of food and tobacco. After they lowered the casket into the ground, they built a fire at the head of the grave and tended it for four days, until the soul began its passage to the sky. After the burial, family members washed themselves with an herbal compound prepared by a medicine man to ease the pain of their loss. Creek Christians abandoned most of these funeral customs, although they still held an all-night service in the church before a burial.

CURRENT TRIBAL ISSUES

Most Creek are members of the Muscogee Nation in Oklahoma. The early groups that made up the Creek were diverse, though, and a few groups desired to be separate from the Muscogee Nation.

In 2011, the Kialegee Tribal Town of Oklahoma bought 300 acres on St. Simons Island along the Georgia coast. The people indicated that they wanted to turn it into a reservation. The Georgia Senate approved the purchase, but the House committee had concerns about whether the band planned to put up a casino on the land. The Bureau of Indian Affairs, which must also approve the creation of the new reservation, also questioned the plans because the land is so far from their Oklahoma reservation.

The Creek are trying to retain their cultural heritage, especially their language and customs. They are also trying to maintain economic independence and gain access to ancestral lands that hold spiritual significance, but are located away from tribal property.

NOTABLE PEOPLE

Chitto Harjo (1846–1911), called Crazy Snake by white settlers, formed a group of Creek known as the Snakes. The Snakes believed that the Creek Treaty of 1832 guaranteed the Creek self-government, and they refused to recognize U.S. authority. In resisting U.S. troops, Harjo was seriously injured and died from his wounds; afterward, the Snake movement quickly weakened.

Opothleyahola, also spelled Opothle Yohola (c. 1798–1863), a skilled Creek orator, negotiated land agreements with President John Quincy Adams, and later with President Andrew Jackson. For a time he resisted the government's enforced removal of the Creek, but he finally accepted relocation. In 1836, he led 2,700 people to Indian Territory. He became head chief and tried to preserve the traditions of his ancestors.

BOOKS

Benton, Jeffrey C., compiler. *The Very Worst Road: Travellers' Accounts of Crossing Alabama's Old Creek Indian Territory, 1820–1847*. Tuscaloosa: The University of Alabama Press, 2009.

Braund, Kathryn E. Holland. *Deerskins and Duffels: The Creek Indian Trade with Anglo-America, 1685–1815*. 2nd ed. Lincoln: University of Nebraska Press, 2008.

Brown, Virginia Pounds, Laurella Owens and Nathan Glick. *The World of the Southern Indians: Tribes, Leaders, and Customs from Prehistoric Times to the Present*. Montgomery, AL: NewSouth Books, 2011.

Jordan, Ann T., and David Lewis Jr. *Creek Indian Medicine Ways: The Enduring Power of Mvskoke Religion*. Albuquerque: University of New Mexico Press, 2002.

Snyder, Clifford Gene. *Ghost Trails: Mythology and Folklore of the Chickasaw, Choctaw, Creeks and Other Muskoghean Indian Tribes*. North Hollywood, CA: JES, 2009.

Snyder, Clifford Gene, ed. *The Muskogee Chronicles: Accounts of the Early Muskogee/Creek Indians*. North Hollywood, CA: JES, 2008.

Sonneborn, Liz. *The Creek*. Minneapolis: Lerner Publications, 2007.

Stone, Amy M. *Creek History and Culture*. Milwaukee: Gareth Stevens Publishing, 2011.

Swanton, John R. *Creek Religion and Medicine*. Lincoln: University of Nebraska Press, 2000.

Swanton, John R. *Early History of the Creek Indians.* Reprint. Greenville, SC: Southern Historical Press, 2006.

Ward, Jill. *Creeks and Cherokees Today.* Hamilton, GA: State Standards, 2010.

Wilds, Mary C. *The Creek.* San Diego, CA: Lucent Books, 2005.

WEB SITES

"Creek Indian." *American Indian Tribe.* http://www.creekindian.com/ (accessed on June 12, 2011).

"Creek Indian Records." *Rootsweb.* http://freepages.genealogy.rootsweb.ancestry.com/~texlance/main.htm (accessed on June 12, 2011).

"Creek Indian War, 1813–1814." *Alabama Department of Archives and History.* http://www.archives.state.al.us/teacher/creekwar/creek.html (accessed on June 12, 2011).

"Creek Indians." *GeorgiaInfo.* http://georgiainfo.galileo.usg.edu/creek.htm (accessed on June 12, 2011).

Muscogee (Creek) Nation of Oklahoma. http://www.muscogeenation-nsn.gov/ (accessed on June 12, 2011).

Poarch Creek Indians. http://www.poarchcreekindians.org/xhtml/index.htm (accessed on June 12, 2011).

Redish, Laura, and Orrin Lewis. "Creek Indian Fact Sheet." *Native Languages of the Americas.* http://www.bigorrin.org/creek_kids.htm (accessed on June 12, 2011).

"Sequoyah Research Center." *University of Arkansas at Little Rock.* http://anpa.ualr.edu/ (accessed on June 12, 2011).

"2011 Oklahoma Indian Nations." *Pocket Pictorial Directory.* Oklahoma City: Oklahoma Indian Affairs Commission, 2011. Available from http://www.ok.gov/oiac/documents/2011.FINAL.WEB.pdf (accessed on June 12, 2011).

Natchez

Name

The name *Natchez* (pronounced NAH-chee, although some people say it NATCH-ez, and the French pronunciation was NOTCH-ay) may have come from the people's main village, Naches, meaning "Great (or Grand) Village." Other possible spellings of the name include Nvce, Nahchee, Natches, Naktche, and Natsches. One early writer listed the Natchez as the "Sunset Indians." The Cherokee called them *Ani'-Na'tsl*. Some sources say the people called themselves *Theloel* or *Thecoel*, but the Natchez Nation gives its name as *W'NvhX'Ce*, which means "fast warrior."

Location

The Mississippi culture, ancestors of the Natchez, stretched from what is now North Carolina to Eastern Oklahoma, and from Minnesota to the Gulf of Mexico. By the time the French arrived in the late 1600s, the Natchez had as many as nine villages along the Mississippi River around St. Catherine's Creek, east and south of present-day Natchez, Mississippi. After the French massacre in the early 1700s, some Natchez joined the Cherokee (see entry) along the Hiwassee River in present-day North Carolina. They later moved to Oklahoma with the Cherokee, where they lived on the western edge of the reservation. Natchez who escaped to the Creek (see entry) also ended up in Oklahoma. Natchez also lived in Four Hole Springs in South Carolina, but some fled from the Catawba in 1744. As of the twenty-first century, most Natchez lived around Gore, Oklahoma, or Columbia and Ridgeville, South Carolina, although a few communities are scattered throughout the southeast, such as in Georgia and as far north as North Carolina.

Population

The Natchez tribe may have numbered about 6,000 people in 1682 at the time of their first contact with the French. Other estimates for the later 1600s were 3,500 to 4,500. Following their conflicts with the French and other tribes, the number of Natchez warriors dropped to 300 in 1731, but that count did not include their family members. The French deported many of the people as slaves, but 180 warriors avoided the attack and

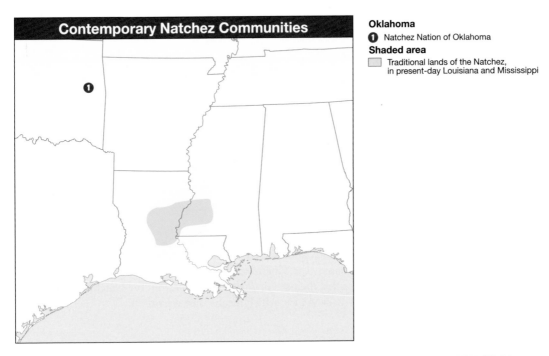

Contemporary Natchez Communities

Oklahoma
❶ Natchez Nation of Oklahoma
Shaded area
Traditional lands of the Natchez, in present-day Louisiana and Mississippi

A map of contemporary Natchez communities. MAP BY XNR PRODUCTIONS. CENGAGE LEARNING, GALE. REPRODUCED BY PERMISSION OF GALE, A PART OF CENGAGE LEARNING.

joined the Chickasaw. Estimates place about 20 to 150 warriors with the Creek; no figures were recorded for those living among the Cherokee. One source suggests a total of 300 Natchez in 1836. Because they were living with other nations, the Natchez population was not counted separately from that time on.

Language family
Gulf.

Origins and group affiliations
The ancestors of the Natchez were the Mound Builders (see entry), specifically the final group of Mississippian culture. In later times, both the Tioux and Grigras were under Natchez protection, but neither were related to them. It is possible that the Taensa and Chitimacha were once united with the Natchez, but the Chitimacha speak a totally different language. During the late 1600s and early 1700s, the Natchez fought with neighboring groups as well as the French. In 1729, the Choctaw

and Quapaw (see entries) attacked the Natchez and almost brought about their destruction. The Natchez scattered and found homes with the Creek, Cherokee, Chickasaw (see entries), and Catawba.

Descended from the Mississippian culture of mound builders, the Natchez were skilled artists, farmers, and traders who developed a unique culture. Unlike most neighboring tribes, which operated in a democratic manner, the Natchez had a strict class system and a theocratic leader who operated as both the political and religious authority. The upper class consisted of "Suns," nobles, and esteemed people; the commoners, or *michmichgupi*, made up the labor force. Although many sources indicate that the French essentially destroyed the Natchez and sold most of the remaining people into slavery, some survivors sought refuge with other tribes. Several groups still exist that claim their heritage: the Natchez Nation (Gore, Oklahoma), Eastern Band Natchez (Columbia, South Carolina), and Edistos Natchez-Kusso (Ridgeville, South Carolina) along with a few small southeastern communities. The Natchez name also lives on in towns in Mississippi, Louisiana, Indiana, and Alabama, as well as a parkway and other sites.

Important Dates

1682: Réne-Robert de La Salle's expedition descends the Mississippi River into Natchez territory.

1713: The French establish a trading post among Natchez.

1716: Natchez have their first conflict with French.

1729: French governor Sieur d'Etchéparre demands Natchez land for a plantation; Natchez revolt begins.

1731: French capture 400 Natchez; some are killed, and others are sold into slavery in Santo Domingo.

1735: Village of Nanne Hamgeh built.

1744: Natchez leave the Catawba who are living in South Carolina.

1965: Last fluent speaker of Natchez language dies.

HISTORY

Early history

Archaeological evidences shows that the Natchez culture may have begun as far back as 700 CE. In addition to their Mississippian ancestry, the people may have also been part of the powerful Quigualtam chiefdom that the Spanish explorer Hernando de Soto (c. 1496–1542) encountered on his 1542 expedition. These Europeans left behind the first diseases to which the Native tribes had no immunity. Measles, smallpox, and bubonic plague drastically reduced the population in the lower Mississippi River Valley over the next century.

At the end of the seventeenth century, the Natchez had settled in several autonomous (self-governing) communities that encompassed some Tunican-speaking refugees. Many people banded together for protection from the British, who came to the area seeking slaves. The hereditary chief of the Natchez, the Great Sun, was the ceremonial leader, but the outlying groups also had chiefs. By the time the French arrived, the Natchez had about nine towns in addition to their main one.

Europeans move into Natchez territory

René-Robert Cavelier de La Salle's (1643–1687) expedition in 1682 was the next Natchez encounter with Europeans. Soon after the La Salle expedition descended the Mississippi, French and English explorers, fur traders, military units, and missionaries visited the area.

The French opened their first trading post in 1713, thus beginning their colonization of the land. The priests who arrived had no success in gaining converts among the Natchez, whose religious beliefs were strongly integrated into their social system. The British fared better at making allies of the Natchez, particularly by befriending Bearded Chief, who was in charge of three of the villages. The Natchez villages, however, were divided in their allegiance. Hickory, White Apple, and the immigrant centers of Tiou and Grigra were anti-French, whereas Great Village and Flour Village supported the Europeans.

Conflicts with the French

After the British and the Natchez (under Bearded Chief) raided their trading post, the French set up military control. To restore peace, the Natchez executed six of their own war chiefs and three other people and sent their heads to the French governor. The Great Sun even sent laborers to help build Fort Rosalie. For the next few years, relations remained friendly. The Great Sun's brother, Tattooed Serpent (d. 1725), and his mother, Tattooed Arm, encouraged an alliance with the French.

When a French sergeant shot a Natchez warrior, however, the men of White Apple Village retaliated, wounding a plantation director. Tattooed Serpent negotiated peace, but the anti-French faction continued their raids. After Tattooed Serpent died in 1725, the Great Sun supported them against France. Three years later, the Great Sun died, and his young successor was no match for the growing power of the White Apple chief. That left Tattooed Arm as France's main ally.

Natchez warriors raid the Fort Rosalie settlement in 1729. © NORTH WIND PICTURE ARCHIVES/ALAMY

Demands for Natchez land

The situation between the Natchez and French worsened in 1729 when Sieur d'Etchéparre (sometimes spelled Chepart, Chépart, de Chapeare, Chopart), the new commandant at Fort Rosalie, ordered the Natchez to move from Great Village so he could have the land for a plantation. Although the Great Sun had no intention of complying, he requested two moons to build a new village elsewhere. Chépart agreed but demanded rent—birds, corn, pelts, and bear oil—for whatever time the Natchez remained. The commandant threatened to imprison the Great Sun if he did not comply.

The Natchez used that time to plot against the French, and at the first frost, they attacked Fort Rosalie and other forts along the river, killing more than 200 French. The Yazoo (Yazou), an upriver tribe the Natchez had enlisted to help them, murdered more. The Natchez captured several hundred woman, children, and slaves as well as Chépart. The warriors refused to touch him with their weapons, so they had a member of the lower class, whom the French called Stinkards, club him to death.

Destruction of the Natchez

After gathering their allies, including the Choctaw and Quapaw, the French attacked the Natchez, who released the prisoners and escaped across the river to Louisiana, where they built a fort on Sicily Island. By the following year the French had forced the Natchez to surrender. The French burned some of their prisoners to death, but the majority of the

Massacre and Destruction of Natchez

Some early sources indicate that the Choctaw (see entry) planned to join the Natchez in the attack against the French. The date was set for December 1, 1729, and the Choctaw and Natchez each had an equal number of *fagots* (bundles of twigs bound together to be used as fuel) that they used to time the attack. One fagot was to be thrown into the fire daily so that they could count down the days. Several stories have been told about why the Natchez attacked several days early rather than on the appointed day in concerted effort with the other neighboring tribes.

One account blames the premature attack on the Great Sun's mother, who remained loyal to the French. She tried several times to warn the French military of the impending attack, but her messages were ignored. She believed that the attack would be less deadly if the Natchez raided alone, and the French could then prepare for the other tribes. It is said she took some of the fagots to hasten the day of the invasion. Another story, given by Dumont de Montigny, a soldier at Fort Rosalie, blames the chief's son.

> Each day from that of the plot, the chiefs of the two nations had each burned one of the fatal fagots; but it happened one day, that the great chief of the Natchez having gone to

the temple, after having thrown into the first one of the fagots, according to custom, had turned round to speak to the guardian of the temple, a young lad, his son, who had come with him, felt an irresistible inclination to imitate what his father had done. He took two of the fagots, therefore, and threw them into the fire, which was the real cause why the Natchez advanced the massacre two days, attacking the French on the 29th of November.

The Choctaw, who were responsible for raiding New Orleans, did not arrive until two days later. They did not gain entry to the capital and returned to their village disappointed. When the Choctaw went to the Natchez villages and were only given a small portion of the goods the Natchez had taken from the French, the Choctaw called the Natchez *dogs* and accused them of attacking early so they could take all the spoils for themselves. Perhaps this was why the Choctaw joined the French in destroying the Natchez a short while later.

SOURCE: "Massacre and Destruction of Natchez." *Colburn's United Service Magazine and Naval and Military Journal.* Part 1. London: H. Hurst, 1847, p. 31–32.

four hundred Natchez, the Great Sun among them, they sold into slavery into Santo Domingo.

A few of the prisoners got away and continued to attack French voyageurs, but most fled to other tribes. The French did not exterminate the Natchez as some sources claimed, but the people scattered among other tribes. About 180 warriors, who were not present during the battle, took shelter with the Chickasaw. In 1735, they built a separate village, Nanne Hamgeh. About fifty Natchez gunmen ended up around Tallahassee Creek, where they occupied a town called Natchez and part of a settlement called Abikudshi. A large number joined the Creek in Alabama; others went to the Cherokee, who were removed to Indian Territory in 1832. Many Natchez ended up near Tahlequah and Muskogee in eastern Oklahoma. Some people moved to South Carolina with the Catawba, but left in 1744 to avoid revenge from their adopted tribe over several murders.

Natchez in twenty-first century

Most accounts of the Natchez end in the early 1700s, but the people did not forget their identity and heritage despite living in far-flung places. Although they lived with other tribes, they kept themselves apart and retained their distinct culture. For example, when they were removed with the Cherokee to Oklahoma, the Natchez maintained their own portion of the reservation.

In the 2000s, the Natchez live in the southern part of the Muscogee (Creek) and Cherokee reservations. Some also make their homes with the other "Five Civilized Tribes," as the Americans in the 1800s called the Cherokee, Chickasaw, Choctaw, Creek, and Seminole (see entries). Other small Natchez communities exist across the Southeast. The state of South Carolina has recognized two of these bands, the Eastern Band Natchez (at one time called the Natchez-PeeDee) and the Edisto Natchez-Kusso. The Natchez living with the Muscogee in Oklahoma operate independently as the Natchez Nation.

RELIGION

Creation story

The Natchez creation story said that the Infinite Spirit created all good things. Some of the little spirits, his helpers, also assisted by making some of the beautiful things in the universe. These spirits were free, but they were as respectful as slaves. The Infinite Spirit tied up the leader of the evil spirits who might do harm in the world. Yet some of the evil one's spirit-helpers still caused trouble. Prayer could prevent them from doing harm. To invoke the good spirits, the people fasted and prayed.

The Infinite Spirit also formed man from clay and breathed life into him. When people went wrong, he sent a man and woman to Earth to teach humans how to live. The man was the sun's younger brother. He instructed the people keep a sacred fire constantly burning in the temple, because fire was a piece of the sun. He also gave the people a code of conduct for daily living. The main rules were to kill only in self-defense, never to commit adultery, not to steal, not to lie or get drunk, and not to be greedy but to give freely and share with those in need.

Religious rituals

The Great Sun was regarded as part god. One of his daily duties was to ensure that the sacred fire stayed burning in the temple. His daily ritual began with greeting his elder brother, the sun, with song and prayer, wailing three times, and blowing smoke from a calumet (pipe) in each of the four directions (east, west, north, south). Then he checked on the fire.

People could not enter the temple, but they left food offerings there for the Great Sun. Two men tended the fire, which was never allowed to go out. The priest, or master of ceremonies, wore a half-crown of feathers and carried a stick with red or white feathers. Every month, the entire tribe went to the temple and paid tribute to the Great Sun. He generally appeared before them wearing a feathered crown and sitting in an ornate chair carried by eight throne bearers.

The Great Sun dressed in rich clothes and was carried from place to place so his feet would never touch the ground. Only certain people were permitted into his presence, and they had to follow strict rules when approaching him (see the Mound Builders entry, "Religion").

Carrying on the traditions

In the 1870s, a Natchez named Creek Sam worked to reorganize the Keetoowah and Four Mothers (see "Government") societies. He formed them around a sacred fire his ancestors had carried from the east. These groups tried to resist the changes that more liberal tribal members wanted to institute. At this time, Creek and his son Watt were two of the five people who still spoke the Natchez language (see "Language").

LANGUAGE

Ancient dialects

The people had two distinct forms of their dialects. One was spoken by the nobles, the other by commoners. Suns and nobles were spoken to in a more formal manner. For example, a Sun visitor to a home would be greeted with the words, "I'm pleased to see you." A commoner would be told to "sit down." Women used slightly different inflections than men.

In addition to these two dialects, the Natchez spoke a common language that was understood by many of the tribes in the area. This common language was useful for trade and planning with other tribal leaders.

Natchez language preservation

The Natchez spoke a unique language that has few ties with other families. At times, it has been considered a dialect of Muskogean. Other linguists labeled it part of the Algonquian family. More recently, it has been called a Gulf language, which places it in a category with Atakapa, Chitimacha, and Tunica. All experts agree that it is not closely related to any other languages, and some have given the dialect its own classification, Natchesan.

Although the Natchez were absorbed into other tribes, they retained their dialect until about 1800. By 1907, only five people who lived with the Cherokee still spoke their language. By 1931, Creek Sam and his son Watt Sam were two of the five people who still used the Natchez language (see "Language"). An anthropologist made wax cylinder recordings of Watt Sam speaking Natchez, and a linguist recorded word lists and stories that he told her a few years later. When he died in 1965, Watt Sam was the last known fluent speaker of the Natchez language.

Nevertheless, some tribal members now use their language on a daily basis. Many people also speak another language in addition to English. Most speak Cherokee or Muscogee because those are the nations where they live. The Natchez language has been preserved on tape, and data can be found as part of the University of Oklahoma's Western History Collections. Some language materials are available online.

GOVERNMENT

Traditional leadership

The Natchez government was intricately tied to the religion. The Great Sun was both the king and the religious leader. He made the decisions for the people, and they followed them slavishly. He did, however, have

Natchez Words	
waˑckup	"dog"
tca	"deer"
tcoˑkop	"wolf"
en	"fish"
hiˑ	"squirrel"
olo	"turtle"
o'oc	"owl"

a council composed of priests, warriors, and other important people to advise him. The Great Sun was responsible for appointing the chiefs, temple guardians, and ceremonial officers, called "Little Suns." Usually he selected his brothers or uncles to serve in these positions. The principal woman Sun, either the Great Sun's mother or sister, chose his successor from among her sons or brothers.

Maintaining traditions

The Natchez Nation considers itself to have one of "the oldest continually functioning governments" in the world. As in the past, four clan mothers, called Law Keepers, are in charge of judicial affairs and tribal life. If tribal members have any business they want to discuss at council meetings, they let their clan mothers know. Tribal leaders are the principal peace chief (Great Sun) and the principal war chief, called first warrior or second chief. They are expected to work together harmoniously, and like clan mothers, they are chosen for their expertise and virtues. The peace chief oversees internal affairs and calls councils of Suns, which make the final decisions. Leaders from other tribes are included in the council. All council decisions are made by consensus, which means everyone must agree.

In the 2000s, the Natchez Nation are a treaty tribe of the Muscogee Nation, and they have maintained their sovereign traditional tribal government. The Natchez-Kusso Indian Tribe of South Carolina has an eleven-member council with a chief, vice chief, and chairman/treasurer. The state recognized the tribe in 2010.

ECONOMY

The Natchez, who subsisted mainly on farming, developed an elaborate social class system. At the top was the Great Sun. People could not get near him, and his feet did not touch the ground. He was carried everywhere in a litter, and others spoke to him only from a distance. Women Suns, his relatives, were more powerful than any other people. Nobles, who were below the Suns, inherited their positions. They held places of honor at village events and war parties. The next level down contained Honored Men and Women. People could earn these designations by doing brave deeds or being pious in their religion. All of these rankings were considered part of the upper class.

On the lowest level were commoners, whom the French called *puants* or "stinkards." The Natchez called them *michmichgupi*. Michmichgupi could improve their status by showing extreme courage during wartime or being very devoted to their religion. Other than that, they remained in their social class all their lives. Michmichgupi did all the work in the village and served the upper classes.

DAILY LIFE

Families

In general, men had higher social ranks than women. They held the leadership positions and took charge of their households. Men also ate first. Women Suns, however, had a greater position than others, and their husbands, who were michmichgupi, were of lesser rank. Women Suns were also responsible for choosing the next Great Sun, so they had great power and political influence (see "Economy" and "Government").

Children belonged to the father, and they lived with him, his wives, and all his other children in the same home. The old man, who was the oldest male in the family, often a great-grandfather, had the greatest authority.

Children who misbehaved by being stubborn or hurting others were threatened with punishment from the old man. Though they were rarely punished, they learned to respect and fear the old man. Families looked to him as a judge, and his word was law. Everyone called him "Father," including nephews. Observers said they never saw the children fight, perhaps because they were told they would be banished if they did. They were taught not to strike back if someone hit them, and they did not even wrestle for fun, so older children and adults did not engage in physical fights. Because of this, the Natchez had no need for courts or judges.

Buildings

At one time, the Natchez had as many as nine villages, each with a temple on top of a mound. The main mound was Emerald Mound. Grand Village had three mounds—the Great Sun's Mound, the Temple Mound, and the Abandoned Mound (so named by archaeologists, because it was not excavated like the other mounds). The mounds stood 8 feet (2 to 3 meters) high, but rose in several stages, revealing that previous structures had been knocked down and replaced. A religious structure, housing bones of past Great Suns and a perpetually burning fire, stood facing the rising sun on the Temple Mound, which was farthest south. This temple had carved birds decorating the roof. The chief's mound was near the center of the village. The Great Sun's home, which measured 45 by 25 feet (14 by 7.5 meters) and 20 feet (6 meters) high, was placed at one end of the mound.

Villages had huts of many different shapes—rectangular, square, or round—but all had high, pointy roofs and rectangular doors. Homes were built of poles that were then covered with a mixture of clay or mud and Spanish moss. The high, 15-foot (5-meter) walls had no windows, and they were covered with split cane mats. The round, arched roof came to a conical point and was covered with thatch.

Inside, platforms for sleeping lined the walls. Covered with woven mats, the platforms had wooden pillows and blankets made of skins. Shelves held mats for sitting around the fire, which was built in the center of the house. Because the huts had no hole in the roof, the smoke either exited through the door or drifted through the thatched roof, killing mosquitoes and other insects as it rose.

Clothing and adornment

Children did not wear clothes until they reached puberty. Then girls donned short, fringed skirts made of mulberry. Their mothers wore knee-length deerskin or fiber skirts. Men dressed in loincloths (flaps of material that covered the back and front and were suspended from the waist). Chiefs and nobles had black loincloths; others wore white. No one wore shirts in warm weather, but when it grew cold, both men and women put on poncho-like tunics that fell below their knees, and men wore leather leggings. Nobles could be distinguished by their feathered capes. Homosexual men wore skirts and braided their hair like the women.

The Great Sun's headdress was made of net covered with black feathers, with an edging of red with white seeds. Long white feathers protruded from the front, and shorter ones were attached behind. Other sources say his crown was made of red-tasseled swan feathers. He wore a feathered mantle.

Men wore their hair in different styles. Some shaved half their heads. Others plucked all their hair except for a scalplock (a small piece that hung down in back). A few wore tonsures like the priests; they removed all the hair except for a strip around the sides and back. Warriors tattooed their whole bodies with serpents, suns, and other designs. A man who had killed an enemy tattooed a war club and a symbol of the enemy's tribe on his shoulder.

Women eventually began covering their bodies with ankle-length white dresses woven from mulberry bark and nettles. Men added deer-skin leather jackets to their outfits.

Food

As a farming people, the Natchez depended on the crops they raised as their main diet. They grew corn, beans, pumpkins, watermelons, and squash that they used in dishes such as cornbread, hominy, and soups. Women had more than forty different recipes for corn, and they made bread from walnuts, chestnuts, and acorns. They also gathered wild grass, nuts, roots, grapes, and berries. Each of their thirteen calendar months, or moons, was based on a certain food (see "Our Calendar Has 13 Months").

Men hunted for small game, turkey, bison, and deer. Fish and birds were also a part of Natchez meals. Hunters smoked bears out of holes in trees and saved the bear fat for oil. To catch deer, large groups of men chased one until it was exhausted. Then they brought it to the Great Sun (see "Economy"), who killed it and divided the meat among them. Individual hunters dressed in deer costumes and made deer calls to attract the animals.

Education

Children were given adult tasks as soon as they could handle them. Females had more responsibilities than males. Girls learned to plant and weed, pound the corn into flour, care for the children, carry wood and feed the fire, and make pottery, mats, clothes, and tools. They were warned that if they were lazy, they would not attract a good husband. Boys learned to hunt, fish, and cut wood. As they grew older, they worked to prepare the fields, dressed skins, and built houses.

Around the age of ten or twelve, children were expected to carry small loads to help their families. About this time, boys received a small bow and arrows. They were trained to shoot by using grass targets attached to a pole. The old man (the oldest man in a family; see "Families") watched and praised them for trying hard rather than for their accuracy.

Although the boys sometimes raced with each other, the old man stopped them before they got overheated. The children bathed daily in the water, and all year round, one of the old men called all the children to swim. Mothers started teaching their youngsters how to swim when they were about three. Children were taught to make loud noises to scare away the alligators and to keep themselves warm when it was cold.

Only certain children were chosen to learn the oral traditions, ancient history, and stories. The Natchez viewed these oral accounts as treasures and entrusted them to those they believed could memorize them and would use them wisely.

Healing practices

To become a healer, a person isolated himself or herself for nine days and ate nothing until after receiving a vision. Shamans (pronounced *SHAH-munz* or *SHAY-munz*), or healers, used owl heads and small stones in the course of their work. They sucked out objects (a piece of wood, straw, or leather) from an incision. In addition to curing illness, some were able to change the weather.

ARTS

Known for their skill in pottery-making, the Natchez incised designs into clay. Swirls and organic shapes, often in sets of parallel lines, showed white or gray against a terracotta background. The ancestors of the Natchez developed the technique of shell tempering, which involved adding small bits of shell to strengthen (temper) the clay. The women were experts at shaping bottles, pots, jars, and plates. The Natchez were also skilled at basketry and woodcarving.

CUSTOMS

Birth and naming

Natchez mothers washed their babies right after they were born and then put them on a prepared cradleboard, which was about 2.5 feet (0.8 meters) long and about 9 inches (23 centimeters) wide. The end piece refolded to make a footboard. Inside the cradle the baby was laid on Spanish moss and a hide pillow stuffed with moss. Two bands of deerskin across the forehead kept the head on the pillow and also made it flat. The Natchez practiced head flattening. The child was tied onto the cradleboard with bindings around its shoulders, arms, legs, and hips. This cradleboard stayed beside the mother in bed or was placed on two pieces of cane so it could be rocked back and forth. Children were rubbed with bear oil to keep their muscles flexible and prevent bugs from biting them.

The Panther and the Crane

Storytelling was important to the Natchez, who had many traditional tales. One of the most important is about the origin of the sacred fire. Other characters that often appear in their folklore are Rabbit, a trickster; Olobit (Olobis, Olo'bit, Olo-Bit), sometimes called the sharp-breasted snake; Tlanuwa, a bird with metal feathers; and Tie-snakes, water spirits shaped like snakes who drag people under the water to drown them. Another common group of stories centers on Lodge-Boy and Thrown-Away (or Wild Boy). These two twins, born after their mother was killed by a monster, cause trouble as they try to slay monsters. Some tales, such this one, are about animals who behave like people.

> Panther and Crane laid a wager. Panther said to Crane, "Let us see who can throw the farthest." "All right," Crane answered. They said, "Let us throw a hammer across a stream." Panther threw first, and he got it across, but when Crane stood ready to throw, he thought, "I can't get it across." The two had agreed that whichever did not succeed in getting the hammer across should be killed.

> "If I do not get it across, he will kill me," thought Crane, and, as he stood there, he whistled. "Why are you whistling?" said Panther. "My elder brother lives way up there where the hammer is going to fall. I am whistling because when I throw this hammer I want him to see it. He is a blacksmith and I think it will be useful to him. That is why I am making a noise." "If that is so, don't throw it. I have some use for it myself. I can't spare it. Let us try something different. Let us see who can eat most of equal quantities of food." They did so. But the Crane had a bag hung about his person and he sat eating a little and putting more into the bag. Panther, however, did not find it out and ate all, and when all was devoured they brought more in. After they had eaten for a while longer Panther got more than enough and fell down dead. So Crane beat Panther.

SOURCE: "The Panther and the Crane." *Internet Sacred Text Archive.* http://www.sacred-texts.com/nam/se/mtsi/mtsi286.htm (accessed on June 20, 2011).

Courtship

Once they reached puberty, teens spent much time together. Women and men in Natchez society could pursue a person who interested them. One French writer expressed surprise that the young, unmarried women were aggressive in courtship. Women Suns could have as many lovers as they desired. Some Natchez women intermarried with the French.

Couples did not need parental approval; they chose their own spouses. Once they decided to marry, the boy had an interview with the old men of the families. They checked to be sure that the bride and groom were not too closely related, and if either of the old men had any objections, the marriage could not take place. The old men set the wedding date. Young men rarely married before age twenty-five.

Marriage

Wedding ceremony The men of the family hunted, while the women cooked corn and furnished the young man's cabin. When all was ready, the old man conducted the bride to the cabin, and the rest of the family followed. The young man's relatives greeted them and allowed the old men to rest on the beds for a while.

The young man wore a tuft on his head hanging over his left ear that symbolized that he was to be the master. A sprig of oak leaves was attached to it, meaning that he would not fear entering the woods to hunt. In his left hand, he carried a bow and arrows to show that he would defend his wife and children. The young woman held a laurel branch to signify that she would be pure and an ear of maize indicating that she would prepare the meals.

The old men brought the couple together and questioned them about their intentions to live together in peace. If they did not get along, they were warned that their families would reject them. The groom then asked the young woman if she wanted to marry him, and she assented and said she was happy. Her husband then gave a present to her father. After the groom grasped the hands of everyone in the bride's family, she did the same with his. A feast and dance followed the ceremony.

Rules governing marriages The Great Sun could only marry partners from the lowest class of the society, the michmichgupi (see "Economy"). The Great Sun's brothers (the Lesser Suns) and his sisters (the Women Suns) also could only marry commoners. The children of the Great Sun and the Lesser Suns did not retain their parents' high rank. The children of the Women Suns, however, kept their mother's social rank, and one of them would usually become the next Great Sun when his uncle died.

Temple.

Pallbearers carry the body of Chief Tattooed Serpent at his funeral procession in Louisiana in 1725. © MPI/GETTY IMAGES.

Our Calendar Has 13 Months

The Natchez calendar has thirteen months (or moons). Each month is named for the food eaten the month before. The year begins in the spring with Deer Moon, which falls around March.

Chv	"Deer"
Oruh	"Strawberry"
Ha'kuyv Cekestanu	"Little Corn"
Yewes Kvyap	"Watermelon/ Squash"
Vpesur/Henn	"Peach/Fish"
Yeweskvyap	"Mulberry"
Ha'kuyv Sel (Pookup)	"Great Corn/Green Corn"
Sorkorser	"Turkey"
Wastanem	"Bison"
Tsokohp	"Bear"
Hakwi	"Cold Meal"
Puilusi	"Chestnut"
Puhelush (Merkv)	"Walnut (and all other nuts)"

SOURCE: "Our Calendar Has 13 Months." *Natchez Nation.* http://www.natchez-nation. com/culture.html (accessed on June 27, 2011).

Michmichgupi who married into the top social class remained commoners all their lives. They could not eat with their spouses and had to stand in their presence. They also praised all their spouses' remarks. If they offended their high-ranking spouses in any way, they could be killed and replaced.

Once they were married, spouses were expected to be faithful. They were told that their hearts were not their own, but belonged to the other. Divorce was rare, but men could separate from their wives. When that happened the children went with the parent of the same sex.

Funerals

The Natchez conducted elaborate funeral ceremonies for their elite. Everyone gathered at the mound plaza for rituals that included sacrifice. When a Sun died, the spouse and several relatives and friends willingly gave up their lives. Servants, too, were sacrificed to give the Sun assistance in the afterlife, and parents offered their children as sacrifices, particularly in honor of the Great Sun. These volunteers would be strangled, and they considered it a privilege to cross into the spirit world with a Sun.

When Chief Tattooed Serpent (see "History") died in 1725, the French prevented his brother, the Great Sun, from giving up his life, but Tattooed Serpent's wife only laughed at their objections. She insisted that it was a joy for her to die with her husband.

Bodies were placed on raised platforms near the village. The Natchez smeared mud on a mat and covered the corpse with it, but they left the head uncovered. They left food next to the body. An arbor placed over the body was plastered to keep the corpse dry until the flesh decayed. The dried bones were then put into a cane basket and carried to the temple. When the Temple Mound of Great Village was excavated in the late 1900s, archaeologists found piles of these bones in the temple area.

Feasts and games

The ceremonies and feasts of the Natchez were both religious and political in nature. They were used to thank the Infinite Spirit for his blessings, and they allowed people to pay tribute to the Great Sun. Most of these feasts were connected to the thirteen moons (see "Our Calendar Has 13 Months").

Deer Moon Festival The year began in March at the time of the Deer Moon. A special enactment of a past event was part of this monthly festival. Long ago, a Great Sun had been ambushed by enemies, but he was rescued by his warriors. In memory of this incident, the warriors divided into two groups with different colored plumes. One group pretended to be the enemy and advanced toward the Great Sun's home. The Great Sun, dressed in finery, emerged, rubbing his eyes to show he had just awakened. The enemy group captured him, but the other warriors came to rescue him. The enemies issued cries of terror and sang death songs. Then the Great Sun, using an ancient war club, made the motion of a blow, and the enemies toppled to the ground. After many enemies fell before the Natchez warriors, the defeated fighters got up and fled to the woods, pursued by the victors. All the people gave cries of joy.

The Great Sun then rested for a while and later reemerged without his crown. He went to the temple, bowed, threw some earth into the air so that it rained down on his head, then he tossed a bit in each of the four direction. Next he spent a half hour with arms outstretched like a cross. The Grand Master of Ceremonies then took his place, and after him came the Great War Chief; both of them stood still in that position. The people stayed silent during these prayers. Finally, the Great Sun came out dressed in his feather crown, with a necklace of pearls and feathers. He sat on his throne, and the warriors put a bison robe around him and pelts over his feet. Women shouted with joy as they gave him presents. After this, the people feasted and danced.

Strawberry and Maize Moons The second moon feast was for strawberries. The women and children gathered many, and the warriors brought skewered ducks that they caught on a special hunting trip. The most solemn feast was that of maize in the seventh moon. Then the people ate new corn in a religious manner. To grow this corn, warriors prepared cornfields by cutting out the brush, peeling back the bark on the lower halves of the trees, and waiting two weeks for all the plant matter to dry. After that they lit a fire that burned out all the trees, roots, and underbrush. They planted and weeded this field. When harvest time neared, they created a sacred granary of cane lined with cane mats. The large cane they used on the outside had a natural varnish that prevented rats from climbing the sides or chewing holes through it.

Cabins were built near the granary for the Great Sun and the Great War Chief. Warriors also built homes from grass and leaves for their own families. On feast day, everyone rose at sunrise. The Great Sun was transported to his temporary cabin on a red litter; this special chair, carried on the shoulders of warriors, was decorated for the occasion with leaves and flowers. The chief saluted the corn, and the people repeated the salute. The warriors distributed corn first to the Women Suns, then to the other women, who prepared it by hulling and crushing it. They threw it into boiling water while the warriors sang war songs, beating on a pot as a drum.

When the corn was cooked, the Great Sun received two plates, one of each kind of corn that they grew. After he offered it to the four directions, he sent it to the Great War Chief and said, "*Pachcou* (Eat)." Everyone then began to eat; the men first, then the boys, after which the women and children had their portion. Singing and speeches followed. At nightfall, they surrounded the area with huge torches made of cane and danced until daybreak.

The next morning, two teams of warriors with different colored plumes on their heads played *pelotte*, a game using a fist-sized ball of deerskin stuffed with moss. The object of the game was to touch the cabin of the Great Sun or the Great War Chief without carrying the ball or letting it touch the ground. Each team tried to prevent the other from reaching their goal. The people continued to feast in this manner until all the corn was gone. If some people had corn and others did not, the ones with extra corn had a tassel hung in their doorway so others could share it. To end the feast, the Great Sun was carried back to his home on the litter.

CURRENT TRIBAL ISSUES

Once a strong and vibrant nation, the Natchez were scattered in the 1700s following a French attack (see "History"). Most joined other tribes but they tried to maintain their customs and identity. Today, some have been absorbed by these other, larger nations, but they still pass along their heritage to their children. Many are members of two nations—the Natchez and one of the other tribes with which they are affiliated. Several of the groups have gained federal or state recognition, and they work hard to combat the common belief that they were exterminated centuries ago.

NOTABLE PEOPLE

Tattooed Arm, mother of the Great Sun who ruled during the French massacre in 1731, favored the French. When her people plotted to attack several French communities, she tried to alert the commandant and other soldiers, but they ignored her warning. It is even said that she removed bundles of sticks, called fagots, from the Natchez store. Several tribes were using those to count the days up to the joint attack against the French (see "Massacre and Destruction of Natchez" sidebar). This meant the Natchez attacked the French alone. In spite of her loyalty, the French imprisoned her in 1731. Tattooed Arm's son, Olabalkebiche (d. 1725), or Tattooed Serpent, was the brother of the Great Sun. He, like his mother, supported the French until the commandant's ultimatum (see "History"). Some sources indicate that the name Tattooed Serpent may have been given to any Natchez war chief, just as the name Great Sun referred to any head chief.

BOOKS

Barnett, James F., Jr. *The Natchez Indians: A History to 1735.* Jackson: University Press of Mississippi, 2007.

Crediford, Gene J. *Those Who Remain.* Tuscaloosa: University of Alabama Press, 2009.

Feldman, George Franklin. *Cannibalism, Headhunting, and Human Sacrifice in North America: A History Forgotten.* Chambersburg, PA: Alan C. Hood & Co., 2008.

French, Benjamin Franklin. *Historical Memoirs of Louisiana: From the First Settlement of the Colony to the Departure of Governor O'Reilly in 1770.* New York: Lamport, Blakeman, & Law, 1853.

Lankford, George E., ed. *Native American Legends of the Southeast: Tales from the Natchez, Caddo, Biloxi, Chickasaw, and Other Nations.* 5th ed. Tuscaloosa: University of Alabama Press, 2011.

PERIODICALS

Elliott, Jack. "Dawn, Nov. 28, 1729: Gunfire Heralds Natchez Massacre." *Concordia Sentinel.* November 5, 2009. Available from http://www.concordiasentinel.com/news.php?id=4321 (accessed on June 27, 2011).

"Massacre and Destruction of Natchez." *Colburn's United Service Magazine and Naval and Military Journal.* Part 1. London: H. Hurst, 1847, pp. 31–22.

Swanton, John R. "Sun Worship in the Southeast." *American Anthropologist.* New Series, Vol. 30, No. 2 (April–June 1928), pp. 206–13.

WEB SITES

Barnett, Jim. "The Natchez Indians." *History Now.* http://mshistory.k12.ms.us/index.php?id=4 (accessed on June 27, 2011).

Conrad, Jim. "The Natchez Indians." *The Loess Hills of the Lower Mississipi Valley.* http://www.backyardnature.net/loess/ind_natz.htm (accessed on June 27, 2011).

"Grand Village of the Natchez Indians." *Mississippi Department of Archives and History.* http://mdah.state.ms.us/hprop/gvni.html (accessed on June 27, 2011).

Lewis, J.D. "The Natchez Indians." *Carolina—The Native Americans.* http://www.carolana.com/Carolina/Native_Americans/native_americans_natchez.html (accessed on June 27, 2011).

"Natchez Indian Tribe History." *Access Geneology.* http://www.accessgenealogy.com/native/tribes/natchez/natchezhist.htm (accessed on June 27, 2011).

Natchez Nation. http://www.natchez-nation.com/ (accessed on June 27, 2011).

"Natchez Stories." *Sacred Texts.* http://www.sacred-texts.com/nam/se/mtsi/#section_004 (accessed on June 27, 2011).

Redish, Laura, and Orrin Lewis. "Natchez Indian Language." *Native Languages of the Americas.* http://www.native-languages.org/natchez.htm#language (accessed on June 27, 2011).

Sayre, Gordon. "L'Histoire de la Louisiane (1758)." *University of Oregon.* http://darkwing.uoregon.edu/~gsayre/LPDP.html (accessed on June 27, 2011).

Seminole

Name

The name Seminole (pronounced *SEH-muh-nole*) may be from the Spanish word *cimmarrón* ("wild one") or from the Creek word meaning "runaway" or "lover of the wild."

Location

The Seminole people originally lived in Alabama and Georgia, but they migrated to Florida in the seventeenth century to escape American colonists and traders. Present-day Florida has six Seminole reservations. The Oklahoma Seminole live in different towns in that state. Other Seminole reside in California, and some are scattered in small groups around the United States.

Population

In 1821, there were an estimated five thousand Seminole. In the 1990 U.S. Census, 15,564 people identified themselves as Seminole. By 2000, that number had dropped to 12,790, but the 2010 census counted 14,080 Seminole. In 2011, the recorded tribal enrollment for the Seminole Nation was 16,338, according to the Oklahoma Indian Affairs Commission.

Language family

Muskogean.

Origins and group affiliations

Seminole was a name given to a group of Creek, Yamasee, Oconee, Apalachicolas, Alabamas, and other Native groups who fled to Florida in the 1700s from several areas of the southeastern United States. In the 1830s, most of the Seminole were forced to leave their homelands and relocate to present-day Oklahoma, where they formed new relationships with other southeastern tribes also relocated there, including the Cherokee, Chickasaw, Choctaw, and Creek (see entries).

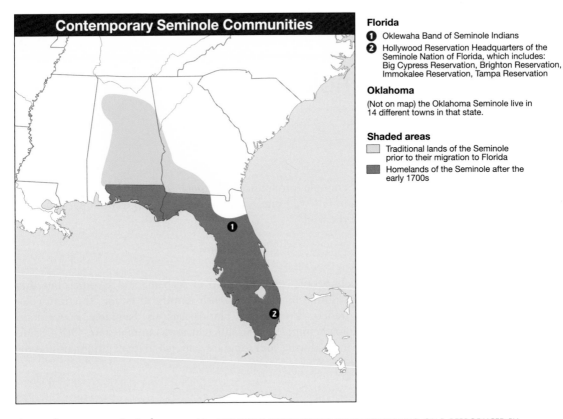

Contemporary Seminole Communities

Florida

❶ Oklewaha Band of Seminole Indians

❷ Hollywood Reservation Headquarters of the Seminole Nation of Florida, which includes: Big Cypress Reservation, Brighton Reservation, Immokalee Reservation, Tampa Reservation

Oklahoma

(Not on map) the Oklahoma Seminole live in 14 different towns in that state.

Shaded areas

☐ Traditional lands of the Seminole prior to their migration to Florida

■ Homelands of the Seminole after the early 1700s

A map of contemporary Seminole communities. MAP BY XNR PRODUCTIONS. CENGAGE LEARNING, GALE. REPRODUCED BY PERMISSION OF GALE, A PART OF CENGAGE LEARNING.

The Seminole did not exist as a tribe until the late 1700s, when a group of Creek moved to northern Florida and settled there to avoid trouble, find better soil, and seek skins for trading. Members of other tribes, as well as runaway slaves, joined this core group to form the Seminole population. The history of the Seminole was marked by conflicts, forced removal to the western United States, and great adversity. Despite these challenges, the people have shown self-sufficiency and a fierce independence.

HISTORY

Move to Florida

The early people whose descendants now make up the Seminole and Creek tribes resided at the fifteenth-century site of Etowah in Georgia. They lived in clans (large groups of related families) and enjoyed an abundant food supply. They also engaged in warfare with the neighboring tribes of Cherokee, Chickasaw, and Choctaw. In the 1700s, some Creek moved to Florida to avoid being caught in these conflicts. They founded communities along river or stream banks and became the new Seminole tribe.

Peace shattered by War of 1812

The eighteenth century was mostly peaceful for the Seminole in Florida. They had good relations with Spanish military troops stationed there. For nearly one hundred years, the people hunted and gathered in the wilds, often trading their goods at the Spanish forts. Runaway slaves from American plantations farther north sometimes hid among the Seminole, who warmly accepted them.

This period of calm ended during the War of 1812 (1812–15; a war in which the United States defeated Great Britain). Although American colonists won independence from Great Britain in 1783, the western boundary of the new United States extended only to the Mississippi River. In 1812, American settlers pushed beyond the Mississippi onto land claimed by the British, thus igniting a war over territory.

Important Dates

1700s: The Creek settle in Florida, forming the core group of a new Seminole tribe.

1817: The First Seminole War occurs when soldiers from neighboring states invade Seminole lands in Florida looking for runaway slaves.

1832: The U.S. government attempts relocation of the Seminole to Indian Territory in Oklahoma, leading to Second Seminole War.

1932: The Florida Seminole move to reservations.

1957: The Florida Seminole Tribe of Florida is established and gains federal recognition.

1962: The Miccosukee Tribe of Florida receives federal recognition.

Creek Wars

During the war, some of the southeastern tribes sided with Great Britain while others sided with the United States. In 1813, a group of Creek Indians captured an American army post near Mobile, Alabama, and massacred the soldiers. The U.S. Army retaliated. In the conflict that followed, called the Creek War of 1813–14, some Creek joined the United States to fight other Creek. Many Native people died, and numerous towns were destroyed. The Creek signed a peace treaty giving all their lands in Georgia and some in Alabama to the U.S. government. Rather than be ruled by the U.S. government, many Creek fled to Florida and joined the Seminole, thereby tripling the Seminole population.

The First Seminole War

Ever-larger numbers of white settlers also moved south, some onto land claimed by the Spanish. A clash between these settlers and the Native inhabitants of the area was unavoidable. Fighting between American settlers and the Seminole caused the United States to declare war on the tribe in 1817 in a conflict called the First Seminole War. U.S. troops invaded Florida (then controlled by Spain) searching for runaway slaves who had sought refuge with the Seminole. Spain was too weak at that time to retaliate against the United States. As a result, U.S. military raids increased, and American troops seized Florida from Spain, burning Native villages and killing their inhabitants. In 1821, Spain gave Florida to the United States. American settlers took over the prime farming land and hunting grounds of the Seminole.

Southern plantation owners continued to travel into what was now American territory in search of the escaped slaves they considered their property. Many of these slaves, who were living under the protection of the Seminole, formed themselves into a black Seminole clan and were adopted into the tribe. Armed soldiers from the southern states accompanied the plantation owners and took many prisoners, not caring if their prisoners were former slaves or full-blood Seminole.

Seminole moved to reservations

In 1823, the U.S. government persuaded the Seminole to move onto reservations in central and southern Florida to make way for settlers. The tribe was promised equipment, livestock, and an annual payment of $5,000 for twenty years. The Seminole gave up 30 million acres of rich farmland for about 5 million acres of sandy, marshy land not well suited for farming. They also agreed to stop protecting escaped slaves.

The move to the reservation took more than a year. Unable to hunt or farm while they waited, the people suffered widespread hunger and had to put up with illegal attacks by those in search of runaway slaves. The Seminole were too exhausted to fight and felt betrayed by the whites with whom they had made the treaty.

Tribe agrees to move to Indian Territory

Over the next ten years, settlers came in great numbers and moved onto former Seminole lands. Soon that land was filled, and the settlers clamored for more. U.S. officials put pressure on some Seminole leaders, and they signed the Treaty of Payne's Landing in 1832, which required them to relocate within three years to Indian Territory. (Indian Territory for the Seminole was the land that now forms most of the state of Oklahoma. During the 1800s, the U.S. government moved many tribes to Indian Territory.) In return for moving, the Seminole would receive annual payments of cash and goods for their former territory. This move, however, would reunite them with the Creek, who by this time had become their bitter enemies.

The Second Seminole War

The move to Indian Territory was to take place in 1835. Before it could begin, Seminole Chief Osceola (1804–1838) started a rebellion that resulted in the Second Seminole War. Although the majority of the tribe moved to Indian Territory, nearly five hundred hid in the Everglades with Osceola. For seven years, the vastly outnumbered Seminole warriors put up a brave resistance, using hit-and-run tactics to resist five thousand U.S. soldiers by striking at them and then disappearing back into the swamps. This conflict developed into the longest and costliest Indian War in the history of the United States. Federal officials became frustrated by the expense and their inability to beat the Seminole. Federal troops captured Chief Osceola under a false flag of truce in 1837. He died in a prisoner-of-war camp shortly thereafter.

Chief Osceola led the Seminole in a rebellion against the U.S. government in the 1830s.
© MPI/STRINGER/ARCHIVE PHOTOS/GETTY IMAGES.

Osceola's successor, Chief Coacoochee (c. 1808–1857), carried on the fight but finally surrendered in 1841. By that time, most warriors had been killed or had submitted to moving west with the rest of their tribe. The Seminole then became part of the movement of the "Five Civilized Tribes" to Indian Territory. The Five Civilized Tribes were the Chickasaw, Choctaw, Seminole, Creek, and Cherokee. The settlers and the U.S. government gave them this name because they had adopted American customs in the late 1700s and early 1800s.

The Third Seminole War

Several hundred Seminole remained hidden deep in the swampy areas of the Florida Everglades. For about ten years, the government largely left them alone. In 1855, land surveyors for the federal government trampled the cornfields and destroyed fruit trees at the Everglades home of Seminole Chief Billy Bowlegs (c. 1810–1859). An angry Seminole war party attacked the surveyors' camp and killed several members of the party, setting off the Third Seminole War (1855–58). In 1858, the U.S. government offered the Seminole money to leave Florida and relocate to Indian Territory. Although Chief Bowlegs and 123 men accepted the offer, a few hundred people did not. Their descendants now make up the Seminole people of Florida.

The Seminole in Oklahoma

In Indian Territory, the Seminole faced many hardships. Forced to live in harsh and unsanitary conditions with their former enemies, many Seminole died. In 1856, the surviving Seminole were given their own reservation.

Settlers soon set their sights on Indian Territory and moved in, although it was illegal. They protested that too much land had been set aside for Native Americans. They also complained that living on isolated reservations, Natives were not assimilating (adopting the ways of the rest of American society) quickly enough.

The U.S. government gave in to settlers' demands. To speed up the process of assimilation, they passed the General Allotment Act (also known as the Dawes Act) in 1887. Allotment divided reservations into small, individual parcels of land. Instead of large plots being tended by an entire tribe, as was their custom, each head of a household received an allotment to tend on his or her own. Leftover land was opened up to American settlement.

In 1906, the government divided 350,000 acres of Seminole land into small parcels. Private ownership of land went against Seminole beliefs. Because they could not live off the land as their relatives had done in the Everglades, many Oklahoma Seminole had to sell part or all of their land for money to buy food and clothing. By 1920, four-fifths of their allotted lands had been sold, or they had been cheated out of it by whites. The now-landless people scattered, and their culture suffered. Tribal self-government was abolished with Oklahoma's statehood in 1906.

The people regrouped in the 1960s, adopted a constitution, and became the federally recognized Seminole Nation of Oklahoma. In 1990, they received $40 million for lands taken from them in Florida. In the early 2000s, fourteen different groups made up the Seminole Nation of Oklahoma. Two of them were Freedman bands, descendants of slaves who found refuge with the tribe before their removal to Oklahoma.

Florida Seminole leave the Everglades

Because their numbers were small and the settlers did not desire the land they inhabited, the Florida Seminole were left alone for nearly seventy-five years after the Seminole Wars ended. More than once, the federal government tried to bribe them to move west, but they ignored the offers. In 1932, the Seminole were finally convinced to move to land reserved for them in central and southern Florida. Some took up cattle herding, while others took jobs for pay.

In the early twenty-first century, the Seminole in Florida live on six reservations throughout the state. They are Brighton Reservation in central Florida; Big Cypress Reservation, north of the Everglades; Hollywood Reservation, southwest of Fort Lauderdale; Immokalee Reservation, southeast of Fort Myers; Tampa Reservation, located on the eastern outskirts of Tampa; and the Ft. Pierce Reservation in St. Lucie County.

RELIGION

The religious beliefs of the Seminole were based upon those of the Creek. The Seminole saw no separation between body, mind, and soul; religion and medicine went hand in hand. They believed in the existence of spiritual beings who were fair and consistent in their dealings with humans. Some of their gods included the Preserver of Life, who gave life and took it away; the Corn Mother, who was the goddess of farming; and Thunder, the god of rain and war. In addition to good spirits, they also believed that water panthers and horned rattlesnakes lived in the water and wrapped around swimmers and drowned them and that "little people" lived in the forest, sometimes helping the tribe members and sometimes tricking them.

Everyone in the tribe practiced daily rituals to make sure the balance of nature was maintained. For example, people would ask forgiveness of an animal before killing it for food. Before eating, they tossed a piece of

Mikasuki Words

Miccosukee is one of two languages spoken by the Seminoles; Creek is the other. These words are from the Miccosukee (Mikasuki) language.

kawayi	"horse"
nokosi	"bear"
cokfi	"rabbit"
cinti	"snake"
i:fi	"dog"
ko:ni	"skunk"

meat into the fire as a sacrifice to the slain animal. Medicine bundles were sacred. They were composed of bits of stone, herbs, dried animal parts, feathers, and other objects that were used in ceremonies to insure the tribe's well-being.

Many Seminole have adopted Christian religions, but others favor the old religion and believe that the fate of the tribe depends upon the balance of nature's forces. The Seminole of Oklahoma call the Stomp Dance their traditional religion. This dance is derived from the Green Corn Dance (see "Customs"), a ceremony brought by the Seminole when they were removed from their Florida homelands.

LANGUAGE

The Seminole spoke two languages of similar origin, Muskogee and Miccosukee. The most common language was Muskogee, the Creek language. Both languages are not traditionally written. When spoken, they have sentence structures and sounds that are very different from English, which makes them difficult for English speakers to master. Although some Seminole elders still speak Muskogee, it is not as common among young people. In the early 2000s, about 500 Seminole people in Florida still spoke Miccosukee, a Muskogean language.

GOVERNMENT

The Seminole shared the governing system of most of the peoples of the Southeast until their escape to the Everglades in the mid-nineteenth century when the system broke down. Previously, each village and tribe had a government headed by a chief. The chief made decisions regarding such matters as food storage, celebrations, building projects, and agricultural planning. The chief's position could be inherited, but tribe members sometimes chose the chief for his wisdom and experience. Advisers and council elders assisted the chief. Military strategy was the responsibility of the war chief. For major decisions, the opinions of all the citizens were sought.

In modern times, the Seminole reservations in Florida are governed by elected tribal councils. In addition, the Seminole Tribe of Florida has a board of directors that is solely in charge of economic development.

The Florida Seminole adopted a constitution in 1957 and voted to officially become the Seminole Tribe of Florida. One small group (who lived in camps along the Tamiami Trail highway) did not want to become part of the new organization. Instead, they created the Miccosukee Tribe of Indians of Florida in 1962 and gained federal recognition. Federally recognized tribes are those with which the U.S. government maintains official relations, and they are entitled to financial or other help. The Miccosukee Reservation is located just south of the Everglades Agricultural Area.

The Seminole Nation of Oklahoma elects a chief and an assistant chief. All decisions about economic matters, social programs, and employment opportunities are the responsibility of a General Council, composed of two representatives from each of the tribe's fourteen groups, who are elected every four years.

Seminole Indians navigate a waterway in their dugout canoe made from a cypress log circa 1800s. © NORTH WIND PICTURE ARCHIVES

ECONOMY

Early economy

Men hunted and fished, constructed buildings, and cleared land for farming. Women raised children, cooked, and made pottery, baskets, and clothing. In Florida, before their retreat to the Everglades, the people took advantage of the abundant wild fowl and game.

Once in the Everglades, the Seminole people had to change their ways. The land was mostly unsuitable for farming, so women gathered wild plants, while men spent their time fishing and hunting game. They were successful in raising pigs and chickens in the hot climate, but cattle did not fare well.

The Seminole used canoes carved from tree trunks to travel the shallow waters of the Everglades. During the 1800s, they hunted deer, otter, raccoon, rabbit, turtle, alligator, fish, and birds for food and pelts. At trading posts, they exchanged pelts, alligator hides, dried fish, beeswax, and honey for supplies such as coffee, tobacco, cloth, metal pots, knives, and liquor.

Between 1870 and 1914, when much of the Everglades was drained by the state of Florida to stop the spread of diseases and aid land development, some Seminole in Florida began working for companies as hunters or fishermen.

Economy today

In the early twenty-first century, Seminole people piloted airboats and served as guides for hunters. Although many still farmed and raised cattle, they also needed other jobs to support their families. The Seminole people in Florida sell arts and crafts, plant grass, engage in logging, and wrestle alligators for tourists, a sport that some of the people want to see go professional, with Freestyle Alligator Wrestling Competitions (FAWC). Some Seminole also work in tribal bingo facilities and casinos that are their most profitable enterprises.

In addition to their casinos, the Seminole Tribe of Florida operates a hotel, citrus groves, smoke shops, hunting operations, a tribal museum, an aircraft company, and the Billie Swamp Safari, among other enterprises. In 2006, the tribe purchased the Hard Rock Cafe restaurant and casino chain for $965 million.

Some of the Miccosukee Tribe enterprises are a casino, a smoke shop, a gas station, a resort, a golf club, several museum attractions, and Indian

Village, where Seminoles demonstrate traditional arts and crafts and tribal lifestyle. Since 2002, they have supported several NASCAR teams.

The Oklahoma Seminole operate a bingo operation, a gaming center (a primary source of income), and two trading posts. Oil production, construction, agriculture, clothing shops, and small manufacturing provide jobs for tribe members.

DAILY LIFE

Families

Several related families usually lived together in one camp. Groups of related families, called clans, were named after an animal such as the bird, otter, wolf, or snake. Children were born into the mother's clan. Families of the Seminole who escaped into the Everglades usually consisted of a husband and wife, their daughters and their husbands, children, and grandchildren.

Seminole villagers gather outside their thatched shelters in the Everglades, circa 1800s. © NORTH WIND PICTURE ARCHIVES

In Seminole families, men tilled the soil and women planted and tended the garden. Although everyone worked together at harvest time, each family was responsible for harvesting its own share of food.

Buildings

Before the Seminole fled to the Everglades, they often lived in villages composed of about thirty families. Each family used two buildings. The first was for sleeping and cooking. The second structure, which was two stories high, served as storage and contained a special room where the head of the family received guests. To construct the buildings, they sank timber posts into the ground and covered the framework with cypress or pine boards to form walls. They used bark shingles, and interior dividers separated the dwelling into rooms.

Life in the damp and hot climate of the Everglades made new types of homes necessary. Called *chickees,* these were open-sided huts with a raised floor and a roof covering of palmetto leaves. The Seminole developed these during the early 1800s when they needed fast, disposable shelters while on the run from U.S. troops. To keep out mud and bugs, the plank floor was raised nearly three feet off the ground. The Seminole used these structures only for sleeping and storing personal items.

To keep the chickees as cool as possible, the Seminole made them without walls, and all cooking took place in a special cookhouse. The roof kept out rain, and a fire that produced dense smoke reduced the number of mosquitoes. The Seminole had no furniture, so they hung their possessions from the rafters. People sat on the floor for eating, sewing, and other activities and slept on mats on the floor. Children slept on animal skins, hoping they would acquire the special qualities of that animal.

Clothing and adornment

Before their move into Florida, the Seminole people wore clothing typical of other southeastern tribes. In warm weather, men wore loincloths (flaps of material that cover the front and back and are suspended from the waist) and women wore knee-length skirts. Both were made from animal pelts or woven from plant fibers. In cooler weather, they draped robes of fur or buckskin over their shoulders. They also made light, warm capes by attaching bird feathers to nets woven from plant fibers. Children often went naked until puberty.

Although women wore nothing on their heads, men wore elaborate headpieces during ceremonial gatherings; sometimes they shaped these to resemble an open bird's wing. They painted their bodies and wore beads, wristbands, and armbands.

The Seminole added their own creative touches to the woven cloth shirts they adapted from the whites. When they acquired sewing machines near the beginning of the twentieth century, they developed the distinctive patchwork designs for which they are famous (see "Stitchery"). In the early twenty-first century, the tribe was also known for the elaborate turban-like headdresses worn by men and the special way women sculpted their hair into a rounded, slightly flat peak or roll above the forehead. Women also wore many layers of brightly colored beads around their necks, wrists, and ankles. This clothing is usually only worn for traditional ceremonies or tourist shows.

Food

When they lived in the northern part of Florida in the early eighteenth century, the Seminole planted tobacco, corn, pumpkins, melons, squash, beans, and other vegetables. They rotated crops each year to give the soil time to replenish. Men hunted and fished; the tribe migrated about the Florida peninsula, finding areas abundant in wild fowl and game as the seasons changed.

Once the Seminole moved to the Everglades, they relied more on fishing and hunting. The women gathered wild plants, such as palmetto, cattail roots, and roots called *coontie* that were pounded and made into flour. The people also ate pineapples, oranges, and bananas. They used palmetto berries to make molasses. In their very limited garden space, they grew sweet potatoes, corn, pumpkins, sugar cane, and beans.

A favorite dish was hominy, made by mixing corn kernels with wood ashes and soaking the mixture overnight. The cooks then removed the hulls and cooked the kernels for several hours before making a thin soup. They were able to raise pigs and chickens in the hot climate, but not cattle. Even though snakes were abundant in the Everglades, the Seminole refused to eat their meat. They believed that doing so would anger the snake spirits.

Education

In traditional times, mothers taught their daughters how to raise children, sew, and run a home. Boys learned by example and participation how to fish and hunt and to make and use canoes. Children shared in the work of the village from an early age and learned to play quietly so as not to attract the attention of the whites.

In the Everglades, children learned to watch for poisonous snakes, insects, and other dangerous creatures. They were shown how to play games. They were told never to try to outdo another person, and this trait of being noncompetitive is retained in the culture even today. Children who misbehaved were sometimes subjected to dry scratching. A wooden implement embedded with fish teeth or bone splinters was used to lightly scratch the wrongdoer, causing more shame than physical injury.

Formal education for Seminole children did not begin until the 1920s, when several elementary schools opened. During the 1930s and 1940s, some children were sent to distant Native American boarding schools, where they often felt lonely and were forced to adopt white ways.

Elementary-age children now attend school on or off the reservation, depending upon where they live. Although children are required to attend school until age sixteen, dropout rates are high. Since 1972, the tribe has worked with the Bureau of Indian Affairs to develop programs to teach preschool children, to preserve the Seminole language and customs, and to provide vocational and financial assistance programs for students wanting to go to college. Increasing numbers of young people are attending college and taking professional jobs as doctors, lawyers, or engineers.

Healing practices

The Seminole used a variety of herbs to heal illnesses. The most important one was red root, the inner bark of a type of willow tree. This root could be soaked in cold water and used as a remedy for nausea, fever, and swellings. It was also used for bathing. The people made a potion by pounding up button snakeroot or bear's grass and mixing it with water to treat serious coughs, snakebites, and kidney troubles. Herbs and roots such as wormseed, horsemint, red cedar, and spicebush were also used to purify the body.

When herbs did not result in a cure, people summoned shamans (pronounced *SHAH-munz* or *SHAY-munz*) who specialized in performing healing rituals. Shamans rubbed the patient's body, sang or recited prayers, or used a comb-like instrument with tiny, sharp teeth to make scratches just deep enough to cause the patient to bleed slightly. The Seminole thought that a person's blood could become too abundant or too heavy, and this condition caused that person to become ill, socially troublesome, or violent. The cause of illness was often thought to be the angry or revengeful spirit of an animal, so the shaman calmed the animal spirit. Some shamans underwent lengthy instruction in the healing arts, while others were born with their talents. They could see and speak with supernatural powers and foresee the future.

Some Seminole people continue to practice traditional medicine. In addition, health care is available at various clinics on or near the reservations. The two types of medicine do not compete with, but supplement each other.

ARTS

Stitchery

Seminole women are known for their artful stitchery, in which they piece together scraps of calico fabric in patchwork designs to produce colorful bands that are attached skirts, shirts, and other items. Some of the designs are traditional, while others are unique creations of the seamstress. The patterns are named for the items they resemble, such as arrows or spools. Complex designs, combining two or more simpler patterns, often are named for the woman who created them. Each Seminole reservation is known for its unique designs. Copying a design is considered an honor by the originator of the design. Seminole women also create dolls from cloth-wrapped palmetto leaves stuffed with cotton that they dress in historically accurate clothing and hairstyles.

Oral literature

Seminole elders often told stories to children late at night, when they were safely tucked under mosquito netting to protect them from insect bites. Seminole tales explain the origin of the world, why certain rituals are performed, and the origins of certain people. At the Green Corn Dance, people told long stories explaining how they came to have corn and why it was important to them.

One of the Seminole origin stories tells how a turtle rose from the depths of the sea to rest. When his back started to crack, people emerged from the cracks. Then the cracks came together in squares, and the people made their homes along the cracks that were streams in the earth.

Men Visit the Sky to See God

This Seminole tale tells of five warriors who desire to see the Great Spirit. They travel a great distance, fall off the edge of the earth, then rise into the sky.

At long last, they landed near the lodge of a very old woman. She spoke to them in a feeble voice, asking, "Tell me, for whom are you looking?" "We are in search of the Great Spirit," they replied. "You may not see him now," the Old Woman said. "You may remain here for the time being."

That evening the five Seminole warriors took a walk away from the Old Woman's lodge. While out walking, they came upon a group of winged, white robed angels. These celestial men were playing a ball game similar to one the Seminoles played on earth. At this sight, two of the five Seminoles decided they would like to become angels and not return to earth. Their desire was granted when the Great Spirit appeared, saying to them, "So be it!"

To prepare the two Seminoles for their new home, the Great Spirit placed them in a large cooking pot with a fire burning beneath it. The two men were cooked until only their bones remained. Then the Great Spirit took the bones out of the pot and put them back into their proper shape. He then placed white robes on both of them and brought them back to life with the touch of his magic stick. They had received their wish to remain and become Men-Angels. At this, the Great Spirit turned to the other three Seminoles and asked them what they wanted to do. "With your permission, we wish to return to our earthly Seminole encampment," they said. "Collect your belongings and go to sleep immediately," ordered the Great Spirit. This they did, and when they awoke, they were once again in their home village. "We have returned," the three warriors told their people. "We will never journey to the sky again for we are happy to be here on earth." These words they spoke to the chief of the Seminoles.

SOURCE: McNeese, Tim. *Illustrated Myths of Native America: The Southwest, Western Range, Pacific Northwest, and California.* London: Blandford, 1999.

CUSTOMS

Festivals

Most Seminole ceremonies had to do with fire or water, both considered sacred. Of the many Seminole customs and rituals, the Green Corn Dance or ceremony was one of the most important and is still performed by some Natives.

The Green Corn Dance or Ceremony

For the Seminole, corn planted in the early spring was ripe and ready to eat by early summer. The Green Corn Dance celebrated the harvest. The ceremony also served as a time to visit friends and family, give thanks, and make amends for past wrongs. Food, including dried corn, was prepared from the past year's harvest and shared by all. Men and boys fasted (went without food) and drank *asi* ("the black drink") to make themselves pure and powerful. They consumed vast quantities of it until they vomited. They believed this gave them the energy to dance all night long.

While the men and boys met, women closed out the year by clearing away all old and unusable items and putting out all the cooking and hearth fires. Spiritual leaders relit the fires as a symbol of the new year.

There were forty different Corn Dances, and both men and women participated in them. The men sang while the women kept the beat with tortoise shell rattles. Villages also played each other in a fierce form of stickball. On the last day, they put out the fires and laid out wood for a new fire. They placed four perfect ears of corn on the fire, then offered prayers, and lit a sacred fire to burn the corn. This fire was used to rekindle all the others in the village. The men then ate the fresh, green corn that the women had prepared. After the fire had completely consumed the four perfect ears of corn and the men had consumed four rounds of *asi,* the ceremony ended. The New Year had begun.

In the early twenty-first century, most Seminole reservations have their own celebrations throughout the year. Some hold powwows and rodeos that are open to the public. A powwow is a celebration at which the main activities are traditional singing and dancing. Many tribes also hold festivals that include Native American drumming, dancing, singing, sampling Native foods, alligator wrestling, airboat rides, and arts and crafts. In February the Big Cypress Reservation reenacts the Seminole Wars at the Kissimmee Slough Shootout and Rendezvous.

Birth and naming customs

Women gave birth at the baby house, a small structure used only for that purpose. The mother and newborn remained there, with the mother preparing all their food, until the baby was four months old. During that time, the mother was thought to be "polluted," and men avoided her for fear of becoming ill. When the time had passed, the mother and new baby rejoined their household.

The Seminole immersed babies in a cold stream right after birth, the first of many purification ceremonies children would experience during their lives. Traditionally, a tribal elder gave Seminole infants names on the fourth day after their birth. When they were twelve, young men received new names at the Green Corn Ceremony to mark their maturity. They were then entitled to all the rights and privileges of adults in the village.

War rituals

The Seminoles were fierce warriors but fair to their enemies, whose lives they spared whenever possible. When men prepared for war, they applied red paint to their faces, necks, and chests. Captured enemies were enslaved, but they were permitted to marry women of the village. The children of these marriages became members of the tribe.

Courtship and marriage

Individuals had to choose a marriage partner from outside their clan (a group of related families). When a young woman wished to marry, usually at about age fourteen, she wore many beads and silver ornaments on her clothing. Sometimes a girl's family chose her marriage partner. Couples often courted one another by playing a gentle form of stickball. When two people wanted to marry, they merely consulted the leader of the woman's clan and went ahead, providing there were no objections. Afterward, they went to live with the bride's family for a few years, until they were able to start a new camp.

The woman was considered the head of the household. It was the husband's duty to provide cooking utensils, beads, blankets, and money, which were given to the bride's family. The Seminole rarely divorced.

Funerals

Seminole burial places were in remote spots in the swamp or woods. They often placed the body in a wooden casket that was set above ground inside a small, thatched structure. They buried all a person's belongings with him or her, because they believed the tools would be needed in the afterlife. It was customary to break the items because only then could they accompany the dead on the journey to the afterlife.

CURRENT TRIBAL ISSUES

Fierce independence, courage, and pride enabled the Florida Seminole to escape the attempted removal to Indian Territory. These same traits still run strong, as the people encourage their children to stay in school through graduation, work to improve health conditions on the reservations, and develop their businesses to provide jobs (see "Economy"). They are also involved in environmental efforts to preserve the Everglades.

The Seminole Tribe of Florida says it will fight if legislation to open five Las Vegas-style casinos in the state goes through. The Seminoles own the only four casinos in the state outside of South Florida. They had signed an agreement for exclusive rights, for which they will pay the state about one billion dollars over five years. The opening of other casinos would be a violation of that agreement.

The Florida tribe has had ongoing difficulties with the Internal Revenue Service (IRS). The IRS has been examining the tax-free bonds the Seminoles use to build casinos, trying to determine if these bonds were, in fact, entitled to the exemption. Under federal law, tribes can use tax-exempt bonds only for "essential governmental functions such as a hospital or a police station."

For the Seminole Nation of Oklahoma, retaining their traditions and reviving their language, maintaining their stomping grounds (where Native ceremonies take place), and raising educational and income levels are current issues of concern.

One other difficulty is the status of the Freedmen. Although the Seminole accepted runaway slaves in the 1700s and 1800s, many of those, called the Freedmen, now find themselves marginalized. When the land settlement money from the U.S. government was disbursed in 1991, 75 percent went to the Seminole of Oklahoma and 25 percent to the Seminole of Florida. The Freedmen received none. In 2000, the Seminole Nation of Oklahoma tried to expel the Freedmen, but the Bureau of Indian Affairs reinstated them in 2003. Being legally considered part of the tribe did not ensure acceptance, however, and many Freedmen still feel the effects of discrimination. They also say they have less access to government assistance, programs, and services.

NOTABLE PEOPLE

Chief Osceola (1804–1838) was a great hunter and fierce warrior. His people respected and valued him for his strong opposition to relocation to Indian Territory. He led Seminole warriors in a two-year campaign in

Independent Group Tries to Retain Traditional Ways

A group of Seminole who call themselves the Independent Traditional Seminole Nation reside about 30 miles (50 kilometers) northeast of Naples, Florida. They are not recognized as a tribe by the federal government and face opposition from many other Seminole people. The group, which numbers about three hundred, insists on living the traditional way. Their spokesperson, Danny Billie, has that said they "represent the original Seminole nation that fought the U.S. government during the 1800s."

In the mid-1990s, the government in Collier County, Florida, backed down from its attempts to make the people move out of their chickees or bring them up to county building codes. In 1997, the Honor the Earth music tour, an effort to raise money and awareness for ecological and Native issues, focused attention on the Independent Traditional Seminole Nation group. They supported the people's efforts to have Florida pass a law that would protect the group from further legal actions for maintaining its way of life.

Early in the twenty-first century, commercial farming encroached on the tribe's traditional lands. The tribe would not accept payment for the land. Seminole Guy Osceola explained, "The Great Spirit put the land here for everybody to live on, We don't believe in accepting money for the land because the land is not ours to sell. It belongs to everybody." The Indian Law Resource Center, however, purchased 2,500 acres to be held in trust for the tribe by the Red Bay Stronghold Foundation. The Seminole will protect this large area of wilderness and will be able to preserve their traditional lifestyle. They also want to continue their traditional way of life in Big Cypress National Preserve, where they have sacred sites, and in 2009, they sent a letter to the preserve planning committee asking to maintain those rights.

the Florida Everglades that cost the U.S. government the death of 1,500 troops and $20 million. He continued to fight until his capture in 1837 and died mysteriously in prison.

Betty Mae Tiger Jumper (1923–2011) was the first Seminole to receive a high school diploma. In the 1960s, she became the first woman elected as tribal chairperson. Active in political affairs, she did much to improve the health, education, and social conditions among her people.

Seminole Donald Fixico (1951–) is a professor of history and Native American studies. He has published many essays on Native American history, as well as a book on the effects on Native Americans of living in cities called *The Urban Indian Experience in America.*

BOOKS

Brown, Virginia Pounds, Laurella Owens and Nathan Glick. *The World of the Southern Indians: Tribes, Leaders, and Customs from Prehistoric Times to the Present.* Montgomery, AL: NewSouth Books, 2011.

Field, Ron. *The Seminole Wars, 1818–58.* New York: Osprey, 2009.

Frank, Andrew. *The Seminole.* New York: Chelsea House, 2011.

King, David C. *Seminole.* New York: Benchmark Books, 2007.

Milanich, Jerald T., and Nina J. Root. *Hidden Seminoles: Julian Dimock's Historic Florida Photographs.* Gainesville: University Press of Florida, 2011.

Mock, Shirley Boteler. *Dreaming with the Ancestors: Black Seminole Women in Texas and Mexico.* Norman: University of Oklahoma Press, 2010.

Pleasants, Julian M., and Harry A. Kersey Jr. *Seminole Voices: Reflections on Their Changing Society, 1970–2000.* Lincoln: University of Nebraska Press, 2010.

Sneve, Virginia Driving Hawk. *The Seminoles.* New York: Holiday House, 1994.

Weisman, Brent Richards. *Unconquered People: Florida's Seminole and Miccosukee Indians.* Gainesville: University Press of Florida, 1999.

West, Patsy. *The Enduring Seminoles: From Alligator Wrestling to Ecotourism.* Gainesville: University Press of Florida, 2007.

Wilcox, Charlotte. *The Seminoles.* Minneapolis: Lerner Publications, 2007.

WEB SITES

Etienne-Gray, Tracé. "Black Seminole Indians." *Texas State Historical Association.* http://www.tshaonline.org/handbook/online/articles/bmb18 (accessed on June 12, 2011).

Miccosukee Seminole Nation. http://www.miccosukeeseminolenation.com/ (accessed on June 12, 2011).

Morris, Allen. "Seminole History." *Florida Division of Historical Resources.* http://www.flheritage.com/facts/history/seminole/ (accessed on June 12, 2011).

Murray, Dru J. "The Unconquered Seminoles." *Florida History: Native Peoples.* http://funandsun.com/1tocf/seminole/semhistory.html (accessed on June 12, 2011).

Redish, Laura, and Orrin Lewis. "Seminole Languages." *Native Languages of the Americas.* http://www.native-languages.org/seminole.htm (accessed on June 12, 2011).

"Seminole Indian Tribe History." *Access Genealogy.* http://www.accessgenealogy.com/native/tribes/seminole/seminolehist.htm (accessed on June 12, 2011).

Seminole Nation of Oklahoma. http://www.seminolenation.com/ (accessed on June 12, 2011).

Seminole Tribe of Florida. http://www.seminoletribe.com/ (accessed on June 12, 2011).

Wilkinson, Jerry. "History of the Seminoles." *Keys History.* http://www.keyshistory.org/seminolespage1.html (accessed on June 12, 2011).

Shawnee

Name

The name Shawnee (pronounced *shaw-NEE*) is from the Algonquian term *sawanwa,* or "southern people." The Shawnee people have been called other names in the past, including Shawano, Savannah, Shawanoe, Shawanese, and Sewanee. The French name for them was *Chaouanons.*

Location

The Shawnee moved frequently, so it is difficult for historians to trace their movements. Prior to the Iroquois Wars in the 1640s, the Shawnee lived in a widespread area from Georgia to New York; they even had settlements as far west as Illinois. When the Europeans arrived in the Americas, they encountered the Shawnee in Ohio, Pennsylvania, West Virginia, Virginia, Maryland, Kentucky, and Indiana. By the late 1600s and early 1700s, the Shawnee resided mostly in eastern Pennsylvania and Ohio. A dispersal occurred during the American Revolution (1775–83), when many Shawnee moved westward into Oklahoma. Some Shawnee also lived in Kentucky, Tennessee, and Illinois until the Indian Removal Act (1830) forced them onto reservations. In the early 2000s, the Shawnee lived mainly in Oklahoma and Ohio.

Population

In the 1660s, prior to contact with Europeans, there were anywhere from 10,000 to 12,000 Shawnee. In 1825, their numbers had dwindled to 2,500. In the 1990 U.S. Census, 6,640 people identified themselves as Shawnee. In 2000, that figure decreased to 6,001. According to the Oklahoma Indian Affairs Commission in 2011, the three Shawnee tribes based in that state had a total tribal enrollment of 8,077.

Language family

Algonquian.

Origins and group affiliations

Although Shawnee oral history relates a move from the South, some scholars believe the Shawnee are one of the Algonquian tribes who moved from

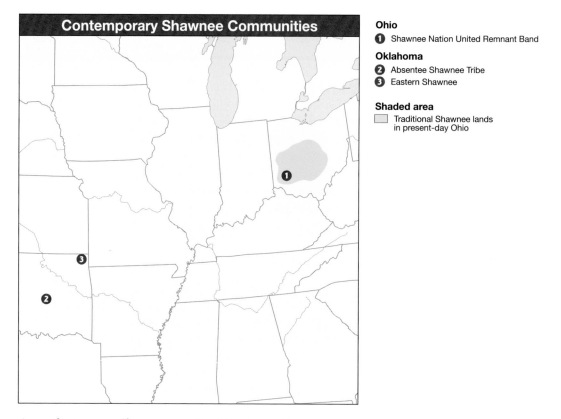

Contemporary Shawnee Communities

Ohio
1 Shawnee Nation United Remnant Band

Oklahoma
2 Absentee Shawnee Tribe
3 Eastern Shawnee

Shaded area
Traditional Shawnee lands in present-day Ohio

A map of contemporary Shawnee communities. MAP BY XNR PRODUCTIONS. CENGAGE LEARNING, GALE. REPRODUCED BY PERMISSION OF GALE, A PART OF CENGAGE LEARNING.

Canada's eastern coast during prehistoric times. They had connections with Sac and Fox (see entries) and Kickapoo tribes. Their closest associations were with the Delaware, Creek (see entries), and Mingo, and they had generally hostile relations with the Iroquois (see entry).

For centuries, the Shawnee wandered from place to place, becoming known far and wide for their skill as warriors. Beginning in the 1600s, they were often invited to settle among other tribes. In exchange for protecting those tribes, they received the use of harvest and hunting grounds. The Shawnee strongly opposed white settlement beyond the original thirteen colonies. Because of their ability to recover after bad times, they are currently one of the more prosperous Native American tribes.

HISTORY

Prehistory

Controversy exists over the ancient history of the Shawnee people. Some scholars have suggested that the Shawnee descended from the prehistoric Fort Ancient culture. This culture flourished from 1000 to 1650 CE along the Ohio River in present-day Ohio, western West Virginia, and northern Kentucky. The Fort Ancient mound-building culture may have developed from the Hopewell culture (100 BCE–500 CE), which constructed earthworks for burial, ceremonies, and nobles' home sites (see the Mound Builders entry). The record is not continuous between the Fort Ancient sites and the Shawnee, who later occupied that area, but some similarities exist in the culture, art, and mythology between the two groups.

Shawnee oral history indicates that their people migrated from Mexico to Florida, and from there to Georgia, where several communities were established. As some of the people moved north, they encountered English settlers, who called them "Savannah Indians," in Charles Town, South Carolina, in 1674. Reports from other early European settlers show them around the Delaware River and in Illinois and Canada. They were also a presence in many mid-Atlantic states and Ohio.

Important Dates

1670: The Shawnee first encounter Europeans.

1774: The Shawnee take on the British in the Battle of Point Pleasant.

1794: U.S. forces defeat the Shawnee at the Battle of Fallen Timbers.

1795: The Greenville Treaty opens Shawnee land to American settlement.

1811: Shawnee settlement of Prophet's Town is destroyed in the Battle of Tippecanoe.

1813: Chief Tecumseh is killed fighting the Americans at Battle of the Thames in the War of 1812.

1830: Most Shawnee leave Ohio.

1936: Two Shawnee groups in Oklahoma organize as one federally recognized tribe.

1937: A third Shawnee group in Oklahoma is federally recognized as the Eastern Shawnee Tribe.

1980: Ohio's Shawnee Nation, United Remnant Band receives state recognition.

2000: The federal government recognizes the Loyal Shawnee.

Scattering of the Shawnee tribe

The Shawnee first made contact with Europeans in the early 1670s, when French trappers and traders came to Tennessee and South Carolina. The Shawnee traded furs and hides to the French, and later to the British, for European goods such as jewelry, glass beads, ribbons, pots, blankets, and steel weapons. By the late 1600s, many Shawnee had moved north into the Ohio Valley and eastern Pennsylvania. There some joined groups of Delaware (see entry) and lived in what is present-day Indiana.

Return to their homeland

In the 1720s, the Wyandot (see entry) offered the Shawnee a section of land in southern Ohio. Shawnee from all directions welcomed the invitation and gathered there. It was excellent land for hunting and farming, and there was plenty of it. By 1730, most Shawnee had returned to this land in Ohio, probably their original homeland. Because they needed huge tracts of open land for their nomadic way of life, they saw the westward expansion by British settlers as a serious threat to their survival.

The French and Indian War

The struggle between the British and French for control of the American colonies developed into the French and Indian War (1754–63; a war fought in North America between England and France involving some Native groups as allies of the French). In 1755, the Shawnee were drawn into the war because of a misunderstanding. Angry British colonists mistakenly believed that the Shawnee were responsible for the murder of British general Edward Braddock (1695–1755) and half of his army of 2,200 men. As a result, when Shawnee representatives went to talk with British officials in Washington regarding another matter, they were hanged. The Shawnee then allied themselves with the French and went to war against the British. Shawnee war parties inflicted great punishment on British settlements. When the British won the war in 1763, the Shawnee knew that the English would retaliate and overrun the Shawnee settlements in the Ohio Valley.

Pontiac's Rebellion

Now firmly in control of the American colonies, the British treated the Natives as a conquered people. They stopped supplying the gunpowder and rum that had become important to the tribes. To express their unhappiness, the Shawnee and other tribes burned settlements and captured colonists. This led in 1763 to the Shawnee's involvement in the famous uprising known as Pontiac's Rebellion. Ottawa chief Pontiac (c. 1720–1769), angry at the British for taking over his people's lands, united a group of warriors from different tribes to terrorize white settlers in Western Pennsylvania, Maryland, and Virginia. The Shawnee division was commanded by the most important Shawnee chief, Hokolesqua (c. 1720–1777), and his primary war chief, Pucksinwah (c. 1727–c. 1774).

In an incident that has gone down in American history as one of the dirtiest tricks of warfare, the British military commander arranged to have smallpox-infected blankets delivered to the tribes. The disease spread quickly, and thousands died as a result.

Pontiac's Rebellion was not a military victory for the Native peoples, but it resulted in an important agreement with the British. Called the Royal Proclamation of 1763, the treaty set limits to the growth of the colonies. It also made all lands west of the Allegheny Mountains in Pennsylvania Indian Territory, where the tribes were to be left "unmolested." The document stated that Native nations had aboriginal title to their lands, and only the British Crown, not the colonists, could buy land from them. The proclamation also described the proper way to make treaties and appointed two ambassadors to handle relations between the British king and Native American leaders. That agreement, however, like many other agreements between Natives and whites over the next century, did not last long. European settlement continued to expand into Shawnee lands.

Settlers adopted by tribe

The Shawnee did not give up their land without a fight. The tribe became feared for its practice of kidnapping and torturing those who tried to move onto Shawnee land. Not all settlers were killed, however. Some learned to appreciate the Shawnee way of life and were adopted by the tribe. One famous captive was the legendary frontiersman Daniel Boone (1734–1820), who stayed with the Shawnee for several months until he escaped.

Battle of Point Pleasant

In 1774, tensions between the Shawnee and the British increased again after the governor of the Virginia colony announced a plan to open land on both sides of the Ohio River to British settlers. The land he meant was the heart of Shawnee territory. The governor sent three thousand soldiers with orders to invade Shawnee land and attack their villages. Before the British could carry out this order, a Shawnee war party led by Chief Pucksinwah and war leader Blue Jacket (c. 1745–c. 1810) attacked the British forces. During the battle, later named the Battle of Point Pleasant, Chief Pucksinwah was killed. The battle ended without a clear victory for either side, and by then all attention had turned to the larger fight between the colonists and the British.

American Revolution divides the tribe

The colonists declared their independence from England in 1776, fueling the American Revolution (1775–83). The Shawnee argued among themselves about which side to support, but they could not agree. To avoid being drawn into the fight, nearly half of the Shawnee moved west into what is now Missouri. The rest decided to support England against the colonists. They believed that the British would reward them after the war by protecting their homelands from settlement. In the spring of 1782, Shawnee and Delaware warriors ambushed and defeated five hundred colonial soldiers and tortured their leader to death. But their support of the British yielded them nothing, because England lost the war.

Victory and retaliation

After the war Blue Jacket and Chief Tecumseh (1768–1813), the son of Chief Pucksinwah, continued the fight against American settlement of Native lands. In 1791 Blue Jacket led a large force composed of several tribes in a surprise attack against American forces along the Wabash River in Indiana. They killed some 630 men and wounded 300 more. Only 21 of Blue Jacket's army were killed, while 40 were wounded. This incident was the greatest victory in the history of Native resistance to American settlement.

In response, President George Washington (1732–1799; served 1789–97) sent another army to put down Blue Jacket's forces in 1794. Under the command of General "Mad" Anthony Wayne (1745–1796), this larger army defeated Blue Jacket and his allies at the Battle of Fallen Timbers near present-day Toledo, Ohio. Wayne and his men burned Shawnee villages and destroyed the crops.

Prophet's Town

With the defeat at Fallen Timbers, Native resistance to white settlement began to crumble. Now facing starvation at the hands of the American army, ninety-one chiefs representing twelve nations were convinced to sign the Treaty of Greenville in 1795. As a result of the treaty, the Shawnee lost more land than any other tribe. Many Shawnee stayed in Ohio and agreed to abide by the terms of the treaty.

Native American warriors battle U.S. troops led by William Henry Harrison at Tippecanoe in 1811. © KURZ & ALLISON, ART PUBLISHERS, CHICAGO, IL/TIME & LIFE PICTURES/GETTY IMAGES.

For the next ten years, the Shawnee, under the leadership of Chief Tecumseh, watched settlers moving into their lands and saw their resources being depleted. In 1805, Tecumseh's younger brother, Lalawethika (c. 1775–1836), started a religious revival that attracted large numbers of followers from various tribes to a community in Ohio he had established. He preached a return to traditional values and a rejection of American ways; he insisted that the whites had no right to the lands they had taken. Lalawethika then changed his name to Tenskwatawa (pronounced *TENS-kwa-TAH-wuh,* meaning "the open door"). He was also known as the Shawnee Prophet.

Tecumseh joined his brother and worked to change this movement from religious to political. He wished to see all remaining Native lands under the common ownership of tribes, and he wanted to form a military and political confederacy to unite many tribes to fight the white invasion. To the concern of government officials, a growing number of warriors moved into the new community. In 1808, Tecumseh built a new village called Prophet's Town near Ohio's Tippecanoe Creek. Native people who wanted to protect their homelands and preserve their culture came to Prophet's Town. Tecumseh traveled far and wide to recruit tribes to join his confederacy to halt the spread of white settlements.

While Tecumseh was away on one of these journeys, William Henry Harrison (1773–1841), who was governor of the Indiana Territory at the time, put pressure on several chiefs to sell three million acres of Native lands for American settlers. As word of this loss spread among the northwestern tribes, a flood of warriors joined Tecumseh's cause. When Tecumseh returned, he told Harrison of his anger and opposition to the sale. Harrison waited until Tecumseh left on another journey and set off with one thousand men to attack Prophet's Town. In the battles that followed, Harrison burned Prophet's Town to the ground.

The death of Tecumseh

After their defeat in the American Revolution, the British retained territory in Canada and claimed a section of land in Maine. Relations between the United States and Britain were uneasy, and war between them broke out again in 1812.

During the War of 1812 (1812–15), the Shawnee again fought on the side of the British. Tecumseh, still hoping the British would preserve his people's homelands against American settlers, led a force of warriors from many tribes. He was defeated and killed in 1813 at the Battle of the Thames in Ontario, Canada. With that, the last major combined Indian resistance to American expansion ended.

Shawnee move to Oklahoma

The Shawnee moved frequently and far after the War of 1812, often splitting up and then coming back together. Finally, most of them settled on reservation land in Oklahoma.

Life in Oklahoma was not easy for the Shawnee people, who tried to make their living by farming and ranching. Gas and petroleum were found on Native American land in the early 1900s, and many Shawnee were pressured into selling their land to whites. They were often paid less than its value, and many ended up in poverty. Tribal unity was disrupted as the people divided into the groups in which they live today. Three federally recognized divisions of the tribe exist in Oklahoma: Eastern Shawnee, Shawnee Tribe, and Absentee Shawnee. The Shawnee Nation, United Remnant Band in Ohio is state recognized, and a splinter group from that band established the East of the River

Shawnee. Two other small Shawnee groups are the Blue Creek Band and the Piqua Shawnee Tribe, which has also received state recognition in Alabama.

Shawnee Words

hileni	"man"
kweewa	"woman"
nepi	"water"
waapa	"white"
mškwaawi	"red"
mkateewa	"black"

RELIGION

The Shawnee recognized a Great Spirit and worshipped the spiritual qualities in all natural things. The people believed they had been created by a female god called Our Grandmother, who someday would gather them up in a huge net and take them to heaven. Each tribal group had a sacred bundle that contained holy objects, and they used it to bring good harvests, success in battle, or help for the sick. Only the most important men and women in the tribe knew the contents of the bundles. The people sought the aid of the spirits through dances, chants, and songs. Later, Baptist missionaries in Oklahoma converted many Shawnee, and the Baptist religion remains a presence there.

LANGUAGE

The Shawnee language is considered endangered, but is still spoken by some Shawnee in Oklahoma, who are teaching it to Shawnee children. The reservations have language classes so that the language can be passed on to future generations.

GOVERNMENT

Tribal chiefs were men and women who had inherited their lifelong positions. Peace chiefs served as spiritual leaders. War chiefs, who were chosen for their skill and bravery in battle, planned raids on the enemy. Decisions were made following discussions that continued until everyone agreed on a matter. Women served as important advisers during war and peacetime, and female elders were often in charge of determining the fate of captives.

In the early 2000s, each of the three Oklahoma tribes had its own elected tribal council that made decisions for the tribe. Each tribe also had a chief who led ceremonies.

The Oklahoma Shawnee

There are three groups of Shawnee in Oklahoma: the Absentee Shawnee, the Eastern Shawnee, and the Shawnee Tribe.

Absentee Shawnee

In 1845, a group of Shawnee left the Shawnee reservation in Kansas. They relocated to Indian Territory (now the state of Oklahoma) and came to be known as the Absentee Shawnee. In 1872, the U.S. government gave the Absentee Shawnee land on a reservation near present-day Shawnee, Oklahoma. The Citizen Band of Potawatomi (see entry) also occupied this reservation. The Absentee Shawnee gradually split into two groups. One group, the White Turkey Band, was more willing to adopt American ways, whereas the Big Jim Band refused to do so. Although relations between the two groups were troubled, they organized as one tribe under the Oklahoma Indian Welfare Act in 1936.

In the early 2000s, the Absentee Shawnee lived in south-central Oklahoma, about 35 miles (56 kilometers) west of Oklahoma City. The tribe remained divided into the Big Jim Band and the White Turkey Band. Members totaled about 3,050 in 2011, and they lived in two different counties in Oklahoma.

Eastern Shawnee

In 1832, most of the Shawnee in Ohio moved to a reservation in Oklahoma where they joined a small group of Seneca (see Iroquois entry) to form the United Nation of Seneca and Shawnee. In 1937, this group of Shawnee officially separated from the Seneca and became the federally recognized Eastern Shawnee Tribe of Oklahoma. They have 2,801 members as of 2011.

Most Eastern Shawnee lands are located in far northeastern Oklahoma near the Missouri border, with headquarters in West Seneca, Oklahoma.

Shawnee Tribe

The Shawnee Tribe, formerly called Loyal Shawnee or Cherokee Shawnee, lived in Kansas when the American Civil War (1861–65; a war between the Union [the North], which was opposed to slavery, and the Confederacy [the South], which was in favor of slavery) began. Some sources say they received their name because of their loyalty to the North during the war. Their loyalty benefited them little, however, because after the war U.S. officials forced them off their Kansas lands.

In 1869, they purchased land from the Cherokee (see entry) in northeastern Oklahoma. They kept their own identity, though, and in 2000, Congress recognized them as a separate tribe. Their tribal headquarters is in Miami, Oklahoma, but tribal members are scattered around the United States.

ECONOMY

The Shawnee lifestyle centered on hunting, farming, and food gathering. Men hunted, traded, and fought in wars. Women gathered food, farmed, and made craft items. In the spring, men cleared fields, and women and children planted and tended the crops. Individual households owned farming fields. During the early eighteenth century, fur trading with the French became important to the economy.

In the early 2000s, many Absentee Shawnee in Oklahoma received income from farming and livestock, oil- and gas-related businesses, and small businesses. A major source of funds was the tribe's Thunderbird Casino. The tribe also owned several manufacturing plants, a medical supplies plant, a shopping mall, smoke shops, and a convenience store. In 2011, the Absentee Shawnee Economic Development Authority (ASEDA) entered a partnership to finance and lease fleet vehicles.

The Shawnee Tribe Development Corporation, started in 2001, handles new business development. In 2008, the Shawnee Tribe announced plans to open a casino and entertainment resort to complement already existing companies, such as a housing authority, tribal smoke shop, gift shop, and gallery. The tribe also issues its own license plate.

The Eastern Shawnee owned casinos, a construction business, a travel center, a recycling center, and a variety of service and retail operations. Proceeds from these industries funded community programs such as health care, childcare, education, and social services for the tribe. The Eastern Shawnee also maintained partial ownership in several oil wells near the reservation.

In 1996, the United Remnant Band purchased the Zane Shawnee Caverns and acreage surrounding it. They opened the cave to the public and constructed a camping and retreat center. In addition, they developed a small settlement, similar to a reservation, on the site. However, because the settlement is not managed by the Bureau of Indian Affairs, it is not officially considered a reservation. A museum and pioneer village were later added along with outreach programs to teach others about the Shawnee culture.

The three Oklahoma groups are striving for economic self-sufficiency and meeting with success. They are better off than many tribes and have better housing. Casinos help to fund programs to improve the lives of tribe members and provide employment for some of their people.

DAILY LIFE

Families

The Shawnee lived in small groups of extended families made up of mothers, fathers, children, aunts, uncles, grandparents, cousins, and in-laws. They lived together in one big dwelling or in houses located near one another.

Buildings

In warm weather, the Shawnee lived in summer villages of twenty to three hundred people. Each village had a large log council house used for religious and political gatherings; it provided protection when villagers came under enemy attack. Palisades, fence-like structures, surrounded the village for protection. Shawnee homes were made of saplings (young trees) tied to form a frame and covered by sheets of bark or animal skins. A hole in the roof allowed smoke to escape.

During the fall and winter, the Shawnee set off on long hunting and gathering trips. Their cold-weather dwellings were much smaller, often holding only one or two persons. Unlike most migrating tribes, the Shawnee did not carry their houses with them, because building materials could be found almost anywhere they went.

Clothing and adornment

The Shawnee wore buckskin clothing. In the winter, men and women wore shirts, leggings, fur cloaks, and moccasins. Summer clothing consisted of simple breechcloths (flaps of material that hung from the waist to cover the front and back) for men and wrap skirts for women. Women also wore moccasins trimmed with bells that jingled when they walked. Children dressed like their parents. Most garments were decorated with dyed porcupine quills, beads, or feathers. After they began to trade for European goods, the Shawnee developed a fondness for silver pins, beads, necklaces, and bracelets. Shawnee men could be recognized by their silver nose rings and earrings.

The tribe painted their faces and bodies for ceremonies. Men wore headbands made of animal fur trimmed with one or more feathers from a hunting bird, such as an eagle, hawk, or owl. The women wore their long hair parted in the middle and rolled into buns, kept in place by silver combs. Some painted small red dots on their cheeks.

Food

Corn, the staple crop, was eaten as a vegetable or used to produce hominy (a hot cereal) or bread flour. The name "johnny cake," still used for corn-bread, probably comes from the name "Shawnee cake." The people grew beans, squash, and pumpkins and gathered wild rice. Women made maple syrup and gathered persimmons, wild grapes, nuts, berries, roots, and honey. They used dried onions to season meat and cooked it over different types of wood. Maple, hickory, or cherry wood smoke added special flavorings.

Men hunted year-round for deer, elk, bear, turkeys, pheasants, and small fur-bearing animals. Shawnee hunters imitated animal calls. They disguised themselves so that they could approach their prey and shoot it with a bow and arrow or knock it on the head with a club. No part of an animal went to waste. Shawnee used the skins for clothing, bones for tools, tendons for thread and bindings, and fat for cooking and skin ointment.

Education

The elders of the tribe were greatly respected. They formed close relationships with the children and taught them Shawnee ways. Children learned that honesty was good, and lying was a crime.

In 1839, an Indian boarding school opened at the Shawnee Mission. Children learned basic subjects for six hours a day and three hours on Saturday. They worked about five additional hours in manual labor every day. Boys farmed or did woodworking. Girls sewed, cooked, and did laundry. The pupils were forbidden to speak their language or practice their customs or religions. After the school closed, most students went to public schools as they do today.

Traditional ceremonies, songs, dances, and crafts are kept alive through education and practice. Tribal members ensure that these rituals and skills are passed down from generation to generation.

Healing practices

Shawnee healers used herbs and rituals to cure illnesses, which they believed were caused by evil spirits. The Shawnee "toughened" babies by briefly dipping them in cold water or snow every day for a few months. Both sexes purified themselves in sweat lodges where steam was produced by pouring water over hot stones. The bathers then jumped into a cold river or stream.

ARTS

Oral literature

During the winter, the Shawnee dressed in animal robes and gathered around the fire to hear elders tell stories of their past triumphs or tales about the gods.

An often-repeated story told of the Shawnee long ago crossing an ocean or "sea of ice." Anthropologists (people who study ancient cultures) believe this could have been one of the Great Lakes or a lake farther north in Canada that they would have crossed as they journeyed south.

The Celestial Sisters

The Shawnee tell of Waupee, or White Hawk, who saw a basket descending from heaven filled with twelve beautiful sisters. To get close to them, he turned himself into a mouse. As the younger sister chased him, he changed back into himself, and the girl became his bride.

> Winter and summer passed rapidly away, and their happiness was increased by the addition of a beautiful boy to their lodge. Waupee's wife was a daughter of one of the stars, and as the scenes of earth began to pall upon her sight, she sighed to revisit her father. But she was obliged to hide these feelings from her husband. She remembered the charm that would carry her up, and took occasion, while the White Hawk was engaged in the chase, to construct a wicker basket, which she kept concealed. In the meantime she collected such rarities from the earth as she thought would please her father, as well as the most dainty kinds of food. When all was in readiness, she went out one day, while Waupee was absent, to the charmed ring, taking her little son with her. As soon as they got into the car [basket], she commenced her song and the basket rose....

> [Waupee] mourned his wife's loss sorely, but his son's still more. In the meantime his wife had reached her home in the stars, and almost forgot, in the blissful employments there, that she had left a husband on earth. She was reminded of this by the presence of her son, who, as he grew up,

Crafts

The Shawnee created baskets that were so tightly woven they could hold water. They also fashioned wampum (beads made from shells) belts about 5 feet (1.5 meters) long and 4 feet (1.2 meters) wide decorated with symbols, designs, and special colors.

CUSTOMS

Social organization

Shawnee society had five divisions, each with its own particular purpose. For example, the Pekowi division took charge of religious duties, whereas the Kishpoko handled war duties, and the Mekoche took care of health and healing practices. Both the Thawikila and Chalaakaatha divisions became anxious to visit the scene of his birth. His grandfather said to his daughter one day, "Go, my child, and take your son down to his father, and ask him to come up and live with us. But tell him to bring along a specimen of each kind of bird and animal he kills in the chase." She accordingly took the boy and descended. The White Hawk ... heard the message of the Star, and began to hunt with the greatest activity, that he might collect the present. He spent whole nights, as well as days, in searching for every curious and beautiful bird or animal. He only preserved a tail, foot, or wing of each, to identify the species; and, when all was ready, they went to the circle and were carried up.

Great joy was manifested on their arrival at the starry plains. The Star Chief invited all his people to a feast, and, when they had assembled, he proclaimed aloud, that each one might take of the earthly gifts such as he liked best. A very strange confusion immediately arose. Some chose a foot, some a wing, some a tail, and some a claw. Those who selected tails or claws where changed into animals, and ran off; the others assumed the form of birds, and flew away. Waupee chose a white hawk's feather. His wife and son followed his example, when each one became a white hawk. He spread his wings, and, followed by his wife and son, descended with the other birds to the earth, where his species are still to be found.

SOURCE: Williams, Mentor L. "The Celestial Sisters." *Schoolcraft's Indian Legends.* East Lansing: Michigan State University Press, 1962.

took care of political matters. Tribal chiefs came from one or the other of these last two divisions.

Birth and naming

Women gave birth in a small hut where the mother and baby remained for ten days until the baby was named at a special naming ceremony. Parents and tribal elders suggested names that would bring the bearer good luck or would guarantee certain skills.

Childhood and puberty

The Shawnee did not physically punish children but encouraged them to behave by praising them for good actions and shaming them for bad behavior.

Many tribes sent boys on a vision quest at puberty, but Shawnee boys undertook their quest at a younger age. A boy on a vision quest went off by himself, usually under strenuous circumstances, to seek the spirit that would guide him through life. In one example of a vision quest, the boy rose each morning at dawn, ran naked through the snowy woods, dove to the bottom of a frigid pond (cracking the ice first if necessary), and then returned to camp. On his last day he was told to grasp the first object he touched at the bottom of the pond, often a stone, and this became his "power object," which he wore around his neck on a string. The object brought him courage, strength, and wisdom.

Festivals

Although drums and gourd rattles often accompanied the dancers, most Shawnee preferred singing to musical instruments. Men attached deer hooves and dewclaws (two horn-like "toes" located on the ankle above the hoof) to the bottoms, sleeves, and shoulder fringes of their shirts and garters to make noise as they moved. The people later used sleigh bells and metal cylinders to decorate costumes and to provide musical sounds while dancing.

Special ceremonies marked the changes in the seasons. The most important was the spring Bread Dance, when women were honored for their farming and gathering skills and everyone prayed for an abundant harvest. At the autumn Bread Dance, the tribe celebrated the man's role as hunter and gave thanks for the crops.

A Green Corn Dance took place in August. During that seven-day celebration of the harvest, dances were performed to music from flutes, drums, and deer-hoof rattles, and all persons accused of minor crimes were forgiven.

War rituals

Warfare was a way to show courage and to gain honor. Shawnee councils gathered to decide whether or not the tribe would go to war. To invite neighboring villages to join a war party, they sent tomahawks covered with red clay. Dances and feasts were held before a battle. If prisoners were taken, they had to "run the gauntlet" past a line of warriors who beat them with guns and sticks as they passed.

Courtship and marriage

Marriage was usually arranged by families, and the only ceremony was a gift exchange. The bride usually went to live with her husband's family. By the 1820s, Shawnee marriages no longer included a gift exchange.

Funerals

After a member of the Shawnee tribe died, attendants dressed the corpse in clean clothes and painted it. As payment, the attendants received some of the deceased's possessions. Mourners grieved for twelve days and did not engage in their normal tasks during that time. A feast was then held, and the people returned to their daily activities. Spouses who lost a mate could not wear jewelry or body paint for a year.

CURRENT TRIBAL ISSUES

Despite the many migrations and upheavals of their history, the three Shawnee tribes in Oklahoma, the Absentee Shawnee, the Loyal Shawnee, and the Eastern Shawnee, are known for their efforts to preserve their culture. In her book, *The Shawnee,* Janet Hubbard-Brown states, "While many other tribes in Oklahoma have completely forgotten their traditional ceremonies, the Shawnees … still know their complete annual cycle of ceremonial dances."

Tenskwatawa, brother of Chief Tecumseh, was a religious prophet who incited his tribe to rebel against American settlers. © MPI/STRINGER/ ARCHIVE PHOTOS/GETTY IMAGES.

By the end of the twentieth century, the Shawnee Nation, United Remnant Band in Ohio had set about purchasing tracts of property associated with Shawnee history. By the early 2000s, they owned 180 acres near their former homelands in Ohio. There they hold meetings, ceremonies, and youth education activities.

In 2010, the Eastern Shawnee filed a lawsuit asking for damages for the mismanagement of the tribe's trust funds held by the federal government. In 2011, however, the Supreme Court overturned a 2009 decision that allowed tribes to sue the federal government and instead ruled that tribes can no longer bring lawsuits for these claims.

NOTABLE PEOPLE

Chief Tecumseh (1768–1813) is best known for organizing and leading the Native resistance to American settlement. An eloquent speaker and statesman, he urged people of all tribes to unite against the threat to their way of life. Tecumseh's younger brother, Tenskwatawa (called the Shawnee Prophet; 1775–1836), began a religious revival that advocated returning to traditional Native American ways. Even though the two brothers won the loyalty and support of more than fifty other tribes, many chiefs among the Shawnee became jealous of the brothers, and they had few followers among their own tribe.

Other notable Shawnee include Tecumseh's father, War Chief Pucksinwah (c. 1727–c. 1774), who fought to help preserve Shawnee lands; Shawnee/Cayuga poet and teacher Barney Furman Bush (1945–), whose books of poetry deal with nature and family; and Shawnee-Sauk/Fox-Creek-Seminole professor Donald L. Fixico (1951–), a national expert on tribal issues and government policy toward Native Americans.

BOOKS

Allen, John W. *Legends and Lore of Southern Illinois.* Carbondale: Southern Illinois University Press, 2010.

Calloway, Colin G. *The Shawnees and the War for America.* New York: Viking, 2007.

Clark, Jerry E. *The Shawnee.* Lexington: University Press of Kentucky, 2007.

De Capua, Sarah. *The Shawnee.* New York: Marshall Cavendish Benchmark, 2008.

Lakomäki, Sami. *Singing the King's Song: Constructing and Resisting Power in Shawnee Communities, 1600–1860.* Oulu, Finland: Oulu University Press, 2009.

Zimmerman, Dwight Jon. *Tecumseh: Shooting Star of the Shawnee.* New York: Sterling, 2010.

WEB SITES

Absentee Shawnee Tribe. http://www.astribe.com/Government.html (accessed on June 12, 2011).

East of the River Shawnee. http://www.eorshawnee.com/About%20The%20EORS.htm (accessed on June 12, 2011).

Eastern Shawnee Tribe of Oklahoma. http://estoo-nsn.gov/ (accessed on June 12, 2011).

"History." *Shawnee Nation Ohio Blue Creek Band.* http://niteowlvisuals.com/BCB/?page_id=2 (accessed on June 12, 2011).

"Our History." *Piqua Shawnee Tribe.* http://piquashawnee.webs.com/ (accessed on June 12, 2011).

Redish, Laura, and Orrin Lewis. "Shawnee (Shawano, Savannah, Sewanee)." *Native Languages of the Americas.* http://www.native-languages.org/shawnee. htm (accessed on June 12, 2011).

"The Shawnee in History." *The Shawnee Tribe.* http://www.shawnee-tribe.com/ history.htm (accessed on June 12, 2011).

"Shawnee Indian Tribe History." *Access Genealogy.* http://www.accessgenealogy. com/native/tennessee/shawneeindianhist.htm (accessed on June 12, 2011).

"Shawnee Indians." *Ohio Historical Society.* http://www.ohiohistorycentral.org/ entry.php?rec=631&nm=Shawnee-Indians (accessed on June 12, 2011).

"The Shawnee Marriage Dance." *AAA Native Arts.* http://www.aaanativearts. com/article889.html (accessed on June 12, 2011).

Shawnee Nation, United Remnant Band. http://www.zaneshawneecaverns.net/ shawnee.shtml (accessed on June 12, 2011).

Sultzman, Lee. "Shawnee History." *First Nations: Histories Site.* http://www. tolatsga.org/shaw.html (accessed on June 12, 2011).

Great Plains

Great Plains

The image of North America's Native population as warriors on horseback who hunted buffalo and lived in tepees is a stereotypical view of just one culture—the Great Plains culture. This culture emerged around 1700 and lasted for nearly two hundred years. It was not wholly native to the Plains but developed around the interactions between the Plains environment and the different groups who lived there. Before the arrival of Europeans, the peoples of the Great Plains were a mixture of semi-sedentary horticulturists (farmers who stayed in one place for enough of the year to be able to plant and harvest the food they grew) and nomadic hunters (people who moved from place to place seeking animals to hunt). The Europeans introduced horses, guns, diseases, and territorial pressures, which changed the ecology, tribal relationships, cultures, and populations of the Great Plains.

The Great Plains culture stretched from Alberta and Saskatchewan in Canada to central Texas in the United States, and from east of the Rocky Mountains to west of the Mississippi River, corresponding to the grasslands ranged by the buffalo before their wholesale destruction at the end of the nineteenth century. The Great Plains are characterized by relatively low precipitation. They received enough moisture to enable prehistoric farming activity around the Missouri and its tributaries. To the west, though, where annual rainfall levels generally fall below 20 inches (50 centimeters), a nomadic hunting lifestyle prevailed.

Some features of life on the Great Plains united the tribes culturally, but beneath the similarities that arose from adapting to similar conditions, the tribes displayed great differences. Although the tribes shared buffalo hunting, the construction of tepees, and other elements of material culture, they demonstrated a diversity of languages, as well as regional and cultural backgrounds. Neither was the Great Plains culture unchanging: nomadic tribes were constantly moving, adapting to their new environment, and absorbing new cultural influences.

INDIAN LODGES AND LAKE OF THE WOODS.

"Two different kinds of Lodges are used by the Indians of the Northwest, viz.: the Conical Buffalo-Skin Lodge, and the Oblong Birch Bark Lodge."

Skin tepees were used by tribes on the Great Plains when on the move during hunts. © NORTH WIND PICTURE ARCHIVES.

of the classic Great Plains culture. The annual migrations of the buffalo were the most important element in the lives of the nomadic hunters and determined their seasonal activities. Nomadic hunters had roamed the Plains for thousands of years. Before the Europeans brought horses, a pedestrian (on foot) buffalo culture existed. The communal spring and fall hunts brought in most of the people's subsistence needs in terms of food, clothing, and shelter. The tribe remained together during the summer months, roaming with the herds and observing its most important ceremonies. Historically the buffalo hunting lifestyle brought a greater level of material conformity to these people.

The semi-sedentary Plains peoples, some of whom were direct ancestors of historic Plains peoples, began moving onto the Plains as early as 900, where the land was more fertile and precipitation higher. They lived in permanent villages near watercourses, dwelling in homes covered with earth, bark, or grass. They cultivated maize, beans, squash, and other crops. The buffalo were also important to their subsistence economies, although they were less dependent on the animal than wholly nomadic groups. For example, the Pawnee left their villages in mid-June for the summer hunt and returned in September to harvest their crops. Once their crops were stored around the end of October, they departed until early April to hunt, returning to sow their new crops. Following the buffalo on their long hunting quests, these peoples lived in skin tepees like the nomadic hunters. Sedentary for part of the year, these groups were able to produce goods absent among the nomadic societies, such as pottery. Village life also enabled them to develop elaborate religious rituals.

Warfare on the Plains Warfare among tribes had influenced the region since prehistory. Societies rewarded brave, successful warriors with prestige, respect, and wealth. Many tribes had separate war and peace leaders, and often the war chief held sway over his peacetime counterpart. In many societies, men could only marry after proving themselves in conflict. Young men acquired glory by achieving such feats as a "counting coup," which meant touching a live enemy during battle. Tribes of the Great Plains practiced scalping as well, although the status gained by such an act varied greatly from tribe to tribe. Supernatural forces were thought to guide war efforts. Not only were war leaders assumed to have divine guidance in deciding whether or not to attack, but a successful war leader could also endow shields and other elements of war with good war medicine.

These beliefs about warfare overlapped with other religious beliefs. The tribes were pantheistic, believing that spirits existed in natural features and events. One of the most important religious ceremonies to develop among the peoples of the Great Plains was the Sun Dance. The ceremony served as an annual initiation rite for young men. It also reaffirmed relationships and signaled the renewal of the tribe and its physical environment.

At the heart of the Great Plains religion lay sacred medicine bundles. Collected in these bundles were sacred items such as medicine pipes. The people believed the items in the bundle held the power to improve hunting and other activities. Some even paid substantial amounts of goods to view the contents of the bundles.

Post–European contact

The vast size of the Great Plains meant that, in some regions, tribes made contact with Europeans much sooner than in others. In the southern Plains, the 1540 expedition of Spanish explorer Francisco Vásquez de Coronado (c. 1510–54) probably interacted with the Wichita. Although the Europeans established a physical presence in the South earlier than in the North, some historians speculate that the diseases that devastated the South made their way to the North long before any European adventurers arrived there. Devastation to Great Plains Indian society from these diseases stands out as one of the most important features of this early interaction. The 1780–81 smallpox epidemic destroyed half of the Great Plains population.

The first record of European contact in the northern region of the Great Plains comes from Henry Kelsey (c. 1667–1724), a fur trader and explorer who documented his contact with the Assiniboin and Gros Ventre he encountered between 1690 and 1691. For more than a century, the fur trade profoundly affected the destinies of tribes on the Great Plains. The new commerce surrounding fur enabled the flow of guns, alcohol, and other European-style commodities into the region.

Horses on the Plains

The introduction of the horse on the Great Plains was revolutionary. Horses spread throughout the area in the middle of the seventeenth century, until all tribes had access to horses by 1800. Besides its influence on warfare, the horse brought other advantages of mobility to the Great Plains tribes. Buffalo hunting became much easier. Not only could the Great Plains hunters kill more buffalo in less time, but they could carry their prey over great distances. This, in turn, encouraged the commercial use of buffalo. Horses could carry heavier gear than pedestrians or dogs, so the people built taller moveable tepees. With horses, the tribes could afford to carry the sick or wounded, whereas before immobilized members of the tribe often had to be left behind. Horses shifted the balance of power somewhat toward the nomadic tribes. The new speeds with which the tribes moved made it nearly impossible to track or catch nomadic tribes. The presence of the horse prompted all of these changes, and the fundamental dynamics of the culture changed forever.

Warfare with guns

The presence of guns produced dramatic swings in power among the region's peoples. For example, the Shoshone stood as one of the most powerful tribes on the Northern Plains around 1700; however, when their rivals, the Blackfeet, Cree, and Assiniboin, acquired guns from traders, the newly empowered groups drove the Shoshone from the Plains by the end of the eighteenth century. Among the European powers, it was the Spanish who traded with the Shoshone, and they refused to trade in weapons. As a result, the Shoshone found themselves at an insurmountable disadvantage.

Intertribal warfare had been part of life on the Plains long before guns were introduced by Europeans. Undeniably, though, interaction with Europeans changed the nature of warfare. Of course, the appearance of guns increased the damage that one warrior could do, but the introduction of the horse had at least an equally profound effect on the way the tribes fought. Success in battle had always brought glory, but with horses, hunting became easier. With the extra time thus allowed, tribes turned their attentions to political struggles more often than previously. Warriors could move across distances easily and quickly, thus putting more foes within reach. Also, whereas before horses most tribes fought in pitched battles, after the advent of the horse, raiding parties and attacks on population centers became easier and more common.

European and American settlement also intensified warfare by displacing Native peoples. As settlers moved west, tribes retreated still farther west onto territory used by other tribes. Formal acts of law occasionally sped up this movement. For example, the 1830 Indian Removal Act generated increased hostility as more tribes vied for an ever-decreasing area of land. Under this act the U.S. government relocated the "Five Civilized Tribes" of the Southeast (the Choctaw, Chickasaw, Cherokee, Creek, and Seminole) to the Great Plains. These five tribes left their Native lands on a government-enforced march to the West called the "Trail of Tears," to find themselves unwelcome on land that Plains Indians had long used for survival.

White settlers on the Plains

European and American contact had many incidental effects, but direct conflict with settlers had an impact just as powerful. The opening of the Oregon Trail in the 1840s brought many American settlers through the Great Plains, increasing friction with the Great Plains tribes. The situation worsened when gold was discovered in California in 1849. As prospectors moved through the area, conflict ensued. In some cases, these newcomers came between warring tribes, but in other cases, the two group attacked one another deliberately. The U.S. government sought to ease the situation and enable their citizens to use the Oregon Trail through the Great Council of Fort Laramie in 1851. Although the council gathered members of many tribes, the government's intention had little to do with Native rights and aimed mainly to make travel safe for the settlers. The agreement sought to demarcate specific areas for Native groups so that settlers could rely on certain areas being free of conflict or hostile parties.

Flaws in the treaty soon showed as both sides violated its terms. Through a series of agreements at Fort Laramie, the government agreed to give the Sioux permanent rights to their Dakota lands including the Black Hills, but non-Natives encroached on this territory as early as the 1860s. The Sioux, who had been driven from their lands in Minnesota, felt threatened and took a stance against the intruders. When prospectors discovered gold in the Black Hills, the government tried to renegotiate the Sioux possession of the Black Hills, but the Sioux refused to give up land they held sacred. This tension coincided with the end of the American Civil War (1861–65), which led to a dramatic increase in people moving West. The U.S. government began to take a more direct hand in local politics.

Battling U.S. military and commercial forces

The Sioux were, at that time, gaining the upper hand on their tribal rivals. In some cases, they formed alliances; along with the Cheyenne and the Arapaho, they controlled the Northern Plains by 1870. In response to Sioux aggression, some groups, such as the Mandan and Hidatsa, sought alliances with the Americans. General warfare prevailed in this period. The hostilities reached a peak in the Battle of Little Bighorn on June 25, 1876, when the Sioux and the Cheyenne defeated Lieutenant Colonel George Custer (1839–1876) and the U.S. Cavalry. This victory stiffened the American government's resolve in battling the tribe. By 1877, the Sioux had lost many military encounters with the U.S. forces, and quite a few of the tribes had moved to reservations.

By the 1870s, commercial hunters were slaughtering three million buffalo a year, driving them to near extinction. The completion of the transcontinental (spanning the nation from coast to coast) railroads divided the buffalo's grazing lands and disrupted their migratory habits. As the U.S. population expanded into the land, the buffalo populations diminished further. Without the buffalo, many Great Plains tribes faced terrible poverty and were forced to depend on the U.S. government for food and supplies.

The confinement of the Great Plains peoples on reservations and the interaction of the U.S. government has been very destructive to their native culture. Although many tribes currently face enormous issues, such as unemployment, there has also been a revival of Native pride and the renewal of ancient cultural traditions.

BOOKS

Brown, Joseph. *The Spiritual Legacy of the American Indian: Commemorative Edition with Letters while Living with Black Elk.* Bloomington, IN: World Wisdom, 2007.

Curtis, Edward S. *The Plains Indian Photographs of Edward S. Curtis.* Lincoln: University of Nebraska Press, 2001.

Doherty, Craig A., and Katherine M. Doherty. *Plains Indians.* New York: Chelsea House, 2008.

Fowler, Loretta. *The Columbia Guide to American Indians of the Great Plains.* New York: Columbia University Press, 2005.

Goodrich, Thomas. *Scalp Dance: Indian Warfare on the High Plains, 1865–1879.* Mechanicsburg, PA: Stackpole Books, 2002.

Haines, Francis. *The Plains Indians: Their Origins, Migrations, and Cultural Development.* New York, NY: Thomas Y. Crowell Company, 1976.

Jennys, Susan. *19th Century Plains Indian Dresses.* Pottsboro, TX: Crazy Crow, 2004.

Kaelin, Celinda R., and the Pikes Peak Historical Society. *American Indians of the Pikes Peak Region.* Charleston, SC: Arcadia Pub., 2008.

Lookingbill, Brad D. *War Dance at Fort Marion: Plains Indian War Prisoners.* Norman: University of Oklahoma Press, 2006.

Lowie, Robert H. *Indians of the Plains.* Garden City, NY: Natural History Press, 1963.

Mails, Thomas E. *Peoples of the Plains.* Tulsa, OK: Council Oak Books, 1997.

Marriott, Alice, and Carol K. Rachlin. *Plains Indian Mythology.* New York, NY: Thomas Y. Crowell, 1975.

McGinnis, Anthony. *Counting Coup and Cutting Horses: Intertribal Warfare on the Northern Plains 1738–1889.* Lincoln: University of Nebraska Press, 2010.

Patent, Dorothy Hinshaw, and William Munoz. *The Buffalo and the Indians: A Shared Destiny.* New York: Clarion Books, 2006.

Robinson, Jane Ewers, ed. *Plains Indian Art: The Pioneering Work of John C. Ewers.* Norman: University of Oklahoma Press, 2011.

Rosoff, Nancy B., and Susan Kennedy Zeller. *Tipi: Heritage of the Great Plains.* Seattle: Brooklyn Museum in association with University of Washington Press, 2011.

Schlesier, Karl H., ed. *Plains Indians, AD 500–1500: The Archaeological Past of Historic Groups.* Norman: University of Oklahoma Press, 1994.

Viola, Herman J. *Trail to Wounded Knee: The Last Stand of the Plains Indians 1860–1890.* Washington, DC: National Geographic, 2004.

Wishart, David J., ed. *Encyclopedia of the Great Plains Indians.* Lincoln: University of Nebraska Press, 2007.

West, Elliott. *The Contested Plains: Indians, Goldseekers, & the Rush to Colorado.* Lawrence: University Press of Kansas, 2000.

WEB SITES

"Indian Arts and Crafts Board: Museum of the Plains Indian." *U.S. Department of the Interior.* http://www.doi.gov/iacb/museums/museum_plains.html (accessed on July 1, 2011).

"Indian Peoples of the Northern Great Plains." *MSU Libraries.* http://www.lib.montana.edu/epubs/nadb/ (accessed on July 1, 2011).

Mitchell, Jon G. "Change of Heartland: The Great Plains." *National Geographic Magazine.* http://magma.nationalgeographic.com/ngm/0405/feature1/index.html?fs=www7.nationalgeographic.com (accessed on July 1, 2011).

Plains Indian Ledger Art. http://plainsledgerart.org/ (accessed on July 1, 2011).

"Plains Indian's Way of Life." *Virtual Museum of New France.* http://www.civilization.ca/cmc/VMNF/premieres_nations/en/plains_indians/waylife.shtml (accessed on July 1, 2011).

Redish, Laura, and Orrin Lewis. "Indian Tribes and Languages of the Great Plains." *Native Languages of the Americas.* http://www.native-languages.org/plains-culture.htm (accessed on July 1, 2011).

Redish, Laura, and Orrin Lewis. "Native American Tribes of North Dakota." *Native Languages of the Americas.* http://www.native-languages.org/ndakota.htm (accessed on July 1, 2011).

Wissler, Clark. "North American Indians of the Plains." 1920. http://www.accessgenealogy.com/native/plains/ (accessed on July 1, 2011).

Arapaho

Name

The Arapaho (pronounced *uh-RAP-uh-ho*) called themselves *Inuna-ina* or *Hinono'eno,* which might mean "our people," "sky people," or "roaming people." The name Arapaho may have been derived from the Pawnee word *tirapihu,* meaning "trader"; the Kiowa name for the tribe, *Ahyato*; or the Crow name for the tribe, *Alappaho.*

Location

In the 1700s, the Northern Arapaho occupied the plains of southern Wyoming and northern Colorado. The Southern Arapaho occupied the plains of west-central Oklahoma and southern Kansas. In the early 2000s, the Northern Arapaho shared the Wind River Reservation in Wyoming with the Shoshone (see entry). The Southern Arapaho lived on the Cheyenne-Arapaho Reservation in western Oklahoma.

Population

The Arapaho population was approximately 3,000 in pre-reservation days. By 1861, the numbers had fallen to 750 (Northern) and 1,500 (Southern). In the 1990 U.S. Census, 5,585 people identified themselves as Arapaho. More specifically, 1,319 people said they were Northern Arapaho and 14 people said they were Southern Arapaho. In 2000, the census showed 7,181 Arapaho; of those, 4,579 were Northern Arapaho. The 2010 census counted 8,014 Arapaho, with a total of 10,861 people claiming some Arapaho heritage. In 2011, the Oklahoma Indian Affairs Commission indicated that tribal enrollment for the Cheyenne-Arapaho had reached 12,185.

Language family

Algonquian.

Origins and group affiliations

The Arapaho probably originated in the Great Lakes region—perhaps in Minnesota or Canada. One group of Arapaho were called Gros Ventre (pronounced *grow VAHNT*) by the French. The reason for the name, which means "Big Bellies," is unknown, but it has stuck. The Gros Ventre settled on the Fort Belknap

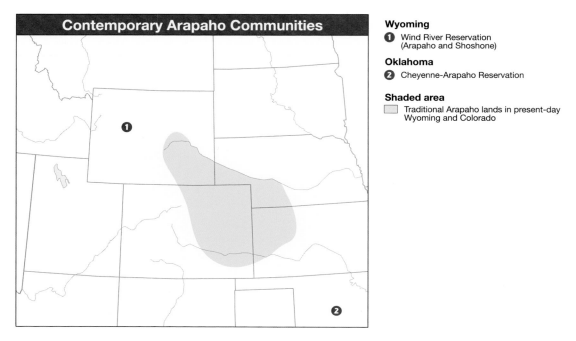

Contemporary Arapaho Communities

Wyoming
❶ Wind River Reservation
(Arapaho and Shoshone)

Oklahoma
❷ Cheyenne-Arapaho Reservation

Shaded area
☐ Traditional Arapaho lands in present-day
Wyoming and Colorado

A map of contemporary Arapaho communities. MAP BY XNR PRODUCTIONS. CENGAGE LEARNING, GALE. REPRODUCED BY PERMISSION OF GALE, A PART OF CENGAGE LEARNING.

Reservation in northern Montana in 1878. The Cheyenne (see entry) and Arapaho shared a similar language and culture but were separate tribes; later a portion of both tribes moved onto a reservation together. The Shoshone, historically an enemy of the Arapaho, lived alongside them on the Wind River Reservation.

The Arapaho were a spiritual, peace-loving people who moved to the Great Plains in the mid-1600s. They gave up their farming lifestyle to roam the plains, hunting buffalo on horseback. When gold seekers and settlers overran the West, the Arapaho offered them safe passage but then lost most of their lands—and their livelihood—to them. In the 1800s, after splitting into two groups to search for increasingly elusive herds of buffalo, the Arapaho were permanently divided and several decades later were moved onto reservations.

HISTORY

From Great Lakes to Great Plains

Around the year 1000 BCE, most Algonquian speakers lived in the Great Lakes region. The Arapaho migrated in a southwesterly direction to the Great Plains and changed their livelihood from farming to hunting.

By the 1700s, the Arapaho had adopted a typical Great Plains lifestyle, living in hide-covered tepees and following the migrations of the great buffalo herds. Spanish explorers introduced horses to the New World, and the Arapaho acquired their own in the 1730s. They quickly became skilled riders and could then hunt far more efficiently than on foot.

Relations with neighbors

The Arapaho established trading relationships with neighboring tribes who relied on farming. They gave surplus meat and hides to the Hidatsa and Mandan peoples in exchange for beans, corn, and squash. At the same time they raided and fought with other tribes, often to accumulate more horses.

In the mid-1800s, a major wave of whites streamed into Arapaho territory. Some planned to stay; others were on their way to find gold in California. The vast wagon trains disrupted the migrations of the buffalo herds, sending the buffalo in different directions and making them harder to find. Plains tribes were forced into competition for game and land. The Arapaho traded with settlers for guns, ammunition, and knives to fight their enemies. As hunting by non-Natives made game more scarce, the tribe began to depend on settlers for food and clothing. Sometimes they acquired these items in payment for escorting wagon trains through the territories of neighboring tribes who were hostile to the invading whites.

Division in the tribe

Around 1835, under increasing pressure from non-Native settlers, the tribe separated. The Northern Arapaho settled at the edge of the Rocky Mountains in present-day Wyoming. The Southern Arapaho settled along the Arkansas River in present-day Colorado. They remained in close contact with one another, a pattern that continues to this day.

Eventually, the Arapaho made peace with several of their former enemies, including the Dakota, Lakota, Nakota, and Cheyenne (see entries).

Important Dates

1600s to mid-1700s: The Arapaho migrate from the Great Lakes region onto the Great Plains and adopt a wandering, hunting lifestyle.

1835: The Arapaho divide into two groups: the Northern Arapaho settle near the North Platte River in Wyoming, and the Southern Arapaho settle near the Arkansas River in Colorado.

1864: At least 130 Southern Arapaho and Cheyenne—many of them women and children—are killed by U.S. Army troops during the Sand Creek Massacre.

1867: The Southern Arapaho are placed on a reservation in Oklahoma, which they share with the Cheyenne.

1878: The Northern Arapaho move onto the Wind River Reservation in Wyoming, which they share with the Shoshone.

Little Raven was head chief of the Southern Arapaho in the mid-1860s. NATIONAL ARCHIVES PHOTO. AMERICAN INDIAN SELECT LIST NUMBER 104.

The Arapaho were one of eleven tribes to sign the Fort Laramie Treaty of 1851, which set aside large tracts of land for the Native nations. Before long, however, settlers wanted that property as well. Although the Arapaho were generally more peaceful than their neighbors, they did take part in several battles over domination of the Great Plains.

Sand Creek Massacre

Continuing conflicts between Plains Indians and settlers who tried to take their lands reached a climax in November 1864. Cheyenne chief Black Kettle (c. 1803–1868) told the U.S. government he wanted peace, and he asked to be directed to a safe place. They sent him with his people and members of the Arapaho tribe to Sand Creek in Colorado. There the people lived peacefully for a few weeks. Then early one morning American troops ambushed them as they lay sleeping. At least 130 people were brutally killed in the Sand Creek Massacre, including many women and children. In retaliation, the Southern Arapaho, led by Little Raven (c. 1810–1889), joined the Cheyenne in an all-out raid against the Americans that lasted six months.

After the war

By 1867, the Southern Arapaho population had been greatly reduced by war, disease, and starvation. Tribal leaders reluctantly agreed to accept placement on a reservation. In exchange for their former lands, the Southern Arapaho agreed to share land in western Oklahoma with the Southern Cheyenne.

The Northern Arapaho resisted the pressure to settle on a reservation. Although they were urged to share the Pine Ridge Reservation in South Dakota with the Sioux, they insisted on receiving their own lands. In 1878, they finally agreed to accept lands on the Wind River Reservation in Wyoming. They had to share the reservation with their former enemies, the Shoshone; for a time, relations were tense. Finally, the two groups reached an understanding. They still live together, but each maintains its own identity, culture, and government.

Once on reservations, the Arapaho faced a great deal of pressure to abandon their traditional lifestyle and assimilate, or become like white Americans. The Northern Arapaho have been more successful in resisting the pressure, in part because Wyoming remains the center of Arapaho religious life. The Southern Arapaho travel to Wind River Reservation each year for powwows (festivals of singing and dancing), rituals, and dances. The most important ceremony is the Offerings Lodge. It is held in the summer and allows participants to express their commitment to the Arapaho community.

RELIGION

Traditionally, the Arapaho were an intensely religious people. All aspects of their lives had spiritual significance, and they looked for signs and wonders everywhere. They believed in a creator who made the world and the Arapaho people. They believed that they would be granted health and happiness if they prayed and offered gifts to the Creator. Their most sacred object was the flat pipe that represented the power of the Creator on Earth.

The main Arapaho religious ceremony was the annual Sun Dance, which involved rituals centering on the sacred wheel or a sacred tree with a rawhide doll tied to the top. Although Arapaho who were to join in the Sun Dance fasted and went without sleep for several days in preparation, they did not include self-torture (piercing and tearing the flesh) in their Sun Dance like some other Plains tribes did.

Missionaries tried to convert the Arapaho to Christianity in the late 1800s. Some converted, but others embraced the Ghost Dance religion when it spread among western tribes during the 1880s. Founded by Wovoka, a Paiute, the religion predicted a new age without whites, when plentiful game and dead ancestors would return to the earth. Today, the Northern Arapaho continue to practice the Sun Dance, and many Southern Arapaho make the annual pilgrimage to the Wind River Reservation to participate.

The Native American Church and the Sweat Lodge Ceremony also found followers among the Arapaho. The Native American Church combines Christian and Native beliefs and practices and features an all-night ceremony composed of chanting, prayer, and meditation. The Sweat Lodge Ceremony is a purification ritual that involves a sweat bath.

Tribe members participate in the Ghost Dance, which became popular among the Arapaho in the 1880s. NATIONAL ARCHIVES AND RECORDS ADMINISTRATION

LANGUAGE

The Arapaho spoke a dialect (variety) of the Algonquian language family, unusual among tribes of the Great Plains but common among those in the Great Lakes region. Few Native speakers remain among the Arapaho. The loss of their native language has been a major problem for the people, and in recent times, the Northern Arapaho have established a language program in reservation schools to encourage its use. Several online resources provide information on both the Southern and Northern Arapaho dialects. The numeral 3 in written Arapaho is pronounced as the *th* sound.

GOVERNMENT

Arapaho men acquired power within their bands by capturing horses in raids. If a man had many horses and displayed qualities such as generosity and competence, he might be chosen the leader of his group.

Leaders, however, had limited powers. Important matters had to be discussed at length by every adult man and some older women in the group before decisions were made. The greatest weight was given to the opinions of leaders and elders.

In the early twenty-first century, two separate general councils, which are made up of members of the Arapaho and Shoshone tribes who are age eighteen or over, hold meetings at the Wind River Reservation. Both tribes are governed by business councils; six members are elected to serve two-year terms, and the council members elect the chairpersons.

A joint tribal business committee operates at the Cheyenne-Arapaho Reservation in Oklahoma. Four members from each tribe are elected to serve four-year terms. The reservation also has a tribal council that includes all members age eighteen and older. The tribal council approves the budget, land leases or changes, and laws about membership. Council members may also propose amendments to the constitution, change district boundaries, and override business committee decisions. To veto committee decisions, at least seventy-five members must vote against them. Every four years, the people elect a governor and lieutenant governor to oversee the various departments of the executive branch, such as education, social services, treasury, and others.

Arapaho Words

bee'ee'	"red"
bii3ih	"eat"
biikousiis	"moon"
he3	"dog"
hiisiis	"sun"
hinen	"man"
hisei	"woman"
nec	"water"
neniitonoot	"see"
niibeiinoo	"sing"
nonoo3oot	"leave"
nowo'	"fish"
siisiiyei	"snake"
wox	"bear"
woxhoox	"horse"

ECONOMY

The Arapaho divided labor according to gender, but the work of men and women was considered equally important. Long ago, the economy was based on farming. After they moved to the Great Plains, the people depended on buffalo for food, clothing, and shelter. Because horses were necessary to hunt buffalo, a person's wealth was measured in the number of horses he owned. By the mid-1800s, though, buffalo had become nearly extinct. Weakened by diseases and food shortages, tribe members were often forced to steal livestock from settlers. When the federal government finally authorized the distribution of food to poverty-stricken Arapaho, the agents in charge of providing the food often cheated them out of the supplies.

The Arapaho gradually began to support themselves by farming, cattle ranching, and selling or leasing reservation land. Both Northern and Southern Arapaho earn income from oil and gas revenues and from small businesses, including smoke shops, casinos, bingo parlors, and convenience stores. The Northern Arapaho also raise cattle and horses, operate tourist attractions, and run NATI, an information and technology firm, all of which bring in additional funds.

DAILY LIFE

Buildings

The Arapaho lived in portable tepees that were easy to assemble and take apart and were owned by the women of the tribe. Each family built its own tepee, which consisted of wooden poles set into the ground and arranged in a cone shape, with a cover of fifteen to twenty buffalo hides stretched over the top. When the buffalo was near extinction, tepees were made of canvas obtained from the U.S. government.

In the winter, the tribe usually scattered into the foothills of the Rocky Mountains, where they were more sheltered from the elements. There they camped in groups of twenty to eighty families. They mounded dirt around the outsides of their tepees for warmth. The inside had a sleeping platform and a fire fueled with buffalo dung. Sometimes they painted the walls with pictures of the man's successes in war. In the summer, when the whole tribe came together to hunt on the prairies, they arranged all the tepees in a large circle.

Food

Before it almost became extinct in the late 1800s, the buffalo was a primary food source. Men also hunted deer, elk, and small game, but they would not eat bear because they considered bears their ancestors.

Arapaho women gathered roots and berries to eat fresh or make into a soup. The most common meal was a stew consisting of meat and wild roots such as potatoes and turnips. The Arapaho also enjoyed a tea made with wild herbs.

Arapaho gather after hanging buffalo meat to dry at a camp near Fort Dodge, Kansas, in 1870. NATIONAL ARCHIVES AND RECORDS ADMINISTRATION

Clothing and adornment

The Arapaho made most of their clothing from deer or elk hides. Women fashioned the skins into long dresses or into moccasins attached to leggings that extended to the knee. Arapaho men wore shirts, breechcloths (garments with front and back flaps that hung from the waist), leggings, and moccasins. In the winter, they added buffalo-skin robes and made snowshoes from strips of rawhide attached to a wooden frame. They decorated much of their clothing with painted or embroidered designs that had religious themes.

The Arapaho adorned themselves with tattoos made by pricking the skin with cactus needles and rubbing charcoal into the wound. A man usually had three small circles across his chest, whereas a woman had a small circle on her forehead.

Healing practices

The Arapaho believed that people could become ill merely by thinking or speaking about disease and death or by failing to show proper respect to the Creator. When a person became sick, his or her relatives would open the person's medicine bundle (a pouch with objects held sacred by the owner) and pray. Sometimes they offered gifts of food, property, or even flesh to make their loved ones well again. If that did not work, they called upon a medicine person called a shaman (pronounced *SHAH-mun* or *SHAY-mun*) for help.

The Arapaho have a special healing ceremony that is performed in extreme cases. It has been held only two times in the twentieth century: in 1918 during a flu epidemic and in 1985 after a rash of suicides by young people on the reservation. Called the Paint Ceremony, it was described in a magazine article by Ted Delaney:

> One by one, people entered the tepee where the elders sat. The ceremony involved steps of cleansing, by prayer, by smoke, then by paint on the face.... When people emerged from the tepee, they left the grounds, silent. Most of the five thousand people of the Wind River Reservation took part.

Education

In the past Arapaho children regarded all adults as their mothers and fathers, and they learned by watching and imitating adults. Parents often invited respected elders to dine and tell stories of their life experiences and successes.

Toys were miniature versions of adult items and helped teach children their expected adult roles. Girls played with tiny tepees and with dolls. Dolls were not treated as babies because the Arapaho believed that even to mention a baby could cause pregnancy. Boys played war and hunting games.

After the Arapaho moved to reservations, their children were sent away to boarding schools. Some boarding schools were located on the reservations, but others were often great distances from home. Children were cut off from their parents and forbidden to use their native language. Children who had never before experienced punishment were often treated harshly.

In recent times On the Wind River Reservation in the early twenty-first century, the custom of elders teaching children survives. Children have little contact with people outside the reservation until they graduate from reservation schools. In 2004, the tribe opened Four Winds Charter School, where students can study traditional academic subjects or receive vocational training.

Arapaho children in Oklahoma mainly attend local public schools, colleges, and vocational-technical centers. The tribe also operates a number of Head Start centers and day cares. Students who want to go on to college receive scholarships. In addition to adult education classes, the reservation has language classes and vocational training.

ARTS

Inspiration for the decorative arts came to the Arapaho in dreams. Highly skilled women artists painted and embroidered their visions onto beautiful containers, medicine bundles, jewelry, and personal belongings.

CUSTOMS

Childhood

The Arapaho believed that the four stages of life corresponded with the four directions of the winds. These stages were childhood, youth, adulthood, and old age; each had special rituals. Immediately after a baby was born, for example, older relatives prayed for it to be strong and healthy and marked its face with red paint. Between the ages of two and five, Arapaho children had their ears pierced in a special ritual that helped the child learn to deal with future pain and hardship. As they approached puberty, boys and girls were separated from one another to prepare for adult life. Boys entered special societies; girls spent considerable time with the older women of the tribe, dressing modestly and learning their future duties.

Societies

Arapaho males progressed through eight military societies, beginning as young boys. As boys became young men, they entered the Kit Fox Lodge. After they reached a certain level of skill and bravery, they progressed into the Star society. Other societies included the Tomahawk, Spear, Crazy, and Dog Lodges. Graduation to each of these societies in turn brought added prestige and new responsibilities.

The Sun Dance Wheel

A Sun Dance was primarily intended as a religious ceremony, and it brought separate Arapaho groups together for a joyous reunion each summer. Its centerpiece was the Sacred Wheel, which was displayed on an altar and included decorations representing the sun, earth, sky, water, and wind. The following story explains the creation of the Sacred Wheel and the meaning of its various parts. The disk in the center of the wheel represented the sun; the band of wood encircling it was painted like a harmless snake and represented the water; the markings on four sides symbolized the Four Old Men who controlled the winds; and the beads and feathers represented the sky and rain. The exact meaning of the constellations mentioned in the story is no longer known.

At one time, water covered all the Earth. No land could be seen in any direction. It was then that a man walked across the water for four days and four nights, thinking. In his arms he carried Flat Pipe, his only companion and good counselor. The man wanted to treat his pipe well and give it a good home. For six days he fasted while he thought how to do this. Finally on the evening of the sixth day he reached a firm conclusion. "To give Flat Pipe a good home there should be land, and creatures of all kinds to inhabit it."

On the morning of the seventh day he resolved to find land. Calling in all directions, he asked the animals to help. And from the four directions came all manner of animals willing to offer their aid. It took a long time, but finally, with their help, he made the Earth a home for Flat Pipe and placed the Four Old Men in the four directions to control the winds. The Earth was also to be the place of the Sun Dance Lodge, where every year the people would gather to worship together, praying for bounty and health for the tribe.

The man saw a tiny snake and said, "Come and sit near me, Garter Snake. You will be a great comfort to the

The seven tribal elders known as the Water-Pouring Old Men were the most respected members of the tribe. Their duties were to direct ceremonies, take care of the sacred flat pipe, and pray for the well-being of the Arapaho people.

In the days of buffalo hunting, Arapaho women had their own society, the Buffalo Lodge. Members performed ceremonial dances to ensure a successful hunt. They wore costumes and painted their faces white to look like buffalo. Then they blew on special whistles to attract the bison.

people in the future and will have an important place in the Sun Dance Lodge. You will be the Sacred Wheel." Then, looking around to the many helpers that had gathered nearby, he said, "We will need material for a wheel."

Many offered, but Long Stick, a bush with flexible limbs and dark red bark, was most suitable. He said, "For the good of all, I offer my body for the wheel. I am anxious to do good. Please accept my offer so my name will live through the ages." All murmured approval, and they made Long Stick into the ring for the Sacred Wheel.

Then the eagle spoke up, saying, "My great strength and power carry me high above the Earth. My holy body and broad wings soar on the winds of the four directions. I offer my feathers as symbols of the Four Old Men. From here on, if anyone should give you eagle feathers to honor and respect, please remember this day and my request. Help them to use my feathers well."

The man then said, "Eagle, the good and faithful one, has asked that his feathers be used to represent the Four Old Men. We will honor his desire and tie four bunches of eagle feathers to the wheel."

After he had shaped the Sacred Wheel, the man painted it in the image of Garter Snake and arranged the eagle feathers in positions of the Four Old Men—northwest, northeast, southeast, and southwest—and tied them carefully. Then on the wheel the man placed Morning Star, the Pleiades, and Lone Star. Next he placed other groups of stars, such as Chain of Stars, Seven Buffalo Bulls, the Hand, the Lance, and the Old Camp. Finally he painted on the Sacred Wheel the symbols of the Sun, the Moon, and the Milky Way. The man thanked Garter Snake, who was pleased to serve the people in this way.

SOURCE: Monroe, Jean Guard, and Ray A. Williamson. "The Sun Dance Wheel." *They Dance in the Sky: Native American Star Myths*. Boston: Houghton Mifflin, 1987.

Hunting rituals

Arapaho men on horseback worked together during a buffalo hunt, chasing down individual animals and cutting them off from the rest of the herd. At first they used bows and arrows made of cedar and sinew; later they used guns. The men butchered the buffalo with flint or bone knives and then brought it back to camp, where women smoked or dried the meat and prepared the skins to make clothing, tepee covers, or containers for water and food.

Marriage

Most Arapaho marriages were arranged by a woman's male relatives. Women had the right to refuse marriage, but few did so. The wedding day began with an exchange of gifts between the bride's and groom's families. The bride's family then hosted a feast, and the couple was allowed to sit together for the first time. Following the wedding, both the bride and the groom avoided contact with the other's parents.

Medicine bundles

Each member of the Arapaho tribe possessed a medicine bundle containing sacred objects that represented his or her personal relationship with the Creator. A vision revealed to a person what should go into the medicine bundle. During times of illness or war, people used their medicine bundles to make special appeals to the Creator.

CURRENT TRIBAL ISSUES

The Arapaho have been involved in a number of issues concerning land and water rights. In 1989, the tribe successfully protested against a U.S. Forest Service plan to turn a sacred site in Big Horn National Forest into a tourist attraction. In 2004, the Wind River Reservation received a $90,000 grant to restore the declining fish population in the creeks and river. The Southern Arapaho have been working to clean up illegal dumping sites, control solid waste, and enhance the environment.

NOTABLE PEOPLE

Black Spot (c. 1824–1881) was a daring warrior and Arapaho chief who learned white ways as a boy. After he was accidentally left behind when his family moved camp in 1831, a white trapper and trader adopted him and renamed him Friday. The young boy was educated in St. Louis. On a trip west in 1838, Black Spot's relatives recognized him and brought him back to the Arapaho tribe. Thanks to his familiarity with white culture, Black Spot acted as a negotiator and interpreter during treaty talks and was part of the group that secured the Wind River Reservation for his people.

A number of other famous Arapaho leaders assisted Black Spot in negotiations with the government. Among them were Black Bear, who was murdered by a group of white settlers in 1871; Medicine Man, a revered healer who died about the same time; his successor, Black Coal; and Sharp Nose, who continued efforts that allowed the Northern Arapaho to remain in Wyoming.

BOOKS

Anderson, Jeffrey D. *One Hundred Years of Old Man Sage: An Arapaho Life.* Lincoln: University of Nebraska Press, 2003.

Burgan, Michael. *The Arapaho.* Tarrytown, NY: Marshall Cavendish Benchmark, 2009.

Carter, John G. *The Northern Arapaho Flat Pipe and the Ceremony of Covering the Pipe.* Whitefish, MT: Kessinger Publishing, 2007.

DeRose, Cat. *Little Raven: Chief of the Southern Arapaho.* Palmer Lake, CO: Filter Press, 2010.

Dorsey, George A. *The Arapaho Sun Dance: The Ceremony of the Offerings Lodge.* Whitefish, MT: Kessinger Publishing, 2006.

Dorsey, George A., and Alfred. L. Kroeber. *Traditions of the Arapaho. Collected under the Auspices of the Field Colombian Museum and of the American Museum of Natural History.* Whitefish, MT: Kessinger Publishing, 2006.

Fowler, Loretta. *Wives and Husbands: Gender and Age in Southern Arapaho History.* Norman: University of Oklahoma Press, 2010.

Mosqueda, Frank, and Vickie Leigh Krudwig. *The Hinono'ei Way of Life: An Introduction to the Arapaho People.* Edited by Susan Scott Hill. Concho, OK: Cheyenne and Arapaho Tribes of Oklahoma, 2008.

Mosqueda, Frank, and Vickie Leigh Krudwig. *The Prairie Thunder People: A Brief History of the Arapaho People.* Edited by Susan Scott Hill. Concho, OK: Cheyenne and Arapaho Tribes of Oklahoma, 2008.

Schelling, Andrew. *From the Arapaho Songbook.* Albuquerque, NM: La Alameda Press, 2011.

Simmons, Marc. *Friday, the Arapaho Boy: A Story from History.* Albuquerque: University of New Mexico Press, 2004.

Smith, Bruce L. *Wildlife on the Wind: A Field Biologist's Journey and An Indian Reservation's Renewal.* Logan: Utah State University Press, 2010.

Sutter, Virginia. *Tell Me, Grandmother: Traditions, Stories, and Cultures of Arapaho People.* Boulder, CO: University Press of Colorado, 2004.

Wiles, Sara. *Arapaho Journeys: Photographs and Stories from the Wind River Reservation.* Norman: University of Oklahoma Press, 2011.

PERIODICALS

Delaney, Ted. "Confronting Hopelessness at Wind River Reservation" *Utne Reader,* January/February 1990: 61–63. Excerpted from *Northern Lights,* October 1988.

Eskin, Leah. "Teens Take Charge. (Suicide Epidemic at Wind River Reservation)." *Scholastic Update,* May 26, 1989: 26.

WEB SITES

Anderson, Jeff. "Arapaho Online Research Resources." *Colby College.* http://www.colby.edu/personal/j/jdanders/arapahoresearch.htm (accessed on July 2, 2011).

"The Arapaho Project: History of the Northern Arapaho Tribe." *University of Colorado.* http://www.colorado.edu/csilw/arapahoproject/contemporary/history.htm (accessed on July 2, 2011).

"The Arapaho Tribe." *Omaha Public Library.* http://www.omahapubliclibrary.org/transmiss/congress/arapaho.html (accessed on July 2, 2011).

"The Early History and Names of the Arapaho." *Native American Nations.* http://www.nanations.com/early_arapaho.htm (accessed on July 2, 2011).

"A Guide to Learning the Arapaho Language Alphabet: Salzmann System." *Wind River Tribal College.* http://www.arapaholanguage.com/language.htm (accessed on July 2, 2011).

Northern Arapaho Tribe. http://www.northernarapaho.com/ (accessed on July 2, 2011).

Redish, Laura, and Orrin Lewis. "Arapaho Language and the Arapaho Indian Tribe (Inuna-Ina, Hinonoeino, Arapahoe)." *Native American Language Net.* http://www.native-languages.org/arapaho.htm (accessed on July 2, 2011).

"The Sand Creek Massacre." *Last of the Independents.* http://www.lastoftheindependents.com/sandcreek.htm (accessed on July 2, 2011).

"Sharp Nose." *Native American Nations.* http://www.nanations.com/arrap/page4.htm (accessed on July 2, 2011).

The Southern Arapaho. http://southernarapaho.org/ (accessed on July 2, 2011).

Wind River Indian Reservation. http://www.wind-river.org/info/communities/reservation.php (accessed on July 2, 2011).

Arikara

Name

Arikara (pronounced *uh-RIH-kuh-rah*) may have meant "horns" or "male deer" in a nearby tribe's language. The name has been spelled several different ways in historical records, including Arickara, Arikaree, and Arickaree. The people have also been called *Ree.* In their own language, the Arikara call themselves *Sahnish* or *Sanish,* which means "the people." In historical records, they are often referred to as the Arikaree or Ree Indians.

Location

At one time, the Arikara lived in an area that spanned South Dakota, Kansas, and Nebraska, reaching as far south as the Gulf of Mexico. They initially lived in the southern drainage area of the Mississippi, but later they moved north and set up villages along the Missouri River, beginning at the mouth of the Platte. By 1770, they were below the mouth of the Cheyenne River. The explorers Meriwether Lewis (1774–1809) and William Clark (1770–1838) saw them at the Cannonball River in the early 1800s. By the time the artist and author George Catlin (1796–1872) arrived in 1833, they had settled by the Grand River. Several years later, they joined the Mandan below the Knife River. They moved to Nebraska to stay with the Pawnee for two or three years but then returned to the Missouri River. They established their homes between the Grand and Cannonball Rivers in present-day northern South Dakota. In 1870, the Arikara moved to the Fort Berthold Reservation in North Dakota, where many of the people still live.

Population

Some estimates place the Sahnish population at more than 50,000 in the early 800s CE. In the mid-1600s, the Arikara numbered about 30,000 in about forty bands. That figure dropped sharply to 3,800 following a smallpox epidemic in 1780. When the Lewis and Clark expedition arrived in 1804, they found only three of the twelve Arikara villages left, with a total population among them of about 2,600. Two more devastating bouts of smallpox in the early 1800s decreased the tribe to 500 by 1888. In 1907, the census recorded only 389 Arikara. The Arikara are now part of the Three

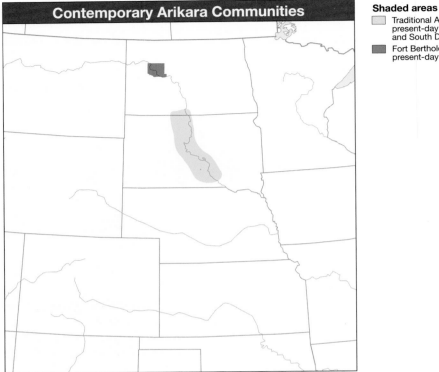

Contemporary Arikara Communities

Shaded areas

Traditional Arikara lands in present-day North Dakota and South Dakota

Fort Berthold Reservation in present-day North Dakota

A map of contemporary Arikara communities. MAP BY XNR PRODUCTIONS. CENGAGE LEARNING, GALE. REPRODUCED BY PERMISSION OF GALE, A PART OF CENGAGE LEARNING.

Affiliated Tribes with the Mandan and Hidatsa. In the early 2000s, the total tribal enrollment for the three groups was 10,400, with about 5,915 of those living on the reservation. The estimate for Arikara alone in 2005 was about 3,400.

Language family

Caddoan.

Origins and group affiliations

The Arikara were an offshoot of the Skidi band of Pawnee (see entry). They traded with the Kiowa and Lakota (see entries) but had many enemies, including the Comanche, Crow, Wichita, Cheyenne, Sioux (see entries), and Apsaroke. At times they also fought with the Mandan and Hidatsa, with whom they currently live.

A populous tribe, at one time the Arikara covered an area that reached from the southern Mississippi River into South Dakota. Over time, they settled along the Missouri River, where the fertile land allowed them to farm. Their main crop was corn, which had sacred significance for them and was the basis for many ceremonies and rituals. Trading crops with neighboring non-farming tribes allowed the Arikara to live in peace even with the more warlike bands, such as the Teton Sioux. After several smallpox epidemics reduced their tribe to a few hundred, the Arikara moved closer to the Hidatsa and Mandan nations. By 1870, all three of these tribes had become the Three Affiliated Tribes and were occupying the Fort Berthold Reservation in North Dakota, which remains home for many Arikara today.

HISTORY

First European contact

Several explorers visited the area during the early 1700s. One of the first French fur traders to arrive, Pierre-Charles Le Sueur (c. 1657–1704), noted that the Arikara lived near present-day Fort Pierre, South Dakota. Étienne de Véniard, Sieur de Bourgmont (1679–1734), who arrived in 1714, lived with the Arikara for several years. According to his accounts, they had three villages on the west side of the Missouri above the Niobrara River in Nebraska as well as forty more communities upstream. By the next decade, the Arikara had moved farther north into South Dakota near the present-day Grand River.

Around 1734, the Arikara broke off from the Pawnee tribe after intertribal warfare. Four years later, the French fur trader Pierre Gaultier de la Vérendrye de Boumois (1714–1755) noted that the Arikara had located their villages close to those of the Mandan near the Cannonball River in southern North Dakota. By the time Jean Baptiste Trudeau (1748–1827), another French fur trader, arrived in 1794, pressure from the Sioux had driven the Arikara farther north. The Arikara people were

Important Dates

1734: Arikara break with Pawnee after intertribal war.

1804: Lewis and Clark expedition arrives in Arikara territory.

1823: Arikara move to northern Nebraska.

1837: Smallpox decimates the Arikara people.

1851: The Fort Laramie Treaty establishes the boundaries of Hidatsa, Mandan, and Arikara land, but most of that property is later taken by the government.

1870: Fort Berthold Reservation becomes the Arikara's home.

1936: The Three Affiliated Tribes—Mandan, Hidatsa, and Arikara—adopt a constitution.

1951–54: Garrison Dam construction floods Arikara lands.

living by the Grand River, which is where Meriwether Lewis and William Clark met them in 1804. By that time, their many villages had been reduced to only three.

Troubles for the Arikara

Over the next decades, the Arikara were engaged in several battles. In 1823, after suffering due to rivalries between trading companies, Arikara warriors attacked and killed American traders. The United States sent in troops, accompanied by Sioux and a group of trappers. This sparked the Arikara War, a brief battle that was the first war fought between the Americans and the tribes in the West.

Although the Arikara signed a peace treaty with the United States in 1825, they still struggled with both the Mandan and Sioux. Following two years of conflict and crop failure, the Arikara moved to Nebraska to live with the Skidi near the Platte River. After a few years, the Skidi asked the Arikara to return to their home on the Missouri River. Sioux raids and smallpox epidemics in 1836 and 1856 that killed many of their people led the Arikara to move closer to the Hidatsa and Mandan in Like-a-Fishhook Village (central North Dakota).

Treaties of Fort Laramie

A treaty signed at Fort Laramie in 1851 guaranteed the Arikara, Mandan, and Hidatsa land west of the Missouri River. They were to receive all the territory from the Heart River to the Little Missouri in North Dakota and west to the Yellowstone River in Wyoming, more than 12.5 million acres. The treaty was never ratified, so in 1868, the Arikara, along with many other tribes, signed the second Treaty of Fort Laramie. This one set North and South Dakota, Wyoming, and Montana as Indian Territory.

In 1870, the federal government took almost eight million acres of the land the Arikara, Mandan, and Hidatsa had been promised. They designated the leftover land as Fort Berthold. A small section was added to the reservation to include Like-a-Fishhook Village. Although the government opened a school for the children, it closed that same year. When gold was discovered in the Black Hills, miners flooded into Indian Territory, violating both treaties. The Commissioner of Indian Affairs tried to persuade the three tribes to move to Oklahoma, but they refused.

In spite of the broken promises, the Arikara maintained good relations with the United States. By 1872, forty Arikara men had become scouts for the U.S. Army. In 1876, they assisted Lieutenant Colonel George Custer (1839–1876) in the Battle of Little Bighorn.

U.S. pressures tribes to assimilate

In 1880, the government took more than a million acres of reservation land without consent. Several years later, the Indian agent burned the earth lodges and cabins to force the tribes to relocate. The people abandoned Like-a-Fishhook Village and moved into communities along the Missouri River.

In 1886, the government banned the practice of Native religions. That year Congress passed the Dawes Allotment Act, which forced the people to give up their usual practice of farming land communally. Instead, each person was given an individual plot of land, and the rest was sold to settlers. The tribes lost almost two-thirds of their remaining land. After 1891, when they were forced to pay taxes, many people had to sell their land to cover the bills. Almost a decade later, the government opened up 320,000 acres of reservation land for homesteaders.

Over the next few years, the three tribes were forced to send their children to schools where they were punished for speaking their Native languages or following traditional customs. Parents who refused did not receive any food or other government support.

Three Affiliated Tribes demand rights

In 1931, the court awarded the Three Affiliated Tribes—Mandan, Hidatsa, and Arikara—money for five million acres, although they had lost eleven million. The Bureau of Indian Affairs subtracted three million from the total, and paid for only two million.

That year, the government began plans for building Garrison Dam. The Three Affiliated Tribes protested, but the project proceeded in spite of their objections. From 1947 to 1954, the tribes were forced to move as the dam flooded their prime farmland. They were offered a payment of $5 million for the loss of land, which they refused. Yet when the representatives for the tribe arrived home, they discovered that the Senate had been told that the tribes had accepted the offer.

The flooding from the dam caused great hardship for the people on the reservation. Eighty percent of the people had to move. Most of them had been farmers or ranchers, but the land where they were relocated was barren. About 94 percent lost their agricultural lands. Many people could no longer earn a living.

The flooding also divided the remaining reservation land into five sections surrounded by water, which meant many tribal members no longer had access to major roads, and they were isolated from their neighbors. In 1992, the Three Affiliated Tribes were awarded $149 million by Congress for their losses. Not until 2005, however, was a new bridge built across the Missouri River to help with some of the transportation problems.

RELIGION

Deities

The main Arikara deity and tribal chiefs were called *Neshán,* or Chief. To the deity, they added the word *Tinachitákuh,* meaning "Above," to distinguish the god from the earthly chiefs. Chief Above created the people and gave them the rites for the medicine lodge through *Atná,* meaning "Mother" or "Corn" (see "Healing practices").

Chief Above also gave the people three things that they were to keep safe—corn, the office of Chief, and secrets of the lodge. He gave them the buffalo for meat. In addition to Chief Above, the Arikara people honored Sun, Wind, Thunder, Night, and She Who Causes Things to Grow.

Creation Story

According to the Arikara creation story, Chief Above made the world. After people laughed at the spirit world, however, he decided to destroy them. He hid corn grains in an underground cave guarded by the animal people. Then he caused a flood that drowned the people on Earth.

Chief Above then made a woman from an ear of corn, and she found the animal people in the cave. The people called her Mother. To get out from underground, several animals—Mouse, Mole, and Badger—took turns digging a hole to the surface. Mouse's nose became sharp and pointy from digging. Mole was blinded by the sunshine when he broke through the ground, and Badger's body has scorch marks from the sun, characteristics that all these animals bear to this day.

As the animals followed Mother through the hole, they became people again. They were told to go west. The people later fought with each other, breaking into four different groups—Assiniboin, Yankton, Ojibway (see entries), and Arikara.

LANGUAGE

By the late 1990s, few elders spoke Arikara, or the Sáhniš language. Most of the fluent speakers had died in the 1970s, so the language was in danger of becoming extinct. Efforts to preserve it began in 1996, when the American Indian Studies Research Institute of Indiana University paired with the White Shield School District in Roseglen, North Dakota, to make recordings of the language. They developed textbooks, a dictionary, lesson plans, podcasts, and CDs to help students learn their language.

The Arikara people suffered a loss when Sahnin Kata', or Yellow Calf Woman, one of the few elders who still maintained the original language, died in 2010. She had been instrumental in passing along her skills to the schoolchildren of the community.

The language, part of the Caddoan language family, is similar to Pawnee, but they are not the same. Members of the Three Affiliated Tribes did not speak similar languages. Both the Hidatsa and Mandan dialects were part of the Siouan language. Once the three tribes shared the Fort Berthold Reservation and children attended schools where they could not speak their native language, most people began to use English as their primary language. In the early days of trade on the Great Plains, the Arikara used sign language to communicate with other tribes. The symbol for the Arikara, who were known as the Corn People or Corn Shellers, was a motion that looked as if the speaker were biting on an ear of corn.

Arikara Words

When researcher and photographer Edward S. Curtis recorded some Arikara words in the early 1900s, he noted that some of the animal names were actually descriptive phrases. For example, the people called the badger "a flat porcupine," and a moose was a "soft-lipped elk." The translation for chipmunk was spotted bone. Some present-day Arikara words are below. (Note: the "š" in Arikara is pronounced like the "sh" sound in English.)

xaátš	"dog"
taáts	"caterpillar"
wáx	"wildcat"
wáh	"elk"
sax	"turtle"
níkus	"bird"
kuúnux	"bear"

GOVERNMENT

Traditional leadership

Experts believe the Arikara were divided among more than forty different bands in the 1600s. By the 1700s, as the population decreased, they were reduced to twelve bands. Each band had a head chief (chosen only from the Awáhu band) and three under chiefs. Chiefs had to keep peace among the members of the tribe, be hospitable to visitors, and set up hunts and migrations. The hunters of the tribe kept the chief supplied with food so that he always had enough to offer to strangers and the needy. The head chief also gave speeches to urge the people to do their duties, which for men meant doing courageous acts and for women meant working hard and being moral.

Decisions were made by consensus among all the men, and discussion continued until they reached an agreement. No one had to follow a decision with which he did not agree. When a chief died, the men of the tribe gathered to choose a successor. After a feast, the chief of each band made a speech nominating a candidate. The person who received the loudest applause was chosen as the new chief.

THREE AFFILIATED TRIBES ADMINISTRATION

After the Arikara moved to Fort Berthold in 1870, they shared the reservation with the Mandan and Hidatsa. Instead of representatives from each village, the people developed a business committee in 1910 made up of members from the various areas. One member each came from Ree (Beaver Creek), Independence, Santee (Lucky Mound), Little Missouri, Elbowoods, and Red Butte. Two members each represented Nishu (formerly called Armstrong) and Shell Creek.

In 1936, the three tribes formed a government under the U.S. Indian Reorganization Act and elected a ten-member council. They had already been operating under a similar government, so the transition was not difficult. Although they have no official status, many other tribal leaders exist who are important to the community. The government leaders and the people depend on the storytellers, sacred bundle carriers, medicine people, and various society members (see "Healing practices") for their wisdom and direction.

ECONOMY

For centuries, the Arikara made their living by farming. They traded excess crops first with other tribes and later with the settlers. In exchange, they received furs, game, tools, horses, guns, blankets, cloth, and cooking utensils. Unlike most tribes, the Arikara refused to trade for alcohol. Women conducted most of the early trade. The men hunted buffalo and small game, and they caught fish to add to their diets.

After the people moved to the reservation and land was allotted, or divided up into individual parcels, many people lost their property and their livelihoods. After the Garrison Dam flooded their best farmland in the 1950s (see "History"), poverty and unemployment became major problems on the reservation.

The economy began to look up when the Four Bears Casino opened in 1993. Over the next decade, the casino expanded, and additional businesses brought more jobs and money for the people. Since the discovery of a wealth of natural resources on the reservation, including coal, oil, and natural gas, the Three Affiliated Tribes have been working to ensure that their people benefit from the exploitation of these fuels.

DAILY LIFE

Families

Children learned from their fathers to hunt and fish. The Arikara were known for their swimming ability, and both boys and girls spent time in the water. The men of the tribe went hunting and off to war, whereas the women farmed, cooked, and tended the children. Men were the only ones who could become chiefs, but women could be healers, storytellers, musicians, and craftspeople.

An earthen lodge typical of those built by the Arikara sits at Fort Abraham Lincoln State Park in Mandan, North Dakoka. © TOM BEAN/ALAMY.

A young Arikara girl named Sweet Scented Grass was the daughter of a chief.
© INTERFOTO/ALAMY.

Buildings

Groups of round earthen lodges clustered around an open space in the center of Arikara villages. One writer counted about sixty homes in a typical village. Two or three families shared each lodge, which was formed from a circular wooden frame of 15-foot (5-meter) logs covered with packed grassy dirt. In the interior, beds surrounded the outer edge of the lodge and were separated from each other by buffalo robes for privacy. A central fire was vented through a hole in the roof.

Large lodges, sometimes 70 feet (20 meters) in diameter, served as medicine and council lodges where people met for dancing, ceremonies, and decision making. Villages also contained several sweat lodges or baths for cleansing before ceremonies. For protection, the people often built their villages on high ground and sometimes surrounded them with moats (water-filled ditches) and palisades (fences of sharpened logs). When the Arikara traveled, such as when the men went hunting, they used small tepees made of buffalo hide.

Clothing and adornment

Women wore long robes made of two deerskins, particularly white ones, of elk or antelope skin. The skirt hems were fringed and scalloped. Mountain-sheep rattles hung at the shoulders. Men wore breechcloths (apronlike pieces of fabric that attached at the waist) and added leggings, buckskin shirts, and buffalo robes in cold weather. Both women's dresses and men's shirts were fringed and decorated with porcupine quills, shells, and elk teeth; some dresses even had strips of ermine on them. Later, beadwork was used. Women's belts were also highly ornamented. As they adopted European ways, the people made their clothes from cloth and used blankets in place of robes.

Both men and women wore their hair long and only cut it when they were in mourning. Men wore two braids that hung down in front, which they wrapped in strips of buffalo fur or otter skin. The hair in front might be cut short, and sometimes on the sides they cut it to shoulder length. At times they curled it with a heated stick. One writer recounted that the men used white clay to roll their hair into a ball on top of their heads. The men often wore blue clamshell earrings. Arikara women wore their hair parted in the middle and either loose or in two braids down their backs, with deerskin wraps decorated with porcupine quills.

Feathers, especially black eagle or swan feathers, formed full headdresses, although some warriors wore only a few individual feathers. Necklaces of bear claws, heel ornaments of foxtails, and deer hoof rattles on their leggings completed most men's outfits. People painted their faces with different designs to signify war, religious occasions, or special ceremonies.

Food

As a farming people, the Arikara were known for their corn, and some experts wonder if the tribe may have brought corn to regions where it had never grown before. Arikara corn was low-growing with multicolored kernels. Some ears were red, black, yellow, purple, blue, or white; others mixed all the colors in one ear. Early writers commented that the Arikara gardens were better tended than any farms they had ever seen.

In addition to many kinds of corn, the Arikara grew beans, squash, pumpkins, melons, sunflowers, and tobacco. They also used wild onions, turnips, celery, milkweed, potatoes, and pigweed (spinach). During the growing season women picked roots, berries, grapes, and cherries. The Arikara also evaporated saltwater to make salt.

Men added to the meals with small game, such as badger, beaver, prairie dog, rabbit, and raccoon. Bison meat came from occasional hunts or from trading with other tribes. The people also ate larger game animals, such as deer, antelope, bear, elk, moose, wolf, coyote, or wildcat. Dogs were also eaten. Because they were near water, the Arikara caught fish and turtles.

PACHTUWA-CHTA.

Arikara warrior Pachtuwa-Chta wears a buffalo robe and leggings typical of what men in his tribe wore in cold weather. © INTERFOTO/ALAMY.

To store their food, the Arikara used deep holes in the ground measuring 4 by 6 feet (1 by 2 meters). They lined these pits with grass or straw, and then layered corn over that, followed by other vegetables. Ceremonies accompanied both the storing of food and taking it out again.

Tools and Transportation

For gardening, women used digging sticks made of deer, elk, or buffalo shoulder blades. They made rakes from reeds tied to a long handle. They ground corn with mortars made of stone or ash wood. The area where they lived had chert, a type of stone that could easily be chipped into points for arrowheads, spear points, and knives. Arrowheads were sometimes made of horn. Men made whistles that imitated the calls of elk or antelope, and they made toys for the children, such as pop guns and flageolets (small flutes).

The Arikara built bull boats, which were round, bowl-shaped crafts. The willow-branch frames were covered with buffalo hide. For ground transportation, the people used travois (pronounced truh-VOI), which were made by attaching long poles to a dog's shoulders. The ends of the poles dragged on the ground. Between the poles, the people inserted a frame of thongs, to which they tied goods. The dogs could pull firewood, meat, possessions, or even babies. One report indicated that most Arikara families owned thirty to forty dogs. After obtaining horses sometime in the early 1800s, the Arikara began keeping large herds of horses, a practice the government discouraged in the 1900s.

Education

Young Arikara children learned their traditional roles from the adults in the tribe. After the Arikara moved to the reservation in the 1870s, the federal government took charge of their education, but schooling was sporadic. Quite a few children attended school when it first opened. As the spring arrived, however, their families needed help with planting, so students did not show up for classes. The school was closed. It was several years before another opened.

Many children were taken from their families and sent to boarding schools run by the Bureau of Indian Affairs (BIA) or by church groups. Most schools severely punished students for speaking their own language or for practicing any of their customs. Those years caused a decline in the Arikara language (see "Language"), because students were not learning about their culture at home but were being trained to speak English and dress and act like the rest of American society.

Changes in government policies in the later 1900s meant that students no longer attended BIA schools. The Garrison Dam construction (see "History") in the 1950s flooded all the schools at Elbowood, so students had to attend new schools in several different communities. These schools are now older and inadequate for the growing population, a concern the Three Affiliated Tribes must deal with as they move into the future.

Healing practices

Herbal potions The Arikara were known among other tribes for their healing powers. They used herbs, roots, and massage along with prayers for healing. Each herb had a special power that the medicine man learned from another healer or through a revelation. Those with great healing knowledge were revered. Before digging up any plant, the healer talked to it, asked for mercy, and prayed that it would make the person better. Like some of the other tribes, the Arikara also got medicines from other bands that had a desired quality or power the healer needed. Healers often sent their wives to request these potions from others.

One of the mixtures the Arikara used was a tea of cedar leaves and berries that women drank before childbirth. Arikara healers awoke unconscious patients using a mixture of sharp-scented roots, dry wood, and tobacco, which caused sneezing. For lung problems, they put the ill person under a robe with a jar of steaming water, dusted him with powder, and then set him or her over a bed of hot coals. When children were sick, the Arikara believed it was an animal taking revenge because their father had killed it.

The usual procedure was for a healer to stay with his patient for four days, praying and smoking. If the patient started to recover by then, the healer remained until the person was well. Before leaving, the healer sang medicine songs to thank the spirit helpers. If the person did not seem to be getting better after four days, another healer was called in.

Medicine Lodge The medicine lodge, one of the largest buildings in the village, was used for various ceremonies. Outside the lodge, Mother (see "Religion") placed a stone, a symbol of eternity, called "Wonderful

Grandfather." She also planted a cedar, the longest-lasting tree, which is called "Wonderful Grandmother." These served as reminders of the Chief Above and Mother. The lodge faced the rising sun in the east. All medicine lodges were built in this manner.

Mother also taught the healers their secrets and gave them sacred bundles. At one time the people had twelve bundles, but now they have seven. Special "keepers" care for the bundles. The objects tied inside the buffalo-skin packages stand for important events in Arikara history.

Healing Societies The Arikara had nine medicine groups: Ghost, Blacktail Deer, Branched Horn (Buck Deer), Shedding (Buffalo), Swamp Bird, Principal Medicine, Big Foot (Duck), Moon, Owl, Mother Night (or Young Dog), and Bear.

The groups sat around the edge of the circular medicine hut in that order. The first four groups were in the southern half; the other four were in the north. Principal Medicine sat in the rear on a raised platform of earth. Above each person's head was a sacred bundle, a buffalo-skin package filled with animal skins and other sacred items, and gourd rattles.

ARTS

Crafts

Arikara artists made baskets of bark woven over a frame. Some say the people taught other tribes to make baskets in this manner. The Arikara also made pottery water jars and cooking pots using clay and sandstone. The cooking utensils were made with holes in the lip, so a stick could be inserted to lift them from the fire. The Arikara were famous for their beadwork and glasswork. They not only learned to make their own glass beads and use them in intricate decorations, but they also supplied many different tribes with beads.

Oral literature

One of the favorite heroes of Arikara legends is Lucky Man, a young man who conquers monsters and negative forces of nature with the help of the spirits. As with many other tribes, Coyote is another character that appears in many stories. He can be both a trickster and a transformer.

CUSTOMS

Social organization

The Arikara had a variety of societies that people could join. Three were military, and three were for women. Some were named for the way their members danced. One, the Shin Raven, was for young people who cut slits in their shins, from which they hung raven feathers when they danced. Men could belong to the organization of their choice and could change groups at any time, but they could only belong to one society at a time. Some of these groups had a specific goal, such as helping others, being hospitable to guests, or caring for the elderly, poor, or orphans.

Sacred Ceremonies

From midsummer into autumn, the various medicine groups participated in sacred ceremonies every afternoon and evening. The rituals began as the group members painted themselves and danced and marched around the cedar and stone at the front of the lodge, singing and calling to Wonderful Grandmother and Grandfather (see "Healing practices").

Each of the different groups then demonstrated their spirit powers. The explorers and traders who witnessed these events called them "performance magic," but they were not sure how these "tricks" were accomplished. For example, one of the Ghosts would swallow a human skull, then lie face down, covered by a robe. When he rose, the skull would be lying on the ground.

The Buffalo men made a buffalo skull bellow. The Swamp Birds leaped into the river, and each came out holding two fish. A member of Mother Night danced on a hot stone that had been pulled from the fire. One of the most dramatic feats was done by a Moon medicine man. After painting his face with a black circle and black spots on his wrists, ankles, and chest, he crawled into a miniature lodge made with sticks and a rush mat. The mat was set on fire, and when it burned away, nothing was left but ashes. The man had disappeared. The people went to the river where the man emerged, beating a drum, and made predictions of the future.

Kinship

Families considered cousins as brothers and sisters, so people could not marry cousins. Aunts and uncles played the same role as fathers and mothers, and in some cases, with so many deaths, the aunts or uncles took over the child care for their deceased siblings.

Brother-in-laws were closer than blood brothers. Men did not talk to their sisters except when it was necessary, and then the exchange would be brief.

Birth and naming

Making smoke offerings with tobacco was an important part of the infant naming ceremony. Tobacco was also used in adoption ceremonies. Rather than using cradleboards, Arikara mothers wrapped their babies in calfskin and then buffalo skin before placing them upright in a narrow sack that swung from the roof timbers of the lodge.

The ceremonial blessing of children took place after the men had gathered a cedar. Women and children placed offerings of cloth on the tree. Then parents brought their children to the priests, who brushed each child with sage to drive away evil and said a prayer.

Marriage

Sometimes couples eloped, but parents usually arranged marriages for their children. The woman had to agree to the union, however. To secure a bride, the man's relatives went to the woman's family and offered to pay for her. Several horses, a gun, and other smaller articles were often exchanged. The first offer was sometimes refused, and negotiations continued until both sides were satisfied. After the family received their goods, the man moved into the home with his wife's family. Sometimes, the couple stayed with her parents for life. Men could have more than one wife, and they had first rights to any of their wives' sisters.

Marriage within bands was acceptable, and children always belonged to their father's band. A man was not allowed to speak to his mother-in-law or even be inside the lodge with her unless he had captured a scalp or many horses for her.

Divorce

If a husband wanted a divorce, he moved out of his in-laws' lodge. If a couple had their own home, the wife returned to her parents.

Spouses who committed adultery were either beaten or abandoned. If the husband knew who his wife had had an affair with, he shot the man's best horse. The wife was beaten.

Death rituals

A dying person decided how his or her belongings would be distributed. Most often the majority of the goods (horse, blankets, and household items) went to the spouse and children, and the rest to close relatives and friends. In the case of a sudden death, the parents of the deceased divided up the property. The children went to a man's parents. If the wife had not fulfilled her duties well, she received nothing.

The parents painted and dressed the body. Then the family hired an old woman to dig the grave. The next afternoon, her relations carried the body on a buffalo robe. Family and friends followed. The body was placed in the pit with its head to the east. The attendants placed a pillow under the head and wrapped the body in the buffalo robe. A special song passed down from the ancestors was sung The old woman then threw a handful of dirt into the grave and said, "This man has gone to a happy place." (The people had no name for the afterlife, but they believed it was pleasant.) Then the grave was filled.

The parents and spouse stayed by the grave until sunset. Wives often slashed their legs. Husbands cut off the tips of their braids and put them inside the robe with the body. On the fourth day after death, the Arikara placed food and water beside the grave to strengthen the soul for its journey. They believed that the soul was the part inside people that was responsible for all their actions and words. They believed that animals also had souls.

In later years, the Arikara used a travois (see "Transportation") to transport the bodies. They continued to mark the four-day period after death, after which the mourners gave a death feast. Tribal elders and family members attended the feast, which lasted late into the night. The family then prepared foods for the dead person to take on the journey to the afterlife.

Hunting rituals

After the men killed a buffalo, they prayed and made offerings. Each person ate a bit of the raw liver and kidney to give them some of the animal's courage and strength. The person who got to the slain animal first took it home to butcher. He then divided the meat among the hunting party, giving the best part to the oldest member. The person who killed the buffalo got the hide and back.

Ceremonies and games

Honoring corn Many Arikara stories and ceremonies were connected with corn, which held a prominent place in the people's lives (see "Religion"). Beginning with planting in spring, the people had rituals, offerings, and feasts for different stages of the corn's growth cycle. One of great importance occurred when the medicine bundle (see "Healing practices") was opened.

An ear of corn was placed on an altar beside weapons and hoes. Four women dipped their fingers in water, moved their hands from their feet to their heads, then raised and dropped their arms to symbolize rain. Following this, four couples danced. As the men mimed protecting the crops and the village, the women acted out hoeing the corn. Other dancers took their places. After the songs ended, the priest, with a Sioux scalp at his feet, held a sword from the bundle and said a prayer. Then cornmeal mush was brought in and divided among the medicine groups. Anyone who received the mush burst out crying.

Games A game called *hánu* (plum seeds) had three men per team. Some seeds were marked with white on one side, black on other. Other seeds had black spots on the reverse side. The seeds were placed in a flat basket, and the men took turns striking the basket so the seeds went flying. The sides that ended on top determined the score. Winners used sticks to keep a running tally of their scores. At the end of the set of games, the person with the most sticks collected the bets.

Women played a ball game with two small deerskin balls joined by a cord. Using sticks, they tried to push the balls over the other team's goal. Another game for women involved trying to toss stones into a buffalo-foot bone.

CURRENT TRIBAL ISSUES

After their lands were flooded in the 1950s, the Three Affiliated Tribes spent decades trying to recover from the financial impact of their losses. Although the court awarded them some compensation, it could not make up for the land that was now underwater; 92 percent of their people lost their farmlands and livelihoods. With so many people out of work and 80 percent of the community members relocated, the people had much rebuilding to do. The reservation also was struggling to recover from heavy spring rains that in 2011 flooded many homes, roads, and newly planted fields.

The Three Affiliated Tribes are working to improve their economy and to gain greater rights over their reservation land and water, especially now that important natural resources, such as oil, coal, and natural gas, have been discovered on their property. To better protect their rights, the business council passed a resolution in 2008 that forbid companies from reselling mineral rights without notifying the council and securing the approval of the people who owned the land and from BIA. Between 2009 and 2010, the reservation increased its number of oil wells from ten to thirty-nine, which brought tribal members almost $180 million. In 2010, the U.S. Department of the Interior also cleared $5 million in back oil royalties owed to the Berthold Reservation.

In recent years, the tribes joined COLT (Coalition of Large Tribes), which includes members such as the Navajo Nation, Blackfeet Tribe of Montana, Sisseton Wahpeton Sioux Tribe, Oglala Sioux Tribe, Rosebud Sioux Tribe, Crow Tribe of Montana, and Spokane Tribe of Washington. The organization formed to address some of the problems these tribes have with law enforcement, land management, energy resources, water sources, and natural resources. They also hope to make changes to the way the government distributes funds, because they say that the formulas do not take into account the difficulties and higher costs of administering programs when tribes are spread across a large geographic area.

NOTABLE PEOPLE

Sitting Bull (1877–1960), or Peter Beauchamp (not the same person as the Sioux warrior Sitting Bull, who died in 1890), was born to a French father and the daughter of a Sahnish chief. Young Sitting Bull lived in Like-a-Fishhook Village until he was sent to the Hampton Institute in Virginia for schooling at the age of eleven. After he graduated, he married a schoolteacher, and he served as tribal chairperson from 1942 to 1944. He spoke both Spanish and English well and helped his people by securing pensions for the Arikara who had worked as scouts. A rancher and farmer, he had many interests, and in later life he became a minister.

Bloody Knife (c. 1840–1876), or Nes-i-ri-pat, had an Arikara mother and a Dakota father. Because of his mixed heritage, he suffered abuse from other young boys. His mother finally returned to her people, but one of his childhood enemies, Gall (see Dakota entry), later became a chief. The two had confrontations over the years, and Gall killed Bloody Knife's two younger brothers. After serving as a mail carrier and a scout for several U.S. expeditions and for the army, Bloody Knife lost his life during the battle of Little Big Horn, when the Dakota, Cheyenne, and Arapaho (see entries) defeated the Americans.

Robert L. Fox (1915–1982) served as a Congregational minister for thirty-two years before becoming active in tribal politics. He served four terms, two as councilman and two as chairman. Fox also served on the State Indian Affairs Commission and the school board, and he was the governor's envoy for the Conference on Indian Affairs for the United States and Canada.

BOOKS

Dorsey, George A. *Traditions of the Arikara.* Washington, DC: Carnegie Institution of Washington, 1904.

Lib, Orin G., ed. *The Arikara Narrative of Custer's Campaign and the Battle of the Little Bighorn.* Norman: University of Oklahoma Press, 1998.

Lowie, Robert Harry. *Societies of the Arikara Indians.* Charleston, SC: Kessinger, 1913; reprint, 2010.

Peters, Virginia Bergman. *Women of the Earth Lodges: Tribal Life on the Plains.* North Haven, CT: Archon Books, 1995.

Straub, Patrick. *It Happened in South Dakota: Remarkable Events That Shaped History.* New York: Globe Pequot, 2009.

Wood, W. Raymond, William F. Hunt Jr., and Randy H. Williams. *Fort Clark and Its Indian Neighbors: A Trading Post on the Upper Missouri.* Norman: University of Oklahoma Press, 2011.

Woods, Marvin. *Custer's Arikara Indian Interpreter (Frederick Francis Gerard).* New York: Vantage Press, 2009.

WEB SITES

"Arikara." *Four Directions Institute.* http://www.fourdir.com/arikara.htm (accessed on June 19, 2011).

"Arikira Indians." *PBS.* http://www.pbs.org/lewisandclark/native/ari.html (accessed on June 19, 2011).

Clark, William. "Lewis and Clark: Expedition Journals." *National Geographic.* http://www.nationalgeographic.com/lewisandclark/record_tribes_020_5_1.html (accessed on June 19, 2011).

Curtis, Edward S. "The North American Indian: The Arikara." *Northwestern University.* http://curtis.library.northwestern.edu/curtis/viewPage.cgi?showp=1&size=2&id=nai.05.book.00000090&volume=5 (accessed on June 19, 2011).

Fausz, J. Frederick. "The Louisiana Expansion: The Arikara." *University of Missouri–St. Louis.* http://www.umsl.edu/continuinged/louisiana/Am_Indians/8-Arikara/8-arikara.html (accessed on June 19, 2011).

Handbook of American Indians, "Arikara Indian Tribe History." *Access Genealogy.* http://www.accessgenealogy.com/native/tribes/nations/arikara.htm (accessed on June 19, 2011).

"The History and Culture of the Mandan, Hidatsa, and Sahnish: Sahnish Creation Stories." *North Dakota Studies.* http://www.ndstudies.org/resources/IndianStudies/threeaffiliated/culture_sahnish1.html (accessed on June 19, 2011).

Mandan-Hidatsa-Arikara Nation. http://www.mhanation.com/main/flash.html (accessed on June 19, 2011).

"Ranching: Community Stories: Fort Berthold." *Canadian Museum of Civilization.* April 1, 2010. http://www.civilization.ca/cmc/exhibitions/aborig/rodeo/rodeo20e.shtml (accessed on June 19, 2011).

Redish, Laura, and Orrin Lewis. "Arikara Indian Fact Sheet. *Native Languages of the Americas.* http://www.bigorrin.org/arikara_kids.htm (accessed on June 19, 2011).

Virtual Archaeologist. "The Like-a-Fishhook Story." *NDSU Archaeology Technologies Laboratory.* http://fishhook.ndsu.edu/home/lfstory.php (accessed on June 19, 2011).

Blackfoot

Name

The Blackfeet, or Blackfoot, call themselves *Niitsitapii,* meaning "the real people." The Crow name for the tribe was *Siksika,* or "blackfeet people," referring to their moccasin soles, which were darkened either by paint or by walking on charred prairie grasses. Although Blackfeet is the official name the government gave the tribe and the reservation, the word is not plural in their language, so most tribe members in Montana prefer to be called "Blackfoot." First Nations in Canada go by the name Blackfoot.

Location

The three tribes in the Blackfoot Confederacy—the Blackfoot proper, the Piikani or Piegan (pronounced *PEE-gun*), and the Blood—occupied the northwestern part of the Great Plains from the northern reaches of the Saskatchewan River in Alberta, Canada, to the southernmost headwaters of the Missouri River in Montana in the United States. As of the early 2000s, Blackfoot people were scattered throughout the United States. Many live in northwestern Montana on the Blackfeet Reservation (bounded by Canada on the north and Glacier National Park on the west), and large numbers live in the states of Washington and California. The Blackfoot people of Canada live in southeastern Alberta.

Population

In the early 1800s, there were an estimated 5,200 Blackfoot. In the 1990s, about 15,000 Blackfoot lived on three reserves in Canada, while about 10,000 lived on the Blackfeet Reservation in Montana. In the 1990 U.S. Census, 37,992 people identified themselves as Blackfoot. In 2000, the U.S. Census showed 28,731 Blackfoot, with 85,750 people claiming to have some Blackfoot heritage, making it the eighth-largest tribal grouping in the United States. In 2007, the Canadian First Nation Profiles indicated that 18,782 Blackfoot resided on and off the reserves. By 2010, the census counted 27,279 Blackfoot in the United States, with a total of 105,304 people claiming some Blackfoot heritage.

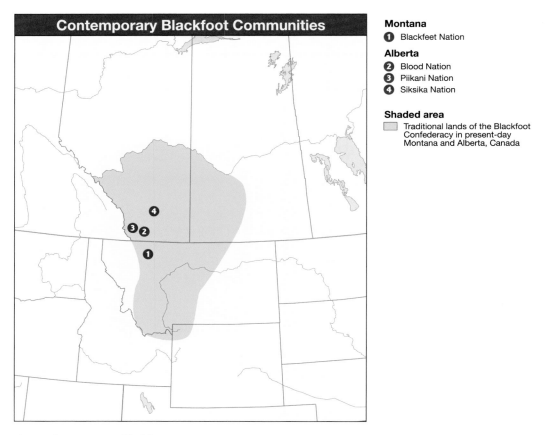

Contemporary Blackfoot Communities

Montana
❶ Blackfeet Nation

Alberta
❷ Blood Nation
❸ Piikani Nation
❹ Siksika Nation

Shaded area
Traditional lands of the Blackfoot Confederacy in present-day Montana and Alberta, Canada

A map of contemporary Blackfoot communities. MAP BY XNR PRODUCTIONS. CENGAGE LEARNING, GALE. REPRODUCED BY PERMISSION OF GALE, A PART OF CENGAGE LEARNING.

Language family

Algonquian.

Origins and group affiliations

The Blackfoot Confederacy is an alliance of three tribes who speak the same language and practice the same culture. Their ancestors may have come to North America thousands of years ago from Asia, crossing a land bridge between Siberia and Alaska. The ancient people probably traveled south, then moved east and north to their present-day region.

The members of the Blackfoot Confederation are the Piikani (or Piegan), meaning "the poorly dressed ones"; the Blood, or Akainawa (also called Kainai), meaning "many chiefs"; and the Siksika, or Blackfoot proper (also known as the Northern Blackfoot). The Blackfoot, along with the Sarcee and

Gros Ventre (see Arapaho entry), were all Algonquian speakers. The tribe's enemies included the Shoshone and Nez Perce (see entries).

For centuries, the Blackfoot wandered the rolling plains that rise westward to the forests of the Rocky Mountains. There they hunted buffalo and gathered wild plants, and they earned the distinction of being, according to the artist and author George Catlin (1796–1872) in 1866, "the most powerful tribe in North America." As American settlers moved west, Blackfoot life was greatly disrupted by the extinction of the buffalo and the devastating diseases the settlers carried with them. In recent years, the tribe has battled poverty and assimilation (the adoption of American ways) by developing their own businesses and passing their traditions down to succeeding generations. One of the few tribes to still live in their traditional homelands, the Blackfoot, who were once called the Lords of the Plains, believe their "true greatness is still yet to come."

Hunters from the Blackfoot tribe ride their horses among a herd of buffalo in Montana in the 1800s. © STOCK MONTAGE/ CONTRIBUTOR/ARCHIVE PHOTOS/GETTY IMAGES.

U•X•L Encyclopedia of Native American Tribes, 3rd Edition

HISTORY

Powerful tribe of Northern Plains

The Blackfoot migrated onto North America's Great Plains from the eastern woodlands before the Europeans arrived. The people followed the enormous herds of buffalo, using tame dogs to carry their belongings. This period before they began using horses and firearms is known as the "Dog Days."

The Blackfoot used arrows and lances in wars with the Shoshone, Plains Cree, Assiniboin, and Flathead (see entries). Most often, their allies were their friendly neighbors, the Gros Ventre (*grow VAHNT*) and Sarcee. After acquiring horses and firearms around the middle of the eighteenth century, the Blackfoot became one of the most powerful tribes of the Northern Plains. By the middle of the nineteenth century, they had pushed their enemies, particularly the Shoshone (see entry), westward across the Rocky Mountains.

Impact of settlers on the tribe

The first known outsiders to visit the region of the Blackfoot were fur trappers who came in the middle of the eighteenth century. They were exploring the West hoping to establish trading relationships with the Native peoples. Among them was British agent and fur trapper David Thompson (1770–1857), who traveled into Blackfoot territory in 1787 and wrote in detail about the tribe. From this date until the buffalo disappeared in the early 1880s, the tribe's relationship with the trading companies became vital to Blackfoot economic and social life.

From their contact with the trading posts, the tribe was introduced to new technologies, such as the gun. They also encountered diseases to which they had no immunity, which led to outbreaks of smallpox in 1781, 1837, and 1869 that killed off many people in the tribe.

Blackfoot protect their territory

In the early 1800s, American explorer Meriwether Lewis (1774–1809) encountered the Blackfoot on one of his journeys. As Lewis discovered, the people he referred to as "strong and honest" could also be aggressive.

Blackfoot horse raiders attacked the party of eight men he led. Lewis and his men escaped and fled the area.

Shortly after 1810, the tribes living near the Blackfoot took sides in the American and British struggle for land. The Blackfoot did everything possible to keep both sides out of their territory, but during the 1820s, there was a new push by trappers who wanted the Blackfoot land. The tribe tried to stop their progress. In 1823 alone, they killed more than twenty-five trappers and stole the guns and supplies of countless more.

By the end of the 1830s, however, overtrapping and the loss of the beaver supply caused most trappers to pull out of the area. In the 1840s, a substantial number of American settlers on their way West traveled through the southern part of the Blackfoot territory. In the mid-nineteenth century, with the discovery of gold nearby, gold seekers flooded the Blackfoot region.

Treaties limit the Blackfoot

Over the years, the Blackfoot were particularly hostile to the whites they encountered, in part due to problems and misunderstandings from earlier days. Settlers moving west heard about the reputation of the Blackfoot as fierce warriors and were terrified of them. The settlers, determined to obtain Blackfoot land, applied to the U.S. government for protection, so the government made treaties with the tribe. In time, the Blackfoot lost much of their territory to the United States through these agreements.

In 1851, the Treaty of Fort Laramie limited the boundaries of the Blackfoot territory in the United States, even though no Blackfoot attended the negotiations. In 1855, the Blackfoot signed their first treaty, known as the Treaty of Lamed Bull for the powerful Piegan chief who signed it. This treaty stated that the U.S. government would pay the tribe $20,000 annually in goods and spend $15,000 each year toward educating and converting the Blackfoot to Christianity. In return, the Blackfoot would give up half of their hunting area and live peacefully with their white neighbors. The tribe also agreed to allow white settlers to build railroads and telephone and telegraph lines.

For a while, relations between the Blackfoot and the settlers improved. The Blackfoot helped the settlers hunt buffalo. They also traded buffalo hides for such supplies as beads, guns, wool, wagons, and food. Within a short time, however, the settlers abused the treaty. They gave the Black-foot spoiled food, damaged wagons, rusty guns, blankets with moth holes, and alcohol, which was to have a long-term negative effect on the people. Feeling disrespected and duped, the Blackfoot responded with anger.

The Baker Massacre

In the 1860s, hostilities with American settlers became so frequent that the Blood division of the Blackfoot, which usually split its time between Montana and the plains of what is now Alberta, Canada, decided to stay in Canada permanently. Its people joined the ranks of the northern Piegan, who had already made the decision to stay in Canada. Most of the Blackfoot who remained in the United States were southern Piegan.

In early 1870, a group of U.S. soldiers attacked the Piegan in an action that is called either the Piegan War or the Baker Massacre (for the U.S. Army major who led the attack). These Piegan had never been involved in aggression against the settlers and had recently undergone a severe smallpox epidemic. The soldiers arrived when most of the Piegan men were away on a hunting trip. The U.S. troops went ahead with their surprise raid and killed two hundred Piegan, mostly women, children, and the elderly. The Americans suffered only one death, probably the result of an accident. The incident drew much criticism from political and media groups.

Later in 1870, the Hudson's Bay Company, a trading operation, gave the area of Alberta where the northern Piegan lived to the Canadian government, which opened it up to settlers. To guard the area, the Canadian government established the North-West Mounted Police ("Mounties"). The Mounties won the respect of the Blackfoot for their fairness and courtesy.

Blackfoot treaties in the United States and Canada

The Blackfoot in the United States signed treaties in 1865 and 1868 that decreased their territory. Although the U.S. Congress never officially confirmed those treaties, an 1874 treaty officially established the Blackfeet Reservation in Montana. The Blackfoot gave up additional land from their reservation in treaties signed in 1887 and 1896. When it was discovered that there was little gold there, the land was made part of Glacier National Park. The conditions of the treaties are still being disputed today.

In 1877, with Treaty No. 7, the Canadian government established reserves in the province of Alberta for the Blood, North Piegan (Piikani), and Siksika (Blackfoot) people. Compared to the removal of Natives to reservations in the United States, the process in Canada went much more smoothly. At that time, the Canadians, wishing to avoid Indian wars like those of their American counterparts, generally treated the Natives more fairly and tried to honor their treaties.

Loss of the buffalo

By the 1880s, the buffalo on the Great Plains had become nearly extinct. Historians blame their disappearance on mass slaughter by white hunters, who killed the beasts for their tongues, which had become a tasty treat in Europe, and for their hides, which were made into fashionable clothing. Some men shot the animals from the windows of passing trains for sport, leaving the carcasses to rot on the Plains. In 1860, when manufacturing firms began using buffalo hide to make machine belts for industry, the price of hides skyrocketed, and the massacre of buffalo increased.

Blackfoot in the twentieth century

In the period following the disappearance of the buffalo, the Blackfoot people in Montana constantly faced starvation. From the late 1870s until 1935, they were dependent on the reservation agent for food and other essential supplies. In addition, they had to learn to adjust to the massive cultural change required by their new agricultural lifestyle.

After 1887, the U.S. government policy called allotment went into effect. Reservation lands in Montana were divided into parcels called allotments, and the Blackfoot were given small plots on which to farm or raise cattle. A drought that took place in 1919 and falling prices for beef forced many Blackfoot to give up their lands for non-payment of taxes.

New laws were passed in the 1930s that lessened the tribe's dependence on government support. Their lands were placed in trust, an arrangement in which the federal government oversees land use. Beginning in 1935 and extending into the 1960s, the Blackfoot became self-sufficient. In the early twenty-first century, the Blackfeet Reservation in Montana remains vital and many of its people support themselves through jobs in ranching, industry, and oil and natural gas. Today, it is home not only to Blackfoot people but to other tribes and non-Natives as well.

Blackfoot Words

Blackfoot words for living things such as animals and people often have the ending "wa" added to them. For example, the people sometimes say the word for buffalo *iinii*, and other times they use *iiniiwa*. Either way is correct.

Some words describe an object rather than giving it a name. An example of this is the word for dried apples (*ohtookiinaattsi*, which means "appear like ears") or for snack (*a'písttaapiksistaki*, which means "move about tasting food").

aakii(wa)	"woman"
ainihkiwa	"sing"
ainima	"see"
asaksiwa	"leave"
ayoohtsiwa	"hear"
ki'sómma	"sun"
ninaa(wa)	"man"
ni't	"one"
oki	"hello"
omitaa	"dog"
ponokáómitaa	"horse"
sipistoo	"owl"
sspopíi	"turtle"

RELIGION

The Blackfoot believed that the physical and supernatural worlds were closely bound together. Animals and natural elements had powers that humans could acquire. This transfer of power usually took place in a dream. An animal in human form appeared to the dreamer and provided him or her with a list of objects, songs, and rituals to use the animal's power. The dreamer gathered the objects and placed them in a rawhide pouch called a medicine bundle. The person then used the medicine bundle along with songs and rituals during social and religious ceremonies. Tribe members sometimes held elaborate ceremonies at which they traded medicine bundles.

The most powerful bundle was the beaver medicine bundle. This was used by the Beaver Men to charm the buffalo and to assist in planting the sacred tobacco. The beaver medicine bundle was also used during medicine pipe rituals, which took place during thunderstorms.

LANGUAGE

The Blackfoot dialect (variety) of the Algonquian language is related to the languages of several Plains, Eastern Woodlands, and Great Lakes tribes. The Blackfoot dialect was influenced by their isolation from other groups who spoke Algonquian and by interactions with speakers of other languages during the tribe's westward move. They did not have written symbols for their language, but they did record their traditional stories and important events, such as wars, in pictographs (picture symbols) on the internal and external surfaces of tepees and on their buffalo robes.

In the 1800s, British clergyman John William Tims developed a written language using symbols to represent sounds. He used his system to translate the Bible into the Blackfoot language. Today, the tribe uses an alphabet like that of the English language, but it has only ten consonants and three vowels; many times these are paired to make other sounds.

GOVERNMENT

The Blackfoot tribes were broken up into a number of hunting bands, each led by both war chiefs and civil chiefs. The war chief was chosen because of his reputation as a warrior, and the civil chief was chosen for his public speaking skills. One of the most important characteristics for a Blackfoot leader, though, was his generosity.

In 1934, the U.S. Congress passed the Indian Reorganization Act (IRA) to stop the damage that the policies of the General Allotment Act of 1887 (also known as the Dawes Act) had done to the people on reservations all over the country. The IRA restored some land to tribes and encouraged a form of self-government on the reservations. For the Blackfoot, the new act stemmed the tribe's land losses by placing most of their land into trust status, an arrangement whereby the federal government oversees land.

In the early 2000s, the affairs of the tribe were run by the Tribal Business Council of the Blackfoot Reservation in Browning, Montana, which had nine members who serve staggered four-year terms. Three of the four districts elect two members to the council, and the Browning District elects three. The council then nominates its own officers, including a chairperson, vice chairperson, secretary, and sergeant-at-arms.

The Blackfoot reserves in Canada are run by a single governing body with one chairperson. As in the past, the Blackfoot still make their decisions by consensus, or agreement among all the members. In 2007, the Piikani Nation, who had been under third-party management for several years due to tribal difficulties, elected a new chief and council.

ECONOMY

Early economy In the early days, the Blackfoot were a wandering people who depended on hunting for their food. The buffalo supplied not only most of their nutritional needs but the raw materials for clothing and shelter. In time the tribe engaged in fur trading, particularly with the British.

Around 1915, the U.S. government stopped urging the Blackfoot on the reservation to engage in farming, as they had for several decades, and suggested they begin raising livestock. However, a 1919 drought and a huge drop in beef prices forced many Blackfoot to give up their land because they were unable to pay their taxes. In the 1920s, a tribal leader encouraged the people to begin small, manageable farms growing grains and vegetables.

Modern economy In the early twenty-first century, many people grow grains and raise livestock. Others make their living in construction, tourism, and the timber industry. About one-third of the people on the reservation are employed by the tribal government. Many of these jobs are linked to federal government programs such as building government-funded housing. Still others work in a variety of professions on and off the reservation.

Pikuni Industries produces and erects modular homes, and in 2009, the company went into partnership to test and develop lightweight materials for missile construction for the government. Small businesses manufacture tepees and canvas carrying bags. The tribe also produces bottled water. Hundreds of retail and service operations provide jobs for the tribe and generate revenue. In addition, the tribe owns Blackfeet Industrial Park. On the Canadian reserves, manufactured items include houses, clothing, moccasins, and Native crafts.

Coal, oil, and natural gas have generated a good income for the Montana tribe in recent years. The Blackfoot lease these fields and receive a portion of the profit. The Blackfeet Coalfield may have as much as thirty to fifty million tons of coal. The reservation has other resources that could be exploited, including gold, silver, lead, and zinc.

DAILY LIFE

Families

Two men, three women, and three children made up the typical Blackfoot family. Perhaps because many Blackfoot men died in battle and there were excess numbers of women, men often had more than one wife. Second and third wives were usually sisters of the first wife. The wives worked together on the daily chores.

Buildings

Because of their hunting lifestyle, the Blackfoot built single-family tepees that were easy to construct and move. The women of the tribe carried and built the houses. They used about nineteen pine poles for the frame,

Tepees stand on a Blackfoot encampment in the 1930s.
NATIONAL ARCHIVES AND RECORDS ADMINISTRATION. REPRODUCED BY PERMISSION.

each averaging 18 feet (5 meters) in length. They covered the poles with six to twenty buffalo skins, often decorated with pictures of animals and geometric designs. Furnishings included buffalo robes for beds and willow backrests.

After the buffalo disappeared and the reservations were created, the Blackfoot replaced their tepees with log cabins. These homes were the symbol of a new, sedentary way of life, in which ranching and agriculture became the primary means of survival.

Clothing and adornment

The Blackfoot used buffalo, deer, elk, and antelope skins to make their clothing. Women fashioned ankle-length sleeveless dresses held up by straps. They decorated them with porcupine quills, cut fringe, and simple geometric designs colored with earth pigments. In the winter, they added separate skin sleeves to the dresses, and buffalo robes provided warmth. After contact with American traders, clothing changed. Women used wool and cloth to make many of their garments. However, the buffalo robe remained an important piece of clothing during the nineteenth century.

Men wore leggings made of antelope skin, as well as moccasins, shirts, and buckskin breechcloths (flaps of material that hung from the waist and covered the front and back). War shirts were fringed and decorated with dyed porcupine quills, beads, and elk teeth. In the winter, men wore long buffalo robes, often decorated with earth pigments or plant dyes and elaborate porcupine quill embroidery. They braided their hair and arranged the front into a topknot on their foreheads.

Most Blackfoot men wore traditional dress until the last decade of the nineteenth century. Faced with pressure from Christian missionaries, they began to wear what was called "citizen's dress." This outfit consisted of a coat and pants, but the Blackfoot replaced the stiff leather shoes of the Americans with moccasins.

Blackfoot men usually wore their hair long and loose, whereas women parted theirs and wore it in long braids. Both men and women frequently washed and brushed their hair and applied buffalo fat to make it shine. They wore necklaces of braided sweet grass. Men also donned necklaces made from the claws and teeth of bears; women's bracelets were of elk or deer teeth.

Food

Buffalo was boiled, roasted, or dried. Pieces of fresh meat were cooked with wild roots and vegetables to make a stew, and intestines were cleaned and stuffed with meat mixture to make sausage. Dried meat was stored in rawhide pouches or was made into pemmican, an important food source during the winter and at other times when buffalo were scarce. Men also hunted other large game, such as deer, moose, mountain sheep, antelope, and elk, but most Blackfoot considered fish, reptiles, and grizzly bears unfit for human consumption.

Blackfoot women gathered roots, prairie turnips, bitterroot, and camas bulbs to supplement buffalo meat. They also picked wild berries,

Strips of buffalo meat are hung to dry to make pemmican, a staple food for many Native tribes. © NORTH WIND PICTURE ARCHIVES.

chokecherries, and buffalo or bull berries, and gathered the bark of the cottonwood trees to use the sweet inside portions.

Education

Traditional learning Blackfoot boys learned to hunt, track game, endure physical pain, and recognize signals from both the physical and spiritual worlds. Girls were trained to prepare food and clothing, sew and do bead work, and tan hides.

Catholic and government schools Beginning in 1859, Roman Catholic missionaries introduced Catholic religious practices and educational systems to the Blackfoot people. Catholic priests started schools to teach the Native peoples to farm and raise cattle. The priests served as go-betweens for the Blackfoot and whites. They also learned the Blackfoot language and helped to preserve it by translating Christian texts into the language.

The Catholic influence lessened in the early 1900s, when the federal government established a boarding school and day schools for the Native Americans. One of the purposes of the government schools was to prevent the children from speaking their native language or from following their traditional ways or religion. Children were punished for singing Native songs or doing tribal dances. These schools were often overcrowded and unsanitary. Canadian officials established similar schools sponsored by the Church of England.

Modern educational programs During the 1960s and 1970s, the Montana Blackfeet encouraged tribal elders to teach the native language and old customs to the young people. Head Start programs on the reservation now teach the Algonquian language and Blackfoot cultural values. Similar programs have also been created for adults at neighboring colleges, including the Blackfeet Community College in Browning, Montana. A Blackfoot dictionary was published in 1989 and a Blackfoot grammar book two years later in Alberta.

Browning, Montana, has schools for students from kindergarten through twelfth grade. The tribe also operates Blackfeet Community College and provides financial assistance to students who wish to attend universities.

The Blackfoot in Montana established a program to reduce alcoholism. Programs teach children to make good choices. Instruction in outdoor skills and crafts involves the children in worthwhile activities and encourages a sense of pride in their traditions.

Many Canadian educational organizations and school districts have programs to include aboriginal language and cultural traditions into their lesson plans. Teachers are making efforts to use these materials in their classrooms. By the early 2000s, most Canadian children were learning about their multicultural heritage and history.

Healing practices

The Blackfoot believed that spirits were an active part of everyday life. Illness was understood as the visible presence of an evil spirit in a person's body. Only a professional medicine person who had acquired the ability to heal the sick in a vision could cure these illnesses. Many of the most popular Blackfoot physicians were women.

During healing ceremonies, a medicine person might remove some object from the sick person's body (an object the healer may have brought with her). The healer presented the object to the patient as proof that the ceremony had been successful. Healers used natural herbs in treating lesser injuries, such as cuts. Patients often offered horses as payment for a medicine person's services.

ARTS

Crafts

The Blackfoot were known for their fine craftwork, and their tepees, weapons, and riding equipment were beautifully designed. On the reservation, the people used supplies from traders, such as brass tacks and bells, to create elaborately beaded headdresses, clothing, and accessories. In the early 2000s, the Museum of the Plains Indian in Browning, Montana, featured Blackfoot pottery, clothing, art, decorative items, moccasins, shields, and jewelry.

Music

Men were the main singers in the Blackfoot tribe, as it was considered inappropriate for women to sing alone. Few instruments accompanied the singers, with the exception of percussion such as drums, rattles, sticks, or bells. Most songs came to the singers in visions and dreams, so they were not necessarily for the purpose of communicating with others. For this reason, many songs are composed of sounds rather than words. Songs with words were often short and used to pass down tribal stories. Children did not have songs except mice songs used in a game or lullabies sung by their mothers.

CUSTOMS

Gender roles

Unlike many other tribes, the Blackfoot were somewhat flexible about what they considered male or female work. Men sometimes sewed their own clothing, and married women could become healers. Before the 1880s, it was common for a young married woman with no children to

Origin of the Medicine Pipe

In this Blackfoot tale, the Thunder has stolen a man's wife. The man begs Raven for help. Raven gives him a raven's wing to make Thunder jump back and an elk-horn arrow to shoot through the Thunder's lodge if that does not work.

So the man took these things, and went to the Thunder's lodge. He entered and sat down by the doorway. The Thunder sat within and looked at him with awful eyes. But the man looked above, and saw those many pairs of eyes. Among them were those of his wife.

"Why have you come?" said the Thunder in a fearful voice.

"I seek my wife," the man replied, "whom you have stolen. There hang her eyes."

"No man can enter my lodge and live," said the Thunder, and he rose to strike him. Then the man pointed the raven wing at the Thunder, and he fell back on his couch and shivered. But he soon recovered and rose again. Then the man fitted the elk-horn arrow to his bow, and shot it through the lodge of rock. Right through the lodge of rock it pierced a jagged hole, and let the sunlight in.

"Hold," said the Thunder. "Stop, you are the stronger. Yours is the great medicine. You shall have your wife. Take down her eyes." Then the man cut the string that held them, and immediately his wife stood beside him.

"Now," said the Thunder, "You know me. I am of great power. I live here in summer, but when winter comes, I go far south. I go south with the birds. Here is my pipe. It is medicine. Take it and keep it. Now, when I first come in the spring, you shall fill and light this pipe, and you shall pray to me, you and the people, for I bring the rain which makes the berries large and ripe. I bring the rain which makes all things grow, and for this you shall pray to me, you and all the people."

Thus the people got the first medicine pipe. It was long ago.

SOURCE: McNeese, Tim. "Origin of the Medicine Pipe." *Illustrated Myths of Native America: The Southwest, Western Range, Pacific Northwest and California.* London, UK: Blandford, 1998.

go along with the men into battle, on a hunt, or on raids. Although these women joined in the duty of preparing food, they also engaged in waging war and herding stolen horses back to their tribe. Some nineteenth-century women, such as Elk Hollering in the Water, became well known as skillful horse raiders. The most famous woman warrior, Running Eagle, led hunting, raiding, and warring parties and could outride and outshoot most of her male companions.

Festivals and ceremonies

The major community religious ceremony, the Sun Dance, was held each year in late summer. Proper preparations by the medicine woman in charge and the dancers determined the success or failure of the Sun Dance. First, the people erected a Sun Dance lodge around a central cottonwood pole in the village. Dancers prepared by making sacred vows and fasting from both food and water. Then the dance, which lasted for four days, began.

Dancers sang sacred songs and chants and called on the sun to grant them power, luck, or success. Some dancers pierced their breasts with sticks, which they then attached to the center pole by rawhide ropes. Summoning their courage, the dancers pulled away from the pole until the skewers tore free. Sometimes men and women would cut off fingers or gouge pieces of flesh from their arms and legs. Government officials forbade the Sun Dance in the late nineteenth and early twentieth centuries, but it never totally disappeared. Some Blackfoot still perform it to this day.

In the early 2000s, Canadian Blackfoot in Alberta sponsored the Blackfoot Indians Art Show at Head-Smashed-In Buffalo Jump, a World Heritage site, where tribes of long ago drove buffalo over the edge of a cliff during their hunts. The show featured Native paintings, beadwork, quillwork, and sculpture along with a selection of Native fare, including frybread, buffalo and venison pemmican, griddlecakes, and jams and jellies from berries found on Blackfoot land. The tribe also offered many other arts-related events throughout the year, such as puppet shows, dancing and drumming, storytelling, and craft instruction.

Every year, the Blackfeet Powwow is held in Browning, Montana. The four-day celebration,

A young member of the Blackfoot tribe dances at a powwow. © STEVE KAUFMAN/ CORBIS.

open to Natives and non-Natives alike, features singing and dancing, storytelling, drumming, and various games. On the menu are Native foods such as boiled beef and deer meat, boiled potatoes, sarvisberry soup, baking powder bread, and fry bread. The powwow also serves to educate non-Natives about Blackfoot ways.

Buffalo hunting

The buffalo was the primary source of food, clothing, shelter, household supplies, and military equipment. The people had more than sixty different uses for parts of the buffalo. Until the near disappearance of the buffalo in the late 1870s, the animals roamed the Plains in huge herds. In earlier times, people chased the buffalo on foot, surrounded the herd, and drove the animals off a cliff. Once they had horses, they preferred to charge the buffalo on fast, well-trained horses called buffalo runners. This method of hunting required courage and skill.

Societies

Blackfoot warrior societies had the duty of protecting the people, keeping order, punishing offenders, and organizing raids and hunts. There were societies for each age group. For example, young boys might belong to the Doves, whereas men who were waiting to become warriors were part of the Mosquitoes, and warriors might belong to the Braves. The most respected societies were the Bulls and the Brave Dogs, made up of men who had proven themselves in battle. Other Blackfoot societies practiced medicine, magic, and dance. An arts society was largely made up of women.

Courtship and marriage

Blackfoot marriages were arranged by the bride's parents when she was still a child or later by close friends or relatives of the couple. Before a wedding could take place, the groom had to convince the bride's father, relatives, or friends that he was worthy. This meant that he had to prove that he was a powerful warrior, a competent hunter, and a good provider. Because of these requirements, very few men married before the age of twenty-one.

Gift exchanging was central to the marriage ceremony. Horses were among the most valuable gifts, and the families of the young couple also gave them household goods and robes. After the wedding, the bride and groom lived either in their own hut or in the home of the husband's family.

Funerals

People who were dying made known their wishes for the distribution of their possessions. When no such arrangement was made, members of the tribe simply took whatever they could gather after the person died.

The face of the dead person was painted, and the body was dressed in fancy clothes and wrapped in buffalo robes. The people either placed the corpse between the forks of a tree or buried it atop a hill or in a ravine. Both men and women mourned the death of loved ones by cutting their hair, wearing old clothes, and smearing their faces with white clay.

When a prominent chief of the Canadian Blackfoot died, his possessions were left within his lodge, and his horses were shot. The Blackfoot believed that the spirit of the deceased did not leave this world but traveled to the Sand Hills, an area south of the Saskatchewan River. Invisible spirits of the dead lived there much as they had in life and often communicated with the living who passed through the region.

CURRENT TRIBAL ISSUES

In 2009, a difficulty arose with a new requirement that people must show passports when they cross the United States–Canada border. The Jay Treaty of 1795 granted North American tribes the freedom to trade and travel between the two countries. In spite of this, many Blackfoot are stopped and questioned at the border, and some have even been denied entry. This is particularly difficult for tribes that have reservations on both sides of the border.

The Blackfoot have always been concerned with their land, which is both sacred and important to their survival. The tribe is working to protect and maintain the natural resources within the boundaries of Glacier National Park. They want to ensure the appropriate use of reservation lands by both members and nonmembers.

The Blackfoot people are concerned about the preservation of their culture. They have established programs to strengthen the sense of community, which may help the tribe overcome such social problems as alcoholism, poverty, and crime. The tribe is also making efforts to further develop industry, the use of oil and natural gas resources, and improve the maintenance of ranches on the reservation.

NOTABLE PEOPLE

At the age of seven, Earl Old Person (1929–) began presenting Blackfoot culture in songs and dances at statewide events. For many years, he served as chairperson of the Blackfeet Tribal Business Council. Under his guidance, recreational, industrial, and housing projects were completed on the reservation. Old Person also served as head of a number of nationally recognized Native organizations. In 1978, Old Person received an honorary lifetime appointment as chief of the Blackfoot Nation. His efforts have made for better relations between Native communities and the larger U.S. society.

Other notable Blackfoot include Canadian architect Douglas Cardinal (1934–); Blood tribal leader Crowfoot (c. 1830–1890); Blood politician James Gladstone (1887–1971); painter Gerald Tailfeathers (1925–1975); and Blackfoot/Gros Ventre novelist James Welch (1940–2003).

BOOKS

Bullchild, Percy. *The Sun Came Down: The History of the World as My Blackfeet Elders Told It*. Lincoln: University of Nebraska Press, 2005.

Dempsey, L. James. *Blackfoot War Art: Pictographs of the Reservation Period, 1880–2000*. Norman: University of Oklahoma Press, 2007.

Eggermont-Molenaar, Mary, and Paul Callens, eds. *Missionaries among Miners, Immigrants, and Blackfoot: The Van Tighem Brothers' Diaries, Alberta 1876–1917*. Calgary, AB, Canada: University of Calgary Press, 2007.

Ewers, John C. *The Blackfeet: Raiders on the Northwestern Plains*. Norman: University of Oklahoma Press, 1958.

Ewers, John C. *Indian Life on the Upper Missouri*. Norman: University of Oklahoma Press, 1968.

Grafe, Steven L. ed. *Lanterns on the Prairie: The Blackfeet Photographs of Walter McClintock*. Norman: University of Oklahoma Press, 2009.

Grinnell, George Bird. *Blackfeet Indians Stories*. Whitefish, MT: Kessinger Publishing, 2006.

King, David C. *The Blackfeet*. New York: Marshall Cavendish Benchmark, 2010.

Lacey, T. Jensen. *The Blackfeet*. New York: Chelsea House, 2011.

Stout, Mary. *Blackfoot History and Culture*. New York: Gareth Stevens, 2012.

Wischmann, Lesley. *Frontier Diplomats: Alexander Culbertson and Natoyist-Siksina' among the Blackfeet*. Norman: University of Oklahoma Press, 2004.

Wissler, Clark, and D.C. Duvall, translators. *Mythology of the Blackfoot Indians*. 2nd ed. Lincoln: University of Nebraska Press, 2007.

WEB SITES

"Blackfeet." *Wisdom of the Elders.* http://www.wisdomoftheelders.org/program208.html (accessed on July 2, 2011).

"Blackfeet (Blackfoot)." *Four Directions Institute.* http://www.fourdir.com/blackfeet.htm (accessed on July 2, 2011).

Blackfeet Nation. http://www.blackfeetnation.com/ (accessed on July 2, 2011).

"Blackfoot History." *Head-Smashed-In Buffalo Jump Interpretive Centre.* http://www.head-smashed-in.com/black.html (accessed on July 2, 2011).

"Blackfoot Indian Nations." *AAA Native Arts.* http://blackfeet.aaanativearts.com/ (accessed on July 2, 2011).

Blackfoot Nation. http://www.blackfoot.org/ (accessed on July 2, 2011).

Kainai—Blood Tribe. http://www.bloodtribe.org/ (accessed on July 2, 2011).

"Treaty 7 Past and Present." *Heritage Community Foundation.* http://www.albertasource.ca/treaty7/traditional/index.html (accessed on July 2, 2011).

Cheyenne

Name

The name Cheyenne (pronounced *shy-ANN*) is derived from the Sioux word *shyela* or *shaiena,* meaning "red talkers" or "people of different speech." Other sources suggest that the Dakota word *s`ahiyenan,* meaning "relatives of the Cree" or "little Cree," gave the tribe their name. The Cheyenne call themselves *Tsitsistas* or *Bzitsiistas,* meaning "beautiful people," "like-hearted people," or "our people." Another name for one of the Cheyenne groups is *Sotaeo'o.*

Location

Originally from the Great Lakes area in present-day Minnesota, the Cheyenne moved westward as other tribes took over their land. They settled in North and South Dakota, but they were later forced into the Black Hills of South Dakota and Wyoming. When the tribe split in the early 1800s, some Cheyenne moved to Colorado along the Arkansas River. In the late 1800s, both Southern and Northern Cheyenne were sent to Oklahoma reservations. The Northern Cheyenne fled to Nebraska and were later moved to Montana. In the early twenty-first century, most Cheyenne people live on the Great Plains, mainly in Montana and South Dakota, and in Oklahoma.

Population

Although early estimates of the Cheyenne population varied widely, one estimate says that 3,500 Cheyenne lived on the Great Plains in 1800. In the 1990 U.S. Census, 7,104 people identified themselves as members of the Cheyenne tribe. By 2000, that number had increased to 11,426, and 19,704 people said they were at least part Cheyenne; in 2010, the census counted 11,375 Cheyenne, with a total of 19,051 people claiming Cheyenne heritage. However, in 2011, the Oklahoma Indian Affairs Commission showed 12,185 enrolled members of the Cheyenne and Arapaho Tribe living in the state. The Northern Cheyenne Nation in Montana had an enrollment of 9,945, with about 4,868 of those members living on the reservation.

Language family

Algonquian.

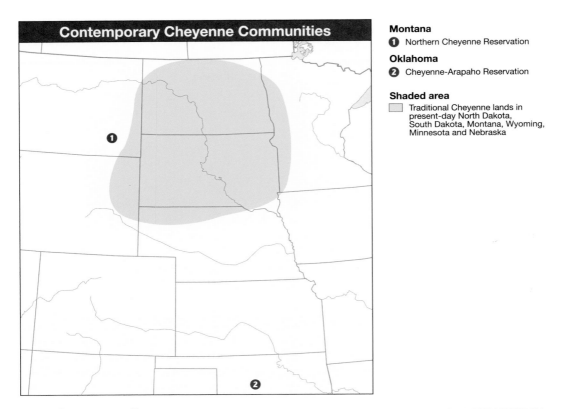

Contemporary Cheyenne Communities

Montana
❶ Northern Cheyenne Reservation

Oklahoma
❷ Cheyenne-Arapaho Reservation

Shaded area
Traditional Cheyenne lands in present-day North Dakota, South Dakota, Montana, Wyoming, Minnesota and Nebraska

A map of contemporary Cheyenne communities. MAP BY XNR PRODUCTIONS. CENGAGE LEARNING, GALE. REPRODUCED BY PERMISSION OF GALE, A PART OF CENGAGE LEARNING.

Origins and group affiliations

The Cheyenne people, who once lived near the Great Lakes, were forced to move west by other eastern tribes who used guns obtained from the Europeans. In the Great Plains, the tribe united with another tribe, the Sutaio, who had also been forced out of their Great Lakes home. The Sioux referred to the new group as *ha hiye na,* meaning "people of alien speech."

The Cheyenne traded with all the Great Plains tribes, but their closest ally was the Arapaho (see entry). Although they often got along well with the Kiowa, the Lakota, and the Comanche (see entries), at other times, the tribes fought. The two main groups of Cheyenne now live on the Northern Cheyenne Reservation in Montana and the Cheyenne-Arapaho Reservation in Oklahoma.

The story of the Cheyenne people is one of relocation. They were forced to move westward by their constant search for stable food sources and by pressure from other tribes who were being pushed into the West by the gradual expansion of the European-American population. The Cheyenne were known for having one of the most highly organized governments among the Native groups. They were also renowned for their mighty warriors, their ethics, and their spiritual ways.

HISTORY

The Cheyenne move west

The Cheyenne probably had their origins in the western Great Lakes region of present-day Minnesota. In the early 1600s, they had occasional contact with French and British fur traders. The first Europeans to encounter them were probably French explorers who were building Fort Crevecoeur at a site on the Illinois River in present-day Minnesota. The Cheyenne lived nearby in farming communities. During the late 1600s, the Cheyenne moved into what is now North and South Dakota

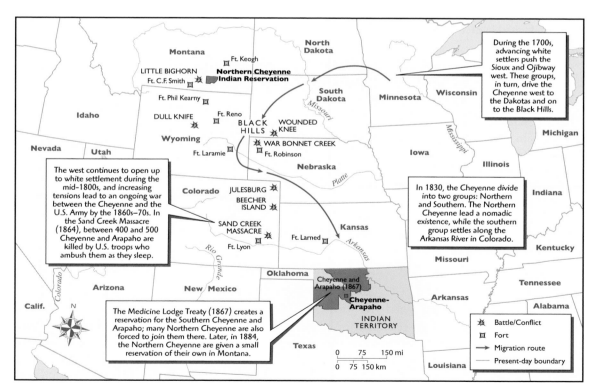

A map of the migrations of the Cheyenne, 1700–1884. MAP BY XNR PRODUCTIONS. CENGAGE LEARNING, GALE. REPRODUCED BY PERMISSION OF GALE, A PART OF CENGAGE LEARNING.

Important Dates

1825: The Cheyenne divide into Northern and Southern groups.

1851: The Cheyenne are one of eleven tribes to sign the Treaty of Fort Laramie, which promises annual payments to the tribes for their land.

1864: More than one hundred sleeping Cheyenne and Arapaho are killed by U.S. soldiers in the Sand Creek Massacre.

1876: The Northern Cheyenne join with the Sioux in defeating Lieutenant Colonel George Custer at the Battle of Little Bighorn.

1884: The Northern Cheyenne Reservation is established in eastern Montana.

1989–90: Passage of the National Museum of the American Indian Act and the Native American Grave Protection and Repatriation Act brings about the return of their burial remains.

2004: Southern Cheyenne Peace Chief W. Richard West Jr. becomes director of the newly opened National Museum of the American Indian in Washington, D.C.

where they built villages of earthen dwellings and farmed the land.

In time, pressure from the Sioux tribes and the Ojibway (see entries) drove the Cheyenne even farther west into the area of the Black Hills. By the 1800s, the Cheyenne were able to hunt for food on horseback. (Horses were introduced to the Americas by the Spanish.) Many left their villages to follow the buffalo herds across the Great Plains. In the first quarter of the nineteenth century, the tribe split into two groups. The Northern Cheyenne preferred to roam the northern country in search of horses and buffalo. The Southern Cheyenne chose to take up permanent residence along the Arkansas River in Colorado.

Conflict

During the mid-nineteenth century, the fortunes of the Cheyenne underwent great change. The United States took much of the land in the West, and settlers streamed westward. They traveled on trails that led through the land of many Great Plains tribes, including the Cheyenne. The increasing white population caused a rapid decline in the number of buffalo. As a result, armed conflicts between the Native groups and settlers (and U.S. soldiers who came to protect them) grew more and more common. The federal government tried to safeguard settlers and to pay tribes for their losses of buffalo and land.

The Sand Creek Massacre

In 1851, the U.S. government and eleven tribes, including the Cheyenne, signed the Treaty of Fort Laramie, which provided that the federal government give annual payments to the Great Plains Indians. It also clearly defined the boundaries of the territory belonging to each tribe. In return, the Native nations agreed that the United States could build roads and military posts in their territories. They also agreed to end warfare among themselves and stop their attacks on settlers. By 1856, though, tensions began again as the numbers of settlers crossing Indian Territory (in present-day Oklahoma) grew. From 1857 to 1879, a war broke out between the Cheyenne and the U.S. Army. The bloodiest encounter of that war was the Sand Creek Massacre.

In 1861, the Southern Cheyenne chief Black Kettle (c. 1812–1868), who tried to secure peace with honor for his people, signed a treaty giving up all their lands to the United States, except the small Sand Creek Reservation in southern Colorado. The barren land could not support the people, so in time many young Cheyenne men had to prey upon the livestock and goods of nearby settlers to survive. After one of the Cheyenne raids, Coloradans sent an armed force that opened fire on the first group of Cheyenne they met.

Black Kettle spoke with the local military commander and was told he and his people would be safe if they stayed at the Sand Creek Reservation. On November 29, 1864, a large group of Cheyenne and Arapaho people lay sleeping at their camp at Sand Creek. In short order, Colonel John M. Chivington (1821–1894) and his Colorado Volunteers slaughtered 105 women and children and 28 men. Women were mercilessly attacked, children beheaded, and old people dismembered.

Chief Black Kettle rode into the gunfire waving his American flag to show he was under the protection of the American government, but his efforts to stop the attack on his people failed. The Cheyenne and Arapaho's horses were scattered across the Plains, and their settlement was destroyed by fire. In the conflict, only nine soldiers were killed and thirty-eight were wounded. Soon after the slaughter, soldiers paraded through the streets of Denver with body parts of the victims displayed on the ends of their daggers. The U.S. Congress later held a series of hearings that led to the formal condemnation of the event and the men who were in charge of the massacre.

Native Americans defeat Custer

The Medicine Lodge Treaty of 1867 created a reservation for the Southern Cheyenne and Arapaho in northern Oklahoma, but the Northern Cheyenne continued fighting the Americans. The conflict peaked with the 1876 Battle of Little Bighorn, when the tribe helped the Sioux defeat Lieutenant Colonel George Custer (1839–1876). In retaliation, U.S. troops rounded up the Northern Cheyenne who had participated in the battle and forced them to move onto the Cheyenne reservation in Oklahoma. The people missed their northern homeland and found conditions on the reservation unbearable. In 1878, they

Cheyenne people travel by horse and foot to their reservation in the 1870s. © NORTH WIND PICTURE ARCHIVES.

escaped and fled north. U.S. troops captured them in Nebraska, and many perished from gunfire and ill treatment by the soldiers. The survivors were sent to Montana, and six years later, in 1884, they were given a small reservation of their own there.

Tribe fragmented

By the 1880s, the buffalo had been hunted to near extinction. As a result, the Cheyenne grew dependent on the government for food, shelter, and clothing. State officials in both Oklahoma and Montana attempted to

A Cheyenne man named Stump Horn poses with his family in the late 1890s. SMITHSONIAN INSTITUTION. BUREAU OF AMERICAN ETHNOLOGY. (1897–1965)/NATIONAL ARCHIVES.

introduce cattle raising and encouraged the Cheyenne to become ranchers. U.S. government officials, however, opposed this. They preferred to make the Cheyenne into farmers, but their plans did not prove successful.

In 1887, the General Allotment Act (also known as the Dawes Act) was passed. Under this legislation, reservations were divided into small plots of land called allotments that were to be owned and farmed by individual Native families; the remaining land on the reservations was opened to American settlement. The breakup of their reservations divided the people and led to the breakdown of the Cheyenne culture. By the end of the 1900s, the Cheyenne people were working hard to revitalize their heritage.

RELIGION

The Cheyenne people believed that plants, animals, and people all had spirits and that they were direct descendants of the creator-god, Heammawihio, who taught the people how to hunt, when to plant and harvest corn, and

Cheyenne Words

emese	"eat"
enemene	"sing"
enesta	"hear"
enoohta	"leave"
epeva'	"It is good."
evoohta	"see"
hetane	"man"
hotame	"dog"
ma'eno	"turtle"
mahpe	"water"
Netonêševehe?	"What is your name?"
vee'e	"tepee"
ve'keso	"bird"

how to use fire. The Cheyenne prayed to the spirit of the earth to keep the crops growing, provide herbs, and heal the sick. The people also prayed to the north, south, east, and west. The west, where the sun set and rain and storms originated, was the most important of the four directions.

The Sun Dance, a ceremony common among many Plains Indians, was the central religious ceremony of the Cheyenne. It lasted eight days. During the first four days, the Cheyenne built the dance lodge and performed secret rites in the Lone Tepee. During the last four days, they held a public dance in the Sun Dance lodge.

In the late 1800s, the U.S. government banned the Sun Dance. The Cheyenne continued to perform the ceremony but renamed it the Willow Dance. In 1911, the Willow Dance was forbidden, and repeated efforts by the Cheyenne to reinstate it were rejected.

LANGUAGE

The Cheyenne spoke a musical language that was part of the Algonquian family. (Other Algonquian languages include Cree, Menominee, Fox, Delaware, and Micmac; see entries.) The language had fourteen letters that the people combined to create very long words. During the time when the Cheyenne nation was strong, its language was widely spoken.

As the tribe was influenced by the Sioux, the Cheyenne language changed and became a mix of the two languages. Because there were so many variations of the language, it is difficult for historians to track the names of groups and determine how many groups of Cheyenne there were. The Cheyenne language is spoken in southeastern Montana, in central Oklahoma, and on the Northern Cheyenne Indian Reservation.

GOVERNMENT

From early times, the Cheyenne had a highly organized government. The governing body of the Cheyenne, the Council of Forty-Four, met annually during the summer. The council was comprised of forty-four men who were elected from ten Cheyenne groups to serve ten-year terms.

Chiefs discussed problems within the tribe and planned how to deal with other tribes. The head of the Council, the Sweet Medicine Chief, performed religious and political duties. He kept the Chief's Medicine, a sacred bundle of grass, and he devised a code establishing how tribal members were to behave. The chiefs shared power; there was no single absolute authority, as all decisions were made by consensus.

In the early 2000s, Montana's Northern Cheyenne tribe was governed by a tribal council made up of the president and twenty-four council members. Council members from five separate districts were elected to two-year terms. The president served a four-year term. In spite of the changes to their government structure over the years, the Cheyenne still believe in making their decisions by consensus.

As of the 2000s, a joint tribal business committee governed the Cheyenne-Arapaho Reservation in Oklahoma. Four members from each tribe were elected to serve four-year terms. The reservation also had a tribal council that included all members age eighteen and older. The tribal council approved the budget, land leases or changes, and laws about membership. They also were responsible for proposing amendments to the constitution, changing district boundaries, and overriding business committee decisions. To veto committee decisions, at least seventy-five members had to vote against the plans.

ECONOMY

Cheyenne women contributed to the tribe by picking berries and digging up edible roots. They cooked and dried meat brought home by hunters. They tanned hides, made tepees, and sewed leather clothing and moccasins. Men hunted antelope, buffalo, deer, elk, and wild sheep. They trapped foxes and wolves for their fur.

In the early twenty-first century, Northern Cheyenne are employed in many fields. Some work on ranches or for coal companies. Others are trained firefighters who help control fires throughout the West. There are also professionals in fields such as law and teaching. More than forty small businesses operate on the reservation, among them laundromats, gas stations, grocery stores, and restaurants. The tribe leases almost all of its rangelands to the Northern Cheyenne Livestock Association, whereas individuals own between twelve thousand and fifteen thousand head of cattle. The Northern Cheyenne also manage a buffalo herd that provides food and draws tourists. In 2001, the tribe formed an economic development administration and adopted a business plan to improve reservation economy. Many tribe members hold jobs in the tribal government, tourism, forestry, mining, construction, manufacturing, or farming.

The Cheyenne-Arapaho people in Oklahoma earn money from leasing farming and grazing lands, from oil and gas royalties, and from casinos and smoke shops. Nevertheless, the reduction of federal funds for Native tribes has become a serious problem for all Cheyenne, who are striving to become financially self-sufficient.

DAILY LIFE

Families

The chief duties of the women of the tribe were to care for their homes, raise their children, and gather food. They made furnishings for their tepees using grass, earth, and buffalo hides. They also packed up belongings when the tribe changed camps. Men hunted and protected their territory from enemies.

Buildings

The Cheyenne lived as farmers in Minnesota and the eastern Dakotas from the 1600s to the early 1800s. They lived in earthen lodges made of wooden frames covered with sod. As they moved to the Great Plains to hunt buffalo, they adopted the tepee. This was a dwelling made of wooden poles and buffalo hides that could be moved easily with the aid of horses. The people built fires in the center of the tepees, and beds of buffalo robes lined the walls. Men sometimes painted their tepees with designs they had seen in a vision. Dome-shaped sweat lodges were used for bathing and purification rituals.

Clothing and adornment

Cheyenne clothing was designed to permit freedom of movement. In warm weather, most men wore only moccasins and breechcloths (material that goes between the legs and fastens at the waist). In colder weather, they also wore leggings and shirts. Women wore dresses and moccasins, adding leggings in winter. In the sixteenth and seventeenth centuries, these items were made of animal skins, usually deer or elk.

Everyday clothing was usually plain, but clothing for ceremonial occasions could be quite elaborate. It might be decorated with beads, quillwork, bells, and fringes. Designs for men's clothing were determined by their status as warriors. The design often told a story about the wearer. The most spectacular pieces of clothing were the knee-length shirts of warriors, adorned with beads and quillwork.

The Northern Cheyenne favored heavily beaded shirts, whereas Southern Cheyenne shirts had dark green fringes and relied more on color for effect. Medicine bags, eagle feathers, and berry beads also provided decoration. Men wore handsome robes during cold weather or to impress visitors.

Tribal leaders wore tall feather headdresses. Only the most well-respected men had long war bonnets with trailing eagle feathers. Men wore their hair either in braids with a topknot or pompadour (high puffed up hair at the forehead). Women braided their hair or left it loose. The Cheyenne painted designs on their faces, and the patterns were different for war than for religious or festive celebrations.

Women work in the community garden on the Northern Cheyenne reservation at Lame Deer, Montana, in 1945. © AP PHOTO.

Food

When the Cheyenne lived in Minnesota and the Dakotas, they raised corn, beans, and squash, supplementing the crops with deer and bear meat. When they moved to the Great Plains, Cheyenne men hunted buffalo. Women used all parts of the buffalo for food, tepee coverings, and other necessities. Later, the Cheyenne traded with Americans for new food items, including coffee, sugar, and flour, plus needles, other metal items, and beads.

Women planted and prepared vegetables from their gardens, such as turnips, which were sliced, boiled, and dried in the sun. They collected fruit from the prickly pear cactus, an especially difficult task because the fruit had sharp spines. The dried fruit was used as a thickener for stews and soups. Women made pemmican balls from dried ground animal meat, dried berries, and animal fat. They made similar balls substituting ground corn for the meat.

Education

Cheyenne girls learned the daily tasks of women by watching their mothers and other women work, and they played with deerskin dolls and had miniature cradleboards to imitate the way their mothers took care of babies. Boys used small bows and arrows and practiced shooting arrows until they never missed a target. They also learned to hunt rabbits, turkey, and fowl. Both boys and girls learned to ride horses, and older boys were taught to tend the tribe's horses. When a boy reached the age of twelve, his grandfather instructed him in men's duties, including buffalo hunting and horse raiding.

In the early 2000s, Chief Dull Knife College, a modern facility on the Northern Cheyenne Indian Reservation in southeastern Montana, served more than three hundred students. It offers associate degrees in arts, applied science, and management. Programs are available in office skills and entrepreneurial training (learning how to create a new business).

Healing practices

Cheyenne medicine men called shamans (pronounced *SHAH-munz* or *SHAY-munz*) performed healing rituals. They sucked out the evil that was causing the illness and spit it out onto the ground. Shamans also said prayers, blew whistles, beat on drums, and used rattles made of gourds, animal bladders, or eagle's heads as part of their healing rituals.

Priests were called in if the shamans were unsuccessful. Priests wore more elaborate costumes and conducted more involved rituals than did shamans. They also practiced minor surgery.

Drums were an important part of the healing process. The round shape of the drum represented the entire universe, and its steady beat symbolized the pulsing heart. Drums soothed tortured minds and healed suffering bodies.

ARTS

Cheyenne women were known for their creativity in decorating objects with horsehair, feathers, and the bones and skin of animals. Traditional crafts included quill embroidery, beadwork, pipestone carving, and pottery. Beginning in the 1800s, they incorporated trinkets, beads, commercial paints, and metal brought by American traders into their clothing and craft designs.

Oral literature

The oral literature of the Cheyenne was made up of war stories, sacred stories, and hero myths. An important figure was Wihio, a trickster who resembled the Coyote trickster of the stories of many other tribes.

CUSTOMS

Birth and naming

When a Cheyenne child was born, a family member sewed a small pouch to hold his or her placenta (an organ that, through a cord attached to the fetus's navel, provides nourishment before the baby is born). The pouches were filled with sweet grass and tied to the child's belt. A girl's navel amulet had a turtle design on it, whereas a boy's had a lizard. Because both these animals had long lives, the families wished this for their newborns. The Cheyenne said that a child who did not have a navel amulet would always be looking for his or her soul.

After a Cheyenne woman had a baby, another woman fed the baby for four days so the mother could rest. If the new baby was healthy, the father gave away his best horse to friends or family. Women did not have a second child until their first one was ten years old. When the parents announced that they were expecting another baby, they had a celebration and the father again gave away a horse.

Puberty

During a girl's first menses, she was painted red and purified with smoke from a fire. Then she joined her grandmother in an isolated hut for four days. The father announced her new status to the village and gave away a horse. Before she returned to the village, she was again purified with smoke.

During her monthly periods, a female could not touch or even be near medicine, shields, weapons, or sacred objects, so most women spent these days in the menstrual hut. If a menstruating woman went into her home, it had to be purified by burning juniper leaves and sweet grass before a warrior could safely enter.

Courtship and marriage

A Cheyenne woman often waited years before accepting a marriage proposal. Those who remained pure were held in high esteem. A man never proposed to a woman directly. Instead, he asked an older female relative to take gifts to the woman's family and make his case for him. If the woman accepted the proposal, the bride was brought to her husband's family. She was placed on a ceremonial blanket, carried into the tepee, and adorned with new clothes and paint. Then a feast was held. A man who was very prosperous sometimes had several wives but was expected to supply a tepee for each one.

Festivals

The most sacred of the Cheyenne ceremonies was the annual renewal of the Sacred Arrows, which took place during the summer solstice (June 21, when the sun is at its highest point). The prophet Sweet Medicine found the sacred arrows in the Black Hills of South Dakota and brought them to the Cheyenne. The arrows' special powers helped the Cheyenne hunt buffalo and defeat enemies in battle.

Only men were allowed to attend the four-day Sacred Arrow ceremony. On the first day, they brought offerings to the Great Spirit, and men were chosen to erect the Sacred Arrow Lodge. On the second day, a man who was painted red and dressed only in a buffalo robe presented a bundle of sacred arrows to the high priest. The unity of each Cheyenne family within the tribe was celebrated on the third day. Sticks representing each family were burned in an incense fire. On the fourth day, the sacred arrows were placed on public view in the sunlight. All the men and boys of the tribe walked past the arrows to obtain their sacred powers. A large tepee called the Sweet Medicine Lodge was then erected over the arrows. That evening, the medicine men went inside the tepee and sang sacred songs. Just before daybreak on the fifth day, all participants went into the sweat lodge for a cleansing.

In the early 2000s, several powwows and celebrations took place each year on the Northern Cheyenne Reservation in Montana. A powwow is a celebration at which the main activities are traditional singing and dancing. Singers and dancers at powwows come from many different tribes. The Cheyenne-Arapaho people in Oklahoma hold an annual Homecoming Powwow during Labor Day weekend in early September.

War rituals

The Cheyenne were organized into five military societies: Bowstring, Dog, Elk, Kit-Fox, and Shield. Four leaders took charge of each society. Two were the war chiefs and decision-makers, and two were peace leaders and ambassadors to other societies. Each group had unique war costumes, rituals, and chants. They each selected a young woman to serve as society sister. These women were respected and held to high standards; for instance, they were forbidden to have babies while they were society sisters.

During the 1800s, the society called the Dog Soldiers, which fought with U.S. government troops, was the most famous and most feared on the Great Plains. A Dog Soldier wore a long sash across his chest made of buffalo hide decorated with beads and dyed porcupine quills. The Dog Soldier pinned one end to the ground with a long, sharp pin to show that he would stay in a battle until the end. To defeat a Dog Soldier, an opponent had to pull the pin from the ground and beat the warrior with a whip to force him to leave.

Pipe smoking

Smoking a pipe is a religious ceremony. Before he smokes, a man touches the bowl of the pipe to the ground four times and honors the spirits who live in the four directions—the holy men of the north, the water creatures of the east, the four-legged creatures of the south, and the birds of the west.

To seal agreements, men smoked a pipe together. A treaty bound in this way was considered sacred. When Custer smoked a pipe with Stone

Forehead in 1869, the chief emptied the ashes onto the general's boots and warned him that if he ever lied to the tribe, he would become like those ashes. Indeed, Custer later went against his word and was killed in the Battle of Little Big Horn in 1876.

Death

A close relative usually prepared the body for a Cheyenne burial by dressing it in fine clothing and wrapping it in blankets. The body was then bound with ropes and carried it to the burial site. Mourners sang and prayed. The deceased person's dearest possessions were placed next to the body. For example, a man might be buried with his gun or knife; sometimes his best horse was shot. His remaining goods were distributed among non-relatives, but his widow was allowed to keep a blanket.

CURRENT TRIBAL ISSUES

Natural resources

Using the rich natural resources on their land in a responsible way is an important issue for many tribes, including the Cheyenne. The discovery of coal in the late 1960s on the reservation in Montana promised an opportunity for economic independence. Supporters of coal mining pointed out that money obtained in this way could pay for educational and health programs to improve living conditions on the reservation. Others feared environmental destruction. They believed coal companies would benefit and leave the tribe in poverty. Those who opposed won the argument, and the land was preserved.

As unemployment affected a large proportion of their population and their small casino failed to draw many visitors, the Northern Cheyenne revisited this earlier decision. Some people still retain traditional values of not disturbing the earth, quoting Sweet Medicine, a Cheyenne prophet, who warned centuries ago that digging up the "black rock" would rob the tribe of its identity. Others forged ahead with plans that they believed would create jobs and help the nation become self-sufficient. In 2011, the Department of the Interior intervened in a proposed venture to swap coal-mining rights between the tribe and a coal mining company. The department did not feel the terms of the agreement were fair to the Northern Cheyenne Nation.

Human remains and sacred sites

In 1986, the Northern Cheyenne discovered that the Smithsonian Institution in Washington, D.C., possessed remains of thousands of Native people and funeral objects (items that had been placed with the dead to accompany them into the next world). Natives started a movement that resulted in passage of the National Museum of the American Indian Act (1989) and the Native American Grave Protection and Repatriation Act (1990).

The first act required that the Smithsonian list all the remains and objects in its possession and then return them to the appropriate tribes. The act also authorized the creation of a Native American Museum. The second act required that all remains held by local, state, or federal agencies had to be returned to the native tribes.

The Cheyenne received and reburied remains of their ancestors. In 2004, when the National Museum of the American Indian opened in Washington, D.C., Peace Chief W. Richard West Jr. (1943–) of the Southern Cheyenne tribe became the museum's first director.

NOTABLE PEOPLE

Women's rights activist Suzan Shown Harjo (1945–), a member of the Cheyenne and Arapaho tribes, is a journalist and poet. She has been a major activist in Washington, D.C., for reshaping federal Native American policy.

In 1992, Ben Nighthorse Campbell (1933–), a member of the Northern Cheyenne tribe, became the first Native American to be elected to the U.S. Senate (R-CO; 1993–2005) in more than sixty years. He was also the first Native person to chair the Senate Committee on Indian Affairs. Of Apache/Pueblo/Cheyenne and Portuguese heritage, he is a U.S. Air Force veteran and a college graduate, and he holds a sixth-degree black belt in judo. He has been a teacher, a horse breeder and trainer, and an award-winning jewelry designer and maker.

BOOKS

Bringing the Story of the Cheyenne People to the Children of Today. Northern Cheyenne Curriculum Committee. Helena, MT: Office of Public Instruction, 2009.

Brown, Dee. "War Comes to the Cheyenne." *Bury My Heart at Wounded Knee.* New York: Holt, 1970.

Coyote, Bertha Little, and Virginia Giglio. *Leaving Everything Behind: The Songs and Memories of a Cheyenne Woman.* Norman: University of Oklahoma Press, 1997.

Dwyer, Helen, and D. L. Birchfield. *Cheyenne History and Culture*. New York: Gareth Stevens, 2012.

Grinnell, George Bird. *The Cheyenne Indians: Their History and Lifeways*. Bloomington, IN: World Wisdom, 2008.

Leiker, N., James Norman, and Ramon Powers. *The Northern Cheyenne Exodus in History and Memory*. OK: University of Oklahoma Press, 2011.

Maddux, Vernon R., and Albert Glenn Maddux. *In Dull Knife's Wake: The True Story of the Northern Cheyenne Exodus of 1878*. Norman, OK: Horse Creek Publications, 2003.

Powell, Peter J. *Sweet Medicine: The Continuing Role of the Sacred Arrows, the Sun Dance, and the Sacred Buffalo Hat in Northern Cheyenne History*. Norman: University of Oklahoma Press, 1998.

Seton, Ernest Thompson. *Sign Talk of the Cheyenne Indians*. Mineola, NY: Dover Publications, 2000.

Sneve, Virginia Driving Hawk. *The Cheyenne*. New York: Holiday House, 1996.

Wagner, Frederic C. III. *Participants in the Battle of the Little Big Horn: A Biographical Dictionary of Sioux, Cheyenne and United States Military Personnel*. Jefferson, NC: McFarland, 2011.

Whiteman, Funston, Michael Bell, and Vickie Leigh Krudwig. *The Cheyenne Journey: An Introduction to the Cheyenne People*. Edited by Susan Scott-Hill. Concho, OK: Cheyenne and Arapaho Tribes of Oklahoma, 2008.

Whiteman, Funston, Michael Bell, and Vickie Leigh Krudwig. *The Tsististas: People of the Plains*. Edited by Susan Scott-Hill. Concho, OK: Cheyenne and Arapaho Tribes of Oklahoma, 2008.

PERIODICALS

Kidston, Martin J. "Northern Cheyenne Break Vow of Silence." *Independent Record*. June 27, 2005. Available online from http://helenair.com/news/state-and-regional/article_fcf44c96-cfb6-56f4-9c57-062e944350ce.html#ixzz1R9UJAuwM (accessed on July 4, 2011).

Linse, Tamara. "Billings Man Captured Culture of Crow, Northern Cheyenne Tribes." *Billings Gazette*. January 16, 2005. Available online from http://billingsgazette.com/news/features/magazine/article_a0eb7a74-aafd-5abb-b7dc-c54c3d1a6f5c.html#ixzz1RIQxEBtH (accessed on July 4, 2011).

WEB SITES

"Black Kettle." *PBS: Public Broadcasting Service*. http://www.pbs.org/weta/thewest/people/a_c/blackkettle.htm (accessed on July 4, 2011).

"Cheyenne Indian." *American Indian Tribes*. http://www.cheyenneindian.com/cheyenne_links.htm (accessed on July 4, 2011).

"Cheyenne Indian History." *Access Genealogy*. http://www.accessgenealogy.com/native/tribes/cheyenne/cheyennehist.htm (accessed on July 4, 2011).

"Cheyenne Visions II." *Denver Art Museum*. http://exhibits.denverartmuseum.org/cheyennevisions2/ (accessed on July 4, 2011).

"The Cheyenne Way of Peace: Sweet Medicine." *Anti-Defamation League.* http://www.adl.org/education/curriculum_connections/Cheyenne_Way.asp (accessed on July 4, 2011).

"Crow/Cheyenne." *Wisdom of the Elders.* http://www.wisdomoftheelders.org/program206.html (accessed on July 4, 2011).

Moore, John H. "Cheyenne, Southern." *Oklahoma Historical Society.* http://digital.library.okstate.edu/encyclopedia/entries/C/CH030.html (accessed on July 4, 2011).

Northern Cheyenne Nation. http://www.cheyennenation.com/ (accessed on July 4, 2011).

"The Red River War. *Texas State Library & Archives Commission.* http://www.tsl.state.tx.us/exhibits/indian/showdown/page3.html (accessed on July 4, 2011).

Redish, Laura, and Orrin Lewis. "Cheyenne Indians Fact Sheet." *Native Languages of the Americas.* http://www.bigorrin.org/cheyenne_kids.htm (accessed on July 4, 2011).

"The Sand Creek Massacre." *Last of the Independents.* http://www.lastoftheindependents.com/sandcreek.htm (accessed on July 4, 2011).

Stands In Timber, John. "Cheyenne Memories." *Northern Cheyenne Nation.* http://www.cheyennenation.com/memories.html (accessed on July 4, 2011).

"2011 Oklahoma Indian Nations." *Pocket Pictorial Directory.* Oklahoma City: Oklahoma Indian Affairs Commission, 2011. Available online from http://www.ok.gov/oiac/documents/2011.FINAL.WEB.pdf (accessed on July 4, 2011).

Comanche

Name

The Comanche (pronounced *cuh-MAN-chee*) called themselves *Numinu* or *Nemene* (the word has various spellings), meaning "people." Their name may have come from the Ute word for the tribe, *Koh-Mahts,* which means "those who are against us" or "those who want to fight us." The Spanish called them *Camino Ancho,* meaning "wide trail." They later altered the spelling to Komantcia, and the Americans changed it to Comanche. Many other tribes had names for the Comanche. For example, the Kiowa called them *Bodalk Inago,* or "snake men," and the Arapaho gave them the name *Catha* ("having many horses").

Location

Before Europeans arrived, the Comanche and Shoshone (see entry) lived along the upper Platte River in eastern Wyoming. Later, they roamed the southern Great Plains, including parts of Texas, New Mexico, Oklahoma, Kansas, Colorado, and Mexico. In the early twenty-first century, descendants of the Comanche shared reservation lands with the Kiowa and Apache (see entries) tribes. The reservation is located 87 miles (140 kilometers) southwest of Oklahoma City, Oklahoma, in Lawton.

Population

At the height of their power in the early 1800s, the Comanche numbered about 20,000. The population declined to 1,500 in 1900 as a result of wars and diseases. In the 1990 U.S. Census, 11,267 people identified themselves as Comanche (170 identified themselves more specifically as Oklahoma Comanche). In 2000, the census reported 10,518 Comanche residing in the United States and a total of 21,852 people who had some Comanche heritage. Of that number, 6,643 resided in Oklahoma, and 3,947 of them lived on the reservation. The 2010 census counted 12,284 Comanche, with a total of 23,330 people claiming some Comanche heritage. Tribal enrollment statistics for 2011 revealed 14,557 members, with about 7,763 of them living in the Lawton–Fort Sill area of southwest Oklahoma.

Language family

Uto-Aztecan.

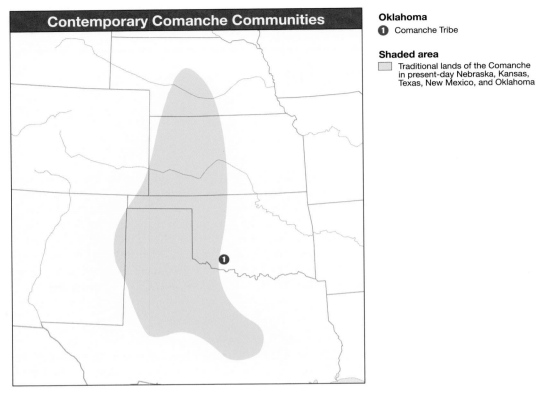

Contemporary Comanche Communities

Oklahoma
① Comanche Tribe

Shaded area
☐ Traditional lands of the Comanche in present-day Nebraska, Kansas, Texas, New Mexico, and Oklahoma

A map of contemporary Comanche communities. MAP BY XNR PRODUCTIONS. CENGAGE LEARNING, GALE. REPRODUCED BY PERMISSION OF GALE, A PART OF CENGAGE LEARNING.

Origins and group affiliations

The Comanche were a branch of the Shoshone tribe until the 1600s. The Comanche then separated from the Shoshone and migrated south from Wyoming and Montana along the eastern slopes of the Rocky Mountains. They took over land occupied by other tribes including the Cherokee, Choctaw, Creek, Crow, and Apache (see entries). They also fought the Kiowa, Kiowa-Apache, Cheyenne, and Arapaho, but eventually made peace with these tribes.

Often referred to as the "Lords of the Southern Plains," the powerful Comanche tribe once controlled a vast expanse of territory known by the Spanish term *Comanchería* ("land of the Comanche"). Loosely organized into nomadic groups of highly skilled horsemen and warriors, the Comanche fought with nearly every Plains tribe at one time or another. They also took on the Spanish, the American settlers, the Texas Rangers, and the U.S. military in a fierce defense of their lands. Comanche resistance is largely responsible for slowing the settlement of the American West during the nineteenth century. They were cunning fighters who learned how their enemies thought, and they added to their population base by adopting captured prisoners into the tribe.

HISTORY

Horses transform lifestyle

The Comanche separated from their relatives, the Shoshone, in the late 1600s. They migrated south from the mountains of Wyoming and Montana onto the Great Plains. Sometime before 1705, they acquired horses from their Ute (see entry) neighbors, who had gotten the animals from the Spanish in Mexico. Horses transformed the lifestyle of these wanderers, who had always hunted on foot. The Comanche became the first Plains people to make extensive use of horses, and by 1750, their men, women, and children were excellent riders. Hunting became easier, and over the next century, the tribe amassed a larger herd of horses than any other Native group.

Comanche warriors sometimes owned as many as 250 horses, and the most prominent members of the tribe might have as many as 1,000. Some horses were taken by conducting raids on neighboring tribes or on pioneer settlements, but the Comanche were also one of the few groups who knew how to breed and train horses. Their mounts responded to verbal commands, and Comanche warriors could lean over their horses' necks and fire arrows from beneath the animals' chins while at a full gallop.

Having horses allowed the Comanche to control a large expanse of territory. Between 1750 and 1875, Comanche groups spread across central and western Texas, eastern New Mexico, southeastern Colorado, southwestern Kansas, and western Oklahoma. This 24,000-square-mile (62,160-square-kilometer) area became known as the Comanchería.

Important Dates

1705: The Comanche acquire horses from the Ute; within the next fifty years they become excellent horsemen and maintain the largest herds of any tribe.

1834: The first official contact occurs between the U.S. government and representatives of the Comanche people.

1838: Thirty-five Comanche are killed when the Texas Rangers attempt to seize a group that had come to conduct a peaceful negotiation.

1867–69: Treaty of Medicine Lodge is signed. Most Comanche give up their lands and move to the reservation.

1874–75: The Comanche make their last stand; Quanah Parker and his followers are the last to surrender and be placed on a reservation.

1939–45: Comanche Code Talkers help the World War II effort.

1967: The Comanche adopt a tribal constitution.

2003: The first official Comanche dictionary is published, compiled entirely by the Comanche people.

Comanche warriors attack a group of white settlers in their covered wagons in 1857. ©ENGRAVING BY SCHOOLCRAFT. BETTMANN. REPRODUCED BY PERMISSION.

Occupied by trade, raids, and war

The Comanchería was situated between territory claimed by Spain in the Southwest and by France in Louisiana. Although the Comanche developed trading relationships with both the Spanish and the French, they had better relations with the French. The Comanche traded prisoners of war to the Spanish to be used as slaves; they traded buffalo hides with the French. In return, they got horses from the Spanish and guns from the French, and thus they acquired even more power. They jealously guarded their territory against Spanish expansion and trespassing by other tribes.

In the early 1800s, events happening in faraway places had a far-reaching effect on the Comanche. In the Louisiana Purchase of 1803, France sold to the United States a huge tract of land, extending from the Mississippi River in the east to the Rocky Mountains in the west and from the Gulf of Mexico in the south to what is now Canada in the north. The lands the United States gained in this agreement doubled the size of the nation. However, these lands were already inhabited by Native people.

With this vast new area now in its control, the U.S. government made room for American expansion by forcing eastern tribes to move west of the Mississippi River. There the relocated tribes competed with the Comanche on the Great Plains for a share of the buffalo herds. American settlers then pressed toward the borders of the Comanchería. In 1821, Mexico gained control of present-day Texas from Spain, and Mexican settlers moved into Texas and took over more Comanche lands.

The Comanche resented this intrusion into their territory and fought the newcomers, sometimes killing American hunters and traders or taking them captives. After 1830, U.S. government officials tried to meet with the Comanche to discuss the possibility of moving eastern tribes onto parts of the Comanchería. The Comanche were a loosely organized people, however, and at first, no spokesmen could be found. When representatives of the tribe finally met with U.S. delegates in 1834, little was accomplished.

Problems in Texas

In 1835, the Texas Revolution freed Texas from Mexican rule. American settlers moved onto isolated ranches and farms in Texas with their cattle and their new breeds of larger horses. They were easy targets for Comanche raids, and the Texas Rangers (a police force) had frequent skirmishes with the tribe. The conflicts came to a head in San Antonio in 1838, when Texas Rangers tried to capture Comanche leaders who had come to conduct a peaceful negotiation. Thirty-five Comanche were killed, and many others were wounded.

Over the next three decades, Texas became part of the United States, and gold was discovered in California. More settlers poured into Texas, and

Divisions of the Comanche Tribe

The Comanche tribe was composed of about eight to twelve independent divisions that generally cooperated with each other but sometimes turned antagonistic. Divisions were further broken down into individual bands. At one time, there may have been as many as thirty-five bands, but by the nineteenth century, there were five major bands—the Penatuka, Yaparuka, Noyuka, Kwaharu, and Kuhtsutuuka.

The Shoshone usually named their groups after foods; some Comanche followed this custom. Most of the other divisions had names related to where they lived.

Hanitaibo	"Corn People"
Hois	"Timber People"
Kotsoteka	"Buffalo Eaters"
Kwahada	"Antelope Eaters"
Parkeenaum	"Water People"
Nokoni	"People Who Return" or "They Travel Around"
Pehnahterkuh	"Wasps"
Penateka	"Honey Eaters"
Sata Teichas	"Dog Eaters"
Tahneemuh	"Liver Eaters"
Tenawa	"Those Who Stay Downstream"
Widyunuu	"Awl People"
Yamparika	"Root Eaters"

gold miners galloped across the Comanchería, spreading diseases and disrupting the migrations of the buffalo herds. Weakened now by diseases and hunger, the Comanche fought on. They had a brief period of relief when the United States was distracted by the American Civil War (1861–65; a war between the Union [the North], which was opposed to slavery, and the Confederacy [the South], which was in favor of slavery). After that war, the U.S. government devoted its attention to ending the violence on the Great Plains.

The Buffalo War

After the Civil War, the Comanche had to contend with the Texas Rangers and the full force of the U.S. military, sometimes under the command of the famous Wild West hero Christopher "Kit" Carson (1809–1868). In the 1870s, professional hunters armed with high-powered rifles began to kill off the remaining buffalo herds for use in eastern industries. One of these hunters could kill hundreds of buffalo in a day.

In 1874, a band of Comanche under the leadership of Chief Quanah Parker (c. 1852–1911) tried to stop this slaughter by attacking a group of buffalo hunters. Though the hunters used their rifles to turn back the Comanche and their allies, this event sparked the Buffalo War (1874–75; also known as the Red River Uprising). After U.S. troops killed hundreds of horses and burned Comanche food and tepees, most of the tribe surrendered.

Quanah Parker and his followers held out until June 1875. After the government placed Parker and his people on a reservation in Oklahoma, nearly two centuries of Comanche domination of the Southern Plains ended.

Hardships of reservation life

The U.S. government wanted to turn the Comanche into farmers and tried to force the people to accept American ways and values. The Comanche had to depend on the Bureau of Indian Affairs for food, clothing, and shelter. Since their move to the reservation, the Comanche have endured hunger, poverty, and legal and illegal takeovers of their land. Though destitution and discrimination remain alive, the Comanche proudly struggle to retain their traditions.

RELIGION

The Comanche people did not believe in a creator god. Instead, they thought they had originated from animals, perhaps wolves. Religion for them involved learning to please the supernatural powers who lived in rocks and animals. They believed that by placating these spirits, they would receive what they needed to survive. Once a person discovered what the powers wanted and provided it, he or she could face the future without fear.

The practice of religion was a private matter, and men established a personal relationship with the supernatural through a vision quest (see "Customs"). The Comanche were one of the few tribes of the Great Plains that did not practice the Sun Dance. In fact, they held few group ceremonies of any kind and had no special class of religious leaders.

The Comanche believed that the spirits of the dead lived through eternity in a land where everyone was young and had plenty of game and fast horses. Almost everyone who died gained an afterlife. The exceptions included warriors scalped in battle. The Comanche scalped their enemies to prevent them from enjoying life after death, and they fought fiercely over a fallen comrade to prevent his scalp from being taken.

Unable to adjust to reservation life, many Comanche took solace in the Peyote (pronounced *pay-OH-tee*) religion, which brought people together for singing, praying, and taking peyote, a drug derived from cactus that causes mild hallucinations. In 1918, the popularity of the Peyote religion led to the founding of the Native American Church, which combined Native and Christian practices. Today, some members of the Comanche tribe still belong to the Native American Church, whereas others have converted to Christianity.

LANGUAGE

The Comanche spoke a Shoshonean dialect (variety) of the Uto-Aztecan language family that was similar to Ute and Paiute (see entry). The language was frequently used during trade because many people on the Plains understood it. The language was used in World War II (1939–45; a war in which Great Britain, France, the United States, and their allies defeated Germany, Italy, and Japan), when seventeen young Comanche men served the U.S. Army as Code Talkers, relaying secret messages in their native language.

In 1989, the tribe began a language preservation project. Forty elders taped stories and tribal history in Comanche. They also organized language classes. By the following year, studies showed that 854 people could speak the language; most of them were older members of the tribe.

Comanche Words

ap	"father"
haa	"yes"
haa marúawe	"Hi!"
haamee	"thank you"
kee	"no"
kuutsuu	"buffalo"
paa	"water"
pia	"mother"
tsaatu, untse?	"Fine, and you?"
unha hakai nuusuka?	"How are you?"
unha hakai nahniaka?	"What's your name?"
ura	"thank you"

In spite of these efforts, by 1993 only about 250 elderly members of the tribe still spoke the language. Many Comanche elders were reluctant to teach the language to outsiders. They believe that to know Comanche is to have power over the tribe.

Concerned their language would die out, some members of the tribe formed the Comanche Language and Cultural Preservation Committee to revitalize it. Their plans included teaching all ages to write, speak, and understand Comanche. In 1994, Dr. Alice Anderton, a language specialist, created an alphabet and a spelling system.

Since then, several books, dictionaries, and other teaching materials have been printed, and the committee has secured grants to produce language materials such as tapes and DVDs as well as to teach additional classes. Intensive language training is offered to families through the Master-Apprentice Team Project. Families commit to speaking only Comanche as they work with a skilled speaker for twenty hours a week for five months.

GOVERNMENT

The Comanche tribal government was democratic, with organized bands led by band chiefs who came together as needed to discuss important issues. The Comanche lived in many separate groups and had no need for elected leaders except during wartime; after a war was over, the war leader's authority ended. Decisions were reached after everyone who wished to speak had his say. Every adult male in the group had to agree with the decision; those who could not agree with the majority left and joined another group. Women had no say in decision making and could not attend meetings unless invited.

The Comanche adopted a tribal constitution in 1967. The tribe set up their government with a Comanche Tribal General Council and a Comanche Business Committee. The tribe elects a chairperson, vice chairperson, secretary-treasurer, and four council members; the officers also hold the same positions on the business committee. Members serve three-year staggered terms. All members of the tribe age eighteen or older are part of the tribal council and meet annually.

ECONOMY

The Comanche economy changed in the eighteenth century. Until then, it had been based on gathering and hunting buffalo on foot, a difficult and dangerous undertaking. After 1700, the economy expanded to include horses, mules, and slaves. The Comanche traded these along with buffalo robes to the Spanish for horses and to the French for guns and luxury items. What they could not get through trading, the Comanche took through raiding.

After moving to the reservation, the Comanche struggled to support themselves by farming (although most of the land was not suitable for agriculture), raising cattle, and working for nearby farmers and ranchers. In modern times, they continue these activities, and they also earn money by leasing mineral and cattle-grazing rights to their lands. Small businesses such as a bingo hall, a snack bar, and a smoke shop operate on the reservation. The tribe owns casinos, which generate almost 85 percent of the tribal budget. This revenue funds education and many social service programs.

Some Comanche have upheld the tribe's warrior traditions by serving in the American armed forces during wartime, and military service remains a popular career option for young Comanche men and women. Many Comanche also work off the reservation in the oil fields of Oklahoma and Texas or in skilled occupations in urban areas.

DAILY LIFE

Families

Families consisted of a husband, wife, children, and close relatives. Because Comanche life was so hard and many children died young, all children were cherished, even children taken in raids, who were often adopted into the tribe.

Adults were always hard at work. The primary tasks of men were hunting, making war, and fashioning their own war shields. When they were too old for this work (many were worn out or dead by the age of thirty), they

Why the Bear Waddles When He Walks: A Comanche Tale

In the beginning days, nobody knew what to do with the Sun. It would come up and shine for a long time. Then it would go away for a long time, and everything would be dark.

The daytime animals naturally wanted the Sun to shine all the time, so they could live their lives without being interrupted by the dark. The nighttime animals wanted the Sun to go away forever, so they could live the way they wanted to.

At last they all got together, to talk things over.

Old Man Coyote said, "Let's see what we can do about that Sun. One of us ought to have it, or the other side ought to get rid of it."

"How will we do that?" Scissor-tailed Flycatcher asked. "Nobody can tell the Sun what to do. He's more powerful than anyone else in the world."

"Why don't we play hand game for it?" Bear asked. "The winning side can keep the Sun or throw it away, depending on who wins and what they want to do with it."

So they got out the guessing bones to hide in their hands, and they got out the crow-feathered wands for the guessers to point with, and they got out the twenty pointed dogwood sticks for the umpires to keep score with. Coyote was the umpire for the day side, and nighttime umpire was Owl.

The umpires got a flat rock, like a table, and laid out their counting sticks on that. Then the two teams brought logs, and lined them up facing one another, with the umpires and their flat rock at one end between the two teams.

That was a long hand game. The day side held the bones first, and they were so quick and skillful passing them from hand to hand behind their backs and waving them in the guessers' faces that it seemed surely they must win. Then Mole, who was guessing for the night side, caught both Scissor-tail and Hawk at the same time, and

made bows and arrows out of wood. Women did every other job; they aged quickly and were usually exhausted by the age of twenty-five from hunger, hard work, and the difficulty of bearing many children at a young age.

Education

Because Comanche parents were often busy, grandparents played an important role in child-rearing. Children learned by observing and imitating adults, and they learned at a young age their most important task: making sure there was enough food to eat.

After the Comanche moved to the reservation, Christian missionaries and government agents opened schools, hoping to convince Comanche

U•X•L Encyclopedia of Native American Tribes, 3rd Edition

the bones went to the night side, and the day people began to guess.

Time and again the luck went back and forth, each team seeming to be about to beat the other. Time and again the luck changed, and the winning team became the losing one.

The game went on and on. Finally the Sun, waiting on the other side of the world to find out what was going to happen to him, got tired of it all.

The game was so long that Bear got tired, too. He was playing on the night side. He got cramped sitting on the log, and his legs began to ache. Bear took off his moccasins to rest his feet, and still the game went on and on.

At last the Sun was so bored that he decided to go and see for himself what was happening. He yawned and stretched and crawled out of his bed on the underneath side of the world. He started to climb up his notched log ladder to the top side, to find out what was happening.

As the Sun climbed the light grew stronger, and the night people began to be afraid. The game was still even; nobody had won. But the Sun was coming and coming, and the night animals had to run away. Bear jumped up in such a hurry that he put his right foot in his left moccasin, and his left foot in his right moccasin.

The Sun was full up now, and all the other night animals were gone. Bear went after them as fast as he could in his wrong moccasins, rocking and waddling from side to side, and shouting, "Wait for me! Wait for me!"

But nobody stopped or waited, and Bear had to go waddling along, just the way he has done ever since.

And because nobody won the game, the day and night took turns from that time on. Everybody had the same time to come out and live his life the way he wanted to as everybody else.

SOURCE: Marriott, Alice, and Carol K. Rachlin. "Why the Bear Waddles When He Walks." *American Indian Mythology*. New York: Crowell, 1968.

children to reject their traditional culture. Comanche parents objected, and few children attended the schools. According to author Willard Rollings, Comanche children who attended Oklahoma's public schools in the 1980s still faced the same problems. He wrote: "Local school boards show little respect for Native Americans and their culture and continue to try to convert their children to the culture of white Americans."

Most children in the early twenty-first century attend public schools or the Riverside Indian School. The Comanche Office of Higher Education visits public schools to promote tribal education and to assist students in preparing for college. Comanche Nation College located in Lawton opened in 2002 to offer a Comanche-centered higher education experience.

Buildings

The Comanche were a wandering tribe that moved when the buffalo did or when they needed new patches of grass for their horses. They required homes that could be quickly put up and taken down. Their tepees consisted of four base poles (most Plains tribes used three poles) stuck into the ground and tied together at the top to form a cone shape. Eighteen to twenty smaller poles gave support. A covering of up to seventeen buffalo hides was stretched tightly around this frame.

Sometimes tepee covers were painted with abstract designs and geometric figures. Inside the tepee, the Comanche lit a fire and slept on a low platform covered with buffalo robes along the rear wall. In the summer, they rolled up the hide covers to let in fresh air. In extremely hot weather, they slept outdoors in brush shelters.

Food

The search for food was constant. Buffalo was the primary food source, but the Comanche also hunted elk, bear, antelope, and deer. When game was scarce, they ate horses. Because they considered dogs and coyotes to be relatives of their ancestors, the wolves, they would not eat them, nor would they eat fish. They ate turtles steamed over the fire, but they did not eat fowl unless they were starving, because they considered it food for cowards. When non-Native ranchers began raising cattle on the Comanchería, the tribe often raided those herds and ate beef.

The Comanche did not practice agriculture but obtained plant foods in other ways. They traded with other tribes for corn and tobacco, and they gathered wild plants such as grapes, currants, plums, mulberries, persimmons, roots, and tubers. A favorite high-energy food was pemmican, which was made of dried buffalo meat, melted fat, and various nuts and berries.

Clothing and adornment

Men's clothing Everyday clothing was plain and practical, but Comanche war regalia was colorful and elegant (see "War and hunting rituals"). Comanche men usually wore a buckskin breechcloth (a piece of material that wrapped between the legs and tucked into a belt); fringed buckskin leggings extending from the belt to the ankles; and buckskin moccasins with tough, buffalo-hide soles. Men did not usually wear shirts. Young boys commonly went naked until they reached the age of nine or ten, when they donned adult attire. Men's clothing was sometimes decorated with fringes made of deerskin, fur, or human hair, but it lacked the elaborate beadwork found among some other Plains tribes.

Comanche men grew their hair long and parted it in the middle. They often painted their scalps where the hair was parted and wore braids (sometimes wrapped with fur or cloth) on each side of their faces. A tiny braid known as a scalplock hung over the forehead and was often decorated with cloth, beads, and a single feather. Comanche men plucked their facial and body hair, including their eyebrows. They adorned themselves with bracelets of leather and metal, and earrings of shell, brass, or silver.

Women's clothing Comanche women wore moccasins and long, one-piece buckskin dresses with wide sleeves, flared skirts, and fringes. Young girls wore clothing from the time they could walk. Women's special occasion clothing was ornamented with beads, fringes, and bits of metal that made sounds. The women usually cut their hair short and painted their faces and bodies in bright colors. In the winter, all members of the Comanche tribe wore heavy buffalo robes and knee-high boots for warmth.

Healing practices

Comanche people suffered from hunger, exposure to the elements, and diseases. Children learned at an early age to endure extreme pain and discomfort without self-pity. Comanche doctors were hunter-warriors who had a little extra influence with the spirit world and demonstrated practical skills. They knew how to apply tourniquets and perform minor surgery, and they used a wide variety of herbal remedies to treat wounds and cure illnesses. They knew how to suck out the poison from snakebites and even how to fill cavities in teeth. Sometimes older women were allowed to practice medicine.

ARTS

The Comanche were wanderers, always searching for food, and had little time to devote to the development of the arts. They had few songs, dances, rituals, or ceremonies. Comanche men did devote particular attention to the creation and decoration of their war shields (see "War and hunting rituals").

CUSTOMS

War and hunting rituals

In preparation for a buffalo hunt, the Comanche prayed to the buffalo spirit for a good catch. They usually hunted by encircling a group of buffalo with their horses and then killing as many animals as possible using lances or bows and arrows. Sometimes, they stampeded a herd of buffalo over the edge of a cliff. When individuals hunted alone, they disguised themselves in buffalo robes to sneak up on the herd.

To prepare for battle, Comanche men performed a war dance and prayed to spirits such as the eagle for strength. They painted their faces and bodies with symbols of their personal power. Warriors wore headdresses with buffalo horns and carried shields painted and decorated with feathers, bear teeth, horse tails, and human hair.

Comanche warriors traveled long distances and attacked their enemies without warning. Male enemies were usually tortured and killed because it was not practical to take them prisoner. A prisoner who displayed exceptional courage under torture was sometimes released. Warriors often returned to camp accompanied by women and children prisoners and dressed in items of European clothing taken from their enemies.

Vision quest

A young man about to embark on a vision quest (a search for spiritual guidance) climbed to the top of a hill, stopping four times along the way to smoke a tobacco pipe and pray. He remained alone on the hill for four days and nights without food or water. In the morning, he prayed to the rising sun for a vision.

A vision might be as simple as hearing the sound of a wolf call. After he received his vision, the young man returned to the tribe to ask the medicine man to explain it. From the explanation, he knew what materials he needed for his medicine bundle, which represented his personal power and his relationship with the supernatural.

Courtship and marriage

A young man became eligible to marry after he completed his vision quest and participated in his first war party. Most Comanche men, however, waited to marry until they had proven themselves to be skilled hunters, able to provide for a wife and children. It was common for men to marry within their group; no group wanted to lose a hunter-warrior.

The man sent his relatives to meet with the chosen woman's family and secure their permission for the match; the woman had no say in the matter. Once these informal arrangements had been made, the man formally proposed marriage by giving the woman's male relatives a gift of horses. If they agreed to the union, there was no actual marriage ceremony; the couple simply went together to the man's tepee. In keeping with the Comanche belief that no woman should be left unattached, a man sometimes married his wife's sister too. If a wife was unfaithful, her husband was allowed to mutilate or kill her.

Children

Children were named by a prominent member of the tribe, who usually chose a name with religious significance. If the child became ill or appeared to suffer from bad luck, the family might go through the naming ceremony again and select a different name.

A group of young Comanche wear traditional dress for a ceremony in Gallup, New Mexico. © DICK DOUGHTY/ HAGA/THE IMAGE WORKS.

Games and festivities

The Comanche still enjoy the hand game that has provided entertainment for many generations. One team passes a button, bone, or other small object from hand to hand. After it stops, the other team tries to guess who has the object.

They also hold an annual Homecoming Powwow during the month of July near Walters, Oklahoma. Powwows are celebrations at which the main activities are traditional singing and dancing. In modern times, the singers and dancers at powwows come from many different tribes. In 1972, a group of Comanche established the Little Ponies, an organization that holds powwows and sponsors other events to help keep tribal traditions alive.

CURRENT TRIBAL ISSUES

Land contamination is the primary concern of the tribe in the early twenty-first century. In 1998, the Environmental Protection Agency (EPA) selected a thirty-acre site to clean up and develop, with the intention of returning the site to productive use. In 2004, the Tribal Office of the EPA began installing air quality monitors on the reservation. The office also monitors groundwater to be sure it is safe to drink and work to clean up illegal dumping sites.

One ongoing program is ensuring that Comanche remains be returned to the nation. Under the Native American Graves Protection and Repatriation Act (NAGPRA), local, state, or federal agencies holding any remains must turn them over to their Native tribes. The Comanche Nation has identified close to 150 possible Comanche remains in twenty-nine different states. In 2009, the nation received a grant for their NAGPRA Program to request these remains and grave objects. They began by contacting the states in their traditional territory and will request remains from other states later. In addition to remains and funerary goods, some objects, such as a lance, were returned. These items will be placed in the Comanche National Museum.

NOTABLE PEOPLE

Quanah Parker (c. 1852–1911) was a Comanche leader, the son of a white woman named Cynthia Parker who had been kidnapped as a child and incorporated into the Comanche tribe. After the death of his father, a Comanche chief, in 1867, Quanah Parker led the Comanche and their allies in many successful battles against U.S. troops until he was finally forced to surrender in 1875. Parker adapted quickly to reservation life, learning the ways of whites and making deals to benefit his people. He was an important symbol of Comanche courage and pride.

LaDonna Harris (1931–) is a Comanche woman who has promoted equal opportunity for Native people on a national level. She was instrumental in the return of the Taos Blue Lake to the people of Taos Pueblo (see entry) and helped the Menominee (see entry) regain their federal recognition. In addition to leading Americans for Indian Opportunity, Harris founded many organizations including the National Indian Housing Council, Council of Energy Resource Tribes, National Tribal Environmental Council, and National Indian Business Association. She is also an advocate for world peace.

BOOKS

Betty, Gerald. *Comanche Society: Before the Reservation.* College Station: Texas A&M University Press, 2005.

Carlson, Paul H., and Tom Crum. *Myth, Memory, and Massacre: The Pease River Capture of Cynthia Ann Parker.* Lubbock: Texas Tech University Press, 2010.

Gwynne, S.C. *Empire of the Summer Moon: Quanah Parker and the Rise and Fall of the Comanches, The Most Powerful Indian Tribe in American History.* New York: Scribner, 2010.

Lacey, T. Jensen. *The Comanche.* New York: Chelsea House, 2011.

Libal, Joyce. *Comanche.* Philadelphia, PA: Mason Crest, 2004.

Neeley, Bill. *The Last Comanche Chief: The Life and Times of Quanah Parker.* New York: Wiley, 1996.

Rollings, Willard H. *The Comanche.* New York: Chelsea House Publications, 2004.

Schach, David. *Comanche Warriors.* Minneapolis, MN: Bellwether Media, 2011.

Southwell, Kristina L., and John R. Lovett. *Life at the Kiowa, Comanche, and Wichita Agency: The Photographs of Annette Ross Hume.* Norman: University of Oklahoma Press, 2010.

Yeagley, David A. *Bad Eagle: The Rantings of a Conservative Comanche.* Cambridge: R&R Publishing, 2007.

WEB SITES

Dickerson, W. E. S. "Handbook of Texas Online: Comanche Indian Reservation." *Texas State Historical Association.* http://www.tshaonline.org/handbook/online/articles/bpc10 (accessed on July 4, 2011).

"Comanche." *Edward S. Curtis's The North American Indian.* http://curtis.library.northwestern.edu/curtis/toc.cgi (accessed on July 4, 2011).

"Comanche Indian History." *Access Genealogy.* http://www.accessgenealogy.com/native/tribes/comanche/comanchehist.htm (accessed on July 4, 2011).

"Comanche Language." *Omniglot.* http://www.omniglot.com/writing/comanche.htm (accessed on July 4, 2011).

Comanche Nation of Oklahoma. http://www.comanchenation.com/ (accessed on July 4, 2011).

"The Comanche War." *Texas State Library & Archives Commission.* http://www.tsl.state.tx.us/exhibits/indian/war/page2.html (accessed on July 4, 2011).

Kavanagh, Thomas W. "Comanche." *Oklahoma Historical Society.* http://digital.library.okstate.edu/encyclopedia/entries/C/CO033.html (accessed on July 4, 2011).

Lipscomb, Carol A. "Handbook of Texas Online: Comanche Indians." *Texas State Historical Association.* http://www.tshaonline.org/handbook/online/articles/bmc72 (accessed on July 4, 2011).

"Native Village Elders, Leaders, Heroes Library." *Native Village.* http://www.nativevillage.org/Libraries/elders.leaders,%20heros%20libraryhtm.htm (accessed on July 4, 2011).

Redish, Laura, and Orrin Lewis. "Comanche Language (Numinu)." *Native Language of the Americas.* http://www.native-languages.org/comanche.htm (accessed on July 4, 2011).

"The Salt Creek Massacre." *Texas State Library & Archives Commission.* http://www.tsl.state.tx.us/exhibits/indian/showdown/page1.html (accessed on July 4, 2011).

Sultzman, Lee. "Comanche History: Part One." *First Nations/First People Issues.* http://www.tolatsga.org/ComancheOne.html (accessed on July 4, 2011).

"2011 Oklahoma Indian Nations." *Pocket Pictorial Directory.* Oklahoma City: Oklahoma Indian Affairs Commission, 2011. Available from http://www.ok.gov/oiac/documents/2011.FINAL.WEB.pdf (accessed on July 4, 2011).

Crow

Name

The name Crow comes from a translation of the tribe's name for itself, *Apsáa-looke* (pronounced opp-sah-loh-kay), which means "children of the long-beaked bird" or "bird people." It is also sometimes spelled *Absarokee*.

Location

When the Europeans arrived, the Crow were roaming the Great Plains of Wyoming and Montana; horses extended their range. Most Crow lived along the Yellowstone River and its branches in Montana. In modern times, many live on the Crow Indian Reservation in Bighorn County, Montana, or in the nearby towns of Billings and Hardin. The 2.2-million-acre Crow Indian Reservation is the largest of the seven reservations in Montana. It is bordered by Wyoming to the south and the Northern Cheyenne Indian Reservation to the east, and it includes the northern end of the Bighorn, Wolf, and Pryor Mountains.

Population

Before 1740, there were about 8,000 Crow. In 1944, the tribe's population had dropped to 2,500. In the 1990 U.S. Census, 9,394 people identified themselves as Crow, making the tribe the twenty-ninth largest in the United States at that time. By 2000, the number of Crow had decreased slightly to 9,174, although 14,703 people claimed to have some Crow heritage. According to tribal records, 5,165 Crow lived on the reservation; 7,560 resided in Bighorn County; and 3,950 lived in Yellowstone County. By 2010, the census counted 10,332 Crow in the United States, with a total of 15,203 people claiming some Crow ancestry.

Language family

Siouan.

Origins and group affiliations

Crow tales say that the tribe originated from a land of many lakes—probably Manitoba, in Canada's Lake Winnipeg area. Historians agree that the origins of the Crow date back to before 1300 at the headwaters of the Mississippi

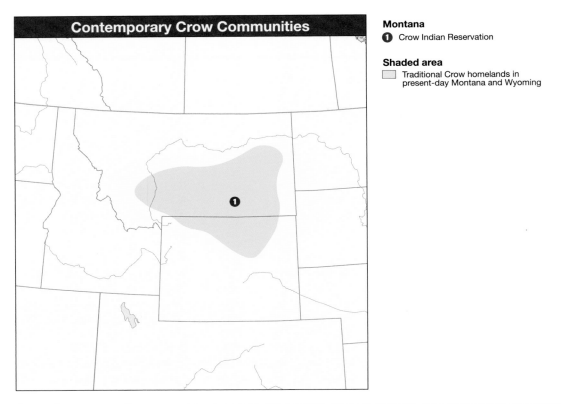

Montana
❶ Crow Indian Reservation

Shaded area
Traditional Crow homelands in present-day Montana and Wyoming

A map of contemporary Crow communities. MAP BY XNR PRODUCTIONS. CENGAGE LEARNING, GALE. REPRODUCED BY PERMISSION OF GALE, A PART OF CENGAGE LEARNING.

River and as far north as Lake Winnipeg, where they formed a part of the Hidatsa tribe. The Crow parted ways with the Hidatsa people, wandering westward and first entering Montana in the 1600s. Their enemies were the Blackfeet, the Sioux, and the Cheyenne (see entries). They sometimes traded with their allies, the Shoshone, the Flathead (see entries), and the Mandan. At times, though, they also fought with the Shoshone.

According to Crow oral history, the tribe went through three transitions. First, they were People of the Earth. During this time animals could talk and were one with humans. Next, they became *Biiluke,* or "Our Side." In this period, they lived in a wooded area while they fished, hunted, and gathered. They lived in lean-tos and wickiups (grass huts) until they migrated to the banks of a big river as they searched for the Sacred Tobacco Plant. At this point, they were called *Awashe,* or "Earthen Lodges." Although they still retained their survival skills, they became farmers. They traveled to Canada twice before finding the plant they sought on the Bighorn Mountain. That was the beginning of the present-day Apsáalooke Nation.

When the Europeans arrived, the Crow were western hunters. The men were known as fierce warriors, but the tribe was hospitable to strangers. Despite their early cooperation with settlers, the Crow were forced to give up their claims to all but a small part of their traditional homeland. In modern times, the Crow people have managed to preserve much of their cultural and language traditions.

HISTORY

Change from farmers to hunters

Early in their history, the Crow were part of the Hidatsa tribe. They stayed in one place and lived as farmers. In the early 1600s, a powerful tribal leader called "No Vitals" had a vision that told him to take his people west into the Rocky Mountains to search for a sacred tobacco plant. He believed that the seeds of the plant would give his people a special identity and make them strong.

Some time during the mid-1600s or early 1700s, about five hundred people separated from the Hidatsa to fulfill No Vitals's vision. They migrated to an area near the Yellowstone River in present-day southern Montana and northern Wyoming. They soon abandoned their former lifestyle in favor of a typical Great Plains existence, living in hide-covered tepees, following the movements of the great buffalo herds, and hunting for the plentiful game in their new homelands. The new tribe took the name the Crow.

In the mid-1700s, the tribe possessed horses, which greatly aided them in traveling, hunting, and warfare. By the early 1800s, they had more horses than any other tribe east of the Rocky Mountains, averaging between twenty and sixty animals per household.

Important Dates

1600s: Part of the tribe splits off from the Hidatsa and begins its westward move.

1825: After a disagreement between two powerful chiefs, the Crow divide into two main groups, the Mountain Crow and River Crow.

1868: The Second Fort Laramie Treaty establishes a reservation for the Crow in Montana, south of the Yellowstone River.

1876: Crow warriors act as scouts for Lieutenant Colonel George Custer before his defeat in the Battle of Little Bighorn.

1934: The Crow people refuse to accept the provisions of the Indian Reorganization Act.

1948: After writing their own constitution, the Crow establish a tribal government.

1961: The tribe receives $9.2 million from the U.S. government for a land claim settlement.

1963: In payment for the Yellowtail Dam and Reservoir property, the Crow receive $2 million from the federal government.

2001: A new, updated constitution is approved.

2010: The Crow Tribe Water Rights Settlement Act is passed.

Crow people split into two groups

When American explorers Meriwether Lewis (1774–1809) and William Clark (1770–1838) encountered them in 1806, the Crow were part of a large group of Native tribes and whites who had gathered to trade near Bismarck, North Dakota. Soon after the Lewis and Clark expedition, more fur traders arrived in Crow territory and constructed forts and trading posts.

In 1825, following a disagreement between two powerful chiefs, the Crow divided into two main groups. Chief Long Hair led the Mountain Crow into the high country south of the Yellowstone River, while Chief Arapooish and the River Crow remained north of the Yellowstone River, along the Musselshell and Judith Rivers that flowed into the larger Missouri River. As settlers pushed westward, the Crow fought with other tribes, including the Sioux and the Blackfoot (see entries), who moved into their territory. Because they were usually outnumbered, the Crow rarely started wars, but they did steal horses from their neighbors.

Peaceful relations with settlers

By the 1850s, many settlers had streamed into Crow country. At times, the Crow conducted raids on the newcomers, but most often, their relationships with the settlers were peaceful.

Wars and smallpox epidemics depleted the Crow population, and experts predicted that the tribe would soon perish. Instead, the Crow established a cooperative relationship with the U.S. Army and settled peacefully on a reservation in Montana. The Crow signed the Fort Laramie Treaty of 1851, which gave them 38.5 million acres in southern Montana, northern Wyoming, and western South Dakota. The Second Fort Laramie Treaty, signed in 1868, established the Crow Reservation south of the Yellowstone River.

In the late 1800s, the Crow leader Plenty Coups (pronounced *Coo*; c. 1848–1932) learned in a vision that his people needed to cooperate with the whites to survive. As a result, he had Crow warriors become allies of U.S. Army troops in several battles against enemy tribes. For example, they fought alongside American soldiers against the Nez Percé and Sioux (see entries) in the 1870s, and they acted as scouts for Lieutenant Colonel George Custer (1839–1876) before his defeat in 1876 at the Battle of Little Bighorn. (For more information on the Battle of Little Big Horn, see Lakota entry.) Crow cooperation with the United States did not earn them any better treatment than the tribes that resisted the Americans in battle. Still, the protection of the U.S. Army may have saved the Crow from perishing at the hands of the Sioux.

Traditional way of life shattered

During the 1880s, many miners, trappers, and settlers moved into Crow country, establishing forts and railroads. Because these newcomers had slaughtered buffalo on a large scale, by 1883, the herds had disappeared. The traditional way of life of the Crow also ended.

The Crow people, suddenly without their main source of food and clothing, were forced to depend on government Indian agents for survival. Over the next few decades, the Crow reservation was reduced in size several times, declining to about 2.2 million acres by 1905. At the same time, the Crow culture began disintegrating as Christian schools were established on the reservation and federal laws were enacted that prohibited traditional Native ceremonies and practices.

Chief Plenty Coups is known for his efforts to align his tribe with the U.S. government in the late 1800s. © THE ART ARCHIVE/GIFT OF FLORENCE SPOHR ESTATE/BUFFALO BILL HISTORICAL CENTER, CODY, WYOMING.

The General Allotment Act of 1887 (also called the Dawes Act) divided reservations into individual plots and opened leftover land to American settlement. The purpose of the act was to force the Native peoples to become more like U.S. citizens, with each one farming a small plot rather than working together on land jointly owned by the whole tribe. Many Crow were not interested in farming and ended up selling their land allotments on the reservation. In time, Crow territory became a checkerboard of Native and non-Native parcels.

Regaining Crow culture

In the late 1800s, Chief Plenty Coups spent much time in Washington, D.C., where he developed good contacts with important people and became shrewd in dealing with the U.S. government. For example, if a government official refused to listen to his demands for aid for his people, Plenty Coups would visit the official's rivals. The adversaries were happy to pay attention. Plenty Coups also learned that when the Crow spoke out about being cheated by government officials or local merchants, Christian church leaders often came to the Native Americans' defense.

In 1911, the Crow formed a business committee to represent the tribe in all its official business (see "Government"). It was headed by a young Crow man who had been educated in government-run schools, Robert Yellowtail (c. 1889–1988). During the 1920s, a general council replaced the business committee. Over time, the Crow attending the council meetings became active participants in the process, along with their elected leaders.

When the tribe refused to adopt the provisions of the Indian Reorganization Act in 1934, a revival of Crow culture began. The act would have allowed the Crow to write a constitution, but only under the supervision of the federal government. The Crow decided to remain independent. In 1948, under the leadership of Chief Yellowtail, the Crow developed their own constitution. The Crow, now more in control of their affairs, practiced their Native religion freely and followed traditional ways without fear of criticism.

The Crow in modern times

During the 1950s, the Crow were forced to sell their land rights in Bighorn Canyon to the U.S. government, which planned to build a dam there. In a strange turn, the officials named the completed project Yellowtail Dam and Reservoir after Chief Robert Yellowtail, who had strongly opposed it.

In the early twenty-first century, the Crow reservation is home not only to the Crow people, but also to several thousand non-Native American residents who have leased or purchased land from the Crow. The tribal government employs many Native people, and money from the federal government has helped to establish health, education, and housing programs.

RELIGION

Crow religion was based on the relationship between each tribal member and the guardian spirit who guided him or her throughout life. The guardian spirit was the source of an individual's power, wealth, and success. Guardian spirits, in the form of animals or features of the natural environment, usually revealed themselves during a vision quest (see "Festivals and ceremonies").

The Crow believed that tobacco had supernatural power and played an important role in their survival. The people who cared for the tobacco plants, the only crop the tribe cultivated, were members of the Tobacco Society. They had the ability to influence events in the natural world. Only men could smoke tobacco, and strict rules surrounded the practice.

Tobacco still plays a role in Crow religious life in modern times, and the people continue to make use of sweat lodges (buildings in which water is poured over hot rocks to produce steam) for purification. Although some belong to Christian churches, others practice the Peyote (pronounced *pay-OH-tee*) religion in special tepees where ritual smoking of peyote takes place. Peyote, which comes from a cactus plant, can cause visions and is used as part of certain Native religious ceremonies, especially those of the Native American Church. (For more information on the Native American Church, see Makah entry.)

LANGUAGE

The Crow speak a dialect (variety) of the Siouan language. Although several Great Plains tribes speak the language, the Crow version is most closely related to that spoken by the Hidatsa, since the two tribes

Crow Words

Many Crow words are descriptions of objects rather than actual names. For example, the word for *key* means "what is used to open doors." The word for *chair* translates as "where one sits" and *table* means "something with four legs."

aasuua	"head"
ahó	"thank you"
baaiihuli	"table"
balealawaache	"chair"
bishké	"dog"
buá	"fish"
deaxkaashe	"eagle"
íaxassee	"snake"
iisashpíte	"rabbit"
iiwilialushtuua	"key"
kaheé	"hello"
xuáhchee	"skunk"

A group of Crow leaders gather in council in 1865. © MARY EVANS PICTURE LIBRARY/THE IMAGE WORKS. REPRODUCED BY PERMISSION.

descended from the same people. Today, the majority of Crow adults and children on the reservation still speak their language, and it is used in reservation schools through the eighth grade.

GOVERNMENT

Each band of the Crow was led by a chief who had earned his position by accomplishing four feats: leading a successful raid against an enemy tribe, capturing an enemy's horses, taking a weapon from a live enemy, and being the first member of a war party to touch an enemy with a coup stick—a practice that was called counting coup. Most bands had more than one chief. The political leader usually demonstrated additional abilities in leadership, influence over the spirits, and public speaking, as well as generosity. When the band experienced a period of bad luck, the people agreed upon a new chief.

In 2001, the tribe adopted a new constitution, which called for three branches of government—the executive, legislative, and judicial—and lengthened the terms of office from two to four years to provide more continuity in government.

A general council—a group that consists of all adult members of the tribe—now leads the Crow. Along with four elected officials and various tribal committees, any person of voting age can provide input at council meetings. A tribal court settles disagreements among tribal members.

ECONOMY

Early livelihood

The Crow economy in traditional times was mainly based on hunting, which required a great deal of moving. Before horses were introduced in the 1730s, the people used tame dogs to carry or pull their belongings as they traveled. Horses provided more mobility and allowed for greater success in hunting. Before European contact, Crow territory was full of large game animals—from huge herds of buffalo to deer, elk, bighorn sheep, and grizzly bear. Hunting supplied most of the tribe's food, clothing, and shelter.

Women prepared the animal carcasses. They also gathered plant foods, collected firewood and water, cooked meals, prepared hides, and made clothing and tepee covers. They set up and disassembled tepees when the tribe moved and cared for the children and the family's horses. Because of their migrations, the Crow did not generally practice crafts such as basketry or pottery.

Modern-day employment

In the early twenty-first century, most of the tribe's income came from leasing land to coal, gas, and oil companies and from federal government grants. Timber, fisheries, and hunting brought in additional money. Although some tribal members tried to make a success of farming and ranching, they often lacked the funds to buy the necessary cattle, tools, and seeds. Instead many people leased out their land to outsiders.

The U.S. government was the largest employer on the reservation. Other workers found jobs as teachers, social workers, police officers, and cowboys, or in the restaurant and coal mining businesses. Finding employment was a challenge for the people on the reservation, and by 2001, the unemployment rate was 60 percent, meaning that six out of every ten people looking for work were unable to find a job.

Tourism helped to boost the economy. The Crow reservation is the site of the Little Bighorn Battlefield National Monument, which commemorates the lives lost during the 1876 Battle of Little Bighorn. Every year, tourists attend reenactments of the battle. The Crow earned profits from the motel and heritage center they built near the site. A casino and a technology business also add to their income.

DAILY LIFE

Families

The Crow lived in bands of various sizes, depending upon the availability of food. The major social unit was the extended family, or clan. Clans are a group of families who trace their families back to a common ancestor. In Crow society, descent followed the mother's clan. People could depend on their clan members to protect, defend, and help them in times of trouble. In fact, being told that "you are without relatives" was the worst possible insult to a Crow.

The Crow had a strict code of behavior for family interactions. Boys paid special respect to their elder male relatives and to their father's kin. Some relatives were to be avoided. For example, married men and women were not supposed to talk with their father-in-law or mother-in-law.

Members of the same clan could not marry one another. The complicated and wide-ranging Crow system of relationships ensured that even as they wandered from their immediate homes, tribe members were sure to encounter people with whom they had special ties and with whom they could ally against common enemies.

Buildings

After separating from the Hidatsa, the Crow adopted the hide-covered tepees used by most tribes of the Great Plains. The tepees had cone-shaped wooden frames made up of twenty poles, each about 25 feet (7 or 8 meters) long, which were covered with buffalo skins. Tepees usually had a fireplace in the center and a hole at the top to allow smoke to escape. Crow families slept on hide mattresses laid along the sides of the tepee. The tribe also built small, dome-shaped sweat lodges, in which men poured water over hot rocks and purified themselves in the steam.

Clothing and adornment

The Crow were known for their striking appearance. Crow men, in particular, were very careful about how they dressed and wore finely made clothes. Their everyday apparel consisted of a shirt, hair-trimmed leggings held up by a belt, moccasins, and a buffalo robe. For special occasions, they wore fancy costumes decorated with dyed porcupine quills or beads. The bridles, saddles, and blankets on their horses were also ornate.

Crow men usually wore their hair long, and they sometimes extended it by gluing human or horsehair to the ends. Some made their hair so long it dragged on the ground. They often hung strings of ornaments in their hair and wore earrings and necklaces of bone, bear claws, or abalone shells. They painted red designs on their faces and applied yellow paint on their eyelids.

Crow women, who spent long hours doing difficult tasks around the camp, tended to be less neat and less elaborately dressed than the men. Women usually wore calf-length dresses made of deer or mountain sheep skins that they often decorated with rows of elk teeth. They also wore leggings and moccasins. Crow women often had short hair. They either pulled it out or cut it short when they were mourning the death of a relative.

Food

As they moved about the countryside on their hunts, the Crow kept alert for available foods. In the spring, they searched for wild turnips, rhubarb, and strawberries. Along with the search for buffalo, summer brought a hunt for chokecherries, plums, and other fruits. Throughout the year, the Crow diet depended on rabbit, deer, elk, grizzly bear, bighorn sheep, and other game.

Education

Although the early Crow had no formal schools, children learned by imitating adults in the tribe. To prepare their sons to become successful hunters and warriors, fathers taught them survival skills, such as hunting and trapping. Mothers taught their daughters to prepare food, make clothing, and take care of a home.

Beginning in 1884, Crow children older than six had to attend a day school near the reservation. Some students were sent away to boarding schools in nearby states, and even as far away as Pennsylvania. Most children in these schools were required to dress like whites and speak only English. Conditions at the boarding schools were harsh, and some were

---

The Importance of Wampum

Chief Plenty Coups supported education because he thought schooling would eventually benefit his people. He made the following statement, which is often translated differently in English:

> *Baaishtashíile ammaaéhche iiwaa awássahcheewailuuk Ammaaéhche éwahkuulak baaawássahcheewiolak baleetáak*

> "With what the whiteman knows, he can oppress us. If we learn what he knows, then he can never oppress us again."

SOURCE: Plenty Coups. "Chapter 3: Historic Apsáalooke Culture: Famous Speeches." *Little Big Horn College Library.* http://lib.lbhc.edu/history/3.09.php (accessed July 5, 2011).

---

so unsanitary that the children there became ill. Despite the pressure for children to assimilate (adopt the ways of the American culture), the Crow made great efforts to keep their families intact and retain their Native beliefs.

In the early twenty-first century, students attended school on the Crow Reservation. The town of Crow Agency is the home of Little Bighorn Community College, a two-year college with a student body that is 90 percent Crow. The college offers associate arts degrees in areas that will contribute to the developing economies of the Crow Indian Reservation community. Because 90 percent of the students are Crow, most student services and business functions of the college are conducted in the Crow language.

Healing practices

The Crow had two types of healers. One treated minor illnesses and injuries using worldly knowledge, such as by rubbing plant products on sores or by lancing swollen areas. The other type, shamans (pronounced *SHAH-munz* or *SHAY-munz*), treated major problems like snakebites or diseases by consulting with the spirits.

Every Crow person also had his or her own medicine bundle, a small pouch containing sacred objects that symbolized the power of the person's guardian spirit. The medicine bundle was thought to be the source of health, luck, and power.

ARTS

Shields

Crow people took special care in decorating the rawhide shields they carried into battle. The images that appeared on them often came from visions experienced by the artist and related to his connection with the supernatural. Shields sometimes had sacred objects such as feathers attached to them. The people believed these protected the user with a special power, and they often passed these items down through the generations. Decorated buckskin covers protected the shields.

Oral literature and crafts

Many Crow stories center on Old Man Coyote, who is often portrayed as a trickster. Old Man Coyote is also recognized as the creator of the world and of the Crow people.

The Crow were known for their skillful quillwork and beading using pastel colors and geometric designs. Men's costumes in particular were elaborately decorated with beads, dyed porcupine quills, dyed horsehair, and paints. Horses, too, wore beaded harnesses. Collectors pay high prices for Crow beadwork from the 1800s and early 1900s. For example, in 1998, a Crow pipebag from the 1800s sold for $19,500 at an auction. Crow carvings are also highly valued.

CUSTOMS

Sodalities

After reaching adulthood, most Crow men were recruited into a *sodality*, or voluntary men's organization. The members of these groups enjoyed a special, family-like bond with one another. Intense rivalries often existed between different sodalities, such as the Lumpwoods and Foxes, the two most popular.

Vision quest

When a young man undertook a vision quest to connect with his guardian spirit, he first purified himself in a sweat lodge. He then traveled to a sacred site on a mountaintop. There he fasted (did not have food or water) for three days and slept uncovered in the cold for three nights. Some visionaries cut off the first joint of one finger and offered it to the rising Sun. On the fourth day, after he had proved his courage and willingness to deprive himself, the young man's guardian spirit would appear to him in a vision.

The spirit gave the man a sacred song or symbol that he could use to appeal for the spirit's help in the future. Another way for a young man to seek a vision was to cut two slits in the skin of his chest and insert a wooden skewer. He then tied each end of the skewer to a tall pole, and ran around the pole or leaned back until the skewer ripped from his flesh. Often in the midst of his pain, he received a vision.

Courtship and marriage

In the Crow culture, girls usually married before their first menstruation. Young men, who could not join the hunt until after they were married, spent most of their time grooming themselves to show off before eligible young women. To propose marriage, the man offered horses to the woman's brothers and meat to her mother.

To show that he would be a good provider, a young boy collected elk teeth over many years of hunting and saved them until he was ready to marry. His mother or sisters then sewed them onto a dress for his bride. Because the only elk teeth used on dresses were the two ivory eyeteeth, it took a long time to obtain them. Many elk teeth on a dress meant great wealth.

Upon marriage, the Crow husband would move in with his new wife's family. Some Crow men had more than one wife. Cheating on one's spouse was common among both men and women.

Crow women were very important and obtained high status in the tribe. Some women even became chiefs.

Berdaches

Another element of Crow society were *berdaches,* men who enjoyed dressing as women. The Crow considered berdaches to be a third gender and believed that they possessed special powers.

Festivals and ceremonies

Of all the traditional Crow ceremonies, the Sun Dance was the most sacred. A Sun Dance was held so a man could receive a special vision, usually to help him cure a sick child or to exact revenge on an enemy for the death of a relative. The man who held the Sun Dance was called the whistler. He enlisted the help of a shaman who possessed a sacred doll. The dolls were considered gifts from the gods and were passed down from one generation to another.

Other men seeking visions could participate in the Sun Dance by fasting and inflicting wounds on themselves (see "Vision quest"). For many years, the U.S. government prohibited traditional Crow ceremonies. William Big Day (born c. 1891) reintroduced the Sun Dance to the tribe in 1941 after learning it from the Shoshone (see entry). Today, the tradition continues, and the Crow hold Sun Dances each summer, drawing up to one hundred participants.

Every year during the third week in August, Crow Agency becomes the "Tepee Capital of the World." At that time, the Crow hold a giant homecoming featuring powwows (celebrations of Native singing and dancing), arts and crafts displays, a rodeo, and a road race. This celebration at the Crow Fairgrounds has been held for more than ninety years. Food booths offer frybread, Indian tacos, and the traditional *menudo,* a mixture of chili and tripe (part of an ox's stomach). Among other popular treats are puffball mushrooms and blueberry pudding.

In the 1990s, tribe members hoped to combat drug and alcohol abuse by involving their youth and adults in activities to instill pride in themselves and their heritage. The tribe started Crow Native Days, during which young people could compete in a variety of events. One of the most grueling is the Ultimate Warrior Challenge, where participants race in three events—canoeing, running, and horseback riding. Although it is similar to an Olympic decathlon, this race starts and ends the same day. Initially only for males, this event is now open to females. Other activities featured during Crow Native Days include basketball games, a rodeo, horse races, relays, a powwow (Native singing and dancing), a parade, and a trail ride. A reenactment of the Battle of the Little Big Horn takes place at the actual site. These events are now held yearly on the anniversary date of the battle.

CURRENT TRIBAL ISSUES

Like many other tribes, the Crow have been involved in a number of land claims and land use disputes over the years. They remain concerned about how their lands are being used and feel that too often non-Natives are profiting from their land. The parcels of land that tribal members received in the early 1900s were not enough to support the growing population. If a father divided his land among his children at his death and they divided their portion among their children, the plots became too small to farm. By the early 2000s, much of the reservation land had been sold or leased to large agricultural or mining interests.

The Crow have had trouble in obtaining what they believe to be a fair proportion of the income from the use of their natural resources. They did, however, receive a $9.2 million land claim settlement from the U.S. government in 1961, plus another $2 million in 1963 for the Yellowtail Dam and Reservoir property. The Crow used the funds to purchase land for industrial development programs and to make loans to tribal members. The tribe also invested in a variety of businesses.

In 2010, the Crow Tribe was given a deadline of November 1 to replace the Little Big Horn Casino in Crow Agency, Montana. The casino, built in the 1970s, no longer met building standards. The Crow were not sure that they could secure financing for the upgrade, given the state of the economy and their financial situation. The Shakopee

Mdewakanton Tribe in Minnesota came to their aid with $2 million in grants and $3 million in loans. Construction on the casino was not completed in 2010 as planned, but the tribe received an extension on the deadline. The 12,000-square-foot (3,700-square-meter) Apsaalooka Nights Casino is situated near tourist spots that attract more than half a million people annually. The Crow hope it will draw customers from that traffic. They intend to add a hotel at a later date.

In December 2010, President Barack Obama (1961– served 2009–) signed the Crow Tribe Water Rights Settlement Act. This act provides $460 million to improve the Crow Irrigation Project, construct a water system, and develop energy projects. The state of Montana will also contribute $15 million. The Crow people are guaranteed most of the water from Bighorn Lake and the other basins—Little Bighorn River, Pryor Creek, and Rosebud Creek. Supporters of the bill say it will ensure the water rights of the tribe for future generations and provide irrigation. They also see it as giving them opportunities for economic expansion. Opponents counter that landowners lost the rights they were granted as allotees under the Dawes Act (see "History"). An even greater concern is that much of the water will be used for a coal-to-diesel plant, which will use large amounts of fresh water and return filthy water in its place, causing environmental damage.

In the early 2000s, the federal government began programs to help tribes reduce unemployment, increase management skills, and boost the economy by training tribe members for jobs in power plants, irrigation facilities, and other water operations as well as working to improve water supplies and environmental recovery. The Crow Tribe has now become one of the participants in this venture.

NOTABLE PEOPLE

Plenty Coups (c. 1848–1932), or Alaxchíiaahush ("Bull That Goes Against the Wind"), was the last traditional chief of the Crow. As a boy, Plenty Coups had a vision that convinced him that the only way to save the Crow people was to cooperate with non-Native settlers and the U.S. government. Plenty Coups effectively represented the interests of the Crow people before the federal government. In 1921, the chief was chosen to represent all Native nations at the dedication of the Tomb of the Unknown Soldier at Arlington National Cemetery near Washington, D.C.

Other notable Crow include Curly (c. 1859–c. 1935), a scout for Custer (see "History"); educator and administrator Barney Old Coyote (1923–); and Janine Pease-Windy Boy (1949–), founding president of Little Big Horn College, who helped overturn a Montana state law that had allowed discriminatory practices against Native voters.

BOOKS

Bauerle, Phenocia, ed. *The Way of the Warrior: Stories of the Crow People.* Lincoln: University of Nebraska Press, 2003.

Beckwourth, James. *The Life and Adventures of James P. Beckwourth, Mountaineer, Scout, and Pioneer, and Chief of the Crow Nation of Indians.* Paris, France: Adamant Media Corporation, 2005.

Crow, Joseph Medicine. *Counting Coup: Becoming a Crow Chief on the Reservation and Beyond.* Washington, DC: National Geographic, 2006.

Crow, Joseph Medicine. *From the Heart of the Crow Country: The Crow Indians' Own Stories.* Lincoln: University of Nebraska Press, 2000.

Keefe, Brian L., compiler. *Red Was the Blood of Our Forefathers: Episodes from Crow Indian Intertribal Warfare.* Caldwell, ID: Caxton Press, 2010.

Linderman, Frank B. *Pretty-shield: Medicine Woman of the Crows.* Toronto, Canada: Bison Books, 2003.

Lobo, Susan, Steve Talbot, and Traci L. Morris, compilers. *Native American Voices: A Reader.* 3rd ed. Upper Saddle River, NJ: Prentice Hall, 2010.

Snell, Alma Hogan. *A Taste of Heritage: Crow Indian Recipes & Herbal Medicines.* Lincoln: University of Nebraska Press, 2006.

Yellowtail, Thomas. *Native Spirit: The Sun Dance Way.* Edited by Michael Oren Fitzgerald. Bloomington, IN: World Wisdom, 2007.

PERIODICALS

Linse, Tamara. "Billings Man Captured Culture of Crow, Northern Cheyenne Tribes." *Billings Gazette.* January 16, 2005. Available online from http://billingsgazette.com/news/features/magazine/article_a0eb7a74-aafd-5abb-b7dc-c54c3d1a6f5c.html#ixzz1RIQxEBtH (accessed on July 5, 2011).

WEB SITES

"The Apsáalooke (Crow Indians) of Montana Tribal Histories." *Little Big Horn College.* http://lib.lbhc.edu/history/ (accessed on July 5, 2011).

"Crow/Cheyenne." *Wisdom of the Elders.* http://www.wisdomoftheelders.org/program206.html (accessed on July 5, 2011).

"Crow Indian Tribe." *Access Genealogy.* http://www.accessgenealogy.com/native/tribes/crow/crowhist.htm (accessed on July 5, 2011).

Crow Tribe, Apsáalooke Nation Official Website. http://www.crowtribe.com/ (accessed on July 5, 2011).

"Lewis and Clark: Crow Indians (Absaroka)." *National Geographic Society.* http://www.nationalgeographic.com/lewisandclark/record_tribes_002_19_21.html (accessed on July 5, 2011).

Medicine Crow, Joe. "Introduction to Native Spirit: The Sun Dance Way." *World Wisdom.* http://www.worldwisdom.com/public/viewpdf/default.aspx?article-title=Intro_by_Joe_Medicine_Crow_to_Native_Spirit_The_Sun_Dance_Way.pdf (accessed on July 4, 2011).

Old Coyote, Barney. "Turtle Island Storyteller Barney Old Coyote." *Turtle Island Storytellers Network.* http://www.turtleislandstorytellers.net/tis_montana/transcript_b_old_coyote.htm (accessed on July 4, 2011).

"Preserving Sacred Wisdom." *Native Spirit and the Sun Dance Way.* http://www.nativespiritinfo.com/ (accessed on July 5, 2011).

Redish, Laura, and Orrin Lewis. "Crow Indian Language (Apsaalooke, Apsaroke, Absarokee)." *Native Languages of the Americas.* http://www.native-languages.org/crow.htm (accessed on July 5, 2011).

Kansa (Kaw)

Name

When the French arrived in the 1700s, they often named tribes after nearby landmarks. Jacques Marquette (1637–1675), who mapped the area in 1674, asked about the river that ran toward the Mississippi and Missouri Rivers. The French took the name they were told, *Koln-Za,* and made it Kanza. The English later changed it to Kansas, a name given to the surrounding area when it became a state. The name for the Kansa people has also been written as Konze, Can, Caw, Ka-anzou, Kancez, Kanissi, Kansies, Kantha, Caugh, Keniser, and Quans. The people call themselves the Kaw Nation, but some say their original name came from the Siouan word *aca,* meaning "south wind," So they are also known as the "people of the south wind." The name has sometimes been translated as "plum."

Location

Some sources say the Kansa may have originated in the Southeast and lived in southern Illinois and Indiana prior to contact with Europeans. According to oral history, the Kansa, as part of the five Dhegiha (pronounced *they-GEE-hah*) tribes, tell of moving west from their home in the Ohio Valley. Perhaps this migration occurred because colonists were pushing many of the coastal tribes farther inland. After the Dhegiha groups separated, the Kansa moved into present-day northeastern Kansas along the Missouri River. In 1724, a French explorer wrote of the Kansa living on a cliff in what would later be Doniphan, Kansas. After the Kansa gave up this village, they settled along the Kansas River before the Discovery Corps expedition, led by Meriwether Lewis (1774–1809) and William Clark (1770–1838), arrived in 1804. At one time, their territory covered most of eastern and northern Kansas, with extensive hunting grounds to the west. Yet during the next decades, encroaching settlers caused the tribe to give up land several times until the Kansa ended up in four villages around present-day Council Grove, Kansas, along the Neosho River. In 1872, Congress forced the Kansa to relocate to Indian Territory (present-day Oklahoma). The people eventually settled on a reservation along the Arkansas River. Today, their reservation is located in Kaw City, Oklahoma.

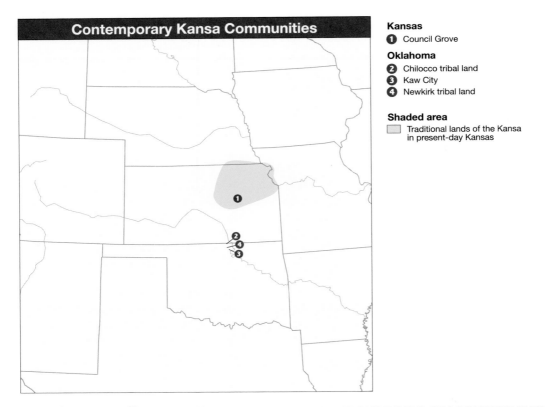

Contemporary Kansa Communities

Kansas
1 Council Grove

Oklahoma
2 Chilocco tribal land
3 Kaw City
4 Newkirk tribal land

Shaded area
Traditional lands of the Kansa in present-day Kansas

A map of contemporary Kansa communities. MAP BY XNR PRODUCTIONS. CENGAGE LEARNING, GALE. REPRODUCED BY PERMISSION OF GALE, A PART OF CENGAGE LEARNING.

Population

The earliest population estimates for the Kansa indicated about 3,000 people in 1780. Disease and starvation decreased those figures rapidly each decade during the 1800s. After beginning with a population of 1,850 in 1822, the number of Kansa went down to 1,588 in 1843; 1,015 in 1857; 718 in 1868; 533 in 1873; 193 in 1887; and 185 in 1897. At the same time, the percentage of settlers in the area almost tripled each decade. During the 1900s, the population figures stayed between 209 in 1905 and 515 in 1937. Not until later in the century did those totals rise. By 1993, Kansa membership had reached 1,678. According to the Kaw Nation, it had 3,167 citizens as of 2011.

Language family

Siouan.

Origins and group affiliations

The Kansa, along with the Omaha, Osage (see entries), Poncan, and Quapaw (see entry), were Dhegiha-Siouan people who lived together in the Ohio Valley in the late 1400s. These groups had all descended from the ancient Hopewell culture (see the Mound Builders entry). Enemies of the Kansa included the Cheyenne, Osage, Pawnee, Sac and Fox (see entries), Iowa, Omaha, and Oto (see Missouri entry). Two years after signing their first peace treaty with the United States in 1815, the Kansa made an official pact of friendship with the Oto.

The Kansa, who may have originated in the Southeast, drifted west across the Great Plains from the Ohio Valley to the Missouri River area. Forced moves later took them to Kansas and Oklahoma. Through all their migrations, one element remained constant in their lives—the wind. The people believed that the south wind lived with them, revealing the whereabouts of the buffalo that they hunted each summer and winter. The south wind showed them who were enemies and who were allies, and it assisted the people as they foraged for food. Later, as the "south wind people" settled far from their traditional lands, the south wind still offered guidance. Present-day Kaw consult the south wind before council meetings, court appearances, or building homes. As they traveled over the centuries, the Kansa left their name behind, revealing the path they traveled. The state of Kansas, the Kansas River, and Kansas City (one in Missouri and one in Kansas) bear their tribal name, as do many other places, including their final destination—their reservation at Kaw City.

HISTORY

Prehistory

From about 150 BCE to 500 CE, the Hopewell culture (see the Mound Builders entry) flourished in the Ohio Valley. The Hopewell people replaced the Adena culture that had lived in the area for thousands of years. Both ancient groups were farming people, as were the Woodland tribes that followed. The Hopewell were also known for their extensive trading with other peoples. They gathered copper from the Great Lakes region, obsidian from the Rocky Mountains, shells and shark teeth from the Gulf of Mexico, and mica from the Carolinas.

In addition to their unique stone tools and pottery, the Hopewell culture was known for their earthworks. As one of the ancient mound-building cultures, the Hopewell constructed huge burial mounds, such as the largest ones in Chillicothe, Ohio, the Mound City Group. Many mounds curved into geometric patterns or other shapes. The large mounds served for burying the Hopewell dead.

In the Late Woodland period that followed, the people built larger villages and traveled less frequently. Perhaps they feared for their safety, because ditches or walls surrounded many villages. These Hopewell people were ancestors of the Dhegiha-Siouan division, which consisted of the Osage, Omaha, Quapaw, Poncan, and Kaw, or Kansa people. These groups lived together in the lower Ohio Valley in the late 1400s.

Separation of the tribes

At some point, these groups, possibly under pressure from stronger eastern tribes, the Dhegiha peoples moved west to the Ohio River, and each tribe went a different way. Four groups went upstream—the Kansa, Omaha, Ponca, and Osage. The Quapaw went past the mouth of the Ohio to the Mississippi River and became known as the "downstream people." The Osage moved southwest into the Ozarks, whereas the Omaha and Ponca took over territory in what is now eastern Nebraska.

The Kansa went up the Missouri River and stopped near the Kansas River. When they tried to go farther upriver, the Cheyenne attacked, and the Kansa were forced to retreat. The Kansa occupied the Kansas River valley, part of which later became Kansas City. By 1674, a map drawn by Jacques Marquette (1637–1675) showed the Kansa along the Kansas River.

Early European contact

Marquette was not the first European to record information about the Kansa. If the Guaes people that Francisco Vásquez de Coronado (1510–1554) mentioned were the Kansa, then the Kansa met their first Europeans in 1541. It is also possible that Juan de Oñate (c. 1550–1626) referred to the Kansa as *Escansaques* as he wrote about his travels through south-central Kansas in 1601.

Some sources indicated that during the 1700s, the Kansa fought among themselves and with other Dhegiha peoples as well as with the Fox, Sauk (Sac), Pawnee, Oto, and Iowa. In 1724, the Kansa received a visit from French explorer Étienne de Véniard, Sieur de Bourgmont (1679–1734). Bourgmont appreciated Kansa hospitality and enlisted their help in his travels to the Padouca in western Kansas. Several Kansa, Oto, Iowa, and Missouri accompanied Bourgmont to his meeting. The Padouca—whom Bourgmont called the Comanche (see entry), but experts say were more likely the Apache (see entry)—were willing to trade horses and listened to Bourgmont's speeches about maintaining peaceful relations among the tribes.

Bourgmont's mission had few results of lasting value, but he left behind a written record of the Kansa settlement on a bluff in Doniphan, Kansas. Although they eventually moved to the Kansas River, the Kansa village was still pointed out as a landmark in the next century. Other writers, too, mention the Kansa. Throughout the 1700s, the Kansa remained one of the dominant tribes on Great Plains west of Missouri, where they had spread throughout most of northern and eastern Kansas.

United States makes Louisiana Purchase

In 1803, the United States bought France's Louisiana Territory, which included the Kansa homeland. This huge parcel of land later became fifteen states and two Canadian provinces. President Thomas Jefferson (1743–1826; served 1801–09) assigned Meriwether Lewis to explore the area. Accompanied by William Clark and the Corps of Discovery, Lewis reached Kansa lands in 1804. The Kansa, though, were not around; they had gone on a buffalo hunting expedition in western Kansas. The expedition noted that the Kansa lived overlooking the Missouri River near where it met the Kansas River.

Within a short time, however, settlers flocked to Louisiana Territory. Some moved onto Kansa lands, and their town later became Atchison, Kansas. The Kansa migrated to where the Big Blue River met the Kansas River, but arriving settlers again took land to the west of them, which became Manhattan, Kansas. The federal government soon began eyeing the land the Kansa occupied.

Kansa give up their lands

In 1825, the Kansa signed a peace treaty with the United States in which they sold most of their land in Missouri, Nebraska, and Kansas for the use of the displaced eastern tribes. The Kansa relocated to an

Important Dates

1804: Lewis and Clark camp at a Kansa village.

1815: The United States signs the first peace treaty with the Kansa.

1825: The Kansa sell a large portion of their land to the United States.

1872: The Kansa are moved to reservation in Kay County, Oklahoma.

1902: The Kaw Allotment Act dissolves the tribe.

1959: The federal government recognizes Kaw Nation.

1960s–70s: Former reservation land floods because of Kaw Reservoir; tribal cemetery and council house need to be relocated.

1990: The Kansa ratify their constitution.

2011: The Kaw Nation Constitution is rewritten.

area near present-day Topeka. A devastating flood in 1844 left the people in dire straits, so in 1846, they again ceded their land to the government and moved along the Neosho River to a place later called Council Grove, Kansas.

By 1860, the Kansa lived in three main villages around Council Grove. Called by the names of the chiefs, the villages were Ishtalasea (Speckled Eyes) on Big John Creek, Kahegahwahtiangah (Fool Chief) near Dunlap, and Kahagawachuffe (Hard Chief) on Kahola Creek. Some Kansa lived in individual lodges outside these communities. Meanwhile, settlers continued to move onto the land set aside for the Kansa. They cut the timber, chopped up the sod, and let their livestock roam across the reservation. Railroad developers and other merchants also wanted this property, so the Kansa were forced to give up all but the poorest land.

Kansa population decreases

During this time, the Kansa population dropped sharply from about 1,700 at Lewis and Clark's arrival to about 500 in early 1870. Many deaths were from smallpox, a disease for which the people had no natural immunity. Others were from attacks by other tribes, such as the Pawnee. Some Kansa died at the hands of traders using the Santa Fe Trail.

The Kansa population plummeted even more after an act of Congress in 1872. In spite of protests from Chief Allegawaho, the people were forced to sell their tribal land and move to an Oklahoma reservation. The Kansa had no say in the matter. The tract they bought, part of Osage land, cost them most of the sale of their Kansas trust lands. By the time the Kansa had lived on this 100,137-acre reservation for little more than a decade, their numbers had dwindled to 193.

Kansa resistance to government intervention

Government actions and policies had caused many difficulties for the Kansa, beginning with the 1825 treaty, which gave property to Kansa half-bloods who supported negotiating with United States, but nothing to the rest of the tribal members. This lead to factionalism, and division developed between those who opposed American ways and those who supported them.

Throughout the 1800s, the government tried to turn the Kansa into an agricultural people, but they resisted. Before they left for the reservation, everyone in the tribe, even the children and the elderly, participated

Representatives from the Kansa tribe meet with the U.S. Commissioner of Indian Affairs in 1857. © CORBIS.

in their last buffalo hunt. Still, most government representatives strongly believed that the Kansa should give up their hunting lifestyle. For example, Luke Lea, the U.S. Commissioner of Indian Affairs, without considering the Kansa's preferences, insisted that the Kansa people needed to be confined to a smaller space:

> It is indispensably necessary that they be placed in positions where they can be controlled and finally compelled by sheer necessity to resort to agricultural labor or starve.... There should be assigned to each tribe, for a permanent home, a country adapted to agriculture, of limited extent and well-defined boundaries; within which all, with occasional exception, should be compelled constantly to remain until such time as their general improvement and good conduct may supersede the necessity of such restrictions.

The government was determined to change the Kansa into farmers and American citizens, but the people themselves worked to keep their traditions intact. This Kansa resistance to changing their culture extended, too, to education. Many other tribes allowed their children to be shipped off to boarding schools run by the federal government or religious institutions, but the Kansa refused. This may have helped to preserve their culture, because children attending government or religious schools were not allowed to speak their languages or practice their religions or traditions.

More troubles for the Kansa

In 1898, the Curtis Act allowed the federal government to allot (give out) or lease tribal land to whomever they pleased without asking tribal authorities. The act also took away many tribal rights, including the Kansa's ability to issue money or operate their own courts. This act was particularly troublesome to many full-blood Kansa, because the author of the bill, Charles Curtis (1860–1936; see "Notable People"), who later served as vice president under Herbert Hoover (1874–1964; served 1929–33), was a mixed-blood Kansa. This led to continuing struggles over tribal affairs and to factions within the community.

The next major blow fell in 1902. With the passage of the Kaw Allotment Act, the Kansa (Kaw) tribe was legally terminated by the federal government. At the same time, the government required the Kansa to give up 160 acres for an Indian agency, a school, and a town called Washungah. The reservation was broken up into individual plots, and the people received 405 acres each. Curtis and his children were each given 1,625 acres of land. Over the next decades, many Kansa sold or lost their land due to taxes. By 1945, only about 13 percent of the reservation was owned by Kansa people. In 1959, the federal government finally recognized the Kansa Nation.

Flooding from Kaw Reservoir

After allotment, the tribe had kept 260 acres near Beaver Creek, but in the mid-1960s, the government authorized the construction of a dam above the mouth of the Arkansas River. Construction began in 1966. Waters from the reservoir were expected to flood Washungah town, the council house, and the cemetery. The Kansa had to negotiate with local and federal officials for permission to move the cemetery. They finally received a 15-acre plot in Newkirk, Oklahoma. An act of Congress later granted them 135 additional acres.

The U.S. Army Corps of Engineers moved the cemetery and the council house. By 1975, the original town was under water. In 2000, the people found more than one hundred bodies that had not been moved from the cemetery. The bodies have since been reinterred in the Kaw Cemetery in Newkirk. Both Newkirk and Kaw City have since become important tribal centers.

Kansa in the twenty-first century

Since before they moved to the reservation, the Kansa struggled with poverty and gradual loss of their culture and traditions. Over time they have worked to establish businesses, including a casino, a travel plaza, tobacco shops, and housing projects, that will benefit the tribe. To prevent their language from dying out, they established the Kaw Language Project in 2001. They also hold traditional dances and powwows to keep their traditions alive.

RELIGION

Creation stories

The Kansa believed that Wakanda (Waucondah or Wakonda), the great Creator God, had put people on Earth. They have several accounts of their people's origins. In one of these stories, men were first created with long tails, but they soon became boastful. The Great Spirit took away their tails and turned the tails into nagging women. Wakanda also sent swarms of mosquitoes to bother the men and remind them to not to brag.

Another variation on the creation story is that Wakanda, or the Master of Life, created men. When the men cried about being lonely, Wakanda made women. Later, as the population grew, the small island where the Kansa lived became overcrowded. The fathers wanted to drown the children, but the mothers prayed for more room. The Master sent animals—turtles, beavers, and muskrats—to dig up mud from under the great waters surrounding the island. The animals added this land to the island until it formed the earth as it is now. The Master used autumn leaves to fill the land with animals. The world was soon filled with plant and animal life and, most of all, beauty.

Traditional religion

The Kansa were very private about their religion, so little is known of their beliefs beyond the fact that they believed in spirits that were a part of the natural world. These spirits were found in rivers, darkness, woods, light, and other aspects of the universe. Some objects were considered sacred—white horses, pipes, clam shells, and medicinal roots used in ceremonies. A sacred fire was lit in newly built lodges.

By the late 1800s, the Kansa may have known of peyote (see Lakota entry), a plant causing hallucinations that was being used for religious purposes by many tribes, but few Kansa used it in the early 1900s. A school supervisor noted in 1909 that only five Kansa used peyote, and he indicated that it had not caused them any harm.

In 1914, Alanson Skinner (1886–1925), an ethnologist who studied Native culture, asked the Kaw about Peyotism. According to his records, it had been popular for about seven or eight years and had replaced older religious practices. Skinner remarked that the way the Kansa followed Peyotism, it had no connections to Christianity. (A typical Peyote ceremony in many tribes often ended with sermon from the Bible.) The people held their gatherings in a large tepee, and used eagle feather fans and gourd rattles. Those who followed the Peyote religion no longer got drunk. Instead, Saturday nights were devoted to Peyote meetings. Skinner concluded that the Peyote religion and the Kansa's newly acquired wealth (cars, phones, and other luxuries) had destroyed previous traditional beliefs. Many people continue to participate in the Native American Church (see Makah entry).

Outside religious influence

Several Protestant groups tried to convert the Kansa. The Methodists set up mission schools from 1850 to 1854, and the Quakers worked among the people from 1869 to 1873. However, the Kansa kept to themselves, and most refused to let their children attend these schools. They felt very strongly that it would be ruinous for their children. The adults also showed little interest in Christianity. Only one Kansa converted during more than two decades of missionary influence.

LANGUAGE

The Kansa speak a dialect of the Dhegiha-Siouian language family called *Kaánze Íe*, or Kanza. The Kanza language is similar to that spoken by the Quapaw (see entry), Omaha, and Ponca, and it is very close to the

Osage dialect. It is also related to the language of the Lakota, Dakota, Nakota (see entries), Ioway, and Otoe-Missouria. Crow (see entry), Biloxi, Hidatsa, and Mandan are also distantly related.

Although the Kansa resisted sending their children to government schools, where students were punished for speaking their native language, over time, the people slowly stopped using their language. By the 1970s, only a few full-bloods still spoke Kansa fluently. In 2001, the Kaw Nation began the Kanza Language Project, which funds research and school classes and produces books and publications for language study. The Kanza Language Project also provides a wealth of online language resources.

Kanza Words	
zhúje	"red"
zíhi	"yellow"
bazóego	"purple"
sábe	"black"
ska	"white"
wéyashkige	"soap"
míonba	"sun"
nánje	"heart"
ho	"fish"

GOVERNMENT

Traditional leadership

The position of chief was hereditary, but he only remained a leader as long as he distinguished himself by bravery in battle and by generosity and exemplary personal character. In addition, the Kansa had several under-chiefs, but none had much authority.

Political struggles within the tribe

After their leader Washunga died in 1908, the people had no formal tribal government. The last full-blood council was held in 1916. Amid continuing political struggles, the tribe reorganized in 1959 and was recognized by the federal government. Federal recognition meant that the U.S. government would maintain official relations with the tribe. It also made the tribe eligible for government services and programs.

In the 1970s, seventeen full-blood members filed a lawsuit for control of the tribe. The court ordered a new tribal election in 1974. The Kansa ratified a new constitution in 1990 and set up a tribal court. The people began working on amending the constitution in 2011. One area under discussion was the amount of Kansa blood tribal leaders must have. The last Kansa full blood died in 2000. The constitution initially

Repayment of Debt at Dances

It was the custom for creditors to allow debtors the privilege of paying off old scores, at a dance of triumph, by standing in the center of the circle and submitting to sound beatings, at one dollar a blow.

An old [Indian woman] had tried in vain to collect the sum of twelve dollars from a young man. Desiring to end her importunities [begging] for money, he advanced and stood, the object of all eyes in stoical forbearance, while she administered, to the full extent of her power, the requisite amount of punishment. As usual, the Kaws had buried their most valuable goods previous to undertaking the foregoing expedition. First, a large cavity had been made in the ground and the articles placed inside. These were covered with sticks and branches, earth being piled on top and stamped down. In a violent effort to bestow the last blow effectively, the old woman caused this structure to give way and sank into the chasm, to the great diversion of spectators—for the Indians, among themselves, on such a day, were prone to cast dignity to the winds.

SOURCE: De Voe, Carrie. "The Kaws and Osages." *The Folk-Lore of the Indians of the Kansas River Valley.* Kansas City, MO: Franklin Hudson Publishing Co., 1904. Available from http://www.kancoll.org/books/kaw/ (accessed on June 17, 2011).

required 1/32 Kansa blood. Some members wanted leadership to stay with 1/8 Kansa blood or more, meaning one of the leader's grandparents would have to be Kansa. Others felt that establishing a blood requirement eliminated some good potential leaders.

As of the 2000s, the Kaw Nation had an executive council with a chairperson, vice chairperson, secretary, and four other members. Council members were elected by a majority vote of the general council composed of all member of the nation of voting age. The Kaw Nation also had reestablished tribal courts (district and supreme) that the U.S. government had closed.

ECONOMY

For half the year, the Kansa lived in their villages, where the women grew corn and gathered wild plants for food. Twice a year, they journeyed to the plains of western Kansas to hunt buffalo. After the arrival of the Europeans, some men turned to trapping so that they could trade furs with the French. In return, they received guns and other goods.

As the Kansa were pushed into increasingly smaller territories by the settlers and government treaties, hunting buffalo became more difficult. The Kansa also had to compete with other Great Plains tribes for a decreasing buffalo supply and to watch for attacks from other tribes, such as the Pawnee and Comanche. Although the Kansa resisted government efforts to get them to turn to farming, they had little choice once the government divided up their land and assigned them small plots. Many people ended up selling or losing their land. By the time the Kansa were moved to the Oklahoma reservation, most were in poverty.

Meach-o-Shin-Gaw, also known as Little White Bear, was a Kansa warrior in the 1800s. © HULTON ARCHIVE/ GETTY IMAGES.

Over the years, the Kansa built up their economy to include a travel plaza, smoke shops, businesses, and the Southwind Casino, all of which generate income for the tribe. The Kaw Nation issues its own license plates and has a housing authority that provides low-cost housing to those who need it. Two other important ventures include Kaw Enterprise Development Authority (KEDA), which seeks new business, and SouthWind Energy, which handles the development of renewable energy sources, such as wind farms.

DAILY LIFE

Families

Men were warriors and hunters. Women tended crops, cared for children, cooked, gathered, made clothing, and preserved meat. They also accompanied the men on bison hunts, where they took care of butchering the meat and preserving it for later use.

Buildings

Kansa homes changed as the people moved to new locations. When they lived near the Ohio and Missouri Rivers, they made homes similar to those of the Eastern Woodland tribes. They used leaves, bark, and mats to cover pole frames. These homes averaged 60 feet (20 meters) long by 25 feet (8 meters) wide. A central opening allowed smoke from the fire to escape. Most homes had two or three fires; each was used by one of the families who shared the lodge.

As they moved west to the Great Plains, the Kansa used dirt and wood for the walls of their round huts. They dug into the ground about 3 feet (1 meter) and set up poles. An inner circle of poles also supported the structure. Beams connected the posts and met at the top. The people laid twigs parallel to each other between each post and laced them together with bark. The Kansa then covered that understructure with grass or reed mats, or with bark sheets. The outside was covered with dirt.

Inside the doorway to the east was a tunnel-like structure leading into and out of the house. An opening in the roof let out smoke. Around the outer edge, the Kansa made raised bunks about 6 feet (2 meters) wide that they cushioned with buffalo robes. Homes were shared by three to five families.

When they traveled for hunting, the Kansa set up tepees of pole frames covered with bison or deer skin. Tepees may also have been used when the people lived at Council Grove (see "History").

Clothing and adornment

Men wore breechclouts dyed blue or red. These apronlike pieces of cloth hung from a belt at the waist. In cold weather, the men added leggings and wrapped a blanket around their shoulders. Women wore knee-length leggings in blue or red along with a skirt and sometimes had a cloth over one shoulder. Both men and women wore moccasins made of deerskin, but unlike those of other tribes, theirs were undecorated. The Kansa

Monchousia, also known as White Plume, was a Kansa chief in the 1800s. © CORBIS.

made robes of the thicker winter fur of the buffalo; they removed the thinner summer fur to make leather.

The men shaved their heads and left only a thin line of hair on the scalp. They had a wire tool that they used to pluck their hair. They also pulled out arm, beard, and eyebrow hair. Men sometimes dyed the small strip of scalp hair vermillion and added an eagle feather. Roaches (headdresses) made of deer tail dyed red or long thin hair pipes were also worn. Women parted their long hair in the center and painted the part with vermillion. Men and women both tattooed their bodies. Men wore beads,

Kansas Blizzards

When there is a blizzard, the other Kansa beg the members of the Tcihaci gens [clan] to interpose, as they are the Wind People.

They say, "Oh, grandfather, I wish good weather. Please have one of your children decorated."

Then the youngest son of one of the Wind People, but one half grown, is selected. He is painted all over with red paint. Then he goes out into the storm and rolls over and over the snow, reddening it for some distance. This stops the storm.

SOURCE: Judson, Katharine Berry. "Kansas Blizzard." *Myths and Legends of the Great Plains.* Chicago: A.C. McClurg, 1913, p. 60. Available from Project Gutenberg. http://www.gutenberg.org/catalog/world/readfile?pageno=1&fk_files=1526911 (accessed on June 17, 2011).

shells, tin trinkets, porcelain sticks, or large metal ornaments in their ears. Necklaces of metal buttons or bear claws hung around their necks or were attached to their leggings.

Food

The main staples of the Kansa diet were corn and bison meat. Corn that was not eaten roasted or used in soups during the summer was dried and stored underground. Bison flesh was preserved by slicing it into strips, braiding the strips together, and drying them on scaffolds. Some meat was wrapped around poles to dry. In later years, the Kansa used salt from the Saline River to cure their meat. The women stored the fat from the meat inside pieces of buffalo intestine.

Women grew a few additional crops, such as beans, muskmelons, watermelons, squash, pumpkins, and prairie potatoes. They also gathered wild plants, roots, nuts, and berries. Men added fish, birds, venison, and small game to the meals.

Education

Children learned to do adult chores at a young age. By the time a girl was ten or twelve, she could carry a one-hundred-pound load on her back for miles. Girls helped with carrying firewood and doing all the jobs their mothers did. Sewing bison hides into clothing or tepee covers, putting up and taking down the tepees, decorating clothes with porcupine quills or beadwork, butchering animals, cooking and processing food, and caring for young children were all skills girls needed to learn.

Boys trained to be warriors. They gained honor by being brave in battle. Raiding enemy tribes helped them gain wealth and prestige. Stealing horses was one way young men could prove themselves. To help boys become more aggressive, their parents did not scold or discipline them.

In the 1800s, when the federal government mandated schools for all Native peoples, the Kansa refused to send their children. They believed that government or religious schools would destroy their culture, so they continued to educate their young themselves.

As of the 2000s, the Kaw Nation has the Kanza Education and Learning Center, which houses a library, Internet center, cultural center, and community information center. They also have a language program for keeping their culture alive. To help students get a higher education, the Nation offers grants and scholarships to students who go on to college. Younger students are also eligible for some assistance and educational support. Adults can take advantage of vocational training programs.

Healing practices

Shamans (pronounced *SHAH-munz* or *SHAY-munz*), or healers, used roots to cure patients. Guardian spirits, which young men obtained during their vision quests, gave them special powers for healing.

ARTS

Music and Dance

Music and dance were an important part of Kansa life. Deer foot rattles and hide drums accompanied chanting and other instruments. Women were usually the creators of the songs. The Kansa performed dances on many occasions; often the dances were held for war, death, thanksgiving, and healing.

Many writers have described the celebrations. In one, the men dressed in dance clothes and painted their faces. They tied hawkbells to their legs and held hatchets in striking position as they danced. Another early writer described a victory dance where the scalps hung from a pole. The men formed a circle and shuffled around in a bobbing motion for long hours. The song continued until all the battle events had been described.

Art

The Kansa were known for their weaving, hide paintings, and beadwork. Some of their beadwork designs were flowing and flowery, depicting plants and leaves. Others were in geometric designs.

In 1994, sculptor Mark Sampsel made bronze busts of the five living full-bloods—Edgar Pepper, Jesse Mehojah Jr., William A. Mehojah Sr., Clyde G. Monroe, and Johnnie R. McCauley. By 2000, all the men had died, but their images live on in the Kaw Museum.

Kansa Gentes

Gentes were clans, groups that were related to each other by birth. These connections were generally through the father's side of the family.

The gentes listed by George Amos Dorsey, curator of anthropology at the Field Columbian Museum, in 1897 were as follows:

Manyinka (earth lodge)
Ta (deer)
Panka (Ponca)
Kanze (Kansa)
Wasabe (black bear)
Wanaghe (ghost)
Kekin (carries a turtle on his hack)
Minkin (carries the sun on his back)
Upan (elk)
Khuva (white eagle)
Han (night)
Ibache (holds the firebrand to
    sacred pipes)
Hangatanga (large Hanga)
Chedunga (buffalo bull)
Chizhuwashtage (Chizhu peacemaker)

In 1999, the South Wind Art & Cultural Foundation planned an exhibit that included a bronze horse and a rider, with arms outstretched to the south wind. The group was unable to raise enough funds for the rest of the exhibit, so the sculpture by Todd Whipple was moved to the front of the Kaw Museum.

CUSTOMS

Social organization

At some point in their early history, the Kansa and the Omaha, who were reportedly close allies, split. The Kansa people then divided into at least two gentes (clans)—the "Keepers of the Pipe" and the "Wind People," groups that later split into about seven gentes. These groups formed the basis for family groupings.

The sixteen clans each had their own sides of a camping circle. People traced their family through the father's side, and a man could only take a wife from the opposite side of the tribal circle.

Puberty

When boys were about twelve or thirteen, they went on vision quests. For four days, they stayed in the wilderness alone and fasted (went without food and drink). During that time they would have a vision that would help them. They painted these visions on their war shields and tepees.

Marriage

Kansa men could only marry women from opposite clans. When the oldest girl in the family married, she took over the lodge. She was in control of her mother and her sisters. A man could marry more than one wife, but his next wives were usually his wife's sisters. If her husband died, the wife married her husband's eldest brother. If her husband had no brothers, she could marry anyone she chose.

When a man was ready to marry, his relatives met with the girl's family to decide on what gifts they would give for her. Then the groom placed his tent near his in-law's lodge. The day of the wedding, the presents for the bride's family were placed inside the groom's tent, and the horses were tied up outside. Four of the groom's female relatives stayed in the tent. The bride, dressed in finery, rode on the family's best horse, which was also richly decorated.

A gun was discharged as she started her journey, and the four women came out to meet her and seated her in the tent. After the groom entered, the couple sat back to back while they ate the wedding feast. The other guests then entered for a feast, and presents were distributed.

Divorce was allowed, but both parties had to agree. Afterward, either spouse could marry again.

Death and mourning

The women prepared the body for burial by painting the face and covering the body with bark and a buffalo robe. After an old man gave the corpse instructions on how to reach the world of the dead, the Kansa placed the body in a grave with goods to help in the afterlife. Weapons, tools, a pipe, clothing, and food went into the shallow pit before they piled dirt and rock slabs on top. Sometimes, the man's horse was strangled and placed on top of the grave. The Kansa believed the spirit of the dead went to live in a previous village.

Families often hired professional mourners. A widow mourned for a year by scarring her face and hands, covering herself with clay, and becoming unkempt. After the mourning period, she became the wife of her husband's eldest brother. Widowers stayed in mourning for up to eighteen months.

War and hunting rituals

Although the Kansa took war seriously, observers told of a time on June 1, 1868, when they staged a mock battle in Council Grove with the Cheyenne. The settlers hid when they saw about one hundred Cheyenne warriors galloping toward the Kansa reservation. The Kansa men responded by painting their own faces and meeting them. Although many bullets and arrows flew and both sides screamed and shouted, when it was over, no one was hurt, and the Cheyenne left with several stolen horses.

Games and ceremonies

Games and sports Competitions such as wrestling, horse racing, and foot racing were popular. Gambling often accompanied these events, with some men betting horses, guns, robes, or other expensive articles. Both boys and girls enjoyed guessing games.

Sacred Drum In the 1880s, three Kansa men took a ceremonial drum to the Waxáxonlin (Pawhuska) of the Osage as a way to preserve their heritage. They stayed there that winter to talk about their dance, Íloshka Wachín, and how the Osage would interpret it. An Osage father accepted the drum for his young son, Ben Mashunkashey. Soon afterward, Ben held the first I-Lo-Skah, as the Osage called the dance. More than a century later, in 1984, the Kaw attended the I-Lo-Skah. A plaque was unveiled to commemorate the event.

The Kansa no longer have their dance, but they hold yearly powwows. The drum is brought into the arena for four songs. Special dancers, called tail dancers, finish each song with a short dance in the Íloshka Wachín style.

CURRENT TRIBAL ISSUES

In 2011, the Kansa began rewriting their constitution. They are also working to revitalize their economy. Strides have been made as bridge and road repairs have been completed, new buildings built, and fledgling businesses started. The casino, smoke shops, and travel plaza continue to bring in money that is being used for social services that the tribe needs. In looking to the future, the Kansa are planning to use renewable energy sources, such as wind power, on tribal trust lands in Chilocco, Oklahoma—a fitting idea for these "people of the south wind."

NOTABLE PEOPLE

Many chiefs were important to the Kansa, but Allegawaho (c. 1820–c. 1897) served as chief from 1867 to 1873, during one of the darkest periods of his people's history. Though he protested, his people were forced into moving to the Oklahoma reservation.

Charles Curtis (1860–1936) served in both the House and Senate, and later as vice president to Herbert Hoover (1874–1964; served 1929–33). Curtis was responsible for sponsoring the Curtis Act of 1898 (see "History"), which took away some Kansa rights.

Maude McCauley Rowe (d. 1978) was one of the last to speak the Kanza language. She recorded hours of tapes to pass on the language and the oral traditions. Rowe has also been credited with reviving the traditional dances in the 1970s. William A. Mehojah, the last Kaw full blood, died in 2000.

Jim Pepper (1941–1992), a saxophonist, composer, and singer, used his Kansa heritage in music. He left behind a legacy of both Creek and Kansa songs, some of them reinterpretations of traditional music.

BOOKS

Brown, Virginia Pounds, Laurella Owens, and Nathan Glick. *The World of the Southern Indians: Tribes, Leaders, and Customs from Prehistoric Times to the Present.* Montgomery, AL: NewSouth Books, 2011.

Blair, Ed. *The History of Johnson County.* Lawrence, KS: Standard Publishing Co., 1915. Available online from http://www.kancoll.org/books/blair/blchapter01.htm (accessed on June 17, 2011).

De Voe, Carrie. Legends of the Kaw: *The Folk-Lore of the Indians of the Kansas River Valley.* Kansas City, MO: Franklin Hudson Publishing Co., 1904. Available online from http://www.kancoll.org/books/kaw/ (accessed on June 17, 2011).

Hobson, Geary, Janet McAdams, and Kathryn Walkiewicz, eds. *The People Who Stayed: Southeastern Indian Writing after Removal.* Norman: University of Oklahoma Press, 2010.

Jeter, Marvin D. *Edward Palmer's Arkansaw Mounds.* Tuscaloosa: University of Alabama Press, 2010.

The Kanza Clan Book. Kaw City, OK: Kanza Language Project, Kaw Nation of Oklahoma, 2002.

Lea, Luke, quoted in Francis Paul Prucha. *The Great Father: The United States Government and the American Indians.* Lincoln: University of Nebraska Press, 1984, 112–13.

Pierson, George. *The Kansa, or Kaw Indians, and Their History, and the Story of Padilla.* Charleston, SC: Nabu Press, 2010.

Sharp, Jim. *Black Settlers on the Kaw Indian Reservation.* Townsend, MA: AG Press, 2008.

Stewart, Omer C. *Peyote Religion: A History.* Norman: University of Oklahoma, 1987.

Unrau, William E. *The Kansa Indians: A History of the Wind People, 1673–1873.* Norman: University of Oklahoma Press, 1971.

PERIODICALS

Parks, Ron. "Selecting a Suitable Country for the Kanza." *The Kansas Free Press.* June 1, 2011. Available online from http://www.kansasfreepress.com/2011/06/selecting-a-suitable-country-for-the-kanza.html (accessed on June 17, 2011).

WEB SITES

Fausz, J. Frederick. "The Louisiana Expansion: The Kansa/Kaw." *University of Missouri-St. Louis.* http://www.umsl.edu/continuinged/louisiana/Am_Indians/3-Kansa_Kaw/3-kansa_kaw.html (accessed on June 17, 2011).

"Kanza Cultural History." *The Kaw Nation.* http://kawnation.com/?page_id=216 (accessed on June 17, 2011).

"Kansa Indian Tribe History." *Access Geneology.* http://www.accessgenealogy.com/native/tribes/siouan/kansahist.htm (accessed on June 17, 2011).

"Kansa (Kaw)." *Four Directions Institute.* http://www.fourdir.com/kaw.htm (accessed on June 17, 2011).

Parks, Ron. "Amidst a Christian and Civilized People." *Kaw Mission.* http://www.kawmission.org/places/kawmission/ron_parks_series.htm (accessed on June 17, 2011).

Redish, Laura, and Orrin Lewis. "Kansa Indian Fact Sheet." *Native Languages of the Americas.* http://www.bigorrin.org/kansa_kids.htm (accessed on June 17, 2011).

Simpson, Linda. "The Kansas/Kanza/Kaw Nation." *Oklahoma Territory.* http://www.okgenweb.org/~itkaw/Kanza2.html (accessed on June 17, 2011).

"Territorial Kansas: Kansa Indians." *University of Kansas.* http://www.territorialkansasonline.org/~imlskto/cgi-bin/index.php?SCREEN=keyword&selected_keyword=Kansa%20Indians (accessed on June 17, 2011).

"Tribal Nations: The Kanza Indians." *Kansas Lewis & Clark Bicentennial Commission.* http://www.lewisandclarkinkansas.com/tribal.html (accessed on June 17, 2011).

"Two Cultures: Kaw." *Kaw Mission.* http://www.kawmission.org/places/kawmission/kansaeverydaylife.htm (accessed on June 17, 2011).

Unrau, William E. "Kaw (Kansa)." *Oklahoma Historical Society.* http://digital.library.okstate.edu/encyclopedia/entries/K/KA001.html (accessed on June 17, 2011).

Weiser, Kathy. "The Kanza (or Kaw) Indians." *Legends of Kansas.* http://www.legendsofkansas.com/kansaindians.html (accessed on June 17, 2011).

Kiowa

Name

The name Kiowa (pronounced *KIE-uh-wuh*) comes from the Comanche word "Kaigwa," meaning "two halves differ," describing Kiowa warriors who cut their hair on only one side and left the other side long. It later evolved into the name Kiowa, which means "the Principal People" to the tribe. Their name for themselves was *kwuda,* which means "coming [or going] out," a reference to their origin story.

Location

The Kiowa's earliest known homeland was in western Montana. In 1700, they were living near the Black Hills of South Dakota, but they moved to the southern Great Plains in 1785. In the 1990s, most Kiowa lived in several small cities in southwest Oklahoma near their former reservation, which no longer exists.

Population

In the early nineteenth century, there were about 1,800 Kiowa. In the 1990 U.S. Census, 9,460 people identified themselves as Kiowa (8,936 Kiowa and 524 Oklahoma Kiowa). The 2000 census showed 8,321 Kiowa (7,853 Kiowa and 467 Oklahoma Kiowa). At that time, 12,398 people claimed to have some Kiowa blood. The 2010 census counted 9,437 Kiowa, with 13,787 people claiming Kiowa heritage. In 2011, according to the Oklahoma Indian Affairs Commission, tribal enrollment for the Kiowa was 12,000, with 8,000 residing in the state of Oklahoma.

Language family

Tanoan-Kiowan.

Origins and group affiliations

Oral history says the Kiowa originated near the sources of the Missouri and Yellowstone Rivers in western Montana. They say their ancestors came into this world from an underworld by passing through a hollow log. On

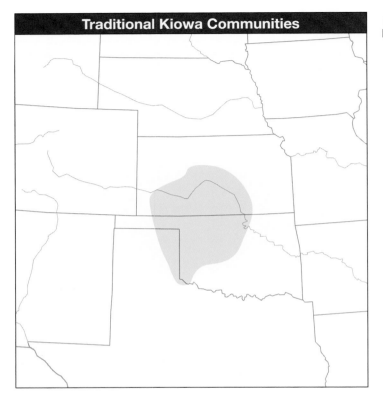

Traditional Kiowa Communities

Shaded area

Traditional lands where Kiowa settled in present-day Kansas, Oklahoma and Texas. (Until the 1700s, the Kiowa lived as nomadic hunters, traveling the northwestern Great Plains as far east as the Black Hills)

A map of traditional Kiowa lands. MAP BY XNR PRODUCTIONS. CENGAGE LEARNING, GALE. REPRODUCED BY PERMISSION OF GALE, A PART OF CENGAGE LEARNING.

the way out, a pregnant woman became stuck, barring the way so those behind her could not exit; this explains why there were so few Kiowa. Some then married Sarci Indians and produced a tribe called the Kiowa Apache.

After 1700, the Kiowa were alternately friends and enemies with the Apache, Crow, and Cheyenne (see entries). The Kiowa mainly traded with the Arikara (see entry), Mandan, and Hidatsa. Cheyenne and Sioux (see entry) drove the Kiowa from the Black Hills into Comanche (see entry) territory, where, following a war, the Kiowa later made peace with the Comanche.

Although they were few in number, the Kiowa were respected across the Great Plains as proud and fierce warriors. Their ferocious resistance to the American settlement of their homeland made them legends. They may have lost their reservation, but they did not lose their traditions.

HISTORY

Early days on the Great Plains

The ancient Kiowa were nomadic hunters who traveled the northwestern Great Plains following the vast herds of buffalo that were their primary food source. Seventeenth-century French explorer René-Robert Cavelier, Sieur de La Salle (1643–1687), was the first European to record information about the Kiowa. Although he did not meet them on his expedition in 1682, he wrote that they possessed many horses that may have been acquired from Spanish settlers in Mexico. Horses made life easier, allowing the Kiowa and other Plains tribes to hunt and kill buffalo more efficiently than they could on foot.

Important Dates

1837: The Kiowa sign the Treaty of Fort Gibson, promising peace with fellow Indian tribes and the United States.

1853: The Kiowa sign the Treaty of Fort Atkinson, making peace with Mexico and renewing peace with the United States.

1865: The federal government assigns the Kiowa to a reservation in Oklahoma.

1901–06: The Kiowa-Comanche reservation is broken into individual allotments and is opened for American settlement.

1968: The Kiowa Tribal Council is formed.

By the 1700s, the Kiowa had roamed as far east as the Black Hills of South Dakota, where the tiny tribe formed a close alliance with the large and powerful Crow nation. Plains Indians gained honor within their tribes by raiding, horse thieving, and warring. The Crow and Kiowa prospered in that way, but they often had to deal with other tribes whose lifestyles were the same. They fought constantly with the Comanche and Shoshone (see entry) in the West, the Cheyenne and Arapaho (see entry) in the North, and the Sioux in the East.

Move to southern Plains

The unending fighting, combined with a disastrous smallpox epidemic in 1781 that killed nearly two thousand Kiowa, led to a decision to leave the Black Hills region in 1785 and migrate to the southern Plains. Soon afterward, the weakened Kiowa made peace with the much larger Comanche tribe. The two tribes agreed to share hunting grounds and often joined forces in raids against other tribes. Together, they took control of the southern Plains from the Apache and Wichita (see entry). They gained a reputation as the fiercest of Plains warriors, especially in Texas and New Mexico, where they met the Spanish, established a trading relationship, and terrorized white settlements—something they continued to do for many years.

American explorers Meriwether Lewis (1774–1809) and William Clark (1770–1838) saw the Kiowa in 1804. By then, the Plains culture was in full flower. The Kiowa had just begun to trade with the French, who were more willing to give them guns than the Spanish were. Lewis and Clark observed the Kiowa among several Native groups attending a large trade fair at one of the French trading posts that had sprung up along the Missouri River. The explorers noted that there was much singing, dancing, and general merriment.

Disasters strike

Smallpox epidemics struck in 1801 and 1816, killing many Plains Indians. Though weak, the Kiowa continued their pattern of fighting and raiding. When vast numbers of settlers began to move across the Great Plains, most of the tribes put aside their differences and joined forces to attack wagon trains. This alliance did not include the Osage (see entry), however. In 1833, warriors from the Osage tribe attacked a group of Kiowa who were gathering food. Many Kiowa were killed and beheaded in what came to be called the Cutthroat Gap Massacre. Some women and children were also taken captive.

In 1834, U.S. soldiers returned to the Kiowa one captive girl taken in the massacre. This generous act marked the first contact between the U.S. government and the Kiowa. When the government suggested a peace conference to put an end to warfare on the Plains and open the area for American settlement, the Kiowa were willing to listen.

In 1837, the Kiowa signed their first treaty with the United States. The Treaty of Fort Gibson gave U.S. citizens the right to travel unhindered through Native lands. The Kiowa were guaranteed hunting rights in the southern Plains, including the territory that would become the state of Texas. Two years later, another smallpox epidemic swept through the Plains. In 1849, half the tribe perished in a cholera epidemic; some committed suicide to avoid being overtaken by the terrible disease.

More treaties

The remaining Kiowa strongly objected to settlers moving into Texas, so they continued raiding there. After Texas became a state in 1845, the U.S. government stepped in to end the trouble in the region. When the U.S. Army could not subdue the Kiowa, they sent a government agent to make peace. In 1853, he convinced the Kiowa, along with their Kiowa

Custer talks with Kiowa chiefs in Oklahoma in 1868. ©THE ART ARCHIVE/BUFFALO BILL HISTORICAL CENTER, CODY, WYOMING/89.69.35.

Apache and Comanche allies, to sign the Treaty of Fort Atkinson. The treaty—never accepted by all the Kiowa chiefs—called for peace in the region and granted the federal government the privilege of building roads and forts in return for annual payments for the next ten years.

Kiowa and Comanche warriors continued their raiding against other tribes and American settlers alike. Finally, the U.S. government called for a new peace council. They held it in 1865 at the mouth of the Little Arkansas River (near present-day Wichita, Kansas), and it resulted in the Treaty of Little Arkansas. By its terms, the Kiowa, Apache, and Comanche would move to a reservation in what was then called Indian Territory (present-day Oklahoma). The tribes were also required to renounce their claims to any other lands. When it appeared the Native nations were not going to sign the treaty, the government agreed to allow them to hunt in western Kansas and Texas, but they still had to make the reservation their home. Two years later, another treaty required the Kiowa and other signers to learn to farm, and they were promised cattle, farming equipment, and clothing.

Resistance to farming

Government officials hoped to transform a warlike, wandering people into peaceful farmers who lived like European Americans, a process called assimilation. The Kiowa resisted this transformation and

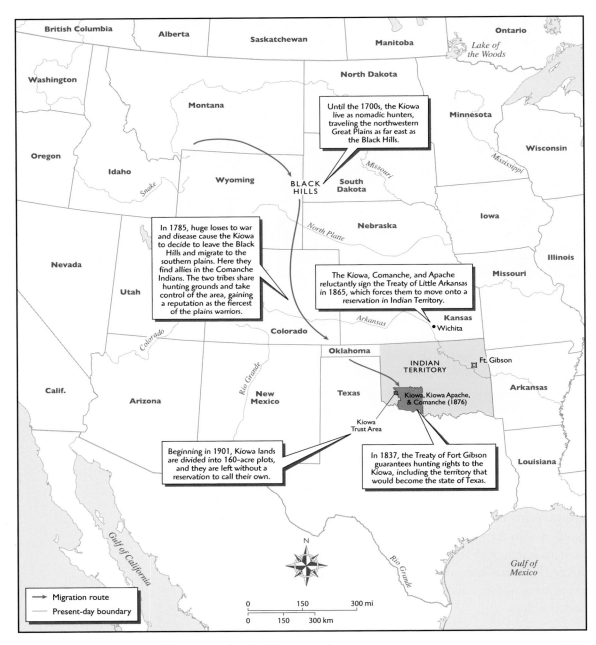

Until the 1700s, the Kiowa live as nomadic hunters, traveling the northwestern Great Plains as far east as the Black Hills.

In 1785, huge losses to war and disease cause the Kiowa to decide to leave the Black Hills and migrate to the southern plains. Here they find allies in the Comanche Indians. The two tribes share hunting grounds and take control of the area, gaining a reputation as the fiercest of the plains warriors.

The Kiowa, Comanche, and Apache reluctantly sign the Treaty of Little Arkansas in 1865, which forces them to move onto a reservation in Indian Territory.

Beginning in 1901, Kiowa lands are divided into 160-acre plots, and they are left without a reservation to call their own.

In 1837, the Treaty of Fort Gibson guarantees hunting rights to the Kiowa, including the territory that would become the state of Texas.

INDIAN TERRITORY

Kiowa, Kiowa Apache, & Comanche (1876)

Kiowa Trust Area

Ft. Gibson

→ Migration route
— Present-day boundary

0   150   300 mi
0   150   300 km

N

A map showing the migrations of the Kiowa at the end of the nineteenth century. MAP BY XNR PRODUCTIONS. CENGAGE LEARNING, GALE. REPRODUCED BY PERMISSION OF GALE, A PART OF CENGAGE LEARNING.

continued with the Comanche to raid other tribes and Texans. Their opposition was finally quashed after a punishing campaign by the U.S. military over the winter of 1868–69. Lieutenant Colonel George Custer (1839–1876) informed the Kiowa that they must surrender or be destroyed.

For the next sixty years, the government pressured the Kiowa on the reservation to give up their ways. Meanwhile, nearby ranchers and farmers wanted Kiowa land and urged the government to permit settlement there. Some simply let their cattle graze illegally. Bolder men built a railroad on reservation land, and towns grew up along the tracks.

In 1887, Congress passed the General Allotment Act. It called for the division of reservation lands into individual plots called allotments; any land left over would be sold to settlers.

Reservation lost

The Kiowa objected to allotment and filed lawsuits that delayed the process. They lost, and the parceling out of their land into small plots began in 1901. By 1906, individual Kiowa people had 160-acre parcels of land and no reservation to call their own. They endured years of poverty and suffering; some left for good. In the early twenty-first century, some Kiowa live on land in Oklahoma that was once part of the vast reservation. Although they are surrounded by white communities, many members of the tribe have worked to preserve their cultural heritage.

RELIGION

The Kiowa believed supernatural forces could give power to human beings. One of the most important of these spirit forces was the sun. They gazed at it during the ceremony called the Sun Dance (see "Customs"). This dance was banned by the U.S. government, and the last Sun Dance performed by the Kiowa took place in 1887.

Another powerful force in Kiowa life was the Grandmothers religion. The Ten Grandmothers were represented by ten medicine bundles, and each had her own tepee, her own horse, and her own dedicated guardian. The Kiowa consulted the Grandmothers and asked them to relay prayers to the Creator. When the last true keeper and guardian of the Grandmothers, Willie Maunkee (Kiowa Bill), died in 1931, the buffalo-hide containers holding the Grandmothers were sewn shut, never to

Kiowa Words

The Kiowa language has been adapted to modern life. For example, the Kiowa word for automobile, *awdlemodlbidl*, is formed from the words *gyesadl* ("it is hot"), *hodl* ("to kill"), and *k'awndedl* ("badly"), literally meaning "bad, hot killing machine." Below are a few simpler Kiowa words:

ant'a	"five"
ch'i	"man"
ma	"woman"
p'ahy	"moon"
pa'o	"three"
pay	"sun"
t'on	"water"
yi	"two"

be opened again. Elders still pass down stories about the Grandmothers to younger members of the tribe.

By 1890, many Kiowa and other tribes were despondent over reservation life. They adopted the Ghost Dance religion developed by Wovoka (c. 1856–1932), a Paiute (see entry) Indian. Wovoka urged the Native nations to perform the dance until the white people were gone and the buffalo were restored.

The late nineteenth century also saw the rise of the Peyote (pronounced *pay-OH-tee*) religion among the Kiowa. Practiced by many tribes, the religion involves consuming part of a small, spineless cactus that grows in the southwestern United States and Mexico. The person then enters a trance state and sees visions. The Kiowa practiced a version known as the Little Moon peyote ceremony, which lasted for one full day. Over the years, peyote use has become part of the religious ritual of the Native American Church, founded in Oklahoma in 1918. Many Kiowa men are members of this church, which is credited with contributing to a revival of traditional ceremonies. (For more information on the Native American Church, see Makah entry.) Women and other members of the tribe are more likely to belong to Christian churches, usually Methodist or Baptist.

LANGUAGE

The language spoken by the Kiowa belongs to the Tanoan-Kiowan family, but it is quite different from most Tanoan dialects spoken by many Pueblo tribes (see entry) and resembles the Uto-Aztecan languages spoken by the Hopi(see entry). The language includes no *r*, and a European observer in 1906 said the language was "full of nasal and choking sounds."

In the modern world, members of the Kiowa tribe are more likely to abandon their Native language in favor of English. Still, some of the older generation speak the language, and young people receive schooling in their Native language.

GOVERNMENT

Each Kiowa band was ruled by a chief, who was chosen for his religious powers or for his outstanding skills in war or healing. Occasionally, all these band chiefs came together to discuss matters of importance to the whole tribe, such as whether to make war or peace or when to hold ceremonies.

On the reservations, the Kiowa were no longer hunters or warriors, and Kiowa men had no opportunity to distinguish themselves as leaders. The people had to obey government policies. One such regulation involved the creation of the Intertribal Business Committee. Government agents chose members from each of the three tribes on the reservation. The Kiowa people were not loyal to these committee members, because they saw them as puppets under the control of the U.S. government.

Federal government policies toward Native nations changed in the 1930s, and new laws were passed that allowed tribes to have more say in their own affairs. Many Kiowa opposed government requirements that they reestablish a reservation, which meant giving up their individual plots of land and allowing the land to be controlled by the tribe as a whole, so they declined to do so.

In 1968, the Kiowa Nation created a governing body called the Kiowa Tribal Council. The council serves to represent both individual

Hides are stacked in a buffalo yard in Dodge City, Kansas, in 1878. By the 1880s, only about one thousand buffalo remained. Without buffalo, the Plains Indians were faced with starvation and had little choice but to move to the reservations. NATIONAL ARCHIVES AND RECORDS ADMINISTRATION.

Kiowa and the tribe as a whole in negotiations with the federal government. Areas of concern are health, education, and economic development. All tribe members age eighteen or older are part of the Tribal Council. In the early 2000s, the seven-member Kiowa Business Committee also handled governmental functions, subject to tribal council approval.

ECONOMY

Before contact with European-American traders, the Kiowa economy was based on hunting and trading with other tribes. The people exchanged horses, mules, and pemmican (dried buffalo meat mixed with fat and berries) for garden goods produced by farming tribes on the Missouri River. They later traded buffalo hides for European goods. What they could not acquire by trading, they took in raids. Favorite targets were horses, food, and captives.

On the reservation, government agents tried to turn them into farmers, but Kiowa hunter-warriors looked down on farming as "women's work." They hated the government's proposal to divide their land into individual farms (allotments) and strongly opposed it. They continued to refuse to farm, and with the buffalo gone by the 1870s, poverty and starvation were common. Within a short time, the Kiowa came to depend on government support.

Those Kiowa who turned to farming found that their farms did not prosper. They were affected by the lack of rain and soil erosion that led to the Dust Bowl of the 1930s, where large parts of the Great Plains suffered from drought and tremendous dust storms. Some Kiowa men left to serve in the military in World War I (1914–18) and World War II (1939–45).

New government policies in the 1950s and 1960s offered money and other incentives to young Natives in rural communities if they relocated to urban areas and learned new skills. Many Kiowa took advantage of the offer and set out for Texas and California, where they took jobs as carpenters and laborers. Some who stayed behind leased their land, but even with that income, the majority of Kiowa lived in a state of relative poverty until the end of the twentieth century. Many supplemented their family income through arts and crafts products.

In 2007, the Kiowa opened the Red River Casino, which employed 575 people, after paying fines and clearing up other issues with the

National Indian Gaming Commission, which had shut down the tribe's previous casino for opening without being in compliance with the 1988 Indian Gaming Regulatory Act. The additional income generated by gaming helped fund many tribal initiatives.

DAILY LIFE

Education

Early efforts to force an American-style education on their children left the Kiowa mistrustful of American authorities, and this led to a condition of undereducation that existed for much of the twentieth century. Over the years, the lack of education contributed to a gradual loss of the Kiowa language and culture. Some trends of the last half century have been promising, though. Today, young people are taught the Kiowan language as part of continuing effort to preserve and renew the tribe's traditional culture. Likewise, many attempts have been made to promote Kiowa art, dance, song, and literature in various publications and on Kiowa land at the Kiowa Nation Culture Museum.

More Kiowa students are completing high school and an increasing number are taking advantage of federal grants to attend college.

Buildings

Tepees Like other nomadic Plains tribes, the Kiowa lived in tepees, cone-shaped tents assembled over a group of sturdy wooden poles tied at the top and enclosed with sewn-together buffalo hides. The entrance was small, perhaps 3 or 4 feet (1 meter) high, and always faced east. Although tepees varied in size according to the number of inhabitants, a large one might measure 20 feet (6 meters) in diameter and stand at least as high. The Kiowa decorated the outside of their tepees with the same symbol that appeared on the warrior's shield or with a special design that identified the family who lived within. Each tepee housed a family of four or five individuals.

The interior was kept quite simple. In the center was a fire hole for cooking and warmth. Beds—made from a small frame of willow rods and covered with buffalo skin—were placed along the perimeter of the tent. The task of erecting the tepee was women's work. The process was fairly simple, allowing the Kiowa to move easily as they followed roaming buffalo herds.

The Passing of the Buffalo

Once buffalo roamed the plains. The Kiowa people honored the buffalo and thanked it when they killed it. In turn, it provided for their needs. However, life changed when the settlers came. They slaughtered the buffalo and destroyed the land with their buildings and railroad tracks.

Soon the bones of the buffalo covered the land to the height of a tall man. The buffalo saw they could fight no longer.

One morning, a Kiowa woman whose family was running from the Army rose early from their camp deep in the hills. She went down to the spring near the mountainside to get water. She went quietly, alert for enemies. The morning mist was thick, but as she bent to fill her bucket she saw something. It was something moving in the mist. As she watched, the mist parted and out of it came an old buffalo cow. It was one of the old buffalo women who always led the herds. Behind her came the last few young buffalo warriors, their horns scarred from fighting, some of them wounded. Among them were a few calves and young cows.

Straight toward the side of the mountain, the old buffalo cow led that last herd. As the Kiowa woman watched, the mountain opened up in front of them and the buffalo walked into the mountain. Within the mountain the earth was green and new. The sun shone and the meadowlarks were singing. It was as it had been before the whites came. Then the mountain closed behind them. The buffalo were gone.

SOURCE: Bruchac, Joseph, and Michael J. Caduto. "The Passing of the Buffalo." *Keepers of the Animals: Native American Stories and Wildlife Activities for Children*. Golden, CO: Fulcrum Publishing, 1991.

Medicine lodges When all of the Kiowa gathered together in the spring for the annual Sun Dance, a special building called a medicine lodge was built. This lodge consisted of seventeen poles arranged in a large circle and inserted into the ground vertically. A roof frame made of similar poles was then extended above. At the central point of this frame hung the sacred Sun Dance fetish, a small human figure carved from green stone called the *tai-me*. The medicine lodge was covered by cottonwood branches that formed the walls of the structure; the roof was left open to the sky.

Food

Like most Plains tribes, the Kiowa relied mainly on buffalo for food, clothing, and shelter. Kiowa men also killed other large hoofed creatures, such as antelope, deer, and elk, and shot turkeys. Women gathered fruits, nuts, and roots to round out the Kiowa diet.

Clothing and adornment

Nearly all clothing and household materials came from the animals of the Plains, primarily buffalo, deer, and other smaller creatures. Men usually wore only leggings and buckskin moccasins in the summer months, with the addition of a deerskin shirt or a buffalo hide robe during the winter season. Women wore dresses of the same materials, along with leggings and moccasins.

The Kiowa adorned themselves with shells, animal bones or teeth, and porcupine quills. Robes were often painted or decorated with embroidery. Animal furs were occasionally worn for warmth. These hides were sometimes thrown over the body with the head still attached, so the head rested over the left shoulder. Warriors painted their shields with figures they saw in the dream visions that told them they were destined to be warriors. Geometric patterns—such as boxes, hourglass shapes, feathered circles, and striped or symmetrical designs—also adorned shields and other items.

Healing practices

The Kiowa believed that natural objects and creatures contained spiritual powers, including the power to heal, bring rain, or see the future. These objects—teeth, animal skins, stones, food, or other items—were gathered together in bundles called personal "medicine." Such medicine was the property of the shaman (pronounced *SHAH-mun* or *SHAY-mun*), who specialized in healing the sick.

Kiowa shamans belonged to the religious society of Buffalo Doctors. Greatly respected by the other members of the tribe, Buffalo Doctors usually received their curing powers in the form of a dream vision—a sign to the dreamer that he was to become a healer. If he was successful in restoring health to the patient, the Buffalo Doctor was handsomely rewarded.

The personal medicine of an especially successful healer became important to the whole tribe. That was the case with ten sacred Kiowa medicine bundles known as the Ten Grandmothers. No one but a specially chosen priest was allowed to open these bundles, so their actual contents were unknown to the Kiowa. Before the last priest died in the 1890s, the bundles were opened annually at a special purification ceremony. The bundles are regarded with deep reverence, and they symbolize the well-being and continuance of the old Kiowa ways. Today, each bundle is guarded by one man and one woman who inherit this honor and continue the tradition. Only nine bundles remain; the tenth was destroyed in a fire in the 1930s. (For more information on the Ten Grandmothers, see "Religion.")

ARTS

For centuries, Kiowa men and women were renowned for their painting. They used colors obtained from earth and rocks to paint geometric designs on clothing and containers, and men covered their tepees with scenes from their personal history and from their battles.

Americans recognized the talent of Kiowa artists when some members of the tribe were imprisoned in Florida by the U.S. military in the 1890s. These prisoners were given drawing materials to pass the time and used the opportunity to record their histories. In 1891, Kiowa artists were asked to paint works for display at international art shows. In the 1930s, five young Kiowa artists were invited to attend the University of Oklahoma School of Art. The group, which consisted of Jack Hokeah (1902–1973), Spencer Asah (1905–1954), James Auchiah (1906–1974), Stephen Mopope (1898–1974), and Monroe Tsatoke (1904–1937), gained fame around the world as the "Five Kiowa Artists."

In a society where most of the honor and glory went to warriors and horse raiders, it was difficult for a woman to gain recognition. Certain Kiowa women belonged to artist societies, whose members knew all the secrets of quillwork and beadwork and would pass the secrets on for a fee. Quilled robes made by these women artists were highly prized; one such robe might be traded for a horse.

In the early twenty-first century, Kiowa men and women are known for their work with buckskin, beads, featherwork, and German silver (nickel). Their work can be seen at the Oklahoma Indian Arts and Crafts Cooperative and other galleries and stores.

CUSTOMS

Sun Dance

The Sun Dance was an annual ceremony held in the spring or early summer. Participants stared into the sun and went without food or water, hoping for a vision. The Kiowa did not include self-torture in their Sun Dances, as many versions of this popular Great Plains celebration did. Violence was a part of the ten-day ceremony, though, because it ended in raiding and warfare. The last Kiowa Sun Dance took place in 1887.

The legacy of the Sun Dance, however, lives on in some present-day Kiowa traditions. The tribe maintains the medicine bundles used in the purification ceremony; some tribal members are responsible for their safekeeping. Several of the dances, such as the Gourd Dance and the Black Leggings Dance, have steps that resemble those of the Sun Dance.

War rituals

The Kiowa were hunters and warriors, and many of their activities featured demonstrations of bravery and strength. Warriors achieved status through individual acts of courage, such as success in hunting or "counting coup," coming close enough in battle to touch but not kill an enemy. Warrior societies were formed based on age and experience. Young boys would be members of the *Polanyup,* or Rabbit Society. Other groups included *Adaltoyuo,* Young Sheep; *Tsentanmo,* Horse Headdresses; *Tonkonko,* Black Leggings; *Taupeko,* Skunkberry People or Crazy Horse; and *Ka-itsenko,* Dog Warriors.

The highest military honor a man could attain was to be named one of the *Koitsenko*; these were the greatest and bravest of the Kiowa warriors and never numbered more than ten.

Rank in society

Social rank was clearly marked out in Kiowa society. At the top were the *onde,* which included the finest warriors, leaders, and priests. The *ondegup'a,* warriors of lesser wealth and stature, were directly beneath them, whereas the *kaan* and *dapone,* poor people, made up most of the tribe.

Not surprisingly in this military culture, women were esteemed far less than men and were obliged to undertake most of the domestic tasks, including building tepees, preparing food, tanning hides, and making and repairing clothing. A small group of older women, however, did belong to the secret and highly respected Bear Women Society.

Social organizations

In addition to warrior societies, the Kiowa had religious societies, healing societies like the Buffalo Doctors or the Owl Doctor Society (whose members could see into the future), and the Sun Dance Shield Society and Eagle Shield Society (whose members guarded the tribe's magical and sacred objects).

By the middle of the twentieth century, all the old societies seemed to have disappeared along with much of the traditional Kiowa way of life. Then soldiers who served in the two World Wars revived the Black Leggings warrior society. Other societies, such as the Gourd Dance Society, the Tia-Piah Society, and the O-Ho-Mah Society, were also revived. People meet in various cities in Oklahoma to perform modern versions of old rituals. Each year the Kiowa travel to Anadarko, Oklahoma, where the Apache tribe is headquartered, to participate in the American Indian Exposition.

Sweat baths

Among the most important Kiowa customs was an emphasis on ritual cleansing, both as the first step in the proper performance of a religious ceremony and as a way of overcoming disease by getting rid of harmful spirits in the body. Those undergoing the cleansing entered a sweat lodge—a wooden structure containing a fire that heated rocks and produced steam vapor from a nearby water vessel.

The Kiowa calendar

The Kiowa believed in the importance of a calendar history. Two times each year the happenings of the past season were recorded in the form of painted illustrations on buffalo hide. The oldest calendar now in existence dates from 1833 and is a valuable chronicle of more than a half century of Kiowa history.

CURRENT TRIBAL ISSUES

In 1998, a U.S. Supreme Court decision in the case of the *Kiowa Tribe of Oklahoma v. Manufacturing Technologies, Inc.* upheld the sovereignty (ability to be self-governing) of Native American tribes. This means that the tribe can operate as a separate, independent nation.

In 2010, the Kiowa struggled with internal factions within the nation. Some members expressed concerns that the Kiowa Business Committee (KBC), which is subject to Kiowa Tribal Council approval, was taking on more responsibility for the direct oversight of the casino without going through the proper tribal council approval process. The KBC claimed the accusations were politically motivated. This situation is a problem on many reservations where the management of gaming income is overseen by the same small governing body that is in charge of tribal administration. This arrangement can lead to corruption and embezzlement because the people approving expenditures are the same people incurring them. It also makes even innocent management subject to questions about integrity from other political candidates who hope to gain office.

NOTABLE PEOPLE

N. Scott Momaday (1934–), of Kiowa, European, and Cherokee ancestry, is one of the most widely recognized Native writers. He is the Pulitzer Prize–winning author of *House Made of Dawn* (1968), the tragic story of a Kiowa man whose life falls apart when he tries to adjust to life in a city. Native issues figure prominently in Momaday's novels and poetry. His book *The Way to Rainy Mountain* (1969) details several centuries of Kiowa history and legend, including the tribe's origins, migrations through the Plains, and contact with American settlers. Momaday is also a well-respected professor of literature, who has received a dozen honorary degrees.

Satanta (1830–1878) was born on the northern Plains, but he later migrated to the southern Plains with his people. Satanta spent much of his adult life fighting U.S. settlers and their military forces. In 1866, as leader of the Kiowa, he favored military resistance against American settlers. In 1867, he spoke at the Kiowa Council at Medicine Lodge Creek, an annual ceremonial gathering, where U.S. observers gave him his nickname, "The Orator of the Plains," because of his eloquent speech. At the council, Satanta signed a peace treaty that obligated the Kiowa to resettle on a reservation in present-day Oklahoma.

Shortly thereafter, however, he was taken hostage by U.S. officials who used his imprisonment to coerce more Kiowa into resettling on their assigned reservation. After his release, Satanta carried out raids against settlers in Texas, including an ambush of a train carrying U.S.

Army general William Tecumseh Sherman (1820–1891). When he attended a peace council a short time later, Satanta was arrested and sentenced to death, but thanks to the protest of humanitarian groups and Native American leaders, he received parole on the condition that he remain on the Kiowa Reservation. Hostilities on the Plains continued, and in 1874, Satanta presented himself to U.S. officials to prove that he was not taking part in them. They rewarded this gesture with imprisonment. Four years later, an ill Satanta jumped to his death from the second story of a prison hospital after being informed that he would never be released.

Other notable Kiowa include: tribal leader Kicking Bird (c. 1835–1875); Kiowa-Delaware playwright, editor, and choreographer Hanay Geiogamah (1945–); attorney and educator Kirke Kickingbird (1944–); and physician and educator Everett Ronald Rhoades (1931–).

BOOKS

Archer, Jane. *The First Fire: Stories of the Cherokee, Kickapoo, Kiowa, and Tigua.* Dallas, TX: Taylor Trade, 2005.

Brown, Dee. "The War to Save the Buffalo." In *Bury My Heart at Wounded Knee.* New York: Henry Holt, 1970.

Chalfant, William Y. *Hancock's War: Conflict on the Southern Plains.* Norman, OK: Arthur H. Clark Company, 2010.

Earenfight, Phillip J., ed. *A Kiowa's Odyssey: A Sketchbook from Fort Marion.* Seattle: University of Washington Press, 2007.

Greene, Candace S. *One Hundred Summers: A Kiowa Calendar Record.* Lincoln: University of Nebraska Press, 2009.

Haseloff, Cynthia. *The Kiowa Verdict.* Unity, ME: Five Star, 1996.

Kiowa & Pueblo Art: Watercolor Paintings by Native American Artists. Mineola, NY: Dover Publications, 2009.

Meadows, William C. *Kiowa, Apache, and Comanche Military Societies: Enduring Veterans, 1800 to the Present.* Austin: University of Texas Press, 2003.

Mooney, James. *Calendar History of the Kiowa Indians.* Whitefish, MT: Kessinger Publishing, 2006.

Owings, Alison. *Indian Voices: Listening to Native Americans.* New Brunswick, N.J.: Rutgers University Press, 2011.

Southwell, Kristina L., and John R. Lovett. *Life at the Kiowa, Comanche, and Wichita Agency: The Photographs of Annette Ross Hume.* Norman: University of Oklahoma Press, 2010.

Yellowtail, Thomas. *Native Spirit: The Sun Dance Way.* Bloomington, IN: World Wisdom, 2007.

PERIODICALS

Rezendes, Michael. "Few Tribes Share Casino Windfall." *Globe.* December 11, 2000. Available online from http://indianfiles.serveftp.com/TribalIssues/Few%20tribes%20share%20casino%20windfall.pdf (accessed on July 4, 2011).

WEB SITES

"2011 Oklahoma Indian Nations." *Pocket Pictorial Directory.* Oklahoma City: Oklahoma Indian Affairs Commission, 2011. Available from http://www.ok.gov/oiac/documents/2011.FINAL.WEB.pdf (accessed on July 4, 2011).

Greene, Candace S. "Kiowa Drawings." *National Anthropological Archives, National Museum of Natural History.* http://www.nmnh.si.edu/naa/kiowa/kiowa.htm (accessed on July 4, 2011).

"Kiowa Indian Tribe." *Kansas Genealogy.* http://www.kansasgenealogy.com/indians/kiowa_indian_tribe.htm (accessed on July 4, 2011).

"Kiowa Indian Tribe History." *Access Genealogy.* http://www.accessgenealogy.com/native/tribes/kiowa/kiowahist.htm (accessed on July 4, 2011).

Kiowa Tribe. http://www.kiowatribe.org/ (accessed on July 4, 2011).

Kracht, Benjamin R. "Kiowa-Comanche-Apache Opening." *Oklahoma Historical Society.* http://digital.library.okstate.edu/encyclopedia/entries/K/KI020.html (accessed on July 4, 2011).

Lassiter, Luke E. "The Power of Kiowa Song: A Collaborative Ethnography." *The University of Arizona Press.* http://www.uapress.arizona.edu/lib/cache/excerpts/KIOWA/kiowasng.htm (accessed on July 4, 2011).

"Meeting of Frontiers: The Kiowa Collection: Selections from the Papers of Hugh Lenox Scott." *Global Gateway: World Culture & Resources (Library of Congress).* http://international.loc.gov:8081/intldl/mtfhtml/mfdigcol/lists/mtfhlsTitles1.html (accessed on July 4, 2011).

Moore, R. E. "The Texas Kiowa Indians." *Texas Indians.* http://www.texasindians.com/kiowa.htm (accessed on July 4, 2011).

Redish, Laura, and Orrin Lewis. "Kiowa Indian Fact Sheet." *Native Languages of the Americas.* http://www.bigorrin.org/kiowa_kids.htm (accessed on July 4, 2011).

"The Salt Creek Massacre." *Texas State Library & Archives Commission.* http://www.tsl.state.tx.us/exhibits/indian/showdown/page1.html (accessed on July 4, 2011).

Weiser, Kathy. "Kiowa—Nomadic Warriors of the Plains." *Legends of America.* http://www.legendsofamerica.com/na-kiowa.html (accessed on July 4, 2011).

Missouri

Name

Missouri (pronounced *mih-ZUR-ee*), or Missouria, was an Illini word meaning "big canoe" or "people with dugout canoes." Some say that this neighboring tribe used this word to describe them to the French, and the name stuck. The word *Missouri* has sometimes been mistranslated as "big muddy." Early writers used many different spellings for the name, including Missourita, Missouris, Massorites, Messorites, Emissourita, Ouemessourit, Missoury, Misuris, and Missuri. The Missouri called themselves *Niútachi,* which means "people of the river mouth." Early explorers sometimes recorded the name as Nau-tat-ci or Peki-tan-oui. The people are now called Otoe-Missouria.

Location

The Missouri descended from the ancient Oneota, who lived around the Great Lakes, so the original homelands of the Missouri were west of Lake Michigan. They later settled in the Missouri River valley, where their territory stretched from present-day Kansas City to the mouth of the Grand River at the Missouri River. The Missouri joined the Otoe along the Platte River in Nebraska in the late 1700s, and half a century later, the two tribes were located on a reservation by the Big Blue River on the Nebraska-Kansas border. After the government sold their reservation, the Missouri divided into two bands. The Quaker Band moved onto a reservation in Pawnee and Noble Counties, and the Coyote Band lived with the Sac and Fox (see entry) but later rejoined the Quakers. The Otoe-Missouria now have their headquarters at Red Rock, Oklahoma, and their land is in Noble County.

Population

The Missouri population has always been small. In 1780, there were an estimated 1,000 Missouri, following a devastating attack by the Sauk (Sac), Fox, and their allies during the 1720s. Another raid in 1798 reduced the population even further. By 1804, only about 300 Missouri remained. That number continued to fall. A count in 1829 indicated 80 Missouri, and by 1910, the population had decreased to 13. The Missouri joined the Otoe in 1829, and figures show an estimated 1,500 Otoe-Missouria living together in 1830. By 1886, only 334 Otoe-Missouria had survived. Later in the twentieth

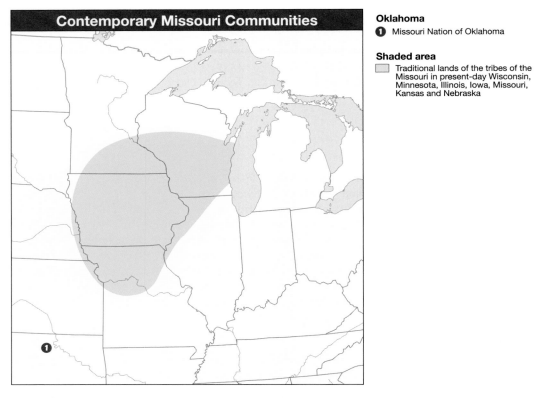

Contemporary Missouri Communities

Oklahoma
❶ Missouri Nation of Oklahoma

Shaded area
Traditional lands of the tribes of the Missouri in present-day Wisconsin, Minnesota, Illinois, Iowa, Missouri, Kansas and Nebraska

A map of contemporary Missouri communities. MAP BY XNR PRODUCTIONS. CENGAGE LEARNING, GALE. REPRODUCED BY PERMISSION OF GALE, A PART OF CENGAGE LEARNING.

century, the population began to rise. In 1995, the combined Otoe-Missouria population was 1,250. The tribe listed 1,449 people in 2004. In 2010, tribal sources noted the population as 2,200.

Language family

Siouan.

Origins and group affiliations

At one time, the Ioway-Otoe-Missouria were all one nation with the Winnebago (Ho Chunk), but they separated into individual tribes. The Missouri traded with other Great Plains tribes, especially the Ponca and Omaha. After the Missouri were almost destroyed by the Sauk and Fox (see Sac and Fox entry) and their allies, the survivors merged with the Osage and Kansa (see entries) or the Otoe.

Originally part of a larger nation composed of the Otoe, Ioway, and Winnebago, the Missouri broke off to live on their own. After the Europeans arrived, the Missouri had a large impact on the fur trade, and they maintained good relations with the French, even intermarrying and traveling to France. Once they lost French protection, the Missouri became vulnerable to attacks from other tribes, particularly the Sac and Fox, who twice almost annihilated them. The remnant of the Missouri joined their kin, the Otoe, for protection. By the end of the 1700s, most of the surviving Missouri had been absorbed into the Otoe tribe, but the Missouri still maintained their identity and their own chiefs. After they were moved to the reservation in the late 1800s, the people took the name Otoe-Missouria, the name by which they are still known. Although the Missouri were always a small tribe, they had a great influence, and the state of Missouri and the Missouri River still bear their name.

HISTORY

Prehistory

Archaeologists have identified an ancient culture, the Oneota, who lived in the upper Midwest in the United States and in Canada. This post-Woodland group was active from about 1000 CE to about 1600. Distinctive pottery, bone tools (such as hoes made of bison shoulder blades and sickles made from deer jawbones), and triangular arrow points were common. Many theories have been proposed for the Oneota origins. Some believe they came from Cahokia, across the Mississippi River from present-day St. Louis. Others say they were descendants of the Late Woodland groups from the upper Mississippi River valley.

The Oneota planted squash, beans, and corn, but they also relied on hunting and gathering to survive. The men hunted bison, deer, and elk as well as birds and fish. Women gathered pigweed and goosefoot, weeds that they cooked with meals. They stored their food in large, underground bell-shaped pits that they lined with grass. Hides and logs over the top kept the food secure. To prevent animals from digging up the food, the Oneota piled dirt on top of the pit.

By 1650, European fur traders had made contact with the Oneota people, because later sites reveal glass beads and silver jewelry that were used as trade items. For many tribes, the arrival of the Europeans meant an increase in new diseases, to which they had no immunity (natural resistance). The Oneota disappeared. Perhaps many died due to these

Important Dates

1720: Sauk (Sac), Fox, and their allies almost destroy Missouri tribe.

1796: Last of the Missouri join the Osage, Kaw, or Otoe after a devastating attack by Sac, Fox, and Ioway.

1817: Missouri and Otoe sign peace treaty with United States.

1854: Big Blue River Reservation is established on the Kansas-Nebraska border.

1898: Curtis Act disbands the tribal government.

1955 and 1964: Otoe-Missouria win settlements for lost lands.

1984: Otoe-Missouria ratify constitution and receive federal recognition.

epidemics, but historians also believe that the Ioway, Otoe, Missouri, and Winnebago are the descendants of this ancient culture. One of the earliest Missouri settlements, the Utz site, dates back to 1450. Other groups that may also have connections to the Oneota include the Osage, Kansa, Quapaw (see entries), Ponca, and Omaha.

Separation of the Tribes

Like their ancestors the Oneota, the four united tribes of the Ioway, Otoe, Missouri, and Winnebago lived by hunting, gathering, and foraging. The buffalo hunt remained an important part of their culture, and families migrated to the plains twice a year. Even women and children went along. These hunts provided food and clothing for the rest of the year. They also supplied the people with buffalo robes for trade. At some point prior to the arrival of the Europeans, however, the groups separated.

The Ioway, Otoe, and Missouri split from the Winnebago and migrated southwest. The Ioway stayed by the mouth of the Iowa River, and the other group continued their westward movement. The Otoe and Missouri, who had remained friendly, supposedly fought over a romantic entanglement. According to the story, the son of the Otoe chief seduced the daughter of the Missouri chief, which caused enmity between these two former allies. The Otoe traveled north along the Missouri River and settled south of the Platte River (now southeast Nebraska). By the 1600s, the Missouri had settled where the Missouri and Grand Rivers meet.

Good relations with the French

The first Europeans to reach the area were Louis Joliet (1645–1700) and Jacques Marquette (1637–1675) in 1673. Following the Europeans' arrival, the Missouri soon became involved in the fur trade. French Canadians established Fort Orleans for the Missouri, and the Missouri and the French got along so well that some tribal members took a trip to France to meet the king. Intermarriage was common between the two groups. The daughter of a Missouri chief married a French nobleman, and another Missouri woman wed a French soldier in Paris at the Cathedral of Notre Dame.

Jacques Marquette and Louis Joliet travel the upper Mississippi River with the aid of Native American guides in 1673. © NORTH WIND PICTURE ARCHIVES/ALAMY.

The Missouri showed an interest in living among the French. The French discouraged that while still maintaining close connections with the tribe. They asked for Missouri help in digging out their cellars and promised them gifts and trade. The two groups continued to coexist peacefully. The Missouri often controlled other tribes' access to the river and to trade, so the French needed to keep the Missouri people as allies.

Attacks on the Missouri

Although the Missouri had an excellent relationship with the French, they were not as fortunate with the Spanish, who plotted to kill them in 1720. The Spaniards planned to arm the Osage with guns and send them against the Missouri, but the Spaniards accidentally entered the Missouri camp and told them the plan. The Missouri waited until the guns were distributed and then turned them on the fifty Spaniards.

Around the same time, the Sauk (Sac) and Fox, who lived in neighboring states, made raids into northern Missouri. They almost decimated the Missouri, whose population had already been greatly decreased by

Hiⁿúñi (My Grandmother)

The Otoe-Missouria told two types of stories. Those called *wórage* were factual accounts based on happenings in the tribe or in people's personal lives, such as the story below. These stories could be told at any time during the year. The *wékaⁿ* were stories from long ago about the sacred. They are set back when people could communicate with animals and always end with the phrase, "That's when I started back home."

The following story is an account of the time when smallpox affected the village. It was recorded from an oral account given in 1936 by Julia Small of the Otoe-Missouria Buffalo Clan. At the time she told the story, she was the last survivor of the Ioway Medicine Lodge.

> The Otoes at the first went out hunting, it seems. They went to shoot buffalo, it seems. My grandmother, my father's mother, married when she was a girl, it seems. They joined the hunt, it seems.

> She and her husband went with them when suddenly disease came and set in, and they were sick, they say.

> They were walking (as) dead, they said. And then they (decided to) come back, they said.

> My grandmother (of) mine, her man together with him those two were sick, they say. Pulling poles the horses were and it is (that) they lay between them, it seems.

> They arrived at a big creek, they said, after they had started back.

> The sick died of thirst, it seems.

> She got up and started for the creek to go look for water, it seems. She went along the creek, (but) there was no water, it seems.

> She met some dogs, she said. "They are wet. Well, they must have discovered some water."

> Again (in turn), she found it, it seems. And there, there was a pool of water, it seems.

> And then, my grandmother got there, it seems. She arrived there, and jumped in, it seems. She drank water, it seems. She drank a lot of water, it seems. And then, she laid down in the water, it seems.

> And then, all day she laid in the water, it seems.

SOURCE: Small, Julia. "Hiⁿúñi (My Grandmother)." *Jimm G. GoodTracks Baxoje-Jiwere Language Project.* http://ioway.nativeweb.org/language/worage_hinkuni.pdf (accessed on June 20, 2011).

smallpox epidemics. Following this attack, the surviving Missouri moved to the west side of the river into Osage territory.

Again in 1798, the Sac and Fox allied with the Ioway to attack the Missouri, who were traveling to St. Louis by canoe to trade. The Missouri suffered devastating losses. No longer able to exist on their own, the remaining Missouri looked to join other tribes for protection. Part of the Missouri went to live with the Kansa and Osage. The rest merged with the Otoe but kept their own clan chiefs and customs. After a few years, some Missouri set up villages south of the Platte River in Nebraska, which is where they were living when the Lewis and Clark expedition arrived.

U.S. makes Louisiana Purchase

In 1803, France sold the United States the Louisiana Territory, which included the Otoe-Missouria lands. This huge parcel of land later became fifteen states and part of two Canadian provinces. President Thomas Jefferson (1743–1826; served 1801–09) assigned Meriwether Lewis (1774–1809) to explore the area. Accompanied by William Clark (1770–1838) and the Corps of Discovery, Lewis reached the area in the summer of 1804. Along the way, they had passed two abandoned Missouri villages.

When they arrived, Lewis and Clark found the villages deserted because most of the people had gone for the summer buffalo hunt. Finally, a week after their arrival, their Shawnee-French scout spotted a Missouri, so the corps sent a message to the chiefs to meet with the Corps of Discovery. Lewis and Clark, who knew the river bore the name Missouri, believed the tribe owned the river. The Missouri were by this time living with Otoe.

The Otoe-Missouria chiefs arrived about a week later with a gift of watermelons. The groups met at Council Bluffs (near present-day Fort Atkinson, Nebraska). Lewis and Clark showed off their corps and handed out presents, including Jefferson peace medals and face paint. They promised protection, more goods, and a trading relationship if the chiefs made peace with the neighboring tribes. The three Missouri chiefs attending this meeting were Black Cat, Hospitality, and Crow's Head, but Lewis and Clark wanted to meet the main chief, Big Horse, as well as Little Thief, who represented the Otoe. Lewis gave his visitors gifts along with a copy of his speech to take to these two important contacts. The Americans met these chiefs a few weeks later as the corps moved upriver. A year later, Little Thief and another Missouri chief went to Washington, D.C., to meet President Jefferson.

U.S. Army major Stephen Harriman Long meets with representatives from the Otoe-Missouria tribe in 1819.
© THE ART GALLERY COLLECTION/ ALAMY.

Signing away land

After an initial peace treaty with the United States in 1817, the Missouri signed several treaties giving up their lands. The first pact in 1830 ceded their land in Iowa and Missouri. In 1833 and 1836, they gave up more land. The 1833 agreement also specified that the Missouri would give up the buffalo hunt and instead settle to farming. The 1836 pact added to the land that the government had taken in 1833. Because the tribes had to move and build new houses during the previous planting season and thus had no crops, the government promised the Otoe and Missouri five hundred bushels of corn the following April. Payment for the land was given in goods. The Otoe received $1,250 worth and the Missouri got $1,000 for all the land "between the State of Missouri and the Missouri River."

In March 1854, the government took the rest of the Otoe-Missouria land, with the exception of 10-mile-wide strip along the Big Blue River. This land along the Kansas-Nebraska border was set aside as a reservation, but the boundaries were later changed when the people discovered the territory they had been assigned lacked trees. Congress later sold 120,000 acres of the Big Blue River Reservation in 1876, and then sold the rest in 1881. Their plan was to move the people to Indian Territory in what is now Oklahoma and Kansas.

Coyotes and Quakers

The Missouri had two different reactions to the changes the U.S. government wanted them to embrace. Some believed the best way to get along with the Americans was to assimilate, or become like them. Others wanted to keep their traditional culture. This disagreement led to a division of the tribe. The Quaker Band, which wanted to embrace American ways, ended up with a small reservation in Indian Territory. The reservation was situated in Pawnee and Noble counties in Oklahoma.

The Coyote Band, which opposed becoming a part of mainstream society, moved to an Iowa reservation with the Sac and Fox. Gradually over the next decade, most of the Coyote Band moved to the Quaker reservation.

Otoe-Missouria in the twentieth century and beyond

In spite of laws forbidding them to have their own government, the Otoe-Missouria opened their own tribal court in 1900. In 1907, the Dawes Act divided their reservation land into allotments, or individual plots of land. The federal government gave one parcel to each head of a household and then opened up the rest of the land to American settlement. In 1912, when oil was discovered on tribal land, the government forced many people off their allotments.

In 1964 and 1967, the people received compensation for some of the land they had lost in the treaties. The 1970s and 1980s brought about an era of construction. The Otoe-Missouria built many houses as well as tribal buildings, a cultural center for dances, games, and other large gatherings. In 1984, the Otoe-Missouria Tribe of Indians ratified its constitution and has its tribal headquarters at Red Rock, Oklahoma. As of 2011, the Otoe-Missouria Tribe had a library and a museum under construction.

RELIGION

The Missouri believed in Wakanda (Wakonda), a universal spirit that was in all objects. Two of the forces of nature that embodied this spirit were the eagle and the snake. People could draw closer to Wakanda through fasting and vision seeking. The Missouri priesthood was hereditary, and the tribe also had curing and dance societies.

The Otoe-Missouria believed the spirits of the dead went to the north to live much as they had on earth, but life there was better because the spirits of the dead had no knowledge of killing. Because they thought the spirits left the bodies in the morning, funeral rituals were held early in the day.

Many members of the Otoe-Missouria belonged to the Native American Church (see Makah entry) in the early 1900s. The church

Chiwere Words

The Missouri spoke a dialect called Chiwere, which is also used by the Ioway and Otoe, although each tribe has their own language. Missouri men used a different greeting than women. Men said "aho," but women said "aha." Like other tribes in the Midwest, the Missouri used Plains Sign Language to communicate with other groups with whom they traded.

bi	"sun"
bi	"moon"
ni	"water"
inake	"woman"
wa^{n}shige	"man"
iyu^{n}ki	"one"
nuwe	"two"
danyi	"three"

faced pressure from state and local officials who wanted to ban the use of peyote in church rituals. Participants use peyote, a druglike plant, to cause trances during certain parts of the church service. In 1914, one of the Otoe of Red Rock, Oklahoma, was instrumental in getting a charter for the Native American Church of Oklahoma, which made it a legally recognized church. In 1944, the church expanded to become the Native American Church of the United States, and in 1955, it broadened its scope to the Native American Church of North America to include Canadians (see Makah entry for more information on the Native American Church). The widespread acceptance of the religion still did not stop the challenges to the use of peyote, and the church as well as other religious peyote users have fought many court battles to keep their rights to practice their religion.

Other religions, introduced by missionaries, were the Baptist Indian Church and the Assembly of God.

LANGUAGE

The Missouri language is part of the Chiwere subgroup of the Siouan family. One of the Mississippi Valley Siouan languages, it is often classified with the dialects of the Iowa and Otoe as the Ioway-Otoe-Missouria (Ba'xoje-Jiwe're-Nyut?achi) language. It is similar to Winnebago (Hochangara). Because the Missouri were absorbed into the Otoe tribe, the differences between the Missouri and Otoe dialect disappeared by the 1900s. Intermarriage between the Otoe and Ioway resulted in a mix of their speech, but people in areas where this did not happen kept their original dialects.

Missionaries started recording the language in the 1830s, and Ioway-Otoe-Missouria books were some of the first published in Kansas. Other than a few studies in the early 1900s, those early sources are the only publications about or in the language. For several decades, Jimm GoodTracks worked on creating files of traditional stories, customs, and songs along with elder interviews. He also created a dictionary. The last fluent speakers died in 1996, and only a few semi-fluent speakers are still living.

GOVERNMENT

At one time a part of a larger nation, which consisted of the Ioway, Otoe, and Winnebago, the Missouri broke away and became a separate tribe. The Missouri people had both clan chiefs and war chiefs. The tribe was patrilineal, which meant inheritance passed down through the father's side, but the leadership position was passed down through the female line. Political leadership was hereditary. The members were from seven to ten clans, and these clan chiefs met to form a tribal council. The Bear clan took the leadership role in the council. Chiefs had limited authority and were expected to care for the orphans, elderly, ill, and poor.

The Otoe-Missouria today are governed by an elected seven-member council who serve for staggered three-year terms. Leaders include a chairperson, vice chair, secretary, and treasurer. The council's duties include making decisions about budgets and investments, enforcing tribal law, providing services to the tribe, and handling specific duties related to their positions.

ECONOMY

When they lived in the East, the Otoe-Missouria maintained a lifestyle similar to the Woodland Indians, who farmed and hunted. The people also did woodworking. After they moved farther west, they became Plains Indians and adopted the buffalo-hunting culture. Once they had horses, the people could range farther across the prairies. Buffalo skins gave them greater wealth, and they spent more time hunting. They traded heavily with other tribes when they had excess hides.

The people had to adapt to a farming lifestyle and give up the buffalo hunt after they moved to the reservation. Once there, the Otoe-Missouria planted more crops—potatoes, wheat, oats—in addition to the staples of corn, beans, squash, and pumpkins they had always grown. Some people planted orchards.

The Otoe-Missouria was one of the first nations to establish bingo halls to generate additional income for the tribe. The tribal council took on the responsibility of economic development, and the Otoe-Missouria have businesses and a casino that are vital to their economy.

DAILY LIFE

Families

Many relatives cared for children, and the family members were called by various names. For example, uncles and aunts were called "fathers" and "mothers." An aunt's children called their older girl cousin "mother." This gave children many close relationships with family members. Because many people died during the smallpox epidemics and attacks by the Sac and Fox (see "History"), these extended relationships made sure that every child had parents to care for him or her. All these relatives shared in child care. One close relationship was between a boy and an uncle (his mother's brother). This uncle gave him a special nickname and provided advice.

Buildings

The ancestors of the Missouri, the Oneota, built the Old Fort in Saline County, Missouri. This earthwork has an irregular shape and double ditches. The earlier Oneota built mounds, but other groups set up regular cemeteries. By the time of the Missouri, homes had become typical dwellings of the Great Plains.

Before they moved to the prairie, the Missouri may have made homes out of bark, similar to those of the Winnebago and Iowa. Once they moved west, Missouri villages usually contained about forty to seventy earth lodges, each about 40 feet (12 meters) in diameter. The lodges were formed of heavy poles stuck in a circular excavated pit. A second smaller inner circle was made with poles that were pushed deeper into the ground. The exterior was of interwoven brush and grass, or rush mats, that was then covered with dirt. Each lodge housed a family and some close relatives. Between fifteen and twenty-five people lived in the house. They sat around a central fire, and an opening in the roof allowed smoke to escape. Doors had wooden frames covered by buffalo skin. An inclined plane measuring 10 to 12 feet (3 to 4 meters) led to the entrance.

Twice a year the Missouri left their villages to go on a bison hunt. For traveling and camping on the plains, the Missouri used buffalo-skin tepees. The tepees for the hunt were placed in a circle with an opening to the east. These portable homes were made of wooden poles that met in a cone shape. The hide thrown over this frame provided shelter, but the tepee could be easily disassembled and moved from one place to another.

Clothing and adornment

Men wore leggings and breechcloths (flaps of deerskin or buffalo hide that hung from the waist and covered the front and back). In the early days, they did not wear shirts, but they later wore hide shirts decorated with beadwork designs. They shaved their heads, often leaving one patch of hair toward the back of the head. Sometimes they attached a roach, or headdress made of a tuft of animal fur, to their hair. Missouri men frequently wore otter-skin turbans. In later years, the turbans were made of cloth.

Women wore deerskin skirts that they topped with ponchos. They kept their hair long and either left it loose or braided it. Both women and men wore moccasins and buffalo robes in winter for warmth.

In later years, after cloth had been introduced, many women made clothing in the European style and decorated the blouses with buttons and their skirts and shawls with ribbon appliqué.

Food

The mainstay of the Missouri diet came from hunting. Small groups brought in deer and small game, but the people greatly depended on the twice-yearly hunt for bison. Everyone from the tribe, including the women and children, moved to the Great Plains for the summer. Another buffalo hunt was planned in the winter. Meat from these hunts were shared equally among all the people in the community.

Both men and women planted and tended the corn, beans, pumpkin, and squash in spring, but most of the duties belonged to the women. To help the plants grow well, the Missouri soaked squash and pumpkin seeds in rainwater for one or two days. Crops were sowed on the fertile land near a creek bed. The women also gathered plants wild plants, nuts, roots, and berries. The men speared fish or caught them in traps made of baskets.

To store extra food, the people dug underground pits that they covered with mats and then dirt to keep animals from digging up the food. Pumpkins were preserved by roasting them on coals and then hanging them on poles. After that, the women flattened and braided strips of pumpkin, similar to the way most Plains tribes braided buffalo meat to dry it. The pumpkin was then left in the sun to dry. This kept it from spoiling.

After the people were moved to the Nebraska and Oklahoma reservations, they added wheat, oats, and potatoes to their individual plots,

Attending Boarding School

In the book *The Otoe-Missouria Elders: Centennial Memoirs, 1881–1981*, Otoe-Missouria Elder John Childs tells about when he was sent away to school.

> I would say that I was about seven or eight and there were about eight kids that went to school here, who lived in the dorm. All government schools are strick with the children. Lots of them used to run away. They would say, "Let's run away and go on home." School just went half a day. The rest of the day, we did painting, carpentry or farming. We had cattle and grew our own food…. At that time we had a watchman whose job was to walk around the school and so forth. If anybody ran away, well he went after them.

SOURCE: Childs, John. *The Otoe-Missouria Elders: Centennial Memoirs, 1881–1981*. Red Rock, OK: The Otoe-Missouria Tribe, 1981, p. 33.

which they often surrounded by fences. Some also tended orchards—walnuts, apples, plums, pears, peaches, and cherries—and vineyards of grapes for fruit and jelly. Following allotment (see "History"), when the land was divided into small plots, the people had to go against their traditional beliefs of owning land as a community. Some Otoe-Missouria tried to keep the land communal by taking away the rocks that marked the boundary lines, but they were ordered to put them back.

Education

Children were supposed to listen and watch adults and then imitate their behavior. In this way, they not only learned survival skills, but they also learned important moral lessons. Grandparents also used storytelling to pass along beliefs and teach children proper behavior, such as respect for animals.

The U.S. government eventually ordered students to go to boarding schools. Students were not allowed to practice their customs, wear their traditional clothing and hairstyles, or speak their language. Later investigations showed that some children were mistreated or abused, but even those who were not often lost their culture. One Otoe-Missouria elder, Truman Dailey, recalled that his grandmother warned him, "You must always try to be an Indian, in your heart and thinking, although you are going to live like a white man."

When the Otoe-Missouria lived on the Big Blue River Reservation in Nebraska, the Quakers were in charge of the school. After the people were forced to move to Oklahoma, the teachers went with them. Red Rock had a school building by 1882, where students learned reading, writing, and mathematics, but pupils also spent half their days learning trades. Boys did woodworking or cared for farm animals. Girls cooked, sewed, and cleaned. Everyone learned to speak English well and practiced American ways of living. By 1918, many parents started sending their children to neighborhood schools instead of boarding schools.

Healing practices

Two of the most important medicine societies were the Buffalo Doctors' Lodge and the Medicine Lodge. The Medicine Lodge was for chiefs and their families. Priests, warriors, and wealthy men and women could also join. They practiced sorcery, and the benefits of membership passed down to the next generations. The Buffalo Doctors' Lodge handled broken bones, wounds, and illness using herbs that were sprayed over the body. The society consisted of six to eight members, who each had a sacred bundle. To become a healer, a person paid to serve an apprenticeship with an experienced healer.

ARTS

Women could not practice any of the arts until they had a vision. Missouri traditional arts included woodworking, porcupine quillwork, parfleche (decorating rawhide containers), and beadwork. Some of the best remaining examples of Missouri abstract floral designs, which were usually outlined in white, can be seen on their moccasins from the late 1800s. Other Missouria-Otoe crafts that have survived are reed mats woven over bark cord, buffalo wool bags, and buffalo-hair wallets.

In June 2002, to celebrate the bicentennial, sculptor Oreland Joe cast bronze sculptures of Lewis and Clark with a Missouri chief, an Otoe chief, an interpreter, and Lewis's dog. The statues were placed where the original council occurred in Council Bluffs, Nebraska. The Otoe-Missouria tribe also had a replica made that they put at the entrance to their First Council Casino in Newkirk, Oklahoma.

To keep their traditional culture alive, the Otoe-Missouria gather for an annual encampment in July. They also hold ceremonies and social gatherings at the Otoe-Missouria Cultural Center.

CUSTOMS

Clan structure

Each clan (or family group) had a sacred bird or animal from which they had descended. That gave the group certain duties and rights, specific rituals and ceremonies, and a set of names for children that came from events and legends. The Bear people, the most powerful clan, took charge in autumn and winter; they also provided the head chiefs. After the spring frog was heard, the Buffalo people led during the spring and summer.

The Buffalo clan was also connected to corn. The Beaver people were in charge of the sacred pipe, whereas the Elk people provided the fire for lighting the pipe. Other early clan names that were recorded by researchers in the 1800s included Pigeon, Owl, Eagle/Thunderbird, and Snake.

Birth and naming

Mothers had their babies in a separate hut and stayed there for fifteen days after the birth. Babies were rubbed with tallow (fat) and tied to a cradleboard. Soon afterward, the infant's ears were pierced during a ceremony where gifts were given out in honor of the child. Special ceremonies were also held when babies received names, when they first walked, and when they got their first pair of moccasins.

Names were significant, and everyone had both sacred and regular names along with nicknames. Most children were named four days after they were born at a feast and gift-giving ceremony. Adults could change their names if they had a vision or performed an important deed.

Puberty

Celebrations occurred for a girl's first menses, when she talked to her first boyfriend, and when she was tattooed. If the girl was a chief's daughter, she received special instruction from an important tattooer before tattoos were placed on the backs of her hands, her forehead, and her breast. Tattoo bundles were passed down.

To become a man, a boy went on a vision quest. After painting his face with charcoal, he carried only a buffalo robe with him as he fasted (went without food and drink) and cried to Wakanda. Receiving power was the most important part of the quest. Boys hoped to get their fathers' special powers.

Status was also important to boys. The top position they could hold was tribal leader. Next was the job of warrior; below that was hunter. Another possible profession was healer or doctor. Boys who were interested in medicine apprenticed with a healer to gain knowledge.

Marriage

Marriages were arranged and had to be between families of the same status. The man's family gave gifts, such as horses, for the bride. The groom's family got gifts of equal value. A man could marry more than one wife, usually his wife's sisters.

Women owed the tepees, all household items, the crops, and even the meat and game. Men's possessions were their hunting equipment, clothes, and personal items. Women took care of the children and the lodge, but men helped carry water and wood.

If a couple wished to divorce, the man returned to his parents' home. After six months to a year, either spouse was free to remarry.

Death and mourning

When a person died, the body was dressed in the best clothes and laid in the lodge for two or three days. Corpses were buried in the ground, sitting upright and facing north, and then covered with logs, a buffalo robe, and earth. The person's horse, decorated with bright colors, was sometimes strangled and left near the grave to give the dead person's spirit transportation. The horse skull was put on the grave, and a piece of mane or tail was attached to pole nearby.

When the weather was too cold for burials, bodies were wrapped in skins, blankets, or bark and tied in the upper branches of a tree. Spirits went north to the spirit world, which was similar to their present life.

The whole village mourned the dead for four days, after which the fires were relit. Relatives might cut their hair, pierce their ears or forearms, or slash their shins. Spouses mourned for one year. Before or after burial, the people might hold competitions such as races or have giveaway contests.

War and hunting rituals

The Otoe-Missouria were more geared for hunting than war, but the 1800s brought settlers and intertribal warfare, so the people were forced into acquiring more aggressive battle techniques. Before they had horses, men painted their faces with charcoal streaks, carried the war bundles that held their power, and used war clubs to fight.

Warriors counted coup (touching an enemy's body with a weapon without getting hurt) to show their bravery. They took the scalps of any enemies they killed. They gave the scalps to their mother-in-laws or sister-in-laws, who danced with them. The warrior then attached the scalp to his war bundle. At the war dance following a victory, each fighter told of his deeds as he struck a post with his weapon. Warriors had a high status and carried out the clan chief's orders. They were also responsible for whipping those who disobeyed the hunt leader.

Buffalo hunts were preceded by a ritual that was led by the Bear clan in the fall and the Buffalo clan in the spring. The people chose a ritual leader, someone with sacred power who would make the hunt successful. Four men reported to this leader and helped keep order

An Otoe-Missouria dancer wears traditional dress at a tribal event in Fort Calhoun, Nebraska, in 2004. © MARK ROMESSER/ALAMY.

during the hunt. Scouts went out in the morning. When buffalo were spotted, the leader spread tobacco on the ground and prayed to the buffalo for a good hunt.

Games and festivals

Men played lacrosse, which was considered sacred. They also enjoyed a game where they tried to throw a javelin (spear) through a moving hoop. Women gambled with seven dice in a wooden bowl and played shinny, a game similar to field hockey. Player used sticks to knock a small wooden ball through the opposite goal post.

Hand games, revived from the past, are conducted to raise money for an honoree or organization. To play, one person from each side is designated as the "guesser." Members of the opposite side hold beaded bone tubes. Guessers figure out which hands the tubes are in. Each player begins with five sticks; the person who gets all ten wins. Between games, the people sing and dance.

An annual Otoe-Missouria encampment is held at Red Rock Creek. Other ceremonies and social gatherings are conducted at the Otoe-Missouria Cultural Center.

CURRENT TRIBAL ISSUES

Although it is one of the smaller Oklahoma tribes, the Otoe-Missouria still holds its own among the larger groups. It was one of the first tribes to make a profit on bingo, and its tribal council continues to look for opportunities for economic self-sufficiency. The Otoe-Missouria Tribe used its gaming revenue to invest in other industries, such as loan companies, convenience stores, hospitality and entertainment industries, and natural resource development. Along with multiple casinos, these businesses provide income to fund many important tribal services and assure the Otoe-Missouria of a brighter future.

NOTABLE PEOPLE

Ignon Ouaconisen (c. 1700–c. 1752) was the daughter of a chief. She had a son with French explorer Étienne de Véniard Sieur de Bourgmont (1679–1734) and traveled to France, where she was hailed as the "Missouri Princess." In France, she traveled and attended the opera along with the five others who had accompanied her, mostly chiefs of various tribes.

Truman Washington Dailey (1898–1996) was the last fluent language speaker in the Otoe-Missouria tribe. Because his father had been a member of the Coyote Band, Dailey learned the traditions that those who assimilated lost. He shared both the language and customs with future generations. Dailey also served as a Roadman and as a leader of the ceremonies in the Native American Church. He also worked in administration for the church when it was the Native American Church of Oklahoma and later when the Native American Church of the United States was formed.

Anna Lee Walters (1946–) is an author, professor, and publisher known for her short stories portraying some of the difficulties of life from a Native perspective. In 1986, she won both the Virginia McCormick Scully Award and the American Book Award. In addition to her fiction, Walters has also written textbooks.

BOOKS

Chapman, Berlin Basil. *The Otoes and Missourias: A Study of Indian Removal and the Legal Aftermath.* Oklahoma City: Times Journal, 1965.

Dickey, Michael E. *The People of the River's Mouth: In Search of the Missouria Indians.* Columbia: University of Missouri, 2011.

Edmunds, David R., Henry F. Dobyns, and John I. Griffin, eds. *The Otoe-Missouria People.* Phoenix: Indian Tribal Series, 1976.

Foster, Lance M. *The Indians of Iowa.* Iowa City: University of Iowa Press, 2009.

The Otoe-Missouria Elders: Centennial Memoirs, 1881–1981. Red Rock, OK: The Otoe-Missouria Tribe, 1981.

Schweitzer, Marjorie M. "Otoe-Missouria Grandmothers: Linking Past, Present, Future." In *American Indian Grandmothers: Traditions and Transitions.* Edited by Margorie M. Schweitzer. Albuquerque: University of New Mexico Press, 1999, pp. 159–79.

WEB SITES

"Art on the Prairies: Otoe-Missouria." *The Bata Shoe Museum.* http://www.allaboutshoes.ca/en/paths_across/art_on_prairies/index_7.php (accessed on June 20, 2011).

Clark, William. "Lewis and Clark: Missouri Indians." *National Geographic.* http://www.nationalgeographic.com/lewisandclark/record_tribes_012_1_9.html (accessed on June 20, 2011).

Fausz, J. Frederick. "The Louisiana Expansion: The Missouri/Missouria." *University of Missouri–St. Louis.* http://www.umsl.edu/continuinged/louisiana/Am_Indians/2-Missouria/2-missouria.html (accessed on June 20, 2011).

Fausz, J. Frederick. "The Louisiana Expansion: The Oto(e)." *University of Missouri-St. Louis.* http://www.umsl.edu/continuinged/louisiana/Am_Indians/4-Oto/4-oto.html (accessed on June 20, 2011).

Fishel, Rich. "The Oneota Culture." *The University of Iowa.* http://www.uiowa.edu/~osa/learn/prehistoric/oneota.htm (accessed on June 20, 2011).

GoodTracks, Jimm. "Ioway, Otoe-Missouria Language." *Native Web.* http://iowayotoelang.nativeweb.org/index.htm (accessed on June 20, 2011).

GoodTracks, Jimm. "These Native Ways." *Turtle Island Storytellers Network.* http://www.turtleislandstorytellers.net/tis_kansas/transcript01_jg_tracks.htm (accessed on June 20, 2011).

May, John D. "Otoe-Missouria." *Oklahoma Historical Society.* http://digital.library.okstate.edu/encyclopedia/entries/O/OT001.html (accessed on June 20, 2011).

Mississippi Valley Archaeology Center at the University of Wisconsin–La Crosse, "Early Cultures: Pre-European Peoples of Wisconsin: Mississippian and Oneota Traditions." *Educational Web Adventures.* http://www.uwlax.edu/mvac/preeuropeanpeople/earlycultures/mississippi_tradition.html (accessed on June 20, 2011).

"Missouri Indian Tribe History." *Access Genealogy.* http://www.accessgenealogy.com/native/tribes/siouan/missourihist.htm (accessed on June 20, 2011).

"Missouri Indians." *PBS: Public Broadcasting Service.* http://www.pbs.org/lewisandclark/native/mis.html (accessed on June 20, 2011).

Oklahoma Humanities Council. "Otoe-Missouria Tribe." *Cherokee Strip Museum.* http://www.cherokee-strip-museum.org/Otoe/OM_Who.htm (accessed on June 20, 2011).

The Otoe-Missouria Tribe. http://www.omtribe.org/ (accessed on June 20, 2011).

Osage

Name

Osage (pronounced "OH-sa-je"). The Osage called themselves the "Little Ones" and *Ni-u-ko'n-ska,* or the "Children of the Middle Waters." At the time of European contact, the Osage were divided into two groups. One group was called the *Tsishu,* or "vegetarians." When the French encountered the second group, the Wazhazhe (pronounced "Wah-sha-she" or "Wah-Zha-Zhi"; translated as "meateaters" or sometimes "upstream people"), they translated this name to "Osage." Osage has been the name that European-Americans have used to identify the tribe ever since.

Location

For hundreds of years, the Osage controlled a vast territory in parts of what are now the states of Missouri, Kansas, and Arkansas. Today, they live on or near the nearly 1.5-million-acre Osage Reservation in Pawhuska, Oklahoma. The town's name comes from the name of an Osage chief.

Population

In the late 1600s, there were possibly 17,000 Osage. In 1815, that number had fallen to 12,000. In 1871, statistics showed a sharp decrease to 3,679 full-blooded Osage and 280 mixed-bloods and intermarried citizens. By 1906, only 2,229 Osage remained, about half mixed-bloods and half full-bloods. In the 1990 U.S. Census, 10,430 people identified themselves as Osage. According to the 2000 census, the population had declined to 7,648; however, 17,831 people claimed they had some Osage heritage. By 2010, the census counted 8,938 Osage, with a total of 18,576 people claiming Osage ancestry. According to 2011 tribal enrollment numbers compiled by the Oklahoma Indian Affairs Commission, 13,307 people were members of the Osage Nation, but only 6,747 of them lived in Oklahoma.

Language family

Dhegiha Siouan.

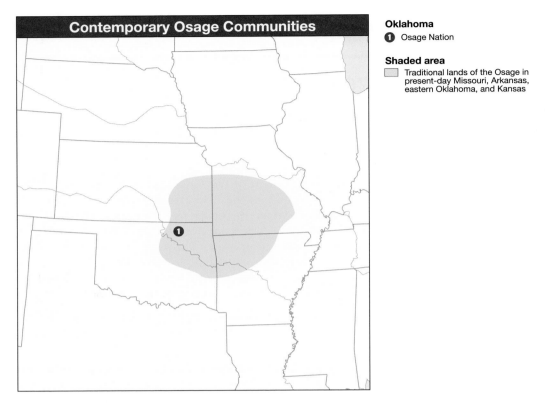

Contemporary Osage Communities

Oklahoma

1 Osage Nation

Shaded area

Traditional lands of the Osage in present-day Missouri, Arkansas, eastern Oklahoma, and Kansas

A map of contemporary Osage communities. MAP BY XNR PRODUCTIONS. CENGAGE LEARNING, GALE. REPRODUCED BY PERMISSION OF GALE, A PART OF CENGAGE LEARNING.

Origins and group affiliations

Long ago, the Osage belonged to a large Siouan group called the Dhegiha. The Dhegiha were mostly farmers who lived in settled towns and cities along the lower Ohio River. Their culture was related to the mound-building communities of the Mississippian culture (see the Mound Builders entry) that flourished from about 700 to 1751. The Dhegiha gradually moved west, broke into five groups, and settled at various spots along the Mississippi and Missouri Rivers.

In 1802, American explorers Meriwether Lewis (1774–1809) and William Clark (1770–1838) identified three groups that made up the Osage tribe: the Great Osage, living on the Osage River; the Little Osage, dwelling farther up the same river; and the Arkansas band, which had settled on the Vermilion River. The group who settled along the Little Osage River became the Osage people. The Osage most likely lived with the Kansa, Quapaw (see entries), Ponca, and Omaha in the Ohio Valley. Later, they drove the Caddo and Wichita (see entries) out of their territory. The Shawnee and Chickasaw (see entries) also feared them. They often fought with other tribes, and in the 1700s, they allied themselves with the French against surrounding tribes, such as the Illinois.

The Osage were a proud, well-organized, adaptable, and often ferocious people who for decades were forced to give up land to the United States. They finally settled in northeastern Indian Territory (present-day Oklahoma). When oil was discovered on their lands in 1906, they became some of the richest people in the world. Wealth brought tragedy and decades of infighting, but it also allowed them to maintain their culture in a way few other tribes have been able to do.

HISTORY

Forced to move westward

The Osage are generally thought of as Plains people, a culture known for its powerful warriors, skilled horsemanship, and buffalo hunting; however, the Plains culture lasted only about two hundred years. It emerged in the late 1700s as a result of tribes being pushed eastward by American pioneers. Osage ancestors had farmed for hundreds of years along the Ohio River before they, like many other Native groups, moved to the Great Plains in the early 1600s. The Osage had settled on the Little Osage River by the mid-1600s.

The French first appeared in Osage territory in 1673 and remained there until the 1760s. The French found a tribe that the famous American writer Washington Irving (1783–1859) later described as "the finest looking Indians I have ever seen." Osage men were of gigantic proportion, often reaching from six feet, five inches to seven feet in height. The Osage (who shaved their eyebrows) called the French "the Heavy Eyebrows." According to Osage author John Joseph Mathews (1894–1979), "The Heavy Eyebrows with their dried sweat and armpit odors made some of the Little Ones sick…. Until recently they have wondered why … white men in general … kept their body odors imprisoned by collars

Important Dates

1693: The French and the Osage begin trading.

1750–1825: The Osage are forced to move west—a move averaging 100 miles (161 kilometers) every ten years. By 1825 the people are settled on a large reservation in southern Kansas.

1871: The Osage move to their reservation in present-day Oklahoma.

1897: Oil is discovered beneath Osage land.

1920s: Fifteen to twenty Osage are murdered during the Osage Reign of Terror.

2004: A bill passes that allows the Osage to set their own rules for tribal membership.

2006: The Osage create a congress.

An illustration shows three Osage warriors circa 1830.
© MARY EVANS PICTURE LIBRARY/THE IMAGE WORKS.

and trousers." The Osage found the Europeans undignified and, therefore, unthreatening.

Plains culture in full flower

The Osage and French got along well together because each group had something the other wanted. The area was rich in fur-bearing animals. The French wanted luxury furs, deerskins, and bearskins to satisfy the growing demand for these products in Europe. Osage skins and furs were especially desirable because the people had an excellent way of preparing the pelts. The Osage liked the items they got in trade from the French: fine fabrics, as well as guns, ammunition, clubs, and axes they could use for hunting and against unwanted Europeans and other tribes.

Before the arrival of the Europeans, Osage warriors had occasionally raided the villages of other tribes to steal horses. Once their appetites were tempted by French trade goods, however, the Osage ranged into land claimed by other tribes to expand their fur trade.

The Osage were known far and wide as fierce warriors and clever traders. Until the end of the 1700s, everyone—other tribes, the French, the Spanish who arrived in the 1760s, and other Europeans—recognized that the Osage were in control of Missouri, Arkansas, eastern Oklahoma, and Kansas. Tribes not aware of Osage control soon learned they were in Osage territory when they saw the severed human heads on stakes that served as territorial markers.

In 1802, just before the Louisiana Purchase (in which the United States purchased a vast area of land from the French) brought the Osage under the control of the United States, nearly half the Osage people left their villages for a new home farther south. This resulted in the tribe being split into two factions that no longer lived close together. The division affected their ability to protect their territory against enemies. It made them less able to withstand the pressure of American settlers heading west.

Under U.S. control

After the Louisiana Purchase, the American government and its citizens forced the Osage to move even farther west. Between 1808 and 1825 alone, the Osage were forced to hand over nearly 100 million acres of their land to the U.S. government in exchange for $166,300, primarily in the form of livestock, horses, farm equipment, and other goods. They were informed that if they wished to be friends and trading partners with the United States, they had to cooperate.

The Civil War (1861–65; a war between the Union [the North], which was opposed to slavery, and the Confederacy [the South], which was in favor of slavery) interrupted Americans' westward push, but when the war was over, migration started up again with renewed vigor. That same year the Osage gave up two more large tracts of land—nearly four million acres—to the U.S. government. They were given six months to relocate to a 12-million-acre reservation in southeastern Kansas, far from their traditional homeland. Three years later, the Osage were forced to sell eight million of their remaining acres to the government, who in turn offered it for sale to settlers.

Even before the land was sold, American settlers moved onto it illegally, claiming squatter's rights. (Squatters occupy a piece of public land to gain ownership of it.) Between 1865 and 1869, more than two thousand settlers had crossed the boundaries of the Osage reservation and were squatting on some of the best farmlands.

Osage author Dennis McAuliffe Jr. discusses one famous squatter family in his book *Bloodland: A Family Story of Oil, Greed, and Murder on the Osage Reservation*: the Ingalls family. Laura Ingalls Wilder (1867–1957) chronicled her life growing up in the American West in the *Little House on the Prairie* series. McAuliffe notes that Wilder described the Osage as skeletal figures who were "beggars and thieves" because she failed to realize the Natives "were hungry because settlers such as her father were burning their fields, forcing them at gunpoint from their homes and threatening them with death if they returned, stealing their food and horses, even robbing their graves—all to force them to abandon their land."

Troubles in Kansas

Settlers demanded that the U.S. government remove the Osage people. Finally, President Ulysses S. Grant (1822–1885; served 1869–77) sent Indian agent Isaac Gibson to resolve the problem fairly. Gibson confirmed

Osage claims that Americans were stealing horses and ignoring Native rights. Gibson reported: "The question will suggest itself, which of these peoples are the savages?"

Meanwhile, the Osage were also being attacked by other tribes, and they could no longer hunt buffalo on the western Plains. Abandoning their reservation seemed their only choice. Osage leaders asked Gibson's assistance, and with his help, laws were passed in 1870 that provided for Osage removal to yet another reservation. Land was available for purchase from the Cherokee (see entry). The U.S. government offered to buy the Osage reservation in Kansas for $1.25 an acre (the government's previous offer two years earlier had been 19 cents an acre). The Osage agreed to sell. While other Oklahoma tribes lost a great deal of land, the nearly $9 million settlement for their land made the Osage the richest tribe in America.

With their money, the Osage bought a new reservation in northeastern Indian Territory (present-day Oklahoma), and they moved there in 1871. Although they were unhappy about leaving the graves of their children behind in Kansas, the people were content with their new reservation. There they had abundant game and buffalo, and no one bothered them.

The Osage refuse allotment

In 1887, Congress decided that Natives were not assimilating (becoming like other Americans) fast enough, and they passed the General Allotment Act to speed up the process. The law allowed the president to divide reservations into parcels called allotments. Each Native head of a household would receive an allotment from land formerly owned by the whole tribe. Leftover acreage would be sold to settlers.

The Osage could not agree among themselves whether to accept allotment. Many mixed-blood members of the tribe pushed for it, but in 1897, before a decision was made, oil was discovered on Osage land. In 1906, the Osage negotiated their own allotment act with Congress. They agreed to accept the policy of individual 160-acre allotments. Because they had paid for their land, however, they refused to make surplus land available to American settlers. The excess land on the reservation after allotment was divided equally and given to each member of the tribe, which then numbered 2,229 people.

Land divided into "headrights"

Each of the 2,229 Osage received an allotment of 657 acres of land; the allotment was called a "headright." Individual ownership applied only to the surface land. It did not extend to mineral (oil) rights. Any underground riches were held in common by all members of the tribe. Each headright was worth 657 acres of land in what is now Osage County, Oklahoma, and one annuity share, or one two-thousandth of the total of all income derived from the production of oil and natural gas beneath the reservation, regardless of who owned the land above. According to the terms of the agreement, the number of headrights would forever remain 2,229. Headrights could be passed on to an owner's heirs, even if they were not Osage, or they could be divided among the heirs. Some Osage might even own more than one headright.

As it turned out, the Osage were living on top of one of the biggest oil fields in the United States. After the fields were tapped, the Osage became some of the richest people in the world. Almost immediately, opportunists began to close in, hoping to cash in on some of the Osage wealth. Some even married Osage headright holders solely to enjoy their newfound riches.

Representatives of the Osage tribe assemble on the steps of the U.S. Capitol building in 1920. LIBRARY OF CONGRESS.

Osage "Reign of Terror"

Between 1921 and 1923, almost twenty people from the Osage Indian Reservation died under suspicious circumstances. The Osage Nation called in the FBI to investigate. Four undercover agents, pretending to be herbal doctors, cattle buyers, and salespeople, discovered the culprit: William Hale, a wealthy rancher often called "King of the Osage Hills." Hale and his nephews, Ernest and Roy Burkhart, had come from Texas to work in the oil fields.

At his uncle's urging, Ernest Burkhart married a full-blooded Osage woman, Mollie Kile (Kyle), who had headrights. She, along with other members of her family, received a percentage of the money generated by the rich oilfields on the reservation. Because those rights could be inherited, Hale and his nephews killed Mollie's mother, sisters, and other relatives for the insurance money as well as headrights to an estimated one-half million dollars a year.

Bill Hale, his nephews, and the ranch hands who assisted in the murders were convicted and sentenced to life imprisonment in 1929. They were not, however, the only ones who resorted to murder to cash in on the wealth brought by oil headrights. Some have estimated that as many as sixty wealthy Osage died during the 1920s, and much of their land ended up in the hands of local American businesspeople and lawyers.

By the 1920s, the Osage were flaunting their wealth. They bought expensive cars and other trappings of rich American society. McAuliffe vividly describes the new lifestyle they embraced, complete with opulently dressed, free-spending men and women who excited the envy and mockery of newspaper readers all around the world. He tells of their "mansions, filled with the finest in furniture, paintings, sculpture, china, and other luxury items—but often no occupants. Many Osage preferred sleeping outside on their lawns, or they continued their nomadic traditions of frequent and seasonal traveling—but this time in style."

Hard times were not over for the Osage, however. In the Osage "Reign of Terror" of the 1920s, which claimed McAuliffe's grandmother as a victim, a string of murders on the reservation finally caught the attention of the Federal Bureau of Investigation (FBI). About two dozen Osage had been killed or had mysteriously "disappeared" from their oil-rich lands. The FBI eventually succeeded in securing sentences of life in prison for the offenders in what became one of its most celebrated cases.

The Osage in the twentieth century

During the twentieth century, oil wealth came and went on Osage lands. During the Great Depression (1929–41), a worldwide economic slowdown during the 1930s, oil income decreased considerably. The international energy crisis of the 1970s renewed interest in Osage oil and brought the tribe new wealth. The boom continued into the 1980s and fell off again in the 1990s. The Osage overspending in the 1920s gave way to a wiser use of oil wealth so it can be drawn upon during hard times.

The Osage have maintained more of their culture than some tribes in Oklahoma have been able to do, partly because of the poverty other tribes have experienced, and because, with their oil income and ownership of their land, the Osage people have been able to remain apart from others.

RELIGION

Traditional beliefs

The Osage creation story speaks of four original groups of people who at some point in the distant past united on Earth into one tribe. They were the Land People, the Sky People, the Water People, and the Isolated Earth People. During a time when there were no enemies to fight and plenty of food had been gathered, certain old men had the leisure to contemplate the meaning of life. These wise men devised a religion for the Osage. From then on, Osage wise men were referred to as the Little Old Men.

The Osage believed the earth was sacred. It is possible that their warlike and ferocious nature, which was often noted by European settlers, was due to their belief in their role as the earth's caretakers.

The ancient Osage discovered the Great Mysteries, which would, according to John Joseph Mathews, "send the wind howling like wolves, and … send down balls of ice to pound their heads, and breathe snow across the land." The Osage did not try to understand these mysteries and the struggles they had endured adjusting to life on Earth (where everything was chaos). Mathews suggested the Osage simply accepted that they were here, as were the sun, the moon, and the stars.

After contact with Europeans

After contact and intermarriage with Europeans, most Osage religious ceremonies had to be abandoned because many clan members had married outside the tribe. Spiritual confusion resulted, leaving the Osage more open to the teachings of Christian missionaries. Many converted to Christianity, both Catholicism and Protestantism.

Some Osage followed the teachings of a Paiute (see entry) called Wovoka (c. 1856–1932), who brought the Ghost Dance religion to them in the 1890s. The Ghost Dance instilled hope that, if it were practiced well, the world would become as it had been before the Europeans came to the Americas—buffalo and other game would return in plenty, dead ancestors would come back, traditional Native values would be restored,

Osage Words

mi	"sun"
mihóⁿdon	"moon"
ni	"water"
ník'a	"man"
shóⁿge	"dog"
wak'ó	"woman"
wiⁿ	"one"

and white men would be gone forever. Wovoka introduced the Osage to peyote (pronounced *pay-OH-tee*), a drug-like substance from the cactus plant that when consumed, it creates visions, which many Native Americans believe are spiritual paths. Some Osage took up the new religion with enthusiasm, and peyote meetings are still held on the reservation.

LANGUAGE

The Osage spoke a branch of the Siouan language called Dhegiha Sioux. The Sioux (see entries) were the largest group of tribes on the Plains, and the term Dhegiha Sioux was used for eastern tribes who had been forced by more aggressive tribes to migrate to the Plains. The Siouan language family had four dialects. The Osage spoke the same dialect as the Kansa, Missouri (see entries), Iowa, Omaha, Oto (see Missouri entry), Ponca, Quapaw, and Winnebago tribes. Classes in the language are held on the reservation.

Because the Plains tribes lived in a widespread area and had come from all over the East, it was rare for groups like the Osage to understand the languages of other groups from the Siouan language family. Because trade among tribes was common, it became necessary for the Plains tribes to develop a sign language, which proved effective in communicating with other groups.

GOVERNMENT

In earlier times, Osage groups were governed by a war chief and a peace chief who guided tribal affairs with advice from the Little Old Men, the wise, elderly warriors who contemplated Osage life and spirit.

In 1881, the Osage people wrote a constitution and established a tribal government loosely patterned after that of the U.S. government. A chief and assistant chief ran the council of three representatives from five districts. The chief had veto power, but a two-thirds vote by the council could override him. Conflicts soon arose when mixed-bloods (the offspring of intermarriages with the French and others) became numerous in the tribe. Their views often clashed with those of full-blood Osage.

In 1900, the U.S. government declared that the Osage tribal government no longer existed, but its members ignored the government's order. In 1906, Congress returned governing authority to the tribal council. It was also decided that only the 2,229 Osage who had headrights (and afterward, their heirs) could vote in tribal elections, hold tribal office, and receive money from oil proceeds. This system created many problems for the tribe, and divisions among members of the tribe grew wider. Tribal membership grew, but an increasing number of people were ineligible to vote. As headright holders died, they passed shares in their headrights to their children. Thus, a mother might leave her headright to her three children, and the three children then would have one-third of a vote in tribal elections. (For more information on headrights, see "Land divided into 'headrights.'") Control of oil wealth was a major issue.

This resulted in a situation where nonvoting Osage, who were often the children of officeholders (and headright holders), attempted to gain a voice in tribal affairs. At the same time, tribal elders and officeholders feared that nonvoters planned to wrest their headrights from them.

A lawsuit in 1991 challenged the tribal voting restrictions. A lower court ruled in 1993 that the Osage had to form a new government and open up voting to include more people. In 1994, only fifty-six people were on the voting list, and the tribal council considered them the entire tribal membership. The 1996 membership roll, though, showed an Osage population of fourteen thousand. An appeal was filed in a higher court, and in 1997, it was decided that only the U.S. Congress can order a change in tribal government. The right to vote in tribal elections was still restricted to headright owners.

Although it had won the case, the Osage Tribal Council announced plans to allow more people to have a say in who represented them on the council. The council, however, stated: "We are equally committed to a protection of the mineral [oil] estate, and will adamantly defend the right of shareholders to have the exclusive control over their mineral assets." So although more people were to be allowed to vote, they would have no say in how oil money was distributed.

In 2006, the Osage Nation created a congress. This legislative branch has twelve members, and all sessions are open to the public. Agendas are posted before each meeting, so the tribe is aware of the issues that will be decided. Congresswoman Debbie Littleton explained this policy by saying, "We need to make sure that this government is driven by the will of the people of the Osage Nation." In addition to the congress, the

Osage Tribe is governed by an elected president and vice-president and the eight-member Osage National Council. A separate Osage Minerals Council deals with headrights and is elected only by headright holders.

ECONOMY

Once the Osage acquired guns and horses from the Spanish and French in the seventeenth century, they no longer depended on farming for their survival. They could travel great distances to hunt buffalo. They eagerly took up fur trading with the French, which changed their way of life. Throughout the year, Osage villages traded with the French and British. The early summer, before the hunt began, was a favorite time for trading. The Osage provided animal skins and dried meat in exchange for brass cooking utensils, whiskey, weapons, ammunition, British cloth, and fine French ribbons and lace.

In the early twenty-first century, in addition to the money from oil, the reservation economy is based on ranching, farming, and the service industry. Many people are employed by the tribal government and in the casinos. The discovery of oil on their reservation land, plus their land-holdings, have combined to make the Osage the wealthiest Native nation in the United States.

DAILY LIFE

Education

In traditional times, the education of Osage children was the responsibility of the entire village. Boys were instructed in hunting and warfare. Girls learned domestic skills, gardening, and the gathering and preservation of food. Grandmothers were responsible for moral instruction. Discipline for unacceptable behavior began with ridicule and progressed to exclusion from the group—the most severe punishment.

Catholic priests and nuns established a mission school for Osage Indians in Kansas in 1847. Boys were instructed in manual labor, and girls were taught to do domestic tasks. After the move to Oklahoma, many Osage children attended government-run boarding schools both on and off the reservation. There they endured a military-style education. They wore uniforms and marched from class to class. Their day began at 5:45 am and ended at 8:30 pm with the playing of "Taps," the bugle call or drum signal that army camps use to signal "lights out." Osage parents were vocal in objecting to this way of educating their children. They especially resented that their children were being forced to perform chores. The boarding schools were finally phased out in favor of public schools.

Buildings

The Osage built two styles of dwellings according to the environment and their activities. On the prairies where they farmed, they built lodges or longhouses—circular or rectangular structures ranging from 30 to 100 feet (9 to 30 meters) long, 20 feet (6 meters) wide, and 10 to 20 feet (3 to 6 meters) high. They built them with frames made of hickory poles that they covered with mats (and later with buffalo skins). They overlapped the mats like shingles to help the buildings shed water. Osage women were responsible for gathering rushes to weave into mats, a task that took a great deal of time. They also used mats to make furniture and beds.

In the center of the lodge was a fireplace, which was vented through a hole in the roof. The fire's central location in the lodge was symbolic of the center of the universe, and the fire served not only for warmth and cooking but also as a communal gathering place. Dried roots, mats, and ears of corn as well as cooking utensils, hunting supplies, and medicine bags were strung about the room. Sacred pipes hung from the walls and were taken down and smoked to welcome visitors. Lodges faced the rising sun so that those exiting in the morning could begin their prayers to Grandfather Sun. Approximately ten to fifteen people occupied the lodge or longhouse.

During the hunting season, the tribe built semi-permanent structures that could be taken down and moved. At times, they carried along some of the building elements from the permanent lodges and used those in the construction. They laid hickory poles in a circle and gathered the ends at the top with flexible branches. Bark rushes, leaves, and moss covered the outside. Later, when horses made buffalo hunting possible, the Osage covered their lodges with buffalo skins.

In some villages, there was a Lodge of Mystery, to which the Little Old Men retired for discussions. This building was built in the same way as the residential lodges, but only the finest animal skins covered it.

Food

The Osage hunted, gathered, and planted gardens. For hundreds of years, whether living in the East or near the Plains, Osage women planted squash, corn, beans, and pumpkins. Once they had planted a garden in spring and the young plants had established themselves, the Osage moved to another environment to take advantage of the available plants and animals. Every healthy man and woman set off on this expedition, leaving behind the old and feeble to watch over the food preserves from the previous year's hunt and harvest.

The travelers gathered wild nuts and berries, persimmons, pawpaws, plums, grapes, roots, and potatoes, which they preserved for winter use. They hunted deer, bear, elk, wild turkey, and small game. When they knew their gardens were ready, the Osage returned to their villages to harvest.

Clothing and adornment

Many of the early traders and travelers who encountered the Osage wrote of their striking appearance. The men were extremely tall and very fond of personal adornment. Osage men wore their hair "roached," a style in which the sides and back of the head are shaved, leaving a lock about two inches high at the top. This strip of hair might be further ornamented with the long hairs from a deer's tail. One or two strands were left long to be decorated with feathers and beads. The Osage also plucked or shaved their eyebrows. Some placed tattoos around their eyes and mouth and painted their shoulders, arms, and chest. Most men pierced their ears; some inserted bones in their ears to make an even larger hole for earrings. They also wore necklaces of wapiti (large deer) teeth and moccasins trimmed with squirrel tails.

Warm-weather wear for men usually consisted of a loincloth (apron-like pieces of fabric) secured by a belt. In cold weather, they wore buffalo-skin capes or trade blankets. The fringes on their deerskin leggings were intended to resemble eagle feathers, because the Osage believed they had originally landed on Earth like an alighting eagle. Warriors decorated their leggings with scalplocks, pieces of scalp with hairs attached that they had removed from an enemy's head during battle.

Osage women favored tattooed breasts, and some wore a long shirt that covered one shoulder. Women and girls might also have worn an apronlike garment made of deerskin. They strung beads into necklaces and wore several long strands. Single women wore their long hair in decorated braids, whereas married women pulled theirs back and tied it with a leather thong. Sometimes a woman painted the part in her hair red to symbolize the sun moving over the earth.

Once trade with the Europeans began, Osage women used cloth, yarn, and colored beads to decorate clothing. They trimmed blankets with silk and satin ribbon work and wore them over their shoulders like shawls. Beadwork, along with animal claws, teeth, and bones, adorned their garments. Beads soon replaced quillwork (designs made with dyed porcupine quills) on moccasins and clothing.

Healing practices

Medicine men or women occasionally served as religious leaders, but they were most highly regarded for their knowledge of extracting drugs from plants and herbs. Medicine men were paid for their services to the sick. When their herbal remedies failed and the patient got no better, medicine men called upon mysterious forces. To get a spirit's attention, they wore special clothing made of bear or snake skins and sometimes decorated with deer hooves. Medicine men generally performed a ritual song and dance over the patient, accompanied by the music of rattles.

One of the medicine man's most important responsibilities was putting together medicine bundles for warriors. These contained herbs and other items to ward off evil spirits and gain the favor of good spirits. A different mixture was required for each warrior. Medicine bags were made from the skins of birds, animals, or reptiles. The renowned painter of Native tribes George Catlin (1796–1872) remarked that "the value of the medicine-bag to the Indian is beyond all price … for he considers it the gift of the Great Spirit."

ARTS

Osage women are known for their beautiful finger weaving and for their ribbonwork. In ribbonworking, the women cut intricate designs of ribbons and then sew them in several layers onto clothing and ceremonial objects such as dance blankets.

CUSTOMS

Clans

Osage society was organized into a complicated system of clans, or family groups. Originally, there were fourteen clans, but these were later expanded to twenty-four. Clans were further divided into Sky Peo-

How the Spider Symbol Came to the Osage People

One day, the chief of the Isolated Earth People was hunting in the forest. He was not just hunting for game, he was also hunting for a symbol to give life to his people, some great and powerful animal that would show itself to him and teach him an important lesson. As he hunted he came upon the tracks of a huge deer. The chief became very excited.

"Grandfather Deer," he said, "surely you are going to show yourself to me. You are going to teach me a lesson and become one of the symbols of my people."

Then the chief began to follow the deer's tracks. His eyes were on nothing else as he followed those tracks and he went faster and faster through the forest. Suddenly, the chief ran right into a huge spider's web that had been strung between the trees across the trail. It was so large and strong that it covered his eyes and made him stumble. When he got back up to his feet, he was very angry. He struck at the spider, which was sitting at the edge of the web, but the spider dodged aside and climbed out of reach. Then the spider spoke to the man.

"Grandson," the spider said, "why do you run through the woods looking at nothing but the ground? Why do you act as if you are blind?"

The chief felt foolish, but he felt he had to answer the spider. "I was following the tracks of the great deer," the chief said. "I am seeking a symbol to give life and strength to my people."

"I can be such a symbol," said the spider.

"How could you give strength to my people?" said the chief. "You are small and weak and I didn't even see you as I followed the great deer."

"Grandson," said the spider, "look upon me. I am patient. I watch and wait. Then all things come to me. If your people learn this, they will be strong indeed."

The chief saw that it was so. Thus the spider became one of the symbols of the Osage people.

SOURCE: Bruchac, Joseph. "How the Spider Symbol Came to the Osage People." *Native American Animal Stories.* Golden, CO: Fulcrum Publishing, 1992.

ple and Land People. The Osage believed all members of a clan were descended from a common ancestor and were related. The common ancestor could have been a plant, animal, or a natural phenomenon. Clan leaders, who inherited their positions through their fathers, shared a limited rule over the entire Osage Nation. Each clan controlled the part of the village in which it lived, and the clan functioned as a military unit during wartime.

Courtship and marriage

When Osage boys and girls reached puberty, they were considered ready for marriage. Osage women usually married immediately, but men waited until they were at least in their late teens. A man's parents chose a mate for him from another clan. The groom's parents asked four "good-men" to determine that the bride was indeed from a different clan and to set up the exchange of gifts that was the main event of a simple wedding ceremony. Divorced and widowed women were outcasts, suitable only as mates for settlers.

In the earliest times, it was the custom for Osage newlyweds to move in with the groom's parents. When the Osage took up hunting and raiding, the custom was reversed, and the couple moved in with the bride's parents. A household that included men from several different clans had an advantage: when some clans left on hunting and raiding expeditions, others could stay behind and contribute to the household.

Babies and children

Osage infants were tied to boards, which their mothers carried on their backs. An infant was bound so tightly to the board that the back of its head was flattened; this was considered an attractive feature.

After the naming ceremony, a young child was considered a "real" person and member of a clan. This was the occasion when a child acquired a special clan hairstyle that he or she wore until puberty.

Festivals and ceremonies

Other than child-naming, important occasions that required elaborate ceremonies included a weeks-long preparation for war, the celebration of a warrior's success in battle, the celebration of peace, and mourning for those who died in battle.

The Osage have held their most important dance every spring since 1884. It is called *I'n-Lon-Schka,* the Playground of the First Son. Each year, they choose a boy to be drum keeper, which is considered a great honor. His family keeps the drum for a year and is in charge of hosting the last dances in the four-day spring event. At those dances, the host family lavishes gifts on their guests.

The Osage were among the first Native peoples to send their men and women off to fight in World War II (1939–45). Before the troops departed, the tribe held a ceremony and bestowed warrior names on them.

CURRENT TRIBAL ISSUES

In the late 1990s, centuries-old remains of the Osages' deceased ancestors were held by the anthropology department at Missouri University at Columbia. The Osage Nation pressed for the return of the remains. The university contended that the remains would give students an opportunity to learn more about Native American history. The Native Graves Protection and Repatriation Act, passed in 1990, however, gives tribes more say in what happens to the remains of their ancestors. The Osage received the remains and grave goods and ceremonially reburied them in September 2007.

Oil wealth has affected the lives of the Osage in ways never experienced by other Native nations. Terry Wilson reported in *Native America in the Twentieth Century* that "Osage politics is still almost completely shaped by the overriding concerns of oil leasing and headright payments."

In the early 2000s, the Osage were involved in two court cases against the federal government. The first, begun in 2000, was to decide whether the Osage should be required to pay taxes. Reservation land is exempt from taxes, but a question existed as to whether Osage land had been terminated as a reservation a century ago. The eleven-year case ended in 2011 with a Supreme Court decision against the Osage. The court declared that their land is no longer reservation land, which means they must pay taxes. Also in the early 2000s, the Osage filed a lawsuit against the government for mismanagement of trust funds. In its first phase, the Osage Trust case won more than $330 million, and the people expected to receive more compensation in the second phase that began in 2011.

NOTABLE PEOPLE

Osage dancer Maria Tallchief (1925–) joined the Ballet Russe, a world-famous Russian ballet troupe, and worked under the renowned choreographer (composer and arranger of dance steps) George Balanchine (1904–1983). In 1946, she married Balanchine and moved to Paris with him. Tallchief was initially treated with disdain in Paris. Her debut at the Paris Opera was the first ever for any American ballerina, but Tallchief's talent quickly won over French audiences. She later became the first American to dance with the Paris Opera Ballet at the Bolshoi Theatre in Moscow. In 1949, she became the first Native American to become prima ballerina at the New York City Ballet, and that year she danced one of her greatest roles in the Balanchine-choreographed version of the

Firebird. In 1965, Tallchief retired from performance to teach ballet. Ten years later, she headed the Chicago Lyric Opera Ballet, and in 1981, she founded the Chicago City Ballet. In 1996, she was inducted into the National Women's Hall of Fame.

Other notable Osage people include Charles Brent Curtis (1860–1936), the first Native American to be elected vice president of the United States in 1929; Corine and Leona Girard, mixed-blood sisters who were active during the 1920s in the fight to obtain voting rights in tribal affairs for Osage women; John Joseph Mathews (1894–1979), the author of the first university-published book to be sold by the Book-of-the-Month Club and a major figure in Osage tribal politics; and Andrew "Buddy" Redcorn (1943–2009), the most-decorated Native American in the Vietnam War.

BOOKS

Bailey, Garrick, Daniel C. Swan, et al. *Art of the Osage.* Seattle: University of Washington Press, 2004.

Bailey, Garrick, ed. *Traditions of the Osage: Stories Collected and Translated by Francis la Flesche.* Albuquerque: University of New Mexico Press, 2010.

Burns, Louis F. *A History of the Osage People.* Tuscaloosa: University of Alabama Press, 2004.

Burns, Louis F. *Osage Indian Customs and Myths.* Tuscaloosa: University of Alabama Press, 2005.

Dorsey, James Owen. *Osage Traditions.* Charleston, SC: General Books, 2010.

Harmon, Alexandra. *Rich Indians: Native People and the Problem of Wealth in American History.* Chapel Hill: University of North Carolina Press, 2010.

Liebert, Robert. *Osage Life and Legends: Earth People/Sky People.* Happy Camp, California: Naturegraph Publishers, 1987.

Mathews, John Joseph. *The Osage: Children of the Middle Waters.* Norman: University of Oklahoma Press, 1961.

McAuliffe, Dennis, Jr. *Bloodland: A Family Story of Oil, Greed and Murder on the Osage Reservation.* Beltsville, MD: Council Oak Books, 1999.

McAuliffe, Dennis, Jr. *The Deaths of Sybil Bolton: An American History.* New York: Random House, 1994.

Simermeyer, Genevieve. *Meet Christopher: An Osage Indian Boy from Oklahoma.* Tulsa, OK: National Museum of the American Indian, Smithsonian Institution, in association with Council Oak Books, 2008.

Stewart, Philip. *Osage.* Philadelphia, PA: Mason Crest Publishers, 2004.

Stowell, John. *Don Coronado through Kansas, 1541, Then Known as Quivira: A Story of the Kansas, Osage, and Pawnee Indians.* Charleston, SC: Nabu Press, 2011.

WEB SITES

French, Mary. "Osage Ceremonial Garments." *University of Missouri Museum of Anthropology.* http://anthromuseum.missouri.edu/minigalleries/osagegarments/osagegarments.shtml (accessed on June 12, 2011).

McCoy, Ron. "Neosho Valley: Osage Nation." *KTWU/Channel 11.* http://ktwu.washburn.edu/journeys/scripts/1111a.html (accessed on June 12, 2011).

Mussulman, Joseph. "Osage Indians." *The Lewis and Clark Fort Mandan Foundation.* http://lewis-clark.org/content/content-article.asp?ArticleID=2535 (accessed on June 12, 2011).

National Museum of the American Indian. "Prairie." *Smithsonian.* http://americanindian.si.edu/searchcollections/results.aspx?regid=60 (accessed on June 12, 2011).

"Native Americans: Osage Tribe." *University of Missouri.* http://ethemes.missouri.edu/themes/1608?locale=en (accessed on June 12, 2011).

"The Osage." *Fort Scott National Historic Site, National Park Service.* http://www.nps.gov/fosc/historyculture/osage.htm (accessed on June 12, 2011).

"Osage Indian Tribe History." *Access Genealogy.* http://www.accessgenealogy.com/native/tribes/osage/osagehist.htm (accessed on June 12, 2011).

Osage Nation. http://www.osagetribe.com/ (accessed on June 12, 2011).

Redish, Laura, and Orrin Lewis. "Osage Indian Fact Sheet." *Native Languages of the Americas.* http://www.bigorrin.org/osage_kids.htm (accessed on June 12, 2011).

Sabo, George III. "Osage Indians." *University of Arkansas.* http://arkarcheology.uark.edu/indiansofarkansas/index.html?pageName=The%20Osage%20Indians (accessed on June 12, 2011).

"2011 Oklahoma Indian Nations." *Pocket Pictorial Directory.* Oklahoma City: Oklahoma Indian Affairs Commission, 2011. Available from http://www.ok.gov/oiac/documents/2011.FINAL.WEB.pdf (accessed on June 12, 2011).

Pawnee

Name

The name Pawnee (pronounced *PAW-nee* or *paw-NEE*) probably comes from the Sioux term *pa-rik-i,* meaning "horn." The word refers to the distinctive hairstyle of the Pawnee warriors, who coated their hair with thick grease and paint so that it stood up and curved like a horn. Some groups of Pawnee called themselves *Ckirihki Kuruuriki,* meaning "looks like wolves," or *Chahiksichahiks,* meaning "men of men."

Location

The Pawnee believe their ancestors came from the Southwest; some historians say they may have come from Mexico. Evidence suggests that the tribe had inhabited the Central Plains for at least five hundred years. The Pawnee once lived in what is now Kansas and Nebraska, concentrating in the valleys of the Loup, Platte, and Republican Rivers. In the early twenty-first century, the Pawnee reservation is located in north central Oklahoma, about 50 miles (80 kilometers) west of Tulsa.

Population

At their peak, the Pawnee probably numbered about 35,000. In 1790, there were about 10,000 Pawnee. In 1900, that figure fell sharply to about 650. In the 1990 U.S. Census, 3,387 people identified themselves as Pawnee. According to the 2000 census, that number had decreased to 2,636; however, a total of 5,205 people claimed some Pawnee background. In 2007, tribal sources indicated a Pawnee enrollment of 3,190. The Oklahoma Indian Affairs Commission showed a total enrollment of 3,240 for 2011.

Language family

Caddoan.

Origins and group affiliations

The Pawnee and other speakers of Caddoan may be descendants of the prehistoric hunter-gatherers who roamed the Great Plains region of North America as many as 7,500 years ago. Some historians believe

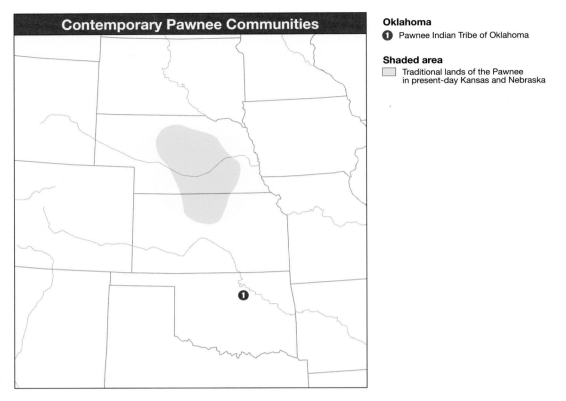

A map of contemporary Pawnee communities. MAP BY XNR PRODUCTIONS. CENGAGE LEARNING, GALE. REPRODUCED BY PERMISSION OF GALE, A PART OF CENGAGE LEARNING.

they came from Mexico but moved northward, and by 1600, they were in control of large parts of the western Plains. The Pawnee say they descended from the Kawarakis Pawnee, ancestors of the Chaui, Kitke-hahki, and Pitahawirata Bands, who settled in southeastern Nebraska in approximately 900.

The Pawnee nation consisted of four related bands: the *Chaui*, or Grand Pawnee; the *Kitkehahki*, or Republican Pawnee; the *Pitahawirata*, or *Tappage* Pawnee; and the *Skidi*, or Wolf Pawnee. The Arikara (see entry) were once considered part of the Pawnee, but they split from the main group long ago and are now considered a separate group. The major enemies of the Pawnee were the Cheyenne and the Sioux (see entries) tribes.

The Pawnee were a peaceful farming people who could be fierce when pushed to defend themselves. Because they stayed in one area, they made easy targets for other wandering Plains tribes. Still, most tribes regarded them as mysterious and were awed by their poetic stories and rituals concerning the heavens and the earth.

HISTORY

Pawnee in ancient times

For centuries, the Pawnee way of life revolved around pursuing the Plains buffalo on foot, stampeding them over cliffs, trapping them in corrals, and killing and butchering them with chipped-stone tools. The Pawnee also farmed part time, raising corn, squash, and beans in the fertile river valleys of the Great Plains.

Sometime around the early thirteenth century, the Pawnee left the Great Plains, perhaps because of a change in climate. Whereas some scholars believe the Pawnee settled in the Southwest, others think they moved into the Southeast near the Mississippi River delta. By 1300, however, the ancestors of today's Pawnee returned to the Great Plains. They settled in the river valleys of modern Kansas and Nebraska between the Apache people to the west and the Sioux people to the east. From the fourteenth through the sixteenth centuries, Pawnee civilization flourished on the Great Plains.

Important Dates

1300: The Pawnee begin their migration to Nebraska.

1541: Francisco de Coronado meets the Pawnee on the Great Plains while looking for treasure.

1817: The Pawnee chief Petalésharo puts an end to the tradition of the Morning Star maiden sacrifice.

1833–72: The Pawnee sign four different agreements giving their land to the U.S. government.

1876: The U.S. government forces the Pawnee to abandon their land in Nebraska for a reservation in Oklahoma.

1960s–1970s: The federal government returns Pawnee reservation lands in Oklahoma to the tribe.

Horses arrive on the Plains

In 1541, about 250 years after the tribe returned to the Great Plains, the Spanish explorer Francisco Vásquez de Coronado (c. 1510–1554) encountered people he called *Harahei* north of the Arkansas River in what is now Kansas. These people were probably the Pawnee. Coronado, then in search of the riches, did not stay among them long.

Sometime before 1680, horses (originally brought from Spain) became a common sight on the Great Plains, and the Pawnee began to use them. Horses allowed the tribe to travel farther in search of buffalo. Although tribes such as the Sioux and the Cheyenne (see entry) used horses to move from place to place, the Pawnee remained primarily an agricultural people.

Tribe faces changes

Many changes occurred among the Pawnee in the nineteenth century. Their lands were overrun, first by eastern settlers who had heard stories of free, fertile land in the West, then by miners heading to California after gold was discovered in 1848. The waves of migrant people, intent on crossing the Great Plains to find riches, frightened the buffalo on which the Pawnee relied for their survival. Sometimes starving Pawnee attacked wagon trains and settlements to stay alive.

The settlers brought European diseases to which the Pawnee had no immunity. A smallpox epidemic (outbreak of disease) in 1831 cut their numbers in half. In 1849, cholera, a deadly disease that spreads rapidly, reduced the tribe by half again. By 1857, widespread measles and tuberculosis had made the Pawnee dependent on aid from the U.S. government. That year, the federal government placed the few remaining members of the tribe on a reservation on the Loup River near what is now Genoa, Nebraska, but on the reservation, the Pawnee were vulnerable to raids from other Plains tribes, particularly the Sioux. In 1864, the government began a campaign to subdue the hostile Sioux, and the

A Pawnee family stands in front of its lodge at Loup, Nebraska, in 1873. NATIONAL ARCHIVES AND RECORDS ADMINISTRATION.

Pawnee volunteered to assist. Pawnee warriors fought bravely alongside the U.S. Army regulars.

Difficulties on the reservation

On the reservation, the Pawnee tried to live as before, hunting and farming in their communal style, whereby all the people shared in the work and divided equally the crops they produced. Federal agents, however, wanted them to farm as individuals. Agents also tried to convince the Pawnee to live in wooden houses and send their children to government schools, where they were forbidden from speaking their native language.

Then more disasters struck, both natural and man-made. A drought resulted in the dehydration and death of most of the buffalo and harmed the crops, and a plague of grasshoppers destroyed the crops that had survived. By this time, after all the disease and disorientation, the Pawnee were very weak. On August 5, 1873, a day when their men were away hunting, a large party of Sioux attacked Pawnee women and children. Between 75 and 115 innocent people died in what came to be called the Battle of Massacre Canyon.

In the face of continuing demands of white settlers for more Pawnee lands, the U.S. government convinced the tribe to move from Nebraska to a reservation in Oklahoma in 1876. The government pushed the Pawnee off their Nebraska lands so quickly that they did not even have time to harvest their crops. The people spent a terrible winter with little food.

Rebirth of a nation

Government acts in 1887 and 1898 further reduced the land holdings of the remaining Pawnee, whose lives by now were full of sickness and misery. In 1893, settlers again pressured the federal government for more land, so most of the Pawnee Reservation was purchased and settled by non–Native Americans.

By the early twentieth century, the Pawnee seemed to all but disappear. In the early 1930s, however, the government tried to right some past wrongs and help the Pawnee become a functioning tribe. The Indian Reorganization Act of 1934 restored some of their rights, but it was not until the mid-1960s that the federal government finally returned Pawnee reservation lands in Oklahoma to the tribe. In 1966, the Indian Claims Commission awarded the tribe $7 million for their original lands in Kansas and Nebraska, which the United States had taken in the nineteenth century. During the 1970s, the Pawnee regained more tribal lands.

In the early twenty-first century, most Pawnee lived in Pawnee, Oklahoma, the site of their tribal government. Although many adapted to mainstream American life, they also still held celebrations of their Pawnee heritage throughout the year.

RELIGION

The sun and stars

The religion of the Pawnee is inspired by the sun and the stars of the Great Plains sky, which they once used to guide them on their travels. Many of the stars and planets were worshipped as gods. The Pawnee believed that after death, human souls followed the Milky Way to heaven and lived out eternity with Tirawa, their Creator.

Pawnee priests served as messengers between the invisible spirit world and the everyday world. They watched the skies during planting and growing season, and if storms or other dangers threatened the crops, they performed rites to drive them away. They used stuffed birds and animals in religious ceremonies.

They also believed that the stars determined the best times for planting crops. In the spring, they began a series of ceremonies to ensure a good harvest. At the summer solstice (June 21, when the sun is at its highest point), they offered a human sacrifice, and following the harvest, they offered maize (corn) and other crops to the gods. Human sacrifices ended in the 1800s.

Sacred bundles and secret societies

Like many of the Plains tribes, the Pawnee had sacred bundles. Sacred bundles are pouches that contained religious tools and symbols and were used in rituals and ceremonies. A hereditary keeper cared for each bundle. Shrines were central to their Pawnee rituals (see "Sacred architecture"). Priests took charge of the ceremonies. The people believed that by pacifying the supernatural powers, they would have food, long life, and prosperity.

Several secret societies were connected with supernatural animals. These societies attracted game, healed diseases, and bestowed special powers. Some Pawnee also participated in the Ghost Dance movement during 1890s.

LANGUAGE

The Pawnee spoke a language that was distantly related to the languages of the Wichita, the Caddo (see entries), and the Arikara, three other tribes whose languages were in the Caddoan family of languages. Caddo was related to the languages of the Sioux and the Iroquois. Caddoan speakers all made use of Great Plains sign language for communicating outside their tribal group.

In modern times, the Chaui, Kitkehahki, and the Pitahawirata speak the South Band dialect (variety of a language), but the Skidi band have their own dialect. Both of these dialects comprise the Pawnee language.

In 1997, the tribe began the Pawnee Language Program. They created computer programs to teach vocabulary and grammar to all ages. With funding from a grant, they also developed a Teacher Training Program and the Language Nest Model to teach Pawnee to young children. Language teachers spend two to four hours every day speaking Pawnee in the classrooms at the Hukasa Child Learning Center. The children receiving this training are infants to five-year-olds; their families can also participate in additional language instruction. In this way, the tribe hopes to revitalize the Pawnee language and pass on their culture to the next generation.

The Major Gods of the Pawnee

The most important Pawnee god is *Tirawa*, who represents the open sky. Tirawa created the universe to relieve his loneliness. He first created the four primary stars: the Evening Star in the west, with the moon as her helper; the Morning Star in the east with the sun as his helper; and the North and South Stars marking the other two directions. Tirawa also created stars for the skies of the northeast, northwest, southeast, and southwest and gave them the task of holding up the earth.

The Evening Star and the Morning Star were responsible for the creation of the earth and the ancestors of the Pawnee. The Evening Star created the earth from a clap of thunder and a flash of lightning. The Morning Star then persuaded Evening Star to marry him, and they produced the first of the Pawnee. Their first-born child, a girl, was lowered to the earth on a whirlwind. Their second-born child, First Man, became Chief of Center Village and of all the Pawnee. First Man had to assemble and bring the important sacred bundles to the various Pawnee villages. Aided by Evening Star and Morning Star, the people developed their ceremonies, symbols, and songs. Bound by their shared gifts, the people then banded together to form a nation.

GOVERNMENT

In traditional times, a Pawnee chief inherited his position from his father. Still, he had to prove he had the necessary knowledge and power to deserve the position. Pawnee leaders were respected for speaking in a quiet tone of voice, for giving freely, and for leading in a wise, patient, and understanding manner.

Pawnee Words

asakis	"dog"
eerit	"see"
kiítsu'	"water"
páh	"moon"
piíta	"man"
raruuku	"sing"
sakuru	"sun"
tsápaat	"woman"
árusa	"horse"
kuúruks	"bear"
katsiki	"fish"
rútki	"snake"

The tribe was organized by villages; each of which had its name, its shrine containing sacred objects, and its priests. It also had a hereditary chief and a council composed of the chiefs and leading men. Each chief had a herald who announced his orders.

Chiefs from the different villages made up a tribal council. Council meetings followed strict rules. Only certain people could speak, and attendance was limited to a few privileged men who watched the proceedings. The council made all major decisions for the tribe as a whole.

Today, the tribe is governed by two eight-member governing bodies: the business council and the chiefs of the Nasharo Council. The bands chose their chiefs, while the entire tribe elects the president, vice president, and secretary/treasurer of the business council.

ECONOMY

The Pawnee relied on two different economies: the farming economy and the hunting economy based on the Plains buffalo. To produce the best crops, it was important to know when the spring planting should take place; this was the focus of the Ground-Breaking Ceremony (see "Ground-Breaking Ceremony").

The Pawnee way of life changed in the early 1700s with the introduction of guns and horses. The people came to rely on hunting to supply things that their crops could not give them, including meat and hides for clothing and shelter. They used all parts of the buffalo. Buffalo hair was braided into rope, horns were made into spoons and tools, and the animals' shoulder blades were used as hoes.

In the early 2000s, the tribe received most of its money from government grants and contracts, as well as from leasing tribal land for agricultural use and for oil and gas exploration. Additional revenue came from their casino and trading post, travel plaza, and deli. The Pawnee Tribal Development Corporation oversees these businesses and works to develop economic opportunities for the tribe and create jobs for the people.

DAILY LIFE

Families

The oldest woman was the most important person in a family or in a household. Women raised the children, did the farming and the cooking, and made bowls, spoons, and other utensils. Men hunted, made war, fashioned weapons such as bows and arrows, went on twice-yearly buffalo hunts, and served as chiefs or healers. Since a Pawnee man could have more than one wife, he did not always live with his children, but it was his job to provide them with food and other necessities. A woman might have more than one husband, but all her children considered themselves brothers and sisters.

Older women of the tribe watched the children while middle-aged women worked. Young single women learned their duties by helping and observing. Pawnee society was matrilineal, so tribal heritage was passed down through the mothers. Men generally had one of the following functions: medicine man and priest, hunter, or warrior. Although men and women had distinct jobs, they shared decision making.

Buildings

The Pawnee built two types of structures: earth lodges and tepees. They lived in earth lodges during the spring and fall while they were planting and harvesting their crops. They carried tepees with them on the buffalo hunt. Tepees were large, with eleven lodge poles, and could house up to eighteen people. They were made from buffalo hide and could be easily carried from place to place.

Earth lodges were made of dirt piled over a wooden framework of cottonwood and willow. They were well suited to the changing climate of the Great Plains, but they only lasted three to six years. They were also hard to build and maintain. It took the timber from four large trees and up to one hundred smaller trees or bushes to build one lodge.

Ten to twelve lodges made up a village, and each could shelter as many as ten related families. A lodge usually had a covered entryway, measuring about 12 feet (3.6 meters) high, 7 feet (2 meters) across, and 8 feet (2.5 meters) long. The entryway led to the main part of the circular dwelling, which was about 40 feet (12 meters) in diameter and about 15 feet (4.5 meters) high at the smoke hole in its center.

Two Pawnee men pose for a portrait wearing boot moccasins, leggings, breechcloths, and medals. DENVER PUBLIC LIBRARY, WESTERN HISTORY COLLECTION, CALL NO X33142. REPRODUCED BY PERMISSION.

Sacred architecture Both the earth lodge and the tepee were built according to Pawnee ideas of sacred architecture. They were miniature models of the universe, with the roof representing the sky overhead and the floor representing the earth underfoot. The four cedar logs holding up the roof stood for the four Pawnee clans, and a star shrine pointed to the west.

Each lodge or tepee had a sacred spot called the *wi-haru,* "the place of wonderful things." The wi-haru represented Pawnee Paradise, where the corn was always ripe and the buffalo were always plentiful. It was always located along the western wall of the dwelling and included an altar with a buffalo skull and the family's sacred bundle (see "Sacred bundles and secret societies").

Clothing and adornment

The Pawnee made most of their clothing from buckskin. Women wore leather dresses or wrap skirts, adding leggings and overblouses in winter. Men wore leather breechcloths (garments with front and back flaps that hung from the waist), loose shirts, and leather leggings. They wore two belts. One held up their clothes; the other held necessities, such as a tomahawk, knife, pipe, and tobacco. Men carried buffalo robes to impress visitors with their power and status. The quality of a man's hide shirt, with its decorations of quillwork, scalps, or skins, also showed his status.

Shirts and robes were decorated with moons, suns, or stars to represent the tribe's special relationship with the heavens. Moccasins made of otter hide were usually left plain, although they might be decorated for special ceremonies, such as burials or warfare. Men sometimes wore turbans of hide or cloth. On special occasions, they wore war bonnets adorned with suns, moons, and stars. Both men and women pierced their ears and wore ornate beaded earrings.

Food

On their farmland in the fertile river valleys of Kansas and Nebraska, the Pawnee raised ten to fifteen different kinds of corn, eight kinds of beans, and seven kinds of pumpkins and squash, as well as watermelons, sunflowers, and tobacco. They also harvested a grain similar to wild rice. The village chief assigned plots of land to various families.

Excellent hunters, the Pawnee shot raccoon, skunk, quail, and prairie chickens with bows and arrows. When they caught buffalo, the people, who in later times were often near starvation, gorged on hunks of the roasted or baked meat. The tribe used all parts of the buffalo, including the stomach lining, which made strong waterproof vessels and water pails.

Education

Grandparents were the primary teachers of Pawnee children, instructing them in the tasks of tribal life. Grandmothers also took care of children's daily needs and gave them toys and treats. Grandfathers joked with their grandchildren and sometimes took the boys outside on a winter morning, occasionally dumping them into the snow or into a stream to "toughen them up." Uncles taught the boys to hunt, fight, and make tools. Girls learned from women how to take care of the lodge and work in the fields.

From childhood, tribal members were treated as independent, respected persons who were expected to be self-reliant. Children were taught to share their goods with others, a lesson that produced adults without a strong sense of personal possessions.

In the early twenty-first century, most Pawnee students attend area public schools. In 2005, the tribe opened the Hukasa Child Learning Center and Pawnee Nation College. A language program plays an important part in the curriculum at both schools (see "Language"), and college students can learn more about their culture through the American Indian Studies Program.

Healing practices

The Pawnee had two separate types of "medicine men": holy men who maintained the tribal relationship with Tirawa, the Creator, and the other gods; and shamans (pronounced *SHAH-munz* or *SHAY-munz*), who maintained the tribal relationship with animals and the natural world. The shamans were organized into eight "doctor groups," and each had its own unique healing ceremonies. Every group conducted at least two healing ceremonies during the year and took part in "mesmerizing contests," where they demonstrated their skills in hypnotizing people. Only members of the doctor groups could practice the healing arts. Others who did so were considered witches and were treated with contempt.

*A child wearing traditional
Pawnee dress dances
at an event in Pawnee,
Oklahoma.* © J. PAT CARTER/
CONTRIBUTOR/GETTY IMAGES
ENTERTAINMENT/GETTY IMAGES.

ARTS

Pawnee people enjoyed decorating their homes, tools, and clothing
with colorful feathers, beads, and paint. Porcupine quills were a favorite
material. Quills were dyed various colors, then woven or sewn into

The Fast Runners

Many tribes told tales to explain why animals had certain physical features. In this story, the Pawnee explain why an antelope has a gall bladder (a small organ near the liver that stores bile for digesting food), whereas a deer does not, and why a deer has dew claws (short hoofs or claws on the back of the leg that do not touch the ground), but an antelope does not. Most versions of this story begin with two children examining the carcasses of the two animals and questioning their mother about the differences.

> Once long ago, the antelope and the deer met on the prairie. At this time both of them had galls and both dew claws: They began to talk together, and each was telling the other what he could do. Each one told how fast he could run, and before long they were disputing as to which could run the faster. Neither would allow that the other could beat him, so they agreed that they would have a race to decide which was the swifter, and they bet their galls on the race. When they ran, the antelope proved the faster runner, and beat the deer and took his gall.

> Then the deer said, 'Yes, you have beaten me on the prairie, but that is not where I live. I only go out there sometimes to feed, or when I am travelling around. We ought to have another race in the timber. That is my home, and there I can run faster than you can.'

> The antelope felt very big because he had beaten the deer in the race, and he thought wherever they might be, he could run faster than the deer. So he agreed to race in the timber, and on this race they bet their dew claws.

> They ran through the thick timber, among the brush and over fallen logs, and this time the antelope ran slowly because he was not used to this kind of traveling, and the deer easily beat him, and took his dew claws.

> Since then the deer has had no gall, and the antelope no dew claws.

SOURCE: McNeese, Tim. *Illustrated Myths of Native America: The Southwest, Western Range, Pacific Northwest, and California.* London: Blandford, 1999.

designs on clothing, hunting shields, and other objects. In later years crafters also used European glass beads. Paintings were done on a variety of surfaces, ranging from buffalo hides to the painter's body. They often depicted important events or battles, as well as images of the land, sky, and stars.

CUSTOMS

Much has been written about Pawnee practices because four Pawnee men—James Murie, Roaming Scout, He Arrives in the Lead, and Mark Evarts—cooperated with American anthropologists (people who study the cultures of various peoples) to record and preserve many Pawnee traditions.

War and hunting rituals

The main objective of most Pawnee attacks was to steal horses. When the men raided enemy villages, they approached quietly in the night and made off with herds of horses. Sometimes they cut off scalps of the enemy as war trophies.

The Buffalo Dance was held to ensure that a hunt would result in a large kill. Painted dancers, carrying spears and wearing large buffalo masks, reenacted a hunt. Moving to the beat of a drum that represented the beating heart of the Pawnee hunter, a dancer circled the fire until a blunt arrow shot by another dancer hit him. Then the buffalo dancer collapsed and was dragged out of the circle. Non-dancing participants pretended to skin and butcher the dead "buffalo," but in the end, they released him.

All Pawnee buffalo hunts were supervised by a society called the Hunt Police, who kept the people in order so the animals would not be frightened and stampede. The Hunt Police seized and beat anyone who disturbed the silence.

Puberty

At the onset of menstruation, a girl moved into a separate lodge with her grandmother. Afterward, the grandmother bathed and clothed the girl, then purified her with cedar smoke. A Pawnee boy did not wear clothes until he reached puberty. At that time he moved in with his uncle's wife, who taught him about sex. The uncle decided when the boy was ready for marriage and sometimes selected the boy's wife.

Courtship and marriage

Girls who had learned how to care for a home and family were considered ready to marry at about age fifteen. Boys often married when they were about eighteen. Marriages were often informal. If a family approved of a boy, he could move into the girl's home. Although a man might have more than one wife, he usually married his wife's sister.

Birth customs

When his wife went into labor, a husband unbraided his hair and went to a lodge for four days. After the placenta (an organ that, through a cord attached to the fetus's navel, provides nourishment before the baby is born) was cut, it was placed in a special buckskin pouch.

Festivals and ceremonies

The Ground-Breaking Ceremony Each year, the time to plant was determined through a Pawnee ritual known as the Ground-Breaking Ceremony. This was the only Pawnee ritual in which women played a major role.

A woman who had a wintertime dream about planting reported it to the priests of the tribe. If they decided the dream was inspired by Tirawa, they pronounced the woman and her family the sponsors of the Ground-Breaking Ceremony.

Shortly after the first budding of the willows in spring, the woman performed a special dance to launch the annual planting. The tribe devoted the following day to ceremonies and rituals describing the process of planting and caring for the crops, especially corn. For the next six days, the entire tribe worked to weed and plant the crops.

Morning Star Ceremony The most famous Pawnee rite was the Morning Star ceremony, in which the Pawnee sacrificed a young girl to the Morning Star god to thank him for creating the tribe. The ceremony began when a warrior had a special dream about Morning Star. He then went before the priests of the tribe, who gave him permission to kidnap a young girl of about thirteen from another tribe—usually a Sioux band, according to tradition.

The warrior carried the girl back to his village, where she was tenderly cared for until the time for the ceremony came. The warrior placed her on a platform. As the sun rose, a priest shot her through the heart with an arrow. Then every male in the tribe, even the youngest, shot the girl's body with arrows. Pawnee chief Petalésharo (c. 1797–c. 1832) ended this practice in 1817. He interrupted a ceremony and freed the young woman before she could be sacrificed, giving her food and a horse so she could return to her own people.

Other festivals Another popular ceremony was the Harvest Festival. It lasted for twenty nights and featured chanting, music, and performances by magicians and clowns. Outsiders who witnessed the performance reported seeing fantastic sights such as the sudden appearance of people dressed as bears and other animals who chased and mangled people to death. The "dead" people were then cured by shamans and arose unharmed.

Every year since 1946, the Pawnee nation has hosted the Pawnee Indian Veteran's Homecoming around the fourth of July, where all members of the tribe are welcome to return to their traditional homelands. Dressed in Native clothing, they play Pawnee games and do tribal dances.

CURRENT TRIBAL ISSUES

Like other Native peoples, after years of poverty and the shattering of traditions by government policy, the Pawnee face such problems as alcoholism, drug abuse, poverty, child neglect, and hunger. The tribe has developed some effective ways to deal with these social problems. These include health, substance abuse, and community services programs, as well as programs that deal with child welfare and the feeding of the elderly.

Dealing with the remains of deceased tribal members that are displayed at museums and in private collections is also an issue. The Pawnee Tribal Business Council has been bringing their ancestors' bones back to the reservation. They see that the remains are buried appropriately.

Beginning in 2003, the Pawnee looked for ways to address its energy issues. A Pawnee Nation Energy Task Force spent time studying possibilities, including solar, biomass, methane capture, and water or wind power. Some of the options were not viable, particularly as enough funding was not available. The task force decided to proceed with a proposed wind energy project at the Chilocco School in northern Oklahoma, where the Pawnee jointly own land with the Kaw and Cherokee (see entries). They also identified projects that will benefit the tribe, including a installing a solar heater and adopting energy-efficient building codes.

NOTABLE PEOPLE

The self-taught Pawnee artist Charles W. Chapman (1944–) attracted attention during the mid-1980s for his dramatic portraits. For many years, Chapman had been employed primarily as a horse breeder, rodeo rider, and construction worker. His artwork draws on his Pawnee heritage, usually depicting shamans, warriors, scouts, and hunters in their Native dress. He has won many awards for his art.

Other notable Pawnee include Chief Petalésharo (c. 1797–c. 1832), who was honored as a great warrior because he tried to make conditions better for all human beings; attorney and Indian rights activist John E. Echohawk (1945–), who serves as executive director of the Native American Rights Fund; and attorney Walter R. Echo-Hawk (1948–), a tribal judge, scholar, writer, and activist.

BOOKS

Fradin, Dennis B. *The Pawnee*. Chicago: Childrens Press, 1988.

Hahn, Elizabeth. *The Pawnee*. Vero Beach, FL: Rourke Publications, Inc., 1992.

Jensen, Richard E., ed. *The Pawnee Mission Letters, 1834-1851*. Lincoln: University of Nebraska Press, 2010.

Kallen, Stuart A. *The Pawnee*. San Diego: Lucent Books, 2001.

Lesser, Alexander. *The Pawnee Ghost Dance Hand Game: Ghost Dance Revival and Ethnic Identity*. Lincoln: University of Nebraska Press, 1996.

Linton, Ralph. *Purification of the Sacred Bundles: A Ceremony of the Pawnee*. Chicago: Field Museum of Natural History, 1923.

Myers, Arthur. *The Pawnee*. New York: Franklin Watts, 1993.

Owings, Alison. *Indian Voices: Listening to Native Americans*. New Brunswick, NJ: Rutgers University Press, 2011.

Spence, Lewis. *Myths and Legends of the North American Indians*. Whitefish, MT: Kessinger Publishing, 1997.

Stowell, John. *Don Coronado through Kansas, 1541, Then Known as Quivira: A Story of the Kansas, Osage, and Pawnee Indians*. Charleston, SC: Nabu Press, 2011.

Van de Logt, Mark. *War Party in Blue: Pawnee Scouts in the U.S. Army*. Norman: University of Oklahoma Press, 2010.

WEB SITES

Kavanaugh, Thomas W. "Reading Historic Photographs: Photographers of the Pawnee." *Indiana University*. http://php.indiana.edu/-tkavanag/phothana.html (accessed on July 6, 2011).

"Pawnee." *Four Directions Institute*. http://www.fourdir.com/pawnee.htm (accessed on July 6, 2011).

"Pawnee Indian Museum." *Kansas State Historical Society.* http://www.kshs.org/places/pawneeindian/history.htm (accessed on July 6, 2011).

"Pawnee Indian Tribe History." *Access Genealogy.* http://www.accessgenealogy.com/native/tribes/pawnee/pawneehist.htm (accessed on July 6, 2011).

Pawnee Nation of Oklahoma. http://www.pawneenation.org/ (accessed on July 6, 2011).

Redish, Laura, and Orrin Lewis. "Pawnee Indian Culture and History." *Native Languages of the Americas.* http://www.native-languages.org/pawnee_culture.htm (accessed on July 6, 2011).

"2011 Oklahoma Indian Nations." *Pocket Pictorial Directory.* Oklahoma City: Oklahoma Indian Affairs Commission, 2011. Available from http://www.ok.gov/oiac/documents/2011.FINAL.WEB.pdf (accessed on July 6, 2011).

Quapaw

Name

The Quapaw (pronounced QUAW-paw) have been called by many different names. They called themselves *O-Gah-Pah,* which means "downstream people." Their name has been recorded as Ugakhpa, Ugákhpa, Ugaxpa, Okáxpa, O-guah-pah, Quappa, Quapois, Quawpaw, and Quyapa. The people have also been called the Accancea, Akansea, Akensas, Arkansas, or Akansa, meaning "southern," or "southern place," which came from their town *Acansa.* The state of Arkansas later took this as its name.

Location

At one time, the Quapaw may have lived as far east as the Allegheny Mountains, but they later moved west to the Mississippi River into the Ohio River Valley. War with the Iroquois caused the Quapaw to move south to the Arkansas River. They settled into four villages at the mouth of the river and were living in the lower Mississippi River Valley by the time the Europeans arrived. The Quapaw's traditional territory encompassed northwest Mississippi, eastern Arkansas, southeastern Missouri, and a tiny bit of southeastern Tennessee before they were moved first to the Red River area in Louisiana, then to a reservation on the Kansas-Oklahoma border, and finally to a smaller reservation in Oklahoma. Since that time, the tribal headquarters has been Quapaw in Ottawa County, Oklahoma.

Population

Some sources say there may have been as many as 5,000 to 7,500 Quapaw people before the Europeans arrived. In 1673, the French believed the Quapaw numbered about 2,500, but because the people traveled and had many villages, that figure may be much too low, because in 1687, a little over a decade later, they estimated the population to be 3,200. The numbers dropped significantly during the 1700s after a smallpox epidemic. By 1750, the Quapaw numbered 1,400. In 1843, the population had decreased to 476 and reached a low of 174 in 1885. In the twentieth century, the population began to rise. The 1910 census showed 307 Quapaw, and by the 1990s, the population had reached 2,600. According to the Oklahoma Indian Affairs Commission, tribal enrollment for the Quapaw was 3,240 in 2011.

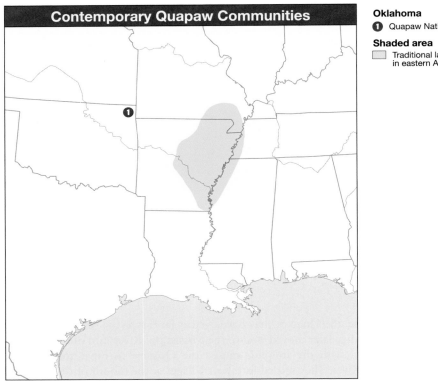

Oklahoma
1 Quapaw Nation of Oklahoma

Shaded area
Traditional lands of the Quapaw in eastern Arkansas

A map of contemporary Quapaw communities. MAP BY XNR PRODUCTIONS. CENGAGE LEARNING, GALE. REPRODUCED BY PERMISSION OF GALE, A PART OF CENGAGE LEARNING.

Language family

Siouan.

Origins and group affiliations

The Quapaw were part of the Dhegihan Sioux, a larger group composed of the Osage, Kansa (see entries), Ponca, and Omaha. Each of these groups went their separate ways after they left the Ohio Valley, but the Quapaw remained allies with their kin, the Omaha. Early records show that the Quapaw had four subtribes: Ugahpahti, Uzutiuhi, Tiwadimań, and Tańwańzhita, which the French called Kappa, Ossoteoue, Touriman, and Tonginga (the names of the towns).

The Quapaw traded with tribes from the Southeast and Great Plains, and they formed a close relationship with the French. That led to the Quapaw almost destroying the Natchez (see entry). The Quapaw also fought other tribes to support the Spanish in their battle against the British. Although the

Quapaw traded with the Chickasaw (see entry) and Tunica, they also spent much time at war with the Chickasaw and the Osage. Yet at certain times, they also allied with the Osage and the Illinois.

Archaeologists debate about when the Quapaw settled along the Arkansas River, but the people had four villages there when the Europeans arrived in the late 1600s. Early explorers described the Quapaw as polite, generous, and cheerful. Although they fought with some of the neighboring tribes, the Quapaw maintained friendly relations with the French, and they later traded with the Spanish and British. The Quapaw remained loyal to the Americans, even while signing treaties giving up their homeland in the early 1800s. The people then moved to the Red River in Louisiana, but they returned to their original territory following floods and starvation. Settlers convinced the U.S. government to move the people to Indian Territory, where they ceded even more land. The shrewd Quapaw avoided federal allotment of their land by dividing up their own reservation in 1893, thus ensuring that their people received larger plots than the government would have allowed. The discovery of lead and zinc deposits made some landowners wealthy, but the profits were short lived, and the toxic waste left behind has created major environmental and health issues for the nation.

HISTORY

Prehistory

An archaeological dig near Little Rock, Arkansas, in the 1930s found the remains of a prehistoric people. The bodies had been buried sitting up. Copper jewelry, ceramic vessels, bone tools, shells, and leather had been placed in the grave. This civilization, called the Menard Complex, existed between 1500 and 1700. Because the Quapaw inhabited the area, some experts believe these may have been early Quapaw people.

The Quapaw, who likely were attacked by the Iroquois (see entry) living to the north of them in the Ohio Valley, may have migrated sometime after 1200. According to the tribe's oral history, the Dhegihan Sioux group to which they belonged split into several distinct tribes. The Osage, Kansa, Ponca, and Omaha went up the Missouri River; the Quapaw went south. The Menard Complex remains indicate that ancestors of the Quapaw may have been living in Arkansas for more than a century before the arrival of the Europeans. Other sources suggest that they did not move to Arkansas until after the Spanish explorer Hernando de Soto (c. 1496–1542) visited the area.

Important Dates

1673: Jacques Marquette meets the Quapaw on the Mississippi River.

1699: Smallpox epidemic decimates the Quapaw people.

1784: Chickasaw and Quapaw sign a peace treaty.

1818–1824: Quapaw sign a treaty giving up all of their land to the United States.

1834: Quapaw people removed to Indian Territory.

1893: Tribe divides up reservation land before Dawes Act takes effect.

1905: Deposits of lead and zinc found on tribal lands.

1954: Quapaw tribe receives almost $1 million for land ceded in 1824 treaty.

2011: Some Quapaw opt out of the Cobell settlement and file the Goodeagle lawsuit to keep payments from land separate from that of Individual Indian Money (IIM) accounts.

First contact with Europeans

The de Soto expedition from 1539 to 1543 may have been the first Quapaw encounter with Europeans. That was, however, the last the Quapaw saw of Europeans for more than a century. The French arrived in 1673, looking for a route to the Pacific Ocean. Louis Joliet (1645–1700) and Jacques Marquette (1637–1675) heard of the Quapaw from their Illini guides, who called the Quapaw *Akansea,* or "people of the south wind." That is the name the French noted on their maps. According to Joliet's account, the Akansea welcomed him and paid attention to his sermons.

Records of René-Robert Cavelier de La Salle's (1643–1687) expedition in the 1680s mention the chiefs Pacaha and Capaha, who may have been ancestors of the Quapaw. These reports describe a walled city with a moat and many cornfields.

Friendly relations with the French

In 1683, Henri de Tonti (c. 1649–1704) built the first post on the Arkansas River, and for more than a century, the Quapaw remained allies of the French, who gave them weapons and other goods. The French wanted access to the Mississippi River so they could conduct trade from Quebec to Louisiana. The Quapaw supported the French, and many traders married Quapaw women.

To protect French interests, the Quapaw went to war with the neighboring Chickasaw. That war, along with a smallpox epidemic in the late 1600s, caused major losses in the Quapaw population. By 1721, the villages of Tourima and Tongigua had combined with Kappa because they had lost so many people. In 1729, the French convinced the Quapaw to help them destroy the Natchez. In 1762, however, when France turned over all land east of the Mississippi to Spain, the Quapaw lost their longtime allies.

Spanish and British rivalry

Upon France's withdrawal, Spain and Great Britain vied for control of the land and the trade. The Spanish rebuilt the fort on the Arkansas River in 1769 and called it Fort Carlos III. When the Spaniards distributed goods, the Quapaw received a large amount, showing the Quapaw's importance to the Europeans.

Around the same time, the British set up a trading post on the Mississippi. The Quapaw, who had fought for the French against the British, were reluctant to trust the English. The British, hoping to win the Quapaw over, plied them with gifts. The Quapaw initially hesitated to make friends with their former enemies, particularly because the Chickasaw, the Quapaws rivals, had always supported the British. By 1784, however, the Quapaw had signed a treaty with the Chickasaw, ushering in a time of peace for the two tribes. The Quapaw managed to stay neutral in the ongoing battles for control of the territory.

American takeover

In 1801, the land along the Mississippi and its major western tributaries reverted to the French after it had conquered much of Europe under the leadership of Napoleon Bonaparte (1769–1821). Two years later, Napoleon decided not to build an empire across the Atlantic, and he sold the Louisiana Territory to the United States. Eventually, this huge parcel of land became fifteen states and part of two Canadian provinces. At that time, the Quapaw were living in three villages south of the Arkansas River.

The U.S. government wanted to relocate the Cherokee, Creek, and Choctaw (see entries) west of the Mississippi, so they wanted the Quapaw homelands. Settlers, too, soon began moving onto these lands. In the treaty of 1818, the Quapaw ceded thirty million acres to the United States for $4,000 in goods and an annual payment of $1,000. An 1824 treaty gave the settlers the Quapaw land around the Arkansas River. The Quapaw, reluctant to break the friendship they had extended to the Americans during the Calumet Dance (see "Festivals and ceremonies"), signed the second treaty, but they begged the government for fair treatment. Instead, they endured a long, devastating march (now called the "Trail of Tears") in winter to the Caddo (see entry) reservation in northwestern Louisiana.

The area where the Quapaw relocated flooded and sixty people starved, so the tribe returned to its previous home. The people squatted on the land that had once been theirs, and some picked cotton or hunted for the settlers to make a living. Many settlers resented the Indian presence, however, and the U.S. government forced the Quapaw to move to Indian Territory in 1834. The reservation the tribe received included 96,000 acres in Oklahoma and Kansas, but when Kansas became a state, more settlers began to arrive in the area. In 1867, the Quapaw ceded most

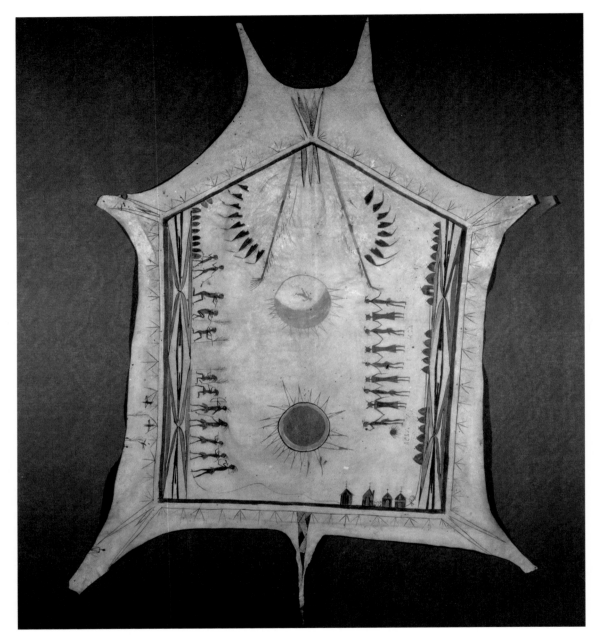

A buffalo skin from the mid-1800s is painted to depict three villages of the Quapaw tribe. © DEA PICTURE LIBRARY/DE AGOSTINI/ GETTY IMAGES.

of their land. They were left with less than 13,000 acres in the northeast corner of Oklahoma, and the tribe's numbers had dwindled to below 250. Many Quapaw moved to the Osage reservation and intermarried.

Reservation land allotted

The Dawes Act of 1887 divided reservation land into individual plots, or allotments. The government then gave a parcel of land to each head of a household. The leftover land was sold to settlers. This act caused much hardship among the tribes on the reservations. Most had always held land in common, so they were unused to farming alone. The land the people received was often too poor to farm, so many lost their land to taxes or sold it.

The Quapaw, however, forestalled the government process by dividing up their own land. In 1893, they gave each family a two-hundred-acre plot and added forty acres to it the following year. This gave them more land than they would have gotten under a government allotment.

Economic boons

In 1905, rich deposits of zinc and lead were found on the reservation. Because the land had been allotted, the wealth was not evenly distributed. Some people became wealthy, but others still lived in poverty. By 1960, all the natural resources had been mined, and the companies had left behind lead dust that caused major health problems for the people (see "Current Tribal Issues").

In the meantime, the Quapaw had petitioned for payment for the land they had given up to the U.S. government. They had submitted claims for the land taken in 1818 and 1824. In 1954, they received almost one million dollars. This money benefited the tribe and gave the people a renewed sense of pride in their heritage. They began to revive their traditions, including dances, naming ceremonies, and mourning feasts. Although not all of these cultural practices lasted, the people continued to hold a regular homecoming picnic that became an annual powwow.

RELIGION

Traditional beliefs

The main spirit in Quapaw religion was Wahkontah (Ouankantaque), the Great Spirit, who was the force behind the universe. This spirit was found in all things, including rocks, stars, animals, plants, and people.

Quapaw Words

mi	"sun"
ni	"water"
miáⁿba	"moon"
nikka	"man"
wax'ó	"woman"
šóⁿke	"dog"

It even resided in objects that the people created, such as pipes and lodges. The Quapaw also honored the sun, moon, and thunder. Guardian spirits were the raven, owl, buffalo, eagle, and snake. Lesser spirits were the thunder people, sky spirits, and mysterious dwarves.

One of the lodges was set aside as a sacred cabin. Masks made of hide and cone-shaped caps created from pelts were stored in one of three largest buildings in the village. The people likely had medicine bundles containing sacred objects.

The Quapaw had both shamans (pronounced *SHAH-munz* or *SHAY-munz*) and priests. The shamans took care of healing. Priests were responsible for relations with the gods and for leading the rituals connected to planting crops. These spiritual leaders, called *Wapinan,* advised the chief and performed rituals sometimes referred to as magic. One writer told of a Wapinan who put a long bone into his throat down to his stomach and then pulled it out again.

Peyote religion

Although most Quapaw had converted to Roman Catholicism by the late 1890s, Caddo John Wilson (also called Moonhead) stirred their interest in the Peyote religion in 1895. They built a permanent roundhouse with a concrete altar that opened to the west. The outer edge, shaped like a crescent moon, represented Jesus Christ's grave. A line running east to west symbolized Wilson's trip to the moon during a vision quest. This line ran through three hearts—heart of the world, heart of Jesus, and heart of goodness. Peyote, a druglike plant that puts people into trances, went on the heart of goodness. Other symbols representing the cross, the sun, stars (days of the week), moon (months), and footprints were placed on the altar. The ritual began with a sweat bath, which was followed by an all-night meeting at which participants drank a tea made of peyote, sang, smoked, spoke, and drummed. They shared a feast at noon the next day.

LANGUAGE

The Quapaw language is a branch of the Dhegihan-Sioux family, which is also spoken by the Osage, Omaha, Kansa, and Ponca. Although the dialects are similar to each other, they are distinct enough to each have their own name. The last speakers of the Quapaw language died in the 1970s, so the dialect is no longer spoken. Rev. James Owen Dorsey published information about it in the 1800s, and linguist (language specialist) Robert Rankin studied it in the 1970s. Some of the youth are now learning their language.

GOVERNMENT

A chief, advised by a council of male elders, headed each village, but when issues concerned the tribe as a whole, the leaders of all the villages met to discuss matters. Decisions were made by consensus, so everyone needed to agree. The role of the chief was to entertain visitors, give feasts, care for the needy, and lead rituals. Some chiefs had orators, or speakers, as well as attendants.

After the Europeans arrived, the French selected one chief to be the head chief, and they negotiated only with him. This chief had received a peace medal, so he was called the "medal chief." This position was passed down through the male line. This form of government, including hereditary chiefs, continued into the 1900s. It ended when the Quapaw leader Tallchief (*Tahíkaŝte*), or Louis Angel, died in 1918. He had no male successor, but his daughter took over the religious duties until she died in 1972.

In 1956, the Quapaw began electing a committee to handle the tribe's business concerns. The seven-member Business Committee has four council members, a chairperson, a vice chairperson, and a secretary-treasurer. Elected to two-year staggered terms, the members meet monthly at the tribe's headquarters in Quapaw, Ottawa County, Oklahoma, to plan administrative and financial matters for the tribe. General Council meetings are held yearly on July 4; these are attended by all members of the tribe. The Tribal Court handles civil and criminal matters that occur on tribal lands.

ECONOMY

Like other Great Plains tribes, the Quapaw depended on the bison hunt. Unlike most bands, only small groups of men hunted at a time. The people used every part of the animal for food, clothing, homes, and tools. They made bedding and winter clothing from the furs and hides. They spun some of the wool into thread to make men's woven bags. Horns were turned into spoons, bones formed tools, and sinew became bowstrings and thread. The Quapaw traded the suet (fat), which they stored in containers made of the intestines.

They traded bison and deer hides with the French, who also taught them to trap beaver. In the late 1600s, the people had such large piles of otter and beaver pelts that they set them on fire. The British later convinced the Quapaw to supply them with slaves, so the Quapaw raided a village on the Yazoo River. In addition to slaves and pelts, they also exchanged bear, bear grease, and bison suet for metal tools, guns, and alcohol.

In time, the Quapaw became an agricultural people. They grew corn, squash, beans, and watermelons. They also had orchard fruits. By the early 1900s, the Quapaw were praised as prosperous farmers who had given up their migratory lifestyle.

The discovery of zinc and lead on some of the allotments brought in a great deal of wealth during the first half of the twentieth century, along with a rash of environmental problems (see "Current Tribal Issues"). A large settlement for the lands they had lost in treaties also aided Quapaw economic development. Casinos, a smoke shop, a motor fuel outlet, and other businesses help fund tribal programs such as health care, educational assistance, elder care, cultural development, and preservation efforts. The Quapaw also make money by issuing their own license plates.

DAILY LIFE

Families

Men hunted and defended their families by going to war when necessary. They also held the political and religious leadership positions. Women cooked, cared for children, transported game, sewed clothes, dressed and painted hides, gardened, and built the homes. Both men and women could tell stories; become artists, musicians, and craftspeople; and serve as healers.

Buildings

An early writer described the villages as walled, equipped with towers, and surrounded by moats. The people set up weirs (small traps made of branches) to catch the fish that flowed from the river into the moats. The writer also remarked on the quantity of grain the people had stored as well as the fields filled with it.

Among the Acconcea (Quapaw)

The La Salle expedition visited the Quapaw in July 1687. One of the members of the voyage, Henri Joutel, kept records of what they observed. He described the Frenchmen's first impressions of an Accancea (Quapaw) village. (Original spelling and capitalization has been kept.)

> The Nation of the Accancea's consists of four Villages. The first is call'd Otsotchove, near which we were; the second Toriman, both of them seated on the River; the third the Accan-Tonginga; and the fourth Cappa, on the Bank of the Missisipi. These Villages are built after a different Manner from the others we had seen before, in this Point, that the Cottages, which are alike as to their Materials and Rounding at the Top, are long, and cover'd with the Bark of Trees, and so very large, that several of them can hold two hundred Persons, belonging to several Families.

The people are not so neat as the Cenis [Caddo group], or the Assonis [Caddo group] in their Houses, for some of them lie on the Ground, without any Thing under them but some Mats, or a dress'd Hide. However, some of them have more Conveniences, but the Generality [most people] has not. All their Moveables [possessions] consist in some Earthen Vessels and oval wooden Platters, which are neatly made, and with which they drive a Trade.

SOURCE: Joutel, Henri. "Among the Acconcea." *Joutel's Journal of La Salle's Last Voyage.* Albany, NY: Joseph Mcdonough, 1906. Available online from http://www.ebooksread.com/authors-eng/henri-joutel/joutels-journal-of-la-salles-last-voyage-1684-7-hci/page-15-joutels-journal-of-la-salles-last-voyage-1684-7-hci.shtml (accessed on June 20, 2011).

Inside the villages, bark-covered longhouses were clustered around an open plaza. The Quapaw often placed their buildings on mounds of dirt to guard against flooding. The lodges were grouped according to clans. To make their homes, the Quapaw drove long poles into the ground, then bent the tops and tied them together, making an arched roof. They wove branches horizontally in between the poles and then covered the lodge with bark sheets. Some sources said they plastered walls made from river cane and thatched their roofs.

Several families shared a longhouse. Each family had its own part of the lodge, with a fire marking its place. An opening in the roof allowed smoke from the fires to escape. The floor was slightly elevated and coated with clay. The interior of the lodge had sleeping platforms covered with woven mats. The people burned reeds for indoor light.

Each village had a community building large enough for all the people to gather for ceremonies, meetings, and dances. An open-sided structure near the plaza was used for public ceremonies and receiving guests. The floor was covered with rush mats. Like the early Mississippians (see the Mound Builders entry), the Quapaw built high mounds. Most were dirt-covered trash piles, but some reached 40 feet (12 meters) high.

Clothing and adornment

In the early years, Quapaw women wore only deerskin skirts when it was warm. Men were either naked or dressed in breechcloths (flaps that hung from the waist and covered the front and back). In colder weather, both men and women wore leggings, moccasins, and buffalo-skin robes. Buckskin shirts for men and long deerskin dresses for women were common. Women decorated these with fringe, porcupine quills, and beadwork.

A married women gathered her hair into a single ponytail that hung down her back, but unmarried women coiled their braids into rolls by each ear. Men shaved their heads, but they kept a scalplock (one long piece in back) to which they sometimes attached a porcupine roach (a headdress made of a tuft of porcupine hair), rings, feathers, and beads. They wore strings of beads in their noses and ears, and some donned the long warbonnets of feathers worn by many Great Plains tribes. The Quapaw had tattoos; they also painted their faces and bodies with black and red in different designs for battle, sacred events, or festivities.

Later, the men dressed in calico shirts with scarlet blankets draped around them. They wrapped handkerchiefs around their heads like turbans. Silver pendants and feathers decorated their outfits.

Food

Before the Europeans arrived, the Quapaw grew crops, such as corn, squash, beans, gourds, pumpkins, sunflowers, and watermelons. In time, they grew peaches, pawpaws, plums, mulberries, wild potatoes, walnuts, wheat, and persimmons, and they gathered other wild plants. They offered visitors dried fruits and made a drink of crushed grapes. The women made flour from wild rice and soup from the nut of the water chinquapin. By the late 1600s, they were raising chickens.

The Quapaw stored their food in large cane baskets or gourds, and they used wooden dishes, including large platters, and pottery plates. They cooked in big earthen pots that they made themselves.

Men hunted and fished along the river. Dugout canoes gave them an advantage in spearing fish. The Quawpaw caught waterbirds by using live decoys. Men swam underwater and grabbed ducks or other birds from below. Bear, turkey, rabbit, and deer were key meats in the people's diet. Hunters sometimes used dogs to track small game.

The bison was extremely important until the late 1800s. Horses changed Quapaw hunting. Until that time, men hunted on foot. Once they had horses, a man rode after a buffalo and speared its hamstring with a strong lance. Then men on foot clubbed it to death.

Tools and Transportation

The Osage Orange bush grew in Quapaw territory, and it had excellent wood for making bows. The French name for the area, *aux arcs,* meant "at the place of the bows." This soon turned into the name *Ozarks,* which is now the name for the mountains of Missouri and Arkansas.

The Quapaw used cypress to make their dugout canoes, but they mainly traveled by land. They kept dogs to pull their travois (pronounced truh-VOI), a type of sled. Poles attached the travois to a dog's shoulders, and as the animals ran, they dragged it behind them. These sleds could carry the Quapaw's belongings as they traveled. Once they acquired horses, the people switched to riding for their transportation and hunting.

Education

Children learned by observing their parents and participating in chores. The Quapaw had always valued education, and they had asked the government to allow them to stay in their original homelands in Arkansas and send their children to school. When Chief Sarasin (see "Notable People") returned from Red River, he sent ten boys to a local school. Four of them later went on to attend the Choctaw Academy in Kentucky.

Soon after that, the Quapaw were removed to Kansas (see "History"). Roman Catholic priests worked among the people there. Although the priests were unsuccessful in getting many converts to Christianity, the Quapaw did send their children to the mission schools.

Healing practices

Shamans (see "Traditional beliefs") were the healers. Several curing societies existed—the Buffalo, Panther, Grizzly Bear, and Beaver. Healers connected with their animal guardian spirits. People relied on their personal sacred objects to keep them healthy and safe. Medicine dances were also held for healing.

ARTS

Crafts

According to the Museum of Native American Artifacts, "Quapaw pottery is considered some of the most artistic and distinct pottery of North America." The people were well known for their red-and-buff pottery. Among some of the more unusual pieces are the head pots, shaped like people's heads. One famous head pot, called the "Screaming Quapaw," depicts a head with an open mouth. The pot is decorated with swirls of paint, resembling face paint, and curled spools in the ears. Some of the pots looked like animals—deer, otters, frogs, and even a two-headed dog. Others were vase-shaped with painted designs, such as swirls, stripes, or abstract floral motifs. Few pots survived intact, so most have been pieced together. After the Europeans arrived, the Quapaw made dishes that were similar to teapots.

Oral Literature

Other tribes praised the Quapaw's skill in painting buffalo hides. The Quapaw also did pipe carving and basket weaving. When beads later became available through trade, the people added beadwork to the list of crafts in which they excelled.

Although the Quapaw had many legends and tales, these were not written down, so no stories were recorded for future generations. The origin tales of the clans have not been passed along, and the only part of the creation story that the elders remembered in the 1980s was that they came from water. The Omaha, kin to the Quapaw, have many legends, many of which are likely to be similar to those of the traditional Quapaw tales.

CUSTOMS

Clan structure

Some sources listed as many as twenty-one clans. Most clan names were animal-related, including Crawfish, Elk, Eagle, Deer, Beaver, Panther, and Crane. Others were connected with the natural world, such as Sun and Thunder Being. The clans were part of two larger groups, Earth

People and the Sky People. Each clan had special ceremonial duties. Sky People handled spiritual concerns, whereas Earth People took care of material and administrative business.

Children traced their clan heritage through their father's line. Although family was the major social unit in the tribe, clans were in charge of educating their members and seeing to their welfare. Thus, they often became more important than a person's birth family.

Birth and naming

Soon after an infant was born, a ceremony occurred at sunrise. A spiritual leader named the babies from a special group of names connected to the clan to which the child belonged. Names were important because they determined whether the child would be successful later in life.

Marriage

A couple needed their parents' permission to marry. If the parents agreed, the couple met around sunrise on their wedding day. The groom presented the bride with a deer leg. She gave him an ear of corn. After separating for the day, they met at sunset to consummate the marriage. The newlyweds moved into the groom's family home, where they set up their own fire pit.

Death and mourning

The dead were buried either under the floor of their lodges or in graves outside heaped with rocks and earth. Sometimes the Quapaw tied the seated body to a stake and covered it with clay before burying it. They put an eagle feather in the corpse's hand and surrounded the body with weapons and tools or hung these goods on a pole nearby. The people believed these objects helped the dead on the journey to the afterlife. If the deceased had acted properly during life, the spirit world was a place of goodness similar to life on earth. If not, the person faced torment. A fire by the grave kept the dead warm on the journey. A four-day mourning period was observed, during which time relatives wailed daily at sunset and sunrise.

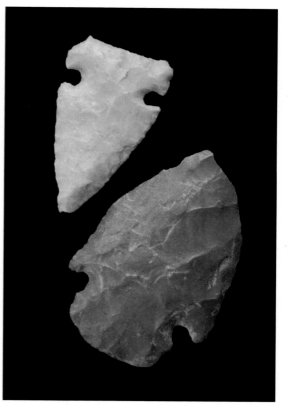

Two arrowheads made by the Quapaw tribe were discovered in northeastern Arkansas. © TERRY SMITH IMAGES ARKANSAS PICTURE LIBRARY/ALAMY.

War and hunting rituals

Originally, war was held for revenge or retaliation. After the French came, the Quapaw added defending the Europeans to their list of reasons for going to war. Later, the people also used raiding and hunting as a means to gain more trade items.

Prior to a battle, a feast was held. At the meal, the chief made a speech to get supporters for the cause. He handed out rods, which may have been a promise of payment. The warriors then painted their war clubs red, invited their allies to a feast, and held a war dance.

The chief fasted, and each warrior checked with his spirit guide for direction. Women helped to recruit additional men. During the war, the Quapaw took scalps and prisoners. In the early years, captives were either tortured and burned to death, or adopted into a family who had lost sons in battle. Later, the prisoners were sold as slaves.

The most important hunting ritual was connected to the buffalo hunt, a major event that occurred once or twice a year. Prior to setting out, the men painted their bodies black and fasted (went without food and drink). After they killed a bison, they painted the head red and covered its body with feathers and tobacco. The men offered some of the meat to the spirits before dividing up the rest.

Festivals and ceremonies

Four main seasonal celebrations were noted in the 1800s. Prayer, singing, dancing, feasting, and thanksgiving were part of each event. A dog sacrifice and a feast accompanied the corn planting. Several other feasts and dances were held, ending with the most important one, the Green Corn Feast.

One of the most important events was the Calumet Dance. The ritual centered on the calumet, a stone pipe attached to a long reed and decorated with feathers, furs, and paints. After the pipe was lit, it was presented to the four cardinal directions (east, west, north, and south) and then passed around to the leaders and guests. The long ceremony included a feast as well as many dances, such as the War Dance, Discovery Dance, and Strike-the-Stick Dance, during which warriors hit a pole with their weapons as they recounted their brave deeds. The Calumet Dance might be held for success in war, good weather for crops, or peacemaking. Guests were often honored with this dance, which was intended to ensure friendship and harmony. Part of this ritual included an adoption ceremony in which one party became the parent and the other the child. Gift-giving played a part in establishing this relationship. The Calumet ceremony was eventually replaced by the French custom of presenting medals.

Another popular event was the Stomp Dance. Men prepared for the dance, held on Sundays, by hunting on Friday and Saturday. Then the women cooked the meat in large iron kettles. Everyone met for feasting and dancing. The Quapaw also had a Stomp Dance connected to the Peyote religion (see "Religion").

For more than a century, the Quapaw have held a yearly homecoming that later came to be an annual powwow, attended by many tribes in Oklahoma. The powwow consists of dancing, races, giveaways, rodeos, ball games, golf tournaments, and communal meals. The Quapaw also hold their general council meeting at this time.

CURRENT TRIBAL ISSUES

One ongoing problem for the Quapaw began in the early 1900s when zinc and lead deposits were discovered on their lands. By the 1960s, those natural resources had been removed, but the mining activities left behind lead dust that covered the city. Lead and zinc also seeped into the water supplies and swimming areas. Children in the area have developed learning disabilities and other problems as a result. The region has been designated as a Superfund site, a name given to an area containing high levels of toxic substances that is designated for cleanup under the direction of the Environmental Protection Agency. Called the Tar Creek Superfund site, the area encompasses land in northeast Oklahoma, southeast Kansas, and southwest Missouri. Concerns include water, air, crop, and fish contamination as well as large piles of chat (mining waste), which includes poisonous chemicals.

In 2010, the Grievance Committee of the Quapaw Tribe accused members of the Business Committee, who hold tribal leadership positions and oversee the casinos, of misuse of funds. The Business Committee denied the allegation, saying that the charges were politically motivated. The Grievance Committee retained a lawyer, contacted the Bureau of Indian Affairs, and demanded a meeting of the General Council, which includes all tribal members who can vote on issues. As of 2011, the issue remains unresolved.

Some members of the Quapaw tribe have opted out of the $3.4 billion Cobell settlement from 2010, in which the government agreed to pay tribes for land held in trust and improper accounting of funds in Individual Indian Money (IIM) accounts. Instead, the Quapaw people have filed the Goodeagle lawsuit, which calls for the separation of land claims from the payments for mismanagement of IIM accounts, which have had millions of dollars go missing over time.

NOTABLE PEOPLE

Two chiefs at the time of removal were Sarasin (d. c. 1832; Saracen, Sarasen) and Heckaton (d. 1842). Sarasin became a legend among Arkansas settlers because he rescued two children who had been captured by Chickasaw raiders. Both he and Heckaton tried to prevent the U.S. government from forcing their people out of their Arkansas homelands. Sarasin had been given a small piece of land for his own use because of his friendship with the Americans. After his people moved to the Red River area, floods destroyed their crops, and sixty people, including his wife, died. Sarasin led some of his people back to his plot of land. Others eventually followed. In 1830, Heckaton brought the rest of the Quapaw back to Oklahoma.

Two important figures born during the twentieth century are Louis W. Ballard (1931–2007), a classical composer and leading figure in developing musical educational materials that reflect the Native heritage; and Geary Hobson (1941–), who served as project director for the Native Writers' Circle of the Americas and as associate editor for *The American Indian Quarterly.* One of Hobson's collections of stories, *Plain of Jars and Other Stories,* was published to critical acclaim in 2011; he is also the author of many other works.

BOOKS

Arnold, Morris. *Rumble of a Distant Drum: The Quapaws and Old World Newcomers, 1673–1804.* Fayetteville: University of Arkansas Press, 2007.

Hobson, Geary. *Plain of Jars and Other Stories.* East Lansing: Michigan State University Press, 2011.

Johnson, Larry G. *Tar Creek.* Mustang, OK: Tate Publishing, 2009.

Williams, C. Fred. *Historic Little Rock: An Illustrated History.* San Antonio, TX: Historical Network, 2008.

WEB SITES

Bogle, David. "Mississippian Period: Quapaw Pottery." *Museum of Native American Artifacts.* http://www.museumofnativeamericanartifacts.org/mississippian.html#Quapaw Pottery (accessed on June 20, 2011).

Handbook of American Indians, "Quapaw Indian Tribe History." *Access Genealogy.* http://www.accessgenealogy.com/native/tribes/quapaw/quapawhist.htm (accessed on June 20, 2011).

McCollum, Timothy James. "Quapaw." *Oklahoma Historical Society.* http://digital.library.okstate.edu/encyclopedia/entries/Q/QU003.html (accessed on June 20, 2011).

"Mississippian, Quapaw, and Caddo Pottery." *ClayHound.* http://www.clayhound.us/sites/miss-qua-caddo.htm (accessed on June 20, 2011).

National Museum of the American Indian. "Southern Plains." *Smithsonian.* http://americanindian.si.edu/searchcollections/results.aspx?regid=61 (accessed on June 20, 2011).

Quapaw Tribe of Oklahoma. http://www.quapawtribe.com/ (accessed on June 20, 2011).

"The Quapaw Tribe of Oklahoma and the Tar Creek Project." *Environmental Protection Agency.* http://www.epa.gov/oar/tribal/tribetotribe/tarcreek.html (accessed on June 20, 2011).

Redish, Laura, and Orrin Lewis. "Quapaw Indian Language (Alkansea, Arkansas, Ogahpah, Kwapa)." *Native Languages of the Americas.* http://www.native-languages.org/quapaw.htm (accessed on June 20, 2011).

"Tar Creek." *Jump the Fence Productions.* http://tarcreekfilm.com/ (accessed on June 20, 2011).

Wilson, Carrie, and George Sabo III. "The Quapaw Indians." *University of Arkansas.* http://arkarcheology.uark.edu/indiansofarkansas/index.html?pageName=The%20Quapaw%20Indians (accessed on June 20, 2011).

Sioux Nations: Dakota

Name

Dakota (pronounced *Dah-KO-tah*) is the tribe's name for itself and may mean "friend" or "ally." It comes from the Santee word *Dahkota,* sometimes translated as "alliance of friends." Another meaning for the name is "those who consider themselves kindred." The Dakota are also known as the Santee Sioux.

The Sioux tribes (Dakota, Lakota, and Nakota) were once given the name *nadowe-is-iw-ug,* which means "little adders (snakes)" by their enemies, the Ojibway. The French mispronounced the Ojibway word as *nadewisou* and shortened it to "Sioux," the name by which the tribes are collectively known. Because the name was intended as an insult, many of the people dislike being called Sioux.

Location

Archaeological evidence indicates that the Dakota occupied what is now western Ontario and eastern Manitoba in Canada prior to 1200. The people later moved south into present-day Minnesota in the United States. Before the arrival of Europeans, they occupied lands east of the Mississippi River along the Minnesota-Wisconsin border. In modern times, they live on reservations in North and South Dakota, Minnesota, Montana, and Nebraska, and on several reserves in Canada.

Population

In 1839, about 3,989 Dakota lived in the Minnesota territory. In the 1990 U.S. Census, 107,321 people identified themselves as Sioux, and 10,999 people as Dakota. About 12,500 Dakota lived on Canadian reserves in 1996. According to the 2000 census, a total of 113,713 Sioux resided in the United States; of those, 22,988 did not specify a specific band. Those who called themselves Dakota numbered 1,771 and the Santee numbered 2,207. Others identified themselves by reservation or community. In 2010, the census counted 112,176 Sioux, with a total of 170,110 people claiming some Sioux ancestry.

Language family

Siouan.

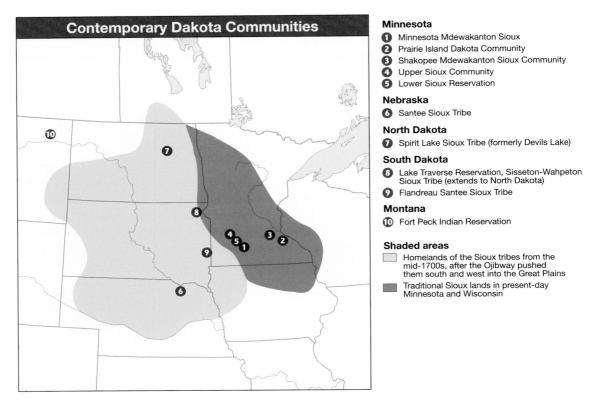

Contemporary Dakota Communities

Minnesota
1. Minnesota Mdewakanton Sioux
2. Prairie Island Dakota Community
3. Shakopee Mdewakanton Sioux Community
4. Upper Sioux Community
5. Lower Sioux Reservation

Nebraska
6. Santee Sioux Tribe

North Dakota
7. Spirit Lake Sioux Tribe (formerly Devils Lake)

South Dakota
8. Lake Traverse Reservation, Sisseton-Wahpeton Sioux Tribe (extends to North Dakota)
9. Flandreau Santee Sioux Tribe

Montana
10. Fort Peck Indian Reservation

Shaded areas
- Homelands of the Sioux tribes from the mid-1700s, after the Ojibway pushed them south and west into the Great Plains
- Traditional Sioux lands in present-day Minnesota and Wisconsin

A map of contemporary Dakota communities. MAP BY XNR PRODUCTIONS. CENGAGE LEARNING, GALE. REPRODUCED BY PERMISSION OF GALE, A PART OF CENGAGE LEARNING.

Origins and group affiliations

The Dakota belong to the Great Sioux Nation, which includes the Lakota and Nakota peoples (see entries). Some Sioux creation stories trace their origins back to the Black Hills of South Dakota, but other accounts give their origination point as the Minnesota woodlands, where they lived at the time of first contact with Europeans. Seven Sioux bands made up the *Oceti Sakowin,* or Seven Council Fires. At some point, the Nakota and Lakota broke away from the Dakota and moved west. There are four Dakota groups: Wahpeton, Mdewakantonwon, Wahpekute, and Sisseton. Dakota enemies were the Ojibway (see entry) to the north, and the Potawatomi, Winnebago (see entries), Mandan, and Sac (see Sac and Fox entry).

The Dakota tribe is considered the parent of the Great Sioux Nation, which also includes the Lakota and Nakota tribes. The people enjoyed a comfortable life among the great natural abundance of Minnesota until American settlers overran their lands in the mid-nineteenth century. The tribe tried to accommodate the newcomers but was forced into the bloody Santee War of 1862. After that, it endured much hardship but worked at keeping its culture intact.

HISTORY

Tribal divisions

Before European contact, the Sioux lived as far north as Mille Lacs in present-day Minnesota. They say they once hunted, fished, and planted on nearly 100 million acres of land in the region. In the distant past, the tribe split into three groups. The Nakota moved to the prairies of South Dakota, and the Lakota moved west of the Missouri River. The Dakota, the largest of the three groups, stayed in Minnesota. All three groups maintained close ties.

In the mid-1700s, the Dakota were pushed south out of Mille Lacs by the Ojibway, who used weapons they had acquired in trade with the French. The Dakota also traded with the French, who arrived in the region in about 1640, but the Ojibway likely received more ammunition and guns. The Dakota moved into the southern half of Minnesota and built villages along the Mississippi and Minnesota rivers. Where they had once lived in villages year-round and planted gardens, they now adopted a Plains lifestyle of gathering wild rice and migrating part of the year to hunt buffalo.

From British to American hands

After England gained control of French lands east of the Mississippi River in 1763, the Dakota traded with the British. When the American Revolution (1775–83; the American colonists' fight for independence from

Important Dates

1805: The Mdewakantonwon band of Dakota signs a treaty with Zebulon Pike.

1837–51: After signing additional treaties, the Dakota lose most of their land and move to a reservation in Minnesota.

1858: The Dakota reservation is cut in half.

1862: Santee War is fought; afterward thirty-eight Dakota warriors are executed.

1863: The Forfeiture Act is passed, taking away all Dakota treaty rights.

1870s: The Dakota move to reservations in North and South Dakota, Nebraska, and Canada; some Dakota attempt to return to Minnesota.

1889: The Sioux Reservation is broken into six small reservations; the remainder of land is opened to American settlers.

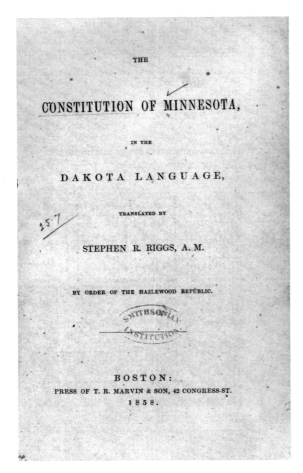

A copy of the Constitution of Minnesota was translated into the Dakota language by Presbyterian missionary Stephen R. Riggs in 1858.
©MPI/GETTY IMAGES.

England) began, the Dakota sided with their trading partners because they believed American expansion posed a greater threat to their way of life than the British did. The British lost the war, and within a few decades, American settlement on Dakota lands began.

In 1805, the American soldier Zebulon Pike (1779–1813) explored the region and obtained land for a fort. Pike signed a treaty with the Dakota to exchange 100,000 acres of land for $2,000 and some presents. In 1819, the U.S. government built Fort St. Anthony (later renamed Fort Snelling) at the mouth of the Minnesota River. Throughout its history, the fort served as a meeting place for Dakota, American soldiers, and government officials.

Meanwhile, settlers poured into Dakota lands in Minnesota. More treaties were signed; soon the Dakota had given up most of their land and were crowded into a small reservation along the Minnesota River. Altogether they yielded control of more than 24 million acres for about 12.5 cents per acre, paid in cash, food, and other supplies. The treaties stated that much of this money would go directly to traders, who deducted large amounts (claiming the tribe owed them money for supplies) before giving the rest to the Dakota people.

Events leading up to Santee War

On the reservation, the Dakota could not hunt or move about as they once had. If they ventured off the reservation to hunt, they had trouble with the settlers. Missionaries arrived, hoping to change Dakota culture and spiritual beliefs. The tribe's resentment grew.

In 1862, the crops failed, and the cash the U.S. government owed the Dakota did not arrive when due. In July of that year, thousands of Dakota gathered outside the headquarters of the Indian agent who was supposed to distribute the money. A rumor spread that the money was not coming because it was being spent on the American Civil War (1861–65; a war between the Union [the North], which was opposed to slavery, and the Confederacy [the South], which was in favor of slavery). When the agent refused to release food from the full warehouse until the money came, the Dakota, by then starving, were furious. One trader said: "So far as I am concerned, if they are hungry let them eat grass or their own dung."

In *Bury My Heart at Wounded Knee* (1970), author Dee Brown described the reaction of Dakota leader Little Crow (c. 1810–1863) to that statement:

> For years he [Little Crow] had tried to keep the treaties, to follow the advice of the white men and lead his people on their road. It seemed now that he had lost everything. His own people were losing faith in him, blaming him for their misfortunes, and now the agents and traders had turned against him. Earlier that summer [his people] had accused Little Crow of betraying them when he signed away their lands by treaties…. In the old days he could have regained leadership by going to war, but the treaties pledged him not to engage in hostilities with either the white men or other tribes.

Soon after, a starving group of young Dakota men shot five white settlers in a dispute over a hen's nest and a few eggs. Tensions escalated into a full-blown battle called the Santee War. By the time the war was over, Little Crow and his Dakota warriors had killed between 450 and 800 settlers and soldiers, but in the end, the Dakota were defeated. On September 26, 1862, they surrendered at their own camp, renamed Camp Release.

Little Crow led the Dakota warriors against the U.S. Army in the Santee War in 1862. DENVER PUBLIC LIBRARY, WESTERN HISTORY COLLECTION, WHITNEY, CALL NO X31803.

Aftermath of Little Crow's War

Hundreds of Dakota were rounded up, imprisoned, and tried in military court. More than three hundred men were found guilty and scheduled to be executed, but President Abraham Lincoln (1809–1865; served 1861–65) reduced the number to thirty-eight. These men were hanged at Mankato, Minnesota, but not before many of them denied participating in the fighting.

The other men were imprisoned, and 1,700 Dakota women and children were sent to Fort Snelling, facing assaults and taunts by angry settlers on the way. Little Crow fled from Minnesota into Canada, but he later returned to Minnesota. On July 3, 1863, he was shot and killed while picking berries with his son, Wowinapa. Little Crow was scalped, and his remains were later displayed at the Minnesota Historical Society. In 1971, his bones were returned to his family and reburied near Flandreau, South Dakota.

Minnesota cries for removal

Even after the thirty-eight Dakota were hanged and Little Crow was killed, settlers still called for the removal of all Dakota from Minnesota. The Minnesota governor, echoing this sentiment, declared that "the Sioux Indians of Minnesota must be exterminated or driven forever beyond the borders of the state." In 1863, the Minnesota legislature passed the Forfeiture Act, which took away the Dakota reservation and the tribe's treaty rights. The Dakota people were also ordered to leave Minnesota.

Many Dakota were transferred to the Crow Creek reservation in present-day South Dakota. The soil was no good for farming, and there was scant rainfall and little drinkable water or wild game to hunt. The people suffered from terrible living conditions, starvation, and disease. Some communities fled to the Devil's Lake reservation in North Dakota and the Sisseton reservation in South Dakota. Still others moved north to Canada in search of safety and land. After three terrible years at Crow Creek, the Dakota living on the desolate reservation moved to the Santee reservation in northern Nebraska.

Over the years, a few families slowly moved back into Minnesota from scattered locations and formed communities at Prairie Island and Prior Lake. The Dakota who ventured back into Minnesota were required to carry papers from the government declaring them to be "peaceful Indians."

Struggle for identity

The Dakota faced many of the same problems on their reservations as had other tribes. They lost much of their land following the General Allotment Act of 1887 (also known as the Dawes Act), which divided reservations into individual plots and opened leftover land to American settlement. (The purpose of the Allotment Act was to force the Native Americans to become more like U.S. citizens, each one farming a small plot rather than owning the property jointly with the whole tribe.)

Missionaries and government officials tried to force the Dakota to give up their religion and customs. Despite the loss of their land and repeated attacks on their cultural and spiritual beliefs, many Dakota maintained strong ties to their communities, the Great Sioux Nation, and their traditional beliefs. Efforts to reclaim their lands and their heritage continue into the twenty-first century.

Dakota in Canada

The Dakota who fled to Canada now live on reserves (the Canadian name for reservations). Some became commercial farmers, producing specialty crops for sale. Other made their living as woodworkers, cattle ranchers, and laborers, Many still have these same professions in the present day.

Because the Canadian government sees the Dakota as an American tribe, the people are treated as immigrants. Whereas other tribes in Canada made treaties with the government, the Dakota were not entitled to any benefits other groups received. This meant less land for reserves and less economic support. The Dakota continue to press for their rights; they banded together and formed an association to represent them politically called the Dakota Nations of Canada. In the late 1990s, this organization initiated a claim against the Canadian government for lands they believed had been unlawfully taken.

RELIGION

The Dakota believed that every aspect of the physical world, including the sun, earth, stars, thunder, rocks, trees, and animals, contained spirits that should be honored and worshipped. All spirits were made and controlled by *Wakan Tanka* (the Great Spirit), who also created the universe. Because Wakan Tanka placed spirits everywhere, the Dakota say that they do not have a religion but a way of life. Spiritual beliefs influenced their everyday activities, from harvesting corn to hunting for elk.

The Dakota performed the Sun Dance, a religious ceremony conducted by many buffalo-hunting tribes (see "Festivals and ceremonies"). Christian missionaries in the United States and Canada banned the ritual. The tribes performed the dance in secret until attitudes toward

Dakota Words

ate	"father"
cistina	"little"
hanhepi	"night"
ina	"mother"
ista	"eye"
kte	"to kill"
mani	"walk"
nape	"hand"
paha	"hill"
siha	"foot"
yanka	"to sit"
waziyatan	"north"

Native American religious freedom changed in the twentieth century, and they were able to perform it publicly again.

In modern times, many Dakota mix traditional practices with Christian beliefs, which were learned from the missionaries who arrived in the 1830s. Others belong to the Native American Church, a mixture of traditional and Christian elements, featuring an all-night ceremony of chanting, prayer, and meditation. (For more information the Native American Church, see Makah entry.)

LANGUAGE

Originally the Dakota, Lakota, and Nakota spoke the same language. As the Lakota and Nakota moved away from the Dakota, the three developed their own forms of the language. All three could still understand each other because the dialects (varieties) remained similar. For example, the word for friend is *koda* in Dakota, *kona* in Nakota, and *kola* in Lakota. All three dialects of the language still survive, although the Nakota branch is less common than the other two.

A Congregationalist missionary named Stephen Return Riggs (1812–1883) began his work among the Dakota in the 1830s. He and his wife, Mary Ann, studied the Sioux language and prepared translations of the Christian Bible in Sioux. The first Bible entirely in Sioux was printed in 1879.

In the mid-2000s the Dakota were making efforts to revitalize their language through community and school programs.

GOVERNMENT

Each of the four Dakota bands was an independent unit, and the band council was the governing body. The council consisted of a chief and representatives from each clan. They discussed important matters and took a vote; then messengers went about the villages announcing the council's decisions.

The council appointed *akicita,* outstanding warriors who served as hunt policemen. During a buffalo hunt, four men took charge, and they

Members of the the Dakota Treaty Council meet at Fort Laramie, Wyoming, in 1868. © TOPHAM/THE IMAGE WORKS.

had absolute power as long as the hunt lasted. They were assisted by the policemen, who made sure no one disrupted the hunt.

Long ago, the chief was chosen for his wisdom, but at some point the position became hereditary (passed down from father to son). In modern times, elected tribal councils govern the various reservations. Although the people are scattered over a wide area, they still consider themselves one people.

ECONOMY

Dakota men and women contributed equally to the survival of their villages. Women made maple sugar, farmed, gathered food, and helped collect wild rice. Dakota men hunted, broke up the soil for planting, collected wild rice, and fished. Observers often commented on the hard lot of Dakota women, and some even called them "slaves" to their husbands. Both men and women played important roles in the economic survival of their communities.

The Dakota traded surplus items with other tribes. Before the Europeans arrived, the people had an extensive trade network. They journeyed to the James River in South Dakota each year to meet and trade with their Lakota and Nakota kinspeople at a gathering known as the Dakota Rendezvous (pronounced *RON-day-voo*).

On the reservations, the Dakota struggled for years to make ends meet. A great number were forced to sell off their land to survive. Today, the Dakota people have learned to adapt to life in cities or on reservations. Many are involved in the tourism industry; others are farmers. Some have moved into a variety of professions both on and off the reservations. A few reservations still have high unemployment rates, but casinos and bingo halls are helping to create jobs and provide funds for cultural revitalization programs.

DAILY LIFE

Families

A Dakota household was usually made up of a maximum of four related families, each consisting of grandparents, their daughters and their daughters' husbands, and grandchildren. The Dakota had a complicated system in which certain aunts and uncles were considered the same as an individual's parents, and the children of these aunts and uncles became additional brothers and sisters. With so many mothers and fathers, few children could become orphans. If they did lose their parents, children were absorbed into the larger family.

The Dakota had strict rules for how different people interacted with one another. For example, daughters-in-law were not supposed to talk directly to their fathers-in-law.

Education

Dakota boys learned from their parents to hunt, make war, or become medicine men, while girls learned to build homes and gather food. Grandparents taught proper behavior and tribal customs and beliefs.

For many years, the Dakota endured a mix of government, church-run, and public schools, where little sensitivity was shown to their culture. Finally, in 1975, the Lake Traverse Reservation Tribal Council drew up plans for two schools that would emphasize tribal values. They opened the Tiospa Zina Tribal School and Sisseton-Wahpeton Community College. The college became recognized as a leader in distance education, offering interactive Dakota language courses and a course in Dakota history and culture via the Internet. Education is also important to the

Dakota people in Minnesota. Two reservations there established their own charter schools, in spite of their small populations. In Nebraska, the Santee Sioux founded Nebraska Indian Community College.

Buildings

Women built and owned the Dakota homes. The tribe lived in two different types of dwellings depending on the season. During warm weather, families resided in villages so the women could cultivate crops. The summer communities consisted of roomy wood and bark homes that families returned to several years in a row. The women built these sturdy homes by setting wooden posts in the ground to create a frame. They covered the posts with elm bark to create walls and a roof. Inside were benches covered with buffalo robes, which served as beds, tables, and chairs.

In colder weather, the Dakota needed portable homes so they could follow wild game. They relied on the cone-shaped tepee. The walls and floors were covered with buffalo or deer hides, and a space was left in the center of the floor for a fire. Tepees were warm and comfortable during the cold, wet months of fall and winter.

Food

The Dakota homeland in Minnesota was filled with abundant resources, and each community enjoyed a healthy, varied diet. The Dakota, who were once primarily farmers, became hunters and gatherers after they moved to the Plains.

In the spring (the Dakota new year), the people scattered from their winter villages and went their separate ways. The women, young children, and elders camped near maple tree groves, where they collected sap for maple sugar. At the same time, the men divided into small hunting parties and left in search of muskrat and buffalo, which they either used for food and furs or traded for other provisions.

In the late spring, Dakota families and friends reunited in their summer planting villages. The women plowed and planted small gardens of corn, pumpkins, and squash. Then the community disbanded again, although members still used the village as a base. The men left on short hunts for deer, duck, turtle, and geese, or to fish in the lakes and streams. The women went off to pick ripe fruits and vegetables, including cherries, plums, and berries, the *psincha* and *psinchicha* (roots found at the bottom of shallow lakes), the *mdo* (potato), and wild turnips. Some women and children remained behind to scare crows away from their cornfields.

In the fall, the women and some of the men collected wild rice from nearby lakes. They stood in canoes and beat the heads of the rice plants with a stick to release the grain. They also harvested corn and dried what they did not need right away. Some men left for the deer hunt. As winter set in, the communities broke up into small groups of one to three families to hunt for deer, buffalo, or other sources of meat, or to ice fish. When spring arrived, the cycle started again.

Clothing and adornment

Long ago, Dakota women relied on buckskin and buffalo hides to make clothing. When trade began with Europeans, they turned to cloth. They made skirts from a single piece of cloth, sewn together at the side and looped over a belt. Cloth leggings reached from their knees to their ankles, where they were tucked into their moccasins. Most of the clothing was decorated with beads and quillwork. Women also wore bead necklaces and earrings. They rarely painted their faces, but did paint a strip of vivid red in the part of their hair. They wore their hair in two or more long braids, sometimes wrapping the braids with otter fur.

In the summer, men wore cotton shirts, leggings, and breechcloths (garments with front and back flaps that hung from the waist). In the winter, they wore long coats that reached past their knees. Their clothes and moccasins were also adorned with beads and quillwork. They cut their hair in the front but wore the rest long in two or more braids fastened with silver ornaments or wrapped with otter fur. Headwear ranged from headdresses made of eagle feathers, to war bonnets. Some men wore sashes as turbans or used hoods to keep out cold or mosquitoes.

Healing practices

The Dakota believed that diseases were caused by spirits, so their *wakan*— medicine men and women—appealed to the spirit world to cure sickness. To bring a patient back into harmony with the spirit world, the wakan used chants, rattles, and dances or sucked on the infected area. They also used various roots, vegetables, berries, and bark to treat ailments.

Medicine men and women were initiated into a medicine lodge, a secret order that could only be joined by those who had earned the honor. Membership was by invitation only. A medicine dance was held, and a period of probation followed, until the men and women proved themselves worthy and learned the secret methods of curing diseases.

CUSTOMS

Festivals and ceremonies

The Dakota did not overuse food-gathering areas. To honor the spirits, they offered feasts and sacrifices before harvesting wild rice or hunting for animals. For example, they held a dance before an elk hunt and made an offering to the spirits after they killed the elk. During wild rice gathering, men and women staged feasts and offerings to the "water god" to ensure that they would not drown during the harvest. Later, after more ceremonial offerings, the rice was harvested and prepared for more feasting and eventual storage.

In addition to these everyday practices, the Dakota conducted important ceremonies throughout the year, such as pipe ceremonies, medicine dances, *Wakan* (spiritual) feasts, and *inipis*, or sweat lodge ceremonies that purified people.

Sun Dances In the summer, the Dakota often gathered with their scattered Lakota or Nakota relatives to perform the sacred Sun Dance. According to the Sun Dance tradition, warriors or others who found themselves facing certain death offered a prayer to the sun for their survival. If they survived, they participated in the Sun Dance the next summer to offer thanks and to atone for their weakness in the face of death. Before the dance, a sturdy pole was set up in a clearing. After the opening ceremonies, participants danced without stopping for a day and night, gazing at the sun, and blowing on an eagle bone whistle. Late in the dance, the participants had incisions made in their chests. Wooden skewers were placed through the cuts and attached with thongs to the pole. The men then pulled until the skewers broke free from their chests. The dancers' sacrifices fulfilled their vows to the sun.

The Dakota still hold Sun Dances and sweating and pipe ceremonies throughout the year. On the anniversary of the hanging of the thirty-eight men at Mankato, the people hold a ceremonial powwow to commemorate their deaths. According to the participants, thirty-eight eagles always appear overhead during the ceremony.

War and hunting rituals

Warfare was an important way for Dakota men to prove their manhood. They earned honor and prestige for their bravery and skill in war. Men organized war parties, carried out frequent raids against their enemies, and remained ever on guard against attacks on their summer planting villages.

A man—and sometimes a woman—usually organized a war party after a dream or vision. The call went forth to form an expedition, and volunteers joined the leader to fulfill the vision. Early observers called Dakota men "savage," but Dakota warriors respected their enemies and showed their strength and bravery by selecting and attacking key enemy warriors, not by destroying everyone in a village. A warrior who faced certain death sang a special death song; the thirty-eight warriors at Mankato sang the song just before they were hanged.

Men made their own weapons for hunting and war, and women were forbidden to touch them. Women made war bonnets to be awarded to successful warriors, but once the bonnets were finished, the makers could never touch them again.

Courtship, marriage, and babies

A young man had to earn his adult name before he could court a young woman. He attracted her by playing sweet music on an instrument made of wood or of a bird's wing or by offering to help with her chores. Once he gained her affection, he gave gifts to her parents to show what a good provider he would be. He might move in with her family for a while, and during that time, the young woman proved she could keep house. If all went well, the young woman and her female relatives built a tepee and held a feast, then the groom took his bride to their new home.

When a child was expected, the husband sometimes left the village to hunt or visit his family until the baby was born. The expectant mother was assisted in the birth by the older women of the village, who tied the newborn onto a wooden board called a cradleboard. Young children slept with their parents or grandparents until they were about four years old.

Naming practices

Dakota people received several different names in their lifetimes. When babies were born, they received a name based on their place in the family. For instance, the first male child was always called *Caske* and the first female child was always named *Winona*. After the child reached five or six years old and had developed a personality, a nickname was given. At the age of twelve, children participated in a naming ceremony, where they accepted a name they had earned.

Death and burial

Old people were respected in Dakota society. When an elderly person sensed that death was near, he or she sometimes left the village to die alone. If the group moved to a new location, a sick or dying person might stay behind so as not to be a burden.

After a person died, family members wailed over the death, cut their skin or hair, and gave away possessions to show grief. Sometimes, a lock of hair was removed from the deceased to make a "spirit bundle." The bundle was hung in the family's lodge, and a dish of food placed under it. After one year, a feast was held, and the spirit bundle was buried.

For the funeral, the deceased was dressed in his or her best clothes and new moccasins for the journey to the Land of Ghosts. The body was then wrapped with blankets or buffalo robes, and prized weapons or items were bound up in the wraps or placed nearby. The Dakota placed the body on a scaffold (a raised platform) so that the remains could fall back to Mother Earth.

CURRENT TRIBAL ISSUES

Despite their separation among various reservations throughout the United States and Canada, Dakota people have shared many similar experiences. They have filed claims against the U.S. and Canadian governments for land losses, and some of these claims have been successful. For example, residents of the Sisseton-Wahpeton Reservation (or Lake Traverse Reservation) received money for some of the land taken from them during allotment. Other land claims are still pending.

In 1980, the U.S. Supreme Court ruled that the Black Hills legally belonged to the Great Sioux Nation. The court awarded the tribes more than $105 million for the Black Hills and over $40 million for lands east of the Black Hills, but the Sioux refused to accept the money. They declared, "One does not sell their Mother." A survey conducted in 1996 revealed that 96 percent of the people agreed with this decision, although many of them were living in poverty. The settlement money set aside for them continues to accrue interest, and by the early 2000s, it was worth more than $863 million, but the still Sioux refuse to touch it. For them, justice will only be served when these lands are restored to their people.

The Dakota and the other members of the Seven Council Fires (Sioux) continue to stress the importance of presenting a united front on land and water rights, gambling, and other issues. For example, in November 1996, the Santee reservation in Nebraska seemed ready to accept money for land lost to the federal government. The other Sioux tribes strongly opposed this move and urged the Santee not to take actions the other nations might have to follow.

The Dakota sometimes call the government's attention these underlying beliefs by engaging in non-violent civil disobedience. To do this they defy local, state, or federal laws that they believe infringe on their sovereignty (right to self-government) as a nation. In 2011, for example, a group of Dakota men netted fish in Cedar Lake in Minneapolis on the day before fishing season officially opened. They gained media attention for their protest and said they wanted to be arrested, so the case would go to court. The men hoped that a trial would bring to light the terms of an 1805 treaty that guaranteed them year-round fishing rights in the area. One of the protestors called for the United States to honor this treaty, the terms of which have been repeatedly broken.

In 2008, the rate of violence on the Standing Rock Sioux Reservation in North Dakota was 8.6 times higher than the national average. The reservation had only nine police officers to patrol 2.3 million acres, so many Dakota and Lakota victims had to wait hours or even days for emergency help. In 2010, President Barack Obama (1961–; served 2009–) signed a Tribal Law and Order Act that may help with some law enforcement reforms. The act gives tribal authorities the ability to lengthen prison sentences, which are presently limited to three years, and gives them access to criminal databases along with strengthening other areas of law enforcement.

NOTABLE PEOPLE

Charles A. Eastman (1858–1939) was born in Minnesota and raised in a traditional Santee setting. He had little contact with American society until he went to school in Flandreau, South Dakota. He received a medical degree in 1890 and became a physician at the Pine Ridge Indian Reservation in South Dakota, the first Dakota in a position of authority there. Eastman wrote about Native culture and the differences between

Native beliefs and those of U.S. society in his autobiographical works *Indian Boyhood* (1902) and *From the Deep Woods to Civilization* (1916). He was active in the Young Men's Christian Association and was one of the founders of the Boy Scouts of America. His other works include *Red Hunters and the Animal People* (1904), *Old Indian Days* (1907), *Wigwam Evenings: Sioux Folktales Retold* (1909), *The Soul of the Indian* (1911), *The Indian Today* (1916), and *Indian Heroes and Great Chieftains* (1918).

Gabriel Renville (1824–1892) was chief of the Sisseton-Wahpeton tribe from 1862 to 1892. He helped establish the Lake Traverse Reservation, where he was a successful farmer, and was instrumental in maintaining traditional Santee customs. William G. Demmert Jr. (1934–2010) was a Tlingit-Dakota university professor and writer of many works on Indian education. He was also the founder of the National Indian Education Association. Hank Adams (1943–) is an Assiniboin-Dakota activist from Montana who joined the struggle over Indian fishing rights in the Northwest.

Santee activist, actor, and musician John Trudell (1947–) was a member of the American Indian Movement (AIM) who joined the group occupying Alcatraz Island. Trudell believes that his appearance in Washington, D.C., to speak out for Indian rights was connected to a fire at his home twelve hours later. His wife and three young children died in the fire; the Bureau of Indian Affairs declared the fire accidental. Trudell expresses his people's goals as follows: "We want to be free of a value system that's being imposed upon us. We do not want to participate in that value system. We don't want change in the value system. We want to remove it from our lives forever.… We have to assume our responsibilities as power, as individuals, as spirit, as people." Sisseton-Wahpeton songwriter and performer Floyd Westerman (1936–2007) played the role of Ten Bears in the film *Dances with Wolves*. Paul War Cloud (1930–1973) was a Sisseton-Wahpeton painter who depicted Dakota culture and tradition in his works.

BOOKS

Brown, Dee. "Little Crow's War." In *Bury My Heart at Wounded Knee*. New York: Holt, Rinehart & Winston, 1970.

Clow, Richmond L., ed. *The Sioux in South Dakota History: A Twentieth-Century Reader*. Pierre, SD: South Dakota State Historical Society Press, 2007.

Custer, Elizabeth B. *Boots and Saddles; or, Life in Dakota with General Custer*. Lincoln: University of Nebraska Press, 2010.

Dahlin, Curtis A., and Alan R. Woolworth. *The Dakota Uprising: A Pictorial History.* Edina, MN: Beaver's Pond Press, 2009.

Eastman, Charles A. *The Essential Charles Eastman (Ohiyesa), Revised and Updated Edition: Light on the Indian World.* Michael Oren Fitzgerald, ed. Bloomington, IN: World Wisdom, 2007.

Eastman, Charles A. *From the Deep Woods to Civilization.* Whitefish, MT: Kessinger Publishing, 2006.

Eastman, Charles A. *The Soul of the Indian.* New York: Dodo Press, 2007.

Erb, Gene, and Ann DeWolf Erb. *Voices in Our Souls: The DeWolfs, Dakota Sioux and the Little Bighorn.* Santa Fe: Sunstone Press, 2010.

Hedren, Paul L. *Great Sioux War Orders of Battle: How the United States Army Waged War on the Northern Plains, 1876–1877.* Norman, OK: Arthur H. Clark Co., 2011.

Keenan, Jerry. *The Great Sioux Uprising: Rebellion the Plains, August–September, 1862.* Cambridge, MA: Da Capo Press, 2003

Miller, David, et al. *The History of the Fort Peck Assiniboine and Sioux Tribes, 1800–2000.* Helena, MT: Fort Peck Community College and Montana Historical Society Press, 2008.

Monjeau-Marz, Corinne L. *The Dakota Indian Internment at Fort Snelling, 1862–1864.* Saint Paul, MN: Prairie Smoke Press, 2005.

Palmer, Jessica Dawn. *The Dakota Peoples: A History of the Dakota, Lakota and Nakota through 1863.* Jefferson, NC: McFarland, 2008.

Stanley, George E. *Sitting Bull: Great Sioux Hero.* New York: Sterling, 2010.

Woolworth, Alan R. *Santee Dakota Indian Tales.* Saint Paul, MN: Prairie Smoke Press, 2003.

WEB SITES

"Dakota Indian Tribe History." *Access Genealogy.* http://www.accessgenealogy. com/native/tribes/siouan/dakotahist.htm (accessed on July 5, 2011).

"Dakota Introduction." *The Dakota Society.* http://www.visi.com/˜vanmulken/ Tutorial/intro.html (accessed on July 5, 2011).

"The Dakota Language Homepage." *The Alliance Project.* http://www. alliance2k.org/daklang/dakota9463.htm (accessed on July 5, 2011).

"Dakota Language Start." *Fort Peck Community College.* http://fpcctalkindian. nativeweb.org/dlintro.htm (accessed on July 5, 2011).

"Dakota Spirituality." *Blue Cloud Abbey.* http://www.bluecloud.org/ dakotaspirituality.html (accessed on July 5, 2011).

Eastman, Mary. "Dahcotah; or, Life and Legends of the Sioux around Fort Snelling." *Access Genealogy.* http://www.accessgenealogy.com/native/ dahcotah/index.htm (accessed on July 5, 2011).

Jones, Susie. "DNR Confiscates Fish Caught by Dakota Indians." *NewsRadio 830 WCCO.* May 13, 2011. http://minnesota.cbslocal. com/2011/05/13/dakota-plan-to-net-fish-in-minneapolis-lake/ (accessed on July 5, 2011).

Mendota Mdewakanton Dakota Community. http://mendotadakota.org/ (accessed on July 5, 2011).

Mni Wakan Oyate: Spirit Lake Dakotah Nation. http://www.spiritlakenation. com/ (accessed on July 5, 2011).

Prairie Island Indian Community. http://www.prairieisland.org/ (accessed on July 5, 2011).

Redish, Laura, and Orrin Lewis. "Lakota and Dakota Sioux Fact Sheet." *Native Languages of the Americas.* http://www.bigorrin.org/sioux_kids.htm (accessed on July 5, 2011).

Shakopee Mdewakanton Sioux Community. http://www.shakopeedakota.org/ (accessed on July 5, 2011).

Sultzman, Lee. "Concerning John Trudell." *First Nations Issues of Consequence.* http://www.dickshovel.com/JTT.html (accessed on July 5, 2011).

Sioux Nations: Lakota

Name

Lakota (pronounced *lah-KOH-tah*) is the tribe's name for itself and may mean "allies" or "friends." It comes from the Teton word *Lakhota,* sometimes translated as "alliance of friends." Another meaning for the name is "those who consider themselves kindred." The people are also known as Teton Sioux. Teton comes from their word *Titunwan,* meaning "prairie dwellers."

The Sioux tribes (Dakota, Lakota, and Nakota) were once given the name *Nadowe-is-iw-ug,* which means "little adders (snakes)" by their enemies, the Ojibway. The French mispronounced the Ojibway word as *Nadewisou* and shortened it to "Sioux," the name by which the tribes are collectively known. Because the name was intended as an insult, many of the people dislike being called Sioux.

Location

At one time, the Great Sioux Nation extended from the Bighorn Mountains in Wyoming to eastern Wisconsin. Their territory stretched from Canada in the north to Kansas in the south. The Lakota occupied an area in western Minnesota around the Great Stone Lake. In the mid-1700s, the Lakota moved from Minnesota to the Black Hills region of western South Dakota, eastern Wyoming, and eastern Montana. In modern times, they live on the Cheyenne River, Lower Brule, Pine Ridge, Rosebud, Crow Creek, and Standing Rock reservations in North and South Dakota, and at Fort Peck Reservation in Montana.

Population

The Indian Bureau estimated that the Teton Sioux (Lakota) numbered about 12,000 in 1842. That figure fell to 8,900 in 1861. The population in 1890 was 16,426, and in 1909, it had reached 18,098 in the United States, with another 100 people living with Sitting Bull in Canada. In the 1990 U.S. Census, 46,943 people identified themselves as members of Lakota Sioux tribes. An additional 44,354 people simply identified themselves as Sioux. The 2000 census indicated that 113,713 Sioux lived in the United States. Of that number, 69,722 lived on Lakota reservations, although the total

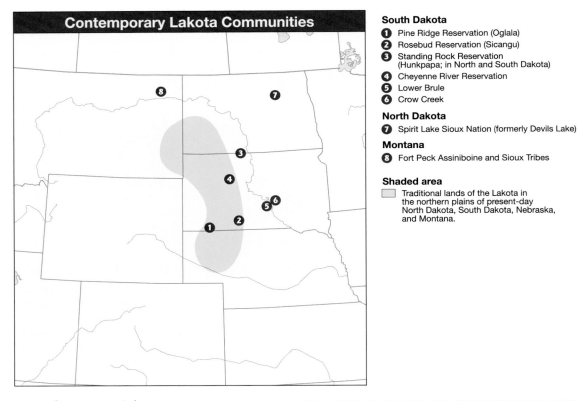

Contemporary Lakota Communities

South Dakota
1. Pine Ridge Reservation (Oglala)
2. Rosebud Reservation (Sicangu)
3. Standing Rock Reservation (Hunkpapa; in North and South Dakota)
4. Cheyenne River Reservation
5. Lower Brule
6. Crow Creek

North Dakota
7. Spirit Lake Sioux Nation (formerly Devils Lake)

Montana
8. Fort Peck Assiniboine and Sioux Tribes

Shaded area
Traditional lands of the Lakota in the northern plains of present-day North Dakota, South Dakota, Nebraska, and Montana.

A map of contemporary Lakota communities. MAP BY XNR PRODUCTIONS. CENGAGE LEARNING, GALE. REPRODUCED BY PERMISSION OF GALE, A PART OF CENGAGE LEARNING.

population on some of these reservations also included people with Dakota or Nakota heritage. Canadian statistics in 2001 showed 3,880 Sioux. In the 2010 census, 112,176 Sioux were counted in the United States, with a total of 170,110 people claiming Sioux heritage.

Language family

Siouan.

Origins and group affiliations

Some Sioux creation stories trace their origins back to the Black Hills of South Dakota, but others say they originated in the Minnesota woodlands, where they and the Nakota (see entry) were part of the Dakota (see entry) tribe. In the mid-1700s, the tribe broke into three groups after wars with the neighboring Ojibway (see entry). The Dakota remained in Minnesota, and the other two groups, calling themselves Lakota and Nakota, moved westward. The Lakota found allies among the Cheyenne and Arapaho (see entries) as they fought with the Kiowa, Crow (see entries), and Omaha.

The Lakota were once the most powerful tribe in North America, controlling a large area of the northern Great Plains. Lakota leaders, including Sitting Bull, Crazy Horse, and Red Cloud, were among the best-known Natives of the nineteenth century, and the tribe was involved in two of the most famous incidents in American history, the Battle of the Little Bighorn in 1876 and the Massacre at Wounded Knee in 1890. In recent times, the Lakota have been at the forefront of the Native rights movement.

HISTORY

Golden Age of the Lakota people

Before their move to the Great Plains in the mid-1700s, the Lakota were part of the Dakota tribe and lived as woodland farmers in present-day Minnesota. Warfare with the Ojibway divided the Dakota into three groups. The group that moved west onto the Great Plains came to be called the Lakota.

The Lakota acquired horses from neighboring tribes and adopted the Great Plains lifestyle. They depended on the buffalo for food, clothing, shelter, weapons, and household objects, and they followed the herds on their annual migrations. Although their migrations differed from their relatives, theNakota and Dakota, who were more settled, the Lakota considered these groups allies and did not fight against them.

During the late eighteenth century, the Lakota divided into seven bands and scattered throughout the region. After forming alliances with the Northern Cheyenne and Northern Arapaho, the Lakota became a powerful force on the Northern Plains. The years from 1775 to 1868 are sometimes called the tribe's "Golden Age."

The Seven Lakota Bands

Shortly after they settled in the Black Hills region, the Lakota divided into seven bands that dispersed throughout the area:

Oglala (which means "They Scatter Their Own"), the largest group, occupying western South Dakota, southeastern Montana, and northeastern Wyoming.

Sicangu or Brule ("Burned Thighs"), occupying northern Nebraska and southern South Dakota.

Miniconjou ("Planters by the Water"), occupying central and northern South Dakota

Oohenonpa ("Two Kettles"), occupying territory just west of the Missouri River in South Dakota.

Hunkpapa ("End of the Entrance"), **Itazipco** or Sans Arcs ("Without Bows"), and **Sihasapa** ("Black Feet") occupying lands farther north.

Explorers Lewis and Clark meet with a group of Native Americans during their travels in the early 1800s. © NORTH WIND PICTURE ARCHIVES.

Troubled American relations

In 1804, American explorers Meriwether Lewis (1774–1809) and William Clark (1770–1838) reached present-day Pierre (pronounced *PEER*), South Dakota. President Thomas Jefferson (1743–1826; served 1801–09) had sent Lewis and Clark to find a waterway to the Pacific Ocean. Lewis had orders from the president to seek out the Sioux, make a good impression on them, and secure them as allies.

The first meeting ended with misunderstandings on both sides. At the second meeting, the Brule band was celebrating a victory over the Omaha tribe and treated Lewis and Clark to a performance of the first scalp dance ever seen by Americans. After the Lakota expressed displeasure at the gifts Lewis and Clark gave them, relations soured. Lewis wrote that he found the Sioux to be "the vilest miscreants [evildoers] of the savage race."

The Sioux did not realize it then, but Lewis and Clark's visit foretold the U.S. intent to claim Sioux territory. Fur traders followed Lewis and Clark, and word spread in the East about the vast new lands. In 1825, the gov-

Important Dates

c. 1770s: The Lakota move to the Black Hills, divide into seven bands, and disperse throughout the region.

1804: The Lakota meet the Lewis and Clark expedition. Trading posts are established in their territory.

1851: Fort Laramie treaties are signed, defining boundaries of Lakota territories and marking the beginning of westward movement by miners and wagon trains on the Oregon Trail.

1866–68: Red Cloud leads a successful fight to close Bozeman Trail, which leads through Lakota hunting grounds to the gold mines of Montana.

1868: The U.S. government gives up its claim to Lakota lands, including the Black Hills, in the Second Fort Laramie Treaty.

1874: Gold is discovered in the Black Hills; prospectors pour in.

1876: Lakota warriors defeat Lieutenant Colonel George Custer in the Battle of the Little Bighorn.

1890: Sitting Bull is murdered. U.S. troops kill more than three hundred Lakota men, women, and children in the Massacre at Wounded Knee.

1973: American Indian Movement (AIM) activists occupy Wounded Knee and engage in a seventy-one-day standoff with government agents.

1980: The Lakota are awarded $105 million for the wrongful taking of their territory. They refuse to accept the money.

2007: Activists declare themselves the Republic of Lakotah, an independent nation from the United States.

ernment sent soldiers to impress the Native nations with American military might and to negotiate treaties.

Treaty era begins

In 1825, treaties were signed with three Lakota bands. The United States claimed the right to control trade in the region and agreed to protect the Lakota and their property against white trespassers. The Americans also agreed "to receive [the tribes] into their friendship" and to grant them "such benefits and acts of kindness as may be convenient" in the eyes of the president. Chief Wabasha (d. 1836) expressed his wish that "this peace will last a long time."

The Lakota enjoyed trading with American companies for goods that made their lives more comfortable, such as guns and cooking utensils. Unfortunately, the newcomers brought diseases and alcohol, or "the water

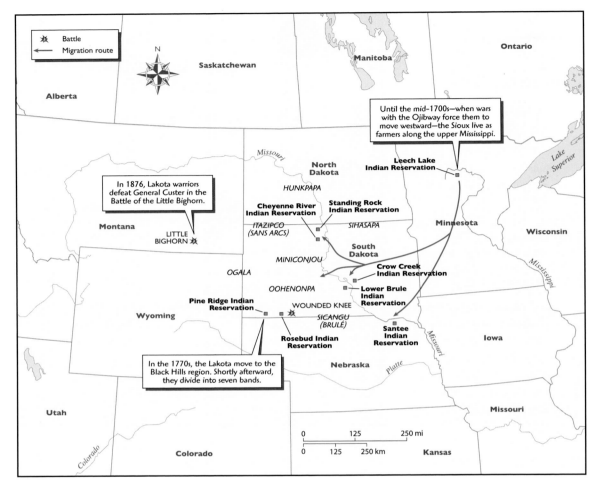

A map showing the migrations of the Lakota Sioux. MAP BY XNR PRODUCTIONS. CENGAGE LEARNING, GALE. REPRODUCED BY PERMISSION OF GALE, A PART OF CENGAGE LEARNING.

that makes men foolish," as the Lakota called it. The tribe grew increasingly dependent on American goods and experienced epidemics (uncontrolled outbreaks of disease).

Wagon trains head west

Until the 1840s, relations between Americans and Native peoples on the Great Plains remained fairly peaceful. Then wagon trains headed west. More and more settlers crossed Lakota territory and drove away the buffalo. The tribe was forced to expand its hunting territory, and this took it closer to the lands of its enemies, the Kiowa and the Crow (see entries), and made it a target for attacks. The tribe tried to discourage the pioneers with threats, robberies, and wagon train attacks, but nothing stopped the westward flow.

In 1850, the U.S. Congress offered to make treaties with "the wild tribes of the prairies." Word was passed among the western tribes that representatives of "the Great White Father" (the American president) wished to talk peace at Fort Laramie, Wyoming. Thousands of people gathered at the fort, many of them starving because the buffalo were nearly gone.

Fort Laramie Treaty made and broken

The Lakota signed the Fort Laramie Treaty of 1851, which recognized their rights to more than 60 million acres of land, including the Black Hills. In return, the tribe guaranteed safe passage of settlers on the Oregon Trail, an agreement that would end their way of life. As author Edward Lazarus put it, "The treaty outlawed many essential aspects of plains life, the raiding, horse thieving, and warring that brought honor and authority to both a man and his tribe."

The terms of the treaty were not kept for long. Violence erupted as tribes battled with each other over trade disputes and access to hunting grounds. Meanwhile, the U.S. Senate changed the terms of the treaty. Instead of annual payments to the tribes for fifty years in the form of cattle, farming implements, seeds, and grains, the Senate decided to make annual payments for only ten years.

To war over a lame ox

For a few years, settlers passed through Lakota lands unmolested. In 1854, a warrior named High Forehead spotted a lame ox at the end of a wagon train and shot it for food. A few days later, the commander of Fort Laramie tried to arrest High Forehead, but he refused to surrender. In the bloody battle that followed, the commander, his troops, and a Lakota chief named Conquering Bear were killed.

The U.S. government sent 1,300 armed troops, who attacked a Brule camp and murdered eighty-six men, women, and children. None of the dead had played any part in the lame ox incident. The Lakota had never experienced a loss of such magnitude. Confused and upset, they headed for the Black Hills.

In 1857, thousands of Sioux gathered in the Black Hills and vowed to protect their lands from the whites. However, gold was discovered in Colorado in 1859, and by 1861, rumors indicated there was gold in Montana, too. Traffic increased on the Oregon Trail and on the Bozeman Trail into Montana. As settlers passed through, many stayed and explored the Great Plains and prairies of the Lakota hunting grounds. War seemed unavoidable.

Red Cloud's War

The Sioux wars began with the Dakota in Minnesota in 1862. Survivors fled to Lakota country, where they joined the battles against U.S. soldiers. Across the West, Native peoples fought American soldiers, who had orders to "attack and kill every male Native over twelve years of age." Women and children were not spared either.

In 1865, Congress decided to build roads into the Montana gold district, where the Lakota hunted, and to make peace with the tribes living there. Some Lakota groups who were starving signed treaties, but many thousands of Lakota warriors remained hostile toward the U.S. government. Their leader was the powerful and respected warrior Red Cloud (1822–1909). When he learned the Americans were talking peace while building forts and planning roads along the Bozeman Trail, the famous warrior declared: "I am for war."

A delegation of Sioux leaders assemble in Washington, D.C., in 1875 to protest the violation of the Fort Laramie Treaty of 1868.
© PRIVATE COLLECTION/PETER NEWARK WESTERN AMERICANA/THE BRIDGEMAN ART LIBRARY.

Red Cloud's War (also known as the War for the Bozeman Trail) lasted from 1866 to 1868. Crazy Horse (c. 1840–1877) and other Lakota warriors led attacks against soldiers in American forts, outsmarting them at every turn. The U.S. government finally admitted defeat. In the Second Fort Laramie Treaty of 1868, the Lakota received the title to the Great Sioux Reservation, which occupied half of present-day South Dakota (west of the Missouri River and including the sacred Black Hills) as well as the Bighorn Mountain region of Wyoming and Nebraska. The Lakota were also given tools, cattle, and other materials designed to convert them into farmers and ranchers.

Gold discovered at Black Hills

Gold was found in the Black Hills in 1874, and miners and settlers again trespassed on Lakota lands. Responding to citizen's demands for more land, the U.S. government tried to buy the Black Hills. Lakota leaders refused to give up the land they held sacred. Crazy Horse said: "One does not sell the Earth upon which the people walk." Hunkpapa Sioux chief Sitting Bull (c. 1831–1890) stated: "We want no white men here. The Black Hills belong to me. If the whites try to take them, I will fight."

In 1876, the U.S. Army tried to force the Lakota to become farmers and to give up land. Intense fighting followed in the war for the Black Hills (also called Sitting Bull and Crazy Horse's War). Some of the most famous battles in American history were fought during this war.

Sitting Bull and Crazy Horse's war

In 1876, the Lakota scored victories at Powder River in Montana, at Rosebud Creek in South Dakota, and in the valley of the Little Bighorn River in Montana. In the battle at Little Bighorn, which came to be known as "Custer's Last Stand," Lieutenant Colonel George Custer (1839–1876) and 250 men attacked a camp of 2,500 Lakota and Cheyenne warriors. Sitting Bull, Crazy Horse, and Gall (1840–1894; Sitting Bull's adopted son) led the counterattack, in which Custer and all his men were killed. This was the last great Native victory on the Great Plains.

Custer's defeat led to calls for the "extermination" of the tribes. Over the next six months, the Lakota were beaten at War Bonnet Creek in Nebraska, Slim Buttes in South Dakota, and Wolf Mountain in Montana. They also lost the Battle of Dull Knife in Wyoming. By mid-1877, many Lakota chiefs had surrendered and were placed on reservations.

Lakota resistance broken

In September 1877, Crazy Horse went to Fort Robinson, Nebraska, to forge a peaceful settlement. Nevertheless, the U.S. Army tried to imprison the great chief; he was killed when he resisted arrest. Sitting Bull and his followers fled to Canada.

The power of the Lakota and their allies over the Northern Plains was broken. On January 31, 1876, the U.S. Congress ordered the Lakota to move away from the Black Hills. When South Dakota became a state in 1889, settlers pressured the federal government for more land. The Sioux Act of 1889 broke the Great Sioux Reservation into four smaller reservations. Under the allotment policy, each Sioux received an individual plot of land; leftover land went to the settlers.

Bodies of Sioux Indians are piled into a mass grave after the massacre at Wounded Knee in December 1890. © MPI/GETTY IMAGES.

Massacre at Wounded Knee

In 1890, Sitting Bull lived at the Standing Rock Reservation, and the U.S. government feared that he might lead another resistance movement. The government became uneasy when the Lakota took up the Ghost Dance (see "Religion") in 1890. A law forbade the dance, but by November 1890, the people performed it anyway. The Indian agent sent a message to Washington, D.C.: "Indians are dancing in the snow and are wild and crazy.… We need protection and we need it now."

In December 1890, U.S. troops under General Nelson Miles (1839–1925) tried to arrest Sitting Bull. A fight broke out, and the chief and seven warriors were killed. The grief-stricken people sought refuge at Pine Ridge Reservation, where Red Cloud was in charge, and at the camp of Lakota leader Big Foot (c. 1825–1890). The U.S. government ordered the arrest of Big Foot. Planning to make peace, Big Foot made his way to Pine Ridge. When American troops intercepted him and tried to disarm his men, a rifle went off. In the battle that followed, more than three hundred people were killed, most of them women and children. This Massacre at Wounded Knee marked the end of the Ghost Dance era and Indian wars.

Reservation years

Many Lakota resisted the allotment policy, but the U.S. government pressured them to turn to farming. People who refused did not receive the government money and goods the treaties had promised. They went hungry, and many died.

The tribe lost more land throughout the early 1900s as reservations were broken into individual allotments. During this period, the Lakota also lost many aspects of their culture. Their children were sent to boarding schools, and missionaries tried to convert them to Christianity. Traditional ceremonies and practices were forbidden until laws passed in the 1930s restored religious freedom.

Lakota in the twentieth century and beyond

The Lakota struggle to regain lost land is ongoing. They never accepted the 1877 order granting ownership of the Black Hills to the United States. Instead, they believe that these sacred lands belong to the tribe as given them by the Creator and promised them by the U.S. government in the Fort Laramie Treaty of 1868.

Lakota ghost dance shirt is on display at the Sioux Cultural Center in Pierre, South Dakota. SOUTH DAKOTA STATE HISTORICAL SOCIETY.

In 1980, the U.S. Supreme Court awarded the Lakota $105 million for the wrongful taking of their territory a century earlier. Despite their dire need for money, the Lakota refused to accept the settlement and insisted that their traditional lands be returned.

RELIGION

The Lakota believe that all life is interrelated. Their god, known as *Wakan Tanka* (the Great Mystery Power, or Creator), includes all elements of nature, so the Lakota have a deep respect for their environment. The spirits of the Sun, Sky, Earth, Buffalo, Bear, and Four Directions of the Winds are particularly important.

According to Lakota sacred lore, a holy woman named White Buffalo Calf Woman gave the people their religious teachings, including the knowledge of the sacred pipe and how to use it in seven ceremonies that made the celebrants one with the universe.

In the 1850s, Catholic priest Father Pierre Jean ("Black Robe") de Smet (1801–1873) lived, preached, and taught among the Lakota. Although many Lakota became members of the Roman Catholic Church and later the Episcopal Church, traditional religion under the guidance of Lakota spiritual leaders remains the primary form of worship.

In 1890, a Paiute (see entry) holy man named Wovoka (c. 1856–1932) taught the Native nations that performing the Ghost Dance would return the earth to a natural state, with huge herds of buffalo and all the dead ancestors returned. No whites would inhabit this world. Tribes conducted Ghost Dance ceremonies as a form of peaceful resistance. Two Lakota medicine men, Kicking Bear (1846–1904) and Short Bull (c. 1852–1935), claimed that dancing and wearing protective Ghost Dance shirts could shield people from white men's bullets. The Ghost Dance offered hope as the tribe faced terrible conditions and starvation. Even after the U.S. government outlawed the ceremony, the Lakota continued to sponsor large gatherings.

LANGUAGE

The Lakota speak one of three dialects (varieties) of the Siouan language family. The other two dialects are spoken by the Dakota and Nakota. Although there are some differences, all three groups understand one another.

The Lakota language is still spoken today by many people on the reservations. It is taught throughout the grade levels at reservation schools and is used in traditional ceremonies. The Lakota represent one of the largest communities of Native language speakers left in the United States. Between eight thousand and nine thousand people use the language.

Lakota men and women use different words to express similar commands or assertions.

Lakota Words

In some American movies, Indians say "How" when they meet someone. This may be a shortened version of the Lakota greeting, *Háukhola*, which means "Hello, friend." Below are some other common expressions and words:

han	"yes"
o han	"okay"
lo wa'cin	"I'm hungry."
to ka ho?	"What's wrong?"

GOVERNMENT

The basic social unit of the Sioux was the *tiyospe,* an extended family group that traveled together in search of game. In the early days on the Great Plains, the Lakota lived in these small groups without designated leaders. They respected older people's opinions, but elders had no special authority. This changed in the 1800s, when settlers threatened the Lakota way of life. The tribe united in larger groups and pledged their allegiance to strong leaders.

On reservations, government agents discouraged having one head chief. Soon, many people declared themselves chiefs, and as people divided their loyalties among the chiefs, they quarreled with each other.

Following the Indian Reorganization Act of 1934, the Lakota established elected tribal councils at several reservations. The U.S. Bureau of Indian Affairs, however, often influenced the selection of leaders. Conflict arose between tribal council leaders and traditional leaders, who sometimes felt the tribal council was corrupt or was controlled by the federal government, so it did not fairly represent the Lakota people.

ECONOMY

Before they moved to the Great Plains, the Sioux economy depended on hunting, fishing, gathering, and farming. After moving and acquiring horses, the people depended on trading in buffalo hides. Lakota raided for horses and drove other tribes away until they dominated much of the Great Plains trade.

After the earliest treaties were signed with the U.S. government, most of the buffalo were gone, and many people became dependent on government handouts. Others became successful farmers and ranchers on the reservations until the Great Depression (1929–41; the period, following the stock market crash in 1929, of depressed world economies and high unemployment). Afterward, many Lakota were unable to recover economically and had to sustain themselves by leasing their lands to white farmers; some still earn money in this way.

Lakota reservations are among the poorest communities in the United States, with up to 80 percent unemployment, meaning that eight out of every ten people who wanted to work could not find jobs. Almost half the people on the Pine Ridge Indian Reservation live below poverty level. Some farming and ranching are done, and tribal government is a major employer. Some small businesses have opened, but because the remote locations of the reservations make the prospects bleak, many people seek work off the reservations. Unemployment rates have dropped on reservations with casinos, and as a result, many tribes are turning to gaming to improve their economies.

DAILY LIFE

Education

Because the Lakota migrated, children learned about geography and plant life. Boys learned from a young age how to be successful competitors. At age three, they raced ponies and participated in games that tested their skill and strength; top spinning and javelin throwing were popular. Later, boys learned survival skills by undertaking long, difficult trips into the wilderness.

Teenage boys could become warriors or buffalo hunters, or join one of several societies (Kit Foxes, Crow Owners, or Brave Hearts, for example), whose members organized buffalo hunts or were in charge of moving the camp.

In the 1880s, Chief Red Cloud petitioned the federal government to allow priests to start schools on the reservations. Generations of Sioux children were educated in Catholic schools begun by the Jesuits. One of the goals of these boarding schools was to change the students' culture. Children were severely punished for speaking their language or practicing their religion or traditions. In 2003, hundreds of former students recounted stories of physical and sexual abuse. Many experts believe the problems of domestic violence and alcoholism on the reservations are a by-product of the treatment the students received in these schools.

Reservation schools now emphasize Lakota language and culture, beginning with Head Start programs for preschoolers and continuing through college. Sitting Bull College on the Standing Rock Reservation has a Native American studies program. More than a dozen private and public schools have been established at Pine Ridge Reservation, including Oglala Lakota College. Cheyenne River Reservation has two campuses for its Si Tanka Huron University, which attracts students from around the world.

Buildings

Like many tribes of the Great Plains, the Lakota lived in tepees, which were easy to assemble and carry. They arranged a framework of wooden poles into a cone shape and covered it with eight to twelve buffalo skins, carefully prepared and stitched together. During the winter, stones held the tepees in place. In the summer, they rolled up the covers to let in fresh air. Lakota men sometimes decorated the outsides of their tepees with paintings that recorded special events in their lives.

The Lakota also built sweat lodges for ceremonial purposes. They believed that sweating rid the body and mind of impurities and made one ready to deal with the spirits.

After about 1900, traditional Lakota tepees were replaced by tents and later by log cabins supplied by the U.S. government.

Food

The great buffalo herds provided food and other necessities for the Lakota. Their diet consisted mainly of buffalo and chokecherries.

Lakota men handled most of the hunting, and women butchered animals, prepared hides, and cooked or preserved meat. The Lakota also hunted deer, elk, and small game. They collected roots and berries and traded for food with farming tribes of the region.

Clothing and adornment

The Lakota were famous for their colorful clothing, mostly made of deer or elk hides. The men wore fringed buckskin shirts and leggings, deco-rated with brightly colored porcupine quills or locks of hair. They also wore buckskin moccasins with tough, buffalo-hide soles. They adorned themselves with earrings, armbands, and bear-claw necklaces. Younger men shaved the sides of their heads and let the hair in the middle grow long. Lakota warriors painted both themselves and their horses with fierce symbols and patterns and wore eagle feathers in their hair as a sign of their acts of bravery.

Women wore buckskin dresses that reached almost to the ankle over leggings that extended to the knee. Their clothing, too, was elaborately decorated with fringes, porcupine quills, or beads. They usually wore their long hair in two braids woven with pieces of cloth or beads. Lakota children of both genders had their ears pierced at age five or six, and from then on, they wore strings of colored beads as earrings.

Healing practices

Many Lakota spiritual leaders and healers learned of their future role when they were children, if a buffalo spoke to them in a dream. Such children were called Buffalo Dreamers. The Lakota people consulted them about a variety of problems, including illnesses and injuries. Healers made medicine from herbs, tree bark, wild fruits, and ground buffalo hooves. They also appealed to the spirits for help in diagnosing and curing illnesses by singing, dancing, and praying in special ways.

ARTS

Oral literature

Some Sioux stories say that the Dakota, Lakota, and Nakota peoples originated in the Black Hills. They were chosen by the Creator to protect the area, which they call *He Sapa*. According to their oral traditions, the Sioux emerged through Wind Cave in the Black Hills, leaving their leader behind. He then came aboveground as a buffalo, offering his body as everything the people needed to survive.

CUSTOMS

Vision quests

When they reached puberty, all Lakota boys (and some girls) participated in a vision quest to connect with the supernatural being who would guide them through life. Young people first purified themselves in a sweat lodge. Afterward, they traveled to a sacred place, accompanied by two helpers who constructed a platform then left them alone. The person seeking a vision paced around on the platform, prayed, smoked a sacred pipe, and fasted (ate and drank nothing). The vision seeker kept careful track of everything he or she saw and heard during this time.

After four days had passed, the helpers returned and brought the seeker back to camp. There spiritual leaders explained the vision and provided special songs, prayers, and objects that represented the seeker's connection with the supernatural. After completing a vision quest, a Lakota gained power and became an adult in the eyes of the tribe.

Rites of passage

At the onset of her first menstrual period, a girl was sent to a special hut outside the camp, where older women visited her to explain her adult responsibilities. A few weeks later, her father hosted a ceremony that celebrated her passage into womanhood. During the ceremony, the right side of the young woman's face and the part in her hair were painted red, a sacred color, and a feather was placed in her hair for good luck in producing children.

When a young Lakota man participated in his first successful hunt or joined his first war party, his family celebrated his passage to manhood with a special ceremony and a feast.

Courtship and marriage

Marriages were usually arranged by a young couple's parents. Sometimes, however, couples fell in love and decided to elope. The couple was formally recognized as husband and wife after gifts were exchanged between the two families and the couple moved into a tepee together. Infidelity in marriage was punished by disfigurement.

Death and burial

The Lakota placed dead bodies on a scaffold (a raised platform) or in the branches of a tree along with possessions and food for the journey to the next world. Although they faced their own death with dignity, they deeply mourned the loss of relatives. Mourners often inflicted themselves with slashes during burial ceremonies.

Keeping of the Soul

One of the seven sacred rites brought to the people by White Buffalo Calf Woman is called Keeping of the Soul. In the old times, it marked the end of a one-year period of mourning following a death. After a year, relatives of the deceased distributed gifts. Such giveaways are still held to celebrate important occasions, including births, marriages, graduations, and acceptance into the U.S. Armed Forces.

War and hunting rituals

A Lakota war chief could be anyone who convinced others to follow him into battle. Upon returning from a successful battle, the tribe held scalp dances to celebrate. The explorer William Clark described a Lakota scalp dance he witnessed in 1804 (the spelling is his):

> A large fire made in the Center, about 10 musitions [musicians] playing on tamberins [tamborines] made of hoops & skin stretched. long sticks with Deer & Goats Hoofs tied So as to make a [jingling] noise and many others of a Similer kind, those men began to Sing & Beet on the Temboren, the women Came forward highly Deckerated in theire way, with the Scalps an Trofies of war of ther father Husbands Brothers or near Connection & proceeded to dance the war Dance. Women only dance—jump up & down.... Every now and then one of the men come out & repeat some exploit in a sort of song—this taken by the young men and the women dance to it.

During the annual *wani-sapa,* or "fall hunt," hundreds of Lakota worked in large groups to supply the tribe with food for the winter. Group hunting methods included surrounding a herd of buffalo with a circle of fire lit on the grass or stampeding a herd over the edge of a cliff or into a corral made of stones and brush. Women and children participated in the stampeding method, shouting from the sidelines to frighten the buffalo.

Sun Dance

Versions of the Sun Dance are performed by many tribes. The dance is one of the seven sacred rites given to the Lakota by White Buffalo Calf Woman, and its name refers to the fact that the dancers gaze into the sun. U.S. authorities prohibited the Sun Dance from the late 1800s to 1935, and some tribes gave it up completely, but the Lakota revived the practice. The three- or four-day ceremony features fasting, dancing, singing, and drumming. Dancers have skewers inserted through the skin of their chests or backs (arms for women), after which they are tied to a center pole. As they dance, they tear their bodies away from the skewers. They believe this sacrifice pleases the Creator.

CURRENT TRIBAL ISSUES

Social concerns

Ongoing issues facing the Lakota today include the poor economic conditions on reservations and land disputes over the Black Hills. Although they could use the money, the Lakota continue to fight for the return of their traditional lands rather than accept a cash settlement. The people are also divided between traditionalists who wish to retain the old Lakota ways and those who prefer to accept the mainstream American culture, government, and economy.

Alcoholism concerns many Native American tribes. In 2007, activists set up a blockade to stop the flow of alcohol into the Pine Ridge Reservation. Tribal police arrested the protestors, including Duane Martin Sr. of the Strong Heart Civil Rights Movement, and Russell Means, an American Indian Movement activist. Nevertheless, these groups remain determined to tackle the problem of alcoholism. Although the Lakota have set up prevention and treatment programs, substance abuse continues to be a serious problem for the tribe, as well as for many other Native people.

In 2008, the rate of violence on the Standing Rock Sioux Reservation in North Dakota was 8.6 times higher than the national average. The reservation had only nine police officers to patrol 2.3 million acres, so many Dakota and Lakota victims had to wait hours or even days for emergency help. In 2010, President Barack Obama (1961–; served 2009–) signed a Tribal Law and Order Act that may help with some law enforcement reforms. The act gives tribal authorities the ability to lengthen prison sentences, which are currently limited to three years, and gives them access to criminal databases along with strengthening other areas of law enforcement.

Environmental initiatives

Some Lakota reservations are still trying to recover from the loss of their lands and forced relocation that occurred in 1944 as a result of the Pick-Sloan Missouri Basin Program. The thousands of levees and dams that were built along the Missouri River system damaged the ecosystems as well. In 2008, representatives from many tribes in the area, including the Cheyenne River, Spirit Lake, and Yankton Sioux tribes, joined forces with federal, state, and local agencies to develop a plan for Missouri River recovery. This Missouri River Recovery Implementation Committee (MRRIC) hopes to restore the environment and give the tribes more say in the planning process.

Declaring sovereignty

In 2007, the Lakota, using the reasoning that the United States had not upheld its treaty promises, declared themselves the Republic of Lakotah and indicated that they wanted to nullify the treaties. Doing so would put the two nations—the Lakotah and the United States—back to their original positions before any treaties were signed; thus, all the land the Lakota ceded would be theirs again. Since that time, the Lakota have worked on being recognized as an independent nation by other countries around the world and by the United Nations. Russell Means, the leader of this movement, explains his intent:

> We need a renewal of the international indigenous revolution, one that does not ask permission from the invaders of our homelands, one that recalls the original message of our ancestors never to surrender, one that advances our natural right to be free and independent peoples, with international personality and dignity and respect.

Along with this bid for autonomy, the Lakota people are facing serious problems with overcrowding (as many as seventeen people per house), inadequate housing, mold infestation, and poverty on the reservations. To alleviate some of these difficulties, they are considering installing renewable energy sources, growing organic crops, and training health-care workers as well as educating the American public and their own people, preserving their culture, and remaining politically active.

NOTABLE PEOPLE

Sitting Bull (c.1831–1890) was a great chief of the Hunkpapa band of Lakota. Born Tatanka Iyotake, he gained a reputation as a fearless warrior from an early age. As a young man, he adopted an orphan boy, Gall (1840–1894), who became his best friend and partner in battle. In 1863, after seeing the deplorable conditions at the Santee Reservation, Sitting Bull believed only force could prevent white settlers from taking over Lakota territory. A medicine man, he inspired the warriors who defeated Custer in the Battle of the Little Bighorn in 1876, but the following year the chief was forced to retreat to Canada. He surrendered to the United States in 1881 and lived at the Standing Rock Reservation, where he continued to resist efforts to Americanize his people. He was killed two weeks before the Massacre at Wounded Knee in 1890.

Billy Mills (1938–) set a world record in track at the 1964 Olympic Games. He then returned to Pine Ridge Reservation and became a role model to Lakota young people. His story was made into a movie, *Running Brave*. In the early 2000s, he was a spokesperson for Native causes and served as director of the charitable organization, Running Strong for Native American Youth.

Among the many other notable Lakota are tribal leader and warrior Red Cloud (1822–1909), known for resisting American settlement in Lakota territory and later for attempts to secure peaceful relations with the U.S. government; spiritual leader Black Elk (c. 1863–1950), subject of a 1932 book *Black Elk Speaks*; military and tribal leader Crazy Horse (c. 1840–1877), called "Our Strange One" by his people because he kept to himself, wore no war paint, took no scalps, and would not boast of his brave deeds; Mary Brave Bird (also known as Mary Crow Dog; 1953–), who dictated two books about how the American Indian Movement gave meaning to her life—*Lakota Woman* and *Ohitika Woman*; American Indian rights activist Russell Means (1939–); imprisoned activist Leonard Peltier (1944–); and political figure Ben Reifel (1906–1990), the first member of the Sioux Nation to serve in the U.S. Congress.

> "You have always noticed that everything an Indian does is in a circle and that is because the Power of the that the earth is round like a ball, and so are all the stars. The wind, in its greatest power, whirls. Even the seasons form a great circle in their changing, and always come back to where they were. The life of a man is a circle from childhood to childhood, and so is everything where power moves."
>
> —Black Elk, Oglala Lakota

BOOKS

Agonito, Joseph. *Lakota Portraits: Lives of the Legendary Plains People*. Guilford, CT: TwoDot, 2011.

Andersson, Rani-Henrik. *The Lakota Ghost Dance of 1890*. Lincoln: University of Nebraska Press, 2008.

Apple, Francis C., Sr. *Iwahokunkiye Wicoiye: Lakota Language Survival Words Spoken by the Old Ones*. Kyle, SD: Wildhorse Publications, 2007.

Baker, Wendy Beth. *Healing Power of Horses: Lessons from the Lakota Indians*. Irvine, CA: BowTie Press, 2004.

Bray, Kingsley M. *Crazy Horse: A Lakota Life*. Norman: University of Oklahoma Press, 2006.

Brown, Dee. *Bury My Heart at Wounded Knee: An Indian History of the American West.* New York: Holt, Rinehart, and Winston, 1970.

Freedman, Russell. *The Life and Death of Crazy Horse.* New York: Holiday House, 1996.

Greene, Candace S., and Russell Thornton, eds. *The Year the Stars Fell: Lakota Winter Counts at the Smithsonian.* Washington DC: Smithsonian National Museum of the American Indian; Lincoln: University of Nebraska Press, 2007.

Johnsgard, Paul A. *Wind Through the Buffalo Grass: A Lakota Story Cycle.* Lincoln, NE: Plains Chronicles Press, 2008.

Larson, Robert W. *Gall: Lakota War Chief.* Norman: University of Oklahoma Press, 2007.

Lazarus, Edward. *Black Hills/White Justice: The Sioux Nation versus the United States: 1775 to the Present.* New York: HarperCollins, 1991.

Marshall, Joseph M. III. *The Journey of Crazy Horse: A Lakota History.* New York: Viking, 2004.

Marshall, Joseph M. III. *The Lakota Way of Strength and Courage: Lessons in Resilience from the Bow and Arrow.* Boulder, CO: Sounds True, 2012.

Marshall, Joseph M. III. *The Lakota Way: Stories and Lessons for Living.* New York: Viking Compass, 2001.

Marshall, Joseph M. III. *To You We Shall Return: Lessons about Our Planet from the Lakota.* New York, NY: Sterling Ethos, 2010.

Nelson, S.D. *Greet the Dawn: The Lakota Way.* Pierre, SD: South Dakota State Historical Society Press, 2012.

Palmer, Jessica Dawn. *The Dakota Peoples: A History of the Dakota, Lakota and Nakota through 1863.* Jefferson, NC: McFarland, 2008.

Peltier, Leonard. *Prison Writings: My Life Is My Sun Dance.* New York: St. Martin's, 2000.

Petrillo, Larissa, Lupe Trejo, and Melda Trejo. *Being Lakota: Identity and Tradition on Pine Ridge Reservation.* Lincoln: University of Nebraska Press, 2007.

Reinhardt, Akim D. *Ruling Pine Ridge: Oglala Lakota Politics from the IRA to Wounded Knee.* Lubbock: Texas Tech University Press, 2007.

Rzeczkowski, Frank. *The Lakota Sioux.* New York: Chelsea House, 2011.

Valandra, Edward Charles. *Not Without Our Consent: Lakota Resistance to Termination, 1950–59.* Urbana: University of Illinois Press, 2006.

Walker, James R. *Lakota Myth.* Lincoln: University of Nebraska Press, 2006.

PERIODICALS

Win, Wambli Sina. "The Ultimate Expression of Faith, the Lakota Sun Dance." *Native American Times.,* July 4, 2011. Available online from http://www.nativetimes.com/index.php?option=com_content&view=article&id=5657:the-ultimate-expression-of-faith-the-lakota-sun-dance&catid=46&Itemid=22 (accessed on July 4, 2011).

WEB SITES

"Birth a New Economy: *Wicohan*—Economic Sustainability and Self-Reliance." *Lakota People's Law Project.* http://lakotapeopleslawproject.org/strategic-objectives/birth-a-new-economy/ (accessed on July 4, 2011).

Cheyenne River Sioux Tribe: Four Bands of the Lakota Nation. http://www.sioux.org/ (accessed on July 4, 2011).

"History—Incident at Wounded Knee." *U.S. Marshals Service.* http://www.usmarshals.gov/history/wounded-knee/index.html (accessed on July 4, 2011).

Hollabaugh, Mark. "Brief History of the Lakota People." *Normandale Community College.* http://faculty.normandale.edu/~physics/Hollabaugh/Lakota/BriefHistory.htm (accessed on July 4, 2011).

"Lakota, Dakota, Nakota—The Great Sioux Nation." *Legends of America.* http://www.legendsofamerica.com/na-sioux.html (accessed on July 4, 2011).

"Lakota Page: The Great Sioux Nation." *Ancestry.com.* http://freepages.genealogy.rootsweb.ancestry.com/~nativeamericangen/page6.html (accessed on July 4, 2011).

"Lakota-Teton Sioux." *Wisdom of the Elders.* http://www.wisdomoftheelders.org/program203.html (accessed on July 4, 2011).

Lower Brule Sioux. http://www.lbst.org/ (accessed on July 4, 2011).

"Massacre at Wounded Knee, 1890." *EyeWitness to History.* http://www.eyewitnesstohistory.com/knee.htm (accessed on July 4, 2011).

Means, Russell. "The Next Chapter." *Republic of Lakotah.* June 4, 2011. http://www.republicoflakotah.com/2011/the-next-chapter/ (accessed on July 4, 2011).

Medicine Crow, Joe. "Introduction to Native Spirit: The Sun Dance Way." *World Wisdom.* http://www.worldwisdom.com/public/viewpdf/default.aspx?article-title=Intro_by_Joe_Medicine_Crow_to_Native_Spirit_The_Sun_Dance_Way.pdf (accessed on July 4, 2011).

National Museum of the American Indian. "Central Plains." *Smithsonian.* http://americanindian.si.edu/searchcollections/results.aspx?regid=58 (accessed on July 4, 2011).

"Overview of the Pine Ridge Reservation: Home to the Oglala Sioux." *AAA Native Arts.* http://www.aaanativearts.com/pine_ridge_reservation.htm (accessed on July 4, 2011).

"Pine Ridge Camp Pictures." *National Geographic.* http://photography.nationalgeographic.com/photography/photos/photo-camp-pine-ridge/ (accessed on July 4, 2011).

Redish, Laura, and Orrin Lewis. "Sioux Culture and History." *Native Languages of the Americas.* http://www.native-languages.org/dakota_culture.htm (accessed on July 4, 2011).

Rosebud Sioux Tribe. http://www.rosebudsiouxtribe-nsn.gov/ (accessed on July 4, 2011).

Standing Rock Sioux Tribe. http://www.standingrock.org/ (accessed on July 4, 2011).

Sultzman, Lee. "AIM, Pine Ridge & the FBI." *First Nations Issues of Consequence.* http://www.dickshovel.com/Aim.Pine.html (accessed on July 5, 2011).

"Teton Sioux Indian Tribe History." *Access Genealogy.* http://www.accessgenealogy.com/native/tribes/siouan/tetonhist.htm (accessed on July 4, 2011).

"Wounded Knee." *Last of the Independent.* http://www.lastoftheindependents.com/wounded.htm (accessed on July 4, 2011).

The Wounded Knee Museum. http://www.woundedkneemuseum.org/ (accessed on July 4, 2011).

Sioux Nations: Nakota

Name

Nakota (pronounced *nah-KO-tah*) is the tribe's name for itself and may mean "friends" or "allies." It comes from the Yankton word *Nakhota,* sometimes translated as "alliance of friends." Another meaning for the name is "those who consider themselves kindred." The two Nakota bands are known as the Yankton and the Yanktonai. *Ihanktunwan* (Yankton) means "end village," and *Ihanktunwanna* (Yanktonai) means "little end village."

The Sioux tribes (Dakota, Lakota, and Nakota) were once given the name *nadowe-is-iw-ug,* which means "little adders (snakes)" by their enemies, the Ojibway (see entry). The French mispronounced the Ojibway word as *nadewisou* and shortened it to "Sioux," the name by which the tribes are collectively known. Because the name was intended as an insult, many of the Nakota dislike being called Sioux.

Location

Both the Yankton and Yanktonai bands of Nakota inhabited the region near present-day Mille Lacs, Minnesota, in the seventeenth century. They traveled westward into parts of modern North Dakota and South Dakota and Iowa over the course of the eighteenth century. Today, many live for at least part of the year on the Yankton Reservation in South Dakota, returning to live in urban areas in South Dakota and Iowa for the rest of the year. Some live with the Lakota people on the Standing Rock and Crow Creek reservations in South Dakota, at the Devil's Lake Reservation in North Dakota, and at the Fort Peck Reservation in Montana.

Population

In the early 1800s, there were about 4,000 Nakota. In the 1990s, Nakota-speakers were no longer counted separately from the Sioux; there were likely at least 10,000 Nakota at that time. In the 2010 U.S. Census, 112,176 people reported that they were Sioux, with a total of 170,110 people claiming some Sioux heritage.

Language family

Siouan.

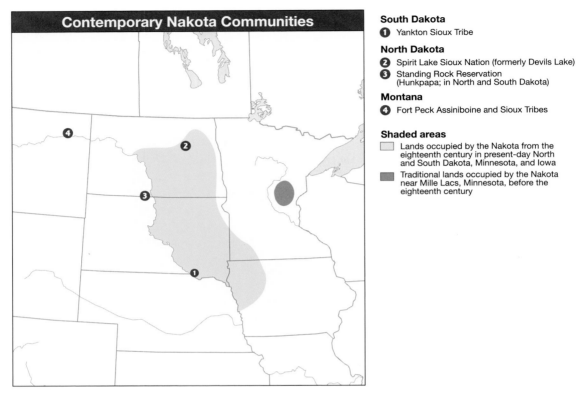

Contemporary Nakota Communities

South Dakota
1. Yankton Sioux Tribe

North Dakota
2. Spirit Lake Sioux Nation (formerly Devils Lake)
3. Standing Rock Reservation
   (Hunkpapa; in North and South Dakota)

Montana
4. Fort Peck Assiniboine and Sioux Tribes

Shaded areas
Lands occupied by the Nakota from the eighteenth century in present-day North and South Dakota, Minnesota, and Iowa

Traditional lands occupied by the Nakota near Mille Lacs, Minnesota, before the eighteenth century

A map of contemporary Nakota communities. MAP BY XNR PRODUCTIONS. CENGAGE LEARNING, GALE. REPRODUCED BY PERMISSION OF GALE, A PART OF CENGAGE LEARNING.

Origins and group affiliations

The Nakota and the Lakota (see entry) peoples were originally part of the Dakota (see entry) tribe; the Nakota were the smallest of the three divisions. The Yankton, Yanktonai, and a third group, the Assiniboin (*uh-SIN-uh-boin;* see entry), called themselves *Nakoda* or (*Nakota*). The Assiniboin left in the sixteenth century and moved north into Canada and west into Montana. The Nakota divided into three bands: Yankton, Upper Yanktonai, and Lower Yanktonai. They fought mostly with the Cree and Ojibway (see entries) in Minnesota but were on good terms with neighboring tribes after their move to the prairies.

The Nakota were the only one of the three Sioux tribes who never officially took up arms against the United States. In spite of the friendly relations between them, the Nakota were forced to give up more than 13 million acres to Americans. On the reservations, the Nakota people managed to retain many of their traditions.

HISTORY

Driven from their homeland

During the 1600s, the Nakota, as part of the larger Dakota tribe that also included the Lakota, occupied the area near Mille Lacs in what is now Minnesota. Explorers in north-central Minnesota noted their location on a map in 1683. In 1700, the French trader-explorer Pierre-Charles leSueur (c. 1657–1704) encountered the Sioux near a quarry in Minnesota, where they may have been collecting stone to make their sacred pipes.

In response to hostility from nearby Cree and Ojibway, the three Sioux groups (Dakota, Lakota, Nakota) moved south and west in the 1700s. The Nakota settled in a region east of the Missouri River in South Dakota. They built their villages along the Missouri and controlled the areas around the Big Sioux, Des Moines, and James Rivers.

Friendship with Europeans

Because of their control of the rivers, the Nakota were ideally situated for trading furs with the French. They quickly became familiar with European ways and enjoyed the goods they acquired in trade.

Their relationship with the French ended with the Louisiana Purchase of 1803, when the United States acquired a vast parcel of land from France, including Nakota territory. The next year, President Thomas Jefferson (1743–1826; served 1801–09) sent Meriwether Lewis (1774–1809) and William Clark (1770–1838) to explore the region. Their orders were to make friends with the Sioux and enlist them as partners in a new American trading system. The Nakota people were the first Sioux encountered by the Lewis and Clark expedition.

Lewis and Clark found the Nakota to be very friendly. They admired their orderly camps and their handsome cone-shaped tepees. They passed out inexpensive presents and designated one of the men as "first chief" in charge of relations with the U.S. government. In spite of the American's insensitivity to their tribal government and the Nakota's displeasure with the presents, the tribe accepted the Americans' offer of friendship.

Important Dates

1700: Pierre-Charles leSueur encounters the Sioux.

1804: Lewis and Clark visit Nakota tribes in the upper Missouri River region and find them friendly.

1858: The Yankton give all lands, except for a reservation on the Missouri River, to the United States.

1865: The Yanktonai sign a peace treaty with the U.S. government and give up lands.

1887–90: Reservation lands are divided into individual allotments (plots).

1932: A tribal constitution is adopted.

1961: Tribal constitution is amended; the Yankton Sioux Tribal Business and Claims Committee becomes the governing body at the Yankton Reservation.

Land giveaways begin

Although the Nakota were friendly toward the Americans, other tribes were not, and the Nakota joined American soldiers in fighting these tribes. In 1830, in an effort to make peace in the area and keep the warring tribes apart, the Yankton band agreed to give up a large piece of their land—about 2.2 million acres—to the U.S. government.

Trading posts sprang up throughout Nakota territory. Visitors came from the East to travel in steamboats along the Missouri River. When they returned home, they spread the word about the wonderful farming land there. Settlers flocked in, and pressure grew for the government to move the Nakota out of the way and place them on a reservation. The Nakota had to decide whether to go peacefully or join the other Sioux tribes in resisting. The Nakota chose peace.

In 1858, more than 11 million acres of Yankton land were turned over the United States in exchange for $1.6 million in money and services to be paid out in installments over fifty years. The tribe retained 430,000 acres of reservation land between the Missouri River and Chouteau Creek in southern South Dakota.

On the reservations

Other Sioux tribes were furious that the Yankton had given up the land. After the Yankton ceded the land in 1830, the Yanktonai claimed ownership of the property and said they had merely loaned it to the Yankton. The Yankton were determined to keep the peace, however. They again displayed their loyalty to the United States in 1862 by refusing to join their kinsmen in the Sioux Wars against settlers in Minnesota. (For more information on the Sioux Wars, see Dakota entry.)

The Yanktonai fought until 1865, when they signed a peace treaty and gave up their lands to the United States. The people were split between the Crow Creek, Devils Lake, and Standing Rock reservations in the Dakotas and the Fort Peck Reservation in Montana.

The Yankton settled on their reservation in 1859, and government agents were sent to teach them farming and ranching methods. Although the Yankton had been friendly to the Americans, many early photos show armed soldiers guarding the people on the reservations. The army also distributed food rations. Because the Native peoples were forbidden from trading or selling food or other goods, they became dependent on government support. Some officers took advantage of this to control the tribes by withholding supplies.

Allotment period

In 1887, Congress passed the General Allotment Act (also known as the Dawes Act). The purpose of this act was to make Native peoples on reservations assimilate (become like American society). It also made vast areas of Native lands available to settlers. The act divided reservation lands into individual farms ranging from 40 to 160 acres in size, to be assigned to Native families. The land left over was sold to settlers. This division of land meant that tribes who had always owned their land communally (as a group) were expected to work on their own separate farms, responsible for themselves. This was a complete reversal of traditional ways.

For the Nakota, the process was completed over the next three years, and by the time it was over, the 435,000-acre Yankton Reservation in South Dakota was reduced to 40,000 acres. For the next several decades, the U.S. government encouraged Native people to abandon their traditional culture. The government hoped that the Yankton and Yanktonai would become productive farmers and ranchers, but the federal policy did not work. Unable to support themselves, many Nakota left the reservation and moved to urban centers in the Great Plains and the West.

Nakota in the twentieth century and beyond

By the 1930s, the U.S. government realized that its policies toward reservation Indians were ineffective. The Indian Reorganization Act (IRA) of 1934 was passed, which encouraged the tribes to adopt written constitutions and establish their own governments. The new tribal governments would be under federal supervision. The Yankton refused to accept the terms of the IRA, and since then, they have been slighted when government funds are being distributed to Native nations. In their search for ways to make a living, the Nakota finally achieved considerable success when they opened the Fort Randall Casino in 1991.

In the early twenty-first century, the Nakota goals and lifestyle are best expressed in these lines from the Vision Statement of the Alexis Nakota Sioux Nation in Alberta, Canada:

> We will walk in both worlds without compromise. We will educate ourselves holistically while protecting the integrity of our inherent and Treaty Rights. Our right to lands, independence and freedom. This right … will exist throughout eternity. As long as the sun shines, the grass grows and the rivers flow our treaties will be sacred.

RELIGION

The Nakota shared many religious customs with the Dakota and Lakota. They worshipped the Great Spirit, *Wakan Tanka,* and performed the Sun Dance. All three Sioux groups conducted the ceremony of the sacred pipe, which was originally taught to the Sioux by a holy woman they called White Buffalo Calf Woman. The Nakota performed the ceremony in a sweat lodge. It began with a period of fasting (not eating or drinking) and consisted of prayers to the Great Spirit for cleansing and guidance. Successful participants of the ritual were rewarded with a dream vision.

Other religious ceremonies that all Sioux groups conducted included the Vision Cry, the Ghost Keeper, the Buffalo Chant, and the Foster-Parent Chant. The most important Nakota ritual was the Mystery Dance, a chance for medicine men to demonstrate their power (see "Healing practices").

The Sacred Pipe ceremony was discouraged by Christian missionaries who arrived in the late 1830s, but many Yakton performed it in secret. In recent years, the ceremony has been held openly on the Yankton Reservation, where some residents also practice the Peyote (pronounced *pay-OH-tee*) Ceremony. In this ceremony, people consume peyote, a druglike substance obtained from cactus; in the trance state peyote induces, users hope to experience visions with spiritual meaning.

By the early 2000s, approximately 90 percent of the population had Christian backgrounds, with the majority being Catholic. At the same time, many people also retain their Native customs and beliefs.

LANGUAGE

Originally, the Dakota, Lakota, and Nakota spoke the same language, but as the Lakota and Nakota moved away from the Dakota, each tribe began to speak its own dialect (form of the language). People from all three tribes could still understand one another because the dialects remained similar. In modern times, five divisions of the original Dakota language exist: Dakota (Santee-Sisseton), Dakota (Yankton-Yanktonai), Lakota (Teton), Nakoda (Assiniboin) and Nakoda (Stoney). The Nakota, or Nakoda, language is also called *Hohe* and is tied to the Assiniboin language. The Nakoda language is spoken in the traditional territories of Saskatchewan and Montana.

Like many Native American languages, Nakota nouns are often more than just names for objects. They describe the object and have special

The Yankton Sioux and the Great Red Pipestone Quarry

The famous writer and painter George Catlin (1796–1872) traveled through Yankton Sioux country in the early 1800s. He heard tales of a quarry where a fantastic kind of red clay stone (called pipestone) could be found, and he decided to see it for himself. As he came upon the area, his party found "great difficulty in approaching, being stopped by several hundred Native Americans who ordered us back and threatened us very hard, saying 'that no white man had ever been to it, and that none should ever go.'" Catlin painted the people at the quarry, wrote about his findings, and sent a sample of the red stone to the nation's capital to be analyzed. The new stone was called *catlinite* in his honor.

The poet Henry Wadsworth Longfellow (1807–1882) heard about the pipestone and mentioned it in his 1855 poem, "The Song of Hiawatha." What Catlin and Longfellow described was the Red Pipestone Quarry in Minnesota, the place, according to Sioux oral tradition, where the Great Spirit sent a flood that cleansed the earth and left behind only the blood of the Sioux ancestors in the form of red pipestone.

The quarry was sacred to the Sioux. Historians say that many different tribes came to it in the summer to quarry stone for use in making their sacred pipes. The Dakota ceded (gave away) the pipestone quarry in a treaty signed with the U.S. government in 1851. The Yankton objected to the giveaway. When they signed over their lands to the United States in 1865, they insisted that 648 acres in Minnesota be handed over to them as the Pipestone Reservation. The tribe sold Pipestone Reservation in 1929 on the condition that it could have access to the stone quarry. In 1937, the land was designated a national monument. The Upper Midwest Indian Cultural Center now located on the site preserves the ancient craft of pipemaking.

meanings. For example, a newborn baby is called *waken yeja,* which means "sacred little one." The Nakota word for water, *mini,* means "my life." When Natives first saw the horse, many tribes called it a "mysterious dog." It was also known as "big-grass-eater-dog-that-runs-on-the-prairie." Descriptive words such as these are chosen with care. The Pulitzer Prize-winning Kiowa novelist Scott Momaday explains:

> At the heart of the American Indian oral tradition is a deep and unconditional belief in the efficacy [power to produce an effect] of language. Words are intrinsically powerful. They are magical. By means of words can one … quiet the raging weather, bring forth the harvest, ward off evil, rid the body of sickness and pain, subdue an enemy, capture the heart of a lover, live in the proper way, and venture beyond death.

Nakota Words

ade	"father"
Dayaya u?	"Are you well?"
Dokenya u?	"How are you?"
gaga	"to make"
hoga	"fish"
ina	"mother"
Mak?u	"Give me"
ni	"life"
peda	"fire"
pinamiya	"thank you"
sunkawakan	"horse"
Tin U!	"Come in!"
washuya	"cookies"

GOVERNMENT

Nakota bands were governed by a council, which consisted of a hereditary chief (the position passed from father to son or another related heir) and other important leaders and warriors from the clans. (A clan is a group of related families who trace their heritage back to a common ancestor.) Once the Nakota people were on reservations, federal agents appointed chiefs to be in charge of distributing goods and money. Agents also set up a tribal police force, formed a new Nakota band whose members were people of mixed blood, and generally oversaw all aspects of Native life. Meanwhile, the Nakota's old chief, Struck-by-the-Ree, encouraged his people to accept this government interference and adapt to American ways.

In the 1930s, the government returned control of their own affairs to the tribes. Congress passed the Indian Reorganization Act (IRA) in 1934. This act allowed the tribe to write a new constitution under the supervision of the federal government. If the Native nation agreed, the people became eligible to receive federal money for development. The tribe at the Yankton Reservation had already adopted their own constitution in 1932 and decided to remain independent.

In the early twenty-first century, the Yankton Reservation is governed by the Yankton Sioux Tribal Business and Claims Committee, whose members are elected to two-year terms. The committee looks for ways to make the reservation an attractive place for members of the tribe to live and work.

ECONOMY

To their early hunting-gathering economy, the Nakota added fur trade with the French and then the Americans in the 1700s and 1800s. They received blankets, cloth, beads, clothing, cooking utensils, tools, and guns in exchange for pelts.

In the early days on the reservations, the Nakota continued many of their old hunting-gathering ways. When there was not enough food, they went off the reservation to hunt buffalo. They slowly adopted

The Legends

Nakota elders told stories to pass on tribal history and teach the young. In this story, Zitkala-Sa explains how much she enjoyed inviting neighbors for dinner when she was a child, knowing that afterward she would enjoy the legends they told.

> I was always glad when the sun hung low in the west, for then my mother sent me to invite the neighboring old men and women to eat supper with us. Running all the way to the wigwams, I halted shyly at the entrances. Sometimes I stood long moments without saying a word. It was not any fear that made me so dumb when out upon such a happy errand; nor was it that I wished to withhold the invitation, for it was all I could do to observe this very proper silence. But it was a sensing of the atmosphere, to assure myself that I should not hinder other plans. My mother used to say to me, as I was almost bounding away for the old people: "Wait a moment before you invite any one. If other plans are being discussed, do not interfere, but go elsewhere."
>
> The old folks knew the meaning of my pauses; and often they coaxed my confidence by asking, "What do you seek, little granddaughter?"
>
> "My mother says you are to come to our tepee this evening," I instantly exploded, and breathed the freer afterwards.

> "Yes, yes, gladly, gladly I shall come!" each replied. Rising at once and carrying their blankets across one shoulder, they flocked leisurely from their various wigwams toward our dwelling.
>
> My mission done, I ran back, skipping and jumping with delight....
>
> At the arrival of our guests I sat close to my mother, and did not leave her side without first asking her consent. I ate my supper in quiet, listening patiently to the talk of the old people, wishing all the time that they would begin the stories I loved best. At last, when I could not wait any longer, I whispered in my mother's ear, "Ask them to tell an Iktomi story, mother."
>
> Soothing my impatience, my mother said aloud, "My little daughter is anxious to hear your legends." By this time all were through eating, and the evening was fast deepening into twilight.
>
> As each in turn began to tell a legend, I pillowed my head in my mother's lap; and lying flat upon my back, I watched the stars as they peeped down upon me, one by one.

SOURCE: Zitkala-Sa. *Impressions of an Indian Childhood.* Washington: Hayworth Publishing House, 1921. Available online at: http://digital.library.upenn.edu/women/zitkala-sa/stories/impressions.html (accessed on September 21, 2007).

European-American ways of farming, but they faced obstacles such as frequent floods, drought, plagues of grasshoppers, and blizzards. Their economy gradually came to rely heavily on farming, but in the 1920s, prices for farm goods fell, and many Yankton could no longer afford to farm. More economic and natural disasters followed. People sold off their plots of land and moved away to work in the non-Native economy. The traditional Nakota way of life seemed to have disappeared.

In the 1960s, the federal government expanded federal funding for Native programs, and some money found its way to the Yankton Reservation. Efforts to modernize the reservation economy using those funds included an electronics industry in the 1960s and the construction of a pork-processing plant in the 1970s. These ventures worked for a time but eventually failed. More people left the reservations in the 1960s to find jobs in cities and towns.

The economy improved when the Yankton Reservation introduced gaming in 1991. The casino was an immediate success in terms of jobs and money, and some people returned to live on the reservation. By the early 2000s, the major employers were the casino, the Indian Health Service, the Bureau of Indian Affairs, the Marty Indian School (Marty is the city in South Dakota where tribal headquarters is located), and the tribal government. Agriculture, fisheries, construction, and tourism also supplied jobs and income.

The Alexis Nakota Sioux Nation operated a variety of businesses including a casino, retail and hospitality businesses, a land management corporation, and forestry. They also received government support for their oil and gas well servicing company and the purchase of new rigs.

DAILY LIFE

Education

Because the Nakota believed children had a close connection with the spirit world, they treated them respectfully. Children were allowed to explore, and parents did not set rules for them except to keep them safe. Adults encouraged children to be individuals. No child was forced to learn something that did not interest him or her; they each developed skills based on their interests. If a child showed a talent in a certain area, adults with expertise in that area helped the child become more proficient. At age seven, boys and girls were taught separately by their aunts and uncles.

Native American boys assemble in front of a government school at the Yankton Sioux Agency in South Dakota in 1890. © NORTH WIND/NORTH WIND PICTURE ARCHIVES. ALL RIGHTS RESERVED.

The first missionary arrived on the Yankton Reservation in 1839, and the first of many religious schools sprang up shortly thereafter. Their goal was to discourage traditional practices and coax the people into accepting white ways. The federal government opened a boarding school in 1882 in nearby Greenwood, South Dakota, and it operated for nearly forty years. School officials removed children from their homes and taught them reading, writing, and arithmetic for half the school day. The other half day, girls learned homemaking skills, and boys were taught to farm and raise livestock. Children were punished for speaking their native language.

In modern times, the Yankton operate their own boarding high school and junior college and teach Nakota culture in buildings originally established by missionaries to erase traditional Nakota ways and beliefs.

Food

The Yankton and Yanktonai adjusted their diet according to the different environments they found as they moved. While living in Minnesota, they built dugout tree-trunk canoes and practiced spearfishing in the nearby lakes and rivers. They also hunted large game, such as moose and deer, and grew grains and vegetables, including corn, squash, and pumpkins.

After they moved to the Great Plains and later acquired horses, the Nakota adopted a Plains lifestyle. They hunted the buffalo that became the major source of food and raw materials for clothing and shelter. They continued to grow some crops, especially corn and squash, and rounded out their diet by gathering wild plums, cherries, and edible roots.

Buildings

In Minnesota, the Nakota lived in houses covered with bark or in small earth-covered lodges. When they moved to the Great Plains to follow the buffalo herd, they built portable buffalo-skin tepees that they painted various colors and sometimes decorated with drawings that recorded special events in their lives.

Healing practices

An important Nakota ceremony was the Mystery Dance of the medicine men. Healers used it to demonstrate their *waka* powers. As the men danced, they struck each other with their medicine bags. The person who was hit fell to the ground to show the other dancer's power, and spectators cheered. New people were initiated during the dance. One of the more experienced healers threw his bag at the novice, who fell to the ground, seemingly unconscious. The older healer then restored him to consciousness.

A person received his medicine either through a revelation or by buying it. He then tested it to be certain it worked by tying a small bag of it to the wrist or moccasin of one of his relatives. If this relative survived in battle, it proved the medicine was powerful. Afterward, the owner of the medicine gave a Sacred Feast for other medicine men and, occasionally, their families. Each attendee brought a large wooden plate that the host piled with food. Following ritual prayers and songs, the host sang rapidly while his guests ate as quickly as possible, emptying their plates.

A warrior hung his medicine bag outside his lodge on a tripod of decorated poles. He covered the bag with a small red blanket or white wolfskin.

CUSTOMS

Birth and naming

In some families, the grandmother is present at the birth to greet each child. When a child is four months old, the parents hold a gathering where family members welcome and offer prayers for the baby. A pipe carrier sends these prayers to God and his helpers. Some children are given spirit names at this ceremony, but others receive theirs later. A spirit name is the name a person is known by in the spirit world. The Nakota believe that because children are pure, they have a closer connection to the spirit world and often receive important teachings and stories.

Puberty

When a girl reached puberty, all her female relatives gathered to honor her. They also taught her womanly duties and responsibilities. She learned how to behave during her "moon time" (menstrual period), when she was expected to avoid attending ceremonies and gatherings.

Boys learned survival skills from their uncles, who also taught them to be honorable and stay on the Red Road back toward the Creator. Some boys went on their vision quests before they reached manhood. For the Nakota, age did not matter in becoming a man. Men proved themselves as hunters or warriors. Taking part in the Sun Dance was also proof of manhood.

Festivals and ceremonies

The Round Dance was a healing ceremony that became a social dance. The Nakota say that the dead join in the Round Dance, which is usually held in the winter. This dance reminds people that their relatives are always with them. Everyone joins hands and forms a circle; people dance clockwise, moving up and down like the Northern Lights. (The Northern Lights are said to be the ancestors dancing.) The drummer and the singers sit in the center of the circle. The drumbeat symbolizes the heartbeat of the community, and all members move as one to show their unity.

The traditional Sioux religious ceremonies are still held; these include the Sun Dance, peyote rituals, and the ceremony of the Sacred Pipe (see "Religion"). They are accompanied by elaborate feasts requiring days of preparation. Large quantities of food and gifts are distributed for people to take home after these feasts. Now instead of ponies and guns, the gifts might include the beautiful star quilts and handcrafted beaded jewelry made by Yankton women.

The Yankton also host large powwows, or celebrations at which the main activities are traditional singing and dancing. In modern times, the singers and dancers at powwows usually come from many different tribes.

CURRENT TRIBAL ISSUES

The Yankton Sioux Tribe was the subject of a Supreme Court decision in 1998 in a complicated case called *South Dakota v. Yankton Sioux Tribe et al.* The case arose after local officials planned to open a solid waste landfill on land that had been part of the 1858 reservation but was later sold to a non-Native. The tribe objected, claiming that asbestos, lime and wastewater sludge, industrial waste, oil, lead-acid batteries, and other toxic waste would endanger their health and the health of their livestock. The tribe also believed that it should have a say in whether such a landfill was built "within the territorial boundaries" of the Yankton Reservation.

The case that went to the Supreme Court did not involve the issue of the landfill. Rather, the issue that was argued was whether the 1858 reservation still existed. The state of South Dakota argued that the reservation ceased to exist when tribal members accepted the 1887 allotment act that divided up their 430,000 acres and sold the leftover land to settlers. The Supreme Court decided that the lands that were sold were indeed no longer part of a reservation, but it refused to make a decision on whether a reservation now existed.

Meanwhile, construction on the site went forward, The Yankton Sioux continue to fight against its location on the lands they consider their own. The court decision gave the state control of the landfill. The Department of Justice indicated that the remaining acreage of the reservation, including extensive nonmember fee lands, is still Indian country. The case against the landfill reached the U.S. Supreme Court in 2011.

Another case where tribal authority has been challenged by the government is in Alberta, Canada. In 2011, the Stony Nakoda Nations were trying to block the installation of a sour gas pipeline near their Eden Valley reserve (the Canadian name for reservation). Sour gas, a form of natural gas, has a high sulfur content that gives it a rotten smell. The sulfur compounds are very harmful and can even be deadly. The Stony Nakoda Nations passed a law forbidding the pipelines within 1 mile (1.5 kilometers) of their property. The province of Alberta fought it, and the initial decision was that the First Nations exceeded their lawmaking ability. The Stony Nakoda have appealed, but the province of Alberta says that First Nations have no right to interfere with provincial government projects.

NOTABLE PEOPLE

Gertrude Simmons Bonnin (1876–1938), also known as Zitkala-Sa or Red Bird, was a writer, educator, musician, activist, and feminist. She was born at the Yankton Sioux Agency in South Dakota and graduated from Earlham College in Richmond, Indiana. An accomplished musician and writer, Bonnin devoted her life to Native reform issues, including speaking out for the employment of Natives in the Indian Service, the preservation of accurate Native history, and citizenship for all Native Americans. Her book, *Old Indian Legends,* was published in 1901. One of her final undertakings was composing an Native American opera with William F. Hanson titled *Sun Dance.*

Other notable Nakota include Yankton ethnologist, linguist, and novelist Ella Cara Deloria (1889–1971); Yankton writer Vine Deloria Jr. (1933–2005); and Yankton artist and professor Oscar Howe (1915–1983).

BOOKS

Chapman, Abraham, ed. *Literature of the American Indians: Views and Interpretations.* New York: New American Library, 1975.

Clow, Richmond L., ed. *The Sioux in South Dakota History: A Twentieth-Century Reader.* Pierre, S.D.: South Dakota State Historical Society Press, 2007.

Dolan, Edward F. *American Indian Wars.* Brookfield, CT: Millbrook Press, 2003.

Farnell, Brenda. *Do You See What I Mean? Plains Indian Sign Talk and the Embodiment of Action.* Lincoln: University of Nebraska Press, 2009.

Gagnon, Gregory O. *Culture and Customs of the Sioux Indians.* Westport, CT: Greenwood, 2011.

Hedren, Paul L. *Great Sioux War Orders of Battle: How the United States Army Waged War on the Northern Plains, 1876–1877.* Norman, OK: Arthur H. Clark Company, 2011.

Maroukis, Thomas Constantine. *Peyote and the Yankton Sioux.* Norman: University of Oklahoma Press, 2004.

Palmer, Jessica Dawn. *The Dakota Peoples: A History of the Dakota, Lakota and Nakota through 1863.* Jefferson, NC: McFarland, 2008.

Sisson, Richard, Christian Zacher, and Andrew Cayton, eds. *The American Midwest: An Interpretive Encyclopedia.* Bloomington: Indiana University Press, 2007.

Sprague, DonovinArleigh. *Standing Rock Sioux.* Charleston, SC: Arcadia, 2004.

Zitkala-Sa. *American Indian Stories.* West Stockbridge, CT: Hard Press, 2006.

Zitkala-Sa. *Impressions of an Indian Childhood.*Kila, MN: Kessinger Publishing, 2004. Available online at http://etext.virginia.edu/etcbin/toccer-new2?id=ZitImpr.sgm&images=images/modeng&data=/texts/english/modeng/parsed&tag=public&part=2&division=div1(accessed on September 21, 2006).

Zitkala-Sa. *Old Indian Legends: Retold by Zitkala--Sa.* Paris: Adamant Media Corporation, 2006.

Zitkala-Sa, Cathy N. Davidson, and Ada Norris. *American Indian Stories, Legends, and Other Writings.* New York: Penguin, 2003.

Zontek, Ken. *Buffalo Nation: American Indian Efforts to Restore the Bison.* Lincoln: University of Nebraska Press, 2007.

WEB SITES

Alexis Nakota Sioux Nation. http://www.alexisnakotasioux.com/ (accessed on June 12, 2011).

Dakota-Lakota-Nakota Human Rights Advocacy Coalition. http://www.dlncoalition.org/dln_coalition/dln_coalition.htm (accessed on June 12, 2011).

"Dakota Language/Nakona Language Lessons." *Fort Peck Indian Community College.* http://fpcctalkindian.nativeweb.org/ (accessed on June12, 2011).

"Lewis & Clark: Yankton Sioux Indians (Nakota)." *National Geographic.* http://www.nationalgeographic.com/lewisandclark/record_tribes_019_2_8.html (accessed on June 12, 2011).

"Pine Ridge Camp Pictures." *National Geographic.* http://photography.nationalgeographic.com/photography/photos/photo-camp-pine-ridge/ (accessed on June 12, 2011).

Redish, Laura, and Orrin Lewis. "Sioux Culture and History." *Native Languages of the Americas.* http://www.native-languages.org/dakota_culture.htm (accessed on June 12, 2011).

"Yankton Sioux." *Wisdom of the Elders.* http://www.wisdomoftheelders.org/program202.html (accessed on June 12, 2011).

Wichita

Name

The name Wichita (pronounced *WITCH-i-taw*) comes from a Choctaw word and means "big arbor" or "big platform," referring to the grass arbors the Wichita built. The Spanish called the people *Jumano,* meaning "drummer," after the Wichita custom of summoning the tribe to council using a drum. The Siouan tribes called them the Black Pawnee because of their skin color and because they are related to the Pawnee. They call themselves *Kitikitish* or *Tawehash.*

Location

In 1541, the Wichita were living in western Oklahoma, but they were pushed south to the Red River area on the Oklahoma-Texas border. Today, most Wichita live in Oklahoma, on or near the Wichita and Affiliated Tribes Reservation.

Population

In 1780, there were about 3,200 Wichita. In 1910, they numbered about 318. In the 1990 U.S. Census, 1,241 people identified themselves as Wichita. By 2000, that number had risen slightly to 1,445, and 2,047 people claimed to be at least part Wichita. In 2011, the Oklahoma Indian Affairs Commission reported a tribal enrollment of 2,564 for the Wichita and Affiliated Tribes.

Language family

Caddoan.

Origins and group affiliations

The Wichita were part of the Caddo (see entry) people who lived in the Oklahoma region for 3,500 years before they encountered Europeans in 1541. The Wichita broke off from the Caddo sometime before this contact to find better farmland. They traveled north to establish their tribe on the Arkansas River in present-day Kansas. The Pawnee (see entry), an offshoot of the Wichita, continued farther north to the North and South Platte Rivers.

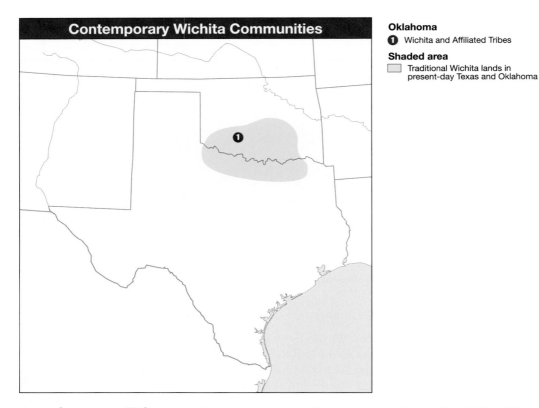

Contemporary Wichita Communities

Oklahoma
1 Wichita and Affiliated Tribes

Shaded area
Traditional Wichita lands in present-day Texas and Oklahoma

A map of contemporary Wichita communities. MAP BY XNR PRODUCTIONS. CENGAGE LEARNING, GALE. REPRODUCED BY PERMISSION OF GALE, A PART OF CENGAGE LEARNING.

A group of Caddoan speakers formed a confederacy, or a group of allied tribes. Nine of the tribes who formed the confederacy have been identified, but the only ones still in existence are the Wichita and a few Waco people. The Wichita were most strongly allied with the Waco and Kichai and were enemies with the Apache and Osage (see entry). In the early twenty-first century, they share a reservation with the Caddo and Delaware (see entry).

The Wichita were a small, peaceful tribe who farmed for centuries in the fertile river valleys of Kansas. Although they acquired horses in the 1700s, they continued to be known as farmers and did not fully adopt the Plains buffalo-hunting culture as other tribes did. They were famous for their unusual dwellings. The Wichita are probably best known today for lending their name to a city in Kansas and to several counties, hills, and rivers in Texas and Oklahoma.

HISTORY

Before European contact

Archaeologists believe the Wichita descended from the Washita River culture, which dates back more than eight hundred years. These people lived in small villages in the valleys of central and western Oklahoma. They built homes of mud plaster, planted gardens, and hunted game. Their tools were made from stone, bone, antler, and wood.

Sometime between 1350 and 1450, the Wichita constructed the large, cone-shaped houses that they are known for today. Some of these homes were fortified. The people traded not only with neighboring tribes, but also with more distant ones. Turquoise pendants, shell beads, and glazed pottery came from the Pueblo tribes (see entries) of New Mexico, whereas engraved pottery and bois d'arc (special wood for making bows) came from the Caddo in Texas. Prior to the European arrival, part of the tribe moved north to the Great Bend of the Arkansas, a place the Spanish later called *Quivira*.

Spanish gold seekers arrive

Early explorers in the New World returned to Spain with tales of the Seven Golden Cities of Cíbola. In 1541, the Spanish explorer Francisco Vásquez de Coronado (c. 1510–1554) set off to find this gold in the then-unknown wilderness north of Mexico, leading a group of hundreds of Spaniards, slaves, and Native peoples, as well as cattle, sheep, and pigs. Instead of golden cities, he found the pueblos of the Zuñi (see entry).

Coronado's hopes flared when a Native slave told him of rich lands to the north, in the "Kingdom of Quivira." This was the territory of the Wichita tribe. Instead of riches, Coronado found twenty-five poor villages. He noted that the people ate raw meat like their enemy, the Apache (see entry). Coronado admired their grass houses, though, and

Important Dates

1541: The Wichita encounter Spanish explorer Francisco Vásquez de Coronado.

1719: The Wichita begin trading with the French.

1758: The Wichita repel a Spanish attack.

1835: A peace treaty is signed by warring Native tribes; the Wichita move to Indian Territory.

1858: U.S. troops kill many Wichita and destroy their property in the Battle of the Wichita Village.

1863: Confederate troops force Wichita to flee to Kansas during the American Civil War.

1872: The Wichita people move to the Oklahoma reservation with the Caddo and other tribes.

1890: The Wichita win a case for lands wrongfully taken by the United States.

1901: Wichita land is divided under the allotment policy.

1961: The Wichita, Keechi, Waco, Tawakoni, and Taovaya tribes organize as the Wichita and Affiliated Tribes.

considered the Wichita more advanced than their neighbors because they grew corn instead of living by raiding. (Coronado's slave later confessed he had invented the story about Quivira gold; he was executed.)

Coronado left Wichita territory without finding the riches he sought, but his companion, the missionary Juan de Padilla (1500–1542), remained with the tribe and converted them to Catholicism. Three years later Padilla began work with another tribe. The Wichita grew jealous and killed him. No more Europeans entered Wichita territory for a long while after that.

Trading and warring begin

In 1719, the Wichita were living along the Canadian River in present-day Oklahoma when the French explorer Bernard de La Harpe (1683–1765) began to trade with them. La Harpe estimated the population to be six thousand people at his first meeting with them. He also wrote that the Wichita had many prisoners of war from a recent conflict with another tribe, and they were preparing to eat them. (Some tribes believed that if you ate the body of a dead warrior, you ingested the warrior's strength.)

The French called the Wichita (and other Caddo) traders *Taovayas,* or *coureurs de bois,* meaning "runners of the woods." Wichita Taovayas acted as go-betweens for the French, trading crops and French tools to the tribes of the West for buffalo robes and furs. The Wichita themselves began to use metal hoes and buckets as well as guns that the French supplied.

In the 1700s, the French and Spanish battled for control of the lands in the American Southeast. Their fighting placed the tribes of the region in a complicated position. The tribes kept changing sides as they traded with both the French and Spanish. Meanwhile, hostile tribes continually forced the Wichita to move farther south.

In 1747, the French persuaded the Wichita to become allies with the Comanche (see entry) in a war against the Apache and the Osage (see entries). Even with the help of the Comanche, however, the Wichita could not withstand the Apache. The Wichita retreated farther south and settled at the present-day border of Oklahoma and Texas in the upper Red River Valley.

War continued, with the Apache, Osage, and the Spanish on one side, and the French, Wichita, Caddo, and Comanche on the other. In 1758, the Wichita were punished for their support of the French side—the Spanish attacked the main Wichita community. Supplied with weapons by the French and flying the French flag, however, the Wichita and their allies repelled the Spanish forces. In 1762, the defeated French gave up their lands in the Southeast to Spain. The Wichita continued to fight the Spanish, carrying out raids against the settlement of San Antonio, Texas. In 1765, the Wichita captured a Spaniard and held him prisoner. Conflicts continued. In 1772 and again in 1778, the Spanish government attempted to formalize peace with the Wichita, but they were unsuccessful.

Battling continues

The Spanish took over trade in the region, and the Wichita Taovayas no longer controlled the trade with other tribes in the West. In 1803, the United States acquired Wichita land as part of the Louisiana Purchase from France. Americans moved there in droves. Like the Caddo, the Wichita were enthusiastic about the American presence at first because the Americans paid more for furs.

Conflicts among the Native tribes, though, continued. The Wichita joined forces with the Caddo and Choctaw (see entry) in the continuing struggle against the Osage. Native populations soon declined from the constant warfare and from European-introduced diseases such as smallpox.

In 1834, U.S. Army colonel Henry Dodge (1782–1867) intervened in the conflicts and arranged a peace among the Wichita, their allied tribes, and the Osage. The following year, the Wichita, Comanche, Caddo, and Choctaw signed their first peace treaty with the U.S. government.

Peace between the Wichita and the United States ended in 1858 with the Battle of the Wichita Village. The Comanche had been carrying out raids against American settlers in Texas at the time. At one point, a peaceful group of Comanche visited the Wichita, and the group was suddenly attacked by U.S. troops. Many were killed, including Wichita women, and the village was completely destroyed. The Wichita lost horses, crops, and homes. The Comanche thought the Wichita had been betrayed them, so they later took their revenge by raiding and stealing Wichita horses.

Suffering hardship

Confederate troops forced the Wichita to flee to Kansas during the American Civil War (1861–65; a war between the Union [the North], which was opposed to slavery, and the Confederacy [the South], which was in favor of slavery). The site where they settled became the future city of Wichita, Kansas. The tribe suffered greatly during the Civil War years, and many died from starvation and disease. Only 822 people returned to Indian Territory in 1867. In 1872, the Wichita agreed to move to a reservation north of the Washita River in Oklahoma, along with the Caddo and other tribes. The U.S. Congress never officially accepted the agreement, so the Wichita never received the title to their land.

Peace was nearly shattered one year later after the Osage killed Wichita chief Isadowa during a buffalo hunt that almost erupted into war. Chief Ches-tedi-lessah succeeded Isadowa, and Tawakoni Jim followed as the next chief.

Struggle for rights

In 1894, 152 chiefs of the Wichita and related tribes signed away their rights to any lands in Indian Territory. The Wichita felt as though they had been forced to sign the agreement, and they protested. They took their case to the U.S. Court of Claims, which ruled in favor of the Wichita. As a result, 965 Wichita received plots of land called allotments, and the remaining Wichita lands were opened to white settlers in 1901.

In the early twenty-first century, the tribe jointly owned about 2,400 acres with the Caddo and Delaware and had 10 acres of its own. Because the tribe is so small, the people have struggled to maintain their culture.

RELIGION

The Wichita believe that the tribe's history is circular. Just as the seasons change and day turns to night, so life revolves from one thing to the next. Golden days of plenty turn to darkness, and the earth is barren. Still, the cycle continues, and the world and the people are renewed through the new creation.

Kinnikasus was the great creator, "Spirit Over All" among the Wichita. His name means "Man Never Known on Earth" or "Not Known to Man." The tribe worshipped many other spirits, including those contained in the sun, called "Man Reflecting Light"; the moon, called "Bright Shining Woman"; the water, called "Woman Forever in the Water"; and many gods, such as Morning Star and Earth Mother. They also believed in spirits that inhabited objects.

The Wichita believed that animals and other guardian spirits could give tribal members power and knowledge. They believed in an afterlife,

Kichai and Waco Tribes

Several tribes were originally part of the Wichita confederacy and have since been incorporated into the group, which organized in 1961 as the Wichita and Affiliated Tribes. Among the groups who shared a language and many customs are the Kichai and Waco.

The Kichai called themselves Kitsash, meaning "going in wet sand." The name Kichai translates from the Wichita language as "red shield." The French called them the "roving nation" because of their nomadic lifestyle.

In 1778, there were two Kichai settlements on the Trinity River in what is modern-day Texas with a total population of about 500 people. By 1849, this number had dropped to about 300, and by 1950, it had slipped to only 150, forty-seven of whom were full-blooded.

The Kichai were expert hunters and guides who killed deer, buffalo, antelope, and other plains animals for tools, clothing, and meat.

The name "Waco" may come from the Wichita word for Mexico, *wéhiko*. The Waco once lived near the Arkansas River in what is now Oklahoma. In modern times, they are probably best remembered for giving their name to a town in Texas. In 1824, the Waco numbered about four hundred. In the years after that, the total population of the tribe was hard to determine because of their close contact with several neighboring tribes. By 1894, there were thirty-seven Waco, and about sixty in the 1950s.

Like the Wichita, the Waco mainly grew corn, but they also hunted buffalo. One of their major rituals was a rain bundle ceremony, which assured the strength of the buffalo herds. They used several other rites to obtain assistance from the natural world, such as the "Surround-the-Fire" ceremony, in which four men sat around the fire and took turns singing and smoking the sacred pipe. Although many tribal customs are no longer practiced, there has been a resurgence of interest in the Waco tribal heritage. This new trend has resulted in a project to record songs and traditional stories so that they might be passed on to future generations.

a spirit world located in the sky, where those who died would lead a life of happiness free of the miseries of earthly life

Religious leaders called shamans (pronounced *SHAH-muns* or *SHAY-muns*) conducted ceremonies and healed those who were ill. Like Caddo shamans, the Wichita shaman performed special rituals that brought spiritual power to cure the sick or wounded.

In modern times, many Wichita are Baptists. Some are practicing members of the Native American Church, formed in Oklahoma in 1918 by John Wilson (c. 1840–1901; see Makah entry). This religion combines elements of Christianity with traditional Native beliefs and practices.

Wichita Words

chi'as	"one"
wits	"two"
taw	"three"
takwits	"four"
iskwi'its	"five"
we'its	"man"
kahika	"woman"
kitsiya	"dog"
sakita	"sun"
waw	"moon"
gits	"water"
wira?a	"bear"
wi:yo:h	"cat"
k?ita:ks	"coyote"
iha:ski:thaw	"monkey"
ic?i:s	"spider"
ko:s	"eagle"

LANGUAGE

Of the many languages in the Caddoan language family, three major languages have survived to the twenty-first century: the Caddo, the Pawnee, and the Wichita. All the tribes in the Wichita group except the Kichai spoke the same Caddoan language as the Wichita, which is similar to Pawnee. There are few speakers of the Wichita language left, but some of those speakers have assisted in the Wichita Documentation Project, a program to keep the language alive by recording it on audio tapes.

GOVERNMENT

The Wichita were part of a larger confederacy of people who spoke the same language and shared many customs and traditions. Each group had its own chief and subchief. Warriors elected the chiefs, whose main job was to handle relations with other groups. The subchief was called "The One Who Locates"; he was responsible for scouting out suitable sites for villages in case a move was necessary.

Chiefs had distinguished themselves in some way, either by bravery, generosity, or through another outstanding trait. They could only make decisions after consulting with everyone in the village.

Once the Wichita were on a reservation, federal Indian agents controlled the people. U.S. policies changed in the twentieth century, and tribes were allowed to form new governments. The Wichita did so in 1961. The people are governed by the Wichita Tribal Council, which empowers the elected executive committee made up of a president, vice president, secretary, treasurer, and three members. A tribal administrator oversees the operation of all tribal programs. Tribal offices are near Anadarko, Oklahoma.

ECONOMY

The Wichita economy was based on agriculture, mostly corn, which they grew and traded to other tribes. The tribe depended less on hunting buffalo and trading buffalo robes than did other Great Plains tribes.

In the early 2000s, most tribal income was derived from leasing farmland, buildings, and mining rights through WCD Enterprises, a business the Wichita own with the Caddo and Delaware tribes. WCD Enterprises also oversees the tribe's land acquisition program and their industrial park. Andarko Industries, a tribally owned business, designs and constructs computer network systems, offers military operations planning, and provides engineering and business services. Other enterprises that bring in income include a casino, smokeshop, and restaurant; the tribe also issues license plates.

DAILY LIFE

Families

Wichita daughters lived with their mothers after they were married. Most families consisted of the parents, their young unmarried children, and their married daughters along with the daughters' husbands and children. The Wichita had a complicated family organization in which some aunts and uncles were regarded as fathers and mothers, and some cousins were regarded as brothers and sisters. A woman's many sisters helped her with the household tasks, and a man's many brothers often accompanied him on hunting or warring expeditions.

Education

Children learned through the examples of their parents and relatives. Mothers had the primary responsibility for teaching both boys and girls until they were about ten years old. Punishment was rare, but if a mother felt she could not handle her child's misbehavior, she might turn the job over to a relative, who was free to choose any suitable punishment. Once she had asked for such assistance, the mother gave up any right to interfere. Only one such request for outside punishment was usually necessary, and the child behaved from then on.

When a boy reached age ten, his father took over his education and taught him to hunt and raid. Today, most Wichita children attend public schools in Oklahoma. Some attend a boarding school at the Riverside Indian School.

Buildings

The Wichita were famous for their sturdy and unusual grass houses. They built them in villages overlooking rivers, and some villages contained as many as one thousand houses. The houses were 15 to 30 feet (4.5 to 9 meters) in

Coyote and Never Grows Bigger

Many tales told by the elders were intended to teach children a lesson. In this one, Coyote learns not to underestimate someone smaller than he is.

One time Coyote met a very small snake called Never Grows Bigger.

"What a ridiculous thing you are," said Coyote. "Who would ever want to be as small as you are? Why are you this small anyway? You ought to be big like me. You can't do anything if you're that small. There must be something wrong with you."

The snake didn't say anything.

"Let me see your teeth," said Coyote.

The snake opened his mouth. Then Coyote opened his mouth and pointed at his teeth. "See? Look at these teeth of mine. What would happen if we bit each other? Your teeth are too small to hurt anyone, but I could bite you in half. Let's bite each other and you'll see what I mean."

So they bit each other and then Coyote said, "Let's move back a little and call out to each other." Coyote knew that he could tell by the way the snake called out how quickly he was dying. The snake gave a cry and then

Coyote called out. Each time the snake called his voice was weaker. Coyote went off a little ways, lay down, and got ready to take a nap. Coyote was still calling out but he could hardly hear the snake. "It's no good to be that small," Coyote thought. "Now he knows."

Soon Coyote noticed that the place where the snake had bitten him was beginning to swell up. The swelling got bad very quickly and Coyote got very weak. He could hardly call out now and he was beginning to feel very dizzy and ill.

By this time the snake's wound had begun to heal. His voice got stronger. Coyote's calls grew weaker and weaker until finally there was no sound out of him anymore. Never Grows Bigger went over to where Coyote was laying down and saw he was dead. "This animal never learns," said Never Grows Bigger. He went away and left Coyote out there on the prairie all blown up like a buffalo bladder from that bite.

SOURCE: Penn, W. S., ed. *The Telling of the World: Native American Stories and Art.* New York: Stewart, Tabori and Chang, 1996.

A Wichita village is dotted with the tribe's unusual cone-shaped grass houses. LIBRARY OF CONGRESS, MISCELLANEOUS ITEMS IN HIGH DEMAND, LC-USZ62-11478.

diameter, were shaped like cones, and were peaked at the top to symbolize the gods of the four quarters of the world. To make these complicated structures, the Wichita covered forked cedar poles with dry grass and carried out a ceremony during the building process. By the 1930s, most Wichita were living in frame houses.

Traditional homes had eight to ten sleeping platforms surrounded by buffalo hide curtains, a central fire that vented through a hole in the roof, and a hollowed-out tree trunk for grinding corn.

Near the grass houses, the Wichita built arbors, which were open-sided grass structures set on raised platforms. They used these buildings for resting in the heat of the summer. They constructed other arbors to store food and laid meat and corn on the roofs to dry. Smaller thatched huts set on platforms held the village's unmarried girls, who were carefully guarded.

Food

The Wichita relied on farm products more than meat, even after horses made hunting more efficient. When they did hunt, they sought out buffalo, deer, antelope, bear, and other wild game. They grew corn, beans, melons, tobacco, pumpkins, squash, and gourds. Cotton and wheat were also grown. Many fruits grew in the area—grapes, persimmons, cherries, plums, blackberries, and elderberries—as well as walnuts, chestnuts, and acorns. The women made use of all of these in their meals. They also gathered wild sweet potatoes and pond-lily bulbs. Although they lived near rivers, the Wichita did not eat fish.

After the harvest had been gathered in the fall, women roasted and dried corn and pumpkin. They ground some of the corn into corn-meal and wove some of the dried pumpkin strips into mats that they traded with the Comanche and Kiowa (see entry) for buffalo meat. They wrapped their dried food in buffalo-hide bags and stored it in under-ground pits. These caches provided food throughout the winter and during times when food was scarce.

Clothing and adornment

French traders used the name *Pani Piqué* for the Wichita, which means "Tattooed Pawnee," or "punctured" or "pricked," because their faces and bodies were tattooed with sharp instruments. Both men and women wore intricate tattoos consisting of dotted and solid lines as well as circles on their faces and bodies. Often referred to as the "raccoon-eyed people," they also had tattoos around their eyes, with either a horizontal line branching from the outside corner of each eye or a line from the bridge of the nose to the upper lip. Women had a chin line tattoo from ear to ear, as well as tattoos on their necks, arms, and breasts. Boys decorated the backs of their hands with claw-like designs after killing their first birds. Other marks were earned as war honors. Men also hung ornaments from four piercings in their ears.

The Wichita were unlike other Plains Indians in that they were shorter, stockier, and had darker skin. In the summer, they wore scanty clothing, perhaps only loincloths (flaps of material that hung from the waist and covered the front and back) and moccasins. In colder weather, the men added leggings, robes, and shirts. Women wore skirts of buck-skin or buffalo hide, usually decorated with ornaments.

CUSTOMS

Life passage rituals

The Wichita had a rich ceremonial life. They had secret societies for both men and women. Each society had its own special ceremonies and dances, such as the singing of songs before a war party set out and when it returned. They observed rituals for childbirth, puberty, marriage, death, and home building.

Marriage, birth, and naming

Marriages were often arranged by relatives, though sometimes marriages were made by mutual consent of the couple. The groom and his family gave gifts to the bride's family and held a feast, but there was no formal ceremony. The couple moved in with the bride's parents, and the man did chores and hunted for his new family. Married couples usually had only one spouse.

Names were chosen for the baby before it was born. These names were usually based on dreams. During childbirth, the mother stayed in a tepee away from the lodge. A husband could not see his wife for four days after their baby was born.

Social ceremonies

The Wichita were fond of dances and held them to mark many occasions. For instance, the entire tribe observed the Deer Dance three times a year—first to celebrate the coming of spring vegetation, then to mark the growth of the plants, and finally to commemorate the harvest of corn. The dance included ritual vomiting and a ceremonial foot race. It was designed to purge the tribe of evil influences and to encourage health, long life, and prosperity.

A more recent tradition is the annual summer visitation between the Pawnee and Wichita. The tribes take turns hosting the two-week event, which consists of a ceremonial gift exchange, stories, and songs along with an opportunity to renew ties and friendships.

War rituals

War was the way a man gained importance in the tribe. Wichita warriors who wished to lead a war party had to convince others to follow them. Although war parties tended to be small, a warrior who was known for his ability—who had counted more coup (pronounced *COO*)—was likely to have more followers than one who was unproven. A coup, touching an enemy's body without causing injury, was a feat of bravery. After warriors returned from a successful raid, there was much singing, dancing, and feasting. Back at home, war leaders resumed their usual position of esteemed warrior; they were no longer in charge, but they were of equal status as all other warriors.

Death and burial

The Wichita placed their dead in shallow graves with the things they would need in the afterlife. Men were buried with weapons and tools; women, with domestic tools. When a loved one died, mourners cut their hair and gave away some of their possessions.

CURRENT TRIBAL ISSUES

In 1872, the Wichita reservation contained 743,000 acres of land. Government policies eventually reduced the tribe's landholdings to ten acres. Individual members, including those of the Caddo and Delaware tribes, owned a total of 2,400 acres. The Wichita have been actively acquiring land. Although most of the land is individually owned, they had increased their holdings to 55,199 acres by 2004.

At the start of the twenty-first century, the tribe's main concerns were air and water quality, pesticide use, abandoned oil wells, and illegal dumping. To deal with these environmental issues, the Wichita have been pursuing funding to assist in the cleanups. The Wichita Department of Environmental Programs is working with the Environmental Protection Agency to monitor and eliminate problems. In 2009, piles of trash, including more than 3,300 tires, were removed from one illegal dumpsite. The tribe was identifying others and working to reduce other environmental hazards on reservation land.

BOOKS

Dolan, Edward. *The American Indian Wars.* Brookfield, CT: Millbrook Press, 2003.

Elam, Earl H. *Kitikiti'sh: The Wichita Indians and Associated Tribes in Texas, 1757–1859.* Hillsboro, TX: Hill College Press, 2008.

Fowler, Loretta. *The Columbia Guide to American Indians of the Great Plains.* New York: Columbia University Press, 2005.

La Vere, David. *The Texas Indians.* Austin: Texas A&M University Press, 2004.

Miles, Ray. "Wichita." *Native America in the Twentieth Century, An Encyclopedia.* Ed. Mary B. Davis. New York: Garland Publishing, 1994.

Patent, Dorothy Hinshaw. *The Buffalo and the Indians: A Shared Destiny.* New York: Clarion Books, 2006.

Smith, F. Todd. *From Dominance to Disappearance: The Indians of Texas and the Near Southwest, 1786–1859.* Lincoln: University of Nebraska Press, 2006.

Southwell, Kristina L., and John R. Lovett. *Life at the Kiowa, Comanche, and Wichita Agency: The Photographs of Annette Ross Hume.* Norman: University of Oklahoma Press, 2010.

Weddle, Robert S. *After the Massacre: The Violent Legacy of the San Sabá Mission with the Original Diary of the 1759 Red River Campaign.* Translated by Carol Lipscomb. Lubbock: Texas Tech University Press, 2007.

WEB SITES

Brush, Rebecca. "The Wichita Indians." *Texas Indians.* http://www.texasindians.com/wichita.htm (accessed on June 9, 2011).

Chapman, Berlin B. "Chronicles of Oklahoma: Dissolution of the Wichita Reservation." *Oklahoma State University.* http://digital.library.okstate.edu/Chronicles/v022/v022p192.pdf (accessed on June 9, 2011).

Curtis, Edward S. "The Wichita." *The North American Indian.* Norwood, MA: The Plimpton Press, 1930. Available online from http://curtis.library.northwestern.edu/curtis/viewPage.cgi?showp=1&size=2&id=nai.19.book.00000048&volume=19 (accessed on June 9, 2011).

Elam, Earl H. "Wichita Indians." *Texas State Historical Association.* http://www.tshaonline.org/handbook/online/articles/bmw03 (accessed on June 9, 2011).

Official Site of the Wichita and Affiliated Tribes. http://www.wichitatribe.com/ (accessed on June 9, 2011).

Redish, Laura, and Orrin Lewis. "Wichita Indian Fact Sheet." *Native Languages of the Americas.* http://www.bigorrin.org/wichita_kids.htm (accessed on June 9, 2011).

"2011 Oklahoma Indian Nations." *Pocket Pictorial Directory.* Oklahoma City: Oklahoma Indian Affairs Commission, 2011. Available from http://www.ok.gov/oiac/documents/2011.FINAL.WEB.pdf (accessed on June 12, 2011).

"Wichita." *Four Directions Institute.* http://www.fourdir.com/wichita.htm (accessed on June 9, 2011).

"Wichita Indian Language (Witchita)." *Native Languages of the Americas: Preserving and Promoting Indigenous American Indian Languages.* http://www.native-languages.org/wichita.htm (accessed on June 9, 2007).

"Wichita Program for the Documentation of Endangered Languages." *University of Colorado at Boulder.* http://www.colorado.edu/linguistics/faculty/rood-old/Wichita/wichlinks.html (accessed on June 9, 2011).

Where to Learn More

Books

Abel, Kerry. *Drum Songs: Glimpses of Dene History.* Montreal, Quebec: McGill–Queen's University Press, 1993.

Adams, Richard C. *A Delaware Indian Legend and the Story of Their Troubles.* Whitefish, MT: Kessinger Publishing, LLC, 2006.

Adamson, Thelma, ed. *Folk-tales of the Coast Salish.* Lincoln: Bison Books, 2009.

Aderkas, Elizabeth, and Christa Hook. *American Indians of the Pacific Northwest.* Oxford: Osprey Publishing, 2005.

Adil, Janeen R. *The Northeast Indians: Daily Life in the 1500s.* Mankato, MN: Capstone Press, 2006.

Agonito, Joseph. *Lakota Portraits: Lives of the Legendary Plains People.* Guilford, CT: TwoDot, 2011.

Agoyo, Herman, and Joe S. Sando, eds. *Po'pay: Leader of the First American Revolution.* Santa Fe, NM: Clear Light Publishing, 2005.

Akers, Donna L. *Culture and Customs of the Choctaw Indians.* Santa Barbara, CA: Greenwood, 2012.

The Aleut Relocation and Internment during World War II: A Preliminary Examination. Anchorage, AK: Aleutian/Pribilof Islands Association, 1981.

Alexander, Annie Lou. *Blood Is Red...So Am I.* New York: Vantage Press, 2007.

Alexie, Sherman. *The Absolutely True Diary of a Part-Time Indian.* Waterville, ME: Thorndike Press, 2008.

Alfred, Agnes. *Paddling to Where I Stand: Agnes Alfred, Kwakwaka'wakw Noblewoman.* Seattle: University of Washington Press, 2005.

Alger, Abby L. *In Indian Tents: Stories Told by Penobscot, Passamaquoddy and Micmac Indians.* Park Forest, IL: University Press of the Pacific, 2006.

Allen, John W. *Legends and Lore of Southern Illinois.* Carbondale: Southern Illinois University Press, 2010.

Andersen, Raoul R., and John K. Crellin. *Miśel Joe: An Aboriginal Chief's Journey.* St. John's, Newfoundland: Flanker Press, 2009.

Anderson, Jeffrey D. *One Hundred Years of Old Man Sage: An Arapaho Life.* Lincoln: University of Nebraska Press, 2003.

Andersson, Rani-Henrik. *The Lakota Ghost Dance of 1890.* Lincoln: University of Nebraska Press, 2008.

Angell, Tony, and John M. Marzluff. *In the Company of Crows and Ravens.* New Haven, CT: Yale University Press, 2007.

Anthony, Alexander E., Jr., David Neil Sr., and J. Brent Ricks. *Kachinas: Spirit Beings of the Hopi.* Albuquerque, NM: Avanyu Publishing, 2006.

Archer, Jane. *The First Fire: Stories of the Cherokee, Kickapoo, Kiowa, and Tigua.* Dallas, TX: Taylor Trade, 2005.

Arnold, Caroline, and Richard R. Hewett. *The Ancient Cliff Dwellers of Mesa Verde.* New York: Clarion Books, 2000.

Aron Crowell, ed. *Living Our Cultures, Sharing Our Heritage: The First Peoples of Alaska.* Washington, DC: Smithsonian Institution, 2010.

Augaitis, Daina, Lucille Bell, and Nika Collison. *Raven Travelling: Two Centuries of Haida Art.* Seattle: University of Washington Press, 2008.

Ayagalria, Moses K. *Yupik Eskimo Fairy Tales and More.* New York: Vantage Press, 2006.

Bahti, Mark. *Pueblo Stories and Storytellers.* 3rd ed. Tucson, AZ: Rio Nuevo Publishers, 2010.

Bahti, Mark, and Eugene Baatsoslanii Joe. *Navajo Sandpaintings.* 3rd ed. Tucson, AZ: Rio Nuevo Publishers, 2009.

Bailey, Garrick, ed. *Traditions of the Osage: Stories Collected and Translated by Francis la Flesche.* Albuquerque: University of New Mexico Press, 2010.

Baker, Wendy Beth. *Healing Power of Horses: Lessons from the Lakota Indians.* Irvine, CA: BowTie Press, 2004.

Ball, Eve, Nora Henn, and Lynda A. Sánchez. *Indeh: An Apache Odyssey.* Reprint. Norman: University of Oklahoma Press, 1988.

Ballantine, Betty, and Ian Ballantine, eds. *The Native Americans: An Illustrated History.* Atlanta: Turner Publishing, 1993.

Bancroft-Hunt, Norman. *People of the Totem: The Indians of the Pacific Northwest.* Photographs by Werner Forman. New York: Putnam, 1979.

Barbeau, Marius. *Huron and Wyandot Mythology.* Ottawa, Ontario: Government Printing Bureau, 1915.

Barbour, Jeannie, Amanda J. Cobb, and Linda Hogan. *Chickasaw: Unconquered and Unconquerable.* Ada, OK: Chickasaw Press, 2006.

Barker, James H., and Ann Fienup-Riordan. *Yupiit Yuraryarait = Yup'ik Ways of Dancing.* Fairbanks: University of Alaska Press, 2010.

Barkwell, Lawrence J. *Women of the Metis Nation.* Winnipeg, Manitoba: Louis Riel Institute, 2009.

Barnett, James F., Jr. *The Natchez Indians: A History to 1735.* Jackson: University Press of Mississippi, 2007.

Barrett, Samuel Alfred. *Ceremonies of the Pomo Indians and Pomo Bear Doctors.* University of California Publications in American Archeology and Ethnology. 1917. Reprint. Whitefish, MT: Kessinger Publishing, 2010.

———. *The Washo Indians.* 1917. Reprint. Charleston, SC: Kessinger Publishing, 2010.

Barron, Donna Gentle Spirit. *The Long Island Indians and their New England Ancestors: Narragansett, Mohegan, Pequot and Wampanoag Tribes.* Bloomington, IN: AuthorHouse, 2006.

Bartram, William, and Gregory A. Waselkov. *William Bartram on the Southeastern Indians.* Lincoln: University of Nebraska Press, 2002.

Basel, Roberta. *Sequoyah: Inventor of Written Cherokee.* Minneapolis, MN: Compass Point Books, 2007.

Bastedo, Jamie. *Reaching North: A Celebration of the Subarctic.* Markham, Ontario: Red Deer Press, 2002.

Bauerle, Phenocia, ed. *The Way of the Warrior: Stories of the Crow People.* Lincoln: University of Nebraska Press, 2003.

Bean, Lowell John, ed. "Introduction." In *The Ohlone Past and Present: Native Americans of the San Francisco Bay Region.* Menlo Park, CA: Ballena Press, 1994.

Bean, Lowell John, and Florence C. Shipek. "Luiseño." In *Handbook of North American Indians.* Vol. 8: *California,* edited by Robert F. Heizer. Washington, DC: Smithsonian Institution, 1978.

Bean, Lowell, Frank Porter, and Lisa Bourgeault. *The Cahuilla.* New York: Chelsea House, 1989.

Beasley, Richard A. *How to Carve a Tlingit Mask.* Juneau: Sealaska Heritage Institute, 2009.

Becenti, Karyth. *One Nation, One Year: A Navajo Photographer's 365-Day Journey into a World of Discovery, Life and Hope.* Los Ranchos, NM: Rio Grande Books, 2010.

Beck, Mary G. *Heroes and Heroines: Tlingit-Haida Legend.* Anchorage: Alaska Northwest Books, 2003.

Beckwourth, James. *The Life and Adventures of James P. Beckwourth, Mountaineer, Scout, and Pioneer, and Chief of the Crow Nation of Indians.* Paris, France: Adamant Media Corporation, 2005.

Behnke, Alison. *The Apaches.* Minneapolis, MN: Lerner Publications, 2006.

Behrman, Carol H. *The Indian Wars.* Minneapolis, MN: Lerner Publications, 2005.

Belting, Natalia. *Whirlwind Is a Spirit Dancing: Poems Based on Traditional American Indian Songs and Stories.* New York: Milk and Cookies Press, 2006.

Bergon, Frank. *Shoshone Mike.* New York: Viking Penguin, 1987.

Berleth, Richard. *Bloody Mohawk: The French and Indian War and American Revolution on New York's Frontier.* Hensonville, NY: Black Dome, 2009.

Betty, Gerald. *Comanche Society: Before the Reservation.* College Station: Texas A&M University Press, 2005.

Bial, Raymond. *The Chumash.* New York: Benchmark Books, 2004.

— — —. *The Cree.* New York: Benchmark Books, 2006.

— — —. *The Delaware.* New York: Benchmark Books, 2006.

— — —. *The Menominee.* New York: Marshall Cavendish Benchmark, 2006.

— — —. *The Tlingit.* New York: Benchmark Books, 2003.

Bibby, Brian. *Deeper than Gold: A Guide to Indian Life in the Sierra Foothills.* Berkeley: Heyday Books, 2004.

Bielawski, Ellen. *In Search of Ancient Alaska: Solving the Mysteries of the Past.* Anchorage: Alaska Northwest Books, 2007.

Birchfield, D.L., and Helen Dwyer. *Apache History and Culture.* New York: Gareth Stevens, 2012.

Biskup, Agnieszka. *Thunder Rolling Down the Mountain: The Story of Chief Joseph and the Nez Percé.* Mankato, MN: Capstone Press, 2011.

Bjorklund, Ruth. *The Cree.* Tarrytown, NY: Marshall Cavendish, 2009.

— — —. *The Hopi.* Tarrytown, NY: Marshall Cavendish Benchmark, c. 2009.

Blackbird, Andrew J. *History of the Ottawa and Chippewa Indians of Michigan.* Charleston, SC: Nabu Press, 2010.

Bodine, John. "Taos Pueblo." *Handbook of North American Indians,* Vol. 9: *Southwest.* Ed. Alfonso Ortiz. Washington DC: Smithsonian Institution, 1979.

— — —. *Taos Pueblo: A Walk Through Time.* Tucson, AZ: Rio Nuevo, 2006.

Bodinger de Uriarte, John J. *Casino and Museum: Representing Mashantucket Pequot Identity.* Tucson: University of Arizona Press, 2007.

Bogan, Phebe M. *Yaqui Indian Dances of Tucson Arizona: An Account of the Ceremonial Dances of the Yaqui Indians at Pascua.* Whitefish, MT: Kessinger Publishing, 2011.

Bonvillain, Nancy, and Ada Deer. *The Hopi.* Minneapolis, MN: Chelsea House Publications, 2005.

— — —. *The Nez Percé.* New York: Chelsea House, 2011.

— — —. *The Zuñi.* New York: Chelsea House Publishers, 2011.

Boule, Mary Null. *Mohave Tribe.* Vashon, WV: Merryant Publishers Inc., 2000.

Bourque, Bruce J., and Laureen A. LaBar. *Uncommon Threads: Wabanaki Textiles, Clothing, and Costume.* Augusta: Maine State Museum in association with University of Washington Press, 2009.

Bowes, John P. *The Choctaw.* New York: Chelsea House, 2010.

Bradley, Donna. *Native Americans of San Diego County, CA.* Mt. Pleasant, SC: Arcadia, 2009.

Bragdon, Kathleen J. *The Columbia Guide to American Indians of the Northeast.* New York: Columbia University Press, 2005.

Braje, Todd J., and Torben C. Rick, eds.*Human Impacts on Seals, Sea Lions, and Sea Otters: Integrating Archaeology and Ecology in the Northeast Pacific.* Berkeley: University of California Press, 2011.

Bray, Kingsley M. *Crazy Horse: A Lakota Life.* Norman: University of Oklahoma Press, 2006.

Breen, Betty, and Earl Mills, Sr. *Cape Cod Wampanoag Cookbook: Wampanoag Indian Recipes, Images & Lore.* Santa Fe, NM: Clear Light Books, 2001.

Brehm, Victoria. *Star Songs and Water Spirits: A Great Lakes Native Reader.* Tustin, MI: Ladyslipper Press, 2010.

Brimner, Larry Dane. *Pocahontas: Bridging Two Worlds.* New York: Marshall Cavendish Benchmark, 2009.

Bringhurst, Robert. *A Story as Sharp as a Knife: The Classical Haida Mythtellers and Their World.* 2nd ed. Vancouver, BC: Douglas & McIntyre, 2011.

Bringing the Story of the Cheyenne People to the Children of Today. Northern Cheyenne Curriculum Committee. Helena, MT: Office of Public Instruction, 2009.

Broker, Ignatia, *Night Flying Woman: An Ojibway Narrative.* St. Paul: Minnesota Historical Society Press, 1983.

Brown, Dee. *Bury My Heart at Wounded Knee: An Indian History of the American West.* New York: Holt, Rinehart, and Winston, 1970.

Brown, James W., and Rita T. Kohn, ed. *Long Journey Home: Oral Histories of Contemporary Delaware Indians.* Bloomington: Indiana University Press, 2008.

Brown, John A., and Robert H. Ruby. *The Chinook Indians: Traders of the Lower Columbia River.* Norman: University of Oklahoma Press, 1988.

Brown, Joseph. *The Spiritual Legacy of the American Indian: Commemorative Edition with Letters while Living with Black Elk.* Bloomington, IN: World Wisdom, 2007.

Brown, Tricia, and Roy Corral. *Children of the Midnight Sun: Young Native Voices of Alaska.* Anchorage: Alaska Northwest Books, 2006.

— — —. *Silent Storytellers of Totem Bight State Historical Park.* Anchorage: Alaska Geographic Association, 2009.

Brown, Virginia Pounds, Laurella Owens and Nathan Glick. *The World of the Southern Indians: Tribes, Leaders, and Customs from Prehistoric Times to the Present.* Montgomery, AL: NewSouth Books, 2011.

Browner, Tara, ed. *Music of the First Nations: Tradition and Innovation in Native North America.* Urbana: University of Illinois Press, 2009.

Bruchac, Joseph. *Flying with the Eagle, Racing the Great Bear: Tales from Native North America*. Golden, CO: Fulcrum, 2011.

Bruemmer, Fred. *Arctic Visions: Pictures from a Vanished World*. Toronto, Ontario: Key Porter Books, 2008.

Brugge, Doug, Timothy Benally, and Esther Yazzie-Lewis. *The Navajo People and Uranium Mining*. Albuquerque: University of New Mexico Press, 2006.

Bullchild, Percy. *The Sun Came Down: The History of the World as My Blackfeet Elders Told It*. Lincoln: University of Nebraska Press, 2005.

Burgan, Michael. *The Arapaho*. Tarrytown, NY: Marshall Cavendish Benchmark, 2009.

— — —. *Inuit History and Culture*. New York: Gareth Stevens, 2011.

Burke, Heather, et al, eds. *Kennewick Man: Perspectives on the Ancient One*. Walnut Creek, CA: Left Coast Press, 2008.

Burns, Louis F. *A History of the Osage People*. Tuscaloosa: University of Alabama Press, 2004.

— — —. *Osage Indian Customs and Myths*. Tuscaloosa: University of Alabama Press, 2005.

Button, Bertha P. *Friendly People: The Zuñi Indians*. Santa Fe, NM: Museum of New Mexico Press, 1963.

Calloway, Colin G. *The Shawnees and the War for America*. New York: Viking, 2007.

Carbone, Elisa. *Blood on the River: James Town 1607*. New York: Viking, 2006.

Carlos, Ann M. *Commerce by a Frozen Sea: Native Americans and the European Fur Trade*. Philadelphia: University of Pennsylvania Press, 2010.

Carlson, Paul H., and Tom Crum. *Myth, Memory, and Massacre: The Pease River Capture of Cynthia Ann Parker*. Lubbock: Texas Tech University Press, 2010.

Carlson, Richard G., ed. *Rooted Like the Ash Trees: New England Indians and the Land*. Naugatuck, CT: Eagle Wing Press, 1987.

Carpenter, Cecelia Svinth, Maria Victoria Pascualy, and Trisha Hunter. *Nisqually Indian Tribe*. Charleston, SC: Arcadia, 2008.

Carter, John G. *The Northern Arapaho Flat Pipe and the Ceremony of Covering the Pipe*. Whitefish, MT: Kessinger Publishing, 2007.

Cashin, Edward J. *Guardians of the Valley: Chickasaws in Colonial South Carolina and Georgia*. Columbia, SC: University of South Carolina Press, 2009.

Cassidy, James J., Jr., ed. *Through Indian Eyes: The Untold Story of Native American Peoples*. Pleasantville, NY: Reader's Digest Association, 1995.

Cassinelli, Dennis. *Preserving Traces of the Great Basin Indians*. Reno, NV: Jack Bacon & Company, 2006.

Castillo, Edward D. *The Pomo*. Austin: RaintreeSteck-Vaughn, 1999.

Chalcraft, Edwin L. *Assimilation's Agent: My Life as a Superintendent in the Indian Boarding School System.* Lincoln: University of Nebraska Press, 2007.

Champagne, Duane, ed. *The Native North American Almanac.* Detroit: Gale, 1994.

Charles, Nicholas and Maria. *Messenger Spirits: Yup'ik Masks and Stories.* Anchorage, AK: N & M, 2009.

Chatters, James C. *Ancient Encounters: Kennewick Man and the First Americans.* New York: Simon and Schuster, 2001.

Chaussonnet, Valerie, ed. *Crossroads Alaska: Native Cultures of Alaska and Siberia.* Washington, DC: Arctic Studies Center, National Museum of Natural History, Smithsonian Institution, 1995.

Chehak, Gail, and Jan Halliday. *Native Peoples of the Northwest: A Traveler's Guide to Land, Art, and Culture.* Seattle: Sasquatch Books, 2002.

Chenoweth, Avery, and Robert Llewellyn. *Empires in the Forest: Jamestown and the Making of America.* Earlysville, VA: Rivanna Foundation, 2010.

Childs, Craig. *House of Rain: Tracking a Vanished Civilization across the American Southwest.* 2nd ed. New York: Back Bay Books, 2008.

Clark, Cora, and Texa Bowen Williams. *Pomo Indians: Myths and Some of Their Sacred Meanings.* Reprint. Charleston, SC: Literary Licensing, 2011.

Clark, Ella E. *Indian Legends of the Pacific Northwest.* Berkeley: University of California Press, 2003.

Clark, Jerry E. *The Shawnee.* Lexington: University Press of Kentucky, 2007.

Clow, Richmond L., ed. *The Sioux in South Dakota History: A Twentieth-Century Reader.* Pierre, SD: South Dakota State Historical Society Press, 2007.

Cobb, Amanda J. *Listening to Our Grandmothers' Stories: The Bloomfield Academy for Chickasaw Females, 1852–1949.* Lincoln: University of Nebraska Press, 2007.

— — —. *Massacre at Camp Grant: Forgetting and Remembering Apache History.* Tucson: University of Arizona Press, 2007.

Cone, Marla. *Silent Snow: The Slow Poisoning of the Arctic.* New York: Grove Press, 2005.

Confederated Salish and Kootenai Tribes. *Bull Trout's Gift: A Salish Story about the Value of Reciprocity.* Lincoln: University of Nebraska Press, 2011.

Cook, Franklin A. "Nunapitchuk, Alaska: A Yup'ik Eskimo Village in Western Alaska." *Anna Tobeluk Memorial School, Nunapitchuk, Alaska.* Lincoln: University of Nebraska Press, 2005.

Cook, R. Michael, Eli Gifford, and Warren Jefferson, eds. *How Can One Sell the Air?: Chief Seattle's Vision.* Summertown, TN: Native Voices, 2005.

Corwin, Judith Hoffman. *Native American Crafts of the Northwest Coast, the Arctic, and the Subarctic.* New York: Franklin Watts, 2002.

Costa, David J. *Narratives and Winter Stories.* Oxford, OH: Myaamia Publications, 2010.

Coté, Charlotte. *Spirits of Our Whaling Ancestors: Revitalizing Makah, and Nuu-chah-nulth Traditions.* Seattle: University of Washington Press, 2010.

Coyote, Bertha Little, and Virginia Giglio. *Leaving Everything Behind: The Songs and Memories of a Cheyenne Woman.* Norman: University of Oklahoma Press, 1997.

Cozzens, Peter. *The Army and the Indian.* Mechanicsburg, PA: Stackpole Books, 2005.

Crediford, Gene J. *Those Who Remain.* Tuscaloosa: University of Alabama Press, 2009.

Crompton, Samuel Willard. *The Mohawk.* Edited by Paul C. Rosier. New York: Chelsea House Publishers, 2010.

Medicine Crow, Joseph. *Counting Coup: Becoming a Crow Chief on the Reservation and Beyond.* Washingon, DC: National Geographic, 2006.

— — —. *From the Heart of the Crow Country: The Crow Indians' Own Stories.* Lincoln: University of Nebraska Press, 2000.

Crowell, Aron L. *Living Our Cultures, Sharing Our Heritage: The First Peoples of Alaska.* Washington, DC: Smithsonian Books, 2010.

Croy, Anita. *Ancient Pueblo: Archaeology Unlocks the Secrets of America's Past.* Washington, DC: National Geographic, 2007.

Cunningham, Kevin, and Peter Benoit. *The Wampanoag.* New York: Children's Press, 2011.

Curtin, Jeremiah. *Myths of the Modocs.* Whitefish, MT: Kessinger Publishing, 2006.

— — —. "The Yanas." In *Creation Myths of Primitive America.* Boston, MA: Little, Brown, and Company, 1903.

Curtain, Jeremiah, and Roland B. Dixon, eds. *Achomawi and Atsugewi Myths and Tales.* Reprint.Sandhurst, UK: Abela Publishing, 2009.

— — —. *The Plains Indian Photographs of Edward S. Curtis.* Lincoln: University of Nebraska Press, 2001.

— — —. "Salishan Tribes." In *The North American Indian.* Vol. 7. Edited by Frederick Webb Hodge. Norwood, MA: The Plimpton Press, 1911. Available online from http://curtis.library.northwestern.edu/curtis/viewPage.cgi?showp=1&size=2&id=nai.07.book.00000075&volume=7 (accessed on August 11, 2011).

— — — "Taos." In *The North American Indian (1907–1930).* Vol. 26. Reprint. New York: Johnson Reprint Corporation, 1970.

— — —. "Umatilla." In *The North American Indian,* edited by Fredrick Webb Hodge. Vol. 8. 1911. Available online from http://curtis.library.northwestern.edu/curtis/viewPage.cgi?showp=1&size=2&id=nai.08.book.00000129.p&volume=8#nav (accessed on August 11, 2011).

— — —. "The Washoe." In *The North American Indian*. Vol. 15. Edited by Frederick Webb Hodge. Norwood, MA: The Plimpton Press, 1926: 89–98. Available online from Northwestern University. http://curtis.library.northwestern.edu/curtis/viewPage.cgi?showp=1&size=2&id=nai.15.book.00000141&volume=15 (accessed on August 15, 2011).

Cushing, Frank H. *Zuñi Folk Tales*. Charleston, SC: Kessinger Publishing, 2011)

Cwiklik, Robert. *King Philip and the War with the Colonists*. Englewood Cliffs, NJ: Silver Burdette Press, 1989.

Dahlin, Curtis A., and Alan R. Woolworth. *The Dakota Uprising: A Pictorial History*. Edina, MN: Beaver's Pond Press, 2009.

Damas, David, ed. *Handbook of North American Indians,* Vol. 5: *Arctic*. Washington, DC: Smithsonian Institution, 1984.

Dangberg, Grace, translator. *Washo Tales*. Reprint. Carson City: Nevada State Museum, 1968.

De Angulo, Jaime. *Indian Tales*. Santa Clara, CA: Heyday Books, 2003.

De Capua, Sarah. *The Shawnee*. New York: Marshall Cavendish Benchmark, 2008.

De Laguna, Fredericæ. "Tlingit." In *Handbook of North American Indians: Northwest Coast*. Vol. 7, edited by Wayne Suttles. Washington, DC: Smithsonian Institution, 1990, pp. 203–28.

Decker, Carol Paradise. *Pecos Pueblo People through the Ages: "—And We're Still Here": Stories of Time and Place*. Santa Fe, NM: Sunstone Press, 2011.

Decker, Peter R. *"The Utes Must Go!": American Expansion and the Removal of a People*. Golden, CO: Fulcrum Publishing, 2004.

DeJong, David H. *Forced to Abandon Our Fields: The 1914 Clay Southworth Gila River Pima Interviews*. Salt Lake City: University of Utah Press, 2011.

Deloria, Vine, Jr. *Red Earth, White Lies: Native Americans and the Myth of Scientific Fact*. New York: Scribner, 1995.

Dempsey, L. James. *Blackfoot War Art: Pictographs of the Reservation Period, 1880–2000*. Norman: University of Oklahoma Press, 2007.

Denetdale, Jennifer. *The Long Walk: The Forced Navajo Exile*. New York: Chelsea House, 2008.

— — —. *The Navajo*. New York: Chelsea House, 2011.

Densmore, Frances. *American Indians and Their Music*. Kila, MN: Kessinger Publishing, 2010.

DeRose, Cat. *Little Raven: Chief of the Southern Arapaho*. Palmer Lake, CO: Filter Press, 2010.

Dial, Adolph L., and David K. Eliades. *The Only Land I Know: A History of the Lumbee Indians*. Syracuse: Syracuse University Press, 1996.

Dickey, Michael E. *The People of the River's Mouth: In Search of the Missouria Indians*. Columbia: University of Missouri, 2011.

Ditchfield, Christin. *Northeast Indians.* Chicago: Heinemann Library, 2012.

— — —. *Plateau Indians.* Chicago: Heinemann Library, 2012.

Doak, Robin S. *Arctic Peoples.* Chicago: Heinemann Library, 2012.

— — —. *Subarctic Peoples.* Mankato, MN: Heinemann-Raintree, 2011.

Doherty, Craig A. *California Indians.* New York: Chelsea House Publications, 2007.

— — —. *Northeast Indians.* Broomall, PA: Chelsea House Publications, March 2008.

— — —. *Southeast Indians.* Minneapolis, MN: Chelsea House, 2007.

Doherty, Craig A., and Katherine M. Doherty. *Arctic Peoples.* New York: Chelsea House, 2008.

— — —. *Great Basin Indians.* Minneapolis, MN: Chelsea House, 2010.

— — —. *Plains Indians.* New York: Chelsea House, 2008.

— — —. *Plateau Indians.* New York: Chelsea House, 2008.

— — —. *Southwest Indians.* Minneapolis, MN: Chelsea House, 2007.

Dolan, Edward F. *The American Indian Wars.* Brookfield, CT: Millbrook Press, 2003.

Donlan, Leni. *Cherokee Rose: The Trail of Tears.* Chicago, IL: Raintree, 2007.

Downum, Christian E. Hisatsinom: *Ancient Peoples in a Land without Water.* Santa Fe: School for Advanced Research Press, 2011.

Dresser, Thomas. *The Wampanoag Tribe of Martha's Vineyard: Colonization to Recognition.* Charleston, SC: History Press, 2011.

Driver, Harold E., and Walter R. Goldschmidt. *The Hupa White Deerskin Dance.* Whitefish, MT: Kessinger Publishing, 2007.

Drury, Clifford M., ed. *Nine Years with the Spokane Indians: The Diary, 1838–1848, of Elkanah Walker.* Glendale, CA: Arthur H. Clark Company, 1976.

DuBois, Cora. *The 1870 Ghost Dance.* Reprint. Lincoln: University of Nebraska, 2007.

Duncan, Kate C. *Northern Athapaskan Art: A Beadwork Tradition.* Seattle: University of Washington Press, 1989.

Dunn, Jacob Piatt. *Massacres of the Mountains: A History of the Indian Wars of the Far West 1815–1875.* Whitefish, MT: Kessinger Publishing, 2006.

Dutton, Bertha P. *Indians of the American Southwest.* Englewood Cliffs, NJ: Prentice-Hall, 1975.

Duval, Kathleen. *The Native Ground: Indians and Colonists in the Heart of the Continent.* Philadelphia: University of Pennsylvania Press, 2006.

Dwyer, Helen, ed. *Peoples of the Southwest, West, and North.* Redding, CT: Brown Bear Books, 2009.

Dwyer, Helen, and D. L. Birchfield. *Cheyenne History and Culture.* New York: Gareth Stevens, 2012.

Dwyer, Helen, and Mary A. Stout. *Nez Percé History and Culture.* New York: Gareth Stevens, 2012.

Eastman, Charles A. *The Essential Charles Eastman (Ohiyesa), Revised and Updated Edition: Light on the Indian World.* Michael Oren Fitzgerald, ed. Bloomington, IN: World Wisdom, 2007.

— — —. *From the Deep Woods to Civilization.* Whitefish, MT: Kessinger Publishing, 2006.

— — —. *The Soul of the Indian.* New York: Dodo Press, 2007.

Eaton, William M. *Odyssey of the Pueblo Indians: An Introduction to Pueblo Indian Petroglyphs, Pictographs and Kiva Art Murals in the Southwest.* Paducah, KY: Turner Publishing Company, 2001.

Ember, Melvin, and Peter N. Peregrine, eds. *Encyclopedia of Prehistory,* Vol. 2: *Arctic and Subarctic.* New York: Kluwer Academic/Plenum Publishers, 2001.

Englar, Mary. *The Iroquois: The Six Nations Confederacy.* Mankato, MN: Capstone Press, 2006.

Erb, Gene, and Ann DeWolf Erb. *Voices in Our Souls: The DeWolfs, Dakota Sioux and the Little Bighorn.* Santa Fe: Sunstone Press, 2010.

Erdoes, Richard. *The Sun Dance People: The Plains Indians, Their Past and Present.* New York: Random House, 1972.

Erickson, Kirstin C. *Yaqui Homeland and Homeplace.* Tucson: University of Arizona Press, 2008.

Erickson, Winston P. *Sharing the Desert: The Tohono O'Odham in History.* Tucson: University of Arizona Press, 2003.

Erikson, Patricia Pierce. *Voices of a Thousand People: The Makah Cultural and Research Center.* Lincoln: University of Nebraska Press, 2005.

Ezell, Paul H. "History of the Pima." In *Handbook of North American Indians,* Volume 10: *Southwest,* edited by Alfonso Ortiz. Washington, DC: Smithsonian Institution Press, 1983.

Falconer, Shelley, and Shawna White. *Stones, Bones, and Stitches: Storytelling through Inuit Art.* Toronto, Ontario: Tundra Books, 2007.

Fariello, Anna. *Cherokee Basketry: From the Hands of Our Elders.* Charleston, SC: History Press, 2009.

Field, Ron. *The Seminole Wars, 1818–58.* New York: Osprey, 2009.

Fitzgerald, Judith, and Michael Oren Fitzgerald, eds. *The Spirit of Indian Women.* Bloomington, IN: World Wisdom, 2005.

Forczyk, Robert. *Nez Percé 1877: The Last Fight.* Long Island City, NY: Osprey, 2011.

Foreman, Grant. *Indian Removal.* Norman: University of Oklahoma Press, 1972.

Foster, Martha Harroun. *We Know Who We Are: Métis Identity in a Montana Community.* Norman: University of Oklahoma Press, 2006.

Foster, Sharon Ewell. *Abraham's Well: A Novel.* Minneapolis, MN: Bethany House, 2006.

Fowler, Loretta. *The Columbia Guide to American Indians of the Great Plains.* New York: Columbia University Press, 2005.

Fradin, Dennis B. *The Pawnee.* Chicago: Childrens Press, 1988.

Frank, Andrew. *The Seminole.* New York: Chelsea House, 2011.

Freedman, Russell. *The Life and Death of Crazy Horse.* New York: Holiday House, 1996.

Gagnon, Gregory O. *Culture and Customs of the Sioux Indians.* Westport, CT: Greenwood, 2011.

Garfinkel, Alan P., and Harold Williams. *Handbook of the Kawaiisu.* Kern Valley, CA: Wa-hi Sina'avi, 2011.

Geake, Robert A. *A History of the Narragansett Tribe of Rhode Island: Keepers of the Bay.* Charleston, SC: History Press, 2011.

Geronimo. *The Autobiography of Geronimo.* St. Petersburg, FL: Red and Black Publishers, 2011.

Giago, Tim A. *Children Left Behind: Dark Legacy of Indian Mission Boarding Schools.* Santa Fe, NM: Clear Light Publishing, 2006.

Gibson, Karen Bush. *The Chumash: Seafarers of the Pacific Coast.* Mankato, MN: Bridgestone Books, 2004.

— — —. *The Great Basin Indians: Daily Life in the 1700s.* Mankato, MN: Capstone Press, 2006.

— — —. *New Netherland: The Dutch Settle the Hudson Valley.* Elkton, IN: Mitchell Lane Publishers, 2006.

Giddings, Ruth Warner. *Yaqui Myths and Legends.* Charleston, SC: BiblioBazaar, 2009.

Gipson, Lawrence Henry. *The Moravian Indian Mission on White River: Diaries and Letters, May 5, 1799, to November 12, 1806.* Indianapolis: Indiana Historical Bureau, 1938.

Girdner, Alwin J. *Diné Tah: My Reservation Days 1923–1938.* Tucson: Rio Nuevo Publishers, c2011.

Glancy, Diane. *Pushing the Bear: After the Trail of Tears.* Norman: University of Oklahoma Press, 2009.

Goddard, Pliny Earle. *Hupa Texts.* Reprint. Charleston, SC: BiblioBazaar, 2009.

— — —. *Life and Culture of the Hupa.* Reprint. Charleston, SC: Nabu Press, 2011.

— — —. *Myths and Tales from the San Carlos Apache.* Whitefish, MT: Kessinger Publishing, 2006.

— — —. *Myths and Tales of the White Mountain Apache.* Whitefish, MT: Kessinger Publishing, 2011.

Goodman, Linda J. *Singing the Songs of My Ancestors: The Life and Music of Helma Swan, Makah Elder.* Norman: University of Oklahoma Press, 2003.

Goodwin, Grenville. *Myths and Tales of the White Mountain Apache.* Whitefish, MT: Kessinger Publishing, 2011.

Gordon, Irene Ternier. *A People on the Move: The Métis of the Western Plains.* Surry, British Columbia: Heritage House, 2009.

Grafe, Steven L. ed. *Lanterns on the Prairie: The Blackfeet Photographs of Walter McClintock.* Norman: University of Oklahoma Press, 2009.

Grant, Blanche Chloe. *Taos Indians.* 1925 ed. Santa Fe: Sunstone Press, 2007.

Grant, Campbell. *Rock Paintings of the Chumash: A Study of a California Indian Culture.* Reprint. Santa Barbara, CA: Santa Barbara Museum of Natural History/EZ Nature Books, 1993.

Gray-Kanatiiosh, Barbara A. *Cahuilla.* Edina, MN: ABDO, 2007.

— — —. *Modoc.* Edina, MN: ABDO, 2007.

— — —. *Paiute.* Edina, MN: ABDO Publishing, 2007.

— — —. *Yurok.* Edina, MN: ABDO, 2007.

Graymont, Barbara. *The Iroquois.* New York: Chelsea House, 1988.

Green, Michael D., and Theda Perdue. *The Cherokee Nation and the Trail of Tears.* New York: Viking, 2007.

— — —. *The Columbia Guide to American Indians of the Southeast.* New York: Columbia University Press, 2001.

Grinnell, George Bird. *Blackfeet Indians Stories.* Whitefish, MT: Kessinger Publishing, 2006.

— — —. *The Cheyenne Indians: Their History and Lifeways.* Bloomington, IN: World Wisdom, 2008.

Guigon, Catherine, Francis Latreille, and Fredric Malenfer. *The Arctic.* New York: Abrams Books for Young Readers, 2007.

Gunther, Vanessa. *Chief Joseph.* Greenwood, 2010.

Guthridge, George. *The Kids from Nowhere: The Story behind the Arctic Education Miracle.* Anchorage: Alaska Northwest Books, 2006.

Hagan, William T. *The Sac and Fox Indians.* Norman: University of Oklahoma Press, 2008.

Hahn, Elizabeth. *The Pawnee.* Vero Beach, FL: Rourke Publications, Inc., 1992.

Haig-Brown, Roderick. *The Whale People.* Madeira Park, BC: Harbour Publishing, 2003.

Hancock, David A. *Tlingit: Their Art and Culture.* Blaine, WA: Hancock House Publishers, 2003.

Handbook of North American Indians, Vol. 6: *Subarctic.* Ed. June Helm. Washington, DC: Smithsonian Institution, 1981.

Harpster, Jack, and Ken Stalter. *Captive!: The Story of David Ogden and the Iroquois.* Santa Barbara, CA: Praeger, 2010.

Harrington, Mark Raymond. *Certain Caddo Sites in Arkansas.* Charleston, SC: Johnson Press, 2011.

Hayes, Allan, and Carol Hayes. *The Desert Southwest: Four Thousand Years of Life And Art.* Berkeley, CA: Ten Speed Press, 2006.

Hearth, Amy Hill. *"Strong Medicine Speaks": A Native American Elder Has Her Say: An Oral History.* New York: Atria Books, 2008.

Hebner, William Logan. *Southern Paiute: A Portrait.* Logan: Utah State University Press, 2010.

Heinämäki, Leena. *The Right to Be a Part of Nature: Indigenous Peoples and the Environment.* Rovaniemi, Finland: Lapland University Press, 2010.

Heizer, R. F., ed. *Handbook of North American Indians.* Vol. 8: *California.* Washington, DC: Smithsonian Institution, 1978.

Hessel, Ingo. *Inuit Art: An Introduction.* Vancouver, British Columbia: Douglas & McIntyre, 2002.

Hicks, Terry Allan. *The Chumash.* New York: Marshall Cavendish Benchmark, 2008.

— — —. *The Zuñi.* New York: Marshall Cavendish Benchmark, 2010.

Hill, George, Robert H. Ruby, and John A. Brown. *The Spokane Indians: Children of the Sun.* Norman: University of Oklahoma Press, 2006.

Himsl, Sharon M. *The Shoshone.* San Diego, CA: Lucent Books, 2005.

Hirst, Stephen. *I Am the Grand Canyon: The Story of the Havasupai People.* Grand Canyon, AZ: Grand Canyon Association, 2006.

Hobson, Geary. *Plain of Jars and Other Stories.* East Lansing: Michigan State University Press, 2011.

Hodge, Frederick Webb. "Dwamish." *Handbook of American Indians North of Mexico.* New York: Pageant Books, 1959.

Hogeland, Kim, and L. Frank Hogeland. *First Families: Photographic History of California Indians.* Berkeley: Heyday Books, 2007.

Holm, Bill. *Spirit and Ancestor: A Century of Northwest Coast Indian Art in the Burke Museum.* Seattle: Burke Museum; University of Washington Press, 1987.

Hooper, Lucile. *The Cahuilla Indians.* Kila, MN: Kessinger Publishing, 2011.

Hoover, Alan L. *Nuu-chah-nulth Voices, Histories, Objects, and Journeys.* Victoria: Royal British Columbia Museum, 2000.

Hopping, Lorraine Jean. *Chief Joseph: The Voice for Peace.* New York: Sterling, 2010.

Houston, James A. *James Houston's Treasury of Inuit Legends.* Orlando, FL: Harcourt, 2006.

Hungrywolf, Adolf. *Tribal Childhood: Growing Up in Traditional Native America.* Summertown, TN:Native Voices, 2008.

Hyde, Dayton O. *The Last Free Man: The True Story behind the Massacre of Shoshone Mike and His Band of Indians in 1911.* New York: Dial Press, 1973.

Hyde, George E. *Indians of the Woodlands: From Prehistoric Times to 1725.* Norman: University of Oklahoma Press, 1962.

Indians of the Northwest Coast and Plateau. Chicago: World Book, 2009.

Indians of the Southwest. Chicago: World Book, 2009.

Inupiaq and Yupik People of Alaska. Anchorage: Alaska Geographic Society, 2004.

Jacknis, Ira. *The Storage Box of Tradition: Kwakiutl Art, Anthropologists, and Museums, 1881–1981.* Washington, DC: Smithsonian Institution Press, 2002.

Jackson, Helen Hunt. *The Indian Reform Letters of Helen Hunt Jackson, 1879–1885.*Edited by Valerie ShererMathes. Norman: University of Oklahoma Press, 1998.

— — —. *Ramona.* New York: Signet, 1988.

James, Cheewa. *Modoc: The Tribe That Wouldn't Die.* Happy Camp, CA: Naturegraph, 2008.

Jastrzembski, Joseph C. *The Apache.* Minneapolis: Chelsea House, 2011.

— — —. *The Apache Wars: The Final Resistance.* Minneapolis: Chelsea House, 2007.

Jenness, Aylette, and Alice Rivers. *In Two Worlds: A Yu'pik Eskimo Family.* New York: Houghton Mifflin, 1989.

Jennys, Susan. *19th Century Plains Indian Dresses.* Pottsboro, TX: Crazy Crow, 2004.

Jensen, Richard E., ed. *The Pawnee Mission Letters, 1834-1851.* Lincoln: University of Nebraska Press, 2010.

Jeter, Marvin D. *Edward Palmer's Arkansaw Mounds.* Tuscaloosa: University of Alabama Press, 2010.

Johansen, Bruce E. *The Iroquois.* New York, NY: Chelsea House, 2010.

Johnsgard, Paul A. *Wind through the Buffalo Grass: A Lakota Story Cycle.* Lincoln, NE: Plains Chronicles Press, 2008.

Johnson, Jerald Jay. "Yana." In *Handbook of North American Indians.* Vol. 10: *Southwest,* edited by Alfonso Ortiz. Washington, DC: Smithsonian Institution, 1983.

Johnson, Michael. *American Indians of the Southeast.* Oxford: Osprey Publishing, 1995.

— — —. "Duwamish." *The Native Tribes of North America.* New York: Macmillan, 1992.

— — —. *Native Tribes of the Northeast.* Milwaukee, WI: World Almanac Library, 2004.

Johnson, Michael, and Jonathan Smith. *Indian Tribes of the New England Frontier.* Oxford: Osprey Publishing, 2006.

Johnson, Thomas H., and Helen S. Johnson. *Also Called Sacajawea: Chief Woman's Stolen Identity.* Long Grove, IL: Waveland Press, 2008.

— — —. *Two Toms: Lessons from a Shoshone Doctor.* Salt Lake City: University of Utah Press, 2010.

Jonaitis, Aldona. *Art of the Northwest Coast.* Seattle: University of Washington Press, 2006.

Joseph, Frank. *Advanced Civilizations of Prehistoric America: The Lost Kingdoms of the Adena, Hopewell, Mississippians, and Anasazi.* Rochester, VT: Bear & Company, December 21, 2009.

Josephson, Judith Pinkerton. *Why Did Cherokees Move West? And Other Questions about the Trail of Tears.* Minneapolis: Lerner Publications, 2011.

Josephy, Alvin M., Jr. *500 Nations: An Illustrated History of North American Indians.* New York: Knopf, 1994.

— — —. *Nez Percé Country.* Lincoln: University of Nebraska Press, 2007.

Kallen, Stuart A. *The Pawnee.* San Diego: Lucent Books, 2001.

Kaneuketat. *I Dreamed the Animals: Kaneuketat: the Life of an Innu Hunter.* New York: Berghahn Books, 2008.

Kavasch, E. Barrie. *Enduring Harvests: Native American Foods and Festivals for Every Season.* Old Saybrook, CT: The Globe Pequot Press, 1995.

Keegan, Marcia. *Pueblo People: Ancient Tradition, Modern Lives.* Santa Fe, NM: Clear Light Publishers, 1999.

— — —. *Taos Pueblo and Its Sacred Blue Lake.* Santa Fe: Clear Light Publishers, 2010.

Keegan, Marcia, and Regis Pecos. *Pueblo People: Ancient Traditions, Modern Lives.* Santa Fe, NM: Clear Light Publishers, 1999.

Kegg, Maude. *Portage Lake: Memories of an Ojibwe Childhood.* Edmonton: University of Alberta Press, 1991.

Kennedy, J. Gerald. *Life of Black Hawk, or Ma-ka-tai-me-she-kia-kiak. Dictated by Himself.* New York: Penguin Books, 2008.

King, David C. *The Blackfeet.* New York: Marshall Cavendish Benchmark, 2010.

— — —. *First People.* New York: DK Children, 2008.

— — —. *The Inuit.* New York: Marshall Cavendish Benchmark, 2008.

— — —. *The Nez Percé.* New York: Benchmark Books, 2008.

— — —. *Seminole.* New York: Benchmark Books, 2007.

Kiowa and Pueblo Art: Watercolor Paintings by Native American Artists. Mineola, NY: Dover Publications, 2009.

Kirkpatrick, Katherine. *Mysterious Bones: The Story of Kennewick Man.* New York: Holiday House, 2011.

Kissock,Heather, and Jordan McGill. *Apache: American Indian Art and Culture.* New York: Weigl Publishers, 2011.

Kissock, Heather, and Rachel Small. *Caddo: American Indian Art and Culture.* New York: Weigl Publishers, 2011.

Koyiyumptewa, Stewart B., Carolyn O'Bagy Davis, and the Hopi Cultural Preservation Office. *The Hopi People.* Charleston, SC: Arcadia Publishing, 2009.

Kristofic, Jim. *Navajos Wear Nikes: A Reservation Life.* Albuquerque: University of New Mexico Press, 2011.

Kroeber, Theodora. *Ishi in Two Worlds: A Biography of the Last Wild Indian in North America.* Berkeley: University of California Press, 2004.

Krupnik, Igor, and Dyanna Jolly, eds. *The Earth Is Faster Now: Indigenous Observations of Arctic Environmental Change.* Fairbanks, Alaska: Arctic Research Consortium of the United States, 2002.

Kuiper, Kathleen, ed. *American Indians of California, the Great Basin, and the Southwest.* New York: Rosen Educational Services, 2012.

— — —. *American Indians of the Northeast and Southeast.* New York: Rosen Educational Services, 2012.

— — —. *American Indians of the Plateau and Plains.* New York: Rosen Educational Services, 2012.

— — —. *Indigenous Peoples of the Arctic, Subarctic, and Northwest Coast.* New York: Rosen Educational Services, 2012.

Lacey, T. Jensen. *The Blackfeet.* New York: Chelsea House, 2011.

— — —. *The Comanche.* New York: Chelsea House, 2011.

Lankford, George E., ed. *Native American Legends of the Southeast: Tales from the Natchez, Caddo, Biloxi, Chickasaw, and Other Nations.* 5th ed. Tuscaloosa: University of Alabama Press, 2011.

Lanmon, Dwight P. and Francis H. Harlow. *The Pottery of Zuñi Pueblo.* Santa Fe: Museum of New Mexico Press, 2008.

Larsen, Mike, Martha Larsen, and Jeannie Barbour. *Proud to Be Chickasaw.* Ada, OK: Chickasaw Press, 2010.

Lenik, Edward J. *Making Pictures in Stone: American Indian Rock Art of the Northeast.* Tuscaloosa: University of Alabama Press, 2009.

Levine, Michelle. *The Delaware.* Minneapolis, MN: Lerner Publications, 2006.

— — —. *The Ojibway.* Minneapolis, MN: Lerner Publications, 2006.

Levy, Janey. *The Wampanoag of Massachusetts and Rhode Island.* New York: PowerKids Press, 2005.

Liebert, Robert. *Osage Life and Legends: Earth People/Sky People.* Happy Camp, California: Naturegraph Publishers, 1987.

Life Stories of Our Native People: Shoshone, Paiute, Washo. Reno, NV: Inter-tribal Council of Nevada, 1974.

Liptak, Karen. *North American Indian Ceremonies.* New York: Franklin Watts, 1992.

Little, Kimberley Griffiths. *The Last Snake Runner.* New York: Alfred A. Knopf, 2002.

Lloyd, J. William. *Aw-aw-tam Indian Nights: The Myths and Legends of the Pimas.* Westfield, NJ: The Lloyd Group, 1911. Available online from http://www.sacred-texts.com/nam/sw/ain/index.htm (accessed on July 20, 2011).

Lobo, Susan, Steve Talbot, and Traci L. Morris, compilers. *Native American Voices: A Reader.* 3rd ed. Upper Saddle River, NJ: Prentice Hall, 2010.

Lourie, Peter. *The Lost World of the Anasazi: Exploring the Mysteries of Chaco Canyon.* Honesdale, PA: Boyds Mills Press, 2007.

Macdougall, Brenda. *One of the Family: Metis Culture in Nineteenth-Century Northwestern Saskatchewan.* Vancouver, British Columbia: UBC Press, 2010.

Mann, John W.W. *Sacajawea's People: The Lemhi Shoshones and the Salmon River Country.* Lincoln, NE: Bison Books, 2011.

Margolin, Malcolm. *The Ohlone Way.* Berkeley, CA: Heyday Books, 1981.

— — —. *The Way We Lived: California Indian Stories, Songs, and Reminiscences.* Reprint. Heyday Books, Berkeley, California, 2001.

Marriott, Alice, and Carol K. Rachlin. *Plains Indian Mythology.* New York, NY: Thomas Y. Crowell, 1975.

Marshall, Ann, ed. *Home: Native People in the Southwest.* Phoenix, AZ: Heard Museum, 2005.

Marshall, Bonnie. *Far North Tales: Stories from the Peoples of the Arctic Circle.* Edited by Kira Van Deusen. Santa Barbara, CA: Libraries Unlimited, 2011.

Marsi, Katie. *The Trail of Tears: The Tragedy of the American Indians.* New York: Marshall Cavendish Benchmark, 2010.

McDaniel, Melissa. *Great Basin Indians.* Des Plaines, IL: Heinemann, 2011.

— — —. *The Sac and Fox Indians.* New York: Chelsea Juniors, 1995.

— — —. *Southwest Indians.* Chicago: Heinemann Library, 2012.

Mcmullen, John William. *Ge Wisnemen! (Let's Eat!): A Potawatomi Family Dinner Manual.* Charleston, SC: CreateSpace, 2011.

Melody, Michael E., and Paul Rosier. *The Apache.* Minneapolis: Chelsea House, 2005.

Merriam, C. Hart. *The Dawn of the World: Myths and Tales of the Miwok Indians of California.* Kila, MN: Kessinger Publishing, 2010.

Michael, Hauser. *Traditional Inuit Songs from the Thule Area.* Copenhagen: Museum Tusculanum Press, 2010.

Miles, Ray. "Wichita." *Native America in the Twentieth Century, An Encyclopedia.* Ed. Mary B. Davis. New York: Garland Publishing, 1994.

Miller, Debbie S., and Jon Van Dyle. *Arctic Lights, Arctic Nights.* New York: Walker Books for Young Readers, 2007.

Miller, Frederic P., Agnes F. Vandome, and John McBrewster, eds. *Nuu-chah-nulth People.* Beau Bassin, Mauritius: Alphascript Publishing, 2011.

Miller, Raymond H. *North American Indians: The Apache.* San Diego: Kid-Haven Press, 2005.

Milner, George R. *The Moundbuilders: Ancient Peoples of Eastern North America.* New York: Thames & Hudson, 2005.

Mooney, James. *Calendar History of the Kiowa Indians.* Whitefish, MT: Kessinger Publishing, 2006.

— — —. *Myths of the Cherokee.* New York: Dover Publications, 1996.

Mosqueda, Frank, and Vickie Leigh Krudwig. *The Hinono'ei Way of Life: An Introduction to the Arapaho People.* Edited by Susan Scott Hill. Concho, OK: Cheyenne and Arapaho Tribes of Oklahoma, 2008.

— — —. *The Prairie Thunder People: A Brief History of the Arapaho People.* Edited by Susan Scott Hill. Concho, OK: Cheyenne and Arapaho Tribes of Oklahoma, 2008.

Mossiker, Frances. *Pocahontas: The Life and the Legend.* New York: Alfred A. Knopf, 1976.

Mundell, Kathleen. *North by Northeast: Wabanaki, Akwesasne Mohawk, and Tuscarora Traditional Arts.* Gardiner, ME: Tilbury House, Publishers, 2008.

Myers, Albert Cook, ed. *William Penn's Own Account of the Lenni Lenape or Delaware Indians.* Somerset, NJ: Middle Atlantic Press, 1970.

Myers, Arthur. *The Pawnee.* New York: Franklin Watts, 1993.

Myers, James E. "Cahto." In *Handbook of North American Indians.* Vol. 8: *California,* edited by R. F. Heizer. Washington, D.C.: Smithsonian Institution, 1978: 244–48.

Neeley, Bill. *The Last Comanche Chief: The Life and Times of Quanah Parker.* New York: Wiley, 1996.

Nelson, Sharlene, and Ted W. Nelson. *The Makah.* New York: Franklin Watts, 2003.

Nez, Chester, and Judith Schiess Avila. *Code Talker.* New York: Berkley Caliber, 2011.

Nichols, Richard. *A Story to Tell: Traditions of a Tlingit Community.* Minneapolis: Lerner Publications Company, 1998.

Nowell, Charles James. *Smoke from their Fires: The Life of a Kwakiutl Chief.* Hamdon, CT: Archon Books, 1968.

O'Neale, Lila M. *Yurok-Karok Basket Weavers.* Berkeley, CA: Phoebe A. Hearst Museum of Anthropology, 2007.

Opler, Morris Edward. *Myths and Tales of the Chiricahua Apache Indians.* Charleston, SC: Kessinger Publishing, 2011.

Ortega, Simon, ed. *Handbook of North American Indians.* Vol. 12: *The Plateau.* Washington, DC: Smithsonian Institution, 1978.

Ortiz, Alfonso, ed. *Handbook of American Indians.* Vols. 9–10. *The Southwest.* Washington, DC: Smithsonian Institution, 1978–83.

Owings, Alison. *Indian Voices: Listening to Native Americans.* New Brunswick, N.J.: Rutgers University Press, 2011.

Page, Jake, and Susanne Page. *Indian Arts of the Southwest.* Tucson, AZ: Rio Nuevo Publishers, 2008.

Page, Susanne and Jake. *Navajo.* Tucson, AZ: Rio Nuevo Publishers, 2010.

Paige, Amanda L., Fuller L. Bumpers, and Daniel F. Littlefield, Jr. *Chickasaw Removal.* Ada, OK: Chickasaw Press, 2010.

Palazzo-Craig, Janet. *The Ojibwe of Michigan, Wisconsin, Minnesota, and North Dakota.* New York: PowerKids Press, 2005.

Peltier, Leonard. *Prison Writings: My Life Is My Sun Dance.* New York: St. Martin's, 2000.

Penny, Josie. *So Few on Earth: A Labrador Métis Woman Remembers.* Toronto, Ontario: Dundurn Press, 2010.

Peoples of the Arctic and Subarctic. Chicago: World Book, 2009.

Perritano, John. *Spanish Missions.* New York: Children's Press, 2010.

Philip, Neil, ed. *A Braid of Lives: Native American Childhood.* New York: Clarion Books, 2000.

Pierson, George. *The Kansa, or Kaw Indians, and Their History, and the Story of Padilla.* Charleston, SC: Nabu Press, 2010.

Pijoan, Teresa. *Pueblo Indian Wisdom: Native American Legends and Mythology.* Santa Fe: Sunstone Press, 2000.

Pritzker, Barry, and Paul C. Rosier. *The Hopi.* New York: Chelsea House, c. 2011.

Riddell, Francis A. "Maidu and Concow." *Handbook of North American Indians.* Vol. 8: *California.* Edited by Robert F. Heizer. Washington DC: Smithsonian Institution, 1978.

Rielly, Edward J. *Legends of American Indian Resistance.* Westport, CT: Greenwood, 2011.

Riordan, Robert. *Medicine for Wildcat: A Story of the Friendship between a Menominee Indian and Frontier Priest Samuel Mazzuchelli.* Revised by

Marilyn Bowers Gorun and the Sinsinawa Dominican Sisters. Sinsinawa, WI: Sinsinawa Dominican Sisters, 2006.

Rollings, Willard H. *The Comanche.* New York: Chelsea House Publications, 2004.

Rosoff, Nancy B., and Susan Kennedy Zeller. *Tipi: Heritage of the Great Plains.* Seattle: Brooklyn Museum in association with University of Washington Press, 2011.

Ruby, Robert H., John A. Brown, and Cary C. Collins. *A Guide to the Indian Tribes of the Pacific Northwest.* Norman: University of Oklahoma Press, 2010.

Russell, Frank. *The Pima Indians.* Whitefish, MT: Kessinger Publishing, 2010.

Ryan, Marla Felkins, and Linda Schmittroth. *Tribes of Native America: Zuñi Pueblo.* San Diego: Blackbirch Press, 2002.

— — —. *Ute.* San Diego: Blackbirch Press, 2003.

Rzeczkowski, Frank. *The Lakota Sioux.* New York: Chelsea House, 2011.

Seton, Ernest Thompson. *Sign Talk of the Cheyenne Indians.* Mineola, NY: Dover Publications, 2000.

Sherrow, Victoria. *The Iroquois Indians.* New York: Chelsea House, 1992.

Shipek, Florence Connolly. "Luiseño." In *Native America in the Twentieth Century: An Encyclopedia,* edited by Mary B. Davis. New York: Garland Publishing, 1994.

Shipley, William. *The Maidu Indian Myths and Stories of Hanc'Ibyjim.* Berkeley: Heyday Books, 1991.

Shull, Jodie A. *Voice of the Paiutes: A Story About Sarah Winnemucca.* Minneapolis, MN: Millbrook Press, 2007.

Simermeyer, Genevieve. *Meet Christopher: An Osage Indian Boy from Oklahoma.* Tulsa, OK: National Museum of the American Indian, Smithsonian Institution, in association with Council Oak Books, 2008.

Simmons, Marc. *Friday, the Arapaho Boy: A Story from History.* Albuquerque: University of New Mexico Press, 2004.

Sita, Lisa. *Indians of the Northeast: Traditions, History, Legends, and Life.* Milwaukee, WI: Gareth Stevens, 2000.

— — —. *Pocahontas: The Powhatan Culture and the Jamestown Colony.* New York: PowerPlus Books, 2005.

Slater, Eva. *Panamint Shoshone Basketry: An American Art Form.* Berkeley: Heyday Books, 2004.

Smith, White Mountain. *Indian Tribes of the Southwest.* Kila, MN: Kessinger Publishing, 2005.

Snell, Alma Hogan. *A Taste of Heritage: Crow Indian Recipes & Herbal Medicines.* Lincoln: University of Nebraska Press, 2006.

Sneve, Virginia Driving Hawk. *The Cherokee*. New York: Holiday House, 1996.

— — —. *The Cheyenne*. New York: Holiday House, 1996.

— — —. *The Iroquois*. New York: Holiday House, 1995.

— — —. *The Nez Percé*. New York: Holiday House, 1994.

— — —. *The Seminoles*. New York: Holiday House, 1994.

Snyder, Clifford Gene. *Ghost Trails: Mythology and Folklore of the Chickasaw, Choctaw, Creeks and Other Muskoghean Indian Tribes*. North Hollywood, CA: JES, 2009.

— — —. *The Muskogee Chronicles: Accounts of the Early Muskogee/Creek Indians*. N. Hollywood, CA: JES, 2008.

Solomon, Madeline. *Koyukon Athabaskan Songs*. Homer, AK: Wizard Works, 2003.

Sonneborn, Liz. *The Choctaws*. Minneapolis, MN: Lerner Publications, 2007.

— — —. *The Creek*. Minneapolis: Lerner Publications, 2007.

— — —. *The Chumash*. Minneapolis, MN: Lerner Publications, 2007.

— — —. *The Navajos*. Minneapolis, MN: Lerner Publications, 2007.

— — —. *Northwest Coast Indians*. Chicago: Heinemann Library, 2012.

— — —. *The Shoshones*. Minneapolis, MN: Lerner Publications, 2006.

— — —. *Wilma Mankiller*. New York: Marshall Cavendish Benchmark, 2010.

Spalding, Andrea. *Secret of the Dance*. Orca, WA: Orca Book Publishers, 2006.

Spence, Lewis. *Myths and Legends of the North American Indians*. Whitefish, MT: Kessinger Publishing, 1997.

Spragg-Braude, Stacia. *To Walk in Beauty: A Navajo Family's Journey Home*. Santa Fe: Museum of New Mexico Press, 2009.

Sprague, DonovinArleigh. *American Indian Stories*. West Stockbridge, CT: Hard Press, 2006.

— — —. *Choctaw Nation of Oklahoma*. Chicago, IL: Arcadia, 2007.

— — —. *Old Indian Legends: Retold by Zitkala--Sa*. Paris: Adamant Media Corporation, 2006.

— — —. *Standing Rock Sioux*. Charleston, SC: Arcadia, 2004.

St. Lawrence, Genevieve. *The Pueblo And Their History*. Minneapolis, MN: Compass Point Books, 2006.

Stanley, George E. *Sitting Bull: Great Sioux Hero*. New York: Sterling, 2010.

Stern, Pamela R. *Daily Life of the Inuit*. Santa Barbara, CA: Greenwood, 2010.

Sterngass, Jon. *Geronimo*. New York: Chelsea House, 2010.

Stevenson, Matilda Coxe. *The Zuñi Indians and Their Uses of Plants*. Charleston, SC: Kessinger Publishing, 2011.

Stevenson, Tilly E. *The Religious Life of the Zuñi Child*. Charleston, SC: Kessinger Publishing, 2011.

Stewart, Philip. *Osage*. Philadelphia, PA: Mason Crest Publishers, 2004.

Stirling, M.W. *Snake Bites and the Hopi Snake Dance*. Whitefish, MT: Kessinger Publishing, 2011.

Stone, Amy M. *Creek History and Culture*. Milwaukee: Gareth Stevens Publishing, 2011.

Stout, Mary. *Blackfoot History and Culture*. New York: Gareth Stevens, 2012.

— — —. *Hopi History and Culture*. New York: Gareth Stevens, 2011.

— — —. *Shoshone History and Culture*. New York: Gareth Stevens, 2011.

Strack, Andrew J. *How the Miami People Live*. Edited by Mary Tippman, Meghan Dorey and Daryl Baldwin. Oxford, OH: Myaamia Publications, 2010.

Straub, Patrick. *It Happened in South Dakota: Remarkable Events That Shaped History*. New York: Globe Pequot, 2009.

Sullivan, Cathie, and Gordon Sullivan. *Roadside Guide to Indian Ruins & Rock Art of the Southwest*. Englewood, CO: Westcliffe Publishers, 2006.

Sullivan, George. *Geronimo: Apache Renegade*. New York: Sterling, 2010.

Suttles, Wayne, and Barbara Lane. "Southern Coast Salish." *Handbook of North American Indians*. Vol. 7: *Northwest Coast*. Edited by Wayne Suttles. Washington, DC: Smithsonian Institution, 1990.

Swanton, John R., and Franz Boas. *Haida Songs; Tsimshian Texts (1912)*. Vol. 3. Whitefish, MT: Kessinger Publishing, 2010.

Sweet, Jill Drayson, and Nancy Hunter Warren. *Pueblo Dancing*. Atglen, PA: Schiffer Publishing, 2011.

Tenenbaum, Joan M., and Mary Jane McGary, eds. *Denaina Sukdua: Traditional Stories of the Tanaina Athabaskans*. Fairbanks: Alaska Native Language Center, 2006.

Tiller, Veronica E. Velarde. *Culture and Customs of the Apache Indians*. Santa Barbara, CA: ABC-CLIO, 2011.

Underhill, Ruth. *The Papago Indians of Arizona and their Relatives the Pima*. Whitefish, MT: Kessinger Publishing, 2010.

Van Deusen, Kira. *Kiviuq: An Inuit Hero and His Siberian Cousins*. Montreal: McGill-Queen's University Press, 2009.

Vanderwerth, W. C. *Indian Oratory: Famous Speeches by Noted Indian Chieftains*. Norman: University of Oklahoma Press, 1979.

Vaudrin, Bill. *Tanaina Tales from Alaska*. Norman: University of Oklahoma Press, 1969.

Viola, Herman J. *Trail to Wounded Knee: The Last Stand of the Plains Indians 1860–1890.* Washington, DC: National Geographic, 2004.

Von Ahnen, Katherine. *Charlie Young Bear.* Minot, CO: Roberts Rinehart Publishers, 1994.

Wade, Mary Dodson. *Amazing Cherokee Writer Sequoyah.* Berkeley Heights, NJ: Enslow, 2009.

Wagner, Frederic C. III. *Participants in the Battle of the Little Big Horn: A Biographical Dictionary of Sioux, Cheyenne and United States Military Personnel.* Jefferson, NC: McFarland, 2011.

Waldman, Carl. "Colville Reservation." In *Encyclopedia of Native American Tribes.* New York: Facts on File, 2006.

— — —. *Encyclopedia of Native American Tribes.* New York: Facts on File, 2006.

Wallace, Mary. *The Inuksuk Book.* Toronto, Ontario: Maple Tree Press, 2004.

— — —. *Make Your Own Inuksuk.* Toronto, Ontario: Maple Tree Press, 2004.

Wallace, Susan E. *The Land of the Pueblos.* Santa Fe, NM: Sunstone Press, 2006.

Ward, Jill. *The Cherokees.* Hamilton, GA: State Standards, 2010.

— — —. *Creeks and Cherokees Today.* Hamilton, GA: State Standards, 2010.

Warm Day, Jonathan. *Taos Pueblo: Painted Stories.* Santa Fe, NM: Clear Light Publishing, 2004.

Waters, Frank. *Book of the Hopi.* New York: Viking Press, 1963.

White, Bruce. *We Are at Home: Pictures of the Ojibwe People.* St. Paul, MN: Minnesota Historical Society Press, 2007.

White, Tekla N. *San Francisco Bay Area Missions.* Minneapolis, MN: Lerner, 2007.

Whitehead, Ruth Holmes. *The Micmac: How Their Ancestors Lived Five Hundred Years Ago.* Halifax, Nova Scotia: Nimbus, 1983.

Whiteman, Funston, Michael Bell, and Vickie Leigh Krudwig. *The Cheyenne Journey: An Introduction to the Cheyenne People.* Edited by Susan Scott-Hill. Concho, OK: Cheyenne and Arapaho Tribes of Oklahoma, 2008.

— — —. *The Tsististas: People of the Plains.* Edited by Susan Scott-Hill. Concho, OK: Cheyenne and Arapaho Tribes of Oklahoma, 2008.

Wiggins, Linda E., ed. *Dena—The People: The Way of Life of the Alaskan Athabaskans Described in Nonfiction Stories, Biographies, and Impressions from All Over the Interior of Alaska.* Fairbanks: Theata Magazine, University of Alaska, 1978.

Wilcox, Charlotte. *The Iroquois.* Minneapolis, MN: Lerner Publishing Company, 2007.

— — —. *The Seminoles.* Minneapolis: Lerner Publications, 2007.

Wilds, Mary C. *The Creek.* San Diego, CA: Lucent Books, 2005.

Wiles, Sara. *Arapaho Journeys: Photographs and Stories from the Wind River Reservation.* Norman: University of Oklahoma Press, 2011.

Williams, Jack S. *The Luiseno of California.* New York: PowerKids Press, 2003.

— — —. *The Modoc of California and Oregon.* New York: PowerKids Press, 2004.

— — —. *The Mojave of California and Arizona.* New York: PowerKids Press, 2004.

Wilson, Darryl J. *The Morning the Sun Went Down.* Berkeley, CA: Heyday, 1998.

Wilson, Elijah Nicholas. *The White Indian Boy: The Story of Uncle Nick among the Shoshones.* Kila, MN: Kessinger Publishing, 2004.

Wilson, Frazer Ells. *The Peace of Mad Anthony: An Account of the Subjugation of the Northwestern Indian Tribes and the Treaty of Greeneville.* Kila, MN: Kessinger Publishing, 2005.

Wilson, Norman L., and Arlean H. Towne. "Nisenan." In *Handbook of North American Indians.* Vol. 8: *California.* Edited by Robert F. Heizer. Washington DC: Smithsonian Institution, 1978.

Winnemucca, Sarah. *Life among the Paiutes: Their Wrongs and Claims.* Privately printed, 1883. Reprint. Reno: University of Nevada Press, 1994.

Wolcott, Harry F. *A Kwakiutl Village and School.* Walnut Creek, CA: AltaMira Press, 2003.

Wolfson, Evelyn. *The Iroquois: People of the Northeast.* Brookfield, CT: The Millbrook Press, 1992.

Woolworth, Alan R. *Santee Dakota Indian Tales.* Saint Paul, MN: Prairie Smoke Press, 2003.

Worl, Rosita. *Celebration: Tlingit, Haida, Tsimshian Dancing on the Land.* Edited by Kathy Dye. Seattle: University of Washington Press, 2008.

Wright, Muriel H. *A Guide to the Indian Tribes of Oklahoma.* Norman: University of Oklahoma Press, 1951.

Wyborny, Sheila. *North American Indians: Native Americans of the Southwest.* San Diego: KidHaven Press, 2004.

Wynecoop, David C. *Children of the Sun: A History of the Spokane Indians.* Wellpinit, WA, 1969. Available online from http://www.wellpinit.wednet.edu/shorthistory (accessed on August 11, 2011).

Wyss, Thelma Hatch. *Bear Dancer: The Story of a Ute Girl.* Chicago: Margaret K. McElderry Books, 2010.

Zepeda, Ofelia. *Where Clouds Are Formed: Poems.* Tucson: University of Arizona Press, 2008.

Zigmond, Maurice L. *Kawaiisu Mythology: An Oral Tradition of South-Central California.* Banning, CA: Malki-Ballena Press, 1980.

— — —. "Kawaiisu." In *Handbook of North American Indians, Great Basin*. Vol. 11. Edited by Warren L. D'Azavedo. Washington, DC: Smithsonian Institution, 1981, pp. 398–411.

Zimmerman, Dwight Jon. *Tecumseh: Shooting Star of the Shawnee*. New York: Sterling, 2010.

Zitkala-Sa, Cathy N. Davidson, and Ada Norris. *American Indian Stories, Legends, and Other Writings*. New York: Penguin, 2003.

Periodicals

Barrett, Samuel Alfred, and Edward Winslow Gifford. "Miwok Material Culture: Indian Life of the Yosemite Region" *Bulletin of Milwaukee Public Museum* 2, no. 4 (March 1933).

Barringer, Felicity. "Indians Join Fight for an Oklahoma Lake's Flow." *New York Times*. April 12, 2011, A1. Available online from http://www.nytimes.com/2011/04/12/science/earth/12water.html (accessed on June 18, 2011).

Beck, Melinda. "The Lost Worlds of Ancient America." *Newsweek* 118 (Fall–Winter 1991): 24.

Bourke, John Gregory. "General Crook in the Indian Country." *The Century Magazine,* March 1891. Available online from http://www.discoverseaz.com/History/General_Crook.html (accessed on July 20, 2011).

Bruchac, Joseph. "Otstango: A Mohawk Village in 1491," *National Geographic* 180, no. 4 (October 1991): 68–83.

Carroll, Susan. "Tribe Fights Kitt Peak Project." *The Arizona Republic.* March 24, 2005. Available online at http://www.nathpo.org/News/Sacred_Sites/News-Sacred_Sites109.htm (accessed on July 20, 2011).

Chief Joseph. "An Indian's View of Indian Affairs." *North American Review* 128, no. 269 (April 1879): 412–33.

Collins, Cary C., ed. "Henry Sicade's History of Puyallup Indian School, 1860 to 1920." *Columbia* 14, no. 4 (Winter 2001–02).

Dalsbø, E.T., "'We Were Told We Were Going to Live in Houses': Relocation and Housing of the Mushuau Innu of Natuashish from 1948 to 2003." *University of Tromsø,* May 28, 2010. Available from http://www.ub.uit.no/munin/bitstream/handle/10037/2739/thesis.pdf?sequence=3 (accessed on May 26, 2011).

Dixon, Roland B. "Achomawi and Atsugewi Tales." *Journal of American Folklore* 21. (1908): 159–77.

Dold, Catherine. "American Cannibal." *Discover* 19, no. 2 (February 1998): 64.

Duara, Nigel. "Descendants Make Amends to Chinook for Lewis and Clark Canoe Theft." *Missourian.* (September 23, 2011). Available online from http://www.columbiamissourian.com/stories/2011/09/23/descendants-make-amends-chinook-lewis-clark-canoe-theft/ (accessed on November 2, 2011).

Elliott, Jack. "Dawn, Nov. 28, 1729: Gunfire Heralds Natchez Massacre." *Concordia Sentinel*. November 5, 2009. Available from http://www.concordiasentinel.com/news.php?id=4321 (accessed on June 27, 2011).

Eskin, Leah. "Teens Take Charge. (Suicide Epidemic at Wind River Reservation)." *Scholastic Update,* May 26, 1989: 26.

Et-twaii-lish, Marjorie Waheneka. "Indian Perspectives on Food and Culture." *Oregon Historical Quarterly,* Fall 2005.

Griswold, Eliza. "A Teen's Third-World America." *Newsweek.* December 26, 2010. Available online from http://www.thedailybeast.com/articles/2010/12/26/a-boys-third-world-america.html (accessed on July 20, 2011).

ICTMN Staff. "Washoe Tribe's Cave Rock a No-go for Bike Path" *Indian Country Today Media Network,* February 10, 2011. Available online at http://indiancountrytodaymedianetwork.com/2011/02/washoe-tribes-cave-rock-a-no-go-for-bike-path/ (accessed on August 15, 2011).

Johnston, Moira. "Canada's Queen Charlotte Islands: Homeland of the Haida." *National Geographic,* July 1987: 102–27.

Jones, Malcolm Jr., with Ray Sawhill. "Just Too Good to Be True: Another Reason to Beware False Eco-Prophets." *Newsweek.* (May 4, 1992). Available online at http://www.synaptic.bc.ca/ejournal/newsweek.htm (accessed on November 2, 2011).

June-Friesen, Katy. "An Ancestry of African-Native Americans." *Smithsonian.* February 17, 2010. Available online from http://www.smithsonianmag.com/history-archaeology/An-Ancestry-of-African-Native-Americans.html#ixzz1RN1pyiD1 (accessed on June 21, 2011).

Kowinski, William Severini. "Giving New Life to Haida Art and the Culture It Expresses." *Smithsonian,* January 1995: 38.

Kroeber, A. L. "Two Myths of the Mission Indians." *Journal of the American Folk-Lore Society* 19, no. 75 (1906): 309–21. Available online at http://www.sacred-texts.com/nam/ca/tmmi/index.htm (accessed on August 11, 2011).

Lake, Robert, Jr. "The Chilula Indians of California." *Indian Historian* 12, no. 3 (1979): 14–26. Available online fromhttp://www.eric.ed.gov/ERICWebPortal/search/detailmini.jsp?_nfpb=true&_&ERICExtSearch_SearchValue_0=EJ214907&ERICExtSearch_SearchType_0=no&accno=EJ214907

Parks, Ron. "Selecting a Suitable Country for the Kanza." *The Kansas Free Press.* June 1, 2011. Available online from http://www.kansasfreepress.com/2011/06/selecting-a-suitable-country-for-the-kanza.html (accessed on June 17, 2011).

Rezendes, Michael. "Few Tribes Share Casino Windfall." *Globe.* December 11, 2000. Available online from http://indianfiles.serveftp.com/TribalIssues/Few%20tribes%20share%20casino%20windfall.pdf(accessed on July 4, 2011).

Roy, Prodipto, and Della M. Walker. "Assimilation of the Spokane Indians." *Washington Agricultural Experiment Station Bulletin.* No. 628.

Pullman: Washington State University, Institute of Agricultural Science, 1961.

Shaffrey, Mary M. "Lumbee Get a Win, But Not without Stipulation." *Winston-Salem Journal* (April 26, 2007).

Shapley, Thomas. "Historical Revision Rights a Wrong." *Seattle Post-Intelligencer.* (December 18, 2004). Available online from http://www.seattlepi.com/local/opinion/article/Historical-revision-rights-a-wrong-1162234.php#ixzz1WBFxoNiw (accessed on August 15, 2011).

"Q: Should Scientists Be Allowed to 'Study' the Skeletons of Ancient American Indians?" (Symposium: U.S. Representative Doc Hastings; Confederated Tribes of the Umatilla Indian Reservation Spokesman Donald Sampson). *Insight on the News* 13, no. 47 (December 22, 1997): 24.

Siegel, Lee. "Mummies Might Have Been Made by Anasazi." *Salt Lake Tribune,* April 2, 1998.

Stewart, Kenneth M. "Mohave Warfare." *Southwestern Journal of Anthropology* 3, no. 3 (Autumn 1947): 257–78.

Trivedi, Bijal P. "Ancient Timbers Reveal Secrets of Anasazi Builders." *National Geographic Today,* September 28, 2001. Available online at http://news.nationalgeographic.com/news/2001/09/0928_TVchaco.html (accessed on June 29, 2007).

Trumbauer, Sophie. "Northwest Tribes Canoe to Lummi Island." *The Daily.* (August 1, 2007). Available online at http://thedaily.washington.edu/article/2007/8/1/northwestTribesCanoeToLumm (accessed on November 2, 2011).

Van Meter, David. "Energy Efficient." *University of Texas at Arlington,* Fall 2006.

Wagner, Dennis. "Stolen Artifacts Shatter Ancient Culture." *The Arizona Republic,* November 12, 2006.

Warshall, Peter. "The Heart of Genuine Sadness: Astronomers, Politicians, and Federal Employees Desecrate the Holiest Mountain of the San Carlos Apache." *Whole Earth* 91 (Winter 1997): 30.

Win, WambliSina. "The Ultimate Expression of Faith, the Lakota Sun Dance." *Native American Times.* July 4, 2011. Available online from http://www.nativetimes.com/index.php?option=com_content&view=article&id=5657:the-ultimate-expression-of-faith-the-lakota-sun-dance&catid=46&Itemid=22 (accessed on July 4, 2011).

Web Sites

"Aboriginal Fisheries Strategy." *Fisheries and Oceans Canada.* http://www.dfo-mpo.gc.ca/fm-gp/aboriginal-autochtones/afs-srapa-eng.htm (accessed on August 15, 2011).

"Aboriginal Peoples: The Métis." *Newfoundland and Labrador Heritage.* http://www.heritage.nf.ca/aboriginal/metis.html (accessed on August 4, 2011).

"About the Hopi." Restoration. http://hopi.org/about-the-hopi/ (accessed on July 20, 2011).

"Acoma Pueblo." *ClayHound Web.* http://www.clayhound.us/sites/acoma.htm (accessed on July 20, 2011).

"Acoma Pueblo." *New Mexico Magazine.*http://www.nmmagazine.com/native_american/acoma.php (accessed on July 20, 2011).

"Acoma'Sky City'" *National Trust for Historic Preservation.*http://www.acomaskycity.org/ (accessed on July 20, 2011).

"Address of Tarhe, Grand Sachem of the Wyandot Nation, to the Assemblage at the Treaty of Greeneville, July 22, 1795." *Wyandotte Nation of Oklahoma.* http://www.wyandotte-nation.org/history/tarhe_greenville_address.html (accessed May 12, 2011).

"The Adena Mounds." *Grave Creek Mound State Park.* http://www.adena.com/adena/ad/ad01.htm (accessed June 7, 2011).

Adley-SantaMaria, Bernadette. "White Mountain Apache Language Issues." *Northern Arizona University.* http://www2.nau.edu/jar/TIL_12.html (accessed on July 20, 2011).

Akimoff, Tim. "Snowshoe Builders Display Their Craft at the Anchorage Museum." *KTUU.* May 5, 2011. http://www.ktuu.com/news/ktuu-snowshoe-builders-display-their-craft-at-the-anchorage-museum-20110505,0,7760220.story (accessed on June 6, 2011).

Alamo Chapter. http://alamo.nndes.org/ (accessed on July 20, 2011).

Alaska Native Collections. *Smithsonian Institution.* http://alaska.si.edu/cultures.asp (accessed on August 15, 2011).

— — —. "Unangan."*Smithsonian Institution.* http://alaska.si.edu/culture_unangan.asp(accessed on August 15, 2011).

"Alaska Native Language Center." *University of Alaska Fairbanks.* http://www.uaf.edu/anlc//anlc/languages/ (accessed on June 4, 2011).

Alaska Yup'ik Eskimo. http://www.yupik.com (accessed on August 15, 2011).

All Indian Pueblo Council. http://www.20pueblos.org/ (accessed on July 20, 2011).

Allen, Cain. "The Oregon History Project: Toby Winema Riddle."*Oregon Historical Society.* http://www.ohs.org/education/oregonhistory/historical_records/dspDocument.cfm?doc_ID=000A9FE3-B226-1EE8-827980B05272FE9F (accessed on August 11, 2011).

"Alutiiq and Aleut/Unangan History and Culture."*Anchorage Museum.* http://www.anchoragemuseum.org/galleries/alaska_gallery/aleut.aspx (accessed on August 15, 2011).

Aluttiq Museum. http://alutiiqmuseum.org/ (accessed on August 15, 2011).

"Anasazi: The Ancient Ones." *Manitou Cliff Dwellings Museum.* http://www. cliffdwellingsmuseum.com/anasazi.htm (accessed on July 20, 2011).

"Anasazi Heritage Center: Ancestral Pueblos." *Bureau of Land Management Colorado.* http://www.co.blm.gov/ahc/anasazi.htm (accessed on July 13, 2011).

"The Anasazi or 'Ancient Pueblo.'" *Northern Arizona University.* http://www. cpluhna.nau.edu/People/anasazi.htm (accessed on July 20, 2011).

"Ancient Architects of the Mississippi." *National Park Service, Department of the Interior.* http://www.cr.nps.gov/archeology/feature/feature.htm (accessed on July 10, 2007).

"Ancient DNA from the Ohio Hopewell." *Ohio Archaeology Blog,* June 22, 2006. http://ohio-archaeology.blogspot.com/2006/06/ancient-dna-from-ohio-hopewell.html (accessed on July 10, 2007).

"Ancient Moundbuilders of Arkansas." *University of Arkansas.* http://cast.uark.edu/home/research/archaeology-and-historic-preservation/archaeological-interpretation/ancient-moundbuilders-of-arkansas.html (accessed on June 10, 2011).

"Ancient One: Kennewick Man." *Confederated Tribes of the Umatilla Reservation.* http://www.umatilla.nsn.us/ancient.html (accessed on August 11, 2011).

Anderson, Jeff. "Arapaho Online Research Resources." *Colby College.* http://www.colby.edu/personal/j/jdanders/arapahoresearch.htm (accessed on July 2, 2011).

"Anishinaabe Chi-Naaknigewin/Anishinabek Nation Constitution." *Anishinabek Nation.* http://www.anishinabek.ca/uploads/ANConstitution.pdf (accessed on May 16, 2011).

"Antelope Valley Indian Peoples: The Late Prehistoric Period: Kawaiisu." *Antelope Valley Indian Museum.* http://www.avim.parks.ca.gov/people/ph_kawaiisu.shtml (accessed on August 15, 2011).

"Apache Indian History." *Access Genealogy.* http://www.accessgenealogy.com/native/tribes/apache/apachehist.htm (accessed on July 15, 2011).

"Apache Indians." *AAA Native Arts.* http://www.aaanativearts.com/apache (accessed on July 15, 2011).

"Apache Nation: Nde Nation." *San Carlos Apache Nation.* http://www. sancarlosapache.com/home.htm (accessed on July 15, 2011).

"Apache Tribal Nation." *Dreams of the Great Earth Changes.* http://www. greatdreams.com/apache/apache-tribe.htm (accessed on July 15, 2011).

"The Apsáalooke (Crow Indians) of Montana Tribal Histories." *Little Big Horn College.* http://lib.lbhc.edu/history/ (accessed on July 5, 2011).

Aquino, Pauline. "Ohkay Owingeh: Village of the Strong People" (video). *New Mexico State Record Center and Archives.* http://www.newmexicohistory.org/filedetails.php?fileID=22530 (accessed on July 20, 2011).

"The Arapaho Tribe." *Omaha Public Library.* http://www.omahapubliclibrary. org/transmiss/congress/arapaho.html (accessed on July 2, 2011).

Arctic Circle. http://arcticcircle.uconn.edu/Museum/ (accessed on June 10, 2011).

"Arctic Circle." *University of Connecticut.* http://arcticcircle.uconn.edu/VirtualClassroom/ (accessed on August 15, 2011).

"The Arctic Is...." *Stefansson Arctic Institute.* http://www.thearctic.is/ (accessed on August 15, 2011).

Arctic Library. "Inuit" *Athropolis.* http://www.athropolis.com/library-cat.htm#inuit (accessed on August 15, 2011).

"Arikira Indians." *PBS.* http://www.pbs.org/lewisandclark/native/ari.html (accessed on June 19, 2011).

"Arkansas Indians: Arkansas Archeological Survey." *University of Arkansas.* http://www.uark.edu/campus-resources/archinfo/ArkansasIndianTribes.pdf (accessed on June 12, 2011).

Arlee, Johnny. *Over a Century of Moving to the Drum: Salish Indian Celebrations on the Flathead Reservation.* Helena: Montana Historical Society Press, 1998. Available online from http://www.archive.org/stream/historicalsketch00ronarich/historicalsketch00ronarich_djvu.txt (accessed on August 11, 2011).

Armstrong, Kerry M. "Chickasaw Historical Research Page." *Chickasaw History.* http://www.chickasawhistory.com/ (accessed on June 16, 2011.

"Art on the Prairies: Otoe-Missouria." *The Bata Shoe Museum.* http://www.allaboutshoes.ca/en/paths_across/art_on_prairies/index_7.php (accessed on June 20, 2011).

"Assiniboin Indian History." *Access Genealogy.* http://www.accessgenealogy.com/native/tribes/assiniboin/assiniboinhist.htm (accessed on June 7, 2011).

"Assinboin Indians." *PBS.* http://www.pbs.org/lewisandclark/native/idx_ass.html (accessed on June 7, 2011).

"Assiniboine History." *Fort Belknap Indian Community.* http://www.ftbelknap-nsn.gov/assiniboineHistory.php (accessed on June 6, 2011).

"Athabascan." Alaska Native Heritage Center Museum. http://www.alaskanative.net/en/main_nav/education/culture_alaska/athabascan/ (accessed on June 6, 2011).

Banyacya, Thomas. "Message to the World." *Hopi Traditional Elder.* http://banyacya.indigenousnative.org/ (accessed on July 20, 2011).

Barnett, Jim. "The Natchez Indians." *History Now.* http://mshistory.k12.ms.us/index.php?id=4 (accessed on June 27, 2011).

Barry, Paul C. "Native America Nations and Languages: Haudenosaunee." *The Canku Ota—A Newsletter Celebrating Native America.* http://www.turtletrack.org/Links/NANations/CO_NANationLinks_HJ.htm (accessed on June 5, 2011).

"Before the White Man Came to Nisqually Country." *Washington History Online.* January 12, 2006. http://washingtonhistoryonline.org/treatytrail/teaching/before-white-man.pdf (accessed on August 15, 2011).

Big Valley Band of Pomo Indians. http://www.big-valley.net/index.htm (accessed on August 11, 2011).

Bishop Paiute Tribe. http://www.bishoppaiutetribe.com/ (accessed on August 15, 2011).

"Black Kettle." *PBS.* http://www.pbs.org/weta/thewest/people/a_c/blackkettle.htm (accessed on July 4, 2011).

"Blackfeet." *Wisdom of the Elders.* http://www.wisdomoftheelders.org/program208.html (accessed on July 2, 2011).

"Blackfoot History." *Head-Smashed-In Buffalo Jump Interpretive Centre.* http://www.head-smashed-in.com/black.html (accessed on July 2, 2011).

Blackfeet Nation. http://www.blackfeetnation.com/ (accessed on July 2, 2011).

Boyer, Ruth McDonald, and Narcissus Duffy Gayton. "Apache Mothers and Daughters: Four Generations of a Family. Remembrances of an Apache Elder Woman." *Southwest Crossroads.* http://southwestcrossroads.org/record.php?num=825&hl=Apache (accessed on July 20, 2011).

British Columbia Archives. "First Nations Research Guide." *Royal BC Museum Corporation.* http://www.royalbcmuseum.bc.ca/BC_Research_Guide/BC_First_Nations.aspx (accessed on August 15, 2011).

Bruchac, Joe. "Storytelling." *Abenaki Nation.* http://www.abenakination.org/stories.html (accessed on June 5, 2011).

Brush, Rebecca. "The Wichita Indians." *Texas Indians.* http://www.texasindians.com/wichita.htm (accessed on June 9, 2011).

"Caddo Indian History." *Access Genealogy.* http://www.accessgenealogy.com/native/tribes/caddo/caddohist.htm (accessed on June 12, 2011).

"Cahto (Kato)." *Four Directions Institute.* http://www.fourdir.com/cahto.htm (accessed on August 11, 2011).

"Cahto Tribe Information Network." *Cahto Tribe.* http://www.cahto.org/ (accessed on August 11, 2011).

"Cahuilla." *Four Directions Institute.* http://www.fourdir.com/cahuilla.htm (accessed on August 11, 2011).

Cahuilla Band of Mission Indians. http://cahuillabandofindians.com/ (accessed on August 11, 2011).

"California Indians." *Visalia Unified School District.* http://visalia.k12.ca.us/teachers/tlieberman/indians/ (accessed on August 15, 2011).

California Valley Miwok Tribe, California. http://www.californiavalleymiwoktribe-nsn.gov/ (accessed on August 11, 2011).

Cambra, Rosemary, et al. "The Muwekma Ohlone Tribe of the San Francisco Bay Area." http://www.islaiscreek.org/ohlonehistcultfedrecog.html (accessed on August 11, 2011).

"Camp Grant Massacre—April 30, 1871." *Council of Indian Nations.* http://www.nrcprograms.org/site/PageServer?pagename=cin_hist_campgrantmassacre (accessed on July 20, 2011).

Campbell, Grant. "The Rock Paintings of the Chumash." *Association for Humanistic Psychology.* http://www.ahpweb.org/articles/chumash.html (accessed on August 11, 2011).

Canadian Heritage Information Network. "Communities& Institutions: Talented Youth." *Tipatshimuna.* http://www.tipatshimuna.ca/1420_e.php (accessed on May 19, 2011).

Carleton, Kenneth H. "A Brief History of the Mississippi Band of Choctaw Indians." *Mississippi Band of Choctaw.* http://mdah.state.ms.us/hpres/A%20Brief%20History%20of%20the%20Choctaw.pdf (accessed on June 12, 2011).

Central Council: Tlingit and Haida Indian Tribes of Alaska. http://www.ccthita.org/ (accessed on November 2, 2011).

Cherokee Nation. http://www.cherokee.org/ (accessed on June 12, 2011).

"Cheyenne Indian." *American Indian Tribes.* http://www.cheyenneindian.com/cheyenne_links.htm (accessed on July 4, 2011).

"Cheyenne Indian History." *Access Genealogy.* http://www.accessgenealogy.com/native/tribes/cheyenne/cheyennehist.htm (accessed on July 4, 2011).

"Chickasaw Indian History." *Access Genealogy.* http://www.accessgenealogy.com/native/tribes/chickasaw/chickasawhist.htm (accessed on June 16, 2011).

The Chickasaw Nation. http://www.chickasaw.net (accessed on June 12, 2011).

"Chief Joseph." *PBS.* http://www.pbs.org/weta/thewest/people/a_c/chiefjoseph.htm (accessed on August 11, 2011).

"Chief Joseph Surrenders." *The History Place.* http://www.historyplace.com/speeches/joseph.htm (accessed on August 11,2011).

Chief Leschi School. http://www.leschischools.org/ (accessed on November 2, 2011).

"Chief Seattle Speech." *Washington State Library.* http://www.synaptic.bc.ca/ejournal/wslibrry.htm (accessed on November 2, 2011).

"The Children of Changing Woman." *Peabody Museum of Archaeology and Ethnology.* http://www.peabody.harvard.edu/maria/Cwoman.html (accessed on July 15, 2011).

"The Chilula." *The Indians of the Redwoods.* http://www.cr.nps.gov/history/online_books/redw/history1c.htm (accessed on August 11, 2011).

Chinook Indian Tribe/Chinook Nation. http://www.chinooknation.org/ (accessed on November 2, 2011).

"Chinookan Family History." *Access Genealogy.* http://www.accessgenealogy.com/native/tribes/chinook/chinookanfamilyhist.htm (accessed on November 2, 2011).

"Chippewa Cree Tribe (Neiyahwahk)." *Montana Office of Indian Affairs.* http://www.tribalnations.mt.gov/chippewacree.asp (accessed on June 3, 2011).

"Chiricahua Indian History." *Access Genealogy.* http://www.accessgenealogy. com/native/tribes/apache/chiricahua.htm (accessed on July 20, 2011).

Chisolm, D. "Mi'kmaq Resource Centre," *Cape Breton University.* http://mrc. uccb.ns.ca/mikmaq.html (accessed on May 15, 2011).

"Choctaw Indian History." *Access Genealogy.* http://www.accessgenealogy.com/ native/tribes/choctaw/chostawhist.htm (accessed on June 21, 2011).

"Choctaw Indian Tribe." *Native American Nations.* http://www.nanations.com/ choctaw/index.htm (accessed on June 21, 2011).

Choctaw Nation of Oklahoma. http://www.choctawnation.com (accessed on June 12, 2011).

"Chumash." *Four Directions Institute.* http://www.fourdir.com/chumash.htm (accessed on December 1, 2011).

The Chumash Indians. http://www.chumashindian.com/ (accessed on August 11, 2011).

Clark, William. "Lewis and Clark: Expedition Journals." *National Geographic.* http://www.nationalgeographic.com/lewisandclark/record_tribes_020_5_1. html (accessed on June 19, 2011).

— — —. "Lewis and Clark: Missouri Indians." *National Geographic.* http:// www.nationalgeographic.com/lewisandclark/record_tribes_012_1_9.html (accessed on June 20, 2011).

"Coast Miwok at Point Reyes." *U.S. National Park Service.* http://www.nps. gov/pore/historyculture/people_coastmiwok.htm (accessed on August 11, 2011).

"Coastal Miwok Indians." *Reed Union School District.* http://rusd.marin. k12.ca.us/belaire/ba_3rd_miwoks/coastalmiwoks/webpages/home. html(accessed on August 11, 2011).

"Comanche." *Edward S. Curtis's The North American Indian.* http://curtis. library.northwestern.edu/curtis/toc.cgi (accessed on July 4, 2011).

"Comanche Indian History." *Access Genealogy.* http://www.accessgenealogy. com/native/tribes/comanche/comanchehist.htm (accessed on July 4, 2011).

"Comanche Language." *Omniglot.* http://www.omniglot.com/writing/coman- che.htm (accessed on July 4, 2011).

Comanche Nation of Oklahoma http://www.comanchenation.com/ (accessed on July 4, 2011).

"Community News." *Mississippi Band of Choctaw Indians.* http://www.choctaw. org/ (accessed on June 12, 2011).

Compton, W. J. "The Story of Ishi, the Yana Indian." *Ye Slyvan Archer.* July 1936. http://tmuss.tripod.com/shotfrompast/chief.htm (accessed on August 11, 2011).

The Confederated Salish and Kootenai Tribes. http://www.cskt.org/ (accessed on August 11, 2011).

Confederated Tribes and Bands of the Yakama Nation. http://www.yakamanation-nsn.gov/ (accessed on August 11, 2011).

Confederated Tribes of the Colville Reservation. http://www.colvilletribes.com/ (accessed on August 11, 2011).

Confederated Tribes of Siletz. http://ctsi.nsn.us/ (accessed on November 2, 2011).

Confederated Tribes of the Umatilla Indian Reservation. http://www.umatilla.nsn.us/ (accessed on August 11, 2011).

"Confederated Tribes of the Umatilla Indians." *Wisdom of the Elders.* http://www.wisdomoftheelders.org/program305.html (accessed on August 11, 2011).

"Confederated Tribes of the Yakama Nation." *Wisdom of the Elders.* http://www.wisdomoftheelders.org/program304.html (accessed on August 11, 2011).

"Connecting the World with Seattle's First People." *Duwamish Tribe.* http://www.duwamishtribe.org/ (accessed on November 2, 2011).

Conrad, Jim. "The Natchez Indians." *The Loess Hills of the Lower Mississipi Valley.* http://www.backyardnature.net/loess/ind_natz.htm (accessed on June 27, 2011).

Cordell, Linda. "Anasazi." *Scholastic.* http://www2.scholastic.com/browse/article.jsp?id=5042 (accessed on July 20, 2011).

"Costanoan Indian Tribe." *Access Genealogy.* http://www.accessgenealogy.com/native/tribes/costanoan/costanoanindiantribe.htm (accessed on August 11, 2011).

Costanoan Rumsen Carmel Tribe. http://costanoanrumsen.org/ (accessed on August 11, 2011).

"Costanoan Rumsen Carmel Tribe: History." *Native Web.* http://crc.nativeweb.org/history.html (accessed on August 11, 2011).

Cotton, Lee. "Powhatan Indian Lifeways." *National Park Service.* http://www.nps.gov/jame/historyculture/powhatan-indian-lifeways.htm (accessed on June 1, 2011).

Council of the Haida Nation (CHN). http://www.haidanation.ca/ (accessed on November 2, 2011).

"A Coyote's Tales—Tohono O'odham." *First People: American Indian Legends.* http://www.firstpeople.us/FP-Html-Legends/A_Coyotes_Tales-TohonoOodham.html (accessed on July 20, 2011).

"Creek Indian." *American Indian Tribe.* http://www.creekindian.com/ (accessed on June 12, 2011).

"Creek Indians." *GeorgiaInfo.* http://georgiainfo.galileo.usg.edu/creek.htm (accessed on June 12, 2011).

"Crow/Cheyenne." *Wisdom of the Elders.* http://www.wisdomoftheelders.org/program206.html (accessed on July 5, 2011).

"Crow Indian Tribe." *Access Genealogy.* http://www.accessgenealogy.com/native/tribes/crow/crowhist.htm (accessed on July 5, 2011).

Crow Tribe, Apsáalooke Nation Official Website. http://www.crowtribe.com/ (accessed on July 5, 2011).

"Culture and History."*Innu Nation.*http://www.innu.ca/index.php?option=com_content&view=article&id=8&Itemid=3&lang=en (accessed on May 19, 2011).

"Culture& History." *Aleut Corporation.* http://www.aleutcorp.com/index.php?option=com_content&view=section&layout=blog&id=6&Itemid=24 (accessed on August 15, 2011).

"Culture and History of the Skokomish Tribe." *Skokomish Tribal Nation.* http://www.skokomish.org/historyculture.htm (accessed on November 2, 2011).

Curtis, Edward S. *The North American Indian.*Vol.13. 1924. Reprint. New York: Johnson Reprint Corporation, 1970. Available online from *Northwestern University Digital Library Collections.* http://curtis.library.northwestern.edu/curtis/viewPage.cgi?showp=1&size=2&id=nai.13.book.00000192&volume=13#nav-Edward (accessed on August 11, 2011).

"Dakota Indian Tribe History." *Access Genealogy.* http://www.accessgenealogy.com/native/tribes/siouan/dakotahist.htm (accessed on July 5, 2011).

"Dakota Spirituality." *Blue Cloud Abbey.* http://www.bluecloud.org/dakotaspirituality.html (accessed on July 5, 2011).

"Dams of the Columbia Basin and Their Effects on the Native Fishery." *Center for Columbia River History.* http://www.ccrh.org/comm/river/dams6.htm (accessed on August 11, 2011).

Deans, James. "Tales from the Totems of the Hidery." *Early Canadiana Online.* http://www.canadiana.org/ECO/PageView/06053/0003?id=986858ca5fbdc633 (accessed on November 2, 2011).

Deer Lake First Nation. http://www.deerlake.firstnation.ca/ (accessed on June 5, 2011).

"Delaware Indian Chiefs." *Access Genealogy.* http://www.accessgenealogy.com/native/tribes/delaware/delawarechiefs.htm (accessed on June 8, 2011).

"Delaware Indian/Lenni Lenape." *Delaware Indians of Pennsylvania.* http://www.delawareindians.com/ (accessed on June 8, 2011).

"Delaware Indians." *Ohio Historical Society.* http://www.ohiohistorycentral.org/entry.php?rec=584 (accessed on June 2, 2011).

The Delaware Nation. http://www.delawarenation.com/ (accessed on June 2, 2011).

Delaware Tribe of Indians. http://www.delawaretribeofindians.nsn.us/ (accessed on June 2, 2011).

DelawareIndian.com. http://www.delawareindian.com/ (accessed on June 2, 2011).

Dene Cultural Institute. http://www.deneculture.org/ (accessed on June 10, 2011).

Deschenes, Bruno. "Inuit Throat-Singing." *Musical Traditions.* http://www. mustrad.org.uk/articles/inuit.htm (accessed on August 15, 2011).

"Desert Native Americans: Mohave Indians." *Mojave Desert.* http:// mojavedesert.net/mojave-indians/ (accessed on July 20, 2011).

Dodds, Lissa Guimarães. "'The Washoe People': Past and Present." *Washoe Tribe of Nevada and California.* http://www.Washoetribe.us/images/ Washoe_tribe_history_v2.pdf (accessed on August 15, 2011).

"Duwamish Indian Tribe History." *Access Genealogy.* http://www.accessgeneal-ogy.com/native/tribes/salish/duwamishhist.htm (accessed on November 2, 2011).

"The Early History and Names of the Arapaho." *Native American Nations.* http://www.nanations.com/early_arapaho.htm (accessed on July 2, 2011).

Eastern Shawnee Tribe of Oklahoma. http://estoo-nsn.gov/ (accessed on June 12, 2011).

Eck, Pam. "Hopi Indians." *Indiana University.* http://inkido.indiana.edu/ w310work/romac/hopi.htm (accessed on July 20, 2011).

Edward S. Curtis's The North American Indian. http://curtis.library.northwest-ern.edu/curtis/toc.cgi (accessed on August 11, 2011).

Elam, Earl H. "Wichita Indians." *Texas State Historical Association.* http://www. tshaonline.org/handbook/online/articles/bmw03 (accessed on June 9, 2011).

Ely Shoshone Tribe. http://elyshoshonetribe-nsn.gov/departments.html (accessed on August 15, 2011).

Etienne-Gray, Tracé. "Black Seminole Indians." *Texas State Historical Associa-tion.* http://www.tshaonline.org/handbook/online/articles/bmb18 (accessed on June 12, 2011).

Everett, Diana. "Apache Tribe of Oklahoma." *Oklahoma Historical Soci-ety.* http://digital.library.okstate.edu/encyclopedia/entries/A/AP002. html(accessed on July 15, 2011).

"Eyak, Tlingit, Haida, and Tsimshian." *Alaska Native Heritage Center Museum.* http://www.alaskanative.net/en/main_nav/education/culture_alaska/eyak/ (accessed on August 15, 2011).

Fausz, J. Frederick. "The Louisiana Expansion: The Arikara." *University of Missouri–St. Louis.* http://www.umsl.edu/continuinged/louisiana/Am_ Indians/8-Arikara/8-arikara.html (accessed on June 19, 2011).

———. "The Louisiana Expansion: The Kansa/Kaw." *University of Missouri-St. Louis.* http://www.umsl.edu/continuinged/louisiana/Am_Indians/3-Kansa_Kaw/3-kansa_kaw.html (accessed on June 17, 2011).

———. "The Louisiana Expansion: The Missouri/Missouria." *University of Missouri–St. Louis.* http://www.umsl.edu/continuinged/louisiana/Am_ Indians/2-Missouria/2-missouria.html (accessed on June 20, 2011).

— — —. "The Louisiana Expansion: The Oto(e)." *University of Missouri-St. Louis.* http://www.umsl.edu/continuinged/louisiana/Am_Indians/4-Oto/4-oto.html (accessed on June 20, 2011).

Feller, Walter. "California Indian History." *Digital Desert.* http://mojavedesert.net/california-indian-history/ (accessed on August 11, 2011).

— — —. "Mojave Desert Indians: Cahuilla Indians." *Digital-Desert.* http://mojavedesert.net/cahuilla-indians/ (accessed on August 11, 2011).

"First Nations: People of the Interior." *British Columbia Archives.* http://www.bcarchives.gov.bc.ca/exhibits/timemach/galler07/frames/int_peop.htm (accessed on August 11, 2011).

"First Peoples of Canada: Communal Hunters." *Canadian Museum of Civilization.* http://www.civilization.ca/cmc/home (accessed on June 10, 2011).

"Flathead Indians (Salish)."*National Geographic.* http://www.nationalgeographic.com/lewisandclark/record_tribes_022_12_16.html(accessed on August 11, 2011).

"Flathead Reservation." http://www.montanatribes.org/links_&_resources/tribes/Flathead_Reservation.pdf (accessed on August 11, 2011).

Flora, Stephenie. "Northwest Indians: 'The First People.'" *Oregon Pioneers.* http://www.oregonpioneers.com/indian.htm (accessed on August 15, 2011).

Forest County Potawatomi. http://www.fcpotawatomi.com/ (accessed on June 5, 2011).

Fort McDowell Yavapai Nation. http://www.ftmcdowell.org/ (accessed on July 20, 2011).

"Fort Mojave Indian Tribe." *Inter Tribal Council of Arizona, Inc.* http://www.itcaonline.com/tribes_mojave.html (accessed on July 20, 2011).

Fort Peck Tribes. http://www.fortpecktribes.org/ (accessed on June 4, 2011).

Fort Sill Apache Tribe. http://www.fortsillapache.com (accessed on July 20, 2011).

"Fort Yuma-Quechan Tribe." *Inter-Tribal Council of Arizona, Inc.* http://www.itcaonline.com/tribes_quechan.html (accessed on July 20, 2011).

Gangnier, Gary. "The History of the Innu Nation."*Central Quebec School Board.* http://www.cqsb.qc.ca/svs/434/fninnu.htm (accessed on May 24, 2011).

Gerke, Sarah Bohl. "White Mountain Apache." *Arizona State University.* http://grandcanyonhistory.clas.asu.edu/history_nativecultures_whitemountainapache.html (accessed on July 20, 2011).

"Geronimo, His Own Story: A Prisoner of War." *From Revolution to Reconstruction.* http://www.let.rug.nl/usa/B/geronimo/geroni17.htm (accessed on July 20, 2011).

"Gifting and Feasting in the Northwest Coast Potlatch." *Peabody Museum of Archaeology and Ethnology.* http://www.peabody.harvard.edu/potlatch/ (accessed on November 2, 2011).

Glenn Black Laboratory of Archaeology. "Burial Mounds." *Indiana University*. http://www.gbl.indiana.edu/abstracts/adena/mounds.html (accessed June 7, 2011).

———. "The Ohio Valley-Great Lakes Ethnohistory Archives: The Miami Collection." *Indiana University*. http://gbl.indiana.edu/ethnohistory/archives/menu.html (accessed on June 7, 2011).

Glover, William B. "A History of the Caddo Indians." Formatted for the World Wide Web by Jay Salsburg. Reprinted from *The Louisiana Historical Quarterly*, 18, no. 4 (October 1935). http://ops.tamu.edu/x075bb/caddo/Indians.html (accessed on June 12, 2011).

GoodTracks, Jimm. "These Native Ways." *Turtle Island Storytellers Network*. http://www.turtleislandstorytellers.net/tis_kansas/transcript01_jg_tracks.htm (accessed on June 20, 2011).

"Grand Village of the Natchez Indians." *Mississippi Department of Archives and History*. http://mdah.state.ms.us/hprop/gvni.html (accessed on June 27, 2011).

Great Basin Indian Archives. http://www.gbcnv.edu/gbia/index.htm (accessed on August 15, 2011).

Great Basin National Park. "Historic Tribes of the Great Basin." *National Park Service: U.S. Department of the Interior*. http://www.nps.gov/grba/historyculture/historic-tribes-of-the-great-basin.htm (accessed on August 15, 2011).

Greene, Candace S. "Kiowa Drawings." *National Anthropological Archives, National Museum of Natural History*. http://www.nmnh.si.edu/naa/kiowa/kiowa.htm (accessed on July 4, 2011).

"Haida." *The Kids' Site of Canadian Settlement, Library and Archives Canada*. http://www.collectionscanada.ca/settlement/kids/021013-2061-e.html (accessed on November 2, 2011).

"Haida Heritage Center at Qay'llnagaay." *Haida Heritage Centre*. http://www.haidaheritagecentre.com/ (accessed on November 2, 2011).

"Haida Language Program." *Sealaska Heritage Institute*. http://www.sealaska-heritage.org/programs/haida_language_program.htm (accessed on November 2, 2011).

"Haida Spirits of the Sea." *Virtual Museum of Canada*. http://www.virtualmuseum.ca/Exhibitions/Haida/nojava/english/home/index.html (accessed on November 2, 2011).

Handbook of American Indians. "Arikara Indian Tribe History." *Access Genealogy*. http://www.accessgenealogy.com/native/tribes/nations/arikara.htm (accessed on June 19, 2011).

Handbook of American Indians.. "Quapaw Indian Tribe History." *Access Genealogy*. http://www.accessgenealogy.com/native/tribes/quapaw/quapawhist.htm (accessed on June 20, 2011).

"History—Incident at Wounded Knee." *U.S. Marshals Service.* http://www. usmarshals.gov/history/wounded-knee/index.html (accessed on July 4, 2011).

"History: We Are the Anishnaabek." *The Grand Traverse Band of Ottawa and Chippewa.* http://www.gtbindians.org/history.html (accessed May 13, 2011).

"History and Culture." *Cherokee North Carolina.* http://www.cherokee-nc.com/ history_intro.php (accessed on June 12, 2011).

"A History of American Indians in California." *National Park Service.* http:// www.nps.gov/history/history/online_books/5views/5views1.htm (accessed on August 15, 2011).

"History of Northern Ute Indian, Utah." *Online Utah.* http://www.onlineutah. com/utehistorynorthern.shtml (accessed on August 15, 2011).

"History of the Confederated Tribes of the Siletz Indians." *HeeHeeIllahee RV Resort.* http://www.heeheeillahee.com/html/about_tribe_history.htm (accessed on November 2, 2011).

Hollabaugh, Mark. "Brief History of the Lakota People." *Normandale Community College.* http://faculty.normandale.edu/-physics/Hollabaugh/Lakota/ BriefHistory.htm (accessed on July 4, 2011).

Holt, Ronald L. "Paiute Indians." *State of Utah.* http://historytogo.utah.gov/ utah_chapters/american_indians/paiuteindians.html (accessed on August 15, 2011).

Holzman, Allan. "Beyond the Mesas [video]." *University of Illinois.* http://www. vimeo.com/16872541 (accessed on July 20, 2011).

———. "The Indian Boarding School Experience [video]." *University of Illinois.* http://www.vimeo.com/17410552 (accessed on July 20, 2011).

Hoopa Tribal Museum and San Francisco State University. http://bss.sfsu.edu/ calstudies/hupa/Hoopa.HTM (accessed on August 11, 2011).

Hoopa Valley Tribe. http://www.hoopa-nsn.gov/ (accessed on August 11, 2011).

"Hopi." *Four Directions Institute.* http://www.fourdir.com/hopi.htm (accessed on July 20, 2011).

"Hopi." *Southwest Crossroads.* http://southwestcrossroads.org/search. php?query=hopi&tab=document&doc_view=10 (accessed on July 20, 2011).

"Hopi Indian Tribal History." *Access Genealogy.* www.accessgenealogy.com/ native/tribes/hopi/hopeindianhist.htm (accessed on July 20, 2011).

"Hopi Tribe." *Inter Tribal Council of Arizona, Inc.* http://www.itcaonline.com/ tribes_hopi.html (accessed on July 20, 2011).

"Hupa." *Four Directions Institute.* http://www.fourdir.com/hupa.htm (accessed on August 11, 2011).

"Hupa Indian Tribe." *Access Genealogy.* http://www.accessgenealogy.com/ native/tribes/athapascan/hupaindiantribe.htm (accessed on August 11, 2011).

Huron-Wendat Nation. http://www.wendake.com/ (accessed May 12, 2011).

Hurst, Winston. "Anasazi." *Utah History to Go: State of Utah.* http://historytogo. utah.gov/utah_chapters/american_indians/anasazi.html (accessed on July 20, 2011).

Indian Country Diaries. "Trail of Tears." *PBS.* http://www.pbs.org/indiancountry/ history/trail.html (accessed on June 12, 2011).

"Indian Peoples of the Northern Great Plains." *MSU Libraries.* http://www.lib. montana.edu/epubs/nadb/ (accessed on July 1, 2011).

Indian Pueblo Cultural Center. http://www.indianpueblo.org/ (accessed on July 20, 2011).

"Indian Tribes of California." *Access Genealogy.* http://www.accessgenealogy. com/native/california/ (accessed on August 11, 2011).

"Indians of the Northwest—Plateau and Coastal." *St. Joseph School Library.* http://library.stjosephsea.org/plateau.htm (accessed on August 11, 2011).

"Innu Youth Film Project." *Kamestastin.* http://www.kamestastin.com/ (accessed on May 24, 2011).

"The Inuit." *Newfoundland and Labrador Heritage.* http://www.heritage.nf.ca/ aboriginal/inuit.html (accessed on August 15, 2011).

"Jemez Pueblos." *Four Directions Institute.* http://www.fourdir.com/jemez.htm (accessed on July 20, 2011).

"Jemez Pueblo." *New Mexico Magazine.* http://www.nmmagazine.com/native_ american/jemez.php (accessed on July 20, 2011).

Jicarilla Apache Nation. http://www.jicarillaonline.com/ (accessed on July 15, 2011).

Johnson, Russ. "The Mississippian Period (900 AD to 1550 AD)" *Memphis History.* http://www.memphishistory.org/Beginnings/PreMemphis/ MississippianCulture/tabid/64/Default.aspx (accessed June 7, 2011).

"The Journals of the Lewis and Clark Expedition: Nez Percé." *University of Nebraska.* http://www.nationalgeographic.com/lewisandclark/record_ tribes_013_12_17.html (accessed on August 11, 2011).

Jozhe, Benedict. "A Brief History of the Fort Sill Apache Tribe." *Oklahoma Historical Society.* http://digital.library.okstate.edu/Chronicles/v039/v039p427. pdf (accessed on July 20, 2011).

"Kansa (Kaw)." *Four Directions Institute.* http://www.fourdir.com/kaw.htm (accessed on June 17, 2011).

"Kanza Cultural History." *The Kaw Nation.* http://kawnation.com/?page_id=216 (accessed on June 17, 2011).

"Kansa Indian Tribe History." *Access Geneology.* http://www.accessgenealogy. com/native/tribes/siouan/kansahist.htm (accessed on June 17, 2011).

Kavanagh, Thomas W. "Comanche." *Oklahoma Historical Society.* http://digital. library.okstate.edu/encyclopedia/entries/C/CO033.html (accessed on July 4, 2011).

— — —. "Reading Historic Photographs: Photographers of the Pawnee." *Indiana University.* http://php.indiana.edu/~tkavanag/phothana.html (accessed on July 6, 2011).

"Kawaiisu." *Four Directions Institute.* http://www.fourdir.com/Kawaiisu.htm (accessed on August 15, 2011).

"The Kawaiisu Culture." *Digital Desert: Mojave Desert.* http://mojavedesert.net/ kawaiisu-indians/related-pages.html (accessed on August 15, 2011).

Kawaiisu Language and Cultural Center. http://www.kawaiisu.org/KLCC_ home.html (accessed on August 15, 2011).

Kawno, Kenji. "Warriors: Navajo Code Talkers." *Southwest Crossroads.* http:// southwestcrossroads.org/record.php?num=387 (accessed on July 20, 2011).

Kidwell, Clara Sue. "Choctaw." *Oklahoma Historical Society.* http://digital. library.okstate.edu/encyclopedia/entries/C/CH047.html (accessed on June 21, 2011).

"Kiowa Indian Tribe History." *Access Genealogy.* http://www.accessgenealogy. com/native/tribes/kiowa/kiowahist.htm (accessed on July 4, 2011).

"Kiowa Indian Tribe." *Kansas Genealogy.* http://www.kansasgenealogy.com/ indians/kiowa_indian_tribe.htm(accessed on July 4, 2011).

*Kiowa Tribe.*http://www.kiowatribe.org/(accessed on July 4, 2011).

Kitt Peak National Observatory. "Tohono O'odham." *Association of Universities for Research in Astronomy.* http://www.noao.edu/outreach/kptour/kpno_ tohono.html (accessed on July 20, 2011).

"Kwakiutl." *Four Directions Institute.* http://www.fourdir.com/kwakiutl.htm (accessed on November 2, 2011).

Kwakiutl Indian Band. http://www.kwakiutl.bc.ca/ (accessed on November 2, 2011).

"Lakota, Dakota, Nakota—The Great Sioux Nation." *Legends of America.* http://www.legendsofamerica.com/na-sioux.html (accessed on July 4, 2011).

"Lakota Page: The Great Sioux Nation." *Ancestry.com.* http://freepages.genealogy. rootsweb.ancestry.com/~nativeamericangen/page6.html (accessed on July 4, 2011).

"Lakota-Teton Sioux." *Wisdom of the Elders.* http://www.wisdomoftheelders. org/program203.html (accessed on July 4, 2011).

Larry, Mitchell. *The Native Blog.* http://nativeblog.typepad.com/the_pota- watomitracks_blog/potawatomi_news/index.html (accessed on June 5, 2011).

"Leschi: Last Chief of the Nisquallies." *WashingtonHistoryOnline.* http://washingtonhistoryonline.org/leschi/leschi.htm (accessed on August 15, 2011).

"Lewis & Clark: Chinook Indians." *National Geographic.* http://www.nationalgeographic.com/lewisandclark/record_tribes_083_14_3.html (accessed on November 2, 2011).

"Lewis and Clark: Crow Indians (Absaroka)." *National Geographic Society.* http://www.nationalgeographic.com/lewisandclark/record_tribes_002_19_21.html (accessed on July 5, 2011).

"Lewis and Clark: Native Americans: Chinook Indians." *PBS.* http://www.pbs.org/lewisandclark/native/chi.html (accessed on November 2, 2011).

"Lewis & Clark: Tribes: Siletz Indians." *National Geographic.* http://www.nationalgeographic.com/lewisandclark/record_tribes_090_14_8.html (accessed on November 2, 2011).

"Lewis & Clark: Yankton Sioux Indians (Nakota)." *National Geographic.* http://www.nationalgeographic.com/lewisandclark/record_tribes_019_2_8.html (accessed on June 12, 2011).

Lewis, J.D. "The Natchez Indians." *Carolina—The Native Americans.* http://www.carolana.com/Carolina/Native_Americans/native_americans_natchez.html (accessed on June 27, 2011).

Lipscomb, Carol A. "Handbook of Texas Online: Comanche Indians." *Texas State Historical Association.* http://www.tshaonline.org/handbook/online/articles/bmc72 (accessed on July 4, 2011).

"The Long Walk." *Council of Indian Nations.* http://www.nrcprograms.org/site/PageServer?pagename=cin_hist_thelongwalk (accessed on July 20, 2011).

"Luiseño." *Four Directions Institute.* http://www.fourdir.com/luiseno.htm (accessed on August 11, 2011).

"Luiseno/Cahuilla Group." *San Francisco State University.* http://bss.sfsu.edu/calstudies/nativewebpages/luiseno.html (accessed on August 11, 2011).

"Lumbee History & Culture." *Lumbee Tribe of North Carolina.* http://www.lumbeetribe.com/History_Culture/History_Culture%20Index.html (accessed on June 4, 2011).

"Métis: History & Culture." *Turtle Island Productions.* http://www.turtle-island.com/native/the-ojibway-story/metis.html (accessed on June 4, 2011).

Métis Nation of Ontario. http://www.metisnation.org/ (accessed on June 4, 2011).

MacDonald, George F. "The Haida: Children of Eagle and Raven." *Canadian Museum of Civilization.* http://www.civilization.ca/cmc/exhibitions/aborig/haida/haindexe.shtml (accessed on November 2, 2011).

"Maidu." *Four Directions Institute.* http://www.fourdir.com/maidu.htm (accessed on August 11, 2011).

"The Maidu." *The First Americans.* http://thefirstamericans.homestead.com/Maidu.html (accessed on August 11, 2011).

"Maidu People." *City of Roseville.* http://www.roseville.ca.us/parks/parks_n_facilities/facilities/maidu_indian_museum/maidu_people.asp (accessed on August 11, 2011).

Makah Cultural and Research Center. http://www.makah.com/mcrchome.html (accessed on November 2, 2011).

The Makah Nation on Washington's Olympic Peninsula. http://www.northolympic.com/makah/ (accessed on November 2, 2011).

Manning, June. "Wampanoag Living." *Martha's Vineyard Magazine.* May–June 2010. http://www.mvmagazine.com/article.php?25216 (accessed on June 9, 2011).

Mashantucket Museum and Research Center. http://www.pequotmuseum.org/ (accessed on June 1, 2011).

Mashpee Wampanoag Tribe. http://mashpeewampanoagtribe.com/ (accessed on June 1, 2011).

"Massacre at Wounded Knee, 1890." *EyeWitness to History.* http://www.eyewitnesstohistory.com/knee.htm (accessed on July 4, 2011).

"Massai, Chiricahua Apache." *Discover Southeast Arizona.* http://www.discoverseaz.com/History/Massai.html (accessed on July 20, 2011).

May, John D. "Otoe-Missouria." *Oklahoma Historical Society.* http://digital.library.okstate.edu/encyclopedia/entries/O/OT001.html (accessed on June 20, 2011).

McCollum, Timothy James. "Quapaw." *Oklahoma Historical Society.* http://digital.library.okstate.edu/encyclopedia/entries/Q/QU003.html (accessed on June 20, 2011).

— — —. "Sac and Fox." *Oklahoma Historical Society.* http://digital.library.okstate.edu/encyclopedia/entries/S/SA001.html (accessed on June 5, 2011).

McCoy, Ron. "Neosho Valley: Osage Nation." *KTWU/Channel 11.* http://ktwu.washburn.edu/journeys/scripts/1111a.html (accessed on June 12, 2011).

McManamon, F. P. "Kennewick Man." *Archaeology Program, National Park Service, U.S. Department of the Interior.* http://www.nps.gov/archeology/kennewick/index.htm (accessed on August 11, 2011).

Media Action. "Excerpt from Youth-led Interview with Phillip Esai." *Vimeo.* http://vimeo.com/15465119 (accessed on June 6, 2011).

— — —. "A Portrait of Nikolai." *Vimeo.* 2010. http://vimeo.com/14854233 (accessed on June 6, 2011).

"Menominee Culture." *Menominee Indian Tribe of Wisconsin.* http://www.mpm.edu/wirp/ICW-54.html (accessed on June 7, 2011).

"Menominee Indian Tribe of Wisconsin." *Great Lakes Inter-Tribal Council.* http://www.glitc.org/programs/pages/mtw.html (accessed on June 7, 2011).

Menominee Indian Tribe of Wisconsin. http://www.menominee-nsn.gov/ (accessed June 8, 2011).

"Menominee Oral Tradition." *Indian Country.* http://www.mpm.edu/wirp/ICW-138.html (accessed on June 7, 2011).

Mescalero Apache Reservation. www.mescaleroapache.com/ (accessed on July 15, 2011).

"Metis Communities." *Labrador Métis Nation.* http://www.labradormetis.ca/home/10 (accessed on June 4, 2011).

"Miami Indian Tribe." *Native American Nations.* http://www.nanations.com/miami/index.htm (accessed on June 7, 2011).

"Miami Indians." *Ohio History Central.* http://www.ohiohistorycentral.org/entry.php?rec=606 (accessed on June 7, 2011).

Miami Nation of Oklahoma. http://www.miaminacion.com/ (accessed on June 7, 2011).

Miccosukee Seminole Nation. http://www.miccosukeeseminolenation.com/ (accessed on June 12, 2011).

"Mi'kmaq Resources" *Halifax Public Libraries.* http://www.halifaxpublicli-braries.ca/research/topics/mikmaqresources.html (accessed on June 1, 2011).

Mississippi Valley Archaeology Center at the University of Wisconsin–La Crosse, "Early Cultures: Pre-European Peoples of Wisconsin: Mississippian and Oneota Traditions." *Educational Web Adventures.* http://www.uwlax.edu/mvac/preeuropeanpeople/earlycultures/mississippi_tradition.html (accessed on June 20, 2011).

"Missouri Indian Tribe History." *Access Genealogy.* http://www.accessgenealogy.com/native/tribes/siouan/missourihist.htm (accessed on June 20, 2011).

"Missouri Indians." *PBS.* http://www.pbs.org/lewisandclark/native/mis.html (accessed on June 20, 2011).

"Miwok." *Four Directions Institute.* http://www.fourdir.com/miwok.htm (accessed on August 11, 2011).

Miwok Archeological Preserve of Marin. "The Miwok People." *California State Parks.* http://www.parks.ca.gov/default.asp?page_id=22538 (accessed on August 11, 2011).

"Miwok Indian Tribe History." *Access Genealogy.* http://www.accessgeneal-ogy.com/native/california/miwokindianhist.htm (accessed on August 11, 2011).

"Modoc." *College of the Siskiyous.* http://www.siskiyous.edu/shasta/nat/mod.htm (accessed on August 11, 2011).

"Modoc." *Four Directions Institute.* http://www.fourdir.com/modoc.htm (accessed on August 11, 2011).

"Modoc Indian Chiefs and Leaders." *Access Genealogy.* (accessed on August 11, 2011). http://www.accessgenealogy.com/native/tribes/modoc/modocindianchiefs.htm

Modoc Tribe of Oklahoma. http://www.modoctribe.net/ (accessed on August 11, 2011).

"Mohave Indian Tribe History." *Access Genealogy.* http://www.accessgenealogy.com/native/tribes/mohave/mohaveindianhist.htm (accessed on July 20, 2011).

"Mohave National Preserve: Mohave Tribe: Culture." *National Park Service.* http://www.nps.gov/moja/historyculture/mojave-culture.htm (accessed on July 20, 2011).

"The Mohawk Tribe." *Mohawk Nation.* http://www.mohawktribe.com/ (accessed on June 7, 2011).

Montana Arts Council. "From the Heart and Hand: Salish Songs and Dances: Johnny Arlee, Arlee/John T., Big Crane, Pablo."*Montana Official State Website.* http://art.mt.gov/folklife/hearthand/songs.asp (accessed on August 11, 2011).

Morris, Allen. "Seminole History." *Florida Division of Historical Resources.* http://www.flheritage.com/facts/history/seminole/ (accessed on June 12, 2011).

Muscogee (Creek) Nation of Oklahoma. http://www.muscogeenation-nsn.gov/ (accessed on June 12, 2011).

Museum of the Aleutians.. http://www.aleutians.org/index.html (accessed on August 15, 2011).

Mussulman, Joseph. "Osage Indians." *The Lewis and Clark Fort Mandan Foundation.* http://lewis-clark.org/content/content-article.asp?ArticleID=2535 (accessed on June 12, 2011).

Muwekma Ohlone Tribe. http://www.muwekma.org/ (accessed on August 11, 2011).

The Myaamia Project at Miami University. http://www.myaamiaproject.com/ (accessed on June 7, 2011).

Myers, Tom. "Navajo Reservation" (video). *University of Illinois.* http://www.vimeo.com/8828354 (accessed on July 20, 2011).

Nametau Innu. "Your First Steps in the Innu Culture." *Musée Régional de la Côte-Nord.* http://www.nametauinnu.ca/en/tour (accessed on May 26, 2011).

Narragansett Indian Tribe. http://www.narragansett-tribe.org/ (accessed on June 1, 2011).

"Natchez Indian Tribe History." *Access Geneology.* http://www.accessgenealogy.com/native/tribes/natchez/natchezhist.htm (accessed on June 27, 2011).

Natchez Nation. http://www.natchez-nation.com/ (accessed on June 27, 2011).

"Natchez Stories." *Sacred Texts.* http://www.sacred-texts.com/nam/se/mtsi/#section_004 (accessed on June 27, 2011).

National Library for the Environment. "Native Americans and the Environment: Great Basin." *National Council for Science and the Environment.* http://www.cnie.org/nae/basin.html (accessed on August 15, 2011).

National Museum of American History—Smithsonian Institution. "Pueblo Resistance: We Are Here." *Mexico State Record Center and Archives.* http://www.newmexicohistory.org/filedetails.php?fileID=23042 (accessed on July 20, 2011).

National Museum of the American Indian. "Central Plains." *Smithsonian.* http://americanindian.si.edu/searchcollections/results.aspx?regid=58 (accessed on July 4, 2011).

— — —. "Prairie." *Smithsonian.* http://americanindian.si.edu/searchcollections/results.aspx?regid=60 (accessed on June 12, 2011).

— — —. "Southern Plains." *Smithsonian.* http://americanindian.si.edu/searchcollections/results.aspx?regid=61 (accessed on June 20, 2011).

"Native Americans: Osage Tribe." *University of Missouri.* http://ethemes.missouri.edu/themes/1608?locale=en (accessed on June 12, 2011).

"Navajo (Diné)." *Northern Arizona University.* http://www.cpluhna.nau.edu/People/navajo.htm (accessed on July 20, 2011).

Navajo Indian Tribes History. *Access Genealogy.* http://www.accessgenealogy.com/native/tribes/navajo/navahoindianhist.htm (accessed on July 20, 2011).

The Navajo Nation. http://www.navajo-nsn.gov/history.htm (accessed on July 31, 2007).

"Nde Nation." *Chiricahua: Apache Nation.* http://www.chiricahuaapache.org/ (accessed on July 20, 2011).

"New Hampshire's Native American Heritage." *New Hampshire State Council on the Arts.* http://www.nh.gov/folklife/learning/traditions_native_americans.htm (accessed on June 5, 2011).

"Nez Percé." *Countries and Their Culture.* http://www.everyculture.com/multi/Le-Pa/Nez-Perc.html (accessed on August 11, 2011).

"Nez Percé (Nimiipuu) Tribe." *Wisdom of the Elders.* http://www.wisdomoftheelders.org/program303.html (accessed on August 11, 2011).

"Nez Percé National Historical Park." *National Park Service.* http://www.nps.gov/nepe/ (accessed on August 11, 2011).

Nez Percé Tribe. http://www.nezperce.org/ (accessed on August 11, 2011).

"Nisqually Indian Tribe, Washington." *United States History.* http://www.u-s-history.com/pages/h1561.html (accessed on August 15, 2011).

Nisqually Land Trust. http://www.nisquallylandtrust.org (accessed on August 15, 2011).

"NOAA Arctic Theme Page." *National Oceanic and Atmospheric Administration.* http://www.arctic.noaa.gov/ (accessed on August 15, 2011).

"Nohwike Bagowa: House of Our Footprints" *White Mountain Apache Tribe Culture Center and Museum.* http://www.wmat.us/wmaculture.shtml (accessed on July 20, 2011).

"Nootka Indian Music of the Pacific North West Coast." *Smithsonian Folkways.* http://www.folkways.si.edu/albumdetails.aspx?itemid=912 (accessed on August 15, 2011).

Northern Arapaho Tribe. http://www.northernarapaho.com/ (accessed on July 2, 2011).

Northern Cheyenne Nation. www.cheyennenation.com/ (accessed on July 4, 2011).

"Northwest Coastal People." *Canada's First Peoples.* http://firstpeoplesofcanada. com/fp_groups/fp_nwc5.html (accessed on August 15, 2011).

"Nuu-chah-nulth." *Royal British Columbia Museum.* http://www.royalbcmuseum. bc.ca/Content_Files/Files/SchoolsAndKids/nuu2.pdf (accessed on August 15, 2011).

"Nuu-chah-nulth (Barkley) Community Portal." *FirstVoices.* http://www. firstvoices.ca/en/Nuu-chah-nulth (accessed on August 15, 2011).

Nuu-chah-nulth Tribal Council. http://www.nuuchahnulth.org/tribal-council/ welcome.html(accessed on August 15, 2011).

"Official Site of the Miami Nation of Indians of the State of Indiana." *Miami Nation of Indians.* http://www.miamiindians.org/ (accessed on June 7, 2011).

Official Site of the Wichita and Affiliated Tribes. http://www.wichitatribe.com/ (accessed on June 9, 2011).

Official Website of the Caddo Nation. http://www.caddonation-nsn.gov/ (accessed on June 12, 2011).

Ohio History Central. "Adena Mound." *Ohio Historical Society.* http://www. ohiohistorycentral.org/entry.php?rec=2411 (accessed June 7, 2011).

"Ohkay Owingeh." *Indian Pueblo Cultural Center.* http://www.indianpueblo. org/19pueblos/ohkayowingeh.html (accessed on July 20, 2011).

*Ohlone/Costanoan Esselen Nation.*http://www.ohlonecostanoanesselennation. org/(accessed on August 11, 2011).

Oklahoma Humanities Council. "Otoe-Missouria Tribe." *Cherokee Strip Museum.* http://www.cherokee-strip-museum.org/Otoe/OM_Who.htm (accessed on June 20, 2011).

Oklahoma Indian Affairs Commission. "2011 Oklahoma Indian Nations." *Pocket Pictorial Directory.* Oklahoma City: Oklahoma Indian Affairs Commission, 2011. Available from http://www.ok.gov/oiac/documents/2011. FINAL.WEB.pdf (accessed on June 12, 2011).

The Oregon History Project. "Modoc." *Oregon Historical Society.* http://www. ohs.org/education/oregonhistory/search/dspResults.cfm?keyword=Modoc &type=&theme=&timePeriod=&region= (accessed on August 11, 2011).

"The Osage." *Fort Scott National Historic Site, National Park Service.* http://www.nps.gov/fosc/historyculture/osage.htm (accessed on June 12, 2011).

Osage Nation. http://www.osagetribe.com/ (accessed on June 12, 2011).

"Osage Indian Tribe History." *Access Genealogy.* http://www.accessgenealogy.com/native/tribes/osage/osagehist.htm (accessed on June 12, 2011).

The Otoe-Missouria Tribe. http://www.omtribe.org/ (accessed on June 20, 2011).

Ottawa Inuit Children's Centre. http://www.ottawainuitchildrens.com/eng/ (accessed on August 15, 2011).

Ottawa Tribe of Oklahoma. http://www.ottawatribe.org/history.htm (accessed May 13, 2011).

"Our History." *Makah Cultural and Research Center.* http://www.makah.com/history.html (accessed on November 2, 2011).

"Pacific Northwest Native Americans." *Social Studies School Service.* http://nativeamericans.mrdonn.org/northwest.html (accessed on August 15, 2011).

Paiute Indian Tribe of Utah. http://www.utahpaiutes.org/ (accessed on August 15, 2011).

The Pascua Yaqui Tribe. http://www.pascuayaqui-nsn.gov/ (accessed on July 20, 2011).

"The Pasqu Yaqui Connection." *Through Our Parents' Eyes: History and Culture of Southern Arizona.* http://parentseyes.arizona.edu/pascuayaquiaz/ (accessed on July 20, 2011).

"Past and Future Meet in San Juan Pueblo Solar Project." *Solar Cookers International.* http://solarcooking.org/sanjuan1.htm (accessed on July 20, 2011).

Pastore, Ralph T. "Aboriginal Peoples: Newfoundland and Labrador Heritage." *Memorial University of Newfoundland.* http://www.heritage.nf.ca/aboriginal/ (accessed on August 15, 2011).

Paul, Daniel N. "We Were Not the Savages." *First Nation History.* http://www.danielnpaul.com/index.html (accessed on June 1, 2011).

"Pawnee." *Four Directions Institute.* http://www.fourdir.com/pawnee.htm (accessed on July 6, 2011).

"Pawnee Indian Museum." *Kansas State Historical Society.* http://www.kshs.org/places/pawneeindian/history.htm (accessed on July 6, 2011).

"Pawnee Indian Tribe History." *Access Genealogy.* http://www.accessgenealogy.com/native/tribes/pawnee/pawneehist.htm (accessed on July 6, 2011).

Pawnee Nation of Oklahoma. http://www.pawneenation.org/ (accessed on July 6, 2011).

"Pecos Indian Tribe History." *Access Genealogy.* http://www.accessgenealogy.com/native/tribes/pecos/pecoshist.htm (accessed on July 20, 2011).

"Pecos National Historical Park." *Desert USA.* http://www.desertusa.com/pecos/pnpark.html (accessed on July 20, 2011).

"Pecos Pueblos." *Four Directions Institute.* http://www.fourdir.com/pecos.htm (accessed on July 20, 2011).

"People of Pecos." *National Park Service.* http://www.nps.gov/peco/historyculture/peple-of-pecos.htm (accessed on July 20, 2011).

"People of the Colorado Plateau: The Hopi." *Northern Arizona University.* http://www.cpluhna.nau.edu/People/hopi.htm (accessed on July 20, 2011).

"People of the Colorado Plateau: The Ute Indian." *Northern Arizona University.* http://cpluhna.nau.edu/People/ute_indians.htm(accessed on August 15, 2011).

"The People of the Flathead Nation."*Lake County Directory.* http://www.lakecodirect.com/archives/The_Flathead_Nation.html (accessed on August 11, 2011).

"Peoples of Alaska and Northeast Siberia." *Alaska Native Collections.* http://alaska.si.edu/cultures.asp (accessed on August 15, 2011).

"Pequot Lives: Almost Vanished." *Pequot Museum and Research Center.* http://www.pequotmuseum.org/Home/MashantucketGallery/AlmostVanished.htm (accessed June 8, 2011).

Peterson, Keith C. "Dams of the Columbia Basin and Their Effects of the Native Fishery." *Center for Columbia River History.* http://www.ccrh.org/comm/river/dams7.htm (accessed on August 11, 2011).

Peterson, Leighton C. "Tuning in to Navajo: The Role of Radio in Native Language Maintenance." *Northern Arizona University.* http://jan.ucc.nau.edu/-jar/TIL_17.html (accessed on July 20, 2011).

"Pima (AkimelO'odham)." *Four Directions Institute.* http://www.fourdir.com/pima.htm (accessed on July 20, 2011).

"Pima Indian Tribe History." *Access Genealogy.* www.accessgenealogy.com/native/tribes/pima/pimaindianhist.htm (accessed on July 20, 2011).

Pit River Indian Tribe. http://www.pitrivertribe.org/home.php (accessed on August 11, 2011).

"Pomo People: Brief History." *Native American Art.* http://www.kstrom.net/isk/art/basket/pomohist.html (accessed on August 11, 2011).

Porter, Tom. "Mohawk (Haudenosaunee) Teaching." *FourDirectionsTeachings.com.* http://www.fourdirectionsteachings.com/transcripts/mohawk.html (accessed June 7, 2011).

"Powhatan Indian Village." *Acton Public Schools: Acton-Boxborough Regional School District.* http://ab.mec.edu/jamestown/powhatan (accessed on June 1, 2011).

"Powhatan Language and the Powhatan Indian Tribe (Powatan, Powhatten, Powhattan)." *Native Languages of the Americas: Preserving and Promoting Indigenous American Indian Languages.* http://www.native-languages.org/powhatan.htm (accessed on on June 1, 2011).

"Preserving Sacred Wisdom." *Native Spirit and the Sun Dance Way.* http://www. nativespiritinfo.com/ (accessed on July 5, 2011).

"Pueblo Indian History and Resources." *Pueblo Indian.* http://www.puebloindian.com/ (accessed on July 20, 2011).

Pueblo of Acoma. http://www.puebloofacoma.org/ (accessed on July 20, 2011).

Pueblo of Jemez. http://www.jemezpueblo.org/ (accessed on July 20, 2011).

Pueblo of Zuñi. http://www.ashiwi.org/(accessed on July 20, 2011).

Puyallup Tribe of Indians. http://www.puyallup-tribe.com/ (accessed on November 2, 2011).

Quapaw Tribe of Oklahoma. http://www.quapawtribe.com/ (accessed on June 20, 2011).

"The Quapaw Tribe of Oklahoma and the Tar Creek Project." *Environmental Protection Agency.* http://www.epa.gov/oar/tribal/tribetotribe/tarcreek.html (accessed on June 20, 2011).

"Questions and Answers about the Plateau Indians." *Wellpinit School District 49 (WA).* http://www.wellpinit.wednet.edu/sal-qa/qa.php (accessed on August 11, 2011).

"Questions and Answers about the Spokane Indians." *Wellpinit School District.* http://wellpinit.org/q%2526a (accessed on August 11, 2011).

Redish, Laura, and Orrin Lewis. *Native Languages of the Americas.*http://www. native-languages.org (accessed on August 11, 2011).

"Research Starters: Anasazi and Pueblo Indians." *Scholastic.com.* http://teacher. scholastic.com/researchtools/researchstarters/native_am/ (accessed on July 20, 2011).

"The Rez We Live On"(videos). *The Confederated Salish and Kootenai Tribes.* http://therezweliveon.com/13/video.html (accessed on August 11, 2011).

The Rooms, Provincial Museum Division. "Innu Objects."*Virtual Museum Canada.* 2008. http://www.museevirtuel-virtualmuseum.ca/edu/ViewLoit Collection.do;jsessionid=3083D5EEB47F3ECDE9DA040AD0D4C956? method=preview⟨=EN&id=3210 (accessed on May 24, 2011).

Sac and Fox Nation. http://www.sacandfoxnation-nsn.gov/ (accessed on June 5, 2011).

"Sac and Fox Tribe." *Meskwaki Nation.* http://www.meskwaki.org/ (accessed on June 5, 2011).

San Carlos Apache Cultural Center. http://www.sancarlosapache.com/home.htm (accessed on July 20, 2011).

"San Carlos Apache Sunrise Dance." *World News Network.* http://wn.com/ San_Carlos_Apache_Sunrise_Dance (accessed on July 20, 2011).

"San Juan Pueblo." *New Mexico Magazine.* http://www.nmmagazine.com/ native_american/san_juan.php (accessed on July 20, 2011).

"San Juan Pueblo O'Kang." *Indian Pueblo Cultural Center.* http://www.indianpueblo.org/19pueblos/ohkayowingeh.html (accessed on July 20, 2011).

"The Sand Creek Massacre." *Last of the Independents.* http://www.lastoftheindependents.com/sandcreek.htm (accessed on July 2, 2011).

"Seminole Indian Tribe History." *Access Genealogy.* http://www.accessgenealogy.com/native/tribes/seminole/seminolehist.htm (accessed on June 12, 2011).

Seminole Nation of Oklahoma. http://www.seminolenation.com/ (accessed on June 12, 2011).

Seminole Tribe of Florida. http://www.seminoletribe.com/ (accessed on June 12, 2011).

"Sharp Nose." *Native American Nations.* http://www.nanations.com/arrap/page4.htm (accessed on July 2, 2011).

"The Shawnee in History." *The Shawnee Tribe.* http://www.shawnee-tribe.com/history.htm (accessed on June 12, 2011).

"Shawnee Indian Tribe History." *Access Genealogy.* http://www.accessgenealogy.com/native/tennessee/shawneeindianhist.htm (accessed on June 12, 2011).

"Shawnee Indians." *Ohio Historical Society.* http://www.ohiohistorycentral.org/entry.php?rec=631&nm=Shawnee-Indians (accessed on June 12, 2011).

Shawnee Nation, United Remnant Band. http://www.zaneshawneecaverns.net/shawnee.shtml (accessed on June 12, 2011).

"A Short History of the Spokane Indians." *Wellpinit School District.* http://www.wellpinit.wednet.edu/shorthistory (accessed on August 11, 2011).

"Short Overview of California Indian History." *California Native American Heritage Commission.* http://www.nahc.ca.gov/califindian.html (accessed on August 15, 2011).

Sicade, Henry. "Education." *Puyallup Tribe of Indians.* http://www.puyallup-tribe.com/history/education/ (accessed on November 2, 2011).

"Simon Ortiz: Native American Poet." *The University of Texas at Arlington.* http://www.uta.edu/english/tim/poetry/so/ortizmain.htm (accessed on July 20, 2011).

Simpson, Linda. "The Kansas/Kanza/Kaw Nation." *Oklahoma Territory.* http://www.okgenweb.org/-itkaw/Kanza2.html (accessed on June 17, 2011).

The Skokomish Tribal Nation. http://www.skokomish.org/ (accessed on November 2, 2011).

Skopec, Eric. "What Mystery?" *Anasazi Adventure.* http://www.anasaziadventure.com/what_mystery.pdf (accessed on July 20, 2011).

Smithsonian Folkways. "Rain Dance (Zuñi)." *Smithsonian Institution.* http://www.folkways.si.edu/TrackDetails.aspx?itemid=16680 (music track) and http://media.smithsonianfolkways.org/liner_notes/folkways/FW06510.pdf (instructions for dance). (accessed on July 20, 2011).

Snook, Debbie. "Ohio's Trail of Tears." *Wyandotte Nation of Oklahoma*, 2003. http://www.wyandotte-nation.org/culture/history/published/trail-of-tears/ (accessed May 11, 2011).

The Southern Arapaho. http://southernarapaho.org/ (accessed on July 2, 2011).

Southern Ute Indian Tribe. http://www.southern-ute.nsn.us/ (accessed on August 15, 2011).

Splawn, A. J. *Ka-mi-akin, the Last Hero of the Yakimas.* Portland, OR: Kilham Stationary and Printing, 1917. Reproduced by Washington Secretary of State. http://www.secstate.wa.gov/history/publications_detail.aspx?p=24 (accessed on August 11, 2011).

"Spokane Indian Tribe." *Access Genealogy.* http://www.accessgenealogy.com/native/tribes/salish/spokanhist.htm (accessed on August 11, 2011).

"Spokane Indian Tribe." *United States History.* http://www.u-s-history.com/pages/h1570.html (accessed on August 11, 2011).

Spokane Tribe of Indians. http://www.spokanetribe.com/ (accessed on August 11, 2011).

Sreenivasan, Hari. "'Apache 8' Follows All-Women Firefighters On and Off the Reservation." *PBS NewsHour.* http://video.pbs.org/video/2006599346/ (accessed on July 20, 2011).

Stands In Timber, John. "Cheyenne Memories." *Northern Cheyenne Nation.* http://www.cheyennenation.com/memories.html (accessed on July 4, 2011).

Stewart, Kenneth. "Kivas." *Scholastic.* http://www2.scholastic.com/browse/article.jsp?id=5052 (accessed on July 20, 2011).

"The Story of the Ute Tribe: Past, Present, and Future." *Ute Mountain Ute Tribe.* http://www.utemountainute.com/story.htm (accessed on August 15, 2011).

Sultzman, Lee. *First Nations.* http://www.tolatsga.org/sf.html (accessed on June 5, 2011).

Swan, Daniel C. "Native American Church." *Oklahoma Historical Society.* http://digital.library.okstate.edu/encyclopedia/entries/N/NA015.html (accessed on August 11, 2011).

"Taos Pueblo." *Bluffton University.* http://www.bluffton.edu/-sullivanm/taos/taos.html (accessed on July 20, 2011).

"Taos Pueblo." *New Mexico Magazine.* http://www.nmmagazine.com/native_american/taos.php (accessed on July 20, 2011).

Taos Pueblo. http://www.taospueblo.com/ (accessed on July 20, 2011).

"Taos Pueblo: A Thousand Years of Tradition." *Taos Pueblo.* http://taospueblo.com/ (accessed on July 20, 2011).

"Territorial Kansas: Kansa Indians." *University of Kansas.* http://www.territorialkansasonline.org/-imlskto/cgi-bin/index.php?SCREEN=

keyword&selected_keyword=Kansa%20Indians (accessed on June 17, 2011).

"Throat Singing." *Inuit Cultural Online Resource.* http://icor.ottawainuitchildrens. com/node/30 (accessed on August 15, 2011).

"Tlingit Tribes, Clans, and Clan Houses: Traditional Tlingit Country." *Alaska Native Knowledge Network.* http://www.ankn.uaf.edu/ANCR/Southeast/ TlingitMap/ (accessed on November 2, 2011).

"Tohono O'odham (Papago)." *Four Directions Institute.* http://www.fourdir. com/tohono_o'odham.htm (accessed on July 20, 2011).

"Totem Pole Websites." *Cathedral Grove.* http://www.cathedralgrove.eu/ text/07-Totem-Websites-3.htm (accessed on November 2, 2011).

"Trading Posts in the American Southwest." *Southwest Crossroads.* http:// southwestcrossroads.org/record.php?num=742&hl=chiricahua:: apache (accessed on July 20, 2011).

"Traditional Mi'kmaq Beliefs."*Indian Brook First Nation.* http://home.rushcomm. ca/-hsack/spirit.html (accessed on June1,2011).

"Tsmshian Songs We Love to Sing!" *Dum Baaldum.* http://www.dumbaaldum. org/html/songs.htm (accessed on August 15, 2011).

"Umatilla Indian Agency and Reservation, Oregon." *Access Genealogy.* http:// www.accessgenealogy.com/native/census/condition/umatilla_indian_ agency_reservation_oregon.htm (accessed on August 11, 2011).

"Umatilla, Walla Walla, and Cayuse." *TrailTribes.org: Traditional and Contemporary Native Culture.* http://www.trailtribes.org/umatilla/home.htm (accessed on August 11, 2011).

"Unangax & Alutiiq (Sugpiaq)." *Alaska Native Heritage Center.* http://www. alaskanative.net/en/main_nav/education/culture_alaska/unangax/ (accessed on August 15, 2011).

Unrau, William E. "Kaw (Kansa)." *Oklahoma Historical Society.* http://digital. library.okstate.edu/encyclopedia/entries/K/KA001.html (accessed on June 17, 2011).

Urban Indian Experience. "The Duwamish: Seattle's Landless Tribe." *KUOW: PRX.* http://www.prx.org/pieces/1145-urban-indian-experience-episode-1-the-duwamish(accessed on November 2, 2011).

The Ute Indian Tribe. http://www.utetribe.com/ (accessed on August 15, 2011).

"Ute Nation." *Utah Travel Industry.* http://www.utah.com/tribes/ute_main.htm (accessed on August 15, 2011).

Virtual Archaeologist. "The Like-a-Fishhook Story." *NDSU Archaeology Technologies Laboratory.* http://fishhook.ndsu.edu/home/lfstory.php (accessed on June 19, 2011).

"A Virtual Tour of California Missions." *MissionTour.* http://missiontour.org/ index.htm (accessed on August 11, 2011).

"Visiting a Maidu Bark House." *You Tube.* http://www.youtube.com/watch?v=fw5i83519mQ (accessed on August 11, 2011).

"The Wampanoag." *Boston Children's Museum.* http://www.bostonkids.org/educators/wampanoag/html/what.htm (accessed on June 1, 2011).

"Washoe." *Four Directions Institute.* http://www.fourdir.com/washoe.htm (accessed on August 15, 2011).

"Washoe Hot Springs." *National Cultural Preservation Council.* http://www.ncpc.info/projects_washoe.html (accessed on August 15, 2011).

"Washoe Indian Tribe History." *Access Genealogy.* http://www.accessgenealogy.com/native/tribes/washo/washohist.htm (accessed on August 15, 2011).

"We Shall Remain." *PBS.* http://www.pbs.org/wgbh/amex/weshallremain/ (accessed on July 20, 2011).

Weiser, Kathy. *Legends of America.* http://www.legendsofamerica.com (accessed on July 20, 2011).

"White Mountain Apache Indian Reservation." *Arizona Handbook.* http://www.arizonahandbook.com/white_mtn_apache.htm (accessed on July 20, 2011).

"White Mountain Apache Tribe." *InterTribal Council of Arizona.* http://www.itcaonline.com/tribes_whitemtn.html (accessed on July 20, 2011).

"White Mountain Apache Tribe: Restoring Wolves, Owls, Trout and Ecosystems" *Cooperative Conservation America.* http://www.cooperativeconservation.org/viewproject.asp?pid=136 (accessed on July 20, 2011).

"Who Were the Lipan and the Kiowa-Apaches?" *Southwest Crossroads.* http://southwestcrossroads.org/record.php?num=522&hl=chiricahua:: apache (accessed on July 20, 2011).

"Wichita." *Four Directions Institute.* http://www.fourdir.com/wichita.htm (accessed on June 9, 2011).

Wind River Indian Reservation. http://www.wind-river.org/info/communities/reservation.php (accessed on July 2, 2011).

Wind River Indian Reservation: Eastern Shoshone Tribe. http://www.easternshoshone.net/ (accessed on August 15, 2011).

WMAT: White Mountain Apache Tribe. http://wmat.us/ (accessed on July 20, 2011).

"Wounded Knee." *Last of the Independent.* http://www.lastoftheindependents.com/wounded.htm (accessed on July 4, 2011).

The Wounded Knee Museum. http://www.woundedkneemuseum.org/ (accessed on July 4, 2011).

Wyandot Nation of Anderdon. http://www.wyandotofanderdon.com/ (accessed May 13, 2011).

Wyandot Nation of Kansas. http://www.wyandot.org/ (accessed May 13, 2011).

Wyandotte Nation of Oklahoma. http://www.wyandotte-nation.org/ (accessed May 13, 2011).

"Yakima Indian Tribe History." *Access Genealogy.* http://www.accessgenealogy. com/native/tribes/yakimaindianhist.htm (accessed on August 11, 2011).

Yakama Nation Cultural Heritage Center. http://www.yakamamuseum.com/ (accessed on August 11, 2011).

"Yaqui." *Four Directions Institute.* http://www.fourdir.com/yaqui.htm (accessed on July 20, 2011).

"Yaqui and Mayo Indian Easter Ceremonies." *RimJournal.* http://www.rimjournal. com/arizyson/easter.htm (accessed on July 20, 2011).

"Yaqui Sacred Traditions." *Wisdom Traditions Institute.* http://www.wisdomtraditions. com/yaqui2.html (accessed on July 20, 2011).

"Yuma (Quechan)." *Four Directions Institute.* http://www.fourdir.com/yuma. htm (accessed on July 20, 2011).

Yuman Indian Tribe History." *Access Genealogy.* http://www.accessgenealogy. com/native/tribes/yuman/yumanfamilyhist.htm (accessed on July 20, 2011).

"The Yup'ik and Cup'ik People—Who We Are." *The Alaska Native Heritage Center Museum.* http://www.alaskanative.net/en/main_nav/education/ culture_alaska/yupik/ (accessed on August 15, 2011).

"Yup'ik Tundra Navigation." *Center for Cultural Design.* http://www.ccd.rpi. edu/Eglash/csdt/na/tunturyu/index.html (accessed on August 15, 2011).

"The Yurok." *California History Online.* http://www.californiahistoricalsociety. org/timeline/chapter2/002d.html# (accessed on August 11, 2011).

"Yurok." *Four Directions Institute.* http://www.fourdir.com/yurok.htm (accessed on August 11, 2011).

The Yurok Tribe. http://www.yuroktribe.org/ (accessed on August 11, 2011).

Zeig, Sande. *Apache 8* (film). http://www.apache8.com/ (accessed on July 20, 2011).

"Zuñi." *Northern Arizona University.* http://www.cpluhna.nau.edu/People/zuni. htm (accessed on July 20, 2011).

"Zuñi." *Southwest Crossroads.* http://southwestcrossroads.org/record. php?num=2&hl=zuni (accessed on July 20, 2011).

"Zuñi Pueblo." *New Mexico Magazine.* http://www.nmmagazine.com/native_ american/zuni.php (accessed on July 20, 2011).

"Zuñi Pueblos (Ashiwi)." *Four Directions Institute.* http://www.fourdir.com/ zuni.htm (accessed on July 20, 2011).

Index

Italics indicates volume numbers; **boldface** indicates entries and their page numbers. Chart indicates a chart; ill. indicates an illustration, and map indicates a map.

F

U•X•L Encyclopedia of Native American Tribes, 3rd Edition

O